Peter A. Cox

THE LARGER RHODODENDRON SPECIES

Timber Press
Portland, Oregon

By the same author

The Smaller Rhododendrons
The Encyclopedia of Rhododendron Hybrids
Cox's Guide to Choosing Rhododendrons

To my sons Kenneth and Raymond. May they get as much interest and enjoyment out of the great genus Rhododendrons as I do.

First edition published 1979, reprinted 1981
This revised edition, with Addendum and
new illustrations, published 1990

First published in North America in 1990 by
Timber Press, Inc.
9999 S.W. Wilshire
Portland, Oregon 97225, U.S.A

ISBN 0 88192 180 7

Printed and bound in Hong Kong

Contents

The Photographs

Between pp. 158 and 159

27 *R. hemsleyanum*. Fortunea subsection
28 *R. orbiculare*. Fortunea subsection, Wolong Panda Reserve, Szechwan
29 *R. vernicosum*. Fortunea subsection, Rilong, Szechwan
30 *R. fulgens*. Fulgensia subsection
31 *R. uvarifolium*. 'Yangtze Bend' A. M. Fulva subsection
32 *R. crinigerum*. Glischra subsection
33 *R. glischrum* ssp. *rude*. Glischra subsection
34 R. kesangiae Bowes Lyon 9703. Grandia subsection (A. D. Schilling)
35 *R. montroseanum* 'Benmore' F.C.C. Grandia subsection
36 *R. macabeanum*. Grandia subsection
37 *R. pudorosum* Ludlow & Sherriff 2752. Grandia subsection
38 *R. sinogrande*. Grandia subsection, Tali Range, Yunnan with Peter Hutchison who has been on all my main plant hunting trips
39 *R. watsonii*. Grandia subsection, Huanglong, Szechwan
40 *R. annae*. Irrorata subsection
41 *R. anthosphaerum*. Sino-British Expedition to China 0163, Irrorata subsection
42 *R. lanatoides*. Lanata subsection, young growth
43 *R. lacteum*. Lactea (Taliensia) subsection
44 *R. beesianum* Rock 107. Lactea (Taliensia) subsection
45 *R. lanatum*. Lanata subsection
46 *R. longesquamatum*. Maculifera subsection, foliage
47 *R. pachysanthum*. Rhododendron Venture 72001, Maculifera subsection
48 *R. pachytrichum*. Maculifera subsection
49 *R. sikangense (cookeanum)*. Maculifera subsection
50 *R. dalhousiae* var. *rhabdotum*. Maddenia subsection
51 *R. formosum* var. *inaequale* Cox & Hutchison 301. Maddenia subsection
52 *R. lindleyi*. Maddenia subsection, Sikkim (W. E. Berg)
53 *R. nuttallii*. Maddenia subsection
54 *R. veitchianum* Peter Valder. Maddenia subsection
55 *R. facetum*. Parishia subsection, Tali Range, Yunnan
56 *R. smirnowii* Apold, Cox & Hutchison 118, Pontica subsection
57 *R. dauricum* 'Hokkaido' A. M. Rhodorastra subsection
58 *R. bainbridgeanum*. Selensia subsection
59 *R. hirtipes* Kingdon Ward 5659. Selensia subsection
60 *R. adenogynum*. Taliensia subsection, Lichiang Range, Yunnan (A. D. Schilling)
61 *R. bhutanense*. Taliensia subsection, Rudong La, Bhutan
62 *R. balangense*. Taliensia subsection, Wolong Panda Reserve, Szechwan (W. E. Berg)
63 *R. bureavii* 'Loch Fyne' A.M., Taliensia subsection
64 *R. bureavii (bureavioides)*. Taliensia subsection, Balang Mountain, Szechwan
65 *R. elegantulum*. Taliensia subsection
66 *R. faberi* ssp. *prattii*. Taliensia subsection, pink form, Balang Mountain, Szechwan

Acknowledgments

Very special thanks are due to the Royal Botanic Garden, Edinburgh. Without the help and co-operation of Mr D. M. Henderson, ex Regius Keeper, Dr J. Cullen and Dr D. F. Chamberlain, this book would never have got off the ground. I owe them my special gratitude for the full use of facilities available in the herbarium, library and garden and for access to their new revision of the genus *Rhododendron*. Thanks are also due to many other members of the staff, especially Dr R. Watling, Mr M. V. Mathew, Mr I. Hedge and Mr K. Grant.

To Mr C. D. Brickell for his foreword, helpful advice and for reading through the manuscript. To my sister for proof reading.

To many friends (too many to list, unfortunately) in Britain, USA, Europe, Australia, New Zealand and Japan who have helped over diverse subjects, from hardiness to lists of nurseries, and allowed me to study their gardens.

My deepest gratitude is extended to Margaret Stones for illustrating yet another book with her beautiful line drawings of species; also to Denise Taylor for the line drawings of leaf and flower shapes and text drawings on pages 89, 90, 91, 154, 155 and 222, and to Sir Peter C. Hutchison, my plant hunting and west Scotland gardening companion, for again producing excellent distribution maps.

Lastly, but above all, to my wife who has patiently (usually!) discussed details and checked the drafts and proofs, and also to my late father, who has always been an inspiration to me in my writing and my love of rhododendrons.

Foreword to First Edition

By C. D. Brickell

Six years have passed since Peter Cox provided the Rhododendron world with his immensely valuable work on Dwarf Rhododendrons and the publication of this companion volume will undoubtedly be received with equal enthusiasm.

Authoritative books on the genus are few and although much has been written on rhododendrons, gardeners frequently find difficulty in obtaining reliable information unless they have the time, energy and patience to consult a number of far-flung references. This comprehensive work gathers together and concisely provides botanical and horticultural detail of the larger species in an easily read and informative manner and is particularly useful in giving the author's very considerable first-hand experience of cultivating the vast majority of the species described.

The Larger Species of Rhododendron is an important milestone in Rhododendron history as it is the first generally available book which adopts the revised classification system put forward by staff at the Royal Botanic Garden, Edinburgh, following their very detailed study of the genus. As an aid to link the older, largely artificial Series classification system of Bayley Balfour and others to the revision a table of equivalent names has been provided which will be extremely useful in equating the new with the old, a feature for which many gardeners will be thankful.

I am delighted to see also that Peter Cox emphasizes the need to preserve and conserve rhododendron species under collectors' numbers. These are rapidly being lost as many of the rich collections formerly maintained by the great rhododendron enthusiasts deteriorate and the unique gene pools which these collections represent disappear into oblivion.

I would fully endorse too the author's plea that a national collection of accurately documented rhododendron species should be established with particular emphasis on populations raised from collectors' seed.

Although this book is entitled *The Larger Species of Rhododendron* those who only have relatively small gardens will still find many species described which can quite comfortably be accommodated in their own planting schemes.

Enthusiasts will need no introduction to the delights of the genus and will find much information to stimulate them further in their quest. Those less well-informed will quickly sense the love and deep knowledge of rhododendrons which Peter Cox instils into this book and can only benefit from his advice and long experience in growing and studying this fascinating and diverse group of plants.

Introduction to First Edition

This is a companion volume to *Dwarf Rhododendrons* (Batsford 1973) and *The Smaller Rhododendrons* (Batsford 1985) and covers all the larger species which were not included in that book, that is all those averaging over 1.50 m (5 ft). I have endeavoured to make it as comprehensive as possible, describing all known species, excluding the Vireya section (Malesian) which was largely but briefly dealt with in *Dwarf Rhododendrons*. Those species not in cultivation have been included in the hope that it may be possible for these to be introduced in the not too distant future.

Most people must by now have heard of the recent change in the naming of the divisions into which rhododendrons are arranged. The old word 'series' disappears and the genus is now divided into subgenera, sections but mostly into subsections. These subsections largely replace the 'series' and while some sub-series have been dropped, others have been elevated to subsection rank. It is hoped that this method of classification will soon become generally accepted and that there will not be any negative arguments for retaining the old system. Sir Isaac Bayley Balfour, himself the originator of the term 'series', fully admitted that a 'change' would have to take place once the majority of species had become better understood. To aid readers with this changeover, a list of the new names with the old series and sub-series in brackets is on page 93.

The descriptions have been lengthened so that they can be used for more positive identification. The old classification of Bayley Balfour, Wright Smith, Tagg, Cowan and Davidian was based largely on morphology and is now outmoded. I have followed the revisions of the Royal Botanic Garden, Edinburgh. (See *Notes from the Royal Botanic Garden, Edinburgh* Vol. 39 *No. 1, Subgenus Rhododendron* (Lepidotes) J. Cullen and *No. 2, Subgenus Hymenanthes* (Elepidotes) D. F. Chamberlain.) These have been worked out on much more scientific grounds than previously, using such new aids as the analysis of chemicals in the leaf waxes and the micro-photography of scales and hairs. We all hope that it will be a more workable classification, though no classification can be perfect or final. With further research and exploration, more changes are sure to be made. Gardeners are apt to bemoan these changes, but they are largely for their own good. The type of change to be regretted is where old and/or unknown names are dug up and substituted for well-known names such as *principis* for *vellereum* and *prinophyllum* for *roseum*.

Certain species, or so-called species, cannot at present be fitted into any subsection. Some may be placed in subsections of their own while others are of such doubtful ancestry that nobody knows whether they are natural hybrids or what. These I have placed at the end of the subsections on their own.

Some plants have more of a story to tell than others, due perhaps to their behaviour in the wild and how much they have been studied there, or their variation or habits in cultivation. I have picked three plants or groups of plants which require additional explanation. These are *R. protistum* (*giganteum*) and its allies, *R. occidentale* in America and the natural hybrids growing in north-east Turkey.

It is hoped that the title *The Larger Species of Rhododendron* does not put off those people who have only very small gardens. Surely everyone who is interested in rhododendrons will have room for one or two of the smaller species included in this book.

Lastly (as mentioned in *Dwarf Rhododendrons* and *The Smaller Rhododendrons* p. 12) I have included a brief description of the climate and conditions at Glendoick, near Perth, east Scotland, where I base most of my comparisons. The conditions are far from ideal for larger species. The winters are relatively mild, never below −18°C (0°F) and the summers cool, rarely over 27°C (80°F). The real bugbear is the frequency of autumn and spring frosts, which can do appreciable damage to buds, flowers, growth and wood. Rain is often inadequate during the growing season. Yearly total is just below 76 cm (30 in.), falling throughout the year, but recently, dry spells of over 1 month have occurred. Snow rarely lies long.

Elevation is between 15–60 m (50–200 ft) above sea-level. There is fairly good shelter from the north-west, north and north-east. Soil is a medium to medium-heavy loam, slightly to moderately acid, very short of organic matter. Drainage is generally good.

The following abbreviations have been used in the text:

AMRS–QB   American Rhododendron Society
            Quarterly Bulletin
RHS–RYB   Royal Horticultural Society
            Rhododendron Year Book
RHS–RCYB   Royal Horticultural Society
            Rhododendron and Camellia Year Book
RHS–RSHB   Royal Horticultural Society
            Rhododendron Species Handbook
SP of RH   *The Species of Rhododendron*, edited by J. B. Stevenson
RBG   Royal Botanic Garden

Introduction to Second Edition

In the ten years plus since I wrote the First Edition, much has happened in the rhododendron species world and many new books have been published on species. In 1980, the first revision was published by the RBG, Edinburgh, of Subgenus Rhododendron (Lepidotes), written by Dr James Cullen, followed in 1982 by the revision of Subgenus Hymenanthes (Elepidotes), written by Dr David Chamberlain. Also in 1980 came the American translation of *Rhododendrons of China*, originally written in Chinese in 1974. H. H. Davidian's first volume, *The Rhododendron Species Volume 1, Lepidotes* was also published in 1982, followed by *Volume 11 Part 1, Elepidotes* in 1989. While these have been the most significant taxonomically, the Chinese have started to produce books full of coloured photographs taken in the wild including two translated into English with descriptions and maps showing locations (see Bibliography).

All these books contain some changes in classification and some descriptions of new species. The two Edinburgh revisions were largely followed in the First Edition of *The Larger Species of Rhododendron* as the Edinburgh taxonomists very kindly kept me up to date on their classifications right up to the time my manuscript was sent to the publishers. Different people and different countries producing classifications and describing new species are bound to lead to conflicts of opinion. For instance, both Davidian and the Chinese have described 'new' species that Cullen and Chamberlain do not accept, while Davidian has religiously maintained the old Bayley Balfour system, despite the fact that the Edinburgh Revisions are being gradually accepted throughout most of the 'rhododendron world'.

The overall numbers of alterations, new descriptions and new information on species already described have not quite warranted the complete rewriting of this volume of the kind undertaken with *Dwarf Rhododendrons*. I have made a few essential corrections and alterations to the main text and have added an addendum to cover the newly described species and any important information on those already described. This has regrettably meant a somewhat disjointed book and extra use will need to be made of the index to locate certain species, especially when they are written about in two places. In many cases it has been impossible to get more information on species newly described by the Chinese but I have deliberately mentioned them all so as to make this book as fully comprehensive as possible and also in the hope that many of these new species will be introduced shortly.

The Chinese are now starting to cultivate rhododendron species in semi-wild areas in different parts of China. When I state that a plant is 'not in cultivation', I mean it has not been introduced into gardens outside China; but some of these could easily now be growing in these new Chinese arboreta. The Chinese interest in their own flora must be a good thing for the future although there is always the danger that transplanting species from one part of China to another may mean the eventual establishment of species in the wild outside their own area and also to many spontaneous hybrids spreading themselves around.

As I stated in *The Smaller Rhododendrons*, I do not totally agree with all the classification changes in the Edinburgh Revisions. Nor for that matter do I reject all Davidian's changes. For instance, I support his placing of *succothii* with *fulgens*. While he has followed a few changes made by Cullen and Chamberlain, the numbers of changes he had not made are indeed astonishing. Whether we shall ever have a classification that satisfies everyone is extremely doubtful. New so-called species based on minute botanical details are not really in anyone's interest and horticulturists with some botanical knowledge, like myself, feel that a much broader look at a plant is essential. So much is lost on a dried herbarium specimen.

Another very different happening hit the rhododendron world in the early 1980s. This was the advent of powdery mildew which reared its ugly head simultaneously in many parts of Britain, to be followed nearly everywhere else in the next year or two among major collections. Only one or two collections in remote parts of Scotland still consider themselves clear at the time of writing this, January 1989. It is now evident in many other countries including the USA. At its worst, particularly as an aftermath of a wet late summer, it can occur on a wide range of rhododendrons and some can be defoliated or even killed. It is something that we are going to have to learn to live with; we must do our best to keep it under control, perhaps by eliminating those species and hybrids that are most susceptible.

1 *Rhododendrons in their natural habitat*

HISTORY OF RHODODENDRON DISTRIBUTION AND EVOLUTION

The reasons for the present world distribution of rhododendrons is a very complex subject and no one to date has proved exactly from where they originated. Various theories are based on data from diverse angles. Continental drift, fossil remains, the association of rust fungus with rhododendrons, climatic changes and the birth of mountain ranges are all involved. As you will see, many ideas are contradictory.

The movement of land masses over the ages is a fascinating subject. There is little doubt that this is one of the most important factors which has led to the odd gaps in rhododendron distribution today and why closely related species occur which are divided by large areas of water.

The theory is that 255 million years ago, the six continents made up a single land mass called Pangaea (see article in Bibliography by Dr A. Kehr, Beltsville, Maryland, on the work of Dr E. E. Leppik). Drifting of the relatively thin Earth's crust divided Pangaea into two definite super-continents called Laurasia in the north and Gondwanaland in the south. The break occurred in the Triassic period about 200 million years ago. This is important because the first rhododendron's ancestral species evolved *after* this break. Therefore age-wise, they are relatively young compared with many other of today's plants. These newly evolved species in Laurasia were prevented from moving south by the ever widening body of water between the two continents.

According to Dr E. E. Leppik of Beltsville, Maryland, USA, (see Bibliography) spruce rust, *Chrysomyxa*, which has a secondary host to complete its life cycle on certain species of rhododendron, occurs only in the northern continents and has a common range in the districts where spruce and rhododendrons grow. This relationship evolved after Gond-wanaland separated with Laurasia and before North America broke from Eurasia. Thus rhododendrons first appeared some time after 200 million years but before 165 million years, when North America separated from Eurasia.

Leppik suggests that the genus *Rhododendron* (including azalea) prob-ably formed on the remains of the Laurasian super-continent during the Tertiary period when both super-continents were separated from each other by the Tethys Sea. A striking fact is the scarcity of rhododendrons on the Indian peninsula, considered part of former Gondwanaland, which later drifted north again. The Himalayas, rich in rhododendrons, were part of former Laurasia and separated from India proper by the immense Tethys Sea. Thus the present geographical distribution of rhododendrons agrees with the theory of continental drift. *R. arboreum* recently migrated southwards to form *nilagiricum* and *zelanicum*. Ancestral rhododendrons must have lived where *Picea* and *Tsuga* were common, on which rust fungi had their secondary hosts. It is probable that *Picea* was more closely associated with *Rhododendron* than it is today.

Fossils are, of course, one of the best means of proving the past distribution of all living things. Unfortunately, rhododendron fossils are comparatively rare and are often hard to identify as rhododendrons, let alone identifying the species. However, enough have been found to throw some light on to past distribution. David Leach says that fossil remains from Europe and North America of 50 million years ago are in substantially the same form as present-day rhododendrons in Asia. The few American survivors today are relics of a lush vegetation when the continent shared many plants with Asia. It is well known that there is a similar flora in China to America, especially south-east USA. There are various theories as to how these continents were attached and by what route these plants migrated: (1) through the Arctic Bering route; (2) a former extension of the Antarctic continent (possibly connected across Australia and South America); or (3) by lands which existed in the tropical Pacific. None of these plants occur along the southern route and this possibility has been largely ruled out, but there is strong evidence that there was once land right across the central Pacific. Many reptiles occur in southwest China similar to those in Central America, also some butterflies, moths and land shells. More creatures, such as birds and mammals, are not common to both, therefore they evolved since America and southwest Asia were separated on the mid-Pacific route. Migration by the Bering Straits route would have been expected to show marked differences that had developed during their long and adventurous journey through northern climates. Their present similarity may indicate that they migrated a long time ago through tropical routes and have lived in a climate of steady conditions. On the other hand, certain sub-arctic living things, such as *R. lapponicum* and *camtschaticum*, have undoubtedly migrated around the Bering Straits as they are so similar in both continents.

A new theory, which is not likely to win instant acceptance, is that 225 million years ago, the world had another continent called Pacifica. This is said to have started north of Australia (the latter was south-east of where it is now), migrated across the Pacific, breaking into smaller continents on its journey and eventually colliding with North and South America, which were advancing in the opposite direction. It was these impacts that threw up the Rockies and the Andes. (Article by Bryan Silcock on the theories of Drs Arnos Nur of Stanford University, California, and Zvi Ben Avraham of Weizmann Institute, Israel, 'An Idea That Moves Mountains', *Sunday Times*, (?) 1977.)

A now widely accepted theory has it that the whole Earth's surface is divided into continent-sized rock plates, which are in constant but slow motion measured in centimetres a year. These plates are seen as 'rafts' on which the continents and other parts move about. It is pointed out that the ranges around the Pacific show remarkable similarities to the collision ranges like the Himalayas. This theory provides another possible link between North and South America and South-East Asia and Australia.

The mountain ranges of the Alps and their offshoots in Europe, the

Caucasus, mountains of northern Iran and the Himalayas, were all upraised at the same period of the Earth's history. The earlier Hercynian mountain systems, including hills (of which only fragments are now left), in Germany, Brittany and parts of England, were made at the same time as the mountain group extending from south-east Tibet to Malesia. There is some doubt whether the Himalayan movements extended round the older mountains of Assam, then southwards through Burma, or whether these are an offshoot of the main Himalayan line, which may have passed across central China and eventually to Kamtschatica. The southward movement probably extended right into New Guinea in the Tertiary period, 20 to 40 million years ago.

Some conclusive evidence, including fossil records, indicates that the present centre of the genus in Asia might have been the gene centre of the genus. European species seem to have migrated to Europe from South-East Asia after the retreat of ice. The presence of rust fungi support this view. Leppik too, favours the idea of several continental bridges over the Pacific, which allowed the movement of plants from east Asia to North America and vice versa.

All this evidence seems to shoot down an odd theory of Leon Croizat (*Manual of Phytogeography*, The Hague, 1952). He maintains that all Ericaceae and Vacciniaceae and their relatives originated in the Indian Ocean area and south Pacific and spread *upwards* from Queensland. By this he presumably means Gondwanaland or that part of the original land mass of Pangaea before the split occurred. Certainly, many members of these families other than *Rhododendron* occur in New Zealand, Australia, Africa and South America. According to him, it is impossible for rhododendrons to have originated in the 'Holarctic' when the whole of Ericaceae on the map is diametrically opposed to this academic figment; and that it seems impossible that one genus could come from 'Holarctic' when all the Angiosperms move around a centre which has nothing to do with this mythical land. One may ask why genera like *Erica* and *Pernettya* in the Southern Hemisphere, did not just as likely spread southwards? Ronald Good in *The Geography of Flowering Plants* rather supports Croizat in stating that it is very rash to maintain that the genus originated in the Himalayas merely on the basis of present distribution. It is certainly true that the high concentration of rhododendrons in the Himalayas and adjacent areas is due to the present ideal conditions and partial isolation.

Occasional fossil remains are found in the Tertiary formations and forty fossil species are listed from this period and one doubtful one from late Cretaceous in the Smithsonian Institute, Washington DC. Some need further substantiation. All known localities are in central areas of distribution in Eurasia and North America. No fossils are known from New Guinea (this may mean no one has looked for them there), Australia, India or in the Miocene plants in the Redwood forests of California. *R. ponticum* can be regarded as a relic species which was once found over a much greater area. Interglacial fossil records were found in the French Alps and Greece. These almost connect present stands in east Bulgaria, European Turkey, north Turkey, the Caucasus and Lebanese mountains with those in the Spanish mountains near Algerciras and Tarifa, and, in Portugal, in Algarbia and Sierra de Monchique. This perhaps discounts the idea that the Iberian *ponticum* may have been distributed by the Moors, Carthaginians or Romans.

The Pontica (Hymenanthes Sleumer) subsection possibly migrated across the Atlantic, unlike azaleas, which probably crossed the Pacific. All this is debatable because there is a similarity in the distribution of Pentanthera (Luteum) azaleas and the Pontica subsection. If we count on all the diverse Pontica subsection as being related, *macrophyllum* and *occidentale* in the west of North America correspond, as do *maximum* and *catawbiense* with the eastern American azaleas, likewise *ponticum* with *luteum* in Eurasia. If *metternichii* (see *pp.* 16 and 247), *brachycarpum* and the others *are* closely connected with the old Ponticum sub-series, then *molle* and *japonicum* correspond nicely with these old Caucasicum subseries members in South-East Asia. Fossil remains of *luteum* have been found in Greece.

Whether rhododendrons originated in the Himalayan region or elsewhere in Laurasia is, we all admit, doubtful. What seems certain is that the original Ericaceae evolved before Gondwanaland split off from Laurasia and therefore rhododendrons evolved independently from the Ericaceae of the Southern Hemisphere. Only the Malaya Peninsula and its continuation down through Sumatra, Java and so on to New Guinea and north Australia have acted as a probable two-way flow of plants. There seems to be no evidence of any rhododendrons other than *lochae* in Australia. The elepidotes (subgenus Hymenanthus) and lepidotes (section Rhododendron) do not appear to have spread farther south than Sumatra for the former and Thailand the latter. On the other hand, the section Vireya has its centre in New Guinea and this appears to have spread north to low elevations in the Himalayan region with species such as *vaccinioides*, *santapauii* and *insculptum* and also *kawakamii* in Taiwan. As no one has so far successfully crossed this northerly group (the old Vaccinioides series) with their apparent relations in New Guinea, they may have evolved separately, or at least independently, over a long period. The obvious conclusion is that all rhododendrons other than the section Vireya have evolved and spread from Eurasia and Vireya, from New Guinea or Borneo, or both. I cannot believe that rhododendrons migrated *from* Australia *after* the Tertiary period.

During an ice age, 18,000 years ago, the sea was 90 m (300 ft) lower than today and both Taiwan and Japan were connected to Asia and to the south-east almost to Australia. This is perhaps the reason for the present distribution of the Obtusum azaleas, which are now found in mainland Asia, Taiwan, Japan, the Philippines and various minor islands. At one time, apparently, Japan drifted quite far north, while Taiwan remained close to the mainland. It is interesting, though, that the rhododendrons in Taiwan and Japan are mostly very different and in both cases have much more in common with the opposite mainland species. The conifer *Taiwania cryptomerioides* is common to Burma and Taiwan and perhaps moved east from Burma, while the Vireya section moved north and west. Dr Hsu, a botanist in Taiwan who associated with the American John Patrick when the latter collected there, believes the non-Vireya rhododendrons of Taiwan are relic populations from an eastward migration through China before the relatively recent geological separation of Taiwan from mainland China.

As mentioned above, the section Hymenathes has reached a southerly point in Sumatra and Malaya. Three species belonging to the subsection Irrorata are found here and have closely related species on the mainland farther north, thus we assume they have spread south. The Vireya section, as shown by Michael Black (who made extensive collections of Malesian rhododendrons on two expeditions), does not apparently occur in east China, not even in warm areas like Hong Kong, but it could have died out there. If the Vireyas migrated south and not north, they may have followed Black's proposed long route by the Philippines, Borneo and Java as well as down the Malaya Peninsula. Other smaller groups from different continents might include *albiflorum* from western North America and the possibly related *semibarbatum* of Japan. The old Canadense (Rhodora Sleumer) sub-series includes species that have failed to be hybridized with each other and are therefore probably not connected.

There are some doubtful fossil remains, which would be valuable if proved to be rhododendrons; one was found in California. Loess is a hopeful source of fossils. It contains innumerable impressions of plants and their roots, animals and land shells. Sir Alexander Hosie in *On the Trail of the Opium Poppy* (Vol. I, *p*. 23) said that loess is the residue of endless generations of living things mixed with sand and dust.

What effect has the climate had on distribution? The answer is a great deal. According to E. Huntingdon in *The Pulse of Asia*, the climate goes in cycles with alternating glacial and warm periods of tens of thousands of years and shorter ones of approximately 36 years – in other words it acts in a sort of pulsation. He goes on to say that most meteorologists agree that although forests conserve moisture once it has fallen, they have no appreciable effect upon the amount of rainfall and where forests have been cleared, students find no evidence that the climate has altered. Many cases have occurred where forests have died through lack of water, such as that around Lop Nor, China. Ice ages have of course wiped out whole plant populations, which often had no chance of returning to apparently suitable locations. Leppik suggests that the reason for the scarcity of rhododendrons in Europe may be due to the occurrence of mountains, which have produced glaciers moving in a northerly direction, thus not giving the plants a chance to escape southwards.

Kingdon Ward collected over a wider area (Bhutan to Szechwan) than any other collector in Asia, therefore his knowledge of rhododendrons in the wild was probably unequalled. He reckoned that *arboreum* must have been one of the earliest rhododendrons to appear in the Himalayas because of its present wide distribution. It has also evolved in such a way as to succeed over a wide variety of habitats and elevation.

This brings us to the question, which of our existing species are the most primitive? Kingdon Ward adopts the view that lepidotes (section Rhododendron) are primitive. Professor and Dr Philipson's nodal research found this group with a simple nodal structure, which supports this theory. Dr J. Hutchinson wrote (RHS–YB, 1946,*p*. 42), 'In primitive groups of plants like in the Grande and Falconeri series there is generally more waste of material in the floral parts than in those of more advanced groups.' He also maintained that there is some resemblance between these species and the family Dilleniaceae, which he considered ancestral to the Ericaceae, where the nodal structures are similar (of a complex or triacular type). Both opinions are of course speculative.

Another interesting piece of research done by Leppik was on pollination. He reckons that successive changes in floral patterns occurred mainly under selective pressure of different pollinators. He reported bird pollination occurring only in Malesia, but, of course, Kingdon Ward saw this method on many occasions in Asia (see Ecology, *p.* 27). Fossil evidence indicates that all showy (to draw pollinators) flowers were radially symmetrical in shape. Later types often show bilateral symmetry (a flower that can only be cut into equal parts vertically) and that evolution corresponded with the changes in evolution of their particular pollinators. Insects are directed in their approach in one way only to reach the nectar in bilateral flowers, while with radially symmetrical flowers, they can enter from various directions and frequently by-pass the stamens and pistil, hence the greater efficiency of the modern flower type. Many other genera have evolved to a similar pattern.

It is of interest that just about the only rhododendrons which repeatedly fail to set seed naturally here at Glendoick are many of the species and hybrids of the Pentanthera subsection of Azalea. Sometimes this is due to lack of pollen, but it is obvious that the long tubes of certain azaleas stop pollination. I have seen whole bushes without a single swollen capsule, except a branch I have hand pollinated. We must have a lack of suitable pollinators here.

Hutchinson puts the groups with few flower parts, such as stamens and corolla lobes as in Azalea and subgenus Pogonanthum (Anthopogon series), as being the most advanced. Yellow is said to be a primitive colour while the old Forrestii sub-series of the Neriiflora subsection is the most advanced in its section. He states quite sensibly that lepidotes probably evolved separately, from elepidotes, as did azaleas. The Maddenia subsection is said to be the most primitive of the lepidotes with extra stamens and ovary chambers. The reduction in stature of species is usually accompanied by a reduction in the inflorescence and stamens. It is hard to believe in his theory that the old Luteum, Tashiroi and Schilippenbachii sub-series evolved from Obtusum, although Tashiroi is perhaps a link between them. Hutchinson rightly says that the so-called primitive, large-leaved group occurs where the largest concentration of species now grows, but surely this is due to the fact that they require the rather specialized conditions that suit the majority of species best. He is also probably correct in considering that azaleas and Triflorums developed independently although they show similarities.

Kingdon Ward reckoned that the large sections are possibly older than the smaller sections, perhaps due to the fact that he thought it would have taken longer to develop the variation in the larger groups. Personally, I doubt this, because the smaller groups often occur in some degree of isolation where they have had less chance to proliferate their characters towards speciation. It is obvious that where the conditions are good, the mountains high, the valleys deep and the habitats varied, a diverse population is going to establish itself over the years. Rhododendrons are still very much in a state of evolution and provided man does not step in and destroy much of their habitat, they will continue to evolve. Man has in certain cases encouraged natural hybridity, and hence evolution and speciation, by clearing areas around rhododendrons, thus allowing populations to become established on ground previously occupied by other genera. This may bring together species not normally closely associated.

Considerable research has still to be done on the reasons for the present world distribution of rhododendrons. The various theories and speculations included here cannot be fitted together to a logical conclusion like the pieces of a jigsaw puzzle. Only by fossil discoveries in new locations and other research into the ancestry of the genus, are we likely to be able to come to any satisfactory answer.

DISTRIBUTION MAPS

The distribution maps are largely self-explanatory. The necessity to include several sections and subsections per map has meant considerable overlapping. It has been impossible to give more precise details and, of course, large areas included in the shading or rings will not have any rhododendrons at all. The sections and subsections included in each map have no botanical significance; they are only placed together for convenience. The sixth map shows the names and positions of the important rhododendron provinces of China and some adjoining countries.

ECOLOGY

In this second part of Chapter 1, I wish to give as vivid a picture as possible of the habitats of rhododendrons in the wild. It is important for the enthusiastic grower of this genus to realize how these plants behave in their native environment and know something about why their environment suits them. Only then may it become clear why rhododendrons do not thrive in mixed shrub borders with no thought given to their rather special ecological requirements. Most wild rhododendrons are found in regions of high rainfall, a humid atmosphere, a temperate climate and with a highly organic acid soil. The often saturated atmosphere, constantly moist soil and lack of sunshine has a very cooling effect on the climate. This in turn leads to the very slow mineralization of organic matter. This organic soil, generally low in elements, favours rhododendrons, which are able to flourish under conditions which are unsuitable to many other plants.

For example, the region of Pemako, south-east Tibet, with its perpetual rain and saturated atmosphere, has a wonderful wealth of flora. In the midst of the rhododendron belt at about 3,700 m (12,000 ft) there are 5 months of rain and 7 months of snow. In alpine Upper Burma at the same altitude, July and August temperatures are definitely cooler than an average English summer. Some rain falls every day in July and some most days in August, but with a little sunshine in between. September is also wet nearly every day with very little sunshine. October has about eighteen rainless days and plenty of sunshine, while November to December are the best months of the year. It so happens that most of the rhododendron

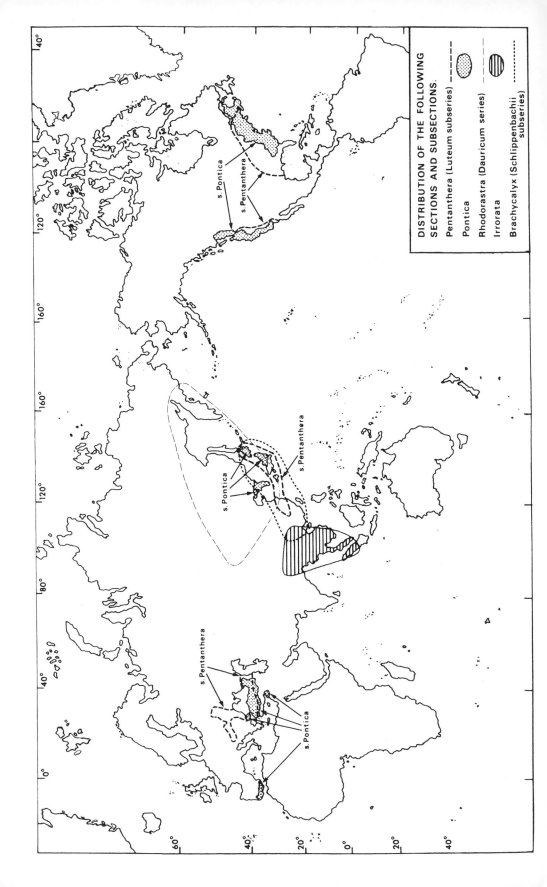

DISTRIBUTION OF THE FOLLOWING
SECTIONS AND SUBSECTIONS:

Pentanthera (Luteum subseries)

Pontica

Rhodorastra (Dauricum series)

Irrorata

Brachycalyx (Schlippenbachii subseries)

s. Pontica

s. Pentanthera

s. Pentanthera

s. Pontica

s. Pentanthera

s. Pontica

s. Pentanthera

s. Pontica

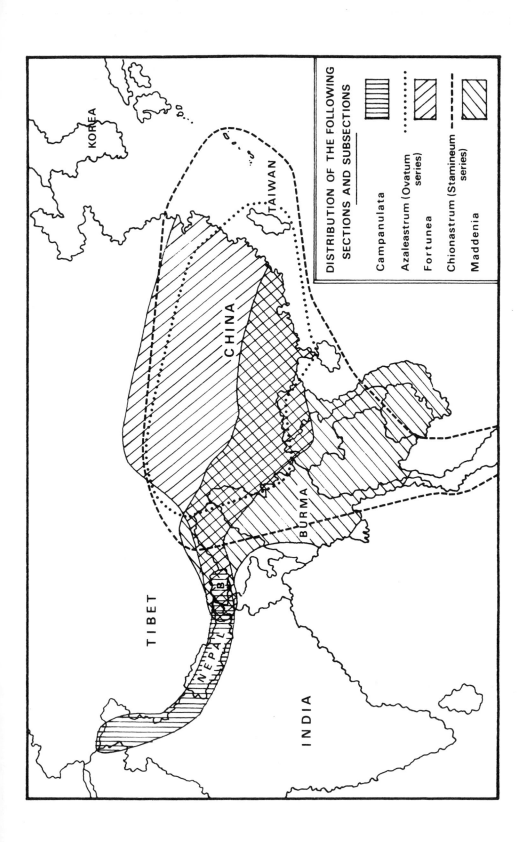

DISTRIBUTION OF THE FOLLOWING
SECTIONS AND SUBSECTIONS

Campanulata

Azaleastrum (Ovatum series)

Fortunea

Chionastrum (Stamineum series)

Maddenia

KOREA

TAIWAN

CHINA

BURMA

TIBET

NEPAL

INDIA

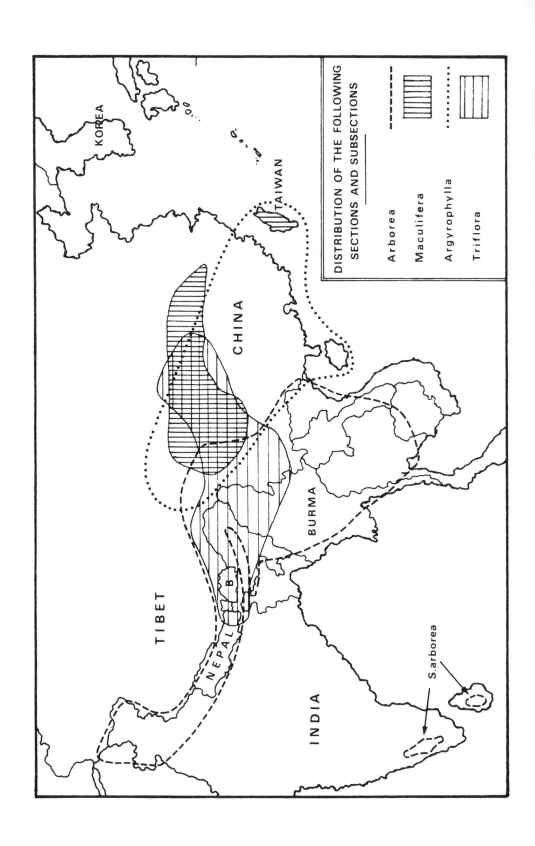

DISTRIBUTION OF THE FOLLOWING
SECTIONS AND SUBSECTIONS

Arborea

Maculifera

Argyrophylla

Triflora

KOREA

TAIWAN

CHINA

TIBET

NEPAL

B

BURMA

INDIA

S. arborea

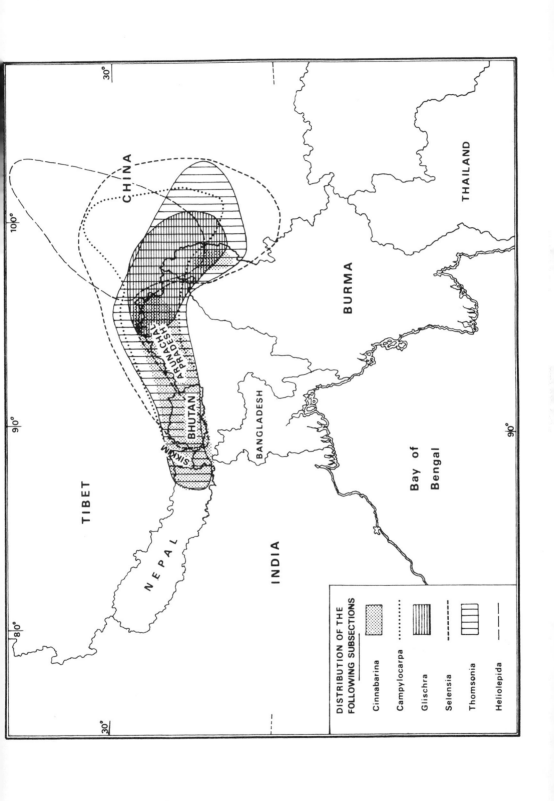

DISTRIBUTION OF THE
FOLLOWING SUBSECTIONS

Cinnabarina
Campylocarpa
Gliischra
Selensia
Thomsonia
Heliolepida

TIBET

NEPAL

CHINA

SIKKIM

BHUTAN

ARUNACHAL
PRADESH

BANGLADESH

INDIA

BURMA

THAILAND

Bay of
Bengal

30°

10°

90°

80°

30°

90°

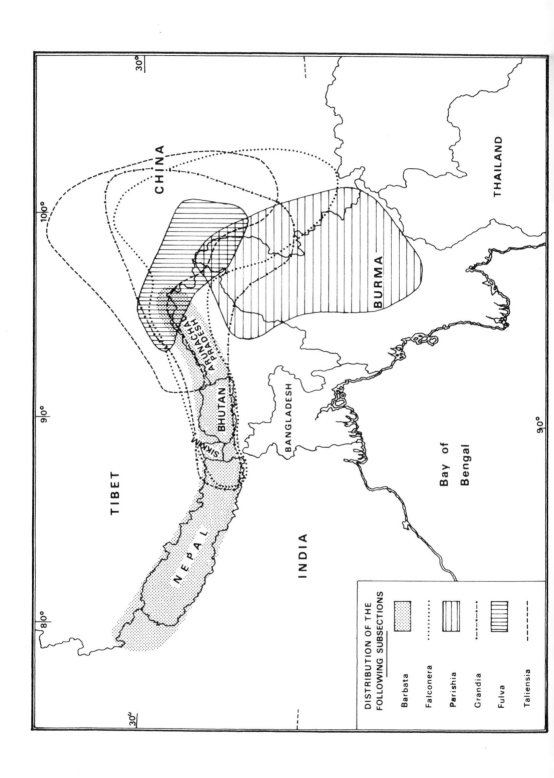

DISTRIBUTION OF THE
FOLLOWING SUBSECTIONS

Barbata ....

Falconera ....

Parishia

Grandia .—.—.—.—.

Fulva

Taliensia –––––––

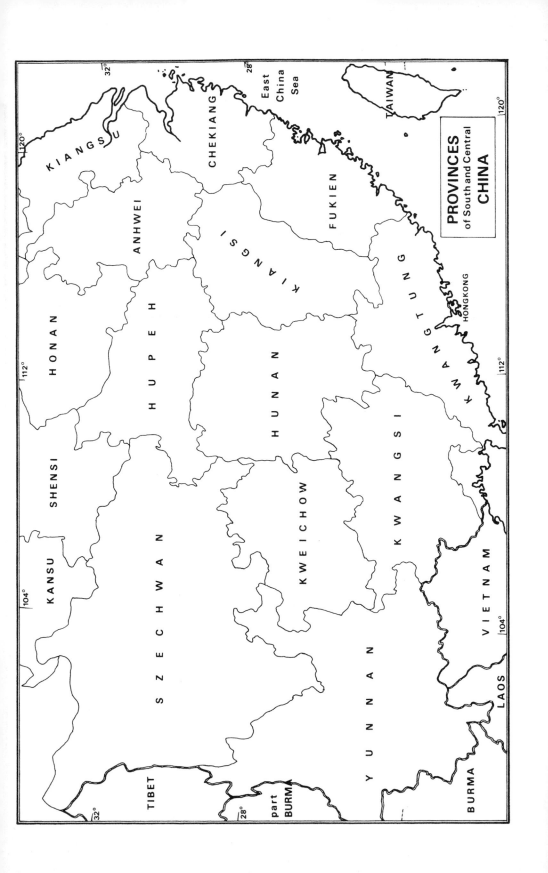

PROVINCES
of South and Central
CHINA

areas of South-East Asia receive the south-west monsoon which strikes chiefly during the period June to September inclusive. In the alpine regions, this covers the whole growing and flowering season.

Plants associated with rhododendrons

J. D. A. Stainton reports that in Nepal, rhododendrons grow in *Abies*, *Tsuga*, *Betula* and upper temperate, mixed broad-leaved forest, or they may form the dominant canopy or upper storey themselves with only irregular trees scattered among them. The same can be said throughout most rhododendron areas in South-East Asia. As in many areas farther east, the big-leaved species may form pure forests. At higher altitudes in most broken forests, several other ericaceous plants occur.

Moss and lichen are commonly associated with forest rhododendrons, and under virgin forest there is often little else. Moss occurs in the wetter regions, while sometimes, in drier areas, trees (including rhododendrons) are covered with lichen, often in long streamers. Our expedition to India in 1965 showed at first hand the tremendous development of moss. In the RHS–RYB, 1966, *p.* 70 we wrote: 'Everywhere, covering everything, was moss; thick wads of it on the upper sides of branches, drapes of it on the lower, long wisps of it hanging from twigs and leaves. In this moss-wrapping of the forest existed a whole plant community of its own.' The epiphytes growing in the moss included several rhododendrons, some of which were scented, and species of *Agapetes*, *Vaccinium*, *Smilax* and many ferns and orchids.

Sir Alexander Hosie found the unusual combination of dwarf rhododendrons and clumps of prickly pears (Opuntia) in Yunnan.

Limestone in China (and other soil)

George Forrest often reported the phenomenon of rhododendrons growing on limestone, much to the surprise of gardeners at home. He reported that the limestone in the Lichiang–Tali area of China has nothing chalky in it, but is apparently a strong magnesium limestone, greyish-white in colour, very hard and durable, such as in the Dolomites. Farther north towards Tibet (Tsarong) the strata, though still limestone, is much freer in composition, disintegrated more readily and is deeply stained ruddy-brown by the presence of minerals. The greatest concentration of rhododendrons is found here. Most rhododendrons in Yunnan grow on limestone according to Forrest, but in organic matter, even on cliffs or boulders.

Growth in relation to altitude and exposure

Various quotations give a very good idea of how rhododendrons respond to different aspects and elevations. Kingdon Ward makes an interesting observation on mountains of different heights in *Return to the Irrawaddy* (*p.* 157). 'It is quickly borne in on the explorer that the plants found on the summit of a mountain 3,700 m (12,000 ft) high are not those found at 3,700 m on a mountain 5,400 m (18,000 ft) high in the same region. On the lower mountain, there is almost certain to be an upward shift and compression of the zones, which on the loftier range are more drawn out. Moreover, the species peculiar to the lower zone may appear in almost any order within that zone, according to local climatic conditions.'

In north Yunnan, the most luxuriant rhododendrons have a north or north-east exposure. Three degrees farther south, the west flanks have the heaviest vegetation due to heavier rainfall. On east flanks over 2,700 m (9,000 ft) the vegetation is dwarf and stunted.

W. R. Sykes, in RHS–RCYB, 1954 (*p*. 62), writes of his experiences in west Nepal. 'Strongest and most vigorous plants occurred on north slopes. High up, melting snow produced enough moisture to prevent complete drying out before the monsoon breaks, in some areas not until July.'

R. E. Cooper noted in Rhododendron Society Notes, Vol. 3, No. 4, 1928 (*p*. 234), that in Bhutan, in the most arid internal valleys, a moist flora develops at 2,700 m (9,500 ft) on the side hills. Therefore, all the tops of the ridges at this elevation are crowned with moist forest containing rhododendrons. I noticed a very similar situation in north-east Turkey with very arid valleys and moist forest starting at about 1,200 m (4,000 ft). There, of course, the mountains are much lower.

It is obvious how high elevations and wind can dwarf species normally attaining much larger proportions in lower, more sheltered positions. On reading Kingdon Ward's writings and studying field notes of herbarium specimens, this is very noticeable. Even tree-like species such as *griffithianum* and *hodgsonii* can be dwarfed in exposed or otherwise unfavourable sites. It is only in sheltered forest, especially in ravines, where species reach their maximum dimensions. We saw a *hodgsonii* near Darjeeling only 90 cm (3 ft) high, full of flower, but of considerable age. The surrounding forest had been destroyed by burning and grazing.

A. D. Schilling suggests in *Rhododendrons 1972* RHS (*p*. 8) that plants close to the main Himalayan range are probably hardier than those in the foothills near the plains, even from the same altitude, because of a harsher climate. This is probably true. Moreover, plants from very high rainfall (and snow) areas tend to be more delicate than those where the snow cover is often light, thus giving less protection from wind and frost in winter.

Kingdon Ward noticed that in the Triangle, Upper Burma and elsewhere, rhododendrons have a tendency to avoid the deep gullies and to crowd on the steep ridges in between. Stainton's statement that pure stands of *grande*, *falconeri* and *hodgsonii* sometimes occur on flat ground, often surrounded by slopes with conifer forest in east Nepal, appears to be the opposite, but this is probably due to the lower rainfall in east Nepal and a different rock or sub-soil leading to better drainage. It is also probable that in the wild, they do better on ridges and slopes so as to avoid frost pockets. It should be pointed out that rhododendrons in the wild must give each other mutual protection to succeed on exposed sites.

Frost damage in the wild and the production of flowers and seeds

Rhododendrons in China and north-east Burma are often found flowering in the snow and the flowers may be frosted. Even the young growth is sometimes damaged. Kingdon Ward saw whole areas of mature-looking tree species without a sign of a flower. He reckoned that they were not able to breed due to some adverse climatic conditions. I would very much doubt this and would suspect the reverse situation in that the conditions were too good for buds to set. In cultivation, it is well known that healthy, vigorous rhododendrons, especially big-leaved species in wet localities, take longer to start to flower than those checked by some adverse effect. Plants at Glendoick tend to start flowering younger and smaller than in Argyll where the rainfall is double. On the other hand, it is possible that certain species do need to attain a given minimum size before flowering, regardless of how fast they grow. *R. sinogrande* grows very slowly at Glendoick and has taken considerably longer than average to begin to flower.

Kingdon Ward also observed that some species do not always set abundant seed after flowering. This could be due to frost or perhaps an unusually wet and cold spring leading to a lack of insect and bird pollinators. He remarked that if a plant flowers freely one year and fails to set seed, it may flower freely the following year. This bears out the value of dead-heading in cultivation.

It is suggested that the curling up of leaves of rhododendrons in cold weather is a natural mechanism, not only to reduce water loss but also to shed snow. Kingdon Ward saw *hylaeum* in full bloom standing in 30 cm (12 in.) of snow with leaves screwed into quills. Presumably this was mostly old snow, although Kingdon Ward said that two snow falls had occurred even at 1,800 m (6,000 ft) shortly before. *R. yunnanense* was observed to be completely frosted (flowers and growth) on 22 April, having snowed for 18 hours. I remember one April snow fall of 10 cm (4 in.) at Glendoick, which thawed almost at once and did practically no damage to fully opened flowers.

The older a rhododendron becomes, the later its growth buds expand. Thus, the older a plant gets, the less it is vulnerable to frost. Kingdon Ward draws attention to the way flower buds delay the breaking of leaf buds. He observed flowering plants of *wardii* with no young growth while non-flowering bushes had fully fledged young leaves. He also mentioned that the growth of young *magnificum* in the Adung Valley, Upper Burma is 2 to 3 weeks earlier than that of mature plants.

Kingdon Ward also draws our attention to the resilience of seeds to the weather when still on the parent plants. In *A Plant Hunter in Tibet*, p. 268, he writes: 'The rhododendron seeds were being frozen hard each night, the stiffened capsules which thawed out under the sun's rays each day. As the frost coated capsule softens, the seeds become soaked with moisture; no sooner do they dry out in the sun than they are frozen again as the sun drops behind the range. This alternate wetting, drying and freezing goes on night after night. I may add that all these seeds, collected in November 1933, germinated readily in England in March or April 1934.' I have even had perfect germination from seed collected off badly winter damaged plants of *lindleyi* and *edgeworthii*.

Kingdon Ward found one year that only one out of 200 to 300 bushes of *principis* (*vellereum*) had flowered. All the rest had flowered the previous year. The one bush with capsules, which were riddled with caterpillars, had but a few fertile seeds.

Lastly Sir J. J. Hooker's observations on flowering to seed ripening. (*Himalayan Journals* p. 419).

	Flowering	Seed ripening	Months	Altitude
nivale	July	September	2	4,900–5,300 m (16,000–17,000 ft)
anthopogon	June	October	4	4,000–4,300 m (13,000–14,000 ft)
campanulatum	May	November	6	3,400–3,700 m (11,000–12,000 ft)
grande	April	December	8	2,400–2,700 m (8,000–9,000 ft)

Bird pollination

I read an article recently (Dr E. E. Leppik, ARS Bulletin, 1972, *p.* 229) that stated that only in Malesia is bird pollination of rhododendrons known. The following reports surely prove otherwise.

Sykes states that the flowers of *arboreum* in Nepal attract many birds such as sunbirds, tits, flycatchers and laughing thrushes. Kingdon Ward makes frequent references to birds' interest in rhododendron flowers. In *A Plant Hunter in Tibet, pp.* 111–12, 'Small birds constantly visited the rhododendron flowers, burying their heads in them to get at the insects which are to be found on the honey and would come out with their heads dusted with pollen and go off to another flower, thereby pollinating it. *R. wardii* and *beesianum* were constantly visited by birds'. In *Plant Hunters Paradise, p.* 117, he says that *kendrickii* (*pankimense*) attracted birds more than any other species, especially sunbirds. Here he says they were after nectar. Other nectar-hunting birds were the Yunnan Sibia, the Yukina and the Yunnan green-backed tit. Pollen was collected on the head and throat. On page 121 he vividly describes the methods of the Nepalese yellow-backed Sunbird. 'This last must have been designed by nature for the purpose of robbing flowers of their honey. Clinging upside down to a flower stalk of *pankimense*, he would thrust his big, curved beak up into the pendant bell, tweeting with pleasure all the while. He also visited the pale almost tropical-looking flowers of *stenaulum*, but his greatest feat was to sip honey in mid-air, hovering with a quiver of gorgeous wings like a humming-bird.' He went on to mention that the clumsy Sibia, not being so well adapted for sucking nectar, was inclined to batter the flowers cruelly. The common Yunnan green-backed tit was also observed to use force and was responsible for perforating the base of the corolla to the extent that the corollas fell off. This is exactly the same type of damage tits do to flowers in Britain, especially red flowered varieties. How interesting that tits should develop the same habit on alien plants imported from almost the other side of the world.

Altogether, Kingdon Ward recognized six species of birds habitually visiting rhododendron flowers and carrying pollen in this area. Only those with large funnel or bell-shaped corollas attract birds and those seen were mainly below 2,100 m (7,000 ft). Most alpine species are ill-adapted to bird pollination. In other areas he saw *arboreum*, *arizelum* and *delavayi* being visited by birds including a spotted woodpecker, nuthatch and a species of parrotbill.

The grotesque shape of trunks

In cultivation, the large species, especially under woodland conditions, tend to form fine, more or less erect trunks. In the wild, this is far from being universal.

I have not had the opportunity when looking at wild rhododendrons to assess how common an occurrence these queer-shaped trunks are, but I do remember noticing that semi-dwarf species in the Alps and north-east Turkey had long, more or less horizontal branches always pointing down the hill. In the Himalayas, nearly all the big species we saw had an erect habit although some plants of *maddenii* had trunks growing horizontally before turning up towards the sky.

Kingdon Ward makes several references in his writings about unusual growth forms. In *Return to the Irrawaddy* (*p.* 166), he writes: 'On the precipitous flanks and narrow crests of the higher hostile ridge, their trunks grow out at any angle between the vertical and the horizontal–often at about 45°. This is curious, because they presently turn erect and bear proudly aloft the great weight of their crown, burdened in spring with an immense load of flowers. . . . All of them, whatever their stature, are massive trees, whose gnarled and knotted limbs indicate their great age. It is as though the weight of years had bowed them down. On a branch of *arizelum* 45 cm (18 in.) in circumference, I counted 75 rings. This gives for a specimen 1.65 m (65 in.) in circumference, an age of over 250 years. No doubt older trees exist!' Elsewhere he mentions the bare red trunks of *arizelum* which grew along the ground before they curved upright. The limbs were almost horizontal, about breast high and were very difficult to climb over or under.

Kingdon Ward suggests that this may be due to the quest for light. This may be so on very steep ridges, but surely the weight of snow is the most likely cause as was obviously the reason on the plants I saw, mentioned earlier. Minor avalanches in the forests might also bend younger plants right over or even uproot them, resulting in growth starting from plants lying at all odd angles.

Reproduction in the wild

Rhododendrons are normally very prolific seed producers. In nature, insects consume a proportion of the seeds before they ripen, but by and large, the majority reach maturity and are scattered widely. The different types of seeds were discussed in *Dwarf Rhododendrons* (*p.* 24). Among the larger species, most belong to the forest and epiphytic types; the former have small-winged large seeds and the latter seeds with large or long wings, which are naturally the more buoyant of the two in the air and have more chance to blow into the mossy crevices of trunks and rocks. This moss is by far the commonest seed bed for rhododendrons and the big-leaved species in particular germinate by the thousand along fallen trunks, on mossy rocks and ground and on horizontal mossy limbs. Kingdon Ward remarks on the abundance of seedlings of *montroseanum*, *sinogrande* and *magnificum* while we saw huge numbers of *grande*.

Many of these seedlings are able to grow for a while in fairly shady conditions under or near their parents, but unless the canopy is broken by falling branches or whole plants, these seedlings have little chance of reaching flowering size.

When man steps in and makes clearings for roads, grazing or other purposes, the whole situation changes. Roadside verges often make excellent seed beds for all sorts of plants and may be the only source of seedlings where roads cut through virgin or secondary growth forest. We found a splendid crop of *falconeri* seedlings on a road verge near Darjeeling. On the other hand, heavy grazing usually halts all natural regeneration of rhododendrons. In Turkey we saw very few small seedlings indeed, while above Darjeeling, there were few if any seedlings in grazed areas.

Disease in the wild

Kingdon Ward gives several examples of disease in the wild. He noticed a form of 'blister blight' on *uvarifolium*. These were nasty leprous, bulging white pustular inflammations, obviously highly infectious, and the blight attacked other ericaceous shrubs, such as *Lyonia ovalifolia*. He also encountered blister blight (*Exobasidium*) in Manipur on *arboreum* and *johnstoneanum*.

Certain fungi attack indumentum, often turning it black. Sir Isaac Bayley Balfour suggested that this frequently abundant fungus may act as a nitrogen fixer for rhododendrons and reckoned it might be connected with some benefit to rhododendrons on limestone.

Different rusts are found on rhododendrons in various parts of the world (see History of Rhododendron Distribution and Evolution, *p*. 11).

The beauty of rhododendrons in the wild

Here are a few vivid descriptions showing the beauty of rhododendrons in their natural habitat.

C. R. Lancaster in *Rhododendrons* 1972, *p*. 30, BLM Expeditions to Nepal: 'In a sheltered gully in the Bagang Khola we walked early one morning through a small wood composed entirely of *hodgsonii*. The majority had superb 6–9 m (20–30 ft) tall trunks with cinnamon and pink-tinged bark peeling in large sheets as the American Paper Birch (*Betula papyrifera*). The ground beneath was patched with freshly fallen snow and this, heightened by the slanting shafts of wakening sun, painted a picture and memory we shall never forget.'

Sir Alexander Hosie states in *On the Trail of the Opium Poppy* (Vol. II, *p*. 104): 'Nowhere have I seen a more magnificent show of flowers than the blossoms of the scarlet and lavender-coloured rhododendrons on the high slopes of the Huo-sheo-p'n valley.' He also reported red and white flowers. This was in Kweichow, a rather ignored Chinese province botanically.

Forrest reports on *traillianum* on a spur of Bei-ma-shan in Yunnan where he saw a belt of 4.8 km (3 miles) of this species on over 305 m (1,000 ft) of altitude, flowering so well as to give a veiled silvery sheen in the distance.

Lastly, on our expedition to north-east India in 1965 'R. grande (*C&H* 431) soon began to appear, magnificent trees in full flower varying from cream to pale yellow, sometimes with a strong pink tinge. The trees were often as much as 15 m (50 ft) high with trunks 60 cm (2 ft) in diameter;

they were a magnificent sight wherever a view could be had, although standing under them one could scarcely see anything but the trusses silhouetted against the sky and well out of reach.'

CONSERVATION IN THE WILD*

It is indeed fortunate for those of us who love rhododendron species, that the majority grow wild in remote mountainous habitats, often unpleasantly wet and therefore in places that are among the last to be disturbed by the greedy and ever destroying hand of man. How often one reads in collectors' field notes of rhododendrons growing on cliffs, among boulders, in ravines and other sites, which are either impossible to get at or at least should be relatively free from depredation.

Another lucky factor in the survival of the majority of species is that nearly all have fairly wide distributions as well as the ability to make use of many different habitats (see Ecology, *p.* 17). Thus if a species is wiped out in one area, due to flooding of a valley for instance, or complete destruction of the forest, there is every chance that it will survive elsewhere although special forms and variations may disappear.

The main reasons for a species being in danger of extinction in the wild, be it a mammal, bird, reptile, or plant, is not from the specific collection or destruction of that individual species, but from the devastation of whole eco-systems. As we all know, this is going on at a most alarming rate throughout the world and to my mind this is the worst result of the appalling increase in the human population coupled with drastic over-exploitation of many of our natural resources.

It is rare that rhododendrons are singled out for any form of deliberate culling in an otherwise little disturbed plant community. There is certainly some truth that the wholesale collection of all plants small enough to handle by plant collectors and nurserymen, has and still is taking place, ·especially in the USA where vast quantities of *catawbiense* were dug for years. Also, there is a tendency for specially selected clones to be dug and moved to gardens. By all means dig if the locality is to be bulldozed for a car park, but surely it is better to collect propagating material if the area is thought to be safe from developers.

Rhododendrons have few known uses other than their horticultural value and natural beauty. Much has been written on the use of rhododendrons in drugs, notably the dwarf *aureum* (*chrysanthum*). Certain dwarfs from the Himalayas have leaves that are used for incense. The indumentum of *lanatum* was used for lamp wicks in Tibet and *aureum* is even used as a tea substitute. The flowers of some species are occasionally eaten in the Himalayas, especially *thomsonii*, while in the Tali area of China, the flowers of *decorum* were eaten under the name of 'white flowered vegetable'. In Tibet they sucked the juices out of the flowers of *cinnabarinum*, which are said (I have not tried!) to taste rather like sorrel. The wood of some large species is sometimes used for woodwork, such as wooden spoons and yak saddles and in World War Two, huge root burls were dug up in America and used by pipe makers as a substitute for briars and

---

* See 'Rhododendron Conservation throughout the World', Peter A. Cox AMRS–QB, Vol. 25, No. 25, April 1971, *p.* 92 and RHS Journal, August 1971, *p.* 362.

thorns and the wood was used for tool handles. Sheep and cattle sometimes eat the less poisonous species.

All these rather minor uses are really of little consequence and even
browsing of wild animals, chiefly deer which are not poisoned by
rhododendron, may just occasionally affect the establishment of young
seedlings. The real threat comes directly from man. In North America,
the forester considers *maximum* takes up too much valuable space which
could be used for silviculture. It is estimated that 1.2 million hectares (3
million acres) of the southern Appalachians are covered with dense
thickets of this species and *Kalmia latifolia. R. maximum* is an aggressive
species (like *ponticum* in parts of Britain) when it comes to seizing and
retaining control of the land and the wind can carry the (approximate)
5,000,000 seeds to 500 g (1 lb.) considerable distances. While it is valuable for its aesthetic appeal and for the protection it offers to wildlife and
watersheds, it is considered a forest weed and many foresters want to limit
this species to much lesser areas than it covers today.

In Europe, shepherds dislike the poisonous Alpine species, which
cover large areas of what they consider would make good grazing ground.
In the Himalayas, many less remote areas are systematically cleared of
forest, largely for grazing. Stainton reports from Nepal that when *Abies*
forest is burnt, dense thickets of bamboo often spring up, thereby pre-
venting the grazing that the trees may have been burnt to create. It is
unfortunate that rhododendrons produce good firewood and I have to admit
to being kept warm in front of a rhododendron fire myself when in India!

The same story is told by collectors and travellers who visit such places
as Malaya and New Guinea. There, the destruction of the virgin and even
secondary forest goes on at an alarming rate. In Malaya, tree species such
as *wrayi* gradually become rarer, while in New Guinea, the adaptable,
normally epiphytic, species often take to ground when the forest is
removed, there to be burnt in grass fires or grubbed up for agriculture. In
the Khasi Hills of north-east India, the scrub, which includes *formosum*, is
cut, placed on potato fields and burnt for its potassium content. In Nova
Scotia much of the most northerly locality of *maximum* has been destroyed by lumbering, while in the eastern USA, a large parking lot was
made by the National Forest Service right in the middle of a splendid
patch of excellent forms of *calendulaceum*. Large clumps of this species at
low elevations have disappeared in recent years. Some are removed for
building sites, some are moved to gardens and some are apparently
removed by the passion of 'clearing out the woods'.

There were reports of white forms of *macrophyllum* being numerous in
the Coos Bay area of Oregon along the coast. Now, only the very
occasional white is to be found. In west Nepal, much of the *arboreum*
forest is being destroyed by indiscriminate burning, felling and grazing
along with the associated *Quercus incana* forest. On the other hand,
Stainton reckons that much of the pure *arboreum* forest now found in
many parts of Nepal may originate because other tree species have been
felled, especially away from the rain-soaked ridges of east Nepal. In the
Adung Valley, Burma–Tibet frontier, Kingdon Ward reported whole
hillsides burnt, with even parts of the fir forest being set alight at 2,700 m
(9,000 ft) – hunters were probably responsible. Many rhododendrons

must have been wiped out in China by the ever-increasing terracing of the hillsides.

Having looked at the black side of the survival of rhododendrons in the wild, let us now examine the brighter side. As I mentioned earlier, rhododendrons are by and large very adaptable and often survive or even benefit from the burning or felling of the surrounding forest canopy. Forrest, on an early expedition, found an area of dense forest with an undergrowth of straggly rhododendrons. Some years later, he discovered that the forest had all been burnt and the rhododendrons had grown away from their roots and made beautiful symmetrical bushes full of flower. In other places, rhododendron seedlings may grow by the thousand as when Kingdon Ward found *magnificum* seedlings 'crammed together like citizens of London in the rush hour'. Dr Frank Mossman makes an interesting observation on *occidentale*. It seems capable of waiting interminable periods for the surrounding vegetation to fall or burn down and may live to be a great age. The above ground parts may be burnt or cut off, but the crown lives on to produce new and vigorous canes, which soon produce a riot of colour. Many of these cleared areas of forest occur in both eastern and western USA. In the east, they are often mountain tops known as 'balds' and in many cases no one seems to know how these patches came to loose their forest canopy, although it is suspected that they result from earlier Indian grazing. The azaleas love these open spaces and flourish and multiply. S. D. Coleman had a theory that by clearing large areas of forest, man encouraged the numerous azalea species to hybridize seminaturally, as natural barriers between colonies are often removed. This could be so as these balds are invariably covered with hybrid swarms in a multitude of different colours. In California and southern Oregon, the best *occidentale* stands are found in openings cleared of forest. In both cases, if the supremacy of the azaleas is to be kept going, steps have to be taken to keep the forest trees from taking over again. Various national forest and state parks have stands of these species inside their boundaries, some especially designated for the preservation of the best colonies.

In other parts of the world, occasional efforts are made at conservation. In Sikkim, where *niveum* is or was down to a handful of plants, a special preservation plot was declared. A large reserve was apparently set up to preserve flora and fauna in Yunnan, China. Some people are trying to save the rarest species from extinction in Hong Kong while on the island of Yakushima in Japan, it is forbidden to collect plants of *yakushimanum*.

Much more can and should be done by creating reserves before it is too late. It so happens that the great majority of rhododendron species come from the heavily populated countries of India, China, Japan and Indonesia. Here, population pressure leads to every available piece of suitable (and sometimes unsuitable) ground being utilized for food production. All we can do is to hope that some people care enough to see that a few areas at least are preserved and any chance we may have to further this enlightenment should be greatly encouraged.

COLLECTING WILD RHODODENDRONS

This is a subject that is hard for me to limit to a few words. Having seen and collected wild rhododendrons myself in India, Turkey, different parts of Europe and very briefly in the USA* and also read many books on collecting, it has been all too easy to become engrossed in the subject. Also, I was lucky enough to know Frank Ludlow and George Sherriff very well. My father had vivid memories of his own expedition to Burma with Farrer. I briefly met Kingdon Ward and Dr Rock when they were old men and I was, unfortunately, only a keen but ignorant adolescent.

Rhododendrons, wherever they grow wild, are such a varied and interesting genus that even the best-known species native to one's own or adjacent countries still deserve considerable study and the searching for special clones and forms. To give an example, *occidentale*, so ably hunted for and documented by Britt Smith and Dr Frank Mossman, still warrants much more work done on it. Every time they search, even in well-trodden areas, they find exciting new variations. On two consecutive days in 1971, they found the nearest to red clones of both *occidentale* and *macrophyllum*. They give much valuable advice on the way to set about collecting *occidentale* and the equipment to take. Search along streams and swampy areas or on hillsides where there are springs or streams. The hardly varying, penetrating, sweet fragrance should be searched for and it is especially obvious in early morning or late afternoon. Wear thick trousers and leather gloves are advisable. Take also a compass, map, whistle, food, camera, polythene bags and notebook. New colonies are still being located of this and the eastern American species. The various different and unusual forms of *occidentale* are often found associated in groups. All persistently double-flowered clones were found by Smith and Mossman within an area of 300 m (330 yds) diameter. Several oddities in other species crop up in the wild and have been reported recently from Japan and other parts of the USA. Many are not, of course, of special horticultural merit. No doubt similar curiosities (such as no corolla) could be found throughout the whole genus.

Unless an area of wild rhododendrons or azaleas is about to be destroyed for development, I cannot support the lifting of any large plants. By all means take natural layers, suckers, scions or cuttings so long as the removal of these is unlikely to have any lasting effect on the health of the parent. Where self-sown seedlings are plentiful and only a few are likely to reach maturity, I see no reason why a limited number should not be collected. Seedlings on roadside verges may of course be collected with no fears of over-exploitation as they will be destroyed sooner or later anyway, except where they are obviously being encouraged for checking erosion. By roadside verges, I mean the area between the road and the permanent vegetation farther back, which is usually kept clean.

If collecting of larger plants is justified, avoid those with large tops where possible, or prune them back to even the balance between shoots and roots. Always dig carefully – an excellent weapon in addition to a spade is an ice axe which is a marvellously versatile tool in wild country. Layers (man-made or natural) and any small plant with poor roots collected in the growing season may have to have their tops reduced but leave some foliage on evergreen species. These may be planted in a shady position and copiously watered or, if small, be potted up and placed under mist, fog, or in a closed frame. Those lifted in the dormant season are, of course, more easily handled, but still require careful looking after. *R*.

* Also collected in Nepal, Bhutan and three times in China.

occidentale can have roots and top pruned in June and be successfully transplanted later having made short new top growth. In August, there is a period of relative dormancy when they can be moved. Some species may not break readily from old wood so cannot be treated in this way.

Michael Black suggests that collecting Malesian rhododendrons involves different techniques from those of temperate regions. There is no question of spending a whole season in the field, watching the plants flower and then gathering the seed harvest in the autumn. Rhododendrons in Malesia flower all the year round and seed can ripen at any time. Also seed of the Vireya section is only viable for a few weeks. So trips of short duration are the order of the day with emphasis being placed on the collection of cuttings, which may be collected off selected plants in flower (most Vireyas root easily) or seedlings. Naturally, all these need to be despatched by air as quickly as possible. As many species will be seen out of flower and the majority in forested areas are epiphytic, one's eye has to be carefully trained into spotting rhododendron foliage.

Wherever collecting is done and for whatever purpose, always make copious notes and give each individual gathering a number. The late Tse Ten Tashi of Sikkim at the end of the 1960s and early 1970s, sent a quantity of wild collected seed through Britt Smith to many rhododendron growers, mostly through the American Rhododendron Society seed exchange. Not only were there no field notes, but none of the seed packets had a collector's number. He took some nice photographs but there was no way of correlating those with the seed packets. As valuable as these collections undoubtedly still are, they have lost so much through this lack of data.

Ideally, every number collected should have details of locality, elevation, habitat and a plant description of characters that will not be noticeable on the herbarium specimen. The description may include such items as colour of the flowers and its various parts, colour of bark and leaves, habit, height and aroma.

A coloured photograph is a valuable addition. Instructions on how to make dried specimens are available from any herbarium, but I should like to point out that it is worthwhile taking trouble to make good specimens. The actual selection of material is important. Try to select an average plant in the area. If there is a great variation, take two or more specimens and either give them separate numbers or make them A, B and so on. If seed, cuttings or plants are to be collected later on, carefully mark those to be gathered with something easily seen.

Collecting wild material for cultivation within the country of origin is obviously simple, compared with transportation over a long distance from overseas. The restrictions for the importation of plants varies enormously from country to country. It is not worth trying to smuggle in collections of wild material and it is nearly always possible (to date) to get permits to import rhododendrons, although in some cases roots need to be washed and even fumigation may be necessary. Export permits and/or health certificates may be needed from the countries of origin. New conservation measures are being introduced in certain countries banning the collecting of certain wild plants and these rules should, of course, be strictly adhered to.

Early importations of rhododendrons from the East were nearly all by seed. Now, with air travel, live plants, cuttings and scions have become possible. Rhododendrons are at present relatively free of disease in cultivation and it is well to consider the fact that there are several diseases and strains of diseases not yet introduced from the wild, such as types of rust, flower blight and galls. These would be all too easily brought in on live material and I sometimes think that restrictions for the importation of plants into Britain are perhaps rather lax.

Few expeditions nowadays manage to spend a full season in the field. This is sad because it is the best way to collect a good representation of what is available. The short trips to Nepal, for instance, either go in spring to see the flowers or autumn to collect seed and both are far from perfect. A pre-monsoon visit to north-east India was made by Peter Hutchison, my wife and myself in 1965. This meant gathering what old seed was still clinging to the opened capsules and transporting seedlings in full growth. As it happened, we were fairly lucky with both. The seed (we managed to get some of most of the species we found) germinated reasonably well when sown without delay. Old seed may be collected fairly successfully as late as April or May, but not after the rainy season has set in. The seedlings were able to be whisked through the heat of Calcutta with remarkably little delay and flown home instead of our luggage, which went by sea. Losses were under 10 per cent.

Naturally, seedlings in full growth have to be handled and watered very carefully. We wrapped the roots of these in a ball of moss tied around with cotton and placed them in trays. Unfortunately, these trays were tipped up and the seedlings finished in a heap at one end. The best way to transport small seedlings is to tie them down to flat bamboo interwoven mats, which fit in layers into a tall basket. Each mat is held in place with wire on route and then taken out again overnight to be watered. The tall baskets can be used for carrying in the wild and for transporting overseas and it does not matter what angle they are subjected to for short periods.

Collectors have different methods of covering territory and collecting seed. The highly organized use of native labour by Forrest and to a lesser extent Rock, is never likely to be repeated. The real object now is to select especially fine or unusual forms, unless the area is botanically virgin country where every species found could be something new or at least different from those in cultivation. Rock generally tried to gather each seed number from one plant only, although his herbarium specimens do not unfortunately always match the seedlings. Kingdon Ward usually took handfuls of seeds off a number of plants and in the case of variable species like *triflorum* 'Mahogany', a multitude of variations have emerged. Of course, even one individual plant can throw a very diverse family of seedlings.

Much has been written of the hazards of collecting plants. Not only are there the rigours of weather, insects, difficult country and illness to put up with, but it is also extremely hard work, before, during and after the expedition. So much research, correspondence and preparation are necessary beforehand. The work in camp after the hard day's travelling and collecting can include pressing new specimens, changing wet paper for dry, drying wet paper (sometimes under soaking conditions), writing notes, treating sores and bites, planning the next day's operations, settling disputes with one's staff and even acting as doctor to their various ailments.

Here are a few other hints on collecting. Some idea of the colour of a flower of a plant in tight bud may be had by cutting a bud open. If the crumpled corolla has a streak or mottle of crimson, it is probably some shade of red to crimson; if orange, the flowers may be yellow; if pale yellow, they may be white. Dwarf species are more likely to lose all their seeds at an early date than the large forest species.

Where are the best places to collect? Parts of China and Tibet are now opening up to tourists and occasional botanical parties, though at present (1989), collecting is officially banned by the Chinese government. Kingdon Ward guessed that there were at least 50 to 100 good species and varieties to be discovered when he wrote 'Collector's Commentary' in *The Rhododendron*, Vol. I (Leslie Urquhart Press, 1958). Seeing that Peter Hutchison, my wife and I collected three of these on one small ridge in 1965, I feel that this is probably an under-estimation, even with the present policy of amalgamating many closely related plants previously recognized as separate species. Kingdom Ward went on to say that far greater areas of Sino-Himalaya remain unexplored than have been botanized. Wilson reckoned that in south-east China, in the interior provinces of Fokien and adjacent mountains of Chekiang, Kiangsi and Kwangtung, the flora is among the least known (to us) of the whole of China. This probably remains so to the present day and an expedition to this region could be well worthwhile. Even though the mountains do not rise above about 2,100 m (7,000 ft), many of the plants should be hardy. Forrest heard that the country north-west and west of Batang, China, was very promising rhododendron territory with a vast undulating plateau everywhere clothed with rhododendrons, to the exclusion of almost everything else.

It is not surprising that certain parts of Arunachal Pradesh (North-East Frontier Agency or north and east Assam) have never been explored as many of these and other untouched areas have the wettest climate and most difficult terrain to traverse. The Lohit district, bordering Tibet and Burma is extremely steep and inaccessible country. Pemako in the Tsangpo Gorge area is exceptionally wet and difficult to reach and, being in Tibet, is hopeless at present. Dapha Bum, Lohit Division of Arunachal Pradesh, was, until recently, in an uninhabited area with no paths. Arunachal Pradesh consists of tribal areas, which were hardly administered by the British, and are now kept strictly out of bounds to foreigners by India.

Understandably, previous collectors often attempted to approach these wet and inhospitable regions from the dry side, coming over the passes from Tibet. In many cases, the high country has been the best explored in China, Burma and the Himalayas. This was not only to collect hardy plants, but to avoid many of the unpleasant aspects of the lower, forested, monsoon-facing slopes infested with leeches, snakes, biting insects, incessant dampness and dangers from disease. Those wishing to find brand new species and varieties must be prepared to brave the rigours of these tormenting mountains to claim their prizes. See also p. 373–4.

2 *Larger species in the garden*

Few people have much choice when it comes to choosing a site for their garden, especially if the only available area is the surrounds of the house. In some localities it is still possible to either buy a plot of derelict woodland or come to some agreement with the owner of such a piece of land.

For the majority of larger species of rhododendron, the first essentials are good shelter and moderate shade. The degree of shade necessary depends entirely on the climatic conditions prevailing. Shade is needed for three related purposes (climate and shade are covered in more detail later in this chapter). The first is to provide shade from the heat of the sun. The second is to modify cold temperatures, especially unseasonable late spring and early autumn frosts. The third is to protect the plants from winter sun, which can be so damaging in cold regions, and from early morning sun after frost during the flowering and growing seasons.

There may be no choice as far as soil is concerned. In many districts there is nothing but heavy clay or neutral loam lacking in organic matter. In these cases, every effort must be made to improve the soil for rhododendrons to enable them to flourish (see Soil preparation and drainage, *p*. 67). A few alkaline areas are lucky enough to have patches of acid 'green sand' and these are well worth searching for. Any soil naturally rich in organic matter (except for a few alkaline peats) is, of course, desirable but may need to be drained, while any type of moderately acid 'medium loams' can be made good with very little trouble.

Most people who start a garden from scratch and wish to build up a collection of rhododendron species find their site falling into two main categories, old woodland or old agricultural ground developed for housing. Some people may of course have an old garden with few, if any, rhododendrons present at the start. For those with an old field site, my advice is, plant trees and other shelter first, then wait *at least* 5 years, preferably longer, before attempting large species. In the intervening years, plant sun lovers, such as the hardiest dwarf rhododendrons, azaleas, hardy shrubs, alpines or annuals. A good suggestion is fairly temporary shrubs, such as brooms.

Woodland will be certain to need some thinning, tidying up and perhaps even draining before the best environment can be made out of the available site.

Generally speaking, the larger the leaves are of the species to be planted, the higher the perfection of shelter and shade conditions must be attained. It is only in very wet and/or mild and relatively sunless areas, like parts of the west of Scotland, that large-leaved species can be grown in open glades with any chance of lasting success. The amount of wind these plants will stand can vary strongly. I have seen several flourishing plantings in various parts of Britain, which were open to the wind from one direction but not to the prevailing wind. Provided that the site is not a real wind tunnel, or where the wind swirls, it may prove satisfactory. Try a few plants to begin with as a trial. Then ask the question, are the leaf petioles frequently broken and the leaves blown off? If so, then the site is unsuitable without additional shelter.

Before any action is taken on felling, clearing and planting, get to know the proposed location intimately. Examine the wind effects from every direction, watch how the sun shines into the area at all seasons and examine the soil during wet and dry periods to see how much it becomes waterlogged or dries out. If there is existing shelter in the form of *ponticum*, laurels, other evergreens or thickets of deciduous scrub, be very careful not to clear too much of this, especially in the early stages of planting. Cut bays in it and gradually cut the scrub back as the plants grow.

Test the soil for depth, consistency, pH and major elements and find out what corrections or additions might be advisable to create ideal conditions for rhododendrons. Check on the species of trees present (if any) and plan to remove those least desirable for rhododendrons where possible (see the later section of this chapter on Shelter, shade and hardiness). Try to decide at an early stage before planting starts, what additional main trees, shrubs and shelter plants are essential for the framework of the garden. Last but not least, watch and test how frost and ground draughts behave. Find out which parts are prone to the lowest temperatures and which to autumn and spring frosts. These are not necessarily one and the same. By a thorough inspection and correlation of all these factors, very many mistakes and even disasters may be avoided. I have to admit that we fell into the trap of planting tender rhododendrons too quickly in our supposedly mild and sheltered west of Scotland plot with dire consequences. Having learned our lesson, I now try to stop others from making the same mistake.

To grow especially tender species (ones that are definitely considered just too tender for your locality), very special micro-climates must be provided. After all the mild winters up to 1977, it was too easy to become progressively bolder over what was tried out of doors. Geoffrey Gorer of Haywards Heath, Sussex, England did much experimenting with the use of walls and favoured corners. Members of the Maddenia subsection are the species he usually tried in these situations but allied species like *camelliiflorum* and such subsections as Choniastrum and Azaleastrum (Stamineum and Ovatum series) are well worth attempting. Gorer advised north and west walls or areas protected by hedges or thick shrubs to the south and east. These appear to be the coldest parts of the garden where the snow lies longest. Sunny, hot sites such as the base of south walls are usually fatal. Overhanging evergreens like hollies are desirable for protection of these often epiphytic species. Although moderately drought resistant, too much overhang, such as house eaves give, leads to over-dry conditions. Walls facing any direction give some protection and provided there is sufficient shade and shelter, even south and east walls may be better than nothing. Plants grown there can be regularly watered by hand. Alas, most of Geoffrey Gorer's tender plants died between 1978 and 1981.

Each subsection, or part thereof, differ in what to it is an ideal situation. The small-leaved Triflora and Heliolepida appreciate a good proportion of sun and can tolerate drier and more windy conditions than most others. The Cinnabarina need rather more moisture and shelter but should not be given too much shade; nor should the Arborea subsection which become leggy in shade and lose their well-clothed appearance. Likewise the Thomsonia, Fortunea and Taliensia subsections should not be grown in much shade and the Thomsonia insist on particularly good drainage. The majority of species lose their shapely habit if not given ample light in our Scottish climate. Exceptions are the more tender species, such as *griffithianum*, *hookeri* and *hylaeum*, which need extra protection in most areas. The Barbata and Irrorata subsections often make their growth early in the season so need special defences against wind and early morning sun. The larger-leaved Grandia, Falconera and Fulva subsections vary considerably in hardiness and times of growth, but protection is essential in most districts for optimum results. The majority of the Campanulata and Lactea subsections do enjoy favoured conditions, while the larger members of the Pontica subsection really do best in some shade. The Maddenia subsection, many being epiphytic in nature, appreciate perfect drainage and abundant or pure organic matter. In damp, mild climates, try planting these in the forks of trees in moss, on old stumps, mossy rocks and cliffs, tree fern stems and logs and cork oak bark (*Quercus suber*). Even in mild, drier climates, old rotten stumps are ideal sites for these species.

When there are a number of plants to spare of some borderline hardy or difficult species, try planting them in as many different sites as are available. One or two only may succeed.

SUITABLE AREAS FOR SPECIES, DISTRICT BY DISTRICT

The following notes on various places where rhododendrons are grown do not necessarily give the same information on each. They are more in the form of random notes about temperatures, rainfall, soil, suitable species and other relevant information.

Britain

Maritime climate, rain falls spasmodically throughout the year.
West of Scotland, north-west England Temperatures rarely below −10°C (15°F) or above 27°C (80°F). A longer growing season than in the east with approximately 6 to 7 frost-free months in favourable sites. Rainfall moderate to heavy, usually 1.27–2.54 m (50–100 in.) or more. Soil usually acid. Wind often a problem and much shelter needed, especially on islands which have less frost than anywhere. Big-leaved and a few of the Maddenia subsection do well. Little snow.
Central Scotland 32 km (20 miles) plus from coasts and estuaries. Growing season often shorter than above and in some areas, frost can occur at any time of the year. Temperatures may drop to below −18°C (0°F). Only

the hardier species are recommended. Snowfall often heavy. In 1978–9 winter, −29°C (−20°F) was recorded in Lanarkshire, the coldest ever recorded in Scotland.

East Scotland, north-east England　Well-sheltered areas near coasts are quite favourable sites. Temperatures down to −18°C (0°F) on a rare occasion. A short growing season, only averaging 5 to 6 months without damaging frosts. Heavy snowfalls are rare. Rainfall sometimes inadequate, 635–889 mm (25–35 in.), with dry spells. Soil sometimes alkaline. Big-leaved species grow slowly. Maddeniis generally not hardy.

West Wales, south-west England　Generally similar to west Scotland, but rainfall rarely as heavy and soil not as acid or peaty, except on moorlands. Favourable areas with regard to frost extend farther inland.

South England　Growing season slightly longer than east Scotland, but minimum temperatures similar, especially in Kent where snow often occurs. Higher summer temperatures, 32°C (90°F) and over on occasion. Soil often clay, limy or chalk, the last being useless for rhododendron culture. Rainfall, 508–762 mm (20–30 in.), often inadequate.

East England and Midlands　Colder winters than south and more danger from unseasonable frosts. Rainfall often inadequate, 508–762 mm (20–30 in.) or less. Soil clay or limy in places, north-east winds a problem near east coasts and low humidity and strong sunshine. Only hardier species recommended. Many areas suffer from atmospheric pollution where the dirty air reduces the strength of the sun. Late flowering azaleas often grow poorly. Plant all rhododendrons in more sun than usual. Soil often light and poor, annual top dressing of organic matter desirable.

Europe

Western and southern Scandinavia　More of a continental climate than Britain except for coastal south Norway where winters are modified by the Gulf Stream. Winters over other parts often severe, down to −30°C (−22°F). Rainfall throughout the year, high on west coast, just sufficient (usually) elsewhere. Much snow. Summers cool. Very few species hardy in the colder areas. Growing season May–October.

North-west and north coastal Europe: Belgium to Germany　Winters rather similar to above with moderate amounts of snow. Summers warmer, up to 38°C (100°F). Growing season as above. Rainfall sometimes inadequate.

East Baltic: north-west Russia to Finland　Permanent frost December onwards, minimum −42°C (−43°F). Stable snow covering throughout winter. 150–180 cloudy days a year, 30–40 cloudless. Soil mostly acid with plentiful peatmoss. Many species are being tested in Latvia, but very few have proved hardy in Finland.

Southern central Europe around Alps　Minimum temperature about −11.9°C (10°F). A few late spring frosts, little snow at lower levels. Many overcast days, rainfall often heavy and usually adequate. Moderate maximum temperatures. This is proving a good area, especially in the foothills. Valleys may be rather warm. Rootrot sometimes a problem.

North-west Spain, north Portugal　Very little frost and moderate summer temperatures. Rainfall mostly in winter with shade and watering necessary in growing season. A good area for Maddeniis and perhaps some Vireyas.

Australia and New Zealand

Australia   There is said to be at least twenty times more rhododendron growing area in the USA than in Australia. The best parts of Australia are the relatively wet mountains situated in the south-east, especially around Melbourne (like the Dandenong Ranges in Victoria with acid, deep red volcanic soil) and inland from Sydney. Little frost with occasional light snowfalls. Rainfall mostly in summer, but this is often inadequate due to high temperatures, droughts and hot winds, 1.27–1.52 m (50–60 in.) annually. Temperatures, 32°C (90°F) or over in mountains, 38°C (100°F) or over on plains. Heavy summer mulches and watering desirable. Early flowering species are the most satisfactory as later ones succumb to the heat.

Tasmania   Very mild climate, particularly suitable for rhododendrons.

New Zealand: North Island   Little frost, but inclined to be rather hot at low levels. The west coast is moist and the east dry where irrigation is needed. The north should suit Vireyas and tender lowland forms of species, while mountain areas like Pukeiti are excellent for large-leaved species and Maddeniis.

New Zealand: South Island   Up to 2 months longer growing season than Britain. Inland areas subject to frosts which are especially damaging in spring. Again the west is wet and the east dry, where extra watering is needed. Unlike Australia, nearly all New Zealand can grow some rhododendrons.

Africa

Parts of Africa with high elevations and a heavy rainfall might suit the Vireyas and species from low elevations in South-East Asia. As rainfall is generally seasonal, adequate provisions for watering would be necessary. Some areas of South Africa favourable.

North America

Most parts south of the Arctic Circle and near coasts can grow at least some rhododendron species successfully. In many eastern and southern regions, the climate and soil conditions make rhododendron cultivation very tricky with much care needed over drainage, shade, watering, pests and diseases.

North-east coastal areas   A good variety of species may be grown in eastern Long Island, while only the hardiest will grow in New Brunswick and Nova Scotia. Temperature, minimum −25°C (−15°F) to −15°C (5°F). Summers seldom over 32°C (over 90°F). Temperatures at Arnold Arboretum down to −23°C (−11°F) once; average −20 to 23°C (−5 to −10°F). pH 5.5, mulching and some summer watering needed. Moderate rainfall over most of the year.

North-east inland   Extremes of cold and heat, −34°C (−30°F) or lower. Only very few species will survive. Choose locations out of winter sun. Mulching (winter) helpful. Moderate rainfall, falling most of the year. Spring planting advised.

South-east   Climate often tricky with extremes of heat and cold. Cold northerly blasts or dry south-west winds. Unreliable snow cover and danger of spring frost. North exposure preferred. Raised beds often essential (see Soil preparation and drainage, *p.* 67), avoid over-watering. High shade desirable. Rainfall moderate to heavy, humidity usually high. Many species as yet untried. Plains very hot. Species (or hybrids from them) from low elevations tend to grow better than those from high elevations.

Gulf region   Variable conditions. Hot inland, temperatures sometimes over 38°C (100°F), dry towards Texas. Soil often alkaline or silty. Maddeniis worth trying along coast. Species largely untried. Very hardy hybrids are at present found to be satisfactory. Raised beds are necessary. Try gravel pads under root balls. Redwood tubs are good. Diseases are a frequent problem. Grow proven disease-resistant varieties and do not plant in polythene containers, which encourage disease.

North-west coastal regions   This is the nearest to our British climate, but summers are hotter and drier; 32°C (90°F) is quite common and most rain falls during the winter. Winters usually mild, not below −12°C (10°F) but the devastating 1955 and 1972 freezes did tremendous damage and in certain areas, many large-leaved and other species were wiped out. These cold blasts came from the north and the east. The temperature dropped as low as −28°C (−20°F) in one place. Summer mulching and/or watering essential. Portland and Eugene districts have stronger sun than Tacoma–Seattle and temperatures occasionally reach 38°C (100°F) in places. The best areas are those where the native *macrophyllum* occurs wild.

North-west inland, east Oregon and Washington   Dry, fairly cold winters and hot summers. Plenty of water and shade needed. Soil often rather alkaline. Raised beds are desirable. Plentiful pine needles. Few species yet tried but those suitable for the eastern seaboard should succeed.

North coastal California, including San Francisco Bay area   Little or no frost. In certain coastal areas, fog keeps the summer cool. Rainfall is low, but around San Francisco the fog drip helps compensate for the lack of rain. Many tender species were lost in the 1972 freeze, but as the previous hard frost was 40 years earlier, all should be worth attempting again. Warm November–December makes buds vulnerable to any frosts in January–February. Colour intensity (yellow especially) is poor due to lack of winter cold and the flowers tend to go over quickly.

California inland   Sacramento Valley. Low −8°C (18°F), high 45°C (113°F). Little or no rain from June to October, very low humidity and almost no fog. Ukiah rather similar, but rainfall heavier. Perfect drainage is needed with raised beds advisable. Plant in as much sun as foliage will stand, mulch thoroughly and do not over water. Several species may be grown with good cultural treatment including shelter from drying winds. Sierra Nevada foothills colder, winters down to about −21°C (−6°F). Fairly heavy snowfall but summers hot and dry.

South coastal California Not generally suitable but some heat-resistant Maddeniis and Vireyas are worth trying. Elepidotes (sub-genus Hymenanthes) not successful.

South America

Southern Chile Winters not severe and summers not too hot. Ample rainfall, mostly in winter. Should be a very good area for a large variety of species, especially the less hardy ones.
Argentina, Buenos Aires area Rainfall all the year round, mostly in summer, which is very hot. Heavier rainfall towards Chilean frontier. Some rhododendrons do well and Maddeniis and Vireyas should be promising.

Asia

India, Himalayan foothills, Khasi Hills and similar areas No frost, abundant summer rains. Lower altitude native species, such as low altitude *arboreum* and Maddeniis, should grow well given woodland conditions and forest litter. Vireyas might do well.
Hong Kong and adjacent south China Little or no frost, very good conditions for tender species in forest areas on peaks. Care should be taken that alien species do not run wild.
Japan Lowland areas in the south very hot. Night temperatures too hot and humidity often too low for all but specially selected or bred heat-resistant varieties. Summer rains in central areas usually abundant. Mountains and Hokkaido good for hardier species.

Other parts of the world

All areas where rhododendrons grow naturally should be suitable for a good range of species of roughly similar hardiness to their own native ones. These areas include parts of east Europe, north Turkey, the Caucasus, Sri Lanka, Burma, Philippines, Taiwan, China, Korea, Indonesia, Malaysia, Papua, north Australia and others.

Many damp mountainous areas in the tropics and sub-tropics would grow fine rhododendrons and I would especially recommend the following: Arborea subsection, Parishia subsection, certain species of the Irrorata subsection, Maddenia subsection, Azaleastrum section (Ovatum series), Choniastrum section (Stamineum series), Vireya section and some of the (old) Azalea series.

Shaded, partially shady, or forest conditions would be necessary almost everywhere and some provision for watering would often be essential especially where prolonged dry seasons are prevalent.

THE WOODLAND GARDEN

What is meant by a woodland garden? Many people consider that the term 'garden' refers only to intensively cultivated ground, such as a vegetable plot or an herbaceous border, while to others, it embraces any area where ornamental plants are grown, even on a relatively small scale. In this book, the meaning falls into the latter category, although the degree to which the ground is planted and cultivated can vary enormously. There may be just occasional large rhododendrons and other trees and shrubs, or whole sweeps of woodland given over to mass plantings of all kinds of shade lovers from bulbs to shrubs and trees. Many woodland gardens tend to have a rather monotonous sameness about them, even some which are quite extensive. It must be admitted that large areas of big rhododendrons, which are not broken up in any way, can be dull and overpowering to anyone but dedicated rhododendron enthusiasts.

In our own rather limited area at Glendoick, in endeavouring to build up the collection, nearly all other genera have been excluded in recent plantings in the rhododendron glen. Our west coast plot, being more extensive, has enabled us to confine rhododendrons to certain parts and even there, to plant other genera among them.

I am all for groups of non-woody plants being placed in bays among rhododendrons if there is someone prepared to look after them properly. What I will not recommend is planting herbaceous and sub-shrubby ground cover over the rhododendron root areas. The only really natural root cover for rhododendrons is fallen leaves, conifer needles or moss plus some lichen. Any others compete with the shallow rhododendron roots for moisture and nourishment and stop any regular mulching which rhododendrons greatly appreciate. Only where the natural leaf fall is sufficient to fulfil their needs, are annual mulches of organic matter unnecessary. In our own woodland gardens, little time is available for cultivating groups of herbaceous or bulbous plants so we try to encourage the most desirable elements of the native flora, while keeping the root areas cleared with handweeding and weedkillers. Occasional pulling, scything and spraying of obnoxious weeds, such as brambles, nettles and willowherb, is virtually all the maintenance required to the spaces between the rhododendrons throughout the season. The only other chores are the occasional pruning of surrounding trees and shrubs, the collection of fallen branches after strong winds, dead-heading, dead-wooding and an annual mulching.

Watering is not often carried out in Britain in woodland gardens, but in the drier eastern parts it is frequently desirable. We do some watering most seasons as soon as the plants show signs of wilting, especially when many have yet to complete their growth. It so happens that the growing season is very drawn out and may extend from March to October, starting with species like *dauricum* and *anthosphaerum* and finishing with *auriculatum*. The majority grow in May and June and therefore it is important to see that adequate moisture is available then. In very dry climates or those with dry summers, it is really essential to have watering points situated to cover the whole garden, without the necessity of hoses if possible (see Watering, *p.* 77).

In North America, especially in the Pacific north-west, the native flora, such as dogwood (*Cornus nuttallii*), resents artificial watering and dies off. I suggest that an area of any garden in that region, however small, should be put aside for the lovely native plants of the immediate district. No watering should ever be done and no cultivation other than the removal of 'weed' species and the planting of such treasures as local iris, trilliums and lilies.

HARDINESS, SHELTER AND SHADE

The question is frequently asked, 'is such and such a plant hardy?' and unfortunately, the answer is seldom just a simple yes or no. One well-known rhododendron authority invariably says that a species is hardy without any qualifying statement. This is not only misleading but most unfair to someone who may spend a tidy sum on a so-called 'hardy' plant, only to have it killed the first winter.

There are so many factors involved in hardiness (here hardiness means cold rather than heat-resistant). First there are the major climatic variations. Each area has its own average winter and summer temperatures, together with the all-important minimum and maximum temperatures recorded. These areas are divided into climatic zones, which in North America for instance, are given numbers. Another most vital factor is the expected number of frost-free days which make the length of a growing season. For example, the coldest inland areas of Scotland can get frost during any month of the year and July is the only month *without* frosts that can cause damage. Here at Glendoick, in a good year, we may get 7 or even 8 months without injurious frost in the favourable parts of the garden, while in a bad year, there may be only four frost-free months. Any year which produces late spring *and* early autumn frosts is sure to be a disastrous growing season, especially if dry or cool weather between inhibits growth recovery early enough for it to ripen.

The mention of favourable areas brings up the all-important subject of micro-climates. This is summed up nicely by A. J. Fordham of the Arnold Arboretum:

> Micro-climate situations are infinite. They can occur on hilltops, slopes, valleys, different sides of a house, either side of a wall, under a tree, over a stone or in a footprint. Areas concerned can be highly localized and sometimes involve distances as little as portions of a centimetre. In the Arboretum, there are differences in temperatures as much as 5.5°C (10°F) on a clear, still, very frosty night. This means that on one particularly cold night, parts of the Arboretum lay from zone 5 to 3 and a less cold night, from zone 7 to 4.

No two seasons are the same and each one affects a plant in a different way from the last. There are very few plants in our gardens that do not at least occasionally show the disadvantageous effects of the weather. We grow a very extensive collection of rhododendrons at Glendoick and a high proportion of this collection suffers some sort of cold damage over the years. This damage may vary from frosted or distorted growth, frosted flowers, to bark-split and die-back. It is extraordinary how few we have actually had killed once established. Maybe one of these days an exceptionally severe winter will strike us, such as those in the Pacific north-west of America in 1955 and 1972. By and large, the vast majority of our plants go on giving us enjoyment from year to year. Some undoubtedly have their setbacks, but this adds to the marvellous interest to be had from comprehensive collections of rhododendrons.

I now go into details of how damage from frost, wind and sun can occur and later deal with how best to minimize the effects of extreme weather conditions.

Cold damage can be roughly divided into two groups, winter injury when the plants are relatively dormant and spring or autumn injury when growth is still active. These types of injury do, of course, overlap, but it is important to realize which plants are most likely to succumb to which type of weather conditions before deciding where to place species of border-line hardiness. There is more detail of this under the species descriptions, but some idea of what to look for is given here.

Early flowering species are naturally the most liable to have their blooms destroyed, but certain species have considerably more frost-resistant flowers than others. A notable example of 'tough' flowers is *dauricum*. Early growth is really a more serious problem. Some species have a much greater ability to renew ruined growth than others. The smaller-leaved species are generally the best at this and the large-leaved the worst. Therefore the early growing large-leaved species are virtually useless in areas with frequencies of late frosts. Early growth means an early rise of sap and killed growth may be accompanied by bark-split (see Chapter 7, *p*. 330). Likewise, late growth may be damaged by early autumn frosts. In our severe drought of 1955, normally late-growing species, unless watered frequently, delayed their growth until a few showers occurred in September. A sharp frost in early October ruined most of this growth with no chance of remaking it that year. Examples were *griersonianum*, *eximium* and *sinogrande*. Some plants actually died; others took years to recover.

In Scotland, we rarely see the result of the combination of winter sun and frost that can be so devastating in more continental climates. The severe leaf burn reported from the latter areas is not often seen here. Tender plants seem to be able to withstand just so much hard winter weather. A few nights of temperatures near $-17.8°C$ (0°F) in mid-winter may cause little or no distress, but an accumulation of cold may result in sudden collapse and death later in the season.

I have not yet mentioned the dreaded combination of wind and frost, which is really the worst killer of all. We often get prolonged spells of cold east winds in early spring and these can be very hard on evergreens in exposed situations. In west North America, cold, frost-laden winds can sweep across from the mid-west or north, often just after a warm spell, with appalling results. The sudden November freeze of 1955 even killed cherry trees and *Magnolia stellata*. The December 1972 freeze killed 40-year-old rhododendrons in the Eugene district. The 1955 freeze was uniform over a large area while the 1972 one did little damage around Seattle; farther south, from Portland to San Francisco, record lows were experienced.

The question arises – will there be other winters to equal those of 1955 and 1972 within the foreseeable future? There is frequent talk of an impending ice age, but surely ice ages take hundreds if not thousands of years to develop. I reckon that it would be worth replanting everything that survived earlier freezes, such as 1948–1949, which was then considered to be the worst for 78 years.

Frost, we all know, flows like water and collects in hollows or at the back of solid obstacles, such as walls and thick hedges. The severest frost is at ground level. Under radiated conditions, temperatures 1.22 m (4 ft) above the ground can be 5.5–8°C (10–15°F) warmer than at ground level. With adequate shelter, tender epiphytic type species could benefit considerably by being perched on a high rock, tree stump or fork of a tree. Likewise, large plants with their heads well above ground level, are also less vulnerable. The late Lionel de Rothschild noted how small plants with flowers close to the ground are more easily frosted than large plants.

In Britain, we benefit from a climate where temperatures do not suddenly fluctuate widely up or down. The annoying thing about our weather is the way the temperature fails to follow the months of the year; it can be warmer in January than June! Mild winters like those of 1971 to 1976 were often followed by the worst frosts of the season in April or May. One of our best flowering seasons came after the cold 1963 winter, when winter changed into spring and did not return to spoil our gardens.

Experiments have shown that rapid freezing causes more damage than rapid thawing and it seems that much damage attributed to the latter is caused by rapid freezing when the sun ceases to shine on the foliage. With the air temperature at $-12°C$ (10°F), the leaf temperature was found to be 11°C (20°F) higher. When suddenly shaded, the leaves cooled at a rate near to that proved damaging in laboratory tests. Gradual freezing allows water to move out of the cells and ice crystals develop between the cells, causing no injury.

Much damage is caused by winter sun and wind when the roots are frozen and therefore unable to take up water. The foliage becomes dehydrated. Whether the plant can recover depends on the degree of dehydration and the ability of the clone to tolerate desiccation. Rhododendrons which are cold-hardened and hardy are able to assimilate water from cold but not frozen soil. Plants are able to take up water at -2.25 to $-1°C$ (28–30°F) and provided they are not shaken, a degree or two lower. Frozen stems and frozen soil contribute to injury. Varieties differ considerably in the percentage of water deficit they can tolerate. How much relationship there is between resistance to freezing injury and desiccation injury is apparently not known.

Winter hardiness is not simply a matter of prolonged or sudden low temperatures. Much depends on the weather for the whole season preceding the cold spell, especially the autumn period of hardening off. Ground moisture and air humidity during winter itself are other factors.

Most rhododendrons reach full resistance for hardiness when about 5 years old. Many big-leaved species are exceptionally tender before the leaves grow to their maximum size and need special winter protection in their juvenile state. Early autumn frosts may create more serious flower bud damage than fairly severe mid-winter or moderate early spring frosts. Gradually cooling autumns are the most satisfactory. Warm weather followed immediately by even a slight frost can cause bud and growth tip damage to certain species. Fluctuating cold and warm spells in late winter do, of course, often destroy or damage flower buds.

Mild areas, like coastal Cornwall and south-west England, chiefly suffer from wind problems, but warm autumn weather keeping the sap running leads to trouble from light frosts that would hardly be noticed in colder districts. Likewise, lath houses are liable to keep growth in a tender unhardened-off state resulting in more winter damage than there would have been if placed in a sunny open position.

A nurseryman in Seattle noticed that some of his stock, which was inadequately watered by sprinklers prior to the 1955 freeze, were the least damaged. Hence, short and harder growth withstood the frost better than more robust growth. Certain relatively wind tolerant species, such as Triflorums and Cinnabarinums, succeed in a position which receives some wind, whereas they may die or be severely damaged by bark-split in a normally warmer sheltered area. It is often noticeable that less frost occurs near the tops of ridges where frost drainage is good and wind disturbs the air.

Special emphasis must be laid on the value of gardening on a slope or plateau, provided adequate shelter is present or can be established. Good frost drainage, does, in most years, mean avoidance of much of the trouble from late spring or early autumn frosts which so bother those poor people with only low-lying sites to play with. Even with the beneficial effects of salt water or large lakes, hollows or valley bottoms are often frost traps. Open valleys have the added disadvantage of wind being funnelled up or down the valley.

Frost affects plants in various ways. People come to us bringing queer, malformed foliage, suspecting some unknown pest or disease. The leaves may be twisted, curled upwards, one sided, puckered or even chlorotic (see photograph No. 53). All these symptoms can be caused by frost when the growth buds are elongating. Severely frosted growth dies and secondary buds (if any) will develop into growth some weeks later. Sometimes, where no secondary buds are present, growth sprouts from the previous season's wood. Growth with the leaves largely destroyed but the stem remaining, usually regrows from the terminal bud of the new shoot. In many cases, it is wise to cut out badly damaged growth. This will encourage fresh shoots to appear more rapidly and give them time to mature. Small-leaved species can be left alone as any frosted growth soon withers and may ultimately drop off but frosted larger foliage may go mouldy and rot off the year old shoot it has developed from.

Bark-splitting (see Chapter 7) resulting from frost when the sap is running, may occur on many parts of the trunk or shoots but most often at ground level. While these splits may heal successfully with no apparent ill health to the plant, later whole branches or even the plant may collapse suddenly and wither.

Winter damage is something we in Britain had almost forgotten about, having had no hard winter for 14 years up to 1976. Either plants collapse or black or brown foliage appears, as a result of desiccation, sun and frost, or both. Severe damage may result in death. Supposedly dead plants may be checked by examining the cambium layer just beneath the bark. Theoretically, if the cambium is green the plant may live and if black or brown it will be dead, but several reports indicate that with the latter, the apparently dead cambium occasionally turns green later in the season and eventually some growth may reappear.

Never be in haste to destroy supposedly dead frost-damaged plants. They may even start growing a year after dying back although this is rare. Weak growth late in the season will need special winter protection as it will be very vulnerable. In Oregon, after the 1972 freeze, this type of re-growth emerged only to be killed off during another cold snap the following winter. This final frosting usually proves fatal.

Rhododendrons in containers (and other plants) are more susceptible to winter damage than those growing in the ground. Likewise plants in boxes. If containers are stood pot thick, the outer ones are the first to suffer because they will be the first to be frozen solid and therefore more prone to desiccation. Pot-bound plants are more at risk than those more recently potted. Late watering plus fertilizer usually increases injury. In certain cases, grafted plants are said to be hardier than those on their own roots. This could be due to two reasons – the stock is hardier than the variety above it and the flow of sap is restricted by the union, resulting in less sappy growth.

Collingwood Ingram makes a novel suggestion to make tender rhododendrons hardier. His idea is to remove all the leaves each autumn to avoid excessive transpiration during cold weather. He does not know of anyone who has tried this over a period of years or what the overall effect would be. I doubt if any evergreen would survive this treatment for long, or that it would be much help in bringing tender buds through the winter and who wants to see evergreens denuded? Many species retain their leaves for more than one year anyway and at least half their beauty is often in their foliage.

Heat tolerance

At the other end of the scale, heat bothers rhododendrons in its own way just as much as cold. As most species came from temperate climates, many, in fact the vast majority, simply cannot live, let alone flourish in high temperatures. Even the south of England is liable to be too hot for some species, especially dwarfs which do not concern us here. Heat tolerant species are listed in the 'Recommended lists' and under individual species, but I mention here that those from really moist mountain areas such as the east Himalayas and north Burma are definitely not tolerant. Only those from hotter, drier foothills may stand more heat.

Heat plus dry air are really the killers and make conditions very difficult even with abundant shading and watering. Heat tolerance may be checked at the end of a long hot spell, say in August. If roots are white and fresh, the variety is tolerant, if pale brown but alive, with little whitish growth, it may have suffered heat damage. Foliage tends to become yellowish during a hot spell with poor thin growth. Darker brown and thoroughly dead roots mean the variety is unsatisfactory in heat. Perfectly heat tolerant species should have white roots throughout the year.

Excessive heat would roughly mean prolonged temperatures of over 32°C (90°F), but, of course, any area which receives an exceptionally hot, dry period compared with normal, like England in 1976, can suffer as plants are not used to it, nor are there the necessary shading and watering facilities available to minimize the damage. We rarely get temperatures of over 27°C (80°F) in Scotland, so any spell of a few days over this can cause trouble in a sunny or dry situation.

Coastal influences

Virtually all the larger species of rhododendron appreciate some degree of protection. We have all seen isolated bushes of *ponticum*, *catawbiense* or *maximum* growing out in almost full exposure and by limiting their height and spreading outwards, they manage to exist. They are only likely to succeed under these conditions if the soil, rainfall and temperatures are really suitable. Otherwise they would die. Here lies a very important point; the nearer to the ideal one's climate and soil conditions are, the less trouble need be taken over shade and shelter, provided there is some protection in areas with severe prevailing winds. These winds, if blowing from salt water, may bring the added hazard of salted wind which can cause considerable leaf burn in many species.

It so happens that it is these very gardens, which are liable to salt damage, that are generally blessed with a maritime climate which modifies the temperature range and thus reduces the risks from frost and heat. Thus, nearly all the islands off the west coast of Scotland (which fall into the path of the Gulf Stream) would be ideal for rhododendron culture *provided* wind and salt can be minimized to a tolerable degree. No doubt similar situations occur with other off-shore islands, such as near North America, Japan and New Zealand. The actual amount and strength of the wind is all important. It is very noticeable from the tree growth on the Pacific north-west coast of USA that there are not nearly the same persistent strong winds as in Britain from Cornwall to Sutherland.

At a short distance inland from the direct influence from a large body of salt (or fresh) water, this modification of the temperature begins to be lost. I have only recently realized (to my own cost) how our so-called west coast area, which is not directly associated with the open Atlantic, may in fact be little milder than Glendoick which is 3.2 km (2 miles) from a salt estuary and 32 km (20 miles) from the North Sea.

Shelter

In Scotland, shelter is often a more important consideration than shade. Being on a latitude with Labrador and Kamtschatica, we do not get excessive sun heat, but many species do appreciate some shade and overhead shelter, if only to protect the young growth from radiation frost and to help the flowers last longer. Shelter is always necessary for a collection of large species. Natural protection from a hill or even a low ridge is of great help but the addition of screens of trees and shrubs always improves the conditions. Netting is good for shelter early on.

Any piece of ground, large or small, needs careful studying over a lengthy period before all the wind problems are discovered. There are few gardens or potential gardens which cannot be improved upon shelter-wise and the position should be reappraised every few years. Shelter belts grow taller and can become bare underneath, thereby letting in draughts. I am always seeking to improve our shelter at Glendoick and of course, in Argyll. We suffered considerable damage in the latter county during the prolonged but not exceptionally severe winter of 1976 to 1977. The temperature did not drop below −7°C (19°F) but there was frost most nights during December, January and February, plus some wind. We had severe foliage, bud and shoot injury to most Maddeniis and some big-leaved species, especially *grande*. I am convinced that much of this damage was due to the very cold east winds to which we are exposed and the lack of ground shelter under our mature hardwoods, which let this cold blast of air through underneath their branches.

Seaside shelter

Only a very few trees and shrubs will grow at all, let alone thrive in the full exposure to the Atlantic. Where this problem exists and there is little shelter already, it will take a while to establish sufficient height and density. The general plan is to plant in belts, naturally with the toughest plants on the windward side. Those on the outside can never be expected to attain any appreciable height and this has to be gradually built up by rows behind. It is a good idea to establish the initial belt a year or two before the next so that there is a little shelter to plant behind. Always plant this shelter small. However securely staked, larger plants will inevitably be blown out of the ground.

On the exposed Scottish island of Colonsay, it was found that salt spray could defoliate large rhododendrons almost completely, but the buds were seldom damaged and grew away. Large rhododendrons needed to be secured with slanting stakes or even guy ropes or wires to hold them firm against the wind. None the less, many fine plants have been success-fully grown on this island. The Isle of Gigha, which lies nearer the west coast, also has its wind problems but is blessed with a low bank along the windward side of the fine garden there. Shelter has been planted on the top of the bank, endeavouring to both raise the wind and lessen its strength.

The majority of seaside gardens use walls, often dry stone ones. These make a good start for one to plant behind. For a high screen, start with *Acer pseudoplatanus* (sycamore) and *Picea sitchensis* (sitka spruce). These can be backed with *Pinus contorta*, *P. radiata*, *P. mugo*, *P. nigra* and *nigra maritima* (Austrian and Corsican pines), × *Cupressocyparis* 'Leylandii', *Olearia traversii* and *Cupressus macrocarpa*.

Together with, or behind these, for ground shelter (in case the outside screen gets bare underneath), plant *Escallonia macrantha*, *E.* 'C. F. Ball', *Griselinia littoralis*, *Elaeagnus* varieties, *Olearia albida* or *macrodonta*, *Cotoneaster* varieties and *R. ponticum*. Most of these are reasonably hardy except *Olearia traversii*. Other suitably tough but low plants for the front line defence are *Phormium tenax* (New Zealand flax), *Senecio* varieties, *Hippophae rhamnoides*, *Rosa rugosa*, *Ulex* sp., *Tamarix* sp., *Ligustrum* varieties (privet), and *Crataegus* varieties (thorns).

Many coastal gardens of any size need interior windbreaks as well. Many of the above are suitable and others would be *Quercus ilex*, *Ilex* varieties, *Phillyrea decora*, *Pieris formosa* and *Crinodendron hookerianum*. While *R. ponticum* makes excellent interior shelter, in western areas it is hard to keep under control. Bamboos can make good screens but avoid the running types.

For other parts of the world, there are no doubt many alternative shelter plants that can be utilized.

Inland shelter

Here, the scope is wider as the wind is not usually so ferocious or salt laden. × *Cupressocyparis* 'Leylandii' is again an excellent fast-growing screening plant and many chamaecyparis, cupressus, thujas, and other evergreens may also be used. Do not make shelter too dense as it is always better to subdue its strength rather than just deviate it with too solid a barrier, only to strike even harder farther on. Also solid barriers tend to act as frost dams in which the frost collects. Laurels form good, vigorous shelter, but tend to become leggy in time and need frequent pruning of side branches. Hollies are excellent but slow. Self-sown tree seedlings can be good against ground draughts but do, of course, need drastic thinning out in time. *Tsuga heterophylla* (hemlock) is a good shade-bearing tree for planting under a canopy. Some of the more vigorous rhododendrons themselves make good interior windbreaks, such as *decorum* and *rubiginosum*.

Unless the soil is highly fertile, these shelter plants will all benefit by an occasional boost with a little application of a balanced fertilizer, say once in 2 to 4 years.

Many other trees and shrubs can be used, such as the larger cotoneasters and evergreen loniceras. We are testing out some rarer shrubs like *Myrica californica* and *Euonymus tingens* which both show promise.

Wind can blow certain species bare of leaves. While they can tolerate this occasionally, more frequent leaf stripping will weaken plants considerably. Wind will damage flowers by knocking and brushing branches against each other; those with white flowers will mark readily.

Shade

The use of shade, as previously stated, is highly critical in hot and very cold climates. Evergreen shade is absolutely essential in many cold areas to stop the sun striking frozen plants and avoid rapid freezing when the sun ceases to shine on the foliage. For the east regions of North America, the following are recommended in descending order of preference: oak, hickory, magnolia, tulip poplar, tupelo, dogwood, linden, locust, ash, sweet gum, hackberry, apple, cherry, birch, poplar, willow, walnut, beech, buttonwood, elm and maple. Many of these are, of course, not evergreen. In very cold parts, only the hardiest species can survive without this winter shade. Black walnuts are said to be toxic to rhododendrons in the USA, producing a chemical known as juglone.

Generally speaking, the hotter and drier the climate, the more shade is needed. Thus while big-leaved species will grow in parts of west Scotland in full sun if sheltered, these same species must have considerable shade to succeed in Oregon and Washington States.

Throughout most of Britain, high pruned trees are ideal when well spaced out to allow at least half sun. Deep-rooted trees are best as are those with smallish leaves and not too dense a canopy. The very high pruned oaks at Mount Congreve, near Waterford in Ireland, create the nearest to perfect conditions I have ever seen.

Quercus sp. (oaks) are our best shade trees here as in America and red oaks particularly, are highly recommended, also *Q. borealis* and *palustris*. Good small trees are small-leaved *Acer* sp. (maples), *Stewartia* sp., *Styrax* sp., the upright growing *Prunus* sp. (cherries), *Sorbus* sp. (rowans), *Liquidamber* sp., *Cercidiphyllum* sp. and *Nyssa* sp. Birch, larch and pines are often suitable for the amount of light they let through but as they are greedy for water, do not plant within their root run unless a good water supply is available. Magnolias (most), *Castania* sp. (Spanish Chestnuts), and *Alnus* sp. (alders), tend to have foliage that is too dense and therefore creates too much shade. Likewise *Fagus* sp. (beech), although it provides excellent leaf mould. *Ulmus* sp. (elm), *Eucalyptus* sp. (see end of chapter) and Douglas fir have huge, greedy root systems which dry out and impoverish the soil while sycamore and horse chestnut are thoroughly bad with large leaves and dense shade. Some evergreen *Nothofagus* sp. (southern beeches) are good but the deciduous sp. are too dense.

Where possible, excess trees should be pulled out by the roots to try to avoid honey fungus (*Armillaria*), but I do like old stumps with rotten centres for planting epiphytic species on.

Magnolias may be planted among rhododendrons in large gardens where there is plenty of room. Magnolias hate their roots disturbed and as these cover a large area when mature, rhododendrons should not if possible be moved or planted within this area. It is all right to plant rhododendrons and magnolias together provided plenty of space is given for both to mature.

The lightest of overhead tree cover is a help against spring frosts, particularly those that occur very late in the season. Even the close proximity of trees may modify the temperature as the air trapped beneath the canopy mixes with the colder air out in the open. It is well worthwhile trying to place early growing as well as early flowering species either partially under a tree or in positions shaded from the early sun. Some species have more frost-resistant young growth than others. In the bad late frost of 15 May 1975, certain species in the middle of our nursery were affected, while others next to them were almost untouched. Worst were *wallichii*, *barbatum*, and *orbiculare* while *souliei* and *campanulatum* var. *aeruginosum* were virtually unscathed.

If space permits, it is an excellent idea to plant the best species in both sunny and shady positions, provided that they can remain healthy in each site. Each has its benefits and drawbacks. The benefits of shade are: better individual leaves, some overhead frost protection, lower summer temperatures, finer and longer lasting flowers which often open much later in the season and for those that prefer it, a loose growing habit. The drawbacks are: leggy growth, less flower; certain species develop soft growth in shade resulting in more growth damage from frost (usually in autumn) and bark-split.

Tall *Eucalyptus regnans* have been found to be suitable shade trees in their natural habitat in Australia. They do not generally grow too thickly but the odd tree may be felled if necessary and surface roots removed before planting. Some trouble has been reported of *Armillaria* (honey fungus) and shedding branches, but provided regular liberal mulches are put on and fertilizer (balanced) is applied each spring and occasional watering in dry weather, rhododendrons can do very well and flower freely. Other *Eucalyptus* sp. are probably just as good in the moister mountain areas.

LANDSCAPING

Large species rhododendrons should be considered primarily as foliage plants from a landscaping point of view. While the flowers should obviously be taken into account, it is the magnificent leaves, bark and form of many species which we shall be looking at for the greater part of the year and the whole of their first few years. Much can be made of steep banks, cliffs and rocks for viewing the plants from different angles. Those species with striking indumentum can be shown to full advantage when seen from below, while large-leaved species look splendid when viewed from above.

Large gardens, of course, have so much more scope for varying vistas. I love to look through an extensive planting where contrasting forms of flower and foliage can be seen in the distance. Add to this the subtle colours of various conifers and the soft pale greens of fresh young growth on deciduous trees, and one has a picture of sheer joy and harmony.

Evergreen conifers make a splendid background for rhododendrons. Deep coloured foliage is best and trees of upright and not too spreading habit interfere less with the rhododendrons themselves. Suggested conifers are *Pinus cembra* (Swiss Stone or Arolla pine), *P. strobus* (Weymouth pine), *P. parviflora* (Japanese white pine), *P. thunbergii* (Japanese black pine), *Sciadoptys verticillata* (Japanese umbrella pine), *Cryptomeria japonica* (Japanese red cedar). Precocious flowering deciduous azaleas and the early *R. dauricum* and *mucronulatum* are shown off to advantage with this coniferous background, particularly when mixed with *Corylopsis* or *Hamamelis* species, which should be selected to flower concurrently with the rhododendrons.

Other suggested combinations are *ririei* with *lutescens*; *mucronulatum* with *Prunus* 'Accolade'; *campylocarpum* with *augustinii*; *reticulatum* in front of a foil of evergreens; *augustinii* under white cherries.

It is important to avoid monotony in large gardens and all too many existing collections tend to suffer this fault. Rhododendrons, if grouped according to their leaf size, bark or flower colour, can create many changes and surprises. Triflorums look silly alongside big-leaved species and the latter are often better grouped together and perhaps segregated in association with trees of corresponding size and dignity. Another unsatisfactory combination is a mixture of deciduous azaleas and evergreen rhododendrons. The former are better grouped together with these further divided into the Pentanthera section (Luteum sub-series) in a moister site than those from South-East Asia, such as *schlippenbachii* and *reticulatum*.

Special characters warrant thought for future plantings. Those species with fine bark can be grouped closely together so that the plants get drawn up and show their trunks fairly quickly. On the other hand, species with mounded habits, glaucous foliage and indumentum on the upper side of the leaf, should be placed well apart in an open position so as to grow into compact bushes. *R. thomsonii* fits into both these categories with a lovely bark and glaucous foliage. The best of both worlds may be achieved by having a short clear trunk and at least one side of the plant having enough light and space to develop and show off good foliage.

Any established garden with an abundance of old specimens is greatly improved by having a succession of youngsters coming on around them. Vigorous young plants have magnificent foliage, especially when planted where they get shade and shelter from their elders and betters. A landscape of only mature specimens, if rather drawn up with bare trunks, tends to look gaunt and empty. One might add 'unnatural' to having no seedlings or young plants, but in actual fact, many climax forests in nature have a closed canopy which does not allow in enough light for seedlings to grow.

Siting of permanent paths is all important. Paths among bushy rhododendrons have a nasty habit of getting narrower and narrower, until there is hardly room to push between encroaching branches. It seems that however far back from the centre of a path the plants are placed, they have this annoying tendency to fill up the space. We have frequently had to move or prune plants to clear a way through. On a steep bank, paths may follow the contours and if made at high and low levels, the same plants may be admired from both below and above. In a large garden, it is always worth having at least one main path through the middle of the area, which is wide and firm enough to be used by a tractor. This facilitates the transportation of leafmould, peat, moving large rhododendrons and the removal of unwanted timber. Also it enables old and infirm people to see at least a part of the garden from a vehicle.

Running or still water always greatly increases the beauty of any garden. The ponds of Blackhills, Morayshire, Scotland, where large rhododendrons may be seen across the still water, perfectly reflected, makes this one of the most beautiful rhododendron gardens that I know. Likewise the rocky gorges and cascading burn of Crarae, Argyll, create an entirely different but no less desirable aspect. Many gardens have hollows or even boggy areas where natural looking ponds could be made. In smaller gardens (or in large) it is now quite simple to make polythene-lined ponds, while on a smaller scale, fibreglass pools soon develop harmony with their environment when surrounded by established plants.

A so-called landscaped garden with the accent on grass, rocks and pools where plants appear to be an afterthought, does not appeal to me personally. What is more, little thought is often given to the well-being of the scattered or dotted trees or shrubs, which are positioned in order to create some sort of design rather than where they will be happy. By all means have grass and open space to show off the rhododendrons, but not rhododendrons to show off the grass!

Large species do not fit into formal landscapes and look horribly out of place if used in this type of garden. If standard rhododendrons must be planted, I suppose this is the place for them as they look so artificial anyway. Another type of landscape I abhor is a collection of island beds planted with an incongruous mass of species and hybrids jostling each other for space. The worst examples of these are where they are made in various shapes such as oblongs, triangles and crescents.

Large rhododendrons are always best associated with trees, not only for their own protection from shade and shelter but also from the landscape angle. A dense wood looks lovely edged by a mass planting of rhododendrons. A different effect is achieved in a thin woodland by planting bold groups and massing them in drifts. A woodland sloping up behind the house allows a deep view into the wood if thinned out. An added attraction is a sudden glimpse of a view into the distance. This may be through bushes, trees or even a gap in a wall or hedge. Distant views of some focal point which appears and disappears, to reappear later much closer, adds to the pleasure and anticipation of touring a garden. It is all too easy, even in large gardens, to over plant and loose the marvellous vistas which may be had looking through or over multitudes of different colours and shades at the height of the flowering season.

Visiting various other gardens, especially those on sloping ground, shows how important the initial planning of a garden is. I have been guilty of neglecting this aspect myself. I inherited an established garden at Glendoick with not much suitable ground to expand so it has largely been a case of replanting positions where something has died or has been unwanted and removed. This tends to lead to over planting. Even the two waterfalls were quite hard to see but the pruning of two plants has made one of them easily seen once more. New areas have been cleared since 1979.

If landscape is considered all important, the following well-known points in the landscape trade need considering. Scale, unity, simplicity, balance, interest, sequence and harmony. Landscape chaps are inclined to hate what they call over planting and spoiling the simplicity of the picture. Is the balance right between house and garden and one part of a garden and another? I agree that all this needs consideration, but I put the health and welfare of my plants first.

Drifts of woodland-loving herbaceous or bulbous plants, such as trilliums, hellebores, erythroniums, lilies (some) and primulas, look splendid in the open spaces *between* groups of rhododendrons. Looking after these plants requires a fair amount of manpower. An alternative is to encourage desirable wildflowers such as bluebells, primroses, campions, foxgloves and forget-me-not which can be kept under control by the occasional hand-weed, scything or weedkiller. Furthermore, these help other wildlife in the form of birds and butterflies and create a haven where rhododendrons and nature live in something approaching peaceful coexistence.

RHODODENDRONS AS SPECIMENS

Rhododendrons in the wild rarely get the chance to grow into what we consider to be fine specimens. Whether in virgin rhododendron forest or forest only partially containing rhododendrons, there is the everlasting competition for light. Only those plants able to occupy a portion of the canopy area are able to survive and only when the canopy is broken by death, natural or man-made damage, do seedlings have a chance to grow into mature specimens, or lateral branches have a chance to develop. The net result is leggy tree-like plants with all the foliage clustered at the top. Fine shapely bushes may be seen after a fire, but once the forest regains its full stature, the previously described state of affairs returns.

In gardens, neglect can ultimately lead to a very similar state of affairs. Where planting has been too close and no thinning out is done, side branches gradually die off until all are dead. While the trunks may now be fully appreciated, the flowers and foliage become virtually obscured and can only be viewed properly from a helicopter. I know of several old gardens where this unhappy situation has been reached and a new owner, or burst of enthusiasm, may wish to bring it all back into something worthwhile. The first task is to go around marking those plants that could be moved into other sites. These should include anything of special value which could perhaps be thrown on its side and have its tips layered (see *p*. 317). The best furnished of the remaining specimens can be left to grow on and with ample clearing all round may either grow new shoots from the trunk, which is rare on most large species, or gradually spread and drop their outer branches into the surrounding empty spaces. Cutting back is successful with some species (see *p*. 75).

Large-leaved species have their greatest value in their ability to be magnificent foliage plants. To maintain the size of leaves and spread of foliage to the ground, a regular check should be made to ensure the plant has ample room and that cultural conditions are kept up to the highest possible standard. If lower branches start to die off, investigate the reasons and try to rectify them.

Rhododendrons do not like sun on their roots and there is no better shade for these roots than that created by their own foliage. Where bare trunks to show off bark are desirable, the young plants may be placed nearer a path than usual so that their canopy soon meets overhead and side branches can be trimmed off on the sides nearest the paths. A word of warning: rhododendrons, however large, do not like a heavy traffic of feet trampling on their roots.

In warm, moist climates, like parts of New Zealand, some rhododendrons are grown as street trees. Ample space is needed to develop large heads that are able to shade the roots, even though the trunk is cleaned up a metre or two. Usually *arboreum* hybrids are used, but the very variable *arboreum* itself can make a beautiful tree-like specimen with an impressive trunk and foliage and flowers surpassing any other street tree likely to be encountered. Other possible street trees are *decorum*, *griffithianum*, *discolor*, *thomsonii* and *stenaulum*.

Specimens in gardens can be planted in such a way as to be viewed from one side only with perhaps a background of conifers or other evergreens, or be placed where people can walk right round them.

It is a good policy when planting isolated specimens in a lawn or in a bed with much smaller companions, to move in well-furnished semi-mature specimens rather than attempt to grow on young plants. Whatever is selected, it is essential to have well-grown, heavily foliaged, vigorous plants and to prepare the ground exceptionally well and to maintain a good mulch on the root areas. Badly grown isolated rhododendrons are a disgrace to any garden and are to me an abomination. An alternative is to plant a group of the same species, say, three to seven plants, very close together. These will help protect each other's roots.

FOLIAGE, BARK, SCENT AND COLOUR

To the uninitiated, the statement that a certain species of rhododendron takes, say, 25 years to start flowering, at once puts them off wanting to grow that particular plant. Far too many gardeners these days insist on instant gardening and some will not even buy plants that are not budded. They complain that their garden is small and that they will not have plants growing there that take ages to flower. What they fail to realize is that in many species, flowers are just an added bonus to an otherwise beautiful plant. In very many cases, the young growth is extremely attractive, for example, the bronze of *lutescens*, silvery-white of *uvarifolium*, the glaucous-blue of *cinnabarinum* Concatenans Group and *campanulatum* var. *aeruginosum*, the bright verdigris green to coppery beetroot of *exasperatum* and the deep mahogany of *argipeplum*. Many species have lovely red or scarlet bud scales such as *strigillosum*, *macabeanum* and *protistum* (giganteum). The red candles of *protistum* are especially fine just before the leaves unfurl.

Many species have indumentum on the upper surface of the young leaves and in certain cases, this remains on for many months, greatly adding to their allure. A notable example is *eximium* with superb rusty coloured indumentum.

The majority of species when well grown, have handsome foliage. If a species is grown chiefly for its foliage it is most important to see that the plant is kept in perfect health, not spoilt by surrounding bushes and given the best degree of shade and shelter to develop a good habit and the best possible foliage. Such species as *orbiculare* and *oreotrephes* should be given plenty of light to avoid legginess.

Those species with interesting indumentum can be more fully appreciated if planted on a bank so that they can be viewed from below. With the added combination of wind and sun, the result can be quite startling. For more information on foliage, see the lists on *p.* 334–5, then look up the descriptions of each species.

Many deciduous azaleas and a few more or less deciduous rhododendrons can produce fine autumn colour on the dying leaves. It is well known that this leaf fall colour varies from season to season and district to district, but the majority of these can be relied upon to perform well most years. The common azalea *luteum* has perhaps the finest colour of all but others such as *vaseyi*, *schlippenbachii*, and *occidentale* are often equally good.

Certain deciduous species have interesting foliage all season; *semibarbatum* often has bronzy tints before turning red while *pentaphyllum* and *quinquefolium* usually have distinctive pale green leaves edged with purple especially when young. Certain selected clones of *occidentale* have purple or reddish leaves all summer.

Bark

Many of the larger and certain middle-sized species have most striking barks of various colours and types. Only gardens with ample space are able to show off groves of tree-like rhododendrons. When contemplating a new planting in open woodland conditions, consider planting in bold clumps of these fine barked species. In this way, the interior plants will be drawn up while the outer ones should remain clothed to the ground. Hence, the flowers can be seen from outside and by walking into the clump, the bark can be seen on the interior. Planting on this scale may rarely be possible these days and of course the desired effect of bare trunks takes many years to attain.

Again, where there is plenty of room, isolated specimens in light woodland can have their branches gradually cleaned up from the foot as the trunk or trunks develop, but only do this occasionally. Select where possible, single stemmed plants for this treatment.

Among the best of the attractive barked species are *barbatum*, reddish-plum to deep purple; *hodgsonii*, creamy, pink, brown, green and mauve; *arboreum*, rough, tan to mauve; *thomsonii*, creamy-brown, pink and green, *subansiriense* and *faucium* (*hylaeum*), silvery to grey-brown, peeled smooth; *triflorum* (western forms), brown to pinky-chestnut; *stenaulum* (tender), rich reddish-mahogany and *falconeri*, red-brown. Several members of the Ciliicalyx Alliance also have fine smooth bark.

While I do not advocate too much sun reaching the bark and hence the root area, shafts of sunshine, especially in winter, show up the bark beautifully.

Scent

It is indeed unfortunate that the majority of species which have strongly sweet-scented flowers are tender or very tender. Only in coastal and insular parts of Britain are a large selection of these tender species able to be grown outside.

Scented rhododendrons are chiefly found in four parts of the genus, the hardiest of course being in the Pentanthera subgenus (Azalea series), section Pentanthera (sub-series Luteum). The best of these are the common yellow azalea *luteum*, itself and a number of the American species, notably *occidentale*, *atlanticum*, *viscosum*, *arborescens*, *canescens* and *prinophyllum* (*roseum*).

The second group is found in the Fortunea subsection. These vary in hardiness but *fortunei* itself is the toughest, while some forms of *decorum* will grow in most parts of Britain. Also fairly hardy is *discolor*, rare in its true form. More tender, but often well scented, are *griffithianum* and *diaprepes*. R. *fortunei* and *decorum* are the only scented evergreen species suitable for planting in woodland conditions throughout most of Britain.

The third and largest group is the Maddenia subsection. R. *maddenii* (including *crassum*) in all its diverse forms gives a delicious perfume around mid-summer. Certain types of *crassum* are reasonably hardy in sheltered woodlands and only loose all their buds in hard winters. The Dalhousiae and Megacalyx Alliances possibly produce the finest scented species in the genus, *lindleyi*, *taggianum* and *megacalyx* being supreme. These are moderately hardy on the western seaboard and worth trying on shaded walls and other favourable sites particularly the Ludlow and Sherriff introduction of *lindleyi*.

The large Ciliicalyx Alliance is odd. Many are well scented while some splendid white flowered species such as *ludwigianum* have no scent at all. To me, *inaequale* and *coxianum* really take some beating with their exquisite scent; *edgeworthii* is another superbly scented species.

Lastly, the comparatively unknown Choniastrum section (Stamineum series) which are surprisingly rare, have some fine scents to be discovered. Admittedly the majority are tender and grow too large for the average greenhouse, but *wilsonae* and *stamineum* (at least in the clones represented at Wakehurst in Sussex) have proved remarkably hardy and *stenaulum* survives in the warmest Cornish gardens. These have a lovely heliotrope type scent and should be more widely grown where the climate allows.

Also some Vireyas are scented, *konori* and *superbum* being outstanding.

Most aromatic foliaged species occur among the dwarfs, but various members of the Triflora and all the Heliolepida subsections are strongly aromatic, although it may be said that the smell from these is not always highly desirable.

Some plants of the Taliensia subsection have been found to have surprisingly strong scented indumentum which is considered pleasant by many people.

Scent can of course be elusive and is generally at its best during warm, damp weather, especially in the early morning or evening. Many of the Ciliicalyx and Dalhousiae Alliances may be grown in pots (see *p.* 61) and brought into the house, while the larger species can usually spare a few flowering shoots to adorn and scent a room in a flower arrangement.

Colour

I just want to make a few remarks about colour, especially blues and yellows and how they seem to vary from place to place and season to season.

Many good blues have come from Tremeer, the garden made by General Harrison near Bodmin, Cornwall. He worked on this group very successfully for many years and has shown some outstanding hybrids. I certainly do not want to belittle his efforts, but we have found that the same plants that he has shown, grown on here, while still good and worth growing, do not show the same clearness or richness of blue shades. Possibly the light intensity in the south of England accentuates the pigments in some way or another. It is also discernible here that in some seasons the blues are better than others and I feel they are usually better in a good flowering season for those particular plants. Also hard frost during the dormant season may intensify the depth of colour and, conversely, climates with little or no winter frosts tend to have poor depths of a colour, such as yellow as in California.

Yellows can behave in a different manner. Geoffrey Gorer of Sunte House, Haywards Heath, Sussex, remarked that climatic conditions which produce good deep yellows, give rather dirty blues and vice versa – 1974 was certainly a good blue year. We have observed here that in a year with poorly developed trusses, which tend to be small and contain a number of aborted buds per truss, the depth of yellow pigmentation is sub-standard. This poor development may not be connected with frost in any way, or, on the contrary, may be due to early autumn frosts. Malformed buds which appear smaller than average often result from drought or may be due to immature plants. The latter may have small trusses of little substance and poor colour at their first flowering. This is seen in big-leaved species quite often.

I confess to being very unscientific, especially on the subject of plant pigments. Many learned articles have been written on the subject, but they are generally in such terms as to be way above my head in my ability to understand them.

Indoors

Cultivation of rhododendrons under glass can be divided roughly into two groups, those grown in containers and those grown in beds, although some plants grown epiphytically hardly qualify for either group.

The great advantage of growing in a container is that this can be moved, plant and all, into the house when in flower and can also be plunged out of doors during the summer months. Whichever method is used, careful management is needed to ensure satisfactory results and we can truthfully admit to our fair share of failures with rhododendrons indoors.

For both beds and containers, good drainage is the first essential and any naturally epiphytic species will be the earliest to show ill-effects of any inadequacy in this sphere. As many tender species are naturally epiphytic, this drainage is of added importance and the growing medium should never be firmed or trampled on.

Beds need a great depth to enable the full complement of drainage materials and growing medium to be housed. New beds in the Temperate House at Kew, were bottomed with 30 cm (12 in.) of broken brick, then clinkers and ash in graded layers, followed by sandy, gravelly sub-soil and finished with 38 cm (15 in.) of a mixture of loam, peat and sand. I made the mistake years ago of using alkaline leafmould and alkaline sand with the disastrous results of severe chlorosis and leaf drop. Latterly, a bed consisting of just peat and good oak and beech leafmould had led to too much leggy and top-heavy growth and a reluctance to set flower buds. Some watering system should be installed which gives as even a covering as possible, which is not always easy with a mass of foliage, and make sure the beds are regularly given a thorough soaking.

Even in the best of horicultural establishments I have seen pockets of trouble in these beds. Obviously, a great difficulty in many areas is finding a source of softish water and where the water is hard, an adequate supply of rainwater is not easy to come by. Our many dry summers of recent years have aggravated the situation.

A new greenhouse in the Royal Botanical Garden, Edinburgh, largely for Malesian Ericaceae, has several raised peat wall beds that look like being ideal for epiphytic species. Plants put in a few months ago already look thoroughly established and healthy. It will be most important to keep the peat wet in summer but never soggy.

It is hoped that rhododendrons in containers may prove to be more easily managed in future with the advent of various growth regulators. Phosfon, Cycocel and B9 have all been used on pot-grown rhododendrons with some degree of success and a newer substance Atrinal looks even more promising. The strength and timing of applications are critical and as tender species are so far of little commercial value, official recommendations are only likely to be available for forced hardy hybrids and Obtusum type (indoor) azaleas. A great variation in response from regulators has been experienced so few definite recommendations can be given.

I have found that the majority of species respond well to an all-pine bark or peat and pine bark compost, with liquid feed during the growing season from February to July, depending on heat and variety. A dilute feed every one or two weeks is generally sufficient and many of the proprietary brands are suitable. Also add a little magnesium limestone.

I still prefer clay pots (if they can be obtained) for permanently potted species. One idea with plastic pots to improve aeration is to make holes up the sides of the pots. Never pot too hard, but avoid air pockets where possible. Do not over pot as the medium can soon become sour and soggy. Never allow pots to dry out.

Pots may be plunged outside during the frost-free period, here from early June to late September. A good site is facing north (Northern Hemisphere), but with plenty of light coming from the north to ripen the wood.

Never let free water stand around the base of a pot if any trouble is experienced from root rot (*Phytophthora*), which is encouraged by a combination of high temperatures and abundant moisture.

For the majority of species, it is only necessary to exclude frost, in fact if minimum temperatures are kept too high, many flower buds will fail to open. A temperature of 3°C (37°F) minimum seems about ideal.

An unusual means of growing relatively tender rhododendrons in cold climates, such as east North America, is in sunken pits. These pits can be made quite deep, 2 m (7 ft) ones have been used with a 60 cm (2 ft) roof above ground level. It is advised to have a north sloping sash and lath shading to fit the sash in sunny weather.

Scent has been covered in the last section and the finest scented species mentioned. Many of the less strongly scented or non-scented tender species are well worth growing. Few people have greenhouses large enough to accommodate such species as the big-leaved groups, Choniastrum section (Stamineum series) or the magnificent red Parishia subsection, but many middle-sized species, especially the Ciliicalyx Alliance are of considerable merit. New introductions have recently been made of the gorgeous *veitchianum* which was a popular plant many years ago. The flowers are very large with the margins of the corolla crinkled. Recently introduced from China are *levinei* and *liliiflorum*, while the rare non-scented *ludwigianum* with huge white flowers is now becoming established in cultivation. Other fine species are *dendricola* (*ciliicalyx*) with large sweetly scented flowers often flushed pink. I do not particularly like *johnstoneanum* 'Double Diamond', which is an almost complete double and seems more tender than the type. The probable hybrid known as *cubittii* is excellent with fairly early flowers, white flushed pink with a yellow throat and some scent.

SHOWING RHODODENDRON TRUSSES AND PLANTS

There is a great deal more in showing rhododendrons than just cutting the odd truss, hurrying it off to a show, shoving it in a vase, and then sitting back and hoping to win a prize. Most people have their own pet methods of cutting, keeping, transporting and staging and there is no doubt that each operation can be done in different ways and produce satisfactory results. I will go through the whole operation from start to finish citing my own and various other people's experiences. Few can admit to not having a great sense of elation when they win an unexpectedly large number of cups and prizes at a show. Never be frightened of showing, however small a collection you have. Some shows cater for beginners with special classes. Showing is great fun, although hard work. It is sad that so few smaller gardens enter the competitive classes in London and the Scottish show.

Cutting should always be done early in the morning if possible, before the sun has a chance to strike the blooms and they should, of course, be put into water quickly in a cool, sunless place under cover and away from any likely damage from wind, birds and so on. The base of the stems can either be split each way with secateurs or hammered. I prefer the former, but does either really help water intake? Cut the stems a little longer than will be necessary for staging.

Try to select trusses or sprays growing upright where possible (even if it means using a ladder or steps) as these stand up much better in a vase and, generally, the larger trusses are on the most vigorous shoots anyway. Select trusses with one or two flowers still in bud and avoid any with missing or bruised flowers, or anything on the point of shedding. Also look out for badly formed flowers, which often result from frost. Get helpers to carry some of the trusses if the quantities warrant it, as trying to carry too much results in damage. Include old wood where possible and collect spare trusses of the best items. Select trusses with good foliage as well as flowers.

Opening trusses indoors rarely works well. The results are usually small, pale-coloured and poorly shaped flowers. I have seldom won prizes with any blooms I have attempted to force out from an inflorescence with no opened buds in it.

Plunge the stems in water as high as you can without the corollas touching the surface. Trusses are best cut the day before the staging time, so they can spend at least 24 hours in water, especially if they are going to be transported out of water. A careful clean-up is worth the time and effort. Remove any badly frosted or eaten leaves, all old seed capsules and, on sprays, any withered or misshapen flowers and the remains of flowers if many corollas have shed.

Many different formulas have been tried to prolong the life of cut blooms or resuscitate drooping ones. Suggested mixtures are 4.5 litres (1 gallon) ginger ale, one teaspoonful naphthaline acetic acid and two teaspoons vitamin B-1. Other substances used include 7-Up, Sprite, Fresca and lemonade, all of which have clearly prolonged the life of cut roses. Another formula is 1 quart 'soda pop', 1.1 litre (1 quart) water and $\frac{1}{2}$ teaspoon of chlorine bleach. The explanation for the success of these concoctions is apparently due to the fact that citric acid and carbonation reduces the growth of bacteria which clog the flower stems and hence water intake. These mixtures can be used after cutting, for transportation, at shows, or all three. Other ways suggested for reviving wilted trusses are placing them in hot water at 43°C (110°F), or putting an aspirin in the water. Various proprietary brands of additives for use in water to prolong the life of cut flowers are now available, such as Chrysal and Substral.

Transportation

There are many ways of actual transportation. Here we are dealing with cut material only, not whole plants. For the London show, I use two methods, one for the train, one for the car. For the train, I use standard flower boxes, as long and as deep as available. When the trusses are removed from water, sphagnum moss (or any moss) is wrapped around the ends of the stems, which are placed in polythene bags and are tightly bound with string (the moss should be previously immersed in water and partially squeezed out). This means that the ends of the stems are virtually still in water, yet the branches can be laid on their sides. Trusses and sprays can be supported with sticks firmly fixed across the box and tissue paper can be gently pushed in to keep the blooms from moving about. Fit as many as possible in a box without actually crushing anything.

With the car, I use old bottles full of water or formula, set upright in drink cartons with the bottle sections left in. The stems should nearly fill the tops of the bottles to stop movement. When the car has been transported on a train, I have had excellent results and everything has arrived in perfect condition.

Other suggestions are to place upright stems in test tubes set in sawdust or styrofoam sheets, or push stems through a good layer of paper into moist sawdust, peat or barkdust in a box. Another method, suitable for short journeys is to place a stick or pole across the top of a box and hang the trusses upside down, ensuring that they do not touch the bottom. Various other containers have been used for the stems, such as milk cartons.

For air transportation or storing for an extra long period, cold stores can be made use of, set at a maximum of 4.5°C (40°F).

If the entries are to be driven all the way to the show, get up early and reach the show before the sun has a chance to heat up the car.

Staging

Certain essentials are a must for an attractive, well-displayed show. These are: plenty of room, well defined classes, good vases, proper cards and labels and nicely shown exhibits. It is such a shame when trusses are overcrowded, classes confused with each other, paper cartons used as vases, messy cards attached to leaves or containers and little trouble taken with cleaning up and properly staging the entries. It is most important to face the blooms the best way round and fix the stem so that the flowers do not flop forwards or sideways. Paper, moss, sand and so on can be used for this purpose.

Another point often overlooked is reading and following the schedules for each particular class. Far too many entries land up in the wrong classes; so-called species are often hybrids and trusses are entered where they should be sprays. A class full of fine sprays almost up to the maximum size allowed can look magnificent. If poorly shown sprays or even single trusses are entered with these large sprays, they spoil the whole effect and never win prizes. It is up to the people organizing shows to have them stewarded properly by someone with knowledge and have clear-cut regulations laid down. Dare I say that some shows have too many cups and trophies!

I saw an unusual way of showing in America once. This show was held outside, which I considered brave. The containers were firmly fixed on to a slatted fence in three rows. I had the impression that it gave competitors a fairer chance than on the usual raised staging. This method, can, of course, be used equally well indoors and helps to save space.

A point that often astounds us when we visit or read about American shows is the enormous attendances compared with ours. The Oakland, California, spring garden show of 1955 had over 100,000 while many have 25,000 to 30,000. We frequently get numbers counted only in hundreds at our shows. Only our annual Chelsea show or big county shows, with numerous other attractions, can equal these figures.

Our award systems are quite different from those in America (see *p*. 92). We can receive awards by simply taking cut trusses, sprays or plants into a committee room. I feel it is perhaps a pity that awards can be given to cut rhododendrons arranged in a vase where the actual habit of the plant cannot be judged. Maybe the answer is to give only preliminary awards at show committee meetings and to start a new standard of awards at the Wisley (Royal Horticultural Society's Garden) trials. To do this properly and fairly, other trial gardens would be needed.

Showing plants (as opposed to cut blooms) is of course simpler in many ways, although it is all too easy to be fooled by the weather either being too hot or too cold. Never try to open rhododendrons (hardy types) entirely under glass as the flower colour will be faded. If forcing is necessary, it is a good plan to swell the buds indoors, then open the blooms outside. Likewise, do not leave half-opened blooms in too dark a shed to hold them back. Plants lifted just before a show and replanted afterwards often suffer a surprisingly bad setback and may need extra water and frost protection. It is really better to lift the plants earlier and either containerize them or burlap them and plunge them in peat. Replunge again after the show and do not plant out until the end of the

growing season. Rhododendrons should not be forced in high temperatures or too much sunlight and the greenhouse should be kept well
dampened down.

PHOTOGRAPHY OF RHODODENDRONS

As I do not claim to be a good photographer, I am not going to attempt
here to go into details of equipment, lighting and fine close-up work, but
just give a few hints from my own experience and that of others.

Single lens reflex cameras are the best and easiest for plant photo-
graphy. Cheap cameras cannot produce good, sharp pictures as shutter
speed, size of aperture and focusing cannot be adjusted.

Rhododendron flowers, particularly those of light shades, reflect sunlight. I have had many poor results by taking shots in full sun resulting in
blurred over-exposed blooms, while the surrounds are sharp and of
correct exposure. It is important to test the exposure meter a few centimetres from the flowers, not necessarily at the distance the photograph
is to be taken from. Full sun interferes with the colour as viewed by both
camera and eye. Either avoid close-ups in full sun, or take the photographs under a white nylon umbrella to make light shadow (shade).

Much time can be wasted trying to photograph in the wind when even a
tripod is not of much help in steadying the camera or the object. Tripods
are certainly desirable for close-up work. If the object is still, the shutter
speed can be greatly reduced, therefore allowing a smaller aperture and
greater depth of focus. It is very hard to get depth of focus early in the
season when light is weak, so tripods at this season are essential. Fast films
do help in this case, but they generally have poorer colour renderings and
produce a coarser-grained finish, which is unsatisfactory in enlargements.

If light flowers are to be photographed and the exposure is set for the
flowers, then the foliage and background will be under-exposed and
therefore dark. When taking single trusses, it may be desirable to make
the background out of focus, thereby maintaining the truss as the only
centre of interest.

A few words of advice on cine-filming of rhododendrons. Do not take
too short a footage of each object, keep the camera as steady as possible
and while a slow steady pan shot of a general view is effective, do not jump
from subject to subject when the camera is still in action.

With some experience, interesting results can be obtained by taking
photographs against or side on to the sun. If taking shots against the sun,
the lens must be shaded. Other unusual shots can be made by taking
close-ups of hairs, indumentum and parts of young growth. Taking these
from odd angles may accentuate the objects leading to most unusual
pictures.

3 *Planting and maintenance*

It cannot be over emphasized how important the initial preparation of the ground is for rhododendrons. It can be said that this makes all the difference to the well-being of the plants for the whole of their lifetime on that site. How often are sickly, under-nourished plants seen that will never flourish however long they are established? Subsequent treatment in the way of top dressings and mulches will never compensate for poor soil preparation.

What preparation is necessary depends entirely on the existing soil on the site to be planted. The ideal to be aimed for is a well-drained, loose, moderately acid, moisture-retentive medium. Disappointment will result if any of these aspects are lacking.

Drainage

No attempt is made here to explain how to drain; this information is readily available elsewhere. Rhododendrons do not object to occasional flooding by surface water, especially during the winter months, but any indication of puddles failing to disappear immediately after heavy rain or snow melt must be looked into. A slope does not indicate adequate drainage. Pockets cut in clay on a slope can hold water. In our west coast garden, three of our wettest areas are on steep slopes. On one, a deep, soaking sponge of sphagnum moss has formed, on the second there is a curious thin layer of sodden black peat lying on solid rock. The third, an uneven slope in half sun, consists of sticky, soaking loam. Another quite common poorly drained site is a cup or cleft between or over rock. Planting directly into these has led to several deaths. In all these cases we now raise the elevation of the planting hole so that the base of the root ball is level with, or above, the original ground level. This results in the plant frequently sitting in a mound of soil, which would be fatal in our dry, well-drained eastern conditions, but has so far proved successful in the west.

Always be suspicious of made-up soil on building sites. This has nearly always been compacted by heavy machinery with disastrous results to the drainage. Heavy clay soils are unsuitable as such for rhododendrons. If the drainage is poor and little can be done to improve it sufficiently, either half- or fully raised beds are essential. Half-raised beds are those with a proportion of the clay incorporated in the prepared planting mixture, while fully raised beds have totally fresh ingredients brought in and set above the level of the clay. This can be surrounded by peat blocks, wooden slabs or stones. Many ingredients are satisfactory, depending on local availability. Acid peat and/or leafmould, conifer needles, ground or shredded bark, bark chips, wood chips, coarse sawdust, forest litter, cones, rotten wood, swamp muck, peanut hulls, chopped bracken (rotted), bracken soil, crushed corn cobs or similar materials are all suitable.

Sawdust has proved satisfactory and sometimes very beneficial in western North America, provided adequate nitrogen is added. Many people advocate several light applications instead of one heavy one of nitrogen. As a rough guide, add 5.4 kg (12 lbs) of ammonium sulphate per 93 sq. m (1,000 sq. ft) for each 2.5 cm (1 in.) of sawdust worked into the soil. Good root systems result where the soil has become half-sawdust over the years. One American gets good results by mixing cow manure and sawdust and working it into the soil. In the eastern USA particularly, it is very difficult to estimate the amount of nitrogen to add. Apparently it causes an imbalance of potassium and magnesium with approximately three times the normal level of potassium and one-third of the magnesium, but this can be corrected. A word of warning. This sawdust must be very coarse. Our British version is not recommended for mixing into the soil, as it is too fine.

Be careful of very dry peat. If well mixed into damp soil, no previous wetting is needed, but if planting is to be done into a high percentage of peat, always damp thoroughly *before* planting.

Preparing the soil

The only sites unlikely to need any preparations or additions are woodlands where there is a deep layer of natural acid leafmould, conifer needles or certain types of peaty soil. Even these are better when well-dug or forked over before planting, in order to mix the different layers of soil, to cut tree roots and to break any hard pan which might be impervious to good drainage.

Any soil without an abundance of organic matter should have a liberal amount added. While any of the materials mentioned above for raised beds will help, coarse peat, acid, oak and bench leafmould, pulverized bark and pine or spruce needles are the best ingredients available in Britain. For individual holes, add at least two large shovelfuls per hole for young or small plants and correspondingly more for anything larger. For beds, apply 18 litres ($\frac{1}{2}$ bushel) per sq. m (11 sq ft). In heavy loam, add well-weathered ashes, sand or gravel to loosen up the soil and be used as an addition to the organic matter, which should be as rough as possible itself. Always mix with the existing soil very thoroughly to at least 30 cm (12 in.) deep and break up all clods as fine as possible. Light soils, while affording a good root run, dry out all too readily. Again incorporate plenty of organic matter and apply a mulch to last over the summer months (see Mulching, *p.* 78). Avoid the use of fresh, lower spit peat. Heavy soils may be improved by adding gypsum (calcium sulphate) which helps to flocculate the clay. Apply 454 g (1 lb) per 9.30 sq. m (100 sq. ft) about every 2 years. Sprinkle it on and either scratch or water it in (do not dig it in).

For moderately alkaline soil, the following preparation has proved satisfactory. Dig out beds 38 cm (15 in.) deep and cover the bottom with

10–15 cm (4–6 in.) of clinker or other rough material. Next add a layer of really coarse lumps of peat and loam, then fill the beds with half-peat and half-local loam, which in this case should not be broken too fine. The beds are not raised where the local water is alkaline, to avoid rapid drying out. This formula has worked quite well in the Glasnevin Botanic Garden, Dublin, especially for Triflorums. For acidifying the soil, see Fertilizers, pH and lime, *p.* 70.

Rotten stumps or logs are often ideal situations in which to plant various species, particularly those of an epiphytic nature. Many establish themselves quicker into rotten wood than the open ground and will withstand dry conditions, with less irrigation necessary. If very rotten, the centres can be dug with a spade and little if any nitrogen need be added. An elevation of over 1.22–1.52 m (4–5 ft) off the ground helps against frost damage, but additional wind protection is appreciated. Peat or other organic matter may be added to fill up a hollow. A very large hollow can be partially filled with stones or other rubbish before adding peat. In mild, wet districts, great fun may be had by placing plants on top of mossy rocks, up-ended logs, hollows and forks in trees and even on the top of wide horizontal branches, provided there is some natural moss already present. The moss can be parted and some organic matter placed in the hole (see Planting, *p.* 73).

In Britain, rotten tree stumps and logs tend to be a plant health hazard owing to honey fungus (*Armillaria* species), see Diseases, *p.* 326. I feel this hazard has to be tolerated and eventually the stumps may be used as described above. Very few people can afford labour or equipment to remove stumps of any size, but I would definitely recommend removing all old rhododendron stumps.

To sum up, whatever your rhododendrons are to be planted in, try to have a medium as loose and friable as possible, yet moisture retentive.

SELECTION OF PLANTS

Before starting a collection of species or taking over and adding to an existing one, ask the question – is the aim to have an authentic collection of true and properly named species, or just an assemblage of chance seedlings or any oddments that can be picked up from diverse sources? In other words, is it a connoisseur's collection or a jumble of seedlings of doubtful parentage? There is no doubt that the latter is cheaper to assemble, but surely the end result is much less rewarding and certainly of much less interest. I am often surprised at owners of fine species collections being satisfied with a motley collection of self sown seedlings as successors to their fine old introductions of say Forrest's or Kingdon Ward's. I do admit that these seedlings are rather fun and worth transplanting into outside woods to watch their progress. No doubt I will be shot at for being a purist, but surely it is more desirable to preserve and add to authentic species by layering and other means of vegetative propagation and bringing in new species forms, than ultimately to replace good species with a host of bastards.

Many gardeners start with a few well-known hybrids, then graduate on to species as they get more enthusiastic. This trait is especially noticeable in the Pacific north-west of North America. Only relatively few nurserymen specialize in species (see *p.* 337) and many of the rarer items may only be available occasionally if at all. In America, vegetatively propagated species are now available to members of the Rhododendron Species Foundation and a scheme in Britain is being worked out to make special clones of species more readily obtainable. Personally, I am confident that species will at least retain their present popularity status or even gain against hybrids as more people realize how much more interesting they are to grow.

Special award clones of species will nearly always be more expensive than those grown from seed. Many species or forms of species are sufficiently uniform in their garden value and variation not to warrant vegetative propagation and the great majority, whether grown from hand-pollinated or wild collected seed, make fine plants that will please 95 per cent of gardeners.

In the case of the Triflora subsection, most are easily rooted from cuttings, which is fortunate, as in this case many inferior forms exist which should ultimately be eliminated (see *p.* 299 and 307). Open pollinated seedlings are almost always better avoided.

Grafted versus own root plants is an oft-repeated argument. Many people still regard *ponticum* as the only understock to be used, while in fact many species or hybrids are frequently made use of. Only special clones of hard-to-root species are normally grafted and so long as *ponticum* is not used, there is little or no danger of suckering. One advantage of grafting is that flowers are often produced at an earlier age, but this advantage is more than cancelled out by the dangers of breaking off and constriction at the union. It has been stated that grafted rhododendrons should never be planted in a really hot climate as the flow of sap is frequently insufficient at the union and the plant wilts, never to recover. I am speaking of prolonged temperatures of the range 35–40°C (95–104°F).

Whether to acquire large or small plants really depends on the depth of one's pocket. Large plants often take that much longer to settle in, especially if the soil is very different from what they were growing in previously and may never make any really worthwhile growth. Large specimens usually have a higher percentage of their roots removed by the nurseryman to facilitate ease of moving and less loss of valuable top soil.

Finally, do not be tempted to grow species that are obviously unsuitable for a given site. Remember the rule that, by and large, the bigger the leaf, the more shelter is needed.

FERTILIZERS, pH AND LIME

Many fine healthy collections of species exist where no fertilizer has ever been added. Generally speaking, the more perfect the environment for rhododendrons, the less attention need be paid to nutrition. I suppose this is obvious, but in America particularly, many gardeners feel they must be doing something for the welfare of their plants, regardless of whether they appear healthy or not.

As a nurseryman, I am naturally anxious to make a saleable plant as quickly as possible without forcing it into too much soft growth. Here lies the secret. In the great majority of cases, a little fertilizer applied occasionally, can produce a better specimen quickly, provided other cultural requirements are taken care of. Fertilizer can never cure inadequate shade, shelter, moisture, drainage and organic matter or poor soil preparation. It should be looked upon as an added luxury to improve on the foliage, growth, number of flowers and increase in hardiness (because of sturdy, not leggy growth).

What I preach for here is moderation whenever applying any chemical to rhododendrons. As explained in Chapter 1, rhododendrons grow naturally on soils poor in most essential elements. Why is it then that people expect them to respond favourably to overdoses under cultivation? At best, this results in too much soft, lanky growth, at worst, leaf scorch, severe chlorosis and death.

Like all other plants, rhododendrons do, of course, need some of all the major elements, nitrogen (N), phosphorus (P), potassium (K), calcium (Ca), sulphur (S), and magnesium (Mg), and the minor (trace) elements, manganese (Mn), boron (B), copper (Cu), zinc (Zn), iron (Fe), and molybdenum (Mo). Here we shall only say something about the major elements, iron and the trace elements combined.

Nitrogen is best applied in the form of ammonium, not nitrate. Ammonium leads to a greater acidity of the leaf tissue, which is beneficial, and less is needed to promote good growth than with nitrate. High nitrate levels can cause chlorosis. It is likely that rhododendrons suffer less from drought when there is a good N level in the soil than when it is adequate. N can either be applied in a proprietary compound fertilizer, or by itself in the form of ammonium sulphate, hoof and horn, cotton seed meal, urea or one of the new slow-acting forms (see below) such as 'Gold N'. N encourages vegetative growth and chlorophyll.

Phosphorus is usually obtainable as superphosphate or in compounds. It is especially beneficial for flower bud production. Heavy applications have been found to bring startling results. As an excess of any chemical is liable to cause upsets in the soil leading to other elements becoming unavailable, these heavy applications cannot be generally recommended. K is apparently not needed in any quantity by rhododendrons. It is best applied in a compound fertilizer or as potassium sulphate. K helps to ripen young growth and prevent disease. All three of these elements are needed for growth and health of the plants.

Deficiencies of the above elements are common and all are shown on a regular soil analysis. Other frequent deficiencies are of Mg, which is important for chlorophyll formation and also probably helps to stop excessive intake of Ca and K which can harm rhododendrons. Ca is usually plentiful enough for rhododendrons, but a few very acid soils, like greensand in southern England and peaty and other soils in west Scotland, do benefit from Ca being added in the form of magnesium limestone (dolomite), ordinary lime or the non-alkaline gypsum (calcium sulphate). Not only does the latter improve heavy soils (see *p.* 68) but it appears to improve growth better than magnesium limestone. It is almost insoluble and the reasons for this response is not apparently known. We find that a handful of gypsum well scattered over the root area is very effective on chlorosis in our Argyll garden. Sulphur is usually abundant, partly due to atmospheric pollution, but alkaline soil can be improved for acid-loving plants by adding a good sprinkling of flowers of sulphur to the peat that is incorporated into the soil. Either add Mg as Epsom salts or in one of the newer compounds. P in late summer ripens wood and sets buds.

Do not apply N fertilizers after June or July, depending on how early or severe autumn frosts are likely to occur. The Americans are keen on an early winter application of N to enhance foliage, buds and spring growth.

I am now doubtful of the value of slow acting fertilizers on rhododendrons as they do not appear to give the right amount of elements at the right time. Some release more during hot weather, which is usually in late summer and can lead to soft late growth, scorch and excessive frost damage.

Several organic fertilizers, such as bonemeal and seaweed extracts, can be used but only in minimal quantities. Fish manure may cause chlorosis and poultry manure is usually too high in N (ammonium). I have seen old cattle manure used with some success but it is inclined to dry out and get scattered in dry weather if used as a top dressing.

I like to add fertilizer (general) twice a year April–May and June–July. For planting or transplanting I mix it well into the beds or individual holes prior to planting. As a top dressing, I only apply it where really considered necessary. The fertilizer must be evenly scattered over the planting or root areas, never apply it in heaps around the stem. I like an organic-based compound, analysis 12 N 6 P 6K for all but the most N sensitive species, such as certain members of the Taliensia subsection. Another good-balanced mixture is 5 N 10 P 10 K, although in both cases less K would probably be more satisfactory.

Many claims have been made on the startling effects lime can have on growth and leaf colour on certain soils, but few of these claims rest on scientific data, such as the types of lime used and the acidity of the soil treated. More research needs to be done on Ca in its many forms and its effects on rhododendrons.

The term pH is a means of measuring soil acidity or alkalinity; pH 7 in neutral, 6 slightly acid and 8 slightly alkaline, 5 is ten times more acid than 6 and 4 a hundred times more acid than 6 and so on. An ideal pH for rhododendrons is around 5–5.5, but 4.5 to 6 are generally suitable. Over 6 may necessitate extra peat or even sulphur to reduce the pH, while under 5 may need gypsum or magnesium limestone and under 4.5 some lime.

A high pH usually means excessive lime in the soil, although if the alkalinity is caused by Mg rather than Ca, it may be tolerated by rhododendrons. It is now apparent that they are very efficient utilizers of Ca in the soil. If Ca occurs to excess, as in chalk, they take up far too much and poison themselves.

Various methods can be used to reduce the pH or make certain elements, usually unavailable to rhododendrons in soil rich in calcium carbonate, become available. Aluminium sulphate, while an effective pH reducer, is not recommended as it harms rhododendrons. Several forms of S are much better, such as flowers of sulphur and ferrous sulphate. Ammonium sulphate marginally helps to increase acidity and annual applications of acid peat to increase acidity can be a good remedy. Chelates (sequestrines) can help on some soils but certain species, notably Vireyas can be severely burnt by the recommended doses. Several experiments at Glendoick on chlorotic plants have produced no positive results on improvements in leaf colour. Rayplex Fe is a cheaper alternative to sequestrine for supplying iron to plants and it is also available with other trace elements. It is apparent that rhododendrons can assimilate the most advantageous balance of elements for their well-being in the pH recommended above (5–5.5).

PLANTING

Nearly everyone is guilty of planting rhododendrons with a lack of foresight. I have yet to visit a garden where the planting has not been too close and certain species are completely out-growing their allotted space. If one is prepared to move say every second plant after about 10 years, well and good, but who can be sure that by that time you or your successor will be able or willing to carry out the necessary work? If there is plenty of space, do give ample room for growth even if it means the initial planting looks very sparse. It is particularly the big-leaved species that need abundant space to expand and they soon spoil each other when their branches meet. Make up your mind whether you are planning for the desired effect to be 10, 20 or 30 years ahead. Do not plant dwarfs or semi-dwarfs among strong growers. They will become over-shaded and die.

It is forever important to press home the golden rule not to plant rhododendrons too deep. Never put more than a bare covering of soil over the top of the root ball, watching carefully the previous soil mark on the stem. If the plant is unhealthy and the soil mark is well up the stem, it was too deep previously. Never mound the soil up the stem. The only exception to this rule is with a grafted plant. This grows away better if the union can sooner or later be buried and the scion is able to form roots itself (except in the case of a top-worked standard). A good method is to plant in a cup with the normal soil level just above the level of the graft.

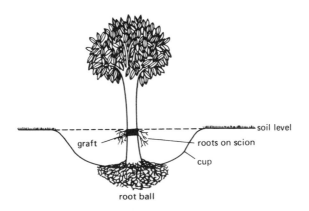

Planting cup

This cup can be gradually filled up over a period of years depending on how high the union is.

Whether to firm or not to firm when planting is always a debatable question. Many Americans advocate no firming, only a good watering in. Americans have two advantages over us. They nearly always have water laid on throughout their gardens and they do not suffer our degree of wind ferocity. Here in Britain, some firming is advisable around the stem even on apparently well-sheltered sites. Only gentle firming with the toes is permitted. Never tamp down hard and never use the heel. The heavier and/or wetter the ground is, the less firming up should be done. In very windy positions, especially with species such as Triflorums and Cinnabarinums, staking may be needed. Always put the stake in before filling in the hole and where possible, avoid pushing a thick stake through the root ball.

Watering in is desirable, particularly in the growing season, dry weather or in the spring. Plants from containers need special care. If planting is done in hot weather, careful attention must be paid to frequent watering. If the root ball is tight and matted, either gently tease open parts of the ball or better still, wash off some of the soil with a jet spray to expose the root tips. This will encourage fresh roots to emerge into the soil as all too often root-bound, container-grown plants never produce fresh roots and eventually languish and die. Also wash roots of plants grown in clay soil.

When planting epiphytic species on to tree trunks (see Soil preparation and drainage, *p.* 69), string may be needed temporarily to hold the moss in place around the roots. For pockets in rocks and trunks, a novel idea is to smear the outside of the pocket after planting with fresh cow dung which has been mixed with a little water in a bucket. This surrounds the pocket with a fairly impervious coating. It helps to retain moisture and has an acid reaction suitable for rhododendrons.

Much nonsense is talked about the benefits of spring planting. Personally, I nearly always encourage people to plant in autumn. The plants get well bedded in by the winter rains and are much more likely to withstand droughts and wind during their first growing season. Only on very cold, windy sites where the leaves may be blown off would I suggest spring planting. But if the site is that bad, they are likely to grow poorly anyway. Another disadvantage of spring planting is where plants are brought from a relatively mild area into one colder, later, and more susceptible to spring frosts. These plants are bound to be further advanced than they would have been if over-wintered on the site, resulting in far worse damage than would have been inflicted on naturally retarded ones. Also, in most seasons, the ground is in a much better condition for planting in the autumn; springs are invariably too wet, too dry or too cold.

PRUNING

As a general rule, rhododendron species should be allowed to grow naturally and provided they are healthy and of good habit, should never have live wood cut off them. All species have individual forms, which they ultimately grow into if they are given adequate light, shelter, soil and space suitable to their individual requirements. Two types of pruning should be carried out regularly, especially with the big-leaved species. These are dead-wooding and dead-heading.

Dead-wooding

This should be an annual winter chore. Dead and dying wood is always ugly and its removal greatly enhances the appearance of any plant where it is easily seen. Cut cleanly and right up flush with the trunk or to the nearest live shoot. Never leave snags and stumps. These are very unsightly and just encourage decay. When large branches are removed, it is advisable to paint the cut with a recommended wound healer. For twigs, this is unnecessary. I usually gather the smaller prunings around the roots of large rhododendrons as these help to trap falling leaves and create a natural mulch. It is suggested that the light and air let in by the removal of dead wood improves growth and checks lichen and moss on the branches.

Dead-heading

Do this as soon as possible after the flowers shed and before the capsules start to swell. It is, of course, hardly possible to dead-head every plant in an extensive collection, or those species with small flowers and capsules like Triflorums. Those species that are liable to develop heavy crops of large capsules, such as the Grandia and Falconera subsections, are those in most need. Much energy is absorbed by a heavy crop of seed that is better diverted into producing new growth and flower buds. The ease in removing the old trusses varies from species to species and care must be taken not to remove growth buds and leaves as well. Usually, the whole inflorescence may be snapped off using finger and thumb, but in some large species, it is easier to take off the individual flower stalks. In certain years, frost takes away the need for this job on at least the early flowering species. Thorough dead-heading is particularly important after a heavy blooming season.

A few people have the mistaken idea that a cool climate leads to little open pollinated seed being set. In our cool east Scotland, nothing could be further from the truth. Nearly all species except certain deciduous azaleas, set abundant seed provided they are not frosted.

Pruning old species

Old neglected plants which have been drawn up by too much shade or too close planting may need drastic treatment. Many species do break successfully from old wood and even some of the smoother trunked species grow away after cutting hard back although they are the ones least likely to do so. Triflorums and other lepidotes usually sprout freely. This severe pruning is best done in March in most areas. Try to cut just above dormant buds, as a cut made where there are no buds can result in no growth, owing to the buds being inhibited by the stump above them.

These buds occur near the top of each annual growth and may be hard to locate.

If old specimens are to be moved, do not prune them until re-established in their new site (at least one year). Certain species are better cut right back to the stump as a better shaped bush will result and there is less likelihood of die-back. There can be no guarantee that the larger-leaved species will sprout and if they are valuable, it would be better to lay them on their sides and layer the tips. Vigorous young growth from the stumps is liable to be very soft and vulnerable to autumn or winter frost injury.

Pruning in mild localities

In very favourable areas only, certain vigorous species of rather straggly habits can be regularly pruned if compact bushes are desired. Species in this category are *griersonianum* and *johnstoneanum*. Pruning should be done soon after flowering. Cut back all long shoots and use shears if necessary. Personally, I feel that these hard pruned plants look rather artificial.

Azaleas

Lichen indicates poor health and growth and in most cases, deciduous azaleas can be revitalized by severe cutting back after flowering. Apply a good feed and/or mulch to encourage strong growth. Pentanthera section (Luteum series) azaleas respond well to a fairly high nitrogen fertilizer, but more discretion must be taken over others.

Hedges

R. ponticum is frequently used as a hedge in good rhododendron areas and can be severely clipped. Other species can be made into a rather looser, informal type of hedge such as the Triflorums, *rubiginosum* and tall forms of *racemosum*.

Pinching and pruning young plants

Young species grown from seed should be allowed to develop naturally. Many large species often form single trunks and these should not be interfered with. A plant whose first growth flush is easily frosted, may not keep a leader and some pruning may be necessary if a new leader is desired. Young plants should be encouraged to retain as much foliage as possible and many should be clothed to the ground for several years, especially those of a bushy habit. If a seedling or rooted cutting is heavily pinched from an early age, too many weak stems can result. Once the bush starts to flower, the shoots may be pulled outwards and downwards by the weight and not rise up again, leaving an ugly hole in the centre which is hard to refurbish. Only the smaller-leaved Triflorum type of plant, especially those propagated vegetatively, may need regular pinching and pruning to avoid lanky, ungainly growth.

WATERING

All rhododendrons appreciate an abundance of moisture in the growing season yet cannot tolerate water-logged conditions. They can put up with a limited amount of surface water in winter, provided it is not stagnant.

Many parts of America and Australia have dry summer seasons and therefore need prolonged artificial watering to ensure satisfactory growth. Even in Britain, a watering system is desirable in drier parts, especially where the soil is light or poor in natural organic matter.

For those who need a constant supply of water for regular watering, it is well worth installing an elaborate system of sprinklers covering the whole rhododendron area. For those who need water only now and then, occasional water points with long lengths of hose should suffice. Many types of excellent, reliable sprinklers are now available, which give an even spread, although many produce a circular rather than a square coverage.

Always give the ground a good soaking with each watering. We leave our sprinklers on for about 3 hours over open ground with small plants and no tree roots, and 5 to 8 hours with large bushes and tree roots present. During hot, dry weather, this usually lasts us a week or more. Try to avoid puddling the ground.

Do not overhead water those rhododendrons in flower, especially late flowering whites, such as *crassum*, *diaprepes* and *auriculatum*, as it turns the flowers brown.

Much has been said and written about the pros and cons of watering on into the autumn. It has now generally been decided that it should be carried on if the soil is very dry, especially with anything newly planted or which makes very late growth. If plants suffer from drought conditions in the autumn, they may fail to develop flower buds properly and go into winter in poor condition.

Do not use water that has had water softener added. The sodium used in the process is poisonous to plants. Water high in soluble salts is bad. It should be de-ionized first and then the desirable liquid fertilizers can be added later if thought necessary. This is rather an expensive process.

The severe drought of 1976 over much of West Europe, England and Wales severely affected many rhododendron gardens and nurseries. Even in Boskoop, Holland where the canals are a mere 45 cm (18 in.) below ground level, the build up of salinity stopped the use of the water for overhead irrigation. Throughout much of England, the use of hoses was banned for several months. The result was many losses.

WEEDKILLERS

The range of weedkillers now available enables us to keep weeds among rhododendrons more easily under control. Rhododendrons do not like a mat of weeds or other plants growing over their roots, which compete for moisture and nourishment. Follow instructions carefully and only spray among one's prize plants oneself. These are a tested selection.

Sodium chlorate is still very useful for killing out weeds on areas of unplanted ground. Heavy applications will kill virtually everything but creeping grasses are rather resistant to lighter doses. Do not plant for at least 6 months.

Carbon 2 (Triclopyr) is a replacement for the old brushwood killer (2, 4, 5-T). This is very useful on many scrubby and broad-leaved perennial weeds, although subsequent applications may be necessary. Spraying is best done about June when most weeds are about full grown. Some brands seem more volatile than others and these should be avoided as young rhododendron growth can be twisted by fumes or drift. It is safe to spray quite close to established plants when growth is hardened, but as growth comes over a long period, this is difficult. Weeds cut over in May will be ready to spray in July–August when most rhododendron growth is hardening.

Prefix (Chlorthiamid) and Casoron G (Dichlobenil) are effective on perennial weeds among rhododendron roots. These act through the roots of herbaceous plants. While they do not often harm rhododendrons, they have caused deaths among shrubs of various kinds and may encourage pathogens like *Phytophthora*. Use at only half-strength on azaleas. Best applied early in the year *before* the weeds emerge.

Asulox (Asulam) is one of the weedkillers successful on docks and bracken. Best applied when the foliage of both weeds is reaching maturity. May need a repeated application.

Ramrod (Propachlor) can be used in the granulated form to control germinating weeds on clean ground among young rhododendrons. Apply in spring and reapply every 6 weeks during growing season. This will not kill weeds that have already germinated. Do not use on plants that have had less than two growing seasons.

Gramoxone or Weedol (Paraquat). This most valuable herbicide burns off the top-growth of most weeds and as it breaks down quickly in the soil, can be applied right up to the trunks or stems of rhododendrons. Avoid touching green wood or foliage where it will cause brown spots. Nettles, ground ivy and cleavers are rather resistant as are shrubby weeds. Apply two to three times a year to give a good control of weeds on root areas.

Glyphosate is excellent for clearing areas prior to planting or careful spot treatment amongst established rhododendrons.

Brushwood killer may be used a bit stronger than usual mixed with diesel oil to kill sprouting stumps. Excellent for killing *ponticum* and *Gaultheria shallon* and other woody subjects. Cut these down to the ground and spray as they are sprouting. Use 0.568 litre (1 pint) 50 per cent 2,4,5–T in 18 litres (4 gallons) of diesel. Large sheets of black polythene are excellent weed suppressors. These can either be left permanently and covered with some weedless mulch, such as old sawdust or shredded bark, or left long enough to kill out patches of weeds. Strong perennial weeds may need at least two seasons.

MULCHING

The purpose of mulching varies according to the climate. In Britain, we mulch largely to feed our rhododendrons. This mulching is especially necessary in positions where the plants quickly exhaust the shallow soil or pockets they are growing in. If no regular feeding is given (using organic matter) in these situations, foliage soon deteriorates, growth becomes weak, die-back sets in and eventually death occurs long before their allotted span of life. It is not only dry and poor climates where this may happen. In heavy rainfall areas of west Scotland, plants can easily become impoverished through neglect.

Mulching is essential throughout most of North America. For instance, in south-east USA, a mulch helps to keep the soil warmer in winter and cooler in summer as well as conserving soil moisture which is so essential during periods of high temperatures.

Natural leaf fall often goes a long way towards keeping rhododendrons in good health, especially if the trees are those which produce the best leafmould, such as oak and beech, or in the case of needles, pines. We often pile twigs and small branches over the root areas to trap these leaves. Unfortunately, there are all too many 'tidy' gardeners who rake out and burn all the leaf mulch under rhododendrons. Like the starved plants mentioned above, these also gradually lose health, starting with a quicker falling of old leaves. A muttering owner then throws out the plants, saying something about his soil being unsuitable for rhododendrons.

Oak and beech leaves can be raked on to the root areas if these are near by or gathered into heaps and left to rot for 2 years. These break down quicker if turned. The placing of V-shaped wire netting enclosures in the path of the wind is an excellent and labour-saving method. These leaves can also be chopped and mixed with wood chips or placed over the roots when fresh, and coarse sawdust, pulverized bark and chips spread out on top of them. Avoid leafmould from alkaline soil.

Conifer needles make an excellent loose mulch. The coarser needled pines are best for large species while those from smaller needled pines, spruce and so on are best for lower growing species. A mulch of 7.6–10 cm (3–4 in.) deep will sink to 5 cm (2 in.) and last the plants 3 to 4 years. It is neat in appearance and the nature of the needles allows good aeration and a reasonable penetration of rain water. Nothing is needed on top to keep the mulch in place and it has excellent insulating and moisture holding properties.

The various waste wood products such as sawdust, shredded bark and wood chips make first-rate mulches provided they are really coarse. Our sawdust in Britain is invariably too fine, mats down into a tight crust and tends to repel water. Even if the rain soaks in a little, it rarely gets through to the roots. Sawdust in particular takes nitrogen out of the soil to rot it down, leaving the plants underneath temporarily deficient, so extra nitrogen should be added, at approximately 5.4 kg (12 lb) of ammonium sulphate per 92.9 sq. m (1,000 sq. ft) for every 2.5 cm (1 in.) of sawdust applied. Sawdust of *Pinus strobus* (white pine) is said to be toxic while that from *P. radiata* is good. One test of soil under sawdust gave a higher pH than an unmulched check plot, contrary to expectations.

Peat itself makes a reasonable mulch and may be used where nothing better is available. It is especially useful when the soil underneath is on the alkaline side. Rhododendrons are grown quite successfully in the University of St Andrew's Botanic Gardens where they have a pH of 7.5. A dressing of 5–7.5 cm (2–3 in.) of peat is added every year as a mulch, together with a good sprinkling of flowers of sulphur. The chief trouble with peat is its inablity to absorb water once it gets really dry. Only a thorough soaking with a sprinkler may eventually soak through, so with a peat mulch, regular sprinkling should be applied in dry weather.

Heavy mulches are also useful for weed control although modern weedkillers and black polythene have perhaps lessened the use of mulching for this purpose.

Mention has been made of the use of mulches in very extreme continental climates. Many people apply their mulch on to partially frozen ground to keep the soil temperature as even as possible through the winter and hold back the warming up of the soil and therefore precocious growth in the spring. However, a heavy mulch reduces the effect the soil has on modifying air temperatures, owing to its insulating properties. Therefore, damage due to cold air in autumn or spring is more likely.

Watering can be rather a tricky operation when used in conjunction with a mulch. Six hours of sprinkling may be needed to penetrate many mulches, but care must be taken not to over-water. Sawdust and too much water can lead to attacks of root rot, *Phytophthora cinnamoni*, especially during high temperatures. I have seen trouble of this nature as far north as Vancouver, BC. Soil moisture can now be measured with special instruments.

Other mulches sometimes recommended are cow manure, ground corn cobs, sugar cane bagasse, wood shavings and peanut hulls. Some people say that they have even used fresh manure with no ill-effects, but I would be wary of this. Also, I have found it liable to dry out and become scattered by birds and wind.

A good alternative to leafmould is rotted chopped bracken. Cut it green but mature, chop it and stack it until rotted. Moisture content is good and the pH is around 4.

Old specimen rhododendrons may need special attention to keep them going. The fine old plants from Hooker's seed at Stonefield Hotel, Argyll are surrounded by rings of wire-netting wide enough to include the whole root areas. Into these goes an annual dressing of leaves, which the netting prevents from blowing away. Do not overdo the application of leaves as the roots may become buried.

4 *Species*

WHAT IS A SPECIES? CHANGES IN CLASSIFICATION

The dictionaries define a species as follows: 'A group of individuals having common characteristics, specialized from others of the same genus'; or 'a group (sometimes rather arbitrarily defined) of closely allied mutually fertile individuals showing constant differences from allied groups, placed under a genus'; or 'the aggregate of all those individuals, which have the same constant and distinctive characters'; or more simply, 'plants classified by qualities which they have in common'.

A more botanical definition which applies to rhododendrons is: 'Within a species there is a continuity of variation while closely related species are separated by correlated discontinuities of at least two independent characteristics; also species usually have a continuous eco-geographical range.'

These definitions may suit some living organisms, but, unfortunately for students of the genus Rhododendron, such words as common and constant rarely hold good. The whole concept of classification is man-made and nature never intended living things to fit neatly into carefully segregated compartments. Dr Frederick Coe (AMRS–QB–April 1960, *p*. 93) summed it up nicely: 'the species idea is one of convenience and means little to the plants'.

Over the years several people have attempted to classify the genus. I think it is true to say that even if a thousand perfectly competent taxonomists tackled the genus as a lifetime's work, quite independently, they would each produce different results.

David Leach refers to the azaleas of south-east USA as a geneticist's dream but a taxonomist's nightmare and the same may be said for the whole genus. Mr Chauncey Beadle of Biltmore Estate, Maryland, gathered together the largest collection of native azaleas. He worked for years on a book, to be illustrated by the stunning water colour paintings of Mrs Luella Porcher Johnson. In the end, he apparently destroyed his manuscript, having become dissatisfied with many of the new species he had described. Leach goes on to say that the species in typical form are often conspicuous by their rarity as they stand out in vast seas of azaleas undergoing introgressive hybridization. The hybrid race does not appear to have any selective disadvantage in their gene combinations and in fact the species so called seem to be less well suited to their environment than their hybrid descendants.

H. F. Tagg of Edinburgh had a different view. 'I think Wilson sent home (mostly from China) seed of many plants not represented in his herbarium collections. Some of the Wilsonian seed plants were probably hybrids-crossed in nature, but not able to establish themselves, but in cultivation here, with no competition they do very well. . . .' J. C. Williams wrote to E. P. Magor in 1919 (RHS–RYB, 1964, *p.* 67): 'When you next come here [Caerhays] you could put in a day doing nothing but examining unmatched rogues and natural hybrids (mostly from Wilson's seed).'

Dr J. M. Cowan reckoned that hybrids do not occur in the Himalayas. Either he must have been unobservant, unable to recognize a hybrid when he saw one, or did little studying of wild species when in the Darjeeling area himself.

This brings us to the question, are new species emerging out of all these hybrids? Before answering this, let us ask, what is a natural hybrid? Again, no taxonomists agree on this one. Personally, I feel that a true natural hybrid should have its parents to be found near by. There are undoubtedly cases where the parents may have died out locally and the hybrids inter-breed. This is surely a case of speciation and once this stage is reached, a specific name may be warranted. This is, of course, perhaps over-simplifying the phenomenon as natural hybrids are often made up of a complex parentage, especially in the case of azaleas.

Many so-called species or groups of sub-species represent unstable populations showing tremendous variations in foliage, habit and other characters in quite small areas. Other species may show a great variation in the colour of their flowers. In the wild, there may be a kaleidoscope of colours in one place while elsewhere the different colours may be segregated individually.

After his first tour of British gardens and herbariums, Leach became especially aware that the majority of species merge into one another. He correctly states that any effort to classify and sort out the genus is at the best a sorry compromise with reality. I certainly confirmed this statement when studying dwarfs in the Edinburgh herbarium prior to writing *Dwarf Rhododendrons*. In certain cases it could be desirable to place a whole subsection (or old sub-series) under one wide spectrum species. This would please some taxonomists, but what about the poor gardener who dislikes losing his specific names and might be left with no means of separating plants he or she considers are horticulturally different? Perhaps the easiest way out is to use the term sub-species more widely although I dislike this arrangement for its clumsiness. Various so-called species are unknown in the wild or are just an obvious variant with a species. If this has horticultural distinctiveness, it may be left with the previous specific name but this is now relegated to a 'Group' cultivar. An example of a variant within a species is *cinnabarinum* Concatenans Group. Both sub-species and the Group cultivar do at least give the gardener a chance to retain the old names and do not compel him to say the full *cinnabarinum* ssp. *xanthocodon* Concatenans Group, every time he wishes to talk about Concatenans. The clonal name 'Copper' can be added after the words Concatenans Group.

Cowan was of the opinion that botanists should compromise on classification and Davidian has more or less followed this pattern in his revisions of the series.

Should we talk about true or typical species? The late Ben Nelson of Seattle draws attention to the point that we should not say, 'I have *thomsonii* or *souliei* but I have a *thomsonii* and a *souliei*.' With a clone of a species or a hybrid it is different. 'I have 'Crest' is correct. Rather than say we have the true *lacteum*, we should say we have an average *lacteum*.

What then are the characteristics used to separate species of Rhododendron? There is no doubt that modern science is helping the taxonomist use additional characteristics previously unavailable, therefore considerably broadening the basis on which classification is founded. In the past, great emphasis was placed on such criteria as the presence or absence of hairs or glands on the style, ovary and calyx. With further examinations of herbarium specimens and living plants, it has now been found that this type of characteristic often does not hold good and tends to vary among siblings from one capsule, or even on one plant. Two or more constant characteristics are now looked for if specific status is to be allowed.

Chemical techniques are now used, such as studying flavonoids. These are used in plants as defence mechanisms against insects and disease. Numerous studies have revealed that flavonoid information is useful in taxonomic investigations and the documentation and analysis of natural hybridization. Species can often be identified by their flavonoid compounds and 'fingerprints'. Hybrids can usually be recognized, since they combine the chemical patterns of their two or more parents. Other chemicals being investigated are triterpane and leaf waxes. Over 60 different chemicals have been identified in the latter. Dr B. A. Knights has done valuable work on these in Glasgow University.

Various other criteria are now used, such as different nodal structures, the number of veins entering the stem from the leaf and features of the cotyledons and seeds. Added to these, much more attention is being paid to natural distribution and variation. One excellent undertaking has been carried out in the Edinburgh Herbarium in making separate distribution maps for every species. It is hoped that all these distinctive qualities will go a long way towards a much more workable and correct classification.

The anxiety of losing well-known specific names as a result of re-classification of plants is nothing new. Many people have tried to introduce rules at botanical congresses whereby names in common use can be retained. Several attempts were made at past International Congresses to bring in *nomina specifica conservanda*, which means retaining well-known names in preference to older (earlier described) unknown names which might take preference over them. Each time the principle of priority of the older names has been considered to be of greater importance by the majority of delegates. Likewise *nomina specifica rejicienda*, which means rejecting older names if ones already in use are well established and widely known, which really means much the same. This proposal was brought up at the Montreal Botanical Congress in 1959 and unfortunately was lost.

Drastic changes in the classification of rhododendrons (as we all know it) are regretfully inevitable. Sir Isaac Bayley Balfour of Edinburgh initiated the term 'Series'. Each series or sub-series was built around a well-known species. This system was devised in a hurry when material was flooding in from Forrest, Kingdon Ward and other collectors. Bayley

Balfour acknowledged at the time that it was only a stop-gap solution and realized that some modification would be necessary. Unfortunately he died before he was able to undertake this revisionary work and all the Rhododendron Handbooks and 'The Species of Rhododendron' have followed the same path. This method of classification has led to many species being misplaced on the basis of one or two characteristics, ignoring the overall features of the species. In other cases, an astonishing assembly of unrelated species or groups of species have been dumped in certain series because they would not fit in elsewhere; examples being the old Campanulatum, Barbatum and Irroratum series.

A very important point is that many of the 'Series' themselves have no nomenclatural validity under the International Code of Botanical Nomenclature.

The German taxonomist, Dr Herman Sleumer, published a classification of the genus involving Subgenera, Sections and Subsections instead of 'Series' and provided all the necessary nomenclatural validation of the names used. Subsequent work in various fields has confirmed the soundness of Sleumer's classification although numerous modifications have and will be made. This work has been largely ignored in Britain and America until recently, but it is now generally accepted by most leading authorities as the basis for present classification and future changes.

In this interim period it has been difficult for me to know which way to angle my own classification. As a compromise, I have added Bayley Balfour's system in brackets so as to act as a transition during the gradual changeover from the old to the new classification.

For fuller details of the history of Rhododendron classification, see J. M. Cowan in RHS–RYB, 1949, Philipson in *Notes from the Royal Botanic Garden, Edinburgh*, 1973, J. Cullen RHS–RCYB, 1977 and the Cullen and Chamberlain revisions (see Bibliography).

CONSERVATION AND THE FUTURE OF SPECIES IN GARDENS

It is sad to consider that every year there are fewer and fewer authentic plants from wild collected seed of the Forrest, Wilson, Kingdon Ward, Rock and Ludlow and Sherriff expeditions left alive in gardens, the great majority of which have never been propagated vegetatively. This is in some way being compensated for by the introduction of new material from China since 1980 and hopefully more parts of China and Tibet will open up shortly.

Much of this loss is due to the neglected or unkept state that many large collections of species have reached through the appalling taxes people with anything of value have to pay these days. Many species do take a long time to flower and show off their real beauty. Dr C. H. Phetteplace gives an example of what happened in America and has also frequently happened in Britain (AMRS–QB, April 1967, *p*. 74): 'For several years most of the plants grown from the Rock (1949) seed appeared quite uninteresting and yet even, after 18 years, half of those I have remaining (50 plants) have yet to set a bud. This of course establishes them as of no value to the commercial nurseryman and perhaps accounts in part why more of them are not grown. Each year however, there are more and more of these plants that excite the interest of those who pass through my garden and quite a number would well deserve a place in the garden even if they never flowered. Also, each year there are more and more visitors who ask if they might be permitted to take cuttings from certain plants.'

Kingdon Ward looked at the nurseryman from another angle. In the 1956 RHS–RCYB (*p.* 48) he wrote: 'Some nurserymen dislike collectors' numbers, claiming that the public wants names, even if they are the wrong names.'

The late Dr Harold Fletcher reckoned that in 1961, 98 per cent of rhododendrons sold in north-west USA were hybrids.

What, the reader may ask, is the future for species and why am I so keen to preserve as many as possible in gardens? One important reason for conserving so many forms of species in cultivation is to have a pool for breeding purposes. Who knows what fine results may emerge from many species as yet never used in hybridizing. As Dr Phetteplace says, many species take years to show their full potential. Nowadays, people are so impatient for quick results. Surely, for sheer interest, delicate beauty and charm, there is nothing among the vast majority of hybrids to equal the species. I would go as far as to say that few species lack some degree of merit and nearly all are worthy of space in large collections. The less-attractive species will always be rare because few people want them, but none the less, for posterity's sake, these should not be allowed to die out in cultivation.

What is being done to conserve species in gardens? The Species Foundation in the USA now seems firmly established in its new home near Tacoma, Washington, after various difficult periods in its history. Let's hope it goes from strength to strength and increases its collection year by year.

Should we have a species project in Britain? Fletcher broached the idea before he retired from the Royal Botanic Garden, Edinburgh, and he even asked for lists of authentic material with collectors' numbers. Personally, I feel that the RBG, Edinburgh could carry out just such a scheme (in fact a start has been made), making full use of their gardens at Edinburgh and Benmore. This work should be carried out by a botanist and horticulturist in close association. All major collections of species should be systematically visited and the desirable propagating material selected. Obviously some rare species may not now exist under collectors' numbers but provided they pass as average for the species, they should be propagated. Only with this type of project will the year by year drain on the total species resources in this country be halted. At present, no other country has more than a small percentage of the species material that we still cultivate here.

The newly regenerated Rhododendron Group is making a valiant effort to have rare rhododendrons more widely propagated and distributed. The idea is to gain co-operation between the owners of the best collections and any nurserymen willing to propagate and sell these plants. In theory, this plan looks promising and I wish it luck, but I am afraid that with the less popular items, it is doomed to failure because people would not pay the extremely high prices the nurserymen would have to charge.

Fine collections do still exist and some of these are still expanding. No individual or nursery can now possibly do more than scratch the surface and any hope of a voluntary body like the American Species Foundation is out of the question here considering the American scheme nearly foundered. Only a government-financed organization could be capable of fulfilling the many years travelling and the study needed for the completion of the task. A new site, complete with the necessary botanical and horticultural facilities, would be ideal but with our country in the state it is at present, this may have to remain a pipe dream. To make a really worthwhile job of this, I cannot overemphasize the need for a botanical–horticultural team to work hand-in-hand in the proximity of the best herbarium collection, which happens to be in Edinburgh.

The best way to make people aware of the beauty of species is to have as many collections as possible open to the public. These should be clearly and correctly labelled and the individual plants should be grown where they can develop into fine specimens and not be overcrowded. It is regretted that owing to human error, most collections have many wrongly named species, even sometimes where they have collectors' numbers attached. Muddles can take place at all stages, from the gathering of the seed onwards. It would be a mammoth but worthwhile task to check numbered plants with the corresponding herbarium specimens. Some collectors were guilty of mixing seed or collecting specimens that were different from the seed. While natural hybrids are commonplace in many batches of seedlings, most mix-ups occur later.

Many of the finest species gardenwise are still very scarce, largely due to difficulty of propagation or their qualities being little known. Others are too delicate for most of the country and it is unfortunate that those people living in favoured localities or with suitable micro-climates, are often reluctant to experiment with the less hardy species. For authentic species collections, rare species should be propagated vegetatively but for general garden use they can be produced much more cheaply and in greater quantities by using hand-pollinated or wild collected seed. Provided good parents are selected, these seedlings should prove to be well up to the average quality for each given species. For comments on self-sown seedlings, see Selection of Plants, *p.* 69.

Do please retain collectors' numbers wherever possible as these are the only way of referring back to where they were collected and by whom. Seedlings off cultivated numbered plants should not keep that number, but can of course be referred to as having come from such a number. So much interest can be inspired by looking into the history of a plant and often quite a little story can be found.

A few enthusiasts have endeavoured to improve certain species by growing generations of hand-pollinated seedlings and selecting clones for hardiness, size and colour of flower and habit. This can only be a long-term project, which requires much space and patience, so that few people have carried out a very worthwhile undertaking. G. G. Nearing of New Jersey, USA has worked on several species including *fortunei*, while Powell Glass worked on making a pure white *catawbiense*. In Britain, Mrs Stevenson (later Mrs Harrison) of Tower Court, bred selections of *concinnum* Pseudoyanthinum Group, *augustinii*, and *diaprepes*. Many generations may be needed to reach a required goal but it would not be too difficult for a few enthusiasts to try one or two species each. Increasing hardiness is perhaps the most useful aim. Seedlings should be grown in substantial quantities and subjected to cold at an early stage. To save room, these seedlings can be closely planted and left for the weather to take its toll. Select the hardiest known forms to start with. Worthwhile species to try in Britain might be many of the Triflorums and some of the hardier scented lepidotes such as *lindleyi*, *crassum* and *edgeworthii*. Most of these flower relatively quickly from seed and one person, provided he or she starts young enough, should be able to grow sufficient generations of seedlings to produce tangible results.

5 Species descriptions

The subsections and sections are in alphabetical order for simple reference. The only exception is the azaleas, which are grouped together under A (see list on *p.* 93). These subsections roughly correspond to the old series. For more details on the reasons for this change, see the previous chapter and the Introduction.

In the descriptions I have attempted to emphasize the best characters for positive identification and in many cases, these are in italics. A little more detail is given than in *Dwarf Rhododendrons*, especially on the petiole, rachis, pedicel, calyx, ovary and style, as this is often still necessary for classifying. Also a few more botanical names for hairs and other characters are used and all are listed in the glossary on *p.* 339. Ten stamens and five corolla lobes are the usual numbers per flower for the majority of species. Generally exceptions only are mentioned.

After the name of the subsection (or section) with the old series name in brackets, (L) = Lepidote or scaly and (E) = Elepidote or non-scaly. The name following the specific name is that of the describer and the year described, where possible.

KEY TO SYMBOLS AND ABBREVIATIONS USED IN SPECIES DESCRIPTIONS

H   Hardiness and constitution.

H4 Hardy anywhere in Britain where conditions are favourable for rhododendrons.

H3 Satisfactory for the west and for the best situated areas near the east and south coasts.

H2 Only for the most sheltered gardens on the western seaboard and very occasionally in the south.

H1 Greenhouse or against the most suitable shaded walls.

A   American hardiness rating: average minimum winter temperature a species can stand in °F.

L   Leaf qualities and leaf description.

F   Flower qualities and flower description.

L4 F4 Excellent.

L3 F3 Good.

L2 F2 Fair.

L1 F1 Of little merit.

Ht Height.

Inflor Inflorescence.

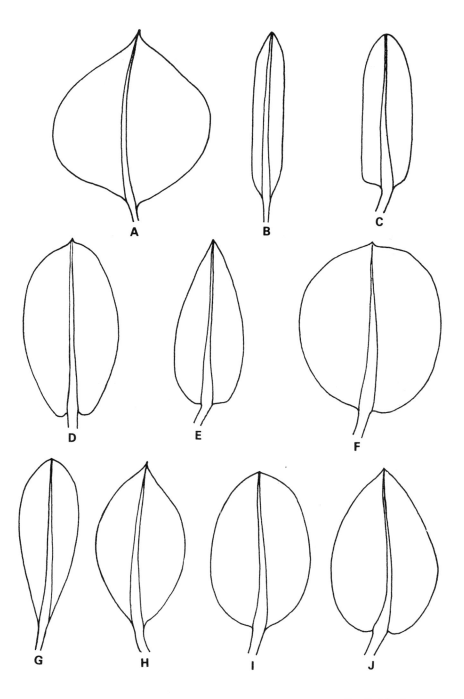

Leaf shapes

A. Rhombic
B. Oblong lanceolate
C. Oblong
D. Obovate
E. Lanceolate

F. Orbicular
G. Oblanceolate
H. Elliptic
I. Oval
J. Ovate

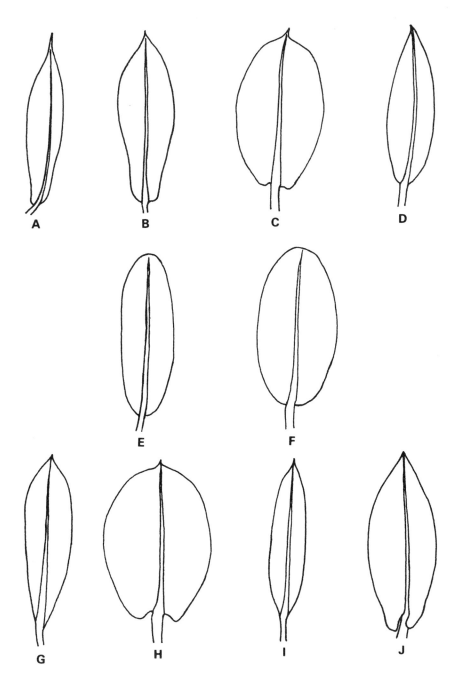

Apex
A. Cuspidate
B. Acuminate
C. Apiculate
D. Acute

E. Obtuse
F. Rounded

Leaf apex and base

Base
G. Narrowed
H. Cordate
I. Cuneate
J. Auriculate

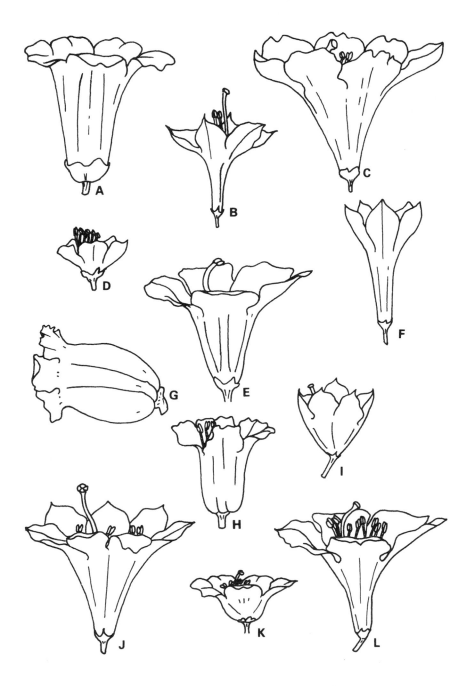

A. Campanulate
B. Funnel-shaped with long tube
C. Widely funnel-shaped
D. Rotate
E. Funnel-campanulate
F. Tubular
G. Ventricose campanulate
H. Tubular campanulate
I. Openly campanulate
J. Funnel-shaped
K. Saucer-shaped
L. Tubular funnel-shaped

Flower shapes

Plant Collectors
F   G. Forrest
KW   F. Kingdon Ward
L&S   F. Ludlow and G. Sherriff
LS&T   F. Ludlow, G. Sherriff and G. Taylor
R   J. J. Rock
SS&W   J. D. A. Stainton, W. Sykes and J. Williams
W   E. H. Wilson
C&H   Cox and Hutchison

Awards

British

FCC First Class Certificate
AM   Award of Merit
PC   Certificate of Preliminary Commendation
AGM Award of Garden Merit
(For information on British Award System, see AMRS–QB, April 1975, *p*. 125)
(For information on American Award System, see AMRS–QB, July 1974, *p*. 150)

Many place names in China and elsewhere have changed since the species were first discovered and described. I have usually followed the old names. The following list gives the old names first and the new ones as found on most modern maps. For further names, see Addendum *p*. 343.

India

North East Frontier Agency (NEFA) = Arunachal Pradesh
Khasi Hills, Assam now in Meghalaya
Ceylon now Sri Lanka
Formosa now Taiwan
Siam now Thailand

China

Tatsien-lu now K'ang-ting
Lower Yangtze Kiang River (Kinsha Kiang) now Chang Chiang
Upper Yangtze Kiang River now Chin-sha Chiang
Mekong River now Lan-ts'ang Chiang
Salween River now Nu Chiang
Shweli River (in Burma) now Nam Mao
Shweli River (in China) now Lung-ch'uan
Tsangpo River now Ya-lu-tsang-pu Chiang
Mupin (Moupin) now Paoksing-hsien
see p. 377

List of sections and subsections (series) as used in this book (old series and sub-series in brackets)

Arborea subsection	(Arboreum series, sub-series Arboreum)
Argyrophylla subsection	(Arboreum series, sub-series Argyrophyllum)
Auriculata subsection	(Auriculatum series)
Azaleas	
Pentanthera subgenus	(Azalea series, sub-series Canadense, Nipponicum and Luteum)
Pentanthera section	(Azalea series, sub-series Luteum)
Rhodora section	(Azalea series, sub-series Canadense)
Viscidula section	(Azalea series, sub-series Nipponicum)
Tsutsutsi subgenus	(Azalea series, sub-series Obtusum and Schlippenbachii)
Brachycalyx section	(Azalea series, sub-series Schlippenbachii)
Tsusiopsis section	(Azalea series, sub-series Tashiroi)
Azaleastrum section	(Ovatum series)
Barbata subsection	(Barbatum series, sub-series Barbatum)
Boothia subsection	(Boothii series)
Camelliiflora subsection	(Camelliaeflorum series)
Campanulata subsection	(Campanulatum series, part)
Campylocarpa subsection	(Thomsonii series, sub-series Campylocarpum and Souliei)
Candidastrum section	(Albiflorum series)
Choniastrum section	(Stamineum series)
Cinnabarina subsection	(Cinnabarinum series)
Falconera subsection	(Falconeri series)
Fortunea subsection	(Fortunei series)
Fulgensia subsection	(Campanulatum series, part)
Fulva subsection	(Fulvum series)
Genestierana subsection	(Glaucophyllum series, sub-series Genestierianum)
Glischra subsection	(Barbatum series, sub-series Glischrum)
Grandia subsection	(Grande series)
Griersoniana subsection	(Griersonianum series)
Heliolepida subsection	(Heliolepis series)
Irrorata subsection	(Irroratum series)
Lactea subsection	(Lacteum series)
Lanata subsection	(Campanulatum series, part)
Maculifera subsection	(Barbatum series, sub-series Maculiferum)
Maddenia subsection	(Maddenii series)
Micrantha subsection	(Micranthum series)
Monantha subsection	(Uniflorum series, part and Triflorum series part)
Mumeazalea section	(Semibarbatum series)
Neriiflora subsection	(Neriiflorum series)
Parishia subsection	(Irroratum series, sub-series Parishii)
Pontica subsection	(Ponticum series)
Rhodorastra subsection	(Dauricum series)
Scabrifolia subsection	(Scabrifolium series)
Selensia subsection	(Thomsonii series, sub-series Selense)
Taliensia subsection	(Taliense series)
Tephropepla subsection	(Boothii series, sub-series Tephropeplum)
Thomsonia subsection	(Thomsonii series, sub-series Thomsonii)
Triflora subsection	(Triflorum series)
Venatora subsection	(Irroratum series, sub-series Parishii, part)

ARBOREA SUBSECTION (ARBOREUM SERIES) SUB-SERIES ARBOREUM) (E)

This is a fairly small group of species but with a very wide geographical distribution in South-East Asia. The most obvious character is the many flowered compact rounded inflorescence; other characters are the thick leathery leaves with indumentum on the upper surface when young, usually dark green and glabrous on maturity; indumentum below usually thin or plastered. Habit often tree-like. Inflor ten to thirty-five, occasionally more, pedicel tomentose. Corolla campanulate to tubular-campanulate with nectar pouches, lobes five-Calyx small, about 2–3 mm with five triangular teeth, hairy and often glandular. Ovary tomentose, white to fawn, sometimes glandular, style glabrous. Stamens ten unequal, filaments glabrous. Capsule about 2 cm × 7 mm with vestiges of tomentum.

These are first-rate garden plants in their better forms, especially when treated as single specimens. Most bloom early in the season. The majority are hardy enough to flourish in our milder British gardens, while *niveum* and the hardier forms of *arboreum* will grow successfully in most sheltered woodlands. Most introductions were severely damaged in the 1972 freeze in Oregon, 1981–2 in northern U.K., 1985–7 in south.

R. arboreum

arboreum Wight 1850 (*windsori* Nutt. *puniceum* Roxb.) H2–4 A −5 to +15 L3–4 F3–4. See Addendum *p.* 343.

Ht to 30 m (100 ft) in the wild down to 1–2 m (3–6 ft) on exposed hillsides; 18 m (60 ft) plus in gardens but rarely over 12 m (40 ft). Habit often tree-like with a single or multiple trunk and almost columnar growth, forming cones or mounds; sometimes with gnarled and twisted trunks in the wild. Bark rough, peeling, plum, tan shading to mauve coloured.

L to 17.7 × 6.3 cm (7 × 2½ in.), usually less, oblong-lanceolate to oblong-oblanceolate to ovate, shades of dark green above, often glossy, indumentum below white to rusty-brown, plastered, mat or of fine woolly texture. L remain for 2 to 3 years. Petiole 1–2 cm, floccose at first.

Inflor around twenty, very compact, rachis about 2 cm. Pedicel about 8 mm ± glandular and hairy.

F blood-red to pink to white, usually spotted, sometimes on all lobes and blotched, about 5 cm (2 in.) long, tubular campanulate, lobes often wavy at margins.

Calyx about 2–3 mm ± glandular and hairy. Ovary white tomentose, ± glandular, style glabrous, about equal in length to stamens.

This is perhaps the most widespread, common and variable species in the world, including its close relatives. Many forms have been and still are being introduced into cultivation. Those from low elevations are invariably blood-red and are naturally the most tender, while those from higher elevations are rosy-red through shades of pink to white and are often much hardier than the American rating of +15 signifies. These high altitude, variable coloured forms are only found in east Nepal, Sikkim and just into west Bhutan. In certain localities, especially Bhutan, Arunachal Pradesh, Khasia Hills and south Tibet, they are closely related to the Chinese *delavayi* which typically has a more woolly indumentum.

In cultivation, *arboreum* has sometimes been cut to the ground and has re-grown again, once three times in 35 years. It also has the ability to occasionally send out new shoots from the trunk when more light is admitted. Most forms flowered successfully in California after the 1972 freeze.

Certain lowland introductions have been found to be very heat resistant, for instance in coastal Japan. Plants collected from close to the main Himalayas seem to be hardier than those from a similar elevation collected near the plains. Leach found 7.6 m (25 ft) trees in the Blue Mountains of Jamaica at about 1,800 m (6,000 ft) where the annual rainfall is 300 cm (120 in.) and the mean temperature between 10–24°C (50–75°F). Nobody seems to know who took them there.

At its best it grows into a most majestic small tree with a splendid trunk and highly ornamental flowers in a rounded truss. It apparently first bloomed in cultivation in 1825. 'Goat Fell' **AM** 1964, F cherry, Brodick; 'Rubaiyat' **AM** 1968 F red, Exbury:

The following are altitudinal and geographical subspecies and varieties of *arboreum*.

R. windsori is possibly a hybrid of *arboreum* × *barbatum* with a large calyx.

arboreum ssp. *cinnamomeum* (ex. Wall.) Lindl 1837 Indumentum a striking dark rusty-brown. F white, sometimes to pale rose; *campbelliae* Hook. f. (now a synonym of ssp. *cinnamoneum*) is very similar with a slightly paler indumentum and with flowers purplish-rose to a pretty pink. The latter comes from a generally lower elevation than *cinnamomeum* and is correspondingly less hardy.

ssp. *cinnamomeum* var. *roseum* (var. *album*) is also fairly hardy. L as above with paler more matted indumentum. F pink to white. These forms come from relatively high elevations, 2,400–4,000 m (8,000–13,000 ft) and usually succeed in the colder parts of Britain.

arboreum ssp. *delavayi* (Franch. 1886) Chamb. (*pilovittatum* Balf.f. & W. W. Sm.) H2–3 L2–3 F2–4. See Addendum *p.* 344.

Ht to 9 m (30 ft). Habit not usually as tree-like as *arboreum*. Young shoots covered with floccose tomentum. Bark rough.
L 7–20 × 2–5 cm (2¾–8 × ¾–2 in.), oblong-lanceolate to oblong-oblanceolate, apex obtuse to acute, base tapered, usually dark and glossy above, white to fawn indumentum below of a thin spongy texture. L remain for 2 to 3 years. Petiole 1.5–2 cm tomentose above, ± glandular. Inflor ten to twenty, rachis about 1 cm. Pedicel about 1 cm densely tomentose, ± glandular.
F blood-red to deep crimson, 4–5 cm (1½–2 in.) long, campanulate, forming a rounded truss.
Calyx about 2 mm tomentose, ± glandular. Ovary densely tomentose, sometimes glandular, style glabrous.

This is the eastern equivalent of *arboreum* but is not nearly so variable. Most forms have very fine red flowers but unfortunately are only suitable for mild localities and can be damaged even in Cornwall. Some introductions are a little hardier and have flowered successfully at places like Howick, Northumberland and Blackhills, Morayshire. Said to be difficult in southern England but it grows well at Wakehurst Place, Sussex. Closely allied to *arboreum* and var. *peramoenum*.

KW's collection from Mt Victoria, south Burma, *KW* 21976, has proved remarkably adaptable in cultivation. While undoubtedly tender, we have flowered it at Glendoick and it bloomed successfully in most Californian gardens after the terrible 1972 freeze. It is an outstanding plant, blooming relatively young with glowing deep scarlet flowers. As seed was collected from a range of over 600 m (2,000 ft), many different forms have emerged with almost flat to erect habits, leaves oval to lanceolate and flowers varying in shade. **FCC** 1936 Margam Castle for an old introduction.

Szechwan, Yunnan, Burma, Thailand and Indo-China in conifer forests, among scrub and thickets and on bouldery slopes, often on a slate formation, often dryish, 1,830–3,350 m (6,000–11,000 ft).

March–May

arboreum ssp. *delavayi* var. *peramoenum* (Balf.f.& Forr.) Chamb. 1920 H2–3 L2–3 F1–3

Ht to 9 m (30 ft), occasionally only 1.2–1.8 m (4–6 ft). Habit as *delavayi*. Young shoots with white tomentum at first.
L to 15 × 3 cm (6 × 1½ in.), narrow-lanceolate, indumentum below very finely woolly as in *delavayi*, generally smoother than *delavayi* on upper surface. Inflor fifteen to twenty, variable in size of truss.
F bright cherry-scarlet to deep rose-crimson, crimson nectar pouches, often spotted deep crimson, 2.5–5 cm (1–2 in.) long, 5 cm (2 in.) across.

Very closely related to *delavayi* of which it seems to be just a narrow-leaved variant. Intermediate forms occur.

Arunachal Pradesh (Cox & Hutchison) and west Yunnan, 1,600–3,400 m (5,200–11,000 ft), open mixed forest, dense rain forest (ours), hillsides, forest margins and thickets. March–April

arboreum ssp. *nilagiricum* Zenker 1836 L shorter and more bullate than *arboreum* type, narrower than *zelanicum* and eglandular. F intense scarlet, crimson to pink. Tender. Given specific status by Cowan. Nilgiri and other Hills south India.

All forms – west Himalayas, Sikkim to Arunachal Pradesh, Khasia Hills, south Tibet and south India, 1,250–4,000 m (4,000–13,000 ft), in and among oaks, hemlock, bamboo, mahonias, pines and rhododendron jungle on open ridges and slopes (often dryish) and banks of rivers. Blood-red types December–March in wild. All forms early February–late May in cultivation.

arboreum ssp. *zelanicum* Booth ex Cowan 1936 (*rollissonii* Hort., *kingianum* Watt ex W. Watson mistakenly synonymous with *zelanicum*) H2–3 A+15 L2–3 F2–3

Ht to 9 m (30 ft) (or more in the wild), usually much less, slow growing. Habit noble gnarled trunks, often branches near the ground. Bark very rough.
L to 13 × 5 cm (5 × 2 in.), elliptic to elliptic-oblong, dark green, apex obtuse, base rounded to slightly cordate, strongly bullate above, convex, dense fawn to tawny indumentum below, midrib glandular. L remain for 3 years. Pedicel glandular.
F usually red to crimson-scarlet or crimson-rose but rich pink forms are reported in the wild. L de Rothschild said the flowers could be white, pink or red but this is doubtful; 3.8–5 cm (1½–2 in.) long.
Calyx small with distinct irregular lobes, glandular.

A fine usually late flowering species near *arboreum*. Most forms in cultivation have crimson-scarlet flowers in July–August. Similar to *nilagiricum* but by no means identical (see Cowan RBG Notes 1936, *p.* 157).

A clone known as 'Noyo Chief' cultivated in America with superb lustrous foliage and glowing long-lasting rose-red flowers in May is most likely a hybrid. Selfed seedlings are very uneven in foliage indicating hybridity. It blooms younger than *zelanicum* and could be closer to *wattii*. Originated in Britain and occurs in old gardens.

Very fine authentic specimens of *zeylanicum* occur at the gardens of Lochinch, Inverewe, Stonefield, Blackhills and especially Arduaine in Scotland. Not for cold gardens. *R. rollissonii* may also be of hybrid origin. Introduced about 1843.

Sri Lanka (Ceylon), 900–2,400 m (3,000–8,000 ft) up to the top of Adam's Peak and other mountains.

Bot. Mag. 7696 (*arboreum* var. *kingianum*) and 9323 (*nilagiricum*) appear to be the same plant and both *zelanicum* as we know it.

Usually July–August

lanigerum Tagg 1930 (*silvaticum* Cowan) H3–4 A+5 L2–3 F3–4

Ht to 6 m (20 ft), usually much less. Habit a rounded shrub or small tree. Small gnarled tree in the wild. Young shoots at first tomentose. Bark rough, partly flaking, greenish, greyish or brownish.

L to 23 × 7.6 cm (9 × 3 in.), oblong-lanceolate to oblong-oblanceolate, sometimes shiny above, indumentum fine woolly, white to olive or cinnamon-brown below. L remain for 1–2 years. Petiole 1.5–2 cm densely tomentose.

Inflor twenty-five to thirty-five or more forming a very compact rounded truss, rachis about 2.5 cm. Pedicel 1–1.5 cm densely tomentose.

F light to deep pink through reddish-purple, cherry-red, rich deep rosy-crimson to scarlet-crimson, 4–5 cm (1½–2 in.) long, broadly campanulate. Calyx about 2 mm fleshy. Ovary densely tomentose, style glabrous.

This very fine species, although variable, is extremely consistent in the high quality of all the clones from wild collected seed. It is indeed unfortunate that the flower buds are very prone to frost damage as soon as they start to swell and that most clones attempt to bloom far too early. The large round flower buds are very distinctive and can look like small green apples.

Closely related to *niveum* but the leaves are usually longer and narrower and the flowers open earlier. Rather tender for really cold areas. The habitat is to the east of *niveum*.

In Seattle, USA, plants from R's 1949 expedition took 22 years to flower and varied from light pink to bright red.

'Chapel Wood' **AM** 1961 **FCC** 1967, *R* 03913 Neyron Rose Crown Lands. 'Round Wood' **AM** 1951 *KW* 6258 crimson Crown Lands. 'Silvia' **AM** 1954 pale crimson, suffused white Logan. 'Stonehurst' **AM** 1961 light cherry Stonehurst. **AM** 1949 Trengwainton.

East Arunachal Pradesh, south and south-east Tibet, north-west Yunnan, has not been found very often but could be common over large areas of unexplored country around the Tsangpo Gorge; 2,600–3,400 m (8,500–11,000 ft) on steep slopes with fir and bamboo, common in places.   February–April

niveum Hook.f. 1851 H3–4 A+5 L2–3 F2–4

Ht medium to large shrub to 6 m (20 ft). Habit often rounded. Young shoots densely white tomentose. Bark pale brown to greyish, slightly flaking.

L to 16.5 × 6.3 cm (6½ × 2½ in.), obovate-lanceolate, largely glabrous on maturity above, with dense indumentum below, at first white, later grey to fawn. L remain for 1 to 3 years. Petiole 1–1.5 cm ± evanescent tomentose.

Inflor about twenty in dense rounded or conical truss, rachis about 2 cm. Pedicel about 1 cm tomentose.

F the colour is variously described as smoky-purple, smoky-blue, parma-violet (best forms), lavender, deep purple or very deep mauve, 3.8–5 cm (1½–2 in.) long, tubular-campanulate.

Calyx very small. Ovary densely tomentose, style glabrous.

I am very fond of this species in its best colour forms. Some people consider the colour dingy or even ugly, but I admire the round trusses contrasting with the near white indumentum and dark leaf upper surface. Very fine at Inverewe, Ross-shire. Hardier than the closely related *lanigerum* but has suffered winter foliage damage at Glendoick. The combination of *niveum* and yellows goes nicely but keep away from reds. L de Rothschild did not like it. **AM** 1951 *F* imperial-purple Tower Court.

It is apparently rare in the wild as it was only found once by *L&S* in east Bhutan although seed, reputedly collected in west Bhutan in addition to Sikkim has been introduced recently. It is in danger of dying out in Sikkim. Sikkim and Bhutan, 3,000–3,700 m (9,500–12,000 ft), bamboo and hemlock forest. April–May

ARGYROPHYLLA SUBSECTION (ARBOREUM SERIES, SUB-SERIES ARGYROPHYLLUM) (E)

This is basically a clearly defined group, which largely comes from China. They are less tree-like than the Arborea subsection. The inflorescence has fewer flowers resulting in a looser truss and the pedicels are relatively longer. The flower colour varies from white to pink to purple and the corolla is generally smaller, usually five lobed. The nectaries of the Arborea subsection are lacking except in *ririei*. Calyx usually small 1–2 mm. Stamens ten to fourteen unequal, usually hairy at base. Ovary usually tomentose and sometimes glandular, style usually glabrous. The leaves have either a plastered or thinnish fine textured indumentum which is often white to grey to fawn. Only *thayerianum* is conspicuously glandular. In the others, minute glands are usually hidden by the indumentum. Leach sees a hair resemblance with some of this subsection and *bureavii*.

Most of this subsection are rare in cultivation or have never been introduced. Few are seen outside Britain and Sweden. Those from northern locations are very hardy and can stand well below −18°C (0°F). Those recently introduced into the USA by the Species Foundation were all relatively unblemished by the 1972 freeze.

Many are very attractive plants with interesting foliage and beautifully shaped flowers of delicate shades. They warrant much wider popularity. As there are so many species not in cultivation, these are listed and briefly described at the end of this subsection. Several may be synonymous with species already in cultivation. Many have leaf chlorosis in cultivation.

adenopodum transferred from Ponticum series, sub-series Caucasicum. See *Dwarf Rhododendrons*, *p*. 149. This species is somewhat intermediate between the more typical membership of ss. Argyrophylla and ss. Pontica though closer to the former.

argyrophyllum Franch. 1886 H4 A−5 L1−3 F3−4

Ht usually 2–3 m but up to 8 m (6½–10 up to 25 ft). Habit fairly erect. Shoots covered at first with thin white to grey tomentum. Bark grey to greenish-brown, roughish, slightly flaking.

R. argyrophyllum

L 6–15 × 1.5–3.8 cm (2½–6×⅜–1½ in.), oblong-lanceolate to oblong, apex acuminate, base usually cuneate, thin, fine textured white to silvery indumentum below. L remain for 2 to 3 years. Petiole 1–1:5 cm glabrescent.

Inflor six to twelve, loose, rachis about 1 cm. Pedicel 2.5–3.5 cm sparsely floccose.

F white through pink to deep rose, sometimes spotted or blotched or striped deep pink, 2–3.8 cm (¾–1½ in.) long and wide, campanulate.

Calyx 1–2 mm. Filaments hairy at base. Ovary white floccose, not glandular, style glabrous.

A fine, hardy species which should be much more grown. The flowers are of a most attractive pure glacé appearance and of a beautiful shape. Some forms are unfortunately slow to start blooming. It has done well in parts of Scandinavia. Liable to become scruffy in cultivation. Very closely related to *hypoglaucum*. **AM** 1934 Wakehurst Place. Now includes var. *cupulare* Rehd. & Wils.

Common in Szechwan. Has been collected by Sven Hedin and Harry Smith in Szechwan and Kansu, also found in Yunnan, 2,000–3,600 m (6,500–11,750 ft). On Mt Omei, it is found on windy cliffs, in thickets, woodlands and in bamboo.   May

argyrophyllum ssp. *hypoglaucum* (Hemsl. 1889) Chamb. (*gracilipes* Franch. *chionophyllum* Diels) H4 A−5 L1–2 F1–3

Ht to 6 m (20 ft). Habit as *argyrophyllum*. Branchlets with evanescent tomentum. Bark rough.

L 6–12 × 2–4 cm (2½–5 × ¾–1½ in.), oblong-elliptic, oblong-lanceolate to oblanceolate, apex triangular-acuminate, base obtuse to semi-rounded, usually smooth and glossy above, thin smooth white to grey indumentum below. L remain for 1 to 3 years. Petiole 1–1.5 cm slight evanescent tomentum.

Inflor four to eight, rachis about 1.5 cm. Pedicel about 2.5 cm whitish floccose.

F white flushed rose to pale pink with numerous deep rose spots, about 3.5 cm (1½ in.) long, funnel-campanulate.

Calyx about 2 mm floccose and ciliate. Filaments less hairy than *argyrophyllum*. Ovary floccose and *glandular*, style *glandular at base*.

An attractive plant with fine white indumentum and nice little white trusses. Very closely related to *argyrophyllum* and may be classed as a geographical variant. Equally hardy. 'Heane Wood' **AM**, buds pink, opening white, faintly suffused red-purple, lightly spotted, Sandling Park.

West Hupeh, 1,500–2,700 m (5,000–9,000 ft), very common in thickets and woods.   May

argyrophyllum ssp. *omeiense* (Rehd. & Wils. 1913) Chamb. See Addendum *p.* 345.

Ht 3–5 m (10–16ft). L smaller and narrower than type and the dun-coloured indumentum is slightly darker. Pedicel slender, drooping. F white, corolla broader than type and less narrowed at base.

Introduced in 1980.

Szechwan, common on Mt Omei at 1,800 m (6,000 ft), growing with *ririei* in forests all along ravines.

argyrophyllum ssp. *nankingense* (Cowan 1953) Chamb. (var. *leiandrum* Hutch.)

L to just over 3.8 cm (1½ in.) wide, more rugose above than type. F larger than type, more than 5 cm (2 in.) across, rich clear pink or lilac-purple with crimson dots.

A fairly distinct geographical variety which is a very fine, hardy plant. 'Chinese Silver' **AM**. Nice young growth with white indumentum on upper leaf surface, later glabrous and lovely pink flowers. Re-introduced 1985.

Kweichow, 2,250 m (7,500 ft) common on rocky slopes.

coryanum Tagg & Forr. 1926 H4 L1–2 F2–3

Ht 3–6 m (10–20ft). Habit freely branches from a low level. Young shoots with thin grey tomentum, soon evanescent. Bark rough.

L 7–17 × 1.8–4 cm (2¾–6¾ × ¾–1¾ in.), four times as long as broad, narrowly elliptic to oblong-lanceolate, apex acute, base wedge-shaped, dark green and leathery above, indumentum below thin buff becoming ash-grey and thinning further with age. L remain for 2 to 3 years. Petiole 2 cm thinly tomentose.

Inflor twenty to thirty in loose truss, rachis 2–3 cm. Pedicel 3–4 cm crimson, sparsely tomentose.
F creamy-white or snowy-white, spotted red, 2.5–3 cm (1–1¼ in.) long, funnel-campanulate.
Calyx 1–2 mm sparsely floccose and glandular. Ovary *glabrous* or with a few hairs, style glabrous.

This is an attractive but not spectacular plant with numerous small, neat flowers.

It is an outlyer in the distribution of the subsection coming from both sides of the Tibet border with Yunnan at 2,300–4,300 m (7,500–14,000 ft) in rhododendron thickets, fir, bamboo, mixed forest and in ravines.   April–May

floribundum Franch. 1886 H4 L2–3 F1–3

Ht 4.6–7.6 m (15–25 ft), only reaches the maximum height when drawn. Habit erect. One year shoots with floccose tomentum. Bark greenish-grey to greyish-brown, not very rough.
L 7–15 × 3–5 cm (3–6 × 1–2 in.), lanceolate, *bullate above*, margins often recurved, apex apiculate, base broadly cuneate, persistent white indumentum below with a loose, felted appearance. L remain for 1 to 3 years. Petiole 1 cm tomentose at first, later glabrescent.
Inflor five to twelve neat but loose trusses, rachis short about 7 mm. Pedicel white tomentose.
F bluish-lilac, *lavender*, pink, dull magenta, pinkish-purple with *large dark blotch and spots*, sometimes streaked, 4 cm (1½ in.) long, widely campanulate.
Calyx tomentose. Ovary covered with white velvety appressed hairs, style glabrous or slightly hairy at base.

Well grown plants of the better forms are good and have handsome, distinctive foliage. The best pink and lavender flowered forms are attractive, the Borde Hill clone being outstanding. Needs good conditions to grow well. Poorly grown inferior forms with chlorotic foliage are of no garden value. Starts to bloom at a relatively young age. Place away from reds. 'Swinhoe' **AM** 1963, Exbury. Re-introduced 1988.

Confined to Mupin, Szechwan at 1,200–2,400 m (4,000–8,000 ft) in woods.   April

formosanum Hemsl. 1895. Only just introduced H4 or 3–4? A −15 to −5

Ht 2–9 m (3–30 ft). Habit often large and tree-like with stout branches. The rigid branchlets are clad with evanescent grey tomentum.
L 7–18 × 1.5–5 cm (2¾–7 × ⅗–2 in.), 4.5–5.5 times as long as broad, *oblanceolate to narrowly lanceolate*, apex acuminate, narrowed to base, often light green above, indumentum below pale buff on young and old leaves, margins recurved, old leaves may turn red. Petiole glabrous.
Inflor seven to twenty, said to be globose, rachis 1.5–2 cm. Pedicel pubescent. F white to pink, spotted, 3–4 cm (1¼–1½ in.) long, widely funnel-shaped, said to be fragrant.

Calyx pubescent. Stamens ten to twelve slightly hairy at base. Ovary densely grey-brown floccose, style glabrous.

This is reckoned to be one of the most beautiful species on Taiwan so it could prove to be a valuable new introduction with apparently little variation. Most seedlings we have grown from three numbers have narrow pointed leaves with a noticeably silvery indumentum. One number is tender. May be closely related to *hypoglaucum* (*W*) and perhaps *simiarum*. Has now flowered. Rather disappointing but flowers young.

Endemic to Taiwan where it is quite common and found in several districts, 800–2,000 m (3,000–6,500 ft), in mixed forest of evergreen oaks and laurels, usually along streams.   March–April (Taiwan)

hunnewellianum Rehd. & Wils. 1913 (*leucolasium* Diels) H4 L1–3 F2–3

Ht 2–7.5 m (6–25 ft). Habit usually a large somewhat rounded bush. Branchlets with greyish floccose evanescent tomentum. Bark brownish-grey.
L 7.6–18 × 1.5–2.5 cm (3–7 × ⅜–1 in.), *narrowly oblanceolate*, apex acuminate, base cuneate, indumentum below snowy-white to grey; young leaves a vivid apple green. L remain for 2 to 3 years. Petiole 1–1.5 cm with thin evanescent tomentum.
Inflor seven to eight, rachis about 1 cm. Pedicel 1.5–2 cm with white hairs.
F white tinged pink to pink with spots, 4–5 cm (1½–2 in.) long, widely campanulate.
Calyx about 2 mm with white hairs. Ovary densely white tomentose, style with a few hairs at base, stigma deep pink.

Quite a nice plant when well grown but the foliage is liable to be chlorotic and the way the rather small, narrow leaves hang, gives the whole bush a rather wind blown appearance. It blooms at a similar time to *oreodoxa*. While the habit can be superior in *hunnewellianum*, it takes longer to reach flowering size. Free flowering on maturity. Generally hardy in Britain but it suffered in Oregon in the 1972 freeze. Inclined to blow over at Benmore, West Scotland.

Probably related to *argyrophyllum* but easily recognized by its very narrow leaves combined with the snowy indumentum.

North-east Szechwan, 1,800–3,000 m (6,000–10,000 ft) in woods and thickets.   March–May

hunnewellianum ssp. *rockii* (Wils.) Chamb. Differs from *hunnewellianum* in its slightly shorter leaves and the upper layer of indumentum turns yellowish instead of remaining white. South Kansu and Szechwan near Kansu border, 2,000–2,400 m (6,500–8,000 ft).

insigne Hemsl. & Wils. 1910 H4 A0 L3–4 F3–4

Ht 1.5–3.7 m (5–12 ft). Habit bushy, slow growing with thickish branches, forms a tight bush in an open situation. Branchlets with evanescent thin tomentum, ash-grey. Bark salmon coloured, for a few years, grey with age.

L 7–13 × 2–4.5 cm (2¾–5 × ¾–1¾ in.), 3–3.5 times as long as broad, oblong-lanceolate to oblong oblanceolate, apex acuminate, base cuneate, *shiny plastered skin-like*, tawny-grey to copper indumentum below. The leaf is *thick, leathery and rigid*. L remain for 3 to 5 years. Petiole 1.5–2 cm with white evanescent tomentum.

Inflor eight to fifteen +, loose to rounded. Pedicel 2–4 cm reddish, sparsely floccose.

F pinkish-white, pale to deep pink with crimson spots and rose coloured lines, to 5 cm (2 in.) long, widely campanulate.

Calyx very small about 1 mm floccose on back. Ovary densely clad with silky hairs, style stout, glabrous.

A remarkable plant, perhaps the best of the subsection. The habit is dwarfer than most and the foliage very distinctive. The seed ripens earlier than all other larger species and the capsules curl back, shedding all the seed quickly. The habit tends to become more upright with age and flowers freely once it starts.

I like Sylvester Christie's description of the foliage; 'stiff spear-like leaves of burnished copper'. The flowers of most forms are very beautiful with lovely markings.

Hardy throughout Britain and parts of Scandinavia. Rare in the Pacific north-west and scarce in the trade. **AM** 1923 Bodnant.

Apparently only found on Wa-shan, west Szechwan, 2,100–3,000 m (7,000–10,000 ft) in woodlands and on limestone bluffs.   May–June

ririei Hemsl. & Wils. 1910 H4 L1–2 F2–3

Ht 3–13 m (10–43 ft). Habit generally erect with long, straight branches. Branchlets with thin whitish tomentum. Bark roughish, brownish-black.

L 7–16 × 2.7–5 cm (2¾–6½ × 1–2 in.), 2.7–3.3 times as long as broad, lanceolate to oblong-lanceolate, apex obtuse to shortly acuminate, base cuneate to narrowly rounded, young leaves soon glabrous above, indumentum below *thin, ± plastered, silvery to grey-green, sometimes almost glabrous*. L remain for 2 to 3 years. Petiole 1–2 cm stout. *Long pointed growth buds.*

Inflor seven to ten, rachis about 5 mm, bud scales and bracts ± persistent during flowering period. Pedicel stout 1 cm.

F very deep purplish-mauve through purplish-red and blue-mauve to pale violet, suffused crimson, nectar pouches violet to crimson-black, glistening, 4–5 cm (1½–2 in.) long, lobes five to seven, campanulate, broad base to tube.

Calyx large about 5 mm a pink ring with unequal lobes. Stamens and stigma ± coloured as the corolla. Ovary with dense grey felty tomentum, style glabrous, reddish towards base.

A very distinct species which always creates interest in early spring and stands out in garden or show. Some call it beautiful, others sombre. Although it takes some years to bloom freely, the flowers are produced over an extended period and are long lasting if frost is avoided. Personally, I like the unusual colour combined with the deep nectar pouches. Some forms grow very early but it is generally easy to please. Flowers large for subsection **AM**, 1931 Bodnant.

Limited to the Mt Omei area of Szechwan, 1,200–2,200 m (4,000–7,250 ft) in forests or thickets and lower slopes, often exposed.

February–March

simiarum Hance 1884 (*fokienense* Franch. *fordii* Hemsl.) H2–4 L1–2 F1–3

Ht 1–4.6 m (3–15 ft). Habit rigid stout branches and crowded leaves. Young leaves with evanescent indumentum. Bark grey.
L 4–15 × 2–4.5 cm (1½– × ¾–1¾ in.), *oblanceolate* to *obovate* to oblong-lanceolate, apex obtuse to rounded, base cuneate, dark green and leathery above, indumentum white, silvered to cork-brown, ± plastered, margins often recurved. L remain for 1 to 2 years. Petiole 1–1.5 cm.
Inflor four to twelve, rachis 1–2 cm. Pedicel 2–3 cm with white to rusty floccose tomentum.
F light rose to white; greyish-yellow, reddish or light violet spots, about 4 cm (1½ in.) long, funnel-campanulate.
Calyx glandular. Ovary covered with hairs and glands, style curving, *glandular at base*. Capsule erect, often rufous tomentose.

Pretty in a quiet way but cannot be rated high class (*W*) but Dr August Kehr says that the flowers are very nice. Very variable in leaf shape and size. While most introductions are only suitable for mild locations, plants have survived for many years in south-west and south England. Seedlings have been slow growing with us but seem reasonably hardy. It promises to be a most useful species for heat tolerance and has already proved to be so in an old Australian garden.

The name *simiarum* should probably cover all related plants found from Kweichow to Fukien, having a very wide distribution. This includes Hong Kong and Hainan but may not spread into Chekiang, 500–1,250 m (1,600–4,000 ft), abundant on steep slopes with oaks, *Schima* and *Sterculia* sp. and other evergreens; may form pure stands, also on rocks, rocky cliffs and thickets.

April–May (Hong Kong)

simiarum ssp. *youngii* Fang. Chief characters: L oblong-elliptic, brownish-grey indumentum. Pedicel densely brown glandular. Ovary coarsely stipitate-glandular *not* brown tomentose as stated in the type description. May be synonymous with *simiarum*.
Szechwan, 1,200–2,000 m (4,000–6,500 ft).

thayerianum Rehd. & Wils. 1913 H4 L2–3 F2–3

Ht 2–4 m (6–13 ft). Habit stout branches, *foliage crowded at ends of branches, bud scales persisting for several years*. Bark shaggy, rough flaking brown.
L 7–15 × 1.5–3 cm (2¾–6 × ⅜–1¼ in.), narrowly oblanceolate, margin recurved, apex acute to acuminate, mucronate, base cuneate, often mottled above, indumentum below ± plastered, fawn: leathery and stiff. L remain for 3 to 6 years. Petiole stout with sparse evanescent tomentum.

Inflor ten to twenty, fairly compact to looser, rachis elongated 3–4 cm.
Pedicel slender, densely glandular (sticky to touch).
F white, white tinged or flushed pink, no spots or blotch or a few spots,
2.5–3 cm (1–1¼ in.) long, funnel-campanulate, bud scales very hairy.
Calyx 2–4 mm with densely glandular unequal lobes. Ovary with dense
whitish glands, sticky, style *whitish glands to tip*.

A very distinct late flowering species with remarkable stiff foliage.
Some have flowers on the small side but those with larger flowers are well
worth having. Slow growing but quite easy. Very hardy including parts of
Scandinavia.

Mupin, west Szechwan, around 3,000 m (10,000 ft) in woodlands.

June–July

Little known species probably not in cultivation

denudatum Levl. 1914 Closely allied to *floribundum* and doubtfully
distinct. The leaves are apparently thinner in texture and also differ in the
thin woolly yellowish upper layer of the indumentum. Probably a form of
floribundum according to Fang. Szechwan and perhaps east Yunnan,
3,000–3,350 m (10,000–11,000 ft).

farinosum Levl. 1914 Closely allied to *floribundum* and *denudatum* but
differs from both in the somewhat hooded leaves and white flowers and
from *denudatum* alone in its dense more persistent indumentum. Doubtfully in cultivation. The same area and altitude as *denudatum*.

haofui Chun & Fang 1955 F white suffused rose. Apparently allied to
floribundum and *denudatum* which differ in having only 10 stamens and
spotted corollas. No specimen in RBG, Edinburgh. Kwangsi 1,450 m
(5,000 ft).

longipes Rehd. & Wils. 1928 Near *hunnewellianum* in leaf shape and also
close to *thayerianum*. Doubtfully worth specific status. Thin compacted
indumentum. See Addendum *p.* 345.

longipes var. *chienianum* (Fang) Chamb. Thicker more spongy indumentum. West Szechwan, 1,200–2,300 m (4,000–7,500 ft). See Addendum
p. 345.

pingianum Fang 1939 May merge with *argyrophyllum*. Also from Mt
Omei. More intensely coloured flowers than *argyrophyllum* and rufous
tomentose eglandular ovary. Introduced in 1980. See Addendum *p.* 345.

versicolor Chung & Fang 1957, Ht 6 m (20 ft). F white to rose. Near
simiarum. Kwangsi 850 m (2,750 ft).

AURICULATA SUBSECTION (AURICULATUM SERIES) (E)

R. auriculatum was originally included with *griersonianum* in a separate series but apart from the long foliar and floral buds, these two have little in common.

Most parts have long- or short-stalked glands making the plant very sticky. It shows some resemblance to the white flowered species of the Fortunea subsection but differs in the hairs and glands on the leaf undersurface and the long buds where the pointed scales protrude some way beyond the bud itself.

auriculatum Hemsl. 1889 H4 A – 5 L2–3 F2–3

Ht 1.80–11 m (6–36 ft). Habit shrub or small tree, often flat-topped or umbrella shaped. Branchlets setose-glandular, foliar and floral buds *long, conical and tapered with long acuminate tips*. Bark roughish, greenish-brown.
L   9.5–32 × 2.8–12 cm   (4–13 × 1–5 in.), oblong, oblong-elliptic to oblong-oblanceolate, apex broadly obtuse to rounded, base rounded, *auricled* with a quantity of hairs and glands below, especially on midrib, pale green, old leaves often almost glabrous above, young leaves ciliate. L remain for only just over 1 year. Petiole 1.3–3.5 cm with long stalked glands.
Inflor six to fifteen, fairly loose, rachis 2.3–5 cm. Pedicel 1–3.5 cm densely long stalked glandular.
F white, creamy-white to rose-pink (rosy-red forms reported by *W*) with greenish blotch, *fragrant*, 6–10 cm (2½–4 in.) long, tubular-funnel-shaped, glandular outside, seven lobed, frilled.
Calyx small 1–3 mm, glandular. Stamens fourteen unequal, glabrous. Ovary densely glandular, style glandular to tip, stigma large, knob-like.

A magnificent late flowering species able to withstand surprisingly harsh conditions such as partial continental climates provide with extremes of heat and cold. It does, of course, need watering if the weather is hot and dry in late summer when its growth is made, but it does appear to appreciate or tolerate sun and dryish conditions. Needs shelter for its large leaves. Has stood more than 50 days of over 32°C (90°F) in Washington DC during June–August. Quite successful in south Sweden but in east Scotland, it can have trouble in ripening the young wood before winter. As the old leaves drop off soon after the young ones have expanded or even earlier, the plant is sometimes rather sparse of leaves and in some areas, inclined to be chlorotic. The huge plant at Arduaine, Argyll is probably the largest individual plant in that fine garden. The parent of several splendid, late hybrids. **AM**, 1922 Bodnant.

From Hupeh, Szechwan and Kweichow, probably quite widespread in central China, 500–2,300 m (1,600–7,500 ft) in light woods, high ridges, rocky slopes in forest and in dense shade.   July–August

chihsinianum Chun & Fang 1957. Allied by the anthers to *strigillosum* (*monesematum*) but the seven-lobed corolla and glandular style suggest a close affinity with *auriculatum* from which it differs in the loosely tomentose young shoots, eglandular pedicels and the smaller corolla.

Forms a small tree to 4 m (13 ft). Inflor *c.* eight flowered. Corolla colour unknown. Not in cultivation. Kwangsi.

PENTANTHERA SUBGENUS (AZALEA SERIES) (E)

This includes the (old) Candense (Rhodora), Pentanthera (Luteum), and Viscidula (Nipponicum) subsections.

These are all deciduous shrubs, some almost tree-like; the majority have hairy leaves and terminal, sometimes multiple flower buds producing several flowers per bud; the branchlets emerge from separate buds below the flower buds.
Calyx usually small, corolla usually funnel-shaped to rotate.
Stamens five to ten, ovary usually hairy. No scales.
Distribution North America, Europe and Asia.
The hairs are always unbranched. Seeds winged.

Azaleas have for a long time been included in the genus Rhododendron but are still generally referred to as azaleas by the gardening public. I have reluctantly included common names (where they exist) for azalea species. This subgenus has not been revised yet.

RHODORA SECTION (CANADENSE SUB-SERIES)

vaseyi A. Gray 1880 Pinkshell Azalea H4 A – 15 L2–3 F2–3

Ht to 3.6 m (12 ft) or more. Habit upright. Branchlets hairy at first, soon glabrous, brown to grey-brown in second year. Older branches flaky or shredding. L scattered on branchlets.
L 5–12.5 × 2–5 cm (2–5 × ¾–2 in.), elliptic to elliptic-oblong, apex acuminate, base cuneate, margins often undulate, dark green and glabrous except midrib above, lighter and largely glabrous below. Petiole slender, 3–8 mm (⅛–⅓ in.).
Inflor five to eight, before leaves. Pedicels 0.5–2 cm (⅛–¾ in.), glandular.
F pale pink, rose-pink to deep pink (sometimes velvety crimson in wild) with red, pink to green spots (sometimes mixed on the same flower) or rarely white, 2.5–3 cm (1–1¼ in.) long, to 5 cm (2 in.) across, widely funnel-shaped, to rotate-campanulate, two lipped, lobes deeply divided. Lacks the long tube of the Pentanthera subsection (Luteum sub-series).
Calyx green, oblique, with glandular hairs. Stamens five to seven, usually six; anthers pinkish to brown; filaments glabrous, white. Ovary glandular-pubescent; style pale green, usually glabrous.

A beautiful, hardy species full of virtues. Should be much more widely grown. Free flowering from a young age. Very distinct and one of the finest American Azalea species. The rather willow-like leaves often turn a rich scarlet to red in autumn. The flowers are not scented. Does not cross (apparently) with any other species so always comes true from seed. Loves moisture and is happiest near a pond or stream, but grows well in a variety of soils and situations. The flowers are frost resistant and it does well in Scandinavia.

This species has no real connection with *canadense* with which it was placed. These two differ strongly morphologically and chemically (flavonoids) and even have different chromosome numbers.

Discovered in 1878 and introduced to Britain about 1880. Only found wild in the mountains of North Carolina, USA, where it is relatively rare in ravines and sometimes in swamps.

'Suva' **AM**, 1969, pink. 'White Find' a very good wild collected white form with yellow autumn colour. Looks well planted with pink forms, rare. **AGM**, 1927.   May–June in wild; April–May

SUBGENUS PENTANTHERA, SECTION VISCIDULA (SUB-SERIES NIPPONICUM)

nipponicum Matsumura 1899 H4 A − 53 L2–3 F1

Ht 1–1.8 m (3–6 ft). Habit upright, rigid branches. Branchlets hairy and glandular when young, later red-brown. Main stems with papery cinnamon-brown shiny bark. Leaves from lateral buds below flower buds. L 5–18 × 3.8–9 cm (2–7 × 1½–3½ in.), obovate to obovate-oblong, apex usually rounded, base cuneate, margins usually notched and densely ciliate. Petiole very short.
Inflor six to fifteen, with or after leaves. Pedicel 1.3–2 cm (½–¾ in.), glandular-hairy, slender.
F *yellowish-white* with greenish spots, 1.5–2.5 cm (⅝–1 in.) long, about 1 cm (⅜ in.) across, *tubular-campanulate* with short sub-erect lobes about ⅓ as long as tube, glabrous, *pendant*.
Calyx small, glandular-hairy. Stamens ten, included. Ovary glandular-hairy, style glabrous, nearly straight, shorter than corolla. Capsule dark, somewhat warty, splitting almost to base.

In many respects this species suggests a relationship with the genus *Menziesia*, while the foliage resembles *schlippenbachii*. The flowers are too small in proportion to the leaves and rather hidden. Handsome foliage with brilliant autumn colour and quite attractive reddish-brown bark. Not widely cultivated.

From Honshu, Japan with limited distribution but fairly common in open country, 900–1,300 m (3,000–4,500 ft), in deciduous forest and on hillsides.   late June–July

PENTANTHERA SECTION (LUTEUM SUB-SERIES)

The Pentanthera section contains the majority of hardy deciduous azaleas and the well-known hybrid strains Knaphill, Exbury and Mollis all come from within this section. Most of these species come from eastern North America, with one from western USA, one from eastern Europe and adjacent parts of west Asia and one each from China and Japan.

Deciduous shrubs with scattered leaves; funnel-shaped flowers, often with a long tube, with no blue or purple shades, usually pubescent and often glandular outside. *Stamens five.*

Leach said (1959) that it is high time that the finer forms of these American species were introduced and distributed in cultivation. This is now happening, especially with *occidentale*.

Leach divides the eastern American species into the following groups:

(1) Early whites, *alabamense, atlanticum.*
(2) Early to midseason pinks, *canescens, periclymenoides (nudiflorum)*, *prinophyllum (roseum)*.
(3) Red-yellow-orange group with little or no scent, *austrinum, flammeum (speciosum), calendulaceum, bakeri, prunifolium.*
(4) Late whites, *arborescens, viscosum, oblongifolium, serrulatum.*

Flavonoids have been found very useful in the classification of the Luteum sub-series. A total of fifty-eight of these chemical compounds have been found in the leaves of these plants. The analysis of these compounds has confirmed (2) as a group and also (3) with the exception of *austrinum* and to some extent *calendulaceum* which may suggest evidence of hybridization with *canescens*. Also *prunifolium* and *bakeri* have a compound in common with some south-eastern populations of *canescens*.

Groups (1) and (4) are closely related morphologically and chemically, especially *alabamense* and *arborescens*. *R. viscosum, oblongifolium, serrulatum* and *atlanticum* make a second group within this relationship. Another most interesting group is formed by *austrinum, occidentale* and *luteum*. Thus with a combination of morphological and chemical characters, the groups turn out as follows:

(1) *alabamense, arborescens.* ⎫
(2) *viscosum, oblongifolium,* ⎬ closely related
   serrulatum, atlanticum. ⎭
(3) *canescens, periclymenoides (nudiflorum), prinophyllum (roseum)*.
(4) *flammeum (speciosum), pruniflorum, calendulaceum, bakeri*.
(5) *austrinum, occidentale; luteum* (not American) (chemical relationship only).

Several collectors have gathered superior forms of these American azaleas and the best of these are now being propagated and distributed and first-rate plants they are. The most comprehensive and perhaps best collections have been made by Dr H. Skinner in the east and Smith and Mossman in the west. Some are being used to create better Exbury-type hybrids.

In eastern North America, this rather complex group of species is further complicated by the presence of multitudes of natural hybrids. Many of these only appear on man disturbed areas. Hybrids between species in different groups mentioned above often occur in these areas and chemical analysis shows that many genes do not function well mixed together in hybrids; the gene flow between these species may be restricted and the species retain their identity. This theory was based on hybrids of *canescens* and *austrinum* but could well hold good in other cases.

Some places contain whole combinations of natural hybrids such as the bare top of a peak called Gregory Bald where there it is thought to be the progeny of *bakeri*, *arborescens*, *viscosum* and *calendulaceum*. In some places these hybrids have inter- or back-crossed for generations producing flowers of every conceivable hue.

These plants enjoy fairly sunny conditions in most rhododendron areas and appreciate plenty of moisture, some relishing in really damp soil like that found at the edge of a pond or stream. Most respond well to fertilizer at a rate that would cause scorch in some rhododendron species. Care must be exercised in the use of the weedkillers Casoron G and Prefix, which must be applied at half the recommended strength or lower to avoid damage. Prone to rabbit and deer browsing.

They are mostly hardy vigorous plants which thrive in good, deep soil in most of Britain. The only exceptions with us are those from south-east USA which grow too long in the autumn and get severely frosted back. Fortunately, these are the ones of least horticultural value.

If these plants become stunted and make little growth for some years, lichens frequently form on the branches. While this may be treated with lime sulphur, or preferably, tar oil (kills insects) when *dormant*, the only real answer is to increase the vigour by a combination of fertilizers, mulches and pruning.

alabamense Rehd. and Wils. 1921 Alabama Azalea H3–4 A – 5 L1 F2–3

Ht 60 cm–2.4 m (2–8 ft). Habit usually low and stoloniferous. Branchlets bristly when young.
L 3–6.3 × 1.3–3 cm (1¼–2½ × ½–1¼ in.), obovate to elliptic to oblong-obovate, often glaucous below. Crushed leaves have a distinct odour. Petiole short.
Inflor six to ten, before leaves, Pedicel 5–10 mm, hairy.
F white, usually with lemon blotch, sometimes snow-white (forms with pale apricot, pink or creamy-yellow flowers are probably hybrids) 2.2–3.5 cm (⅞–1⅜ in.) long, tube narrow, jasmine or lemon scent.
Calyx small, unequal, densely setose, stamens twice as long as tube. Ovary hairy.

A dainty species with fragile looking velvety flowers, deliciously scented and of a good size. Bean (1976) says it is perfectly hardy which I consider doubtful. Not as stoloniferous as *atlanticum*; hybrids tend to be less stoloniferous and taller. The 'best' form only occurs in a limited area around north-central Alabama, while less typical variations are found into Georgia and Florida and these approach *canescens*. Blooms later than *canescens*.

Dry hillsides and tops and richer ravines, often in shade.

April–May

arborescens (Pursh) Torrey 1824 (*verticillata* Lodd.) Sweet Azalea. H4 A – 15 to – 5 L1–2 F2–3.
Ht variable to 6 m (20 ft). Habit from low spreading bushes in the open to tall and leggy in shade. *Not* stoloniferous. *Branchlets smooth and glabrous*. F buds ovoid, glabrous, light brown.

L 3.8–8.8 × 1.3–3 cm ($1\frac{1}{2}$–$3\frac{1}{2}$ × $\frac{1}{2}$–$1\frac{1}{4}$ in.), usually obovate, apex acute to obtuse, base cuneate, usually glabrous, dark lustrous green above, glaucous or green below. Fragrant when bruised. Petiole 3–6 mm, usually glabrous.
Inflor three to six, after leaves are fully developed. Pedicel 1–2 cm ($\frac{1}{3}$–$\frac{3}{4}$ in.).
F *white*, sometimes with yellow blotch or tinged pink, 3.8–5.5 cm ($1\frac{1}{2}$–$2\frac{1}{4}$ in.) long, long tubed, sparsely glandular outside, usually pubescent within, fragrant, heliotrope scented.
Calyx 3–6 mm, glandular ciliate, unequal. Stamens twice as long as tube. Ovary with reddish glands. Style pale to deep *purplish-red*, usually glabrous.

A useful, hardy late flowering species which rarely gives much of a display but the larger flowered forms show up well against the glossy foliage. The poorer forms have small flowers rather hidden by the young growth. The scent is good. 'Ailsa' **AM**, 1952, white, yellow blotch Adams Atton. Needs summer heat to ripen growth.

New York and Pennsylvania to central Georgia and Alabama at 800–1,500 m (2,500–5,000 ft), among scrub oaks and vacciniums, in rich damp woods often along upland stream sides.   July–August

atlanticum Rehd. and Wils. 1921 Coast, Coastal or Atlantic Azalea H4 A–10 L1–2 F2–3

Ht 0.30–1.5 m (1–5 ft). Habit *stoloniferous*, forms arching sprays when well established. Branchlets usually glabrous, occasionally glandular. F buds glabrous.
L 3–6.3 × 1.5–2 cm ($1\frac{1}{4}$–$2\frac{1}{2}$ × $\frac{2}{5}$–$\frac{3}{4}$ in.), obovate to oblong-obovate, apex rounded or acute, base cuneate; often *glaucous-blue* above, sometimes light green and glaucous to bright green below, glabrous or sometimes glandular. Petiole 1–5 mm slightly hairy.
Inflor four to ten, shortly before or with the leaves. Pedicel 1–1.3 cm ($\frac{1}{3}$–$\frac{1}{2}$ in.), hairy.
F *white to white flushed pink, tube usually deeper*, sometimes magenta to purplish tinged or occasionally tinged yellow, 2.8–4 cm ($1\frac{1}{8}$–$1\frac{5}{8}$ in.) long, about 3.8 cm ($1\frac{1}{2}$ in.) across, tubular-funnel-shaped, very fragrant, rather pungent.
Calyx 2–4 mm, usually glandular-ciliate. Stamens twice as long as tube. Ovary hairy, style longer than stamens.

One of the dwarfest deciduous azaleas, this makes an effective plant once it forms a large clump. These smaller flowered azalea species have a most attractive light and airy nature in contrast to the often heavy, over-powering opulence of the Exbury and Mollis hybrids.

This species enjoys wet soil conditions even to the extent of water filling the hole a plant is removed from but it will succeed on deep sandy soil.

A hybrid group called 'Cote' raised at Towercourt, Berkshire, has a high proportion of *atlanticum* blood in it.

R. atlanticum is closely related to *periclymenoides* and *canescens*. Plants with pink flowers are mostly hybrids with *periclymenoides*. One unusual form has flower buds in the axils of the leaves. 'Seaboard' **AM**, 1964 white, pale pink tubes Crown Lands.

Found along the Atlantic coast from eastern Pennsylvania and Delaware south to South Carolina. Knee-high and stoloniferous often spreading to such an extent that a single plant may cover an acre. It makes a splendid sight as an understory in open pinewoods and among ferns and hollies and it quickly recovers from a brush fire, trimming or grazing. Hybrid swarms also occur with *canescens*. May–June

austrinum Rehd. 1917 Florida Azalea H3 (–43) A0 L1–2 F2–3

Ht to 3–3.6 m (10–12 ft). Habit usually stiff and upright. Branchlets often glandular (red). F buds ovoid, large, greyish pubescent.
L 3–8.8 × 2–3.8 cm (1¼–3½ × ¾–1½ in.), elliptic to oblong-obovate, apex usually acute, base cuneate, pubescent above and below and often glandular as well. Petiole 3–8 mm, pubescent and glandular.
Inflor eight to fifteen forming a rounded truss, before or with leaves. Pedicel 5–10 mm, pubescent and glandular.
F *yellow to orange*, tube *deep orange or red* to plum-coloured or occasionally clear yellow; 2.5–3 cm (1–1¼ in.) long, tubular-funnel-shaped, tube glandular, fragrance variable.
Calyx about 2 mm, unequal, pubescent and glandular. Stamens long, nearly three times the length of the tube. Style slightly longer than stamens.

A handsome and free-flowering species. The protruding stamens give a rather feathery appearance while these plus the rather small flowers combine to produce a spidery effect. Not stoloniferous. Mixes and hybridizes with *alabamense* and *canescens*. Growth does not ripen in Scotland.

A restricted range from north-west Florida to south-east Mississippi where it is common in woodland and small stream sides. May

bakeri Lemmon and McKay 1948 (*cumberlandense* E. L. Braun) Cumberland Azalea H3–4 A – 15 L1–2 F2–3

Ht to 2.4 m (8 ft) but *rarely over 1.8 m (6 ft)*. Habit low and twiggy, often stoloniferous. Branchlets with stiff bristles. Buds and leaves similar to *calendulaceum*.
Inflor four to seven after leaves.
F usually *orange to red*; the fine scarlets and blood reds often lose their rich colours when brought into cultivation; 3–4.5 cm (1¼–1¾ in.) long, tubular-funnel-shaped, not fragrant.

This is really just a diploid variation of *calendulaceum*, which has a lower habit and generally smaller flowers. We find it less vigorous than *calendulaceum* and very pretty, making a more compact plant. Rather tender here as a young seedling. 'Alhambra' a superb clone with brilliant orange-red flowers. Other good clones are 'Camps Red' and 'Kentucky Colonel'.

Eastern Kentucky to Tennessee to north Georgia and Alabama. Open woods at high elevations. June–July

calendulaceum (Michx.) Torrey 1824 (*flammea* Bartr., *aurantiaca* Dietr.)
Flame or Fiery Azalea, Flame Flower; H4 A − 20 L1–2 F2–4

Ht to 3.6 m (12 ft) or more. Habit often stiff and upright, vigorous, not
stoloniferous, branchlets pubescent. F buds ovoid, glabrous except for
some white hairs.
L 3.8–8 × 1.3–3.8 cm (1½–3¼ × ½–1½ in.); broadly elliptic to elliptic-oblong
to obovate, finely pubescent above and more so below, especially when
young. Petiole 2–5 mm, pubescent.
Inflor five to seven with or shortly after leaves. Pedicel 0.6–1.3 cm
(¼–½ in.), hairy.
F usually *various shades of orange to red*, more rarely yellow or brilliant
red, 3.8–6.3 cm (1½–2½ in.) long, 4–5 cm (1½–2 in.) across, funnel-shaped,
tube usually pubescent and glandular outside; little or no fragrance.
Calyx 1–4 mm, glandular and hairy. Stamens nearly three times the length
of tube. Ovary glandular and hairy.

This is perhaps the best known and also one of the finest eastern
American azaleas and several well-known Ghent azaleas, such as 'Coc-
cinea Speciosa', are hybrids or even forms of this species. The glowing
bright shades of orange and also the excellent yellows are among the
showiest of all azaleas and the largest flowered forms, which are often
yellow, may rival the Exbury azaleas.

Like the very closely related *bakeri*, the deepest colours found in the
wild are inclined to be less intense in cultivation although this can vary
from season to season and garden to garden. Like *occidentale*, *calendulaceum* produces several queer forms in the wild, such as semi and near
doubles and even one with no corolla but additional stamens. The
filaments are a little deeper than the usual and the occasional one is partly
petaloid. The overall effect is quite pleasing and not unlike a *Callistemon*
(bottlebrush).

High elevation colonies tend to have smaller than average flowers and
bloom later in the season, while the best forms have globular trusses. This
species is a tetraploid and is now thought to be a fairly recent species
which has evolved from the more basic species.

Does well in all parts of Britain, south Scandinavia and other cold
climates.

There is perhaps less hybridizing of this species with its diploid neighbours than was previously considered, but hybrids with *periclymenoides*
and *prinophyllum* make very variable populations of every colour.

'Burning Light' **AM**, 1965 Crown Lands; 'Smoky Mountaineer'
Arnold Arboretum, nearly scarlet.

Pennsylvania to Georgia, Carolina and Virginia at moderate to high
elevations, 550–1,500 m (1,800–5,000 ft) in woods, on cliffs and open
hillsides. May–June

canescens (Michx.) Sweet 1830 (*bicolor* Pursh.) Florida Pinxter, Hoary or
Piedmont Azalea. H3–4 A+5 to 0 L1–2 F1–3

Ht to 4.6 m (15 ft). Habit medium to tall, usually upright, sometimes
stoloniferous. Branchlets hairy. F buds ovoid, densely greyish-pubescent.

L 4.5–8.8 × 1.3–3.8 cm (1¾–3½ × ½–1½ in.); usually oblong-obovate to oblong, apex usually acute, base cuneate, felty-pubescent below. Petiole 2–8 mm, hairy.

Inflor six to fifteen, before or with leaves in almost round, closely packed trusses. Pedicel 5–8 mm, hairy.

F usually pale to deep pink, more rarely salmon-pink, white or deep purplish-red with yellow blotch; 2.5–3.5 cm (1–1⅓ in.) long, tubular-funnel-shaped, usually fragrant, tube glandular, longer than lobes.

Calyx 1 mm, unequal, ciliate. Stamens nearly three times as long as tube.

From a horticultural viewpoint, this is very similar to *prinophyllum* and *periclymenoides*, except that it is often not as hardy and generally has paler coloured flowers. While some forms are good and underrated, the average is inferior to that of *prinophyllum* and the latter is the best of the trio for British gardens.

It is an aggressive species in the wild, covering large areas of south-eastern USA in about ten states from South Carolina and Florida to eastern Texas and Tennessee. Grows on mounds in low-lying woods, often moist, on rocks and on stream sides. Usually blooms earlier than *periclymenoides* and *prinophyllum*.   April–May

flammeum (Michx.) Sarg. (*speciosum* (Wild.) Sweet *fulva* (Michx.) Oconee Azalea. H3–4 A0 L1–2 F2–3.

Ht about 2 m (6–7 ft). Branchlets pubescent and hairy. F buds glabrous.

L 3–6.3 × 1.3–2.5 cm (1¼–2½ × ½–1 in.), obovate to elliptic to oblong, apex usually acute, base broadly cuneate, evanescent pubescent. Petiole 3–5 mm, hairy.

Inflor six to fifteen, opening with the leaves or before. Pedicel 0.6–1.3 cm, hairy.

F a wide colour range, scarlet to reddish-orange to orange to coral-pink, salmon and yellow, about 4 cm (1⅔ in.) across, funnel-shaped tube pubescent, not glandular, not fragrant.

Calyx 1–3 mm, usually pubescent. Stamens more than twice as long as tube. Ovary not glandular, style slightly longer than stamens.

A highly rated species in America which is rare in Britain. Flowers have some of the finest colours, according to Leach, with incandescent reds, luminous yellows and soft pastel shades. Free flowering in cultivation in USA, less vigorous than *calendulaceum*, leaves slightly smaller, thinner branches and more graceful character. Best forms bloom before the leaves. Coming from the southern states, it could well prove unsatisfactory in Britain. As expected, I have found it useless in central Scotland, never ripening its growth. Is this really a good species or a hybrid swarm? Non-glandular. Needs shelter and south exposure in Pennsylvania and is heat resistant in Georgia.

Has a limited distribution in Georgia and south Carolina. The average plant inhabits fairly shady red clay bluffs, open woods and wooded slopes. Blooms between *austrinum* and *calendulaceum* and hybridizes with *alabamense* and *canescens* and probably *austrinum* and *calendulaceum*. The earliest of the red shades.   May *japonicum** Suringar 1908 (*sinense* Maxim., *glabrius* Nakai) H4 A − 25 to − 15 L1–2 F3–4

Ht 1–3 m (3–10 ft) Habit upright.
L 5–10 × 2–3 cm (2–4 × ¾–1¼ in.), mostly oblanceolate, sometimes to obovate; apex obtuse, base cuneate, scattered hairs above, light green and glabrous below but sometimes waxy-glaucous. Petiole 3–8 mm, scattered hairs or glabrous.
Inflor two to twelve, before or with the leaves. Pedicel 0.8–2 cm (⅓–¾ in.), scattered hairs.
F usually orange-red to red, also pink, orange to scarlet and rarely deep yellow, 5–15 cm (2–6 in.) across, widely funnel-shaped, sometimes sweetly scented, pubescent outside.
Calyx small, with grey hairs. Stamens shorter than corolla. Style glabrous, longer than stamens.

This can be quite equal in size of flowers and floriferousness to its so-called hybrids. The usual strains of seedling 'Mollis' appear to be very similar to this species and have an equivalent colour range. As the other so-called parent is apparently no longer in cultivation (*molle*), there seems to be some doubt of what it is like or how hardy it is. It would be interesting to grow quantities of seedlings from mixed seed of *japonicum* from various wild Japanese sources and compare the results with 'Mollis' seedlings. The deep yellow form is commonly cultivated in Japan but is rare in the wild.

Does well in south Scandinavia and is tolerant of less acid conditions than the American species. Also good in eastern North America. Leaves and flowers are poisonous to man and some animals.

Widely distributed in Japan from south-west Hokkaido, south to mountains of Shikoku and mid-Kyushu. From sun-baked grassy plains, open places, among reafforested larch, scrub woodland and moorland, sea cliffs and often scattered throughout bogs up to the very edge of pools. It is vigorous, locally common and gregarious. Pale colours are usually found on the hotter lower southern habitats and the deeper shades from northern parts and the high mountains.   May

luteum Sweet 1830 (*flavum* G. Don, A. *pontica* L.) Common yellow azalea. H4 A − 25 L2–3 F3–4

Ht to 3.6 m (12 ft) usually less in the open. Habit densely branched, spreading, often stoloniferous. Branchlets glandular hairy when young. F buds sticky.
L 5–10 × 1.3–3 cm (2–4 × ½–1¼ in.), oblong to oblong-lanceolate, apex acute to obtuse, base cuneate, pubescent above and below when young and also glandular appressed bristly. Petiole 3–8 mm glandular-pubescent.
Inflor seven to twelve before leaves. Pedicel 0.6–2 cm (¼–¾ in.) long, glandular-pubescent.

---

* Now confirmed as the correct name for the azalea.

F yellow about 3.8 cm (1½ in.) long, 4.5–5 cm (1¾–2 in.) across, glandular-pubescent outside, scented.
Calyx 2–6 mm lobes unequal, glandular-pubescent. Stamens as long or longer than corolla. Style slightly longer than stamens.

Our common yellow azalea is almost as easy to please as *ponticum* in Britain and will grow under trees and close to trunks provided the soil is suitable and does not dry out. Not too successful in eastern North America where the summers are probably too hot; 100-year-old specimens on the lawns at Royal Lodge are 3.6 m (12 ft), while it grows remarkably well on the windswept shores of Loch Ossian, Corrour, Rannoch Moor, one of the bleakest parts of Scotland. It is a common but first-rate garden plant being lovely in flower or covered in its scarlet autumn tints. Very fragrant. Was used frequently as an understock for named Ghent and other hybrid azaleas but readily suckers like *ponticum*. Is naturalized in some parts of Britain. Like other azaleas, the first flowers in a truss often shed before the last ones open, but this gives a long flowering season. Very glandular (sticky) in all parts. Is included in the parentage of many of the hybrid groups. **AGM**, 1930.

From east Europe through Turkey to the Caucasus north to Poland and Lithuania, north-east Yugoslavia, Austria, central and west Russia, from sea level to 1,200 m (4,000 ft). Found in dense forest, open beech forest, with scattered pines, beech and mixed scrub and open grassland, sometimes gregarious.   May–June

molle G. Don 1834 (*sinense* Sweet and also Lodd., *A. mollis* Bl.) Chinese azalea. H2–4? L1–2 F3–4?

Ht about 1 m (3–4 ft). Habit upright. Buds pubescent, glabrous in *japonicum*.
L 6.3–15 × 2–5.5 cm (2½–6 × ¾–2¼ in.), oblong to oblong-elliptic, apex obtuse, base cuneate, *greyish pubescent* below, sometimes only on veins. Petiole 2–6 mm pubescent.
Inflor many flowered, before leaves. Pedicel 1.3–2.5 cm (½–1 in.), hairy.
F soft golden yellow to orange, 5–8.8 cm (2–3½ in.) across, broadly funnel-shaped, fragrant.
Calyx small, smaller than *japonicum*, hairy.

There is some doubt whether the true plant is still in cultivation and just how hardy it is. One report says it is tender while the Handbook and Bean (1976) state it is H4 (hardy). It is said to be less hardy and less vigorous than *japonicum* in east North America where it dislikes the hot summers and cold winters. Was used to produce at least some of the 'Mollis' hybrids along with *japonicum*. Introduced several times. It would seem from its wild locations and altitude that both hardy and tender forms may have been introduced.

Abundant in east China, especially Chekiang, also Kiangsi, Anhwei, Hunan and Hupeh where Wilson thought the western limit of the species is near Ichang, but Fang found it later in Szechwan. Rock found it in Yunnan, apparently wild on the Mekong–Yangtze divide, but as it had been long cultivated there, it may have been a garden escape.

100–2,400 m (330–8,000 ft) on thinly wooded slopes, thin pine wood and open country.   April–June

oblongifolium (Small) Millais 1917 Texas azalea. H3 A0 L1–2 F1–2

Ht to 1.8 m (6 ft). Habit upright, somewhat stoloniferous. Branchlets slightly pubescent and hairy. F buds ovoid, greyish pubescent.
L   3.8–10 × 1.5–3.8 cm   ($1\frac{1}{2}$–4 × $\frac{2}{3}$–$1\frac{1}{2}$ in.),   obovate   to   oblong-oblanceolate, apex acute, base cuneate, glabrous above except for hairy midrib or hairy, similar below. Petiole 2–3 mm, finely pubescent.
Inflor seven to twelve, after leaves are fully developed. Pedicel 1.5–2 cm ($\frac{2}{3}$–$\frac{3}{4}$ in.) hairy.
F white to pink, 3 cm ($1\frac{1}{4}$ in.) long, 2.5–3 cm (1–$1\frac{1}{2}$ in.) across, tubular-funnel-shaped, thinly pubescent outside and deliciously fragrant.
Calyx 2–3 mm, unequal, hairy. Stamens about twice as long as tube. Ovary hairy and glandular, style longer than stamens.

One of the poorest American species with small flowers. Makes a larger bush than the somewhat similar *atlanticum* but with inferior flowers and is rather tender.

From Arkansas, south-east Texas and eastern Oklahoma in moist valleys (mostly white flowers) and drier hill slopes (mostly pinks), also sandy bogs and along streams, sometimes on limestone. Opens shortly after *alabamense*.   June–July

occidentale A. Gray 1876 Western or Pacific Azalea. H4 A − 5 L1–3 F2–4

Ht usually 1–4.6 m (3–15 ft) but occasionally to 7.6 m (25 ft) in the wild. Habit usually rounded, occasionally upright or low. F buds glabrous to finely pubescent, sometimes multiple. Branchlets and foliage sparsely pubescent (from dry areas) to more heavily pubescent (in moist areas).
L 1.5–9.6 × 0.5–4 cm ($\frac{2}{3}$–$3\frac{3}{4}$ × $\frac{1}{4}$–$1\frac{1}{2}$ in.), usually oblanceolate but also linear, elliptic, lanceolate, obovate to almost orbicular, apex acute to obtuse, base cuneate, margins sometimes wavy, light to dark green to reddish to plum coloured to coppery to deep rusty-brown above, shiny or not shiny. Petiole 2–5 mm.
Inflor more than six, often twenty to twenty-five to fifty, one clone fifty-four. A few open before the leaves, later ones with leaves and new growth. Pedicel 0.5–1.5 cm ($\frac{1}{4}$–$\frac{3}{4}$ in.).
F commonly white with a yellow blotch or flare but often tinged pink or red on some or all lobes, some are all pink or nearly all red or even nearly all yellow. The flare varies from yellow to yellow-orange to orange-maroon or maroon and is sometimes on all lobes or absent. To 10 cm (4 in.) across, broadly funnel-shaped, tubular-campanulate to tubular-salverform, lobes commonly five, often six or more, lobe surface flat or crêpe-like and the lobes usually entire, rarely frilled, notched or serrated. Sweetly fragrant.
Calyx 2–5 mm, ciliate. Stamens five, rarely six to ten, about as long as corolla, sometimes petaloid. Style as long or longer than stamens, white

pink to red; stigma small to large knob-like, yellow, green, red, deep red or grey. Capsule 1.3–3.2 cm ($\frac{1}{2}$–1$\frac{1}{4}$ in.), green, yellow-green to deep red.

This superb azalea has probably been studied in the wild more thoroughly than any other species of Rhododendron, hence the amount of information available on it is prodigious. To show how much one species can vary and to indicate some of the types that are or will come on to the market, I have gone into more detail than with any other species.

Many individuals have studied and collected special clones in the wild but three people have done the bulk of this noble work, travelling down from their native Washington State to southern Oregon and northern California where the finest forms grow. Leonard Frisbie pioneered this work, so ably and thoroughly carried on by Britt Smith and Frank Mossman. The latter two collectors have numbered selected clones since 1966; several hundred have been numbered and many of these have been propagated and distributed. They were extremely kind and generous in sending me several of these to try out, plus hand-pollinated seed between some of the best clones. Some of the best clones are 28–2 double cream; 33 pink, orange flare; 186 white, yellow flare and 189 white and pink, orange flare. Many others are of considerable horticultural value, such as the highly coloured SM 502 which is nearly red. Several have been numbered because of their curious characters such as extra lobes, petaloid stamens, coloured foliage, dwarf habit and even the near or total absence of the corolla. These have been named 'Miniskirt', 'Pistil Pete', and 'Pistil Packin Mama'! Some have been found with variegated or partly variegated foliage. A few plants have been discovered sporting, throwing coloured, variegated and/or dwarf canes amongst the others. Some people consider the highly coloured forms rather gaudy.

These selected clones are generally proving excellent plants in cultivation but some take a while to develop their full potential of flower size and colour and one should not be disappointed in them for their first year or two of flowering. It is suspected that the forms used in the ancestry of the Knaphill and Exbury azaleas were inferior to many of these new finds and that the latter should lead to further improvements in these hybrid groups as should the selected clones of other azalea species. Use *occidentale* as a seed parent, as few seeds are normally produced when used as a pollen parent. It crosses readily with eastern American azaleas and various hybrids have been accomplished with elepidote rhododendrons plus one or more natural hybrids with *macrophyllum*.

It grows well in gardens throughout Britain and also southern Scandinavia and is said to survive in eastern USA but does not appreciate the type of summers experienced there. The hardiness of the coastal collections is not fully tested although they came through the 1972 freeze in Oregon well. A variety of soil conditions are tolerated but not where static water exists throughout the year. Where ground is flat it tolerates water-logging in winter only. Use fertilizers cautiously (by American standards!). Blooms in 3 to 4 years from seed. Autumn colour varies from yellow to scarlet to almost blue while some drop their leaves green.

Young plants may remain partly evergreen. **AM** 1944 Kew, white heavily flushed pink, yellow blotch. Small plants vulnerable to spring frosts.

Found over a wide area geographically, approximately 1127 × 80 km (700 × 50 miles), hugging the coast from north of Bandon, Coos County, Oregon to south boundary of Santa Cruz County, California. Isolated colonies occur south almost to Mexico and north into Washington State. South and east of San Francisco it occurs only at over 1,200 m (4,000 ft). Overall at elevations from sea-level to 2,700 m (9,000 ft).

It grows well on exposed sites along the ocean with a high humidity; in lower humidity areas it seeks partial shade. Found on moist ground by streams and edges of swamps, marshy plateaux and even grows where water runs for 7 to 8 months of the year and also on steep hillsides, usually where there are springs. Sometimes it seems that there is only the winter rains to provide moisture. The best forms have been found near the coast, while those found in the mountains have almost universally small white, pale yellow blotched flowers and are usually seen along river banks like those in the Yosemite National Park.

Common associated plants are *Gaultheria shallon*, *Ceanothus* sp., *Vaccinium* sp., *Arctostaphylos* sp., and grass while the trees are douglas fir and coastal redwood. The former tree is liable to spread over the azalea areas and eventually kill them out in places. The natural soil varies too; clay, medium loam, light sand, gravel with some organic matter and even alkaline magnesium rich soil. Susceptible to powdery mildew in the wild.

First discovered in 1827, first introduced before 1857, probably about 1851. Mid-March to mid-August in the wild, peak about 30 May. Mostly June–July in cultivation.

periclymenoides (Michx.) Shinners (*nudiflorum (L)* Torrey *periclymena* Pers.). Pinxterbloom or Honeysuckle Azalea. H4 A – 15 to 25 L1–2 F1–2

Ht to 2.7 m (9 ft) to 4.5 m (15 ft) in the wild. Habit usually tall, vigorous and much branched, sometimes stoloniferous. F buds glabrous, brown.
L 3–8.8 × 1.3–3 cm (1¼–3½ × ½–1¼ in.), elliptic to oblong-obovate, apex acute, base cuneate, bright green, nearly glabrous. Petiole 2–4 mm, hairy.
Inflor six to twelve, shortly before leaves. Pedicel 5–10 mm, hairy.
F usually pale to deep pink, often with deep maroon tubes, also such variations as vivid pinks or white; sweetly fragrant to no scent, 2.5–3.8 cm (1–1½ in.) long, about 3.8 cm (1½ in.) across, funnel-shaped, hairy outside.
Calyx 1–2 mm, unequal, ciliate. Stamens nearly three times as long as tube.

A very hardy species, but the average forms are not such good garden plants as either *atlanticum* or *prinophyllum*. Merges with these two species and is the northern counterpart of *canescens*. The best forms are well worth growing, free flowering and easy. Is involved in the parentage of many Ghent hybrids. Happy in wet or dry conditions. In Bean (1976) the name has been changed to *periclymenoides*.

From the Carolinas and Atlantic seaboard to Tennessee, Ohio and Massachusetts. Common and widespread in rich, damp soil, stream sides and also dry or rocky woods and wooded slopes.   April–May *prinophyllum* (Small) Millais (*roseum* (Loisel.) Rehd. and Wils); Roseshell Azalea. H4 A − 10 to − 25 L1–2 F2–3

Ht medium. Habit upright, well branched, rarely stoloniferous. Flower buds pubescent. Branchlets pubescent and slightly hairy when young, greyish to light brown second year.
L 3–7 × 1.3–3.5 cm (1¼–2¾ × ½–2¼ in.), elliptic to obovate-oblong, apex acute, base cuneate, soft pubescent below, sometimes glandular (Virginia), dull lightish green above. Petiole 3 to 5 mm.
Inflor five to nine, opening with leaves. Pedicel 0.5–1.5 cm (⅕–⅔ in.), hairy and glandular.
F *usually a vivid warm pink*, pale to deep pink, about 4.5 cm (1¾ in.) across, tubular-funnel-shaped, lobes pointed, fragrance spicy.
Calyx unequal, 2 mm, pubescent and glandular. Stamens about twice as long as tube. Ovary tomentose and glandular, style exceeding stamens.

A very good, hardy and valuable species, superior to the average *canescens* and *periclymenoides* to which it is closely related. Leaves greyer or more glaucous. The best forms are excellent. Does well with us at Glendoick. Also good in southern Scandinavia. Makes a neat shrub and produces its lovely pink flowers from a young age. Needs protection from rabbits. *Highly glandular.* Bean changed the name from *roseum* to *prinophyllum* 1976. **AM**, 1955, Towercourt.

From southern Quebec southwards through New England to Virginia and west as far as Missouri, in open woods, edges of sphagnum bogs, swampy woods and thickets in the foothills and mountains, sometimes on limestone.   May

prunifolium (Small) Millais 1917 Plumleaf Azalea H3–4 A − 15 L1–2 F2–3

Ht to 3.6 or even 5.5 m (12–18 ft) in the wild. Habit tall, rounded topped, non-stoloniferous. F buds glabrous. Branchlets almost glabrous.
L 3–12.5 × 2–3.8 cm (1¼–5 × ¾–1¼ in.), usually elliptic, apex acute, base cuneate, dark or bright green above, paler below, usually glabrous with hairs on veins. Petiole 3–6 mm, almost glabrous.
Inflor four to five, after leaves. Pedicel 5 mm, hairy.
F red, orange-red, apricot to orange-yellow, yellow to deep red and scarlet red, 3.8–5 cm (1½–2 in.) across, tubular-funnel-shaped, no hairs on tube, not fragrant.
Calyx about 1 mm, unequal, hairy. Stamens nearly three times as long as tube. Ovary hairy, not glandular, style longer than stamens.

A nearly glabrous species, distinctive for its late red flowers. Reckoned by some to be the finest American species. Is said to be a vigorous grower and comes easily and quickly from seed but I have found it difficult from seed and hard to grow on although two plants flowered nicely for me this year. Slow to bloom but flowers freely on reaching maturity. May need more summer heat than we can give it to do well. Interesting observations have been made on the colour which varies from season to season. A dry, cold year, flowers bright orange; very hot, flowers extremely dark red; also the colour deepens a day or two after opening, the opposite to most species. Often grows best in some shade where it can have a long flowering period and it requires a more than average acid soil and plenty of moisture. Closest to *bakeri* in affinity. Not too hardy at Winterthur. 'Summer Sunset'. **AM** 1950, Crown Lands.

Found on the Georgia–Alabama border where it is restricted to ravines cut by meandering streams in low, moist sites and also pine forest. In danger of extinction in the wild with few young seedlings to be seen.

Mid-June–November in the wild, July–August in cultivation.

serrulatum (small) Millais 1917 Hammock-sweet Azalea. H3 A+5 to 0 L1–2 F1–2

Ht to 3 or even 6 m (10–20 ft) but usually lower. Habit tall, rounded or straggly. Branchlets *rust coloured, hairy*. F buds ovoid, glabrous with distinctive pale scales with dark margins.
L 3.8–8 × 1.5–3.8 cm (1½–3¼ × ⅔–1½ in.), elliptic to obovate-oblong, apex usually acute, base cuneate, margin *serrulate-ciliate*, often pubescent below. Young leaves reddish. Petiole 1–4 mm, hairy.
Inflor six to ten, after leaves are fully grown and some winter buds are formed. Pedicel glandular and hairy, pale green to deep red.
F white, about 3.8 cm (1½ in.) long, funnel-shaped, tube slender, glandular and slightly hairy outside, lobes small, fragrant.

Calyx about 1 mm, glandular-ciliate. Stamens about one and a half times as long as tube. Style much exceeding stamens.

While useful for its lateness, this is the smallest flowered of all American species except possibly *canadense*. Rather similar to *viscosum* but generally inferior and not as hardy. We found that it grows on far too late for Scotland and gets frosted and killed back. Could be useful for hybridizing, perhaps with late clones of *occidentale* or *arborescens*.

From Mississippi, Louisiana, Florida and Georgia in coastal plains on the edges of wooded swamps, cypress islands and thickets and on bog tussocks. One of the latest to flower in the whole genus.

July–October or later

viscosum (L) Torrey 1824 Swamp Azalea or Swamp Honeysuckle. H4 A − 5 to − 25 L1–2 F2–3

Ht to 4.6 m (15 ft), often much dwarfer. Habit large and upright to dwarf and stoloniferous. Branchlets pubescent and bristly. F buds glabrous or pubescent.
L 2–3.8 × 1–2 cm (¾–1½ × ⅓–¾ in.), ovate to oblong-lanceolate, apex acute to rounded, base cuneate, pubescent and bristly. Petiole 1–3 mm, hairy.
Inflor four to nine, after leaves are fully developed. Pedicel 0.5–1.3 cm (⅕–½ in.), hairy.
F white to white suffused pink, about 3.8 cm (1½ in.) across, narrowly tubular-funnel-shaped, glandular sticky and hairy outside, fragrant strong spicy scent.
Calyx about 1 mm, unequal, glandular and hairy. Stamens somewhat longer than tube. Ovary usually glandular, style exceeding stamens, not coloured and usually pubescent.

Useful for its lateness and hardiness but not particularly showy in all but carefully selected forms. Prefers considerable moisture, sandy with organic matter. Easily grown. Can look nice backed by old-fashioned roses. Does well in southern Scandinavia. **AM**, 1921 South Northwood, **AGM**, 1937. There are some excellent new hybrids of this species raised in Holland.

Natural hybrids between *viscosum* and *arborescens* occur in some northern areas. Much more variable than *serrulatum*. Semi-evergreen in the marshes of South Carolina, tall grey leaved and large flowered on pond margins of Cape Cod. *R. coryi* Shinners is probably a variety or form of *viscosum*.

Widespread from Maine southwards to South Carolina, Tennessee and Georgia and even on the island of Martha's Vineyard. On moist pine barrens, wet hummocks, bogs, swampy woods, mucky swamps, river sides and rocky islets in river beds with the roots sometimes growing into the water.   Early June–late July

viscosum var. *aemulans* Rehd.

Low habit. F buds densely grey-pubescent.
L bristly, not pubescent. Inflor many. F small, corolla tubes softly pubescent. Lies botanically between *viscosum*, *serrulatum* and *oblongifolium*, probably closest to the last named. From Georgia and Alabama into Mississippi in drier woods.   May

SUBGENUS TSUTSUTSI SECTION BRACHYCALYX (AZALEA SERIES, SUB-SERIES SCHLIPPENBACHII)

A distinct group of azaleas with whorled leaves, mostly deciduous (subpersistent in *farrerae*, evergreen in *tashiroi*). Corolla more or less rotate. *R. albrechtii* and *pentaphyllum* have been added to this section as they are undoubtedly closely related although they have floral buds, which do not produce leafy shoots, unlike the others where the flowers and shoots come from the same buds. Nor are the leaves so obviously in whorls in *albrechtii*. All come from East Asia from Japan to east Szechwan.

These are generally hardy, sun loving plants and are only seen at their best in climates with warm summers. While we can grow most of them in Scotland, they grow very slowly and take many years to bloom and are not entirely happy. Two exceptions are *schlippenbachii* and *albrechtii* which come from the coldest parts of the range of this group. Both are hardy and bloom well, provided that the rather early young growth is not repeatedly frosted.

Probably divided into two groups (combined research by Sleumer, Philipsons and Seithe).

(1) *schlippenbachii*, *pentaphyllum*, *quinquefolium* and possibly *albrechtii*.
(2) the rest of the old Schlippenbachii sub-series plus possibly *tashiroi* which shows the same hair type and hybridizes readily with this group.

There are unnamed specimens in the herbarium of the RBG, Edin-burgh of one or two interesting looking azaleas from China which could be new species.

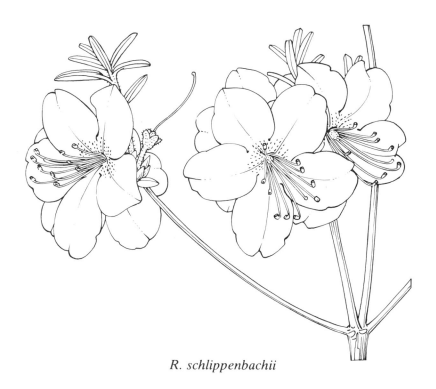

R. schlippenbachii

albrechtii Maxim. 1871 Albrecht's Azalea H4 A – 15 L1–2 F2–4

Ht 1–3 m (3–10 ft). Habit usually upright, twiggy. New shoots come from below the terminal flower bud. Branchlets with glandular (sticky) hairs at first, soon glabrous and purple-brown. Young foliage bronzy.
L   3.8–11.3 × 1.3–6.3 cm   (1½–4½ × ½–2½ in.),   obovate   to   oblong-lanceolate, apex acute, narrowed to shortly winged petiole, margin cili-ate, hairy above and below. Leaves usually in 5s at ends of weaker shoots, spaced on longer shoots.
Inflor four to five, before, or with leaves especially non-flowering shoots. Pedicel 1.3–2 cm (½–¾ in.), hairy.
F bright rose-purple through deep rose to rose, 1–2 cm (⅓–¾ in.) long, 3–4 cm (1¼–1½ in.) across, rotate-campanulate, glabrous.
Calyx small, ciliate. Stamens ten, unequal. Ovary hairy and glandular, style glabrous, longer than corolla.
  A very fine species, best in its deeper coloured forms. These are of a really striking colour, which give a wonderful vibrant glow on large established bushes. This colour makes it difficult to place so it is best planted away from other plants which bloom at the same time

although an under planting of small flowered yellow daffodils might be effective.

While very winter hardy, the early young growth is easily frosted but this is readily replaced. Good in southern Scandinavia. Not too happy in eastern North America where the summers are probably too hot. 'Michael McLaren' **FCC**, 1962, Bodnant.

From mid-Honshu north to central Hokkaido, Japan, in the mountains at about 1,000 m (3,300 ft) in sub-alpine regions, often growing among *brachycarpum*. May–June in the wild, March–May in cultivation

amagianum Makino Mt Amagi Azalea. H4 A − 5 L2–3 F2–3

Ht to 5 m (17 ft). Habit usually erect, old plants with a habit reminiscent of *Cornus florida*. Branchlets rather slender, densely white pubescent when young, glabrous when mature. F buds about 2.5 cm (1 in.) long with dense hairs.

L in threes, 4.8–11.5 × 3–9 cm (2–4½ × 1¼–3¾ in.), broadly ovate-rhombic, apex widely acute, base widely cuneate, scattered long brown hairs above and rusty-brown appressed-pubescent below, margins ciliate, *not* shiny above. Petiole 5–10 mm, hairy.

Inflor two to four. Pedicel 0.4–1.3 cm (⅙–½ in.), stout, erect, with dense appressed rusty pubescence.

F bright orange-pink, red to orange-red, spotted brown, 4 cm (1½ in.) long, 4.5–6 cm (1¾–2½ in.) across, funnel-shaped.

Calyx minute. Stamens ten. Ovary densely tomentose, style crimson, white pubescent at base.

This rare species, only found on two Japanese mountains, is highly rated by most people who have seen it in flower. While it has done quite well at Glendoick, we are disappointed with the flower so far but we are probably too cool in summer. It is said to have large and extremely handsome flowers like a large, late flowered *weyrichii* to which it is closely related. *R. amagianum* has larger, broader leaves, hairy petiole and lower part of midrib. Slow to bloom freely. The large leaves are quite impressive for an azalea. Difficult in Great Lakes region with poor to fair bud hardiness. **AM**, 1948, Bodnant.

Very local on Mt Amagi and Mt Higane in Idzu Province, Honshu, Japan. June–July

farrerae Tate ex Sweet 1831 (*squamata* Lindl.) H1–2 L1–2 F1–2

Ht about 50 cm (1¾ ft). Habit low, densely branches, branches in characteristic whorls. Young leaves with long rusty hairs.

L 2.5–3 × 1.3–2 cm (1–1¼ × ½–¾ in.), ovate, apex usually acute, base rounded, sometimes semi-evergreen, ciliate at first, soon glabrous, smooth and green above on maturity. Petiole very short, hairy.

Inflor one to two, usually single from axillary buds.

F lavender to pale to darker purplish-pink with red or crimson flecks, spots or blotch, about 3 cm (1¼ in.) or more across.

This tender species was first introduced in 1829 and by Fortune in 1844 but is doubtfully hardy anywhere in Britain and is rarely cultivated elsewhere. Of doubtful horticultural value. Related to *mariesii*.

From Victoria Peak, New Territories and Lantau Island, Hong Kong also nearby islands and adjacent parts of Kwangtung, on slopes of mountains to 2,000 m (6,500 ft) on bare, exposed hillsides and cliffs or richly wooded; often in poor soil.   Mid-December onwards in Hong Kong

mariesii Hemsl. and Wils. 1907 (*shojoense* Hayata, *gnaphalocarpum* Hayata) Maries Azalea. H3–4 L1–2 F1–2

Ht 1–6 m (3–20 ft). Habit lean, rather narrow. Branchlets with appressed yellowish silky hairs, soon glabrous, yellow to brown, later pale grey.
L to 10 × 4.5 cm (4–1¾ in.), usually ovate-lanceolate, apex acute, base cuneate, two to three at ends of branchlets, with silky appressed evanescent hairs, dark green above, paler beneath, reticulate. Petiole 0.4–1.3 cm (⅙–½ in.), purplish, glabrous.
Inflor usually one to two, rarely to five, before leaves. Pedicel 4–8 mm, hairy.
F rose to rose-purple, spotted darker, about 5 cm (2 in.) across, rotate-funnel-campanulate.
Calyx minute with appressed hairs.

This has been recently reintroduced from Taiwan and is at present almost unknown in cultivation. Of doubtful garden value and hardiness. One small plant at Glendoick was cut to the ground in 1977, and some seedlings killed. First cultivated indoors at Kew in 1886. Leaves larger than *farrerae* and usually makes a bigger shrub.

Common and widespread in east and south-east China with southern limits in north Kwangtung northwards to Szechwan (rare), Hupeh and Anhwei. Has a foothold in Taiwan. 350–1,200 m (1,200–4,000 ft) in China, 1,600–1,900 m (5,300–6,300 ft) in Taiwan.

pentaphyllum Maxim. 1887 (*nikoense* Nakai) Fiveleaf Azalea. H4 A − 5 L2–3 F2–3

Ht 3–5 m (10–17 ft) in the wild often forming a small tree twice as broad as high. Usually much lower in cultivation, especially in the north, much branched. Branchlets soon glabrous, shiny, red-brown first year, later grey to pale grey-brown, slender.
L five whorls at ends of branchlets, 3–6.3 × 1.5–3 cm (1¼–2½ × ⅔–1¼ in.), broadly elliptic, ciliate at margins, often red tinged at edge as in *quinquefolium* but every variation of reddish colour occurs, small plants more inclined to maroon as edging or over much of the leaf. Mature trees mostly green. Petiole 3–8 mm, sparsely hairy and glandular.
Inflor one to two, before leaves. Pedicel glabrous or glandular-hairy (var. *nikoense*)
F pale pink, rose-pink, deep rose to pale mauve, rarely white, paler with age, 4–6 cm (1½–2⅓ in.) across, rotate-funnel-shaped, glabrous.
Calyx 2–5 mm, *glabrous*. Stamens ten. Ovary and style glabrous. Capsule 1.5–2 cm (⅔–¾ in.), larger than *quinquefolium*, spindle-shaped.

This and the similar *quinquefolium* have a grace and delicacy seen in few other species. Both have superb autumn colour and perfectly placed most attractive leaves. Very slow growing at first and rather difficult in Scotland. Takes a number of years to flower and even then may only do so spasmodically. The earliest azalea to bloom. Likes woodland conditions. Still rare in cultivation, but seeds have been distributed by the American Rhododendron Society in recent years including white forms of var. *nikoense*. Difficult as a seedling.

Differs from *quinquefolium* in its pink flowers and that its leafy shoots spring from separate buds below the terminal floral buds. Sleumer considered this an important character but the Philipsons (I think quite rightly) have placed it in this section for all other morphological characters including the similarities of the seedlings' cotyledons. **AM**, 1942, Bodnant.

Common in parts of mid-Honshu south-west to south Kyushu and Shikoku, here and there on the mountains in the upper deciduous woodlands and may colonize disturbed ground.

April–May in the wild, March–April in cultivation

quinquefolium Bisset and Moore 1877 Cork Azalea. H4 A − 5 L2–3 F2–3

Ht 4–6 m (13–20 ft). In the wild, usually much lower in cultivation. Habit as *pentaphyllum*. Bark grey-brown, corky. Branchlets glabrous, shiny the first year. Outer leaf bud scales with long appendage at the top.
L in fours and fives, 3.8–5 × 2–3 cm ($1\frac{1}{4}$–2 × $\frac{3}{4}$–$1\frac{1}{4}$ in.), broadly elliptic to obovate, apex obtuse to rounded, base cuneate, hairy on midrib above and below and margins, often margined with red-purple. Petiole very short, about 2 mm, hairy.
Inflor one to three, with the leaves or before, rather pendulous. Pedicel 1.3–2 cm ($\frac{1}{2}$–$\frac{3}{4}$ in.), hairy and glandular.
F white, olive-green spotting or eye, to 5 cm (2 in.) across, rotate-campanulate to funnel-shaped, glabrous.
Calyx green, deeply lobed, hairy. Stamens ten, unequal. Ovary and style glabrous.

A most dainty species that does well in south-east England in woodland conditions in light shade, but is very slow growing and rather tricky in Scotland. Lovely foliage and autumn colour. The flowers are often partly hidden by the foliage, especially when young and some forms have very much superior flowers to others of a beautiful bell-like shape which dangle amongst the thin twigs. Prone to rabbit damage.

Apparently successful in south Sweden. Poor bud hardiness in Great Lakes region. Also difficult as a seedling.

Differs from *pentaphyllum* in its white flowers, that the flowers and leaves often spring from single buds, later flowering often with the leaves and the hairy calyx. 'Five Arrows' **FCC**, 1967, Exbury, **AM**, 1931 Dowager Countess Cawdor.

From north Honshu south to the higher mountains of Shikoku at about 1,000 m (3,300 ft), growing in great thickets and forms a portion of open woodland with *degronianum* underneath and it often intermingles with *pentaphyllum*.   May–June in the wild, April–May in cultivation

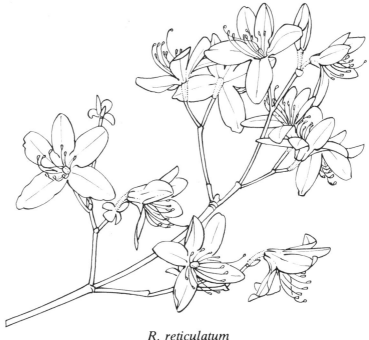

R. reticulatum

reticulatum D. Don ex G. Don 1834 Rose Azalea. H4 A − 15 to − 5 L1–3 F1–3

Ht 1–6 m (3–30 ft) in the wild, not as tall in cultivation. Habit rather erect to spreading, twiggy to loosely branched. Branchlets hairy when young, soon becoming brown, grey second year. Buds rich brown.

L 3.8–6.3 × 2.5–5.5 cm (1½–2½ × 1–2¼ in.), broadly ovate, oval to lanceolate apex acute, base broadly cuneate, reticulate beneath; young leaves with hairs at first, soon glabrous above, pubescent on veins below. Petiole 3–6 mm, flattened.

Inflor one to two, rarely to four, before leaves although leaves are sometimes produced with flowers on separate shoots. Pedicel 4–8 mm with appressed hairs.

F lavender, lilac to purple and deep purple to violent magenta, rarely white, usually unspotted, 2.5–5 cm (1–2 in.) across, rotate-funnel-shaped.

Calyx with minute teeth Stamens usually ten, anthers purple. Ovary usually hairy, style glandular lower half to glabrous.

This extremely variable species has been given a multitude of names by botanical splitting Japanese and these names are listed alphabetically below with small descriptions.

While attractive in its richer coloured, larger flowered forms, all are of some shade of purple (except white) and therefore do not quite have the appeal of those species with more popular colours. We have grown many forms at Glendoick and while they grow reasonably well, they are not contented enough to make good garden plants. All take some years to bloom and definitely do better in southern England than up here though we find they grow quite well in our Argyll garden. Needs careful placing in the garden on account of its colour.

It is very widespread in Japan but it avoids the wet winters of north-west Honshu and the cold Hokkaido and it undoubtedly enjoys warm summers both in its native haunts and elsewhere. Is resistant to heat and cold in a continental type climate, being successful in south Sweden and Winterthur, Delaware but is barely hardy enough for the Great Lakes region with poor to fair bud hardiness. The flowers are fairly frost hardy. Autumn colour is often good, being frequently purple, maroon, red to yellow. Very prone to rabbit damage.

The Yakushima form, perhaps near *nudipes*, is of special interest. It grows on windy slopes, making a small tree of 2–3 m (7–10 ft) with pale lilac to much deeper flowers and variable leaves, some plum coloured like a copper beech with golden hairs.

Wide distribution in Japan from Yakushima to north-east Honshu from 15–1,800 m (50–6,000 ft), often forming thickets 6 m (20 ft) high at around 1,200–1,500 m (4,000–5,000 ft), also rocky slopes, edges of forest, shrubby hillsides and by streams, frequently on rather dry sites.

April–June

decandrum Makino

Branchlets glabrous from the first. L broadly rhombic. Petiole glandular. Stamens ten. Possibly only a geographical variant of *dilatatum* (Ohwi). Ise and Kii provinces and west to Shikoku and Kyushu.   March–April

dilatatum Miq

Branches grey-brown. L and petiole glandular-punctate, glabrous or sometimes hairy above. F 1–3, purplish or white. Stamens five. Ovary glandular. White form said to come true from seed although some I tried all came out a dirty pale mauve. Pure white forms (*leucanthum*) are very attractive. Mid-Honshu on low mountains.   April

glacilescens
L broadly ovate. F pinkish-rose-purple. Near *reticulatum*.

kiyosumense
Branchlets slender. L midrib glabrescent or short hairy below, often small and narrow. F purple to reddish-purple before or with leaves, narrow tube. Capsule broad-cylindric, 4–5 mm across. Mid Honshu.

April–May

lagopus Nakai

L small but size variable. F solitary, rose-purple, 4 cm (1½ in.) across. Ovary pubescent, style glabrous. Very near *wadanum*. Mid and west Honshu, Shikoku.   April?

mayebarae

L glabrous below from the first. Pedicel densely hairy. F purple, before leaves. Calyx densely hairy. May be treated as a variety of *nudipes* (Hara). Mid Kyushu.   April–May

nagasakianum Nakai

L juvenile hairy. Stamens five. Ovary pubescent.

nudipes Nakai

Large shrub, branchlets glabrous.
L 4–8 × 3–6 cm (1½–3¼ × 1¼–2½ in.), broadly rhombic, long brown hairs above, midrib hairy near base below. Petiole 4–8 mm, glabrescent. Pedicels 0.6–1 cm (¼–⅓ in.).
F deep rose, rose-purple, red to purple, 3–8 cm (1¼–3 in.) across.
Calyx minute. Stamens ten. Ovary woolly, pale brown, style glabrous. Capsule narrow cylindric, 2–3 mm across.

This may deserve specific status more than any of the other forms of *reticulatum*. It is reported to be a very good plant with flowers similar to *albrechtii* but larger, more floriferous, more easily grown, more beautiful, and should be grown in every garden. This may be so in warm summer climates, but I would suspect that *albrechtii* will remain the better plant for the north. Said to be quite distinct in colour from other *reticulatum*. Has not proved successful in Scotland.

From west Honshu and Kyushu, 200–1,000 m (660–3,300 ft), along winding stream beds.   May

pentandrum Wils. = (*pentamerum* ? Wils.) five stamens.

rhombicum Miq. A synonym not apparently used by Japanese.

viscistylum

Branchlets hirsute at first. L ovate-acute. Petiole covered with long, soft hairs.
Inflor one to two. Flowers purple. South Kyushu only.   June

wadanum Makino

L base of midrib with softish white hairs. Petiole with similar hairs.
F rose-purple, 3–4 cm (1¼–1½ in.) across, before leaves. Stamens ten. Ovary pubescent, style glandular below middle. Capsule.

This is often given specific status, even in the 1967 RHS Handbook, but it is doubtfully different from *reticulatum*. Evidently common in the wild and cultivation. Mid and north Honshu at high elevations, 1,100–1,500 m (3,500–5,000 ft), in mixed beech and oak forest often growing singly.
                                                                        May

sanctum Nakai 1932 Shrine Azalea. H(3?)–4 L2–3 F1–2

Ht to 5 m (17 ft). Habit tree-like in the wild. Branches rusty-brown pubescent.
F buds separate from leaf buds.
L usually in threes, 4–8 × 3–6 cm ($1\frac{1}{2}$–$3\frac{1}{4}$ × $1\frac{1}{4}$–$2\frac{1}{3}$ in.), broadly rhombic to broadly ovate-rhombic, thick, *shiny* above with long rusty-brown hairs. Petiole 0.5–1 cm.
Inflor three to four. Pedicel 5–8 mm.
F deep aniline-rose, purplish red to rosy-purple, about 3.8 cm ($1\frac{1}{2}$ in.) across, 2.5 cm (1 in.) long, glabrous outside, funnel-shaped.
Calyx small. Ovary hairy, style glabrous.

This recently introduced species has grown moderately well with us and started blooming in 1975 with rather small flowers, reminiscent of an Obtusum azalea. As with other members of this group, this may be a better garden plant in climates with warmer summers. The large, lustrous leaves are handsome and these often colour beautifully in autumn. Related to *amagianum* and *weyrichii* but it is distinctive in flower and leaf and does not seem to merge with other species.

From south Honshu, Tokai and Ise provinces from a limited area in the mountains.   May–June

schlippenbachii Maxim. 1871 Royal Azalea H4 A–25 L2–3 F3–4

Ht 1–4.6 m (3–15 ft). Habit often densely branched with rigid shoots forming a rounded bush. Branchlets glandular-pubescent and pale brown the first year, grey and glabrous second year.
L in whorls of five, to 10 × 7 cm (4 × $2\frac{3}{4}$ in.), *obovate, rounded or notched at apex*, base cuneate, largely glabrous when mature. Petiole 2–4 mm, flattened, hairy.
Inflor three to five, before or with leaves. Pedicel 1.5 cm ($\frac{5}{8}$ in.), glandular-hairy.
F pale pink to rose-pink, occasionally white; spotted red-brown, 4.5 cm ($1\frac{3}{4}$ in.) long, 5.5–8.8 cm ($2\frac{1}{4}$–$3\frac{1}{2}$ in.) across, broadly rotate-funnel-shaped, fairly fleshy.
Calyx 7 mm, margins ciliate-glandular. Stamens ten, unequal. Ovary glandular style glandular-hairy in lower half.

This is often considered to be the finest azalea species and is particularly successful in areas with cold winters and hot summers such as parts of eastern North America. It does well in much of Britain including Scotland, provided the rather early growth is not damaged which is *not* readily replaced by second growth. Prefers light shade. Fully hardy in southern Scandinavia. Flowered perfectly in New York state after − 29°C (−20°F). Good autumn colour. Best grown from seed. 'Prince Charming' **FCC**, 1965, Leonardslee **AM**, 1896, J. Veitch & Son. A very distinct species.

From Korea and north-east Manchuria; wrongly reported from two isolated mountains in north Japan. Occurs in tens of thousands in open woodlands in Korea and the flowers appear in great abundance in late May, early June. In the open, seldom more than 1.5 m (5 ft), much taller and more spindly in woodland.   May

weyrichii Maxim. 1870 (*shikokianum* Makino) Weyrich Azalea H4 A – 5
L1–2 F2–3

Ht 1–4.6 m (3–15 ft). Habit often tree-like in the wild, ascending
branches. Young shoots reddish-pubescent turning to grey and glabrous,
finally dark purple.
L usually two to three at ends of shoots, 3.8–8 × 2–6 cm (1½–3¼ ×
¾–2⅓ in.), sub-orbicular to rhombic-ovate, apex sub-acute to obtuse, base
broadly cuneate. Young leaves with rufous-brown hairs, soon glabrous.
Petiole 0.6–1.3 cm (¼–½ in.), soon glabrous.
Inflor one to four, before or with leaves. Pedicel 6–8 mm, with rufous-
brown hairs.
F rich salmon-pink to brick-red or white, often flushed and marked
mauve or purple, 3.8–6.3 cm (1½–2½ in.) across, rotate-funnel-shaped.
Calyx with minute teeth, rufous hairy. Stamens six to ten, filaments
glabrous or hairy. Ovary densely rufous hairy, style glabrous, a few hairs
at base.

Like the closely related *amagianum*, this has flowers of a queer shade of
brick-orange-rose, although there are different shades in cultivation.
Flowers are smaller and earlier than *amagianum*. Does not do very well at
Glendoick. Not very free flowering at Winterthur, and rather difficult in
the Great Lakes area with poor to fair bud hardiness. The plant called
shikokianum in Japan, regarded as a synonym here, is said to be hardier,
dwarfer and earlier to flower from seed.

From Kyushu, Shikoku and Honshu, Kii and Ise provinces, also Cheju
(Quelpart or Jeju) Island, Korea.

Japan late April–early May, cultivation April–May–June

SECTION TSUSIOPSIS (SLEUMER) BUT WILL PROBABLY BE MOVED TO BRACHYCALYX (SCHLIPPENBACHII SUB-SERIES)

tashiroi Maxim. 1887 Cherry Azalea (south Japanese name) H3–4 L1–2
F1–3

Ht to 4.3 m (14 ft) in the wild. Habit forms a shapely, twiggy bush in the
sun, much branched. Young shoots with appressed brown hairs, soon
glabrous. F buds with brown pubescence.
L *evergreen* in twos or threes at ends of shoots, 3.8–6.3 × 2–3.2 cm
(1½–2½ × ¾–1⅓ in.), elliptic-obovate to rhombic-obovate to oblong-
elliptic, apex acute, base broadly cuneate, appressed grey-brown hairs at
first, soon glabrous and shiny above. Petiole 3–6 mm with appressed
brown hairs.
Inflor two to five. Pedicel 0.6–1.3 cm (¾–½ in.) with dense grey-brown
appressed hairs and sub-persistent bud-scales.
F ivory-pink, very pale pink to pink, deeper from lower elevations,
reddish to maroon-purple spots, 2.5–6.3 cm (1–2½ in.) across,
campanulate-funnel-shaped, more fleshy than most azaleas.
Calyx lobes very small, hairy. Stamens usually ten. Ovary with appressed
shining brown hairs, style glabrous.

This interesting azalea has only recently been introduced into Europe. It appears to vary somewhat in hardiness. Our first plant proved rather delicate and probably came from a low elevation, but other forms are doing well at Boskoop, Holland. The better, hardier forms are attractive, not unlike *yunnanense* of the subsection Triflora in flower. It could be worthy of being extensively cultivated in Britain if it proves to be free flowering. The Japanese think highly of this species and consider the flowers to have incomparable delicacy in shape and colour. It crosses freely with all the *reticulatum* and *weyrichii* groups. Stands drought and hot temperatures successfully, especially plants collected near sea-level, and produces free-flowering hybrids which could be invaluable for hot climates. Probably needs more heat than we can give it.

It is a possible link between the Anthodendron and Brachycalyx sections (Obtusum and Schlippenbachii sub-series). Hara thinks it should be retained in the former while Wada considers it should be in the latter section.

From south Kyushu, south to Yakushima, Riukiu (Ryukyu) Islands and Taiwan at 60–1,800 m (200–6,000 ft). Quite common on Okinawa and Yakushima. Fairly compact to 3 m (10 ft) on the former island in mixed woods and thickets. Taller and leggier on Yakushima; trunks with girths of 1 m (3 ft) at breast height, often epiphytic on cryptomerias.

April in the wild, May in cultivation

AZALEASTRUM SECTION (OVATUM SERIES) (E)

Generally small shrubs with erect or spreading habit and slender branches. L evergreen, glabrous except midrib. Inflor axillary, one flower per bud. F with spreading lobes. Calyx lobes large and broad. Stamens five exserted. Ovary bristly, style usually glabrous. Capsule very short with persistent calyx.

A distinctive group related to azaleas. They bear some resemblance to the Choniastrum section (Stamineum series) but differ in the smaller leaves, shorter corolla tube, the larger calyx, five stamens and the shorter capsules. This section has not been revised yet.

These are pretty little plants, often with attractive foliage and flowers but the latter may be shyly produced in cultivation. Not suitable for the coldest parts of Britain.

bachii Lévl.

L 3–7 × 1.5–3 cm (1¼–2¾ × ⅗–1¼ in.), ovate to broadly elliptic.
Calyx fringed with glands (not in type specimen)
This is almost certainly synonymous with *ovatum* (confirmed by Sealy, *Bot. Mag.* 5064 and 9375), but could be a link between *leptothrium* and *ovatum*. It has the leaf of *ovatum* and calyx of *leptothrium* according to *The Species of Rhododendron*. The plant we grew under *F*9341 was probably *leptothrium* by its leaf shape. The chief characters are the ovate leaf and glandular calyx; for other details see *ovatum*.

From west Hupeh, Kiangsi, Kweichow, borders of Kwangsi and north Szechwan, 500–1,820 m (1,500–6,000 ft), common in forests, thickets and on cliffs.

hongkongense Hutch. 1930 (*Azalea myrtifolia* Champion 1851) Recently introduced

Ht 1.5 m (5 ft). Habit rather leggy. F bud scales *glabrous* outside.
L 2–7.5 × 1–1.5 cm ($\frac{3}{4}$–3 × $\frac{1}{2}$–$\frac{3}{5}$ in.), elliptic, oblanceolate to obovate-oblanceolate, glabrous, midrib red below. Pedicel red.
F white, violet specks, lobes 2–2.5 cm (about 1 in.) long.
Calyx fringed with glands, lobes smaller than *ovatum*.

Herklotts says that this is the most beautiful Rhododendron species in Hong Kong; very free flowering and attractive with a delicate pleasing fragrance. This was confirmed by seeing two plants covered in pretty flowers in containers in the RBG, Edinburgh, early April, 1978. Young leaves often purplish. Reported to be winter flowering in the wild but this means nothing botanically and it is probably synonymous with the variable *ovatum*. Presumably too tender for all Britain.
Hong Kong 1,200 m (4,000 ft) on Black Mountain on rocks.

March or earlier in the wild; March–April

leptothrium Balf.f. & Forr. (*australe* Balf.f. & Forr.) H2–3 L2–3 F1–3

Ht 0.60–7.6 m (2–25 ft). Habit often upright but sometimes dense. Branchlets white pubescent into second year, brown later. Young foliage rich bronze-green, shining at first.
L 2–11 × 1–3.5 cm ($\frac{3}{4}$–4$\frac{1}{2}$ × $\frac{1}{2}$–1$\frac{1}{2}$ in.), *narrowly elliptic, lanceolate to oblong-lanceolate*, thin texture. Petiole 0.5–1.3 cm white pubescent.
Inflor axillary, one per bud, usually two to four per shoot. Pedicel 1–1.2 cm glandular-pubescent.
F pale to *deep rose*, soft to rich purplish-rose to magenta-rose, with or without olive-brown markings, lobes *oblong* (not orbicular), scentless, about 4.5 cm (1$\frac{3}{4}$ in.) across.
Calyx slightly longer than *ovatum*, 9 mm glandular-hairy. Style glandular in Burmese collections crimson.

An attractive little plant for mild gardens in a cool, sheltered site. Growth comes early so is easily frosted. While rather slow to bloom it may flower freely with age. Some forms are superior to others and the flowers tone in nicely with the greeny-brown young foliage. Closely related to *ovatum* but deserves some botanical status.

From central and occasionally north-west Yunnan, north Burma and the Szechwan–Yunnan border. A plant found by *KW* in the Tsangpo Gorge could be a new species in this section. Grows at 1,200–3,400 m (4,000–11,000 ft). A common species in the wild in open and dense thickets, among scrub, in and on margins of conifer and deciduous forest, cliffs, slopes of gullies, on volcanic mountains and by streams.

April–May

ovatum Maxim. (*lamprophyllum* Hayata) H3–4 L1–3 F1–3

Ht 0.9–3.7 m (3–12 ft). Habit erect or bushy. Branchlets glandular and hairy, evanescent. Bark pale, glabrous. Young leaves often bright red and pink.

L 2.5–5 × 1–2.5 cm (1–2 × ½–1 in.), *broadly ovate* to elliptic, apex acute, *mucronate*, base rounded, glabrous above except midrib, margins often with bristle-tipped teeth. Petiole 1.5 cm hairy.

Inflor axillary one per bud. Pedicel 1.5 cm glandular and mealy.

F white, white spotted pink or spotted deep crimson-purple, sometimes with yellow blotch; also pink to light mauve, spotted, 2.5–3 cm (1–1¼ in.) across, rotate, flat when fully opened, glabrous outside, pubescent within. Calyx lobes large, mealy and glandular outside. Ovary bristly, style glabrous.

A neat and airy plant with nicely poised foliage and flowers. The habit is usually good but the flowers may be sparsely produced. While moderately hardy in most gardens, the growth is sometimes frosted. Is said to be difficult at Caerhays, Cornwall. We find the foliage liable to chlorosis for no apparent reason. Is really more suitable for warmer climates than ours and is said to be very heat resistant in Georgia, USA.

The leaves and flowers are usually smaller than *leptothrium* and the leaves more ovate; while the calyx is not hairy and the lobes are broadly ovate. Young foliage often coloured.

First discovered by Fortune on Chusan Island and is very widespread in east China. Most cultivated plants probably come from Hupeh.

Found in Kiangsi and Anhwei southwards to Kwangtung, also Szechwan and Taiwan (central ranges only), open slopes, margins of forest, stream sides, thickets, in the shade of dense forests and rarely on cliffs.   March–April, Hong Kong, May–June in cultivation

vialii Delavay & Franch. Not in cultivation?

Ht 1.80–3 m (6–10 ft). Branchlets shortly pubescent.

L 3.5–10 × 1.5–3.8 cm (1½–4 × ⅗–1½ in.), obovate-lanceolate to obovate, apex often emarginate, base cuneate. Petiole to 2 cm hairy.

Inflor axillary one flowered.

F pink to crimson and perhaps deep lilac, 2 cm (¾ in.) long, narrowly funnel-shaped.

Calyx 5 mm bristly and glandular, lobes crimson.

A distinct species with much narrower flowers than *ovatum*. May be in cultivation but plants grown under this name are doubtfully true.

Only Delavay, Cavalerie and Henry collectors' numbers. From south Yunnan, 1,200–1,800 m (4,000–6,000 ft).

BARBATA SUBSECTION (BARBATUM SUB-SERIES) (E)

A Himalayan group to which *exasperatum* has been added from the old Glischrum sub-series. I have taken the liberty of transferring *shepherdii* as cultivated from the Irrorata subsection.

The chief characters are the plum, purple to reddish peeling bark and the compact rose to scarlet to crimson inflorescences. These are medium to large shrubs, generally branched from the base with medium to dark green leaves (above), glabrous on maturity and often rugose. The truss contains ten to twenty tubular-campanulate flowers, fleshy, with deeper coloured nectar pouches. The calyx is 0.5–1.5 cm long, glabrous or slightly glandular. Stamens usually ten, filaments usually glabrous. The style is glabrous.

These make fine woodland plants, suitable for most of Britain.

barbatum Wall. 1849 (*imberbe*, Hutch., *lancifolium* Hook.f. H3–4 A+5 to +10 L2–3 F2–4

Ht 2–9 m (7–30 ft). Habit generally upright, branched from the base. Bark lovely reddish-plum to deep purple, peeling. Buds sticky. Pretty red bud scales.
L 10–20 × 4–7 cm (4–8 × 1½–2¾ in.), elliptic-lanceolate, apex acute, base obtuse to slightly cordate, sea to deep green above. Loose evanescent indumentum at times, otherwise glabrous below. L remain for 1 to 2 years. Petiole with *several, few or no long bristles*.
Inflor many flowered, rounded, compact, rachis about 2 cm. Pedicel 1–1.5 cm glabrous.
F light to bright scarlet to crimson-scarlet, to 5 cm (2 in.) long, tubular-campanulate.
Calyx 0.5–1.5 cm glabrous. Ovary clad with long-stalked glands, style glabrous.

One of the finest large early flowering species for all but the coldest gardens. Some forms are definitely superior to others; those with deepest coloured flowers are best. The glowing scarlet trusses are a great feature of Argyll gardens. Plants were killed in the 1972 freeze in Oregon and Washington states, while in Britain some bud damage occurs in severe winters and the flowers are often attacked by birds. Some shelter is desirable as the leaves are easily blown off. A few original Hooker plants probably still survive in some old gardens. The plant known as *imberbe* is just a hairless cline of *barbatum*. This is now quite plentiful in cultivation and is found wild throughout most of the distribution of the hairy forms. There seems to be little evidence of natural hybridity in this instance and this example bears out how apparently unimportant the presence or absence of hairs or bristles is in the classification of certain species. **AM**, 1954, Winterfold House.

From Kumaun, Nepal, Sikkim and Bhutan, 2,400–3,700 m (8,000–12,000 ft). A common species of the Himalayas which grows among *Tsuga dumosa, arboreum, campanulatum, hodgsonii, Acer, Sorbus* and *Betula* sp. and occasionally forms large thickets on its own.
Variable flowering time February–April

erosum Cowan 1937 H3–4 L2–3 F2–3

Ht to 6 m (20 ft).
L to 10 × 7.5 cm (4 × 3 in.), obovate to oblong-oval, little or no cordate base, evanescent soft woolly indumentum below. Petiole 1 cm, bristly.
Inflor twelve to fifteen, rachis 0.1 cm. Pedicel 1 cm stipitate glandular.
F rose-pink to deep rich crimson, 3.8 cm (1½ in.) long and broad.
Calyx deep crimson to deep pink, very irregular. Ovary stipitate glandular, style glabrous.

Rather similar to *argipeplum* and *exasperatum* but less hairy. Little difference from *argipeplum* horticulturally. Possibly a hybrid.

This comes from the extreme north-east distribution of the *barbatum* group (excluding *exasperatum*) in south Tibet only, at 3,000–3,800 m (10,000–12,500 ft) in rhododendron and birch forest or in thickets amongst firs, common in places.   March–April

exasperatum Tagg 1931 H3–4 L2–4 F1–2

Ht 1–4.5 m (3–15 ft). Habit low and compact to more open in favourable areas. *Persistent shaggy bud-scales*. Branchlets densely clad with coarse glandular bristles. Bark peeling, partly smooth, reddish-brown to purplish-grey or pinky.
L to 17 × 10 cm (7 × 4 in.), broadly ovate to subovate, midrib bristly below, stalked glands on rest of underside. L remain for 1 to 2 years. Young leaves *verdigris-green to beetroot*, very spectacular. Petiole bristly. Inflor ten to twelve neat and compact. Pedicels about 1 cm.
F brick-red, occasionally to dusty pink, 3.4–4 cm (about 1½ in.) long, funnel-campanulate.
Calyx glabrous, 4–5 mm. Ovary glandular, style glabrous.

When doing well, this is one of the best foliage plants in the genus with the most striking young leaves. As the growth comes early, it needs shelter and overhead protection from frost. Frequently frosted plants become stunted with small leaves. The flowers, while quite pretty, are rarely produced and are rather small in contrast with the foliage. One plant at Windsor, possibly a natural hybrid, has no persistent bud-scales. A very distinctive species, worthy of some trouble to satisfy its needs.

While only found so far in small areas of south-east Tibet and adjoining Arunachal Pradesh, it is probably widespread in surrounding unexplored areas. Grows at 2,900–3,700 m (9,500–12,000 ft) on open ridges, dense thickets and in lower *Abies* forest.   March–May

shepherdii Nutt. 1853

There is quite a muddle over this species. It was originally collected by Booth between Tenga Chu and Dirang Chu, Kameng Division of Arunachal Pradesh with *eximium*. The capsules were all mixed up with those of *hookeri*. The type is a wild collected specimen in fruit. *The Species of Rhododendron* doubts if the so-called true plant is in cultivation, but anyway Chamberlain says it is probably synonymous with *kendrickii*. It first flowered at Nutgrove, Cheshire. The cultivated herbarium specimen came from Lochryan House, Wigtownshire in 1932 and the Glenarn and RBG, Edinburgh stock originated from there. To me these are just large-leaved *barbatum* and are certainly not *kendrickii*. They do not agree with the original description over such characters as the number of flowers in the inflorescence, the calyx, ovary and size of leaves.

smithii Nutt. ex Hook. 1859 (*argipeplum* Balf.f. & Cooper) H3–4 L2–3 F2–3 (see Addendum for recent changes in names *p*. 346.)
Ht 3–7.6 m (10–25 ft). Habit similar to *barbatum* although some forms may be more compact. Bark as *barbatum*.

L 9–20 × 3–10 cm (3½–8 × 1¼–4 in.), oblong-lanceolate to oblong-oval, apex acute to rounded, base obtuse to cordulate. The indumentum below varies in thickness but is always loose, whitish at first turning to pale to deep buff to rufous or greyish-white with age. L remain for 1 to 2 years. Petiole usually bristly.

Inflor compact ten to sixteen, rachis 1.5–2.5 cm. Pedicel glandular.
F bright rose to rich scarlet, 4–5 cm (1½–2 in.) long, tubular-campanulate.
Calyx about 1 cm, irregular sometimes glandular. Ovary as *barbatum*.

This is very similar to *barbatum* but with a loose indumentum. Forms formerly included in *argipeplum* have smaller flowers but larger, more impressive foliage. The copper-plum-coloured young growth is among the loveliest in the genus. This form requires special wind shelter as the leaves break off easily. Certain earlier introductions have foliage closely resembling *barbatum* and very fine scarlet flowers. **AM**, 1978, Borde Hill.

From Sikkim, Bhutan, Arunachal Pradesh and south-east Tibet, 2,400–4,000 m (8,000–13,000 ft), *Abies* and rhododendron forest, common in places.   March–April

BOOTHIA SUBSECTION (BOOTHII SERIES) the rest described in *Dwarf Rhododendrons* and *The Smaller Rhododendrons* (L)

micromeres Tagg H2–3 L1–2 F1. See Addendum *p.* 346.

Ht 0.90–1.80 m (3–6 ft). Habit usually epiphytic in the wild, rather straggly and untidy. Bark dark mahogany-brown on older wood, peeling.
L 3–8 × 1.5–3.6 cm (1½–3 × ⅜–1½ in.), oblong-elliptic, apex obtuse, base obtuse to cuneate, scaly above; grey to greenish-brown below, densely scaly, variable in size, ½–1½ times their own diameter apart.
Petiole 5–10 mm densely scaly.
Inflor terminal, sometimes with multiple buds, three to eight; rachis 2–7 mm. Pedicel slender 2–4 cm (¾–1½ in.) longer than corolla, lengthening in fruit, scaly ± hairy.
F usually pale yellow, sometimes creamy-yellow or white, 1–1.4 cm (⅜–½ in.) long, rotately campanulate, densely scaly outside.
Calyx 2–4 mm often reflexed, scaly outside. Stamens ten unequal, hairy near base. Ovary densely scaly, style very short, stout and sharply bent.
Calyx persistent on capsule.

A tender usually epiphytic species of little horticultural value. The flowers are very small in comparison with the leaves and plant size and are usually a rather sickly yellow. Old leaves may turn scarlet and yellow and capsules crimson in autumn. *KW* reckoned it the only rhododendron not worth growing. Rare in cultivation and likely to remain so. The high altitude forms are probably not in cultivation. Has many features in common with *sulfureum*.

From south-east Tibet, Yunnan, Upper Burma, Arunachal Pradesh and Bhutan where it is common and widespread at 2,400–4,300 m (8,000–14,000 ft); epiphytic on mossy trunks in rain forest including other rhododendrons and conifers, sometimes semi-pendulous, and on rocks and cliff ledges.   May, perhaps June

CAMELLIIFLORA SUBSECTION (CAMELLIIFLORUM SERIES) (L)

Probably only one species, related to the Maddenii Group of the Maddenia subsection. F small, shortly and broadly tubular, white to red, stamens twelve to sixteen. L very densely scaly. East Himalayas only.

camelliiflorum Hook.f. 1853 (*sparsiflorum* Nutt., *cooperi* Balf.f.) H2–3 L1–2 F1–2

Ht 60 cm–3 m (2–10 ft). Habit usually epiphytic, loose, often drooping habit in the wild, loose to fairly compact in cultivation. Young shoots covered with small brown scales. Bark reddish, peeling.
L 3.8–10 cm × 2–3 cm (1½–4 × ¾–1¼ in.), elliptic, oblong, broadly elliptic, narrowly obovate to oblanceolate, apex bluntly acute, base shortly rounded, dark green above with brown scales at first, soon evanescent; *very densely brown-scaly below, contiguous or overlapping*. L remain for 1 to 2 years. Petiole 1 cm densely scaly.
Inflor one to three. Pedicel 1 cm densely scaly.
F usually white or white marked pink but also white inside, pink outside, cream, yellow centre; pale rose-pink through pinkish-red to red, to deep wine-red, also pinkish-red with white ring at base, 6–8 mm (¼–⅓ in.) long, about 3.8 cm (1½ in.) wide, *very broadly tubular with a wide-spreading limb*, hairy in throat, scaly outside, fleshy.
Calyx 6 mm deeply five lobed, a few scales. Anthers orange to brown, *stamens twelve to sixteen* pubescent towards base. Ovary densely scaly, style stout, glabrous, capsule 1.3 cm (½ in.) long.

An unusual and interesting species but the flowers are small in contrast to the leaves. Easily identified by the dark green pointed leaves, densely brown scaly beneath and the flattish camellia-shaped flowers. Needs excellent drainage to succeed. Hardy enough for the mildest British gardens. Some survived the 1976–79 winters at Glendoick but were killed in 1981–2. Several new introductions.

From east Nepal, Sikkim, Bhutan and probably Arunachal Pradesh, 2,700–3,700 m (9,000–12,000 ft), epiphytic on many trees including hemlock, rowan, maples, firs, *arboreum*, oaks and on moist rocks, boulders and cliff ledges in mixed forest, often shady and also dry hillsides.

June–July

lucidum Nutt. 1853 Not in cultivation

L said to be near *maddenii* while the flowers are near *camelliiflorum*. Scales about their own diameter apart.

Found by Booth, so probably from the Kameng Division of Arunachal Pradesh, farther east than the typical *camelliiflorum*. Most likely *camelliiflorum* according to Cullen. Found among pines and other plants of the higher regions.

CAMPANULATA SUBSECTION (CAMPANULATUM SERIES) (E)

This was formerly used as a dumping ground for species that would not fit in anywhere else. *R. sherriffii*, *miniatum* and *fulgens* have now all been moved to the new Fulgensia subsection, while *succothii* has gone to the Thomsonia subsection. Even this is a far from satisfactory arrangement as *fulgens* is closely related to *succothii* and *sherriffii* to *lopsangianum*. R. *lanatum* and *tsariense* also have their own subsection.

The only remaining species are *campanulatum* and *wallichii*.

This subsection comes from the Himalayas as far east as south Tibet and the adjacent parts of Arunachal Pradesh.

These are dwarf to tall evergreen shrubs. All have a moderate to thick indumentum, except a few forms of *wallichii*. The broadly campanulate flowers are in loose to compact trusses of five to fifteen and vary from white to pink to purplish-red. Stamens ten. All are eglandular. They are generally hardy and often have attractive foliage and flowers.

R. campanulatum

campanulatum D. Don 1821 (*edgarii* Gamble, *mutabile* Webb ex Royle) H3–4 A − 5 to + 5 L2–4 F1–4

Ht 60 cm–11 m (2–35 ft). Habit usually a tall multi-stemmed bush but occasionally tree-like. Branchlets glabrous or sometimes hairy. Bark grey to fawn, roughening with age.
L 5–18 × 2.5–9 cm (2–7 × 1–3½ in.), elliptic, obovate, oval to oblong-elliptic, leathery, apex obtuse, base obtuse, rounded or semi-cordate,

upper surface ± glossy, indumentum below usually *dense*, variable in thickness and colour, fawn to rusty-brown. L remain for 1 year. Petiole 0.8–3.4 cm glabrous or hairy.

Inflor six to twelve loose to fairly compact, rachis 0.6–3.4 cm. Pedicel 0.9–3.6 cm glabrous or hairy.

F white, rosy-white, pink, purplish-red, various shades of rosy-purple to blue-lavender, spotted to a greater or lesser extent, 2.8–4.5 cm (1¼–1¾ in.) long, broadly campanulate.

Calyx minute 0.5–2 mm glabrous outside, ± ciliate margin. Ovary glabrous or with a few hairs, style glabrous. Seed long, variable in size and shape.

This common and widespread Himalayan species is exceptionally variable. Horticulturally there are some forms of value for foliage, some for flowers, some for both and some for nothing. A garden could have dozens of different introductions and yet still not cover the whole range of variation. Differs from the closely related *wallichii* in its dense, felted indumentum. Most forms are hardy and long lived in cultivation. Superior forms are some whites introduced by *SS&W* from central Nepal, the near blue flowered 'Knaphill' form, 'Roland Cooper' **AM**, 'Waxen Bell' **AM**, both from the RBG, Edinburgh, and T. Spring Smyth's introductions with beautiful thick rusty indumentum. Unfortunately, some of the special clones are very scarce owing to difficulties in propagation. Several have fine glaucous young foliage. Western introductions have large leaves.

Some forms do well in Sweden and Philadelphia, while others can be damaged even in Oregon or the colder parts of Scotland. Leaf burn is reported from San Francisco. A few plants from Hooker's original collection still survive. These were selling for 5 guineas each in 1841!

White-flowered variations are often found in Kashmir and west Nepal, while Roy Lancaster tells of miles of uniform colour in east Nepal imparting a blue haze to distant hills, some perhaps as good as the 'Knaphill' clone. *R. campanulatum* overlaps with *wallichii* in east Nepal and Sikkim, those found above Darjeeling are mostly *wallichii*. *R. nobile* is probably a *campanulatum* hybrid and *batemanii* is almost certainly a *campanulatum × arboreum* natural hybrid. **AM**s, 'Knaphill' fine blue-mauve 1925 Exbury; 'Roland Cooper' 1964; 'Waxen Bell' 1965 both RBG Edinburgh.

From Kashmir, Punjab, Kumaon to east Nepal, 2,700–4,600 m (9,000–15,000 ft) in dense thickets, mixed with other rhododendrons or in pure stands, by rocks, in *Abies*, *Betula*, *Salix*, *Juniperus* and other forest.   March–May

campanulatum ssp. *aeruginosum* Hook.f. described in *Dwarf Rhododendrons* (*p.* 91), *The Smaller Rhododendrons* (*p.* 155). See Addendum *p.* 346.

It is now apparent that all *campanulatum* from Bhutan plus some from Sikkim are referable to this sub-species. Some *L&S* collections from east Bhutan are undoubtedly natural hybrids. A zone of overlap between ssp. *campanulatum* and ssp. *aeruginosum* occurs in east Nepal and Sikkim.

wallichii Hook.f. 1849 H4 A − 5 L1–2 F1–3

Ht 2–6 m (6–20 ft) or more. Habit as *campanulatum*. Branchlets glabrous or floccose. Bark pinkish-brown to grey, fairly smooth to rough.
L leathery, 5.2–14 × 2.2–5.8 cm (2–5½ × ¾–2¼ in.), elliptic, obovate to oblong, apex obtuse to rounded, base cordate to obtuse, dark and often shiny above, glabrous at maturity, numerous or few *dots of hair tufts, not continuous* below, loose, black to brown or almost glabrous. L remain for 1 to 2 years. Petiole 0.4–2.8 cm glabrous or sometimes tomentose.
Inflor six to ten, rachis about 2 cm. Pedicel 1.5–2.5 cm glabrous or slightly floccose.
F cream flushed mauve, lilac, lavender, violet, rose-purple, blue-mauve, pink or white, ± spotted, 4–5 cm (about 2 in.) long, broadly campanulate. Calyx minute. Ovary and style glabrous.

Closely related to *campanulatum* but differs in the indumentum with its different hair structure. A few forms, especially those with the bluest flowers are as good as the best *campanulatum* but the absence of or uninteresting indumentum tends to make it an inferior foliage plant. Overlaps with *campanulatum* in east Nepal and Sikkim. Above Darjeeling, we found the occasional white form, about equal in rarity to our white heather in Scotland. Occurs at a lower altitude than *campanulatum* ssp. *aeruginosum*.

East Nepal, Sikkim, Bhutan, south Tibet and Arunachal Pradesh, 2,900–4,300 m (9,500–14,000 ft), common; under junipers, among spruce, fir, birch and scrub.   March–May

CAMPYLOCARPA SUBSECTION (THOMSONII SERIES, SUB-SERIES CAMPYLOCARPUM AND SUB-SERIES SOULIEI) (E)

This subsection is now an amalgamation of the old Campylocarpum and Souliei sub-series of the Thomsonii series. These are small to medium-sized evergreen shrubs with somewhat leathery leaves, which appear to the naked eye to be glabrous above and below but a few species have some small hairs, mostly evanescent. Leaf shape is orbicular to elliptic. The flowers are in loose trusses, saucer-shaped to campanulate, yellow, white, pink to rose, sometimes blotched but not spotted, calyx 5–12 mm, stamens ten, ovary glandular and the style glabrous to glandular. The formation of glands is generally marked.

This now small subsection (many have become synonyms) contains some of the finest species horticulturally in the genus and are well known and popular in all species collections.

The distribution stretches from east Nepal to Szechwan. These plants often grow better in the drier, colder east of Britain than the wetter, milder west. All appreciate excellent drainage and light woodland conditions.

campylocarpum Hook.f. 1851 H3–4 A − 15 to − 5 L1–2 F3–4

Ht 1.5–6 m (5–20 ft). Habit bushy, often leggy with age, occasionally tree-like. Bark grey to brown.

L 4–10 × 2.3–5.4 cm (1½–4 × 1–2¼ in.), elliptic to oblong-elliptic to ovate, shape variable; apex broadly obtuse to rounded, base truncate, cordate, rarely rounded, glabrous above, pale glaucous below, ± glabrous. L remain for 1 year. Petiole 0.8–2.4 cm, glandular.
Inflor six to ten loose, rachis 3–8 mm. Pedicel 1.5–3.5 cm glandular.
F pale to bright yellow with or without a faint basal blotch, rarely white tinged yellow or pure white, 2.5–4 cm (1–1½ in.) long, 6.3–7.5 cm (2½–3 in.) across, *campanulate*, sometimes slightly scented. Those with or without blotch seem to occur in equal numbers.
Calyx minute 0.5–1.5 mm glandular. Ovary densely glandular, *style glandular at base or to half its length or eglandular*. Capsule slender.

One of the finest medium-sized yellow flowered species, hardy enough for all but the coldest gardens in Britain. Some forms are much superior to others. These can roughly be divided into two forms which have no real botanical status. (1) Hooker's original form from Sikkim, more compact and bushy, often with deeper yellow flowers which, according to L. de Rothschild, throws mostly pale yellows when hybridized.
(2) var. '*elatum*' a bigger, lankier grower with flowers sometimes tipped orange, said to be more valuable for hybridizing as it throws ivories and pinks tinged yellow as well as pale yellows. There is every grade between the two forms. It has been much used in hybridizing but the results have not been so spectacular as with *wardii*.

Has not proved very hardy in north-west North America as it suffered from being cut back and having damaged foliage in the 1955 and 1972 freezes. Difficult in Scandinavia. Not proving heat resistant. Grows best in western gardens such as Inverewe, Ross-shire. Avoid too much shade.

Differs from *wardii* in the more campanulate flowers, which usually open earlier, but chiefly with the style not being glandular to the tip. *R. campylocarpum* has a larger calyx where it meets *wardii* at Doshong La pass. Ssp. *caloxanthum* and *telopeum*, which come from farther east, are dwarfer and were described in *Dwarf Rhododendrons*. **FCC**, 1892, Hooker's form Veitch of Chelsea.

From east Nepal, Sikkim, Bhutan, Arunachal Pradesh and south Tibet, 2,900–4,300 m (9,500–14,300 ft), often abundant, usually mixed with other species such as *campanulatum*, also in oak, birch or conifer forest, among bamboos, on open or rocky slopes or in scrub jungle.

April–May

souliei Franch. 1895 (*cordatum* Lévl.) H4 A – 5 L2–3 F2–4

Ht 1.2–5 m (4–17 ft). Habit fairly open, can be leggy with age. Bark slightly rough, grey-brown.
L 3.5–8.2 × 2.2–5 cm (1½–3¼ × 1–2 in.), ovate to ovate-elliptic to oblong-elliptic to almost orbicular, apex rounded to broadly obtuse, base truncate, cordulate to rounded, dark green and glabrous above, glaucous when young, glabrous below. L remain for 1 year. Petiole 1.5–2.5 cm ± sparsely glandular.
Inflor five to eight fairly loose, rachis 0.3–1 cm. Pedicel 1.8–4.3 cm

glandular and sticky. F *pink, pink flushed rose* or pink in bud opening white or white flushed pink, 2.5–3.5 cm (1–1½ in.) long, 5–7.5 cm (2–3 in.) across, *openly cup- or saucer-shaped*.
Calyx 2–8 mm, usually glandular. Ovary densely glandular, style *glandular to tip*.

This superb plant is perhaps my favourite species. It has beautiful glaucous young leaves but the saucer-shaped, delicately flushed flowers are quite outstanding. These are produced freely from a relatively young age, often 4 to 5 years from seed on a 60 cm (2 ft) bush. As it has proved impossible to root from cuttings (so far) and is not easy to graft, we have propagated many hundreds from hand-pollinated seed. About 90 per cent of these come true to the colour of the pink and white forms that we grow. One exquisite deep pink seedling bloomed in 1976 which we are endeavouring to layer, but at the best this will never provide many plants. While we find it quite easy at Glendoick, it sometimes develops marginal chlorosis. It is most unfortunate that many gardens in south-west England as far east as Exbury, Hampshire and parts of west Scotland have found this species very hard to grow. The leaf tips may turn brown and the whole plant gradually dies off. Try a really well-drained site in a fairly open situation, but avoid draughts as the growth comes rather early. Survives and often flourishes in the coldest of Scottish gardens and in parts of Scandinavia. There was little or no damage at −20°C (−6°F) in Oregon in the 1972 freeze. Many hybrids are still masquerading under *souliei* in America. **FCC**, 1909, Veitch of Chelsea pale rose, flushed deeper. **FCC**, 1936 Exbury deeper than the above. **FCC**, 1951, Crown Lands white flushed pink flushed deeper to margins.

Pink forms from central Szechwan, white from Yunnan–Szechwan border, 2,700–4,300 m (9,000–14,000 ft) in oak and spruce forest and among boulders where it covers large areas. Was collected in 1903 and 1908 by *W* and was also found by Maire, *R* and McLaren.   May

wardii W. W. Sm. 1914 (*astrocalyx* Balf.f. & Forr., *croeceum* Balf.f. & W.W. Sm., *gloeoblastum* Balf.f. & Forr., *litiense* Balf.f. & Forr., *oresterum* Balf.f. & Forr., *prasinocalyx* Balf.f. & Forr.) H4 A−5 to 0 L2–3 F2–4

Ht 90 cm–7.6 m (3–25 ft). Habit fairly compact to open with age. Young leaves glaucous at first. Bark roughish, greyish-brown.
L 3–12 × 1.8–6.5 cm (1¼–4¾ × ¾–2⅗ in.), more or less orbicular to ovate, oblong-elliptic and oblong, apex rounded to broadly obtuse, base cordulate, truncate to rounded, glabrous above and below with minute punctulations, pale green to glaucous below, sometimes tinged purple. L remain for 1 to 2 years. Petiole 1–3.3 cm glandular to eglandular.
Inflor five to fourteen fairly full to loose, rachis 0.3–2.2 cm. Pedicel 1.5–4.8 cm usually glandular.
F *yellow* in various shades, with or without crimson blotch, 2–4 cm (¾–1½ in.) long, *widely campanulate to saucer-shaped*, sometimes slightly scented.
Calyx 0.4–1.2 cm usually glandular. Ovary densely glandular, *style glandular to tip*.

This is the best yellow species for general planting and is a superb plant in its larger flowered forms. Very variable as the number of synonyms indicates. *R. litiense* which has recently been made synonymous has glaucous leaf undersides but merges completely with *wardii*. *R. wardii* has had more influence in creating yellow hybrids than any other species and most of the best larger elepidote hybrids have *wardii* in their blood.

Most forms are free flowering from a fairly young age, especially those from *L&S* 5679 which has a blotch and blooms and grows later than average. We find this form absolutely first rate, reliable and hardy but a few reports have come from places as wide apart as north-west and south-east England and Oregon that all the flower buds regularly abort. This may be due to a magnesium deficiency, try spraying with Epsom salts. Some other forms grow rather early when young and can loose their first growth to frost but become much more reliable with age when growth comes later, usually after flowering. This species is variable in hardiness but most are reasonably tough, *L&S* 5679 being especially good in Scandinavia and north Germany. No damage reported from 1972 freeze in Oregon to any forms. Like its relations, plant in a well drained site in at least half sun. **AM**, 1926 (*croeceum*) bright yellow, crimson touch **AM**, Williams Launceston; **AM**, 1926 (*astrocalyx*) clear lemon-yellow **AM**, Williams Launceston; **AM**, 1931, *KW* 4170 Exbury bright yellow, flushed green; **AM**, 1959, 'Ellesstee' probably *LS&T* deep crimson blotch Benenden; **AM**, 1963, 'Meadow Pond' *LS&E* 15764 primrose-yellow, deep blotch, Crown Lands. Recently re-introduced.

An exceedingly common and widespread species in the wild, occurring over wide areas of Yunnan, Szechwan and south-east Tibet where it has a long flowering season and the colour varies from ivory to sulphur-yellow, sometimes flushed pink. KW called the Doshong La plant 'Yellow Peril' on account of the impenetrable thickets it forms. Generally, the blotched forms cover the west end of distribution and the unblotched the east but these are sometimes all mixed together; 2,700–4,300 m (9,000–14,000 ft), open hillsides, rocky slopes, open or dense conifer, mixed or oak forest, among bamboo, by streams, in swampy ground, rhododendron thickets and limestone cliffs.   May–June

wardii var. *puralbum* (Balf.f & W.W. Sm.) Chamb. 1978 H4 L2–3 F2–3

Ht 2.4–4.6 m (8–15 ft). Habit as *wardii*. Branchlets glandular.
L 5–12 × 2.4–5 cm (2–5 × 1–2 in.). Inflor five to eight fairly loose.
F *white* in type to white tinged yellow to tinged pink.

This now classed as a white variant of *wardii* and is usually grown under the type number of *F* 10616. It is doubtful if any of the *L&S* numbers from south-east Tibet were introduced. These were recorded as much smaller plants than the type.

Hardiness about equal to the average *wardii*. Shoots and foliage were lost in the 1955 freeze in Seattle. Succeeds in parts of Scandinavia.

From north-west Yunnan and south-east Tibet, 3,400–4,300 m (11,000–14,000 ft), in rhododendron thickets and mixed scrub, open slopes, in rocks above forest and in dense forest.   May

The remaining species in this subsection, *callimorphum* and its variety *myiagrum* and the two sub-species of *campylocarpum*, *caloxanthum* and *telopeum* were described in **Dwarf Rhododendrons**.

CANDIDASTRUM SECTION (ALBIFLORUM SERIES) (E)

Said to be closely related to the Azaleastrum section (Ovatum series). The chief characters are; ten stamens, much shorter than the white, usually unspotted corolla. Flowers scattered along the branches. Leaves deciduous. Western North America. Not much horticultural value.

albiflorum Hook. 1834 (*Azalea albiflora*, *Azaleastrum albiflorum*) H4 A – 25 L1 F1

Ht 90 cm–2.10 m (3–7 ft). Habit erect and ascending in the wild, long fastigiate branches in cultivation. Branches light crimson-brown, young shoots with loosely appressed brown hairs. Bark light grey or greyish-brown after second year.

L deciduous, scattered or clustered at ends of short branchlets, 2.5–7 × 1–2.5 cm (1–2¾ × ⅔–1 in.), elliptic-oblong to oblong, margins somewhat undulate, bright green above, evanescent appressed long brown hairs above and on midrib below. Petiole 1.2–3.2 mm with appressed hairs.

Inflor one to two from axillary buds along branches of previous year, appearing after leaves, nodding. Pedicel 5–10 mm glandular-pubescent. F white, rarely spotted yellow or orange, about 2 cm (¾ in.) across, rotate campanulate, tube hairy inside.

Calyx 8–13 mm glandular-ciliate and hairy. Ovary glandular-hairy, style straight, lower half hairy. Capsule shorter than the persistent calyx lobes.

Very slow growing for the first few years from seed in cultivation and is rather difficult. A fairly sunny site with poor stony soil inclined to dry out in summer seems to suit it, but it never flowers freely enough to give much of a show. A double form has apparently existed. First introduced 1828, first flowered 1837.

I have seen how beautiful and free flowering it is in the wild, but it is known in British Columbia as 'Mountain Misery' because the horizontal branches trip people up.

Alberta to British Colombia and Oregon to Colorado, 1,200–2,200 m (4,000–7,200 ft), in alpine woods and open places, often where conifers are stunted near the tree line. Common.

July–August in the wild, June–July in cultivation

CHONIASTRUM SECTION (STAMINEUM SERIES) (E)

Shrubs or trees to 15 m (50 ft). L evergreen, usually glossy, glabrous or bristly. Young leaves often tinged red. F axillary one to several per bud, white, rose to various shades of purple, often fragrant, funnel-shaped with narrow tube. Calyx very small contrasting with the large calyx in the

Azaleastrum section (Ovatum series). Stamens ten. Ovary glabrous or rarely tomentose, style glabrous. Capsule long, often beaked. This section has not been revised yet.

Found in Burma, south China, Indo-China, Thailand, Arunachal Pradesh and Taiwan.

This much neglected section deserves much more horticultural attention. These plants should flourish in climates like the milder parts of New Zealand, south-east Australia and coastal California. The majority make vigorous small trees with handsome foliage, magnificent bark and fine, often strongly scented flowers, freely produced on maturity but inclined to be short lasting. Effort should be made to introduce those not in cultivation. A few are proving surprisingly hardy.

cavaleriei Lévl. 1903. Not in cultivation

Ht 1.8–2.7 m (3–9 ft). L to 10 × 3 cm (4–1¼ in.). Inflor about three. F white to rose, 3 cm (1¼ in.) long.

There is a mix up of specimens in the RBG, Edinburgh under this name. From Kweichow, Kwangsi, 500 m (1,800 ft) scattered in light woods, fairly common in dry silt.

championiae Hook. 1851 H1–2 L2–3 F2–3

Ht 1.8–7.6 m (6–25 ft). Branchlets hairy (bristly). F bud scales sticky.
L 7.5–15 × 2.5–5 cm (3–6 × 1–2 in.), oblong-oblanceolate, strongly veined and scabrid above, pubescent and loosely bristly below. Often tinged deep reddish-purple. Two rows of hairs on margin, one vertical, the other horizontal. Petiole very hairy.
Inflor five.
F pale rose-pink in bud opening to white, white to pinkish with yellow to orange markings, 10–11.3 cm (4–4½ in.) across.
Calyx unequal, bristly margin.

A tender species, which survived many years in Cornwall. It was recently killed at Caerhays but proved reasonably hardy on a wall at Lamellan where it was slow growing and shy to flower. Obviously more sunshine is needed. Rare in cultivation. Fine large flowers and ornamental foliage. Was the first rhododendron discovered wild in China according to W. Introduced 1881. Easily recognized by the long glandular bristles on branches, petiole, pedicel, calyx and capsule and bristles on both leaf surfaces. Not as fragrant as *westlandii*. Reintroduced recently.

Common in Kwangtung and south Chekiang, rare in Fokien and Hong Kong. Grows in ravines on Mt Victoria, Hong Kong in dense shade among rocks, also dense or half wooded slopes and stream sides.

April in Hong Kong, April–May in cultivation

ellipticum Maxim. 1888 (*leptanthum* F. Muell., *leptosanthum* Hayata, *tanakai* Hayata) Recently introduced. H3?

Ht to 4.6 m (15 ft). Habit slender rigidly branched. Shoots glabrous. Winter buds clustered, glabrous, acute.
L 6–12.5 × 2–4.5 cm (2½–5 × ¾–1¾ in.), oblanceolate to oblong to

oblong-lanceolate, glabrous, lustrous green above, paler below. Petiole 0.5–1.5 cm glabrous.

Inflor axillary, two to three per bud, clustered around ends of branches (one flowered in *tanakai*). Pedicel 2.5–3.5 cm glabrous.

F white, pink and probably rose-purple, 5–6 cm (2–2½ in.) long and across, funnel-shaped, deeply lobed.

Calyx glabrous 2–4 mm, unequal. Stamens hairy lower half. Ovary glabrous, style stout, length equal to stamens, glabrous.

While the habit is rather ungainly due to long internodes, there are good reports on the flowers from California. Several seedlings were undamaged in our nursery in the winter of 1976–1977 when the temperature dropped to −11°C (12°F) but some suffered in 1977–1978 at −15°C (5°F). Mostly killed 1978–1979. Cuttings root easily. I am going to try planting some on walls. First imported into California about 1969, from Taiwan. All eventually failed (1990).

R. leiopodum is very closely related and probably synonymous with *ellipticum*. The flowers of the former are reported to be smaller and one flowered. Said to be similar to *latoucheae*.

From Taiwan, Liukiu to south China (Fukien); Taiwan 50–2,500 m (165–8,300 ft), common in forests throughout the island, by streams and on gravelly slopes; often pioneering new roadside banks with an abundance of seedlings.   March–May (Taiwan)

esquirolii Lévl. 1913 Not in cultivation

Shrub. L 3.8–6.3 × 1.3–2 cm (1½–2½ × ½–¾ in.). Inflor one to two. F rose-violet rather small. Yunnan. No *F* or *R* specimens.

feddii Lévl. 1913 Not in cultivation

One specimen only in RBG, Edinburgh.

hancockii Hemsl. 1895 Not in cultivation

Ht 1–3 m (3–10 ft). Inflor are flowered. F white yellow blotch.

Nice large flowers or smaller. Szechwan, south Yunnan, 1,500–2,000 m (5,000–6,500 ft), open slopes or thickets or in forest.

henryi Hance 1881 (*dunnii* Wils.) Not in cultivation

Ht 1–13 m (3½–43 ft). L glabrous, lustrous. Inflor three to four flowered, numerous. F pink, 3.8 cm (1½ in.) long.

Possibly close to *westlandii*. Obviously worth introducing into cultivation. Pleasing and free flowering according to *W*. South-east Fokien, Szechwan, Chekiang and Kwangsi, common.

latoucheae Finet & Franch. 1899 Not in cultivation

Ht 2–3 m (7–10 ft). F purplish. Chekiang, Fukien, Kwangtung, common in thickets and mixed woods.

leucobotrys Ridley Not in cultivation. Perhaps a synonym of *moulmainense*

Inflor several flowered. F white. Malaya, Kedah Peak, 850–1,200 m (2,800–4,000 ft).

moulmainense Hook. 1856 (*siamense* Diels, *klossii* Ridley) H1 L1–2 F1–2?

Branchlets glabrous. Pinkish young foliage.
L 6.3–13 × 2.5–5 cm (2½–5 × 1–2 in.), elliptic-lanceolate, acute at both ends, glabrous. Petiole 1.3 cm slightly winged.
Inflor two to five, four to five buds per shoot. Pedicel 2.5 cm glabrous.
F white yellow blotch (red in *Species of Rhododendron* very doubtful) 2.5–5 cm (1–2 in.) long, narrowly funnel-shaped, scented.
Calyx very small. Ovary and style glabrous.

Recently reintroduced by Valder who says that the flowers, though small, occur in clusters of up to sixteen to twenty and that the scent is like jonquils. Flowered 1979 in RBG, Edinburgh.

Thailand, Malay Peninsula, perhaps wrongly said to occur in south Burma 900–1,500 m (3,000–5,000 ft), in low *Quercus-Vaccinium* and other evergreen forest.   March–April?

nematocalyx Balf.f. & W.W. Sm. 1917 Not in cultivation?

Ht 2.4–3 m (8–10 ft). L with ciliate margins. F white yellow blotch, 5–6 cm (2–2½ in.) across, fragrant.

Looks an attractive plant from the specimens and photograph of F 26304. Two possible cultivated specimens from Caerhays, Cornwall. Not in *Species of Rhododendron* or *Species Handbook*.

Yunnan, 2,100–2,400 m (7,000–8,000 ft), open situations, thickets, bouldery slopes, among scrub on cliffs, mixed and conifer forest.

oxyphyllum Franch. 1898 H1 L1–2 F1–2?

Ht 3–6 m (10–20 ft). Bark smooth purplish-brown.
L 8.8–12.5 × 2.5–5 cm (3½–5 × 1–2 in.), oblong-oblanceolate, apex acute, base shortly cuneate, glabrous. Petiole 2 cm glabrous.
Inflor several flowered.
F white to white flushed rose, pale pink to pink, violet?, yellow blotch, 5 cm (2 in.) long, fragrant.

Probably similar to *stenaulum* but the latter is one-flowered. Has been cultivated including the USA.

Thailand, Burma north of Myitkina, south Yunnan, Kwangsi, 300–2,100 m (1,000–7,000 ft), common in evergreen jungle, in thickets and open situations among scrub and on steep slopes; often in dry sandy soil.   April?

pectinatum Hutch. 1937 H1 L1–2 F2–3

A chance seedling from *F* 26022 (*stamineum*), no wild specimen. Differs in its ciliate leaves and strange clusters of five to six axillary trusses of three to four flowers giving a very interesting result (Hanger). F white, pale yellow blotch, fragrant. **AM**, 1935, Exbury, probably lost in the war.

stamineum French. 1886 (*chaffanjonii* Lévl. *pittosporifolium* Hemsl.) H2–3 L1–2 F2–3

Ht 3–13 m (10–43 ft). Habit small tree in the wild, usually grows rather untidily in cultivation. Branchlets glabrous.
L 7.5–13.8 × 2.5–4.5 cm (3–5½ × 1–1¾ in.), whorled, narrowly elliptic to obovate-oblanceolate, long acuminate apex, base cuneate, thin, glossy and glabrous, dark green, rather pendulous. Petiole 1 cm glabrous.
Inflor axillary, several flowered, totalling about twenty to twenty-two. Pedicel 1.3–3.8 cm glabrous.
F white, pinkish-white or white flushed yellow-orange, yellow blotch, 3 cm (1¼ in.) long, 3.8–5 cm (1½–2 in.) across, tubular at base, lobes narrow, strongly scented.
Calyx small green, stamens very prominent. Ovary and style glabrous.

Certain introductions are reasonably hardy as a plant has survived at Wakehurst, Sussex, for many years. Growth comes rather early. Not very free flowering. **AM**, 1971, Crown Lands (indoors).

From Yunnan, Szechwan, Hupeh, Hunan, Kweichow, Anhwei and Kwangsi, very widespread and the commonest of the subsection in the wild, 350–2,700 m (1,200–9,000 ft), in pure forest by itself, mixed broad-leaved or open deciduous forests and thickets. May–July

stenaulum Balf.f. & W.W. Sm. 1917 (*mackenzianum* Forr.) H1–2 L1–3 F2–4

Ht 9–15 m+(30–50 ft+). Habit thin tree to compact shrub in an open site. Long annual growth. Buds long and pointed. Bark variously described as red, tawny, mahogany, tawny-purple, copper-red, rich ruddy-brown, smooth or peeling.
L 7.5–17 × 2.5–5 cm (3–6½ × 1–2 in.), narrowly to broadly elliptic to oblong-lanceolate, apex acuminate, whorled at ends of branches, bright glossy green, margins occasionally bristly, especially when young, later glabrous.
Petiole 1.3 cm glabrous.
Inflor axillary, one per bud, ten or more in top few leaves, loose, bud scales persistent. Pedicel 2 cm long, slender.
F white to pale lilac, rose, blush-pink to deep rose-magenta, pale yellow to brownish throat, the tube often deeper coloured than the lobes, 5 cm (2 in.) long, about 6.3 cm (2½ in.) across, very fragrant.
Calyx very small, glabrous. Stamens rather short. Ovary long, glabrous, style much longer than stamens, glabrous.

This splendid plant should be widely grown in suitable climates. It has everything; large scented flowers, fine glossy foliage and a beautiful smooth trunk like an *Arctostaphylos* (manzanita). The finest forms are those with white or dark flowers. Very free flowering in the wild smothering itself in blooms with a strong jasmine or *maddenii*-like scent. The flowers are a little floppy and may shed rather quickly. Young plants often have deep claret-red bristly leaves while old leaves may turn scarlet in the wild. I saw magnificent specimens with white flowers in north-east India which stood out from the forest from afar. Alas, this form was not introduced.

Only just possible to grow outside in Britain being none too hardy at Caerhays, Cornwall and was nearly wiped out in 1917 and 1987. Has also been grown at Lamellan, Cornwall, Headfort, Ireland and indoors.

Close to *oxyphyllum*, differs from *stamineum* in the larger flowers and included style and stamens. Unfortunately, the name may become a synonym. **AM**, 1937, flowers silvery-lilac Exbury.

From south-east Tibet, north Burma, Arunachal Pradesh, and west Yunnan, 1,500–3,000 m (5,000–10,000 ft), a very widespread and common species in openings in forest, shady thickets and ravines, dense mixed and conifer forests.

March Burma, April–May Arunachal Pradesh. April

taiense Hutch. 1938 Not in cultivation

tutcherae Hemsl. & Wils. Not in cultivation

Ht 12 m (40 ft). Branchlets bristly. L. 7.5–10 × 1.6–2.5 cm (3–4 × ⅔–2.5 in.), narrowly lanceolate, hairy below. Petiole 1.3 cm very bristly. Inflor one-flowered. F violet 3.8 cm (1½ in.) long, narrowly funnel-shaped. Ovary tomentose, style glabrous. Southern Yunnan, 1,800 m (6,000 ft) in forests.

westlandii Hemsl. 1889 Recently introduced

Ht 1.5–8 m (5–26 ft). Branchlets glabrous.
L 6.3–12.7 × 2.5–3.8 cm (2½–5 × 1–1½ in.), broadly oblanceolate, apex acuminate, base cuneate, deep green and glossy above. Petiole 1.3 cm glabrous, often red.
Inflor five to six. Pedicel 2 cm glabrous.
F lilac to clear orchid-purple, occasionally white, orange spots or flair, 7.5–8.8 cm (3–3½ in.) across, narrowly funnel-shaped, glabrous, very fragrant.
Calyx obsolete, glabrous. Ovary and style glabrous.

Another beautiful species, lovely in full flower. Habit and foliage suggest certain species of *Pittosporum* while the young growth is often a fine pinkish-red like a pieris. Near *henryi*. Unlikely to be hardy in Britain.

Hainan, Kwangtung and Hong Kong (Lantau Peak and mainland), 800 m (2,500 ft), in mixed woods, margins of forest and sides of ravine.   March–April (Hong Kong) *wilsoniae* Hemsl. & Wils. 1910 H1–3 L1–2 F2–3

Ht to 1.8 m (6 ft) at Wakehurst, Sussex. Habit low, spreading. Bud scales persistent.
L whorled, to 12 × 4.4 cm (4¾ × 1¾ in.), stiff textured, narrowly elliptic to elliptic, dark green and glossy. Petiole to 1.3 cm rounded.
Inflor terminal and axillary one-flowered, totalling four to six. Pedicel to 3 cm.
F pale mauve, lavender-pink, light pink to flesh-pink with brown blotch or spots, slightly to strongly scented, 1.8–3.8 cm (¾–1½ in.) long, and about 5 cm (2 in.) across, widely funnel-shaped.
Calyx pale green, unequal. Ovary and style glabrous.

Has succeeded out of doors at Caerhays, Cornwall and also Wakehurst Place, Sussex in an exposed position. Growth comes rather early. The flowers have been reported as being very pretty and charming and the scent delightful and strong like *luteum*. Survived the 1976–1979 winters to −15°C (5°F) at Glendoick but died 1981–2 to −18°C (0°F) **AM**, March 1971, Crown Lands (indoors).

From west Hupeh, Kwangtung and north-east Kweichow in densely shaded ravines.   Late March

CINNABARINA SUBSECTION (CINNABARINUM SERIES) (L)

A distinctive subsection with very scaly leaves and fleshy tubular flowers which have a quantity of nectar, the only subsection of the subgenus Rhododendron (lepidote series) to do so. Even noticeable on herbarium specimens. Calyx small, stamens ten slightly pubescent, style pubescent, capsule to 1.3 cm (½ in.) long. East Himalayas. The nearest relative is *oreotrephes* of the Triflora subsection, but this does not have the quantity of nectar present. In the wild, the farther east, the more the flowers become purple.

All make beautiful garden plants when covered with their tubular pendant to semi-pendant flowers, but all take a few years to reach a free flowering size. Several forms have fine glaucous foliage which is always aromatic. All are of slightly borderline hardiness and subject to bark-split in east Scotland. Badly damaged in 1972 freeze in Oregon.

cinnabarinum Hook.f. 1849 H3–4 A+5 L2–3 F2–4

Ht to 4.5 m (15 ft) or more. Habit typically upright and often spreading with age. Young branches often purplish. Bark shaggy light brown with age, peeling.
L to 11.5 × 5.5 cm (4½ × 2¼ in.) 1½–3 times longer than broad, obovate-elliptic, broadly lanceolate, broadly to narrowly elliptic apex rounded mucronate, base usually rounded, deep to pale green above, often glaucous, sometimes shiny; densely scaly and glaucous below, scales small and barely their own diameter apart. L remain for 1 year but are sometimes almost deciduous. Petiole about 1.3 cm scaly.

E.M.S.

R. cinnabarinum

Inflor terminal, two to nine, pendant or semi-pendant. Pedicel variable length.

F extremely variable, yellow-orange, apricot, red, reddish-salmon, pink, dark red, plum-crimson, reddish-mauve, pinkish-mauve, rich plum-purple, white and various combinations of these colours giving bi- or tri-colour effects or even a different colour inside and out. Some multicolours are flame rimmed yellow, orange-red tipped light orange, light red over apricot, and orange tipped greenish cream; 3.8–5 cm (1½–2 in.) long, tubular, tubular-campanulate to funnel-shaped, usually widening towards lobes.

Calyx unequally lobed, sometimes rim-like. Ovary scaly, style a little longer than stamens, hairy towards base.

An extremely variable species in all characters such as habit, leaf colour and shape, flower colour and shape and flowering dates. While all make good garden plants, a few take years to bloom freely. If space is available, it is worth growing a wide selection of forms, either of selected clones or from wild seed. Several sources of the latter have been introduced lately from Nepal and Sikkim. Seed collected by myself near Darjeeling produced a remarkable selection of foliage and flower forms. In the wild, one area may have a uniform flower colour while in another the colours may be thoroughly mixed. Very uniform bio-chemically.

Also variable in hardiness. The majority are suitable for sheltered lowland gardens throughout Britain but even at Glendoick we find some subject to bark-split and die-back. Young growth sometimes gets frosted.

Damaged or killed by 1972 freeze in Oregon and Washington State. Unsuitable for hot summers. Plant in a fair degree of sunshine to avoid legginess and a lack of flowers. Considered universally poisonous to goats and cattle including the wood; even the wood smoke causes the eyes to inflame and the cheeks to swell. Very susceptible to powdery mildew, especially orange flowered forms. 'Postling **AM**, 1975 (Roylei x Blandfordiiflorum) Sandling Park; Nepal' **AM**, 1975, *LS&H* 21283 Hydon. See Addendum *p.* 349.

This species is now divided into three sub-species, *cinnabarinum*, *xanthocodon* and *tamaense*. All old names can be retained for horticultural purposes and become Group cultivars.

From east Nepal, Sikkim, Bhutan, south-east Tibet, 2,100–4,000 m (7,000–13,000 ft), common in scrub jungle, open rocky dry and steep hillsides, open woodland, conifer and mixed rhododendron forest, oak or bamboo forest, occasionally forming thickets of its own and on cliffs.

R. cinnabarinum ssp. *cinnabarinum*

cinnabarinum ssp. *cinnabarinum* (var. *aestivale*, var. *blandfordiiflorum*, var. *roylei*) L relatively narrow, length/breadth ratio at least 2.2 times as long as broad, usually non-scaly above. Corolla usually tubular. Western distribution, east Nepal, Sikkim, Bhutan with intermediaries in Bhutan.

For gardeners, it is necessary to give some details of the old species and varieties individually.

'Aestivale' probably equals Blandfordiiflorum. A late flowering clone from Borde Hill.

Blandfordiiflorum Group usually bi- or tri-coloured flowers, commonly tubular. Most forms are late flowering and are amongst the most popular of the species, plus often being the hardiest. **AM**, 1945, Bodnant.

May–July

Roylei Group *F* plum-crimson with a bloom on the corolla, tubular-campanulate. L usually dark green, often shiny above on maturity. This is one of the best-known forms of *cinnabarinum* having been originally collected by Hooker in 1849. Large plants laden with flowers make a fine sight. Var. *roylei* 'Magnificum' is reputed to have flowers larger than average. This name was given to a group of seedlings (not a clone as stated in the 1967 Species Handbook) growing at Crarae, Argyll which are really just good average examples of Roylei Group; a plant under this same name received an **AM** when shown by Reuthe in 1918. 'Vin Rosé' also an **AM**, 1953, Crown Lands; 'Crarae Crimson' **PC**, 1975 Benenden.

R. cinnabarinum ssp. *xanthocodon*

cinnabarinum ssp. *xanthocodon* (Hutch. 1934) Cullen 1978 (*concatenans*, var. *pallidum*, var. *purpurellum*) L relatively broader, length/breadth ratio less than 2.2 times as long as broad, usually persistently lepidote above, corolla usually campanulate. Eastern distribution with intermediaries in Bhutan but chiefly Bhutan to south-east Tibet. Seems fairly resistant to powdery mildew.

Concatenans Group Habit usually lower and more compact than the average *cinnabarinum*. While *KW* 11568, 13758 and *L&S* 6560 were all formerly listed under Concatenans, only *KW* 5874 can be regarded as the real thing. The rest are best considered as normal variants of *cinnabarinum*. *KW* 5874, firmly established in cultivation, is a splendid plant with beautiful glaucous foliage and striking near orange flowers. Should be planted in a fairly open site to retain a compact habit and the best foliage effect. **FCC**, 1935, Nymans.

Collected in the relatively unexplored Tibetan province of Pemako. Nobody knows if this is a stable form in the whole district or not. *KW*'s description of finding his 'Orange Bill' has been written more than once in his books. Except for ssp. *tamaense*, this is the westernmost discovery of *cinnabarinum* forms so far.

Pallidum Group F rose to pale pinkish-purple, widely campanulate.

Purpurellum Group F rich plum-purple to bright pinkish or reddish-purple, funnel-shaped to campanulate. L often smaller than average. There are several different forms of this in cultivation, probably from three *L&S* numbers. While some are pretty, the colour is not usually comparable with most other forms and hardly lives up to the *L&S* description of 'a most beautiful rhododendron'. Possibly shows a relationship with *oreotrephes* and is close to *tamaense*. **AM**, 1951 as *L&S* 6349 Benenden. Fairly resistant to mildew.   April–June *xanthocodon* The plant formerly grown under this name is usually a distinct plant with less glaucous, paler foliage than Concatenans Group and cream to yellow campanulate to funnel-shaped flowers. Usually a pretty, clear pale yellow but with flowers often on the small side to give a really good show.

cinnabarinum ssp. *tamaense* (Davidian) Cullen 1978

Closely related to both *cinnabarinum* ssp. *xanthocodon* Purpurellum Group and *oreotrephes* and probably acts as a bridge between the two subsections Cinnabarina and Triflora although both chemically and morphologically it lies closer to *cinnabarinum* and is therefore placed here.
L deciduous or semi-deciduous with scales wider apart than usual for *cinnabarinum*, usually two to five times, rarely their own diameter apart.
F deep royal-purple to pale lavender, tubular.

Collected by *KW* under three numbers in 1953 from the Triangle, Upper Burma and still rare in cultivation.   June

keysii Nutt. 1855 H3–4 L1–2 F2–3

Ht to 6 m (20 ft). Often rather straggly or leggy. Bark fairly smooth to roughish, fawn to brown.
L 7.5–10 × 2–3 cm (3–4 × ¾–1¼ in.), narrowly elliptic to oblong-lanceolate, scattered on the young shoots, usually light green, densely scaly on both surfaces, unequal sized below. Petiole about 1.3 cm.
Inflor from *lateral* and *terminal* buds often forming *dense clusters* of flowers. Pedicels about 1 cm.
F usually *bicolor*, various shades of red, scarlet, flame to salmon or tinged orange to green with yellow or red lobes; in var. *unicolor* the flowers are all red. The latter is an eastern form from Pemako, *KW* 6257, possibly hardier than average than the type. Both forms have flowers about 2 cm (¾ in.) long, *tubular*, slightly ventricose.
Calyx small, glabrous outside. Ovary densely glandular scaly, style pubescent in lower third.

An unusual species with generally bicolor narrow tubular rather small flowers; not impressive on a small plant but can be very effective en masse. Keep away from crimson hybrids that might flower at the same time. May need pruning to develop a shapely bush and can be trained as an espaliered wall shrub. Easily separated from *cinnabarinum* with its clusters of narrowly tubular lateral and terminal flowers, thinner textured leaves, slender growth and more willowy habit. Some forms are only suitable for mild gardens and all may be cut back in most areas in cold winters. Hardy enough for Pacific coast in all but exceptional winters. Young growth often frosted. **AM**, 1933 to var. *unicolor*, *KW* 6257 Exbury. This var. *unicolor* is probably now classed as a Group so would become *keysii* Unicolor Group but its exact status remains uncertain.

From Bhutan, west Arunachal Pradesh and south-east Tibet, 2,400–3,700 m (8,000–12,000 ft), not to 16,000 ft as stated in the RHS–SHB. Often common on steep hillsides, conifer forest, dense rhododendron jungle and thickets, forest margins and even epiphytic on conifers.   May–July

FALCONERA SUBSECTION (FALCONERI SERIES) (E)

Large shrubs with large, usually heavily indumentumed leaves and large fairly compact trusses of heavily textured, often ventricose, long lasting flowers. This subsection is very closely related to the Grandia subsection. The apparent distinction based on the funnel- or cup-shaped hairs does not really hold good although the majority of the Falconera subsection have a woolly indumentum while the Grandia subsection have more of a plastered one. The two subsections merge in the close alliance between *basilicum* and *praestans*.

Other characters are the leathery leaves, seven to ten lobed corolla, small calyx, twelve to eighteen stamens and the ovary is usually tomentose.

Distribution stretches from east Nepal eastwards through south-east Tibet, Sikkim, Bhutan, Arunachal Pradesh, Yunnan and Burma into Szechwan, mostly in very wet areas.

All are fine foliage plants, well worth growing for foliage alone until the flowers are produced; this takes several years. The young growth is very decorative.

With the exception of the aberrant *galactinum*, all these species are vulnerable to sudden cold spells in north-west North America. Many were lost in both the 1955 and 1972 freezes although some did survive in the more favourable areas. These were either near salt water or parts not too severely effected, such as around Eugene in 1955 and Seattle in 1972.

None of these plants will tolerate very high temperatures, such as those of Melbourne, Australia, or stand very hot sun. The hot sun plus the drought of 1976 caused scorch in southern England even where watering was adequate. Experiments are being made on growing some of these species in south-east USA but the chances of success are not great.

basilicum Balf.f. & W.W. Sm. 1916 (*megaphyllum* Balf.f. & Forr., *regale* Balf.f & Ward) H3–4 L2–3 F2–3.

Ht 3–9 m (10–30 ft). Habit usually flat topped as in *arizelum*, now a subspecies of *rex*. Branchlets rufous tomentose. Bark generally greyer than *arizelum*.
L 13–32 × 7.5–17 cm (5–13 × 3–6½ in.), 1.8–2.4 times as long as broad, ovate to oblanceolate, apex rounded, *base tapered from broadest part*, indumentum below deep cinnamon to fawn with broadly cup-shaped hairs, somewhat spongy, sometimes evanescent leaving a grey skin-like under surface. L remain for 2 to 3 years. Petiole 2–3.5 cm, *widened at base* and flat above with marginal *wings and ridges*.
Inflor fifteen to twenty-five, rachis 3.5 cm. Pedicel 2.5–3 cm pale cinnamon tomentose.
F less variation than *arizelum*, usually white to cream with a prominent blotch but also cream to pale yellow to rich flesh-rose, often flushed, stained, lined or veined pink or purple, about 3.5 cm (1½ in.) long, broadly campanulate, fleshy, lobes eight.

Calyx small tomentose. Stamens sixteen. Ovary densely tomentose, style glabrous.

This species makes a fine specimen with handsome foliage and beautiful young growth. Some with veined and flushed flowers are of a muddy tone, the cream, blotched ones being the more desirable.

There are many cultivated plants and herbarium specimens that lie half-way between this species and *praestans*. In the latter species, the petioles have more pronounced wings and the indumentum is plastered rather than spongy. Many plants occur with thin or dotted indumentum; the newly named *rothschildii* probably fits in here or with *semnoides* to which 30 to 40 herbarium specimens have been transferred from *basilicum*. Hairs less distinctly cup-shaped than *coriaceum* & *hodgsonii*.

The leaves are often larger and the indumentum is usually paler than in *arizelum*. Farrer reported that these two merged and this is noticeable on dried specimens. Did this species in fact emerge from the hybridization of *arizelum* and *praestans*?

Killed in central Oregon in 1972 freeze. **AM**, 1956, Minterne Abbey.

From west Yunnan and upper Burma, distribution generally south of *arizelum* and *semnoides*, 2,700–4,000 m (9,000–13,000 ft) in rhododendron forests, bamboo and open mixed thickets and open situations on rocky hillsides.   March–May

coriaceum Franch, 1898 (*foveolatum* Rehd. & Wils.) H3–4 A+5 L2–3 F1–3

Ht 3–7.6 m (10–25 ft). Also often flat topped, sometimes tree-like. Branchlets grey-white, relatively thin. Bark rough, flaking, brownish-grey. L10–25 × 3–7.5 cm (4–10 × 1¼–3 in.), *narrowly* oblanceolate to *narrowly* elliptic, 2.5–4 times as long as broad, apex obtuse to rounded, base cuneate to rounded, indumentum below white, fine-textured ash-grey to pale fawn in two layers, upper one ± evanescent, and made up of broadly cup-shaped hairs. L remain for 3 to 4 years. Petiole 2.5–3 cm.

Inflor fifteen to twenty, fairly loose, rachis 1–1.5 cm. Pedicel 2 cm fawn tomentose.

F white, white flushed rose, creamy-pink, with crimson blotch, ± spotted, very variable in size, the best forms being over 3.8 cm (1½ in.) long, funnel-campanulate, lobes five to seven.

Calyx minute, tomentose. Stamens ten to fourteen. Ovary glandular or glabrous, style glabrous.

The best forms with larger flowers from *F* 25622 and 25872 are attractive and well worth growing. The rest are worthless with miserably small trusses in comparison with the leaves. The white, kid-glove like young growth is fine on all forms.

Bud and leaf damage may occur in Britain in hard winters and plants were killed in Oregon in the 1972 freeze.

Shows some relationship with *fictolacteum* and could be related to *galactinum*. **AM**, 1953 'Morocco', Crown Lands.

From south-west Tibet and north-west Yunnan, 3,000–4,000 m (10,000–14,000 ft), in conifer and rhododendron forests, thickets and among rocks.   April–May

1 *R. arboreum*. Arborea subsection,
Annapurna South, central Nepal
(A.D. Schilling)

2 *R. arboreum*. Arborea subsection,
Nepal (A.D. Schilling)

3 *R. arboreum* ssp. *delavayi*. S.B.E.C.
0120, Arborea subsection, Tali Range,
Yunnan

4 *R. lanigerum.* Arborea subsection

5 *R. niveum.* Arborea subsection

6 *R. argyrophyllum* ssp. *nankingense* 'Chinese Silver' A.M. Argyrophylla subsection

7 *R. atlanticum* and *R. calendulaceum,* subgenus Pentanthera, section Pentanthera (Azalea)

8 *R. occidentale*. Smith & Mossman 28-2 'Crescent City Double', subgenus Pentanthera, section Pentanthera (Azalea)

9 *R. occidentale*. Smith & Mossman 502 'Humboldt Picotee', subgenus Pentanthera, section Pentanthera (Azalea)

10 *R. argipeplum*. Barbata subsection

11 *R. albrechtii*. Subgenus Tsutsutsi, section Brachycalyx (Azalea)

12 *R. barbatum*. Barbata subsection, bark

13 *R. campanulatum* ssp. *aeruginosum*. Campanulata subsection

14 *R. campylocarpum.* Campylocarpa subsection, Milke Danda, east Nepal

15 *R. souliei.* Campylocarpa subsection, deep-pink selection

16 *R. wardii.* Campylocarpum subsection, Doshong La, south-east Tibet (W.E. Berg)

17 *R. wardii*. Campylocarpum subsection, Li-ti-ping, Yunnan from the other end of the distribution of the species (A.D. Schilling)

18 *R. cinnabarinum*. Cinnabarina subsection, Milke Danda, east Nepal, showing different forms

19 *R. cinnabarinum*. Cinnabarina subsection, Milke Danda, east Nepal

20 *R. cinnabarinum.* Cinnabarina subsection, Milke Danda, east Nepal

21 *R. galactinum.* Falconera subsection, Wolong Panda Reserve, Szechwan

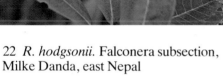

22 *R. hodgsonii.* Falconera subsection, Milke Danda, east Nepal

23 *R. hodgsonii.* Falconera subsection, bark

24 *R. semnoides.* Forrest 21870, Falconera subsection

25 *R. decorum*. S.B.E.C. 1059, Fortunea subsection, Tali Range, Yunnan

26 *R. decorum* and *R. yunnanense*. Tali Range, Yunnan

27 *R. hemsleyanum.* Fortunea subsection

28 *R. orbiculare.* Fortunea subsection, Wolong Panda Reserve, Szechwan

29 *R. vernicosum.* Fortunea subsection, Rilong, Szechwan

30 *R. fulgens.* Fulgensia subsection

31 *R. uvarifolium.* 'Yangtze Bend' A.M. Fulva subsection

32 *R. crinigerum*. Glischra subsection

33 *R. glischrum* ssp. *rude*. Glischra subsection

34 *R. kesangiae* Bowes Lyon 9703.
Grandia subsection (A.D. Schilling)

35 *R. montroseanum* 'Benmore' F.C.C.
Grandia subsection

36 *R. macabeanum.* Grandia subsection

37 *R. pudorosum* Ludlow & Sherriff 2752. Grandia subsection

38 *R. sinogrande.* Grandia subsection, Tali Range, Yunnan with Peter Hutchison who has been on all my main plant-hunting trips

39 *R. watsonii*. Grandia subsection, Huanglong, Szechwan

40 *R. annae*. Irrorata subsection

41 *R. anthosphaerum*. Sino-British Expedition to China 0163, Irrorata subsection

42 *R. lanatoides*. Lanata subsection, young growth

43 *R. lacteum*. Lactea (Taliensia) subsection

44 *R. beesianum* Rock 107. Lactea (Taliensia) subsection

45 *R. lanatum*. Lanata subsection

46 *R. longesquamatum*. Maculifera subsection, foliage

47 *R. pachysanthum*. Rhododendron Venture 72001, Maculifera subsection

48 *R. pachytrichum*. Maculifera subsection

49 *R. sikangense (cookeanum)*. Maculifera subsection

50 *R. dalhousiae* var. *rhabdotum*. Maddenia subsection

51 *R. formosum* var. *inaequale* Cox & Hutchison 301. Maddenia subsection

52 *R. lindleyi*. Maddenia subsection, Sikkim (W.E. Berg)

53 *R. nuttallii*. Maddenia subsection

54 *R. veitchianum* Peter Valder. Maddenia subsection

55 *R. facetum.* Parishia subsection, Tali Range, Yunnan

56 *R. smirnowii* Apold, Cox & Hutchison 118. Pontica subsection

57 *R. dauricum* 'Hokkaido' A.M.
Rhodorastra subsection

58 *R. bainbridgeanum.* Selensia subsection

59 *R. hirtipes* Kingdon Ward 5659. Selensia subsection

60 *R. adenogynum.* Taliensia subsection, Lichiang Range, Yunnan (A.D. Schilling)

61 *R. bhutanense.* Taliensia subsection, Rudong La, Bhutan

62 *R. balangense.* Taliensia subsection, Wolong Panda Reserve, Szechwan (W.E. Berg)

63 *R. bureavii* 'Loch Fyne' A.M. Taliensia subsection

64 *R. bureavii (bureavioides)*. Taliensia subsection, Balang Mountain, Szechwan

65 *R. elegantulum*. Taliensia subsection

66 *R. faberi* ssp. *prattii*. Taliensia
subsection, pink form, Balang Mountain,
Szechwan

67 *R. phaeochrysum*. Taliensia subsection,
Mongbi Mountain, Szechwan

68 *R. principis.* Taliensia subsection, Doshong La, south-east Tibet (W.E. Berg)

69 *R. rufum.* Jiuzhaigou, Szechwan (P. de Spoelberch)

70 *R. rufum (weldianum)*. Mongbi Mountain, Szechwan

71 *R. faucium*. Thomsonia subsection,
Doshong La, south-east Tibet (W.E. Berg)

72 *R. cerasinum*. Thomsonia subsection

73 *R. taliense*. Sino-British Expedition to China 0555

74 *R. hookeri*. Thomsonia subsection

75 *R. eclecteum* yellow form. Thomsonia subsection

76 *R. meddianum.* Thomsonia subsection

77 *R. thomsonii.* Jaljale Himal, east
Nepal, Thomsonia subsection

78 *R. thomsonii.* Jaljale Himal, east Nepal,
Thomsonia subsection, trunks

79 *R. augustinii* ssp. *hardyi*. Triflora subsection

80 *R. concinnum*. Triflora subsection, Szechwan (W.E. Berg)

81 *R. yunnanense.* Triflora subsection, Tali Range, Yunnan

82 *R. venator.* Ventora subsection

decipiens Lacaita 1916

Very poor type specimen. Undoubtedly a natural hybrid between *falconeri* and *hodgsonii*. My wife and I saw numerous natural hybrids of these two species when in north-east India in 1965 and D. Chamberlain saw several groups when in the same area in 1975. Also common in parts of adjacent Sikkim at 3,000–3,400 m (10,000–11,000 ft). Plants growing under this name in cultivation are similar to those hybrids I saw in the wild. There is the same man-made hybrid named 'Hodconeri'.

falconeri Hook.f. 1849 H3–4 A+10 L3–4 F3–4

Ht may eventually reach 12 m (40 ft) in favourable locations. Habit often tree-like with a large head. Branchlets stout, grey-fawn tomentose. Bark *red-brown*, rough but peeling or flaking.
L thick 20–30 + × 5–15 cm (8–18 + × 2–6 in.), oblong-oval to elliptic to broadly obovate, apex obtuse to rounded, base rounded to subcordate; *dark mat green above on maturity, rugose*; thick rust-coloured indumentum below with *narrowly* cup-shaped hairs. L remain for one year or occasionally 2 to 3 years. Petiole 4–6 cm with thin greyish-white tomentum. Inflor twenty or more, fairly compact to compact, rachis 3–4 cm. Pedicel 4–5 cm buff to pinkish tomentose and sometimes glandular.
F creamy-white to almost yellow, purple blotch, no spots, very heavy substance, 4–6 cm (about 2 in.) long, lobes eight, rarely to ten, oblique campanulate, sometimes slightly fragrant.
calyx small ± tomentose and glandular. Stamens twelve to sixteen. Ovary ± numbers of glands and hairs, style stout, glabrous or glandular-tomentose at base, stigma yellow, occasionally jade-green.

One of the monarchs of the genus or even the plant world. A hundred-year-old plus specimens are still to be found in cultivation. A very well known and much admired species. The flowers last longer than any other hardy rhododendron and can remain in full beauty for as much as a month. Always a grand foliage plant but some forms have superior flowers to others. Could be a useful parent.

Grows best on the western seaboard but succeeds in sheltered eastern and southern gardens near the coast. Killed or severely damaged by 1972 freeze in Oregon and mostly killed at Glendoick 1981–2.

Closely related to *arizelum*. Differs from ssp. *eximium* in the flower colour, lack of persistent indumentum on the upper leaf surface and is larger in all parts, **AM** 1922 Gill's Nursery.

Extreme east Nepal, Sikkim, Bhutan and west Arunachal Pradesh, 2,700–3,400 m occasionally to 3,800 m (9,000–11,000 to 12,500 ft), in mixed forest, sometimes fairly open, often forming colonies, common; hybridizes readily with *hodgsonii* in the wild.   Late April to late May

falconeri ssp. *eximium* (Nutt. 1853) Chamb. H3–4 A+5 L3–4 F2–3

Ht 3–9 m (10–30 ft). Habit usually flat topped. Branchlets stout, rusty tomentose. Bark pale to dark reddish-brown, peeling.

L 15–30 × 5–15 cm (6–12 × 2–6 in.), oval to obovate-elliptic, apex obtuse to rounded, base rounded to obtuse, dark green and *rugose* above with ± *persistent indumentum* for the first year, deep cinnamon to rust coloured below, usually thick and woolly. L remain for 2 to 4 years. Petiole 4–5 cm rusty tomentose.

Inflor twelve to twenty, fairly compact, smallish for subsection at times, rachis 3–4 cm. Pedicel about 4.5 cm densely glandular and tomentose.

F cream heavily flushed rose, pale lilac, pink rim, pink to rose or cream, about 4.5 cm (1¾ in.) long, fleshy.

Calyx short, glandular and tomentose. Stamens ten to fourteen. Ovary densely glandular, style glabrous or glandular at base.

One of the finest foliage plants of the genus. The flowers are commonly shades of pink which fade. Cream forms are probably referable to *arizelum* even if the indumentum is rather persistent on the upper leaf surface. Some of our *C&H* 427 open a most attractive shade of pink. Very closely related to *arizelum* and can be considered to lie botanically between *falconeri* and *arizelum* which is where it lies geographically. The size of plant, leaf and flower is generally smaller than *falconeri*.

As growth comes late, a moist shady situation is needed for good growth. Most handsome throughout the year, especially when the leaves are young. Killed in Oregon by the 1972 freeze.

Bhutan and Arunachal Pradesh at 2,650–3,400 m (8,800–11,000 ft). The form we found in 1965 under *C&H* 427 grew in pure stands on top of a ridge.   March–May

galactinum Balf.f. 1926 H4 A−10 L1–2 F1–3

Ht 3.6–8 m (12–26 ft). Habit usually tree-like. Young shoots with evanescent grey tomentum, sparse on young leaves above. Bark roughish, grey-brown. *Terminal foliage buds distinctive, ovoid, densely tomentose.* L 12–21 × 5–8 cm (5–8½ × 2–3¼ in.), oblong-ovate to lanceolate to oblanceolate, apex acuminate to obtuse, base broadly cuneate to rounded, dark grey-green above, glabrous, buff-grey to pale cinnamon below, velvety with two layers of indumentum, upper layer cup or funnel-shaped hairs. L remain for 2 to 4 years. Petiole about 3.5 cm.

Inflor about fifteen fairly loose, rachis 1 cm. Pedicel 2.5 cm thin white tomentose.

F white, white flushed pink, pale pink to pale rose, ± spotted, crimson blotch, about 3 cm (1¼ in.) long, campanulate.

Calyx short 1 mm. Stamens fourteen. *Ovary* and style *glabrous*.

Different from the rest of the subsection with unusual shaped buds, shorter bud scales and glabrous ovary. It lacks the grandure of the rest of the subsection with thinner growth and lighter textured leaves and flowers. Only collected once by *W* in fruit only, *W* 4254 and he reported it as being rare. Plants in cultivation are fairly uniform and unlike any other species. It might be more satisfactorily placed in its own subsection. The wild, fruiting specimen shows some affinity with *rex*. I saw some fine plants in Wolong panda reserve, Szechwan in 1986 and 1989.

It is the hardiest of the subsection and will grow in any sheltered garden in Britain. Reasonably hardy in south Sweden. Some forms are quite pretty in flower but it is basically a rather dull plant. Several may be seen in the old collection at Dawyck, Peeblesshire.

West Szechwan, 2,300–3,300 m (7,500–10,800 ft) in woods.

April–May

hodgsonii Hook.f. H4 A0 L2–3 F2–4

Ht 6–9 m (20–30 ft). Habit rounded, sometimes as wide as it is tall, to erect. Shoots stout with greyish felted tomentum. Bark creamy, mauve shot green, pink to cinnamon, peeling in large sheets. Foliage buds *conical*, outer scales with *long acuminate tips*, green to purple.
L leathery, 18–38 × 7–12 cm (7–12 × 3–4¾ in.), oblong-elliptic to oblong-lanceolate, apex and base obtuse to rounded, loose evanescent indumentum above on younger leaves giving a *hoar-like almost metallic look*. Indumentum below grey to buff, variable in colour and thickness with *broadly* cup-shaped hairs. L remain for 2 to 3 years. Petiole about 5 cm.
Inflor fifteen to thirty compact to fairly compact, rachis 5 cm. Pedicel 3–4 cm densely tomentose.
F pink to deep rose, rosy lilac, lavender, cerise-pink to dark reddish-purple or deep magenta, cherry-red or claret, all forms liable to fade with age, 3–4 cm (about 1½ in.) long, tubular-ventricose-companulate, lobes six to ten.
Calyx short fleshy cup. Stamens fifteen to eighteen. Ovary tomentose, style glabrous.

A fine species with bold foliage, lovely bark and often beautiful flowers. Early introductions generally had dark coloured flowers which faded to a dirty colour but many collected recently have lovely pink to rose flowers, usually reported from lower elevations. Sometimes sweetly scented.

Hardier than most of its relatives and therefore suitable for most sheltered British gardens. Not much damage in Oregon and Washington in 1972 freeze. I find it advisable to protect it as a small seedling up to 3 or 4 years old. Botanically quite distinct from the rest of the subsection.

The favourite firewood of sherpas and porters in east Nepal. Also used for cups, spoons and yak saddles while the leaves are used for plates and for lining baskets.

The pink and magenta forms sometimes grow mixed up in the wild or may form separate stands. One report states the pink form has larger loose trusses while the darker form has tight trusses. 'Poets Lawn' **AM**, 1965 Crown Lands, 'Harp Wood' **PC**, 1971 Sandling Park.

East Nepal, Sikkim, Bhutan and west Arunachal Pradesh, 2,900–4,300 m (9,500–14,000 ft), dominant in some areas, often on east facing slopes, thickets, conifer forest, bamboo and mixed with *arboreum* and *barbatum*. Hybridizes naturally with *falconeri*.   March–May

preptum Balf.f. & Forr. 1920 H3–4 L2–3 F2–3

Doubtfully distinct from *rex* spp. *arizelum*. Leaves a little narrower and indumentum paler with typical *arizelum* hairs. Otherwise as *arizelum*. It probably lies between ssp. *arizelum* and ssp. *fictolacteum*. North-east Upper Burma.

rex Lévl. 1914 H4 A−5 L3–4 F3–4

Ht 3–13.7 m (10–45 ft). Habit large rather erect shrub to tree-like. Young shoots stout, grey-white tomentose. Bark roughish, grey-brown.
L to 46 × 13 cm (18 × 5 in.), oblanceolate, apex broadly obtuse, base narrowly obtuse, dark often shiny above, grey to pale buff indumentum, thickish, below. L remain for 2 to 4 years. Petiole 4–4.5 cm grey tomentose.
Inflor twenty to thirty, usually full, rachis 2 cm. Pedicel 1.5–2 cm tomentose.
F white, pale lilac, pale pink to mauve-pink, with crimson blotch and spots, serrated rather frilled margins, 5–7 cm (3–2¾ in.) long, tubular-campanulate.
Calyx small. Stamens sixteen. Ovary with greyish hairs, style glabrous.

A very fine species, suitable for cold sheltered gardens as well as more favourable sites. This is really just a large edition of ssp. *fictolacteum* with which it merges. Many cultivated plants would fit the description of either as the leaves and flowers may be intermediate in size. The indumentum of *rex* is usually paler. *R* 03800 was the first cultivated number to be recognized as *rex* but *KW* 4509 was included under *rex* later. The latter grows on limestone ranges only, on damp heavily wooded shaded slopes with limestone outcrops. There is an apparent east–west cline of ssp. *fictolacteum* and ssp. *rex*. 'Quartz' **AM**, 1955 *R* 03800 flowers white tinged pinkish-blue, blotch and spots, Crown Lands; **FCC**, 1935 *KW* 4509, Embley Park; **AM**, 1946 *KW* 4509, Bodnant.

Very common in south-west Szechwan above 3,000 m (10,000 ft) sometimes forming pure forests. Also north Yunnan.   April–May

rex ssp. *arizelum* (Balf.f. & Forr.) Chamb. 1920 H3–4 A+5 L3–4 F2–3

Ht 3–7.6 m (10–25 ft). Habit usually flat topped. Branchlets with cinnamon to greyish tomentum. Foliage buds conical. Bark pink, pinkish-brown to reddish-brown, peeling.
L to 25 × 12 cm (10 × 4¾ in.), thick, oval, obovate to oblanceolate, apex rounded, notched or retuse, base obtuse to slightly cordate; dark green and rugose above, thick woolly rusty-red, cinnamon, brown to fawn indumentum below with *strongly fimbriated* cup-shaped hairs, shorter than those of *falconeri* and *eximium*.
L remain for 1 to 4 years. Petiole 2.5–3 cm, fawn tomentose, *not tapered*.
Inflor fifteen to twenty-five fairly compact, rachis 2.5–3.5 cm. Pedicel 2.5 cm fawn tomentose.
F cream to clear yellow, yellow flushed rose, cream tipped rose or mauve, salmon rose, warm apricot, deep soft rose to rosy-crimson, about 4.5 cm (nearly 2 in.) long, lobes eight, obliquely campanulate.
Calyx short, tomentose. Stamens sixteen. Ovary densely tomentose, style glabrous.

A fine foliage plant. Many colour forms are lovely but all are inclined to fade out, often to a dingy pale washy colour. Usually flowers at a younger age than *falconeri* of which it is the eastern equivalent. *R. arizelum* lacks the glands on the ovary and style of *falconeri* and is usually a smaller plant with smaller leaves and flowers. It appears to merge with *fictolacteum* in the wild but not in gardens and is not so hardy.

It would seem that some of the very many colour forms are not in cultivation although many are found in gardens. It is apparent that nearly all plants that differ from the plain cream to yellow flower colour also have untypical foliage. This may indicate some hybrid ancestry, perhaps with species like *praestans*. Uniform and mixed populations probably occur in the wild.

Killed in 1972 freeze in Oregon. **AM**1963, Brodick.

Arunachal Pradesh, south-east Tibet, west Yunnan and Upper Burma, 3,000–4,400 m (10,000–14,500 ft), steep slopes, exposed or sheltered, under conifers or dominant above the forest, rhododendron forest, open situations, bamboo forest. Sometimes forms a sort of gnarled elfin woodland.

March–May

arizelum Rubicosum Group

A form with dark coloured flowers originally described from a plant growing at Lochinch, Wigtownshire of *R* 59550.
F very strong cerise with deeper blotch. Other dark coloured forms occur in gardens, some from other introductions. Several of R's *arizelum* were described as red flowered, others as yellowish-red, orange-red to pure white, but his colours were often from native collectors' notes and unreliable. May be of hybrid origin. The indumentum is usually of a deeper than average colour. **AM**, 1963, Lochinch.

rex ssp. *fictolacteum* (Balf.f. 1916) Chamb. (*lacteum* var. *macrophyllum*)
H4 A−5 L2–3 F3–4

Ht to 12 m (40 ft) under ideal conditions, usually much lower. Habit fairly erect. Young shoots cinnamon tomentose, growth buds with long tails to the scales. Bark *roughish, greyish-brown*.
L to 30+ × 12 cm (12+ × 4¾ in.), 1.5–3.8 times as long as broad, *oblong-obovate to oblanceolate*, apex obtuse to rounded, base tapered, cuneate to subcordate, slightly rugulose above, *very dark green, often smooth and shiny; thick buff to rusty-brown indumentum below*. L remain for 2 to 5 years. Petiole 2.5–4 cm.
Inflor twelve to twenty-five, variable in size, rachis 1.5–2 cm. Pedicel about 3 cm greenish or pinkish, white to fawn tomentose.
F snowy-white through blush-pink, pale lilac to rose, often heavily flushed or margined pink or rose; always blotched and often heavily spotted, frequently frilled; the commonest form is white, blotched; 3–5 cm (1¼–2 in.) long, oblique-campanulate, lobes seven to eight.
Calyx small, 1–2 mm tomentose. Stamens fourteen to sixteen. Ovary densely tomentose, style glabrous.

One of the best larger species, suitable for cooler areas. Very fine for foliage and flowers. While it may take several years to bloom, young plants are always extremely handsome. When mature, it may bloom exceptionally freely, especially the earlier introductions with the smaller leaves and flowers. A few dwarf forms occur in cultivation but as with runts of a litter, they lack vitality and rarely flower if ever. See Addendum *p.* 350.

Just survives in parts of south Sweden, but was undamaged in Oregon in the 1972 freeze. Is hardy enough for all sheltered gardens in Britain but do not plant in a frost pocket as growth when young comes rather early. A little tender when young.

Various geographical variations occur from across the wide areas of distribution. Some seem to merge with *arizelum* (including the type specimen of Delavay's unfortunately). In cultivation the rough greyish-brown bark, the narrower shinier leaves, the unusual growth buds, and the rather different, thinner textured flowers, separate it from *arizelum*. *R. rex* is larger in all parts and the indumentum is usually less dark. **AM**, 1923 Reuthe, **AM**, 1953 'Cherry Tip', Minterne flowers white flushed pink.

Yunnan, Szechwan, south-east Tibet, 3,000–4,300 m (10,000–14,000 ft), very common and widespread in mixed forest and edges of conifer forest.   Mostly April–May

rothschildii Davidian 1972 H3-4 L2–3 F2–3

Ht 2.75–6 m (9–20 ft). Habit shrub or tree-like. Branchlets thin fawn to brown, tomentose. Growth buds large, deep crimson-purple. Bark rough.
L 21–36 × 6–14 cm (8¼–14 × 2¼–5½ in.), oblong-obovate, apex rounded, base tapered to obtuse, slightly rugulose above, glabrous, *thin granular discontinuous indumentum* below, *with an under layer of thin, plastered indumentum with rosulate hairs, yellowish to fawn*. Petiole 1.5–3 cm flat above, *winged margins*, tomentose.
Inflor twelve to seventeen, rachis 2 cm. Pedicel 2.8–4 cm densely fawn tomentose.
F pale yellow to creamy-white, blotched, 3.5–4.3 cm (about 1½ in.) long, obliquely-campanulate, lobes eight.
Calyx minute, tomentose. Stamens thirteen to fifteen. Ovary densely tomentose, style glabrous.

Very closely related to *basilicum* and *semnoides*. Distinguished by its thin granular indumentum, hair structure and yellowish indumentum on young leaves. Is in cultivation. Probably a natural hybrid, perhaps between *basilicum* or *semnoides* and *fulvum* (*fulvoides*).

North-west Yunnan and Yunnan–Tibet border, 3,850 m (12,600 ft), fir forest.   April–May

semnoides Tagg & Forr. 1926 H3–4 L2–3 F2–3

This is closely related to *basilicum* but differs from that species in its more fimbriated but still cupped hairs of the indumentum. 30–40 herbarium specimens have been transferred from *basilicum* to this species. It comes from farther north than *basilicum* in south-east Tibet and north-west Yunnan–south-east Tibet border. It varies little from *basilicum* horticulturally.

sinofalconeri Balf.f. 1916 Not in cultivation (probably)

This species is the most southerly recorded of the subsection. It is totally distinct from the others, has little to do with *falconeri* itself but may perhaps have affinity with *arizelum*. The indumentum is different, not very thick, pale cinnamon, soft spongy and woolly. A plant under this name at Wakehurst is not correct.
Mengtsz, Yunnan, 2,700 m (9,000 ft).

FORTUNEA SUBSECTION (FORTUNEI SERIES)

This subsection, together with most of the Campylocarpa and Thomsonia subsections are the only three large groups with mostly ± glabrous leaves. The majority of this subsection have larger foliage. Most come from China and are in the main vigorous, hardy and valuable garden plants.

The flowers are often glandular (sticky), somewhat fleshy, the corolla often more than five-lobed, the calyx usually small and the stamens more than ten. The capsules are generally large. Several have scented flowers and the corolla is never red or yellow. Most grow to large proportions with a non-peeling bark. The majority of the species come from the drier uplands. Species of the Thomsonia subsection sometimes equal the Fortunea subsection in stature but the former mostly have a large cup-like calyx. Of the species well known in cultivation, *griffithianum* and *orbiculare* are the most aberrant. All species are now placed in the one subsection which Chamberlain considers to be primitive.

These are perhaps the most heat-tolerant rhododendrons after the Pontica subsection and this is endorsed by their reported resistance to heat and sun in the San Francisco area. Most were undamaged by the 1972 freeze in western North America. The late white-flowered species have flowers prone to weather damage.

calophytum Franch. 1886 H4 A−15 L2–4 F2–4

Ht 4.6–9 m (15–30 ft). Habit wide spreading large bush or tree, shapely. Bark roughish, brown. Young foliage with sparse evanescent silvery tomentum.
L coriaceous, 20–30 × 4–8 cm (8–12 × 2–4 in.), oblong-lanceolate, apex acuminate narrowing to cuneate base, glabrous or vestiges of indumentum below, especially on midrib, margins often recurved. L remain for 1 or more commonly 2 years. Petiole 1–2 cm.
Inflor fifteen to thirty, loose, rachis 1.2–2.5 cm. Pedicel *very long* 3–7 cm ± glabrous *red*.
F white to pink, rose or pale mauve-pink flushed purple in cultivation (also purple in the wild), always with deep blotch and spots, 5–6 cm (2–2½ in.) long, openly campanulate, ventricose below, lobes five to seven.
Calyx *c*. 1 mm, very small disc-like glabrous. Stamens *fifteen to twenty very small* compared with style. Ovary and style (stout) glabrous, stigma yellow-green, large.

R. calophytum

One of the hardiest large species, the better forms making a wonderful sight in early spring in sheltered gardens. Takes some years to bloom but is an easy long lived plant. The white forms appear to be commoner in Britain while in the USA, most are pale pink to pale lavender. Both are equally fine and the red pedicels greatly add to their attraction. Hardy throughout Britain and even grows in parts of south Sweden and eastern USA. The leaves curl up like cigarette papers during hard frost. Regenerates freely in a Northumberland garden.

While showing some relationship with *sutchuenense*, this species has strong affinities with the Grandia subsection with its large leaves, long pedicels and especially the ventricose corolla. **AM**, 1920, Reuthe white, flushed pink, **FCC**, 1933, pale-pink South Lodge.

From central west, and east Szechwan and north Yunnan, being the dominant species of the Mt Omei region at 1,800–4,000 m (6,000–13,000 ft) where it is very constant, in woods, thickets and bamboo. (W). All cultivated plants said to be from W 3979.

February–March–April

calophytum var. *openshawianum* (Rehd. & Wils. 1913) Chamb.

Usually a tree 4–12 m (13–40 ft). L smaller and narrower than *calophytum*.
Inflor about eight, rachis 1–1.5 cm. F white to purplish-white, blotched.
Is probably just an elfin form of *calophytum*. W 3414 from western

Szechwan on Wa Wu Shan, 1,400–2,800 m (5,000–9,250 ft) in wood-lands mixed with *Lithocarpus* sp. and growing near *davidii*.

davidii Franch. 1886 H4? L2–3? F2–3? These ratings are from the *Rhododendron Handbook* but all efforts to locate this species in cultivation have failed.
Ht 3–8 m (10–26 ft). Bark grey.
L coriaceous 10–17 × 2–3 cm (4–7 × about 1 in.), 3.2–5.2 times as long as broad, oblanceolate, apex usually long acuminate, base cuneate, whitish-green below, margin recurved. Petiole about 2 cm.
Inflor eight to twelve, *rachis 2.5–6 cm (1–2½ in.), elongated*. Pedicel about 1 cm densely glandular.
F pink, rosy-red, lilac to purplish-blue, spotted purple, about 5 cm (2 in.) long, openly campanulate, lobes seven to eight.
Calyx 1–2 mm densely glandular. Stamens fourteen to sixteen glabrous. Ovary densely glandular, style ± glabrous.

Any plants under this name in cultivation are most likely wrong. The leaves are longer and narrower than *oreodoxa* and also more pointed, while the long rachis is distinctive. Fang says it is very beautiful.

W 1531 from west Szechwan. Also from central and south Szechwan and north-east Yunnan, 1,800–4,000m (6,000–13,000ft), in open situations, bamboo and thickets. Probably February–March.

April (wild)

R. decorum

decorum Franch. 1886 (*franchetianum* Lévl. *giraudiasii* Lévl., *spooneri* Hemsl. & Wils.) H3–4 A–5 to +5 L2–3 F2–3

Ht to 9 m (30 ft). Habit fairly erect, occasionally straggly. Young shoots with glaucous evanescent bloom. Bark rough with broad fissures, brownish-grey or greenish.
L 7–18 × 2.2–7.6 cm (3–7 × ¾–3 in.), two to three times as long as broad, oblanceolate to elliptic, apex blunt to rounded, base rounded *not* cordulate, glabrous to naked eye but has minute hairs below. L remain for 1 to 2 years. Petiole 1.5–4 cm glabrous.
Inflor seven to fourteen, usually open topped, rachis 1.5–3 cm. Pedicel 3.5–4 cm glandular.
F white, pale rose, lavender-rose, with yellow or green or crimson tinge at base, with or without markings, variable in size to 7.5 cm (3 in.) long, 8.5–11 cm (3½–4½ in.) across, openly funnel-campanulate, six to seven lobed, fragrant.
Calyx small about 2 mm glandular. Stamens *twelve to fifteen puberulous at base*. Ovary and style glandular.

An excellent, vigorous, easily grown species which varies much in hardiness. The smaller leaved and flowered forms of *W* and *KW* are hardy enough for most parts of Britain and even survive in the most favourable parts of Scandinavia. Large leaved and flowered forms are closely related to *diaprepes* and are definitely tender. White flowered forms seem to be the commonest in cultivation. Different clones flower at different times giving a long season. The hardiest introductions flower freely from a comparatively young age while the more tender ones are slower. Farrer 979 is tender and approaches *diaprepes*. Merges with *diaprepes* and possibly *vernicosum*, related to *fortunei*. Differs from *vernicosum* chiefly in the puberulousness at the base of stamens and its fragrance.

R. serotinum Hutch. 1920 is very similar to *decorum*. Apart from its later flowering and the blotched corolla, there is little to separate them. It was raised in France from Delavay's seed from the same area as *decorum* and it should probably be placed here at group cultivar status. Its provenance is uncertain as is its existence in the wild. **AM**, 1925, Kew. August–September.

R. decorum is one of the hardiest scented species and also one of the most tolerant of different soil conditions. 'Cox's Uranium Green' is a natural hybrid between *decorum* and *wardii*.

An exceedingly common and widespread species found in Szechwan, Yunnan and north-east Burma, the hardiest forms coming from the more eastern localities, 1,800–4,000 m (6,000–13,000 ft), rarely over 3,400 m (11,000 ft), chiefly from drier areas especially in pine forests, also open and dense thickets, dry open situations, margins of mixed and deciduous forest, dry rocky hillsides and limestone cliffs.   Late April–July

diaprepes Balf.f. & W.W. Sm. 1917 (*rasile* Balf.f. & W.W. Sm.) H3 A+10 L2–3 F2–3. See Addendum *p*. 351–2.

Ht 6–14 m (20–45 ft). Habit often straggly. Bark rough.
L 12–30 × 4.4–11 cm (5–12 × 1¾–4½ in.), elliptic or oblong to ovate,

apex ± rounded, base rounded to cordulate, pale glaucous green below with minute hairs. L remain for 1 to 2 years. Petiole stout 2.4–4 cm glabrous.

Inflor five to ten loose, rachis 1–3 cm. Pedicel 1.5–4 cm stout ± glandular.

F usually white, occasionally slightly flushed pink, heavily scented, as much as *10 × 13 cm (4 × 5 in.)* across, open-funnel-campanulate, fleshy. Calyx about 5 mm glandular. Stamens *eighteen to twenty* hairy at base. Ovary and style densely glandular.

A splendid large species where it can be grown successfully. Flowers much larger than the hardiest *decorum* but botanically they merge with similar locations and elevations. It just deserves specific rank. Only really suitable for the mildest British gardens. Its bark can be split in nearly any locality and its growth comes surprisingly early considering its late flowering season. Grows very large in suitable gardens. 'Gargantua' **AM**, 1953, **FCC**, 1974 (Crown Lands) from selfed seed of *F* 11958 at Towercourt. This triploid clone is hardier than the type and very fine.

From Yunnan, Upper Burma and Laos, 1,800–3,400 (6,000–11,000 ft), margins of shady dense mixed forest and open thickets, deciduous and pine forests and rocky places.   June–July

faithii Chun 1934 Not in cultivation

Ht 4 m (13 ft). L to 21 × 8 cm (8½ × 3¼ in.). F 7.5 cm (3 in.) long. Only known from the type specimen collected in Kwangtung from the Botanic Institute, Canton. Closely resembles *diaprepes* but differing in its glabrous filaments. In woods near stream.

fortunei Lindl. 1859 H4 A−15 L1–3 F2–3

Ht to 9 m (30 ft), usually much less. Habit usually upright and fairly rigid. Young shoots at first glandular. Bark roughish, grey-brown.

L 7–17 × 3.5–8 cm (3–7 × 1½–3 in.), 1.7–4 times as long as broad, broadly oblanceolate to obovate, apex subrounded to acute, base rounded to cordulate, dark green above, pale glaucous-green below with minute punctulate hairs. L remain for 1 to 2 years. Petiole 2–3 cm, usually *purplish*, *bluish* or *reddish*.

Inflor five to twelve loose, sometimes rather pendulous, rachis 1.5–5 cm. Pedicel 2–4 cm densely glandular or glabrous.

F pale lilac-white to pale lilac-pink to pink, fragrant, 4–5 cm (about 2 in.) long, 7–9 cm (3–3½ in.) across, open to funnel-campanulate, seven lobes, often wavy.

Calyx small, glandular. Stamens fourteen to sixteen, glabrous. Ovary and style densely glandular, stigma knob-like.

A popular plant in North America but never common in Britain although a few authentic plants do still exist. Has been much used in hybridizing in America where it is invaluable for its hardiness, heat resistance and being the hardiest scented species. Not in my mind as attractive as *decorum* and it has the undesirable character of new growth with the flowers, which are easily damaged by rain. Also heat resistant in Japan. Needs shelter in south Sweden. Seems to be hardy in Iceland. A particularly fine large flowered, sweet scented clone was used as the seed parent of the original 'Loderi' grex. 'Mrs Butler', a *fortunei* seedling, is finer than the original Fortune introduction. 'Rubra' is probably a hybrid. Introduced by Fortune in 1856 and later found by W.

R. discolor has now been made a sub-species of *fortunei*. The latter has wider leaves but intermediaries do occur.
L obovate 1.7–2.5 times as long as broad: ssp. *fortunei*.
L oblanceolate 2.8–4 times as long as broad: ssp. *discolor*.
The latter now includes *houlstonii*.

Appears to be widespread in south-east and central China but fresh collections are badly needed to ascertain its variability and whether *houlstonii* should be retained at some rank.

Common in the mountains of Chekiang and Lushan Range of Kiangsi, also Hupeh, Kwangtung, and Kiukiang, 600–900 m (2,000–3,000 ft), often on deforested areas where it continues (or did) to flourish, especially alongside torrents.   May–early June

fortunei ssp. *discolor* (Franch.) 1895 Chamb. (*houlstonii* Hemsl. & Wils. 1910, *mandarinorum* Diels, *kirkii* Hort.) H4 A − 5 L2–3 F2–4

Ht 2–7 m (2–23 ft). Habit more open than *fortunei* and perhaps more upright than *diaprepes*. Bark roughish, grey-brown.
L 10–20 × 2.5–7 cm (4–8 × 1–3 in.), sometimes larger, oblong-elliptic to oblong-oblanceolate, apex obtuse, base cuneate, glabrous above and below. L remain for 2 years. Petiole stoutish, 2–3.5 cm.
Inflor about ten, loose, rachis 3–5 cm. Pedicel 3–5 cm ± glandular.
F white to pale pink, shell to quite rosy-pink, fragrant, 5–8 cm (2–3 in.) long to 10 cm (4 in.) across, funnel-campanulate, lobes seven.
Calyx small 3–5 mm distinctly lobed, glandular and ciliate. Stamens fourteen to sixteen glabrous. Ovary and style densely glandular, stigma large.

A fine flowering sub-species, especially for southern districts. Takes many years to bloom freely as do several of its hybrids. Liable to barksplit in Scotland. The true sub-species seems to be rare in cultivation. It is fast growing but inclined to grow leggy. Growth like *diaprepes* and *fortunei* often comes before the flowers. Likes soil that is not too damp. Satisfactory in sheltered parts of Scandinavia and does quite well in many parts of eastern USA including the Great Lakes area.

Comes from a more western area than ssp. *fortunei* but some overlap in distribution of wider and narrower leaf forms occurs in Hupeh and Chekiang. Now includes *houlstonii* which is placed here rather than under ssp. *fortunei* on account of its narrow leaves. The calyx size character difference is not even borne out by the type specimens. Plants grown under *houlstonii* should be given some horticultural distinction from *discolor* because most cultivated clones bloom much earlier in the season, generally in May. One of these received an **AM**, in 1977, 'John R. Elcock' Crown Lands and was very floriferous although it usually has the reputation of being rather shy flowering. Awards under *discolor* **FCC**, 1922, white, slightly tinged pink, Kew. **AM**, 1922, pale pink, blotched, Bodnant.

Common in western Hupeh, Szechwan and Anwhei, 1,100–2,100 m (3,500–7,000 ft) in thickets and woodlands. June–July

glanduliferum Franch. 1886 Not in cultivation

Said to be close to *fortunei* but much more glandular. Elongated leaves and large stigma may show affinity with *calophytum* but it has a glandular ovary and style. Corolla glandular outside. Quite obviously a case where material is grossly inadequate to determine whether this is a good species or not. Also, locality descriptions are inadequate. Specimen collected by Delavay in Yunnan. The long stipitate glands on the pedicels and outside of corolla are unusual in this subsection suggesting that it is a distinct species.

griffithianum Wight 1850 (*aucklandii* Hook.f. *oblongum* Griff.) H2–3 A + 15 L2–3 F3–4

Ht to 6 m (20 ft +) in cultivation, 12–15 m (40–50 ft) in the wild. Habit erect or more spreading, often rather sparse. Bud scales often red. Bark flaking and peeling, usually smooth olive and tan, cinnamon, fawn and glaucous-grey.
L 10–30 × 4–10 cm (4–12 × 1½–4 in.) or more, 2.6–3.8 times as long as broad, oblong to oblong-elliptic to oblong-ovate, apex acute to rounded, base rounded, glabrous above and below. L remain for 1 to 2 years. Petiole 2.5–5 cm.
Inflor *three to six on long, stout rachis to 8 cm (over 3 in.)*. Pedicel 3.5–4 cm usually sparsely glandular.
F white, white with green spots or green base, white tinged or veined red or pink, blush to deep rose-pink or even yellowish; often scented, *3.5–7 cm (1½–3 in.)* and to *15 cm (6 in.)* + across, widely campanulate.
Calyx *large 1–2 cm* green or pink tinted, irregular, glabrous. Stamens twelve to eighteen glabrous. Ovary and style glandular, stigma very large greenish-yellow.

This is a truly marvellous species when well grown. It has among the largest flowers in the genus. While only suitable for favoured areas, it is hardier than its very low elevation in the Himalayas would indicate and grows with some success in many gardens in Sussex, Hampshire and even Blackhills, Morayshire in north-east Scotland. Avoid frost pockets. Considerable shelter and some shade is appreciated, especially when young. There is a possibility that the more easterly collections are the hardiest. Some forms are definitely more beautiful than others and the amount of scent is also variable. *KW*'s favourite species in the wild. Good forms are Hooker's and *L&S* 2835.

This is a very distinctive species that might be better placed in a subsection of its own. It differs from other members of the Fortunei subsection in its large calyx, glabrous rachis and pedicels, very long rachis and large flowers. Some people still consider *aucklandii* worthy of some separate status. It is the parent or is in the parentage of a multitude of popular hybrids including 'Loderi', 'Penjerrick', 'Pink Pearl', and 'Jean Marie Montague'. FCC, 1886, Elmclon. Several new introductions.

From east Nepal, Sikkim, Bhutan, south Tibet to east Arunachal Pradesh, 1,800–2,900 m (6,000–9,500 ft), very common in places, especially Bhutan, in moist forest, oak, rhododendron, magnolia and deciduous forest.   May

hemsleyanum Wils. 1910 (*chengianum* Fang) H3–4? A + 5 L3–4 F2–3?

Ht 3–6 m (10–20 ft). Habit stout and fairly erect branches. Bark roughish, flaking greyish-brown.
L 10–27 × 4–13 cm (4–11 × 1½–5 in.) or more, ovate to ovate-elliptic, 1.7–2.5 times as long as broad, apex rounded, *base deeply auricled-cordate, margins often undulate*, minute hairs and glands towards base below. L remain for 2 years. Petiole 3–6 cm. F buds long and pointed.
Inflor five to ten or more, rachis 4–5 cm, stout not hairy. Pedicels 2.5–4 cm, very glandular and sticky to touch or occasionally glabrous.
F white or white tinged rose-pink on outside, throat yellow-green, 4.5–6 cm (1¾–2⅖ in.) long, 7.5–12.5 cm (3–5 in.) across, widely campanulate, glandular outside, lobes six to seven, fragrant.
Calyx *c.* 1 mm ± glandular or glabrous. Stamens fourteen to sixteen glabrous. Ovary and style densely glandular.

A splendid new introduction which first flowered in cultivation in the American Rhododendron Society's Test Garden, Portland, Oregon in 1963. First flowered with us in 1975. The foliage is the best in the subsection and the plant seems to be hardy. The flower buds, at least on young plants, can get blasted with cold and drying winds. Survived the 1972 freeze in Oregon and may be hardy as far north as Philadelphia. Has a spreading tree-like habit and blooms comparatively young.

From west Szechwan. Only found on Mt Omei by *W* where he found it rare in woods and thickets. He said it is one of the largest and most handsome of Chinese species. Is said to stand strong winds in the wild. Collected by Professor Hu, Hu 8823. Seed was sent to the Arnold Arboretum who sent plants to San Francisco and Seattle. 1,100–2,000 m (3,500–6,500 ft).   June–July–August

huianum Fang 1939 Not in cultivation. See Addendum *p.* 352.

Allied to *davidii* but differing in the larger calyx and glandular style. F pale red to purplish-lilac, corolla seven lobed. Little is known about this plant. Szechwan, 1,000–2,700 m (3,250–9,000 ft).

kwangfuense Chun & Fang 1957 Not in cultivation

Ht 3–4 m (10–13 ft). F rose.
Perhaps related to *oreodoxa* with a similar glabrous style but apparently closer to *fortunei* ssp. *discolor*. No specimen in RBG, Edinburgh. Kwangsi.

orbiculare Decaisne 1877 (*rotundifolium* David 1873 Nomen nudum)
H4 A − 5 L3–4 F1–3

Ht to 3 m (10 ft) usually much wider than high. Sometimes taller in the wild. Habit low and very compact in open positions, can be leggy in shade. Bark grey to greenish-brown.
L 4–10 × 4–8 cm (1½–4 × 1½–3 in.), *1.2–1.5* times as long as broad, ovate to orbicular, *apex rounded, base cordate-auriculate, bright mat-green above*, glaucous below with minute hairs. L remain for 1 to 2 years. Petiole 3–5 cm.
Inflor seven to ten loose, sometimes pendulous, rachis 2–3 cm. Pedicel 4–6 cm with a few glands and minute hairs, bright red.
F deep pink, rose, deep rose to purplish-pink or purplish-rose, no markings, 3.5–5 cm (1½–2 in.) long, campanulate, lobes seven.
Calyx small *c.* 0.5 mm, gland fringed. Stamens fourteen glabrous. Ovary whitish glandular, style glabrous. Capsule curved.

One of the finest foliage plants in the genus which needs plenty of light to retain its compact habit which is a large part of its charm. Plant it as a specimen and never allow it to be crowded by other plants. It is hard to place in a garden colourwise on account of its bright 'icing sugar' pink flowers. One American authority places it in the top ten species for all round garden use, but caution is necessary in selecting good forms. Some have flowers that are too pendulous and/or have too much blue in the colour while in America particularly, many hybrids are masquerading under this species. All plants with leaves at all elongated are hybrids.

Quite hardy, being fairly successful in south Sweden and Long Island. Was undamaged by the 1955 and 1972 freezes in north-western North America. Not very heat resistant. Not closely related to the rest of the Fortunea subsection and is only placed here on account of its seven-lobed corolla and small calyx. **AM**, 1922, Bodnant.

Quite common over a limited area of west Szechwan on Opien-hsien near Mt Omei and Mupin at 2,000–4,000 m (6,500–13,000 ft) in woodlands, thickets, coniferous forests and on rocks.   April–May

orbiculare ssp. *cardiobasis* (Hand.-Mazz. 1935) Chamb. H4 L2 F2

Ht 3 m (10 ft) in the wild.
L 7.5–12.5 × to 8.8 cm (3–6 × to 3½ in.), elliptic to ovate.
Inflor six to seven, looser than *orbiculare*.
F white to red (wild), about 5 cm (2 in.) long, funnel-campanulate.

Geoffrey Gorer of Sussex who cultivated two plants under this name, received three seedlings from Exbury. He said that they appreciate drier, sunnier conditions than *orbiculare*, but this does not necessarily apply elsewhere. The leaves of these plants are longer and more heart-shaped than *orbiculare* while the flowers are similar. So far, they have been accepted as true at the RHS shows, but it would be interesting to know their source at Exbury. The Gorer plants look like many of the *orbiculare* hybrids I have seen in America, but the type locality of ssp. *cardiobasis* in China is some way apart from that of *orbiculare*.

Found in Kwangsi, 1,700 m (5,400 ft).   May

R. oreodoxa var. *fargesii*

oreodoxa Franch. 1886 (*haematocheilum* Craib, *limprichtii* Diels, *reginaldii* Balf.f.) H4 A − 15 to − 5 L1−3 F2−3

Ht 6 m (20 ft) or more in cultivation, 2−5 m (7−17 ft) in the wild. Habit rounded if allowed room to develop but usually becomes leggy. Young shoots with thin tomentum. Bark roughish, grey-brown.
L 5−10 × 2−4.5 cm (2−4 × ¾−1¾ in.), 2−3.2 times as long as broad, narrowly elliptic to oblanceolate-elliptic, apex obtuse to rounded, base similar, glaucous below with minute, sparse indumentum. L remain for 1 year. Petiole 1−2 cm glabrescent.
Inflor six to twelve, rachis short, about 0.5−1 cm. Pedicel shortish 0.5−2.5 cm ± glandular.
F white, white flushed pale lilac to pink or rose, with or without purple spots, 3−5 cm (1−2 in.) long, openly campanulate, lobes five to eight.
Calyx minute less than 1 mm ± glandular. Stamens twelve to fourteen. *Ovary* and style *glabrous*.
 This is a very useful plant, hardy, vigorous, accommodating and free flowering from a fairly young age. The foliage and flowers give a graceful effect compared with some of the larger leaved and flowered species and less shelter is needed for satisfactory results. Some authorities advocate regular dead-heading of this species but once they get big, this is very laborious. Ours are never done and they survive and flower regularly. The flower buds are very frost resistant, even when swelling. Very hardy in the

milder parts of Scandinavia, even as a small seedling. Bears some resemblance to *vernicosum*, especially out of flower and there may be a close relationship here. The leaves are not so waxy and the glabrous style of *oreodoxa* and glandular style of *vernicosum* do divide them. Also the growth is stouter in the latter. **AM**, 1937, Exbury, pale rose with darker stripe. *R. dabanshanense* Fang and S. X. Wang 1978 from Sining, Kansu, may fit in here.

A widespread and variable species from west Szechwan, Mupin, Kansu and Hupeh at 2,100–3,000 m (7,000–10,000 ft) in woodlands.

March–April

oreodoxa var. *fargesii* (Franch. 1895) Chamb. (*erubescens* Hutch.)

L often wider than *oreodoxa*. F lilac-pink to deep pink, heavily speckled inside. Ovary *glandular*, style glabrous.

An easily grown plant even on relatively poor sites such as stiff, wet clay. Some authorities say that this is an easier plant than *oreodoxa* itself, but I doubt if there is much difference as their distinctions are largely botanical, in var. *fargesii* having a glandular ovary. Difficult in the Philadelphia area. The foliage curls up very readily in either sunny or frosty weather, quicker than any other species. **AM**, 1926, Wakehurst Place pale rose-pink, spotted. **AM**, 1969, 'Budget Farthing' Bodnant. Found in fir forest and woodlands.

platypodum Diels 1990 Not in cultivation. See Addendum *p.* 352.

The winged and widened petiole shows some resemblance to certain forms of *eclecteum* but the stouter growth, thicker leaves and longer rachis probably bring it nearer *decorum* although the leaves are rather small on the herbarium specimens. Could be an interesting species with no close allies. From south-east Szechwan (Namchuan Hsien), collected by Bech and Rosthorn and also by Fang at 1,800–2,100 m (6,000–7,000 ft) in thickets.

praeteritum Hutch. 1922 H4 L1–3 F2–3

Ht 3 m (10 ft) or more.
L 6–8 × 2.5–3.2 cm (2½–3 × 1–1¼ in.), *c.* 2.5 times as long as broad, usually oblong, apex and base rounded, glabrous. Petiole *c.* 1.5 cm at first floccose, later glabrous.
Inflor seven, rachis 3–10 mm. Pedicel *c.* 1 cm glabrous.
F white flushed pink to pale pink with flecks but no blotch, 3–4 cm long, *lobes five*.
Calyx 1–2 mm glabrous. Stamens ten glabrous. Ovary and style glabrous.

Very close to *oreodoxa*, differing in the five-lobed corolla, the floccose petioles and probable nectar pouches. Named from one plant at Kew and seed from *W* 1800, normally *wasonii*. It is interesting that both this and *erubescens* came from *W* seed mixed with other species. The smaller number of stamens and five lobes of the corolla tend to make this an aberrant member of the subsection but I have my suspicions that this may be a natural hybrid. Garden value similar to *oreodoxa*.   March–April

praevernum Hutch. 1920 H4 L2–3 F2–3

Ht to 3.7 m (12 ft) or more. Habit often compact. Bark grey-brown, rough.
L 10–18 × 2.5–6 cm (4–7 × 1–2½ in.), 3–4 times as long as broad, elliptic-oblanceolate, apex acuminate narrowed to cuneate base, pale green below, *entirely glabrous*. L remain for 1 to 2 years. Petiole 1.5–2.5 cm.
Inflor eight to fifteen open topped, rachis 1 cm. Pedicel stout 2 cm glabrous.
F white, pale to deep pink, white with pinkish-blue blush, pinkish-lilac, with large deep blotch, 5–6 cm (2–2½ in.) long, campanulate, five-lobed.
Calyx minute glabrous. Stamens fifteen lower half puberulous. Ovary and style glabrous.

Very closely related to *sutchuenense* with which it hybridizes in the wild. *R. praevernum* is smaller in all parts and has a glabrous leaf underside in contrast to *sutchuenense* which has indumentum on the midrib. **AM** Minterne 1954.

Came from the same seed numbers of *W* 509 and 1232. Even *W* considered *praevernum* and *sutchuenense* just variations within one species.   February–April

sutchuenense Franch. 1895 H4 A − 15 L2–3 F2–4

Ht 4.6–10 m (15–35 ft). Habit often a large umbrella-shaped shrub. Young shoots at first tomentose, stout. Bark rough, greyish-brown.
L coriaceous up to 30 × 7.6 cm (12 × 3 in.), 3.2–4.2 times as long as broad, oblong-lanceolate to narrowly oblong-oval, apex acuminate to cuspidate narrowed to cuneate to rounded base, dark green above, midrib below with ± loose indumentum, margin recurved. L remain for 1 to 3 years. Petiole stout, 1.5–3 cm.
Inflor *c.* ten, usually open at top, rachis 1.5–2.5 cm. Pedicel stout, 1.5–2.5 cm, sparsely floccose.
F pale pink, pale pinkish-lilac to pale mauve-pink with or without blotch, 5–7.5 cm (2–3 in.) long, widely campanulate, lobes five to six.
Calyx 1–2 mm disc-like ± glabrous. Stamens thirteen to fifteen. Ovary and style glabrous, stigma knob-like, reddish.

One of the finest large early flowering species with long lasting flowers of good substance. While very hardy, it grows best under favourable woodland conditions. Starts blooming younger than *calophytum*. Some forms have inferior flowers in poor trusses and objectional forms with bright magenta flowers were introduced but these were eliminated according to L de Rothschild. Hardy throughout Britain where sheltered, the milder parts of Scandinavia and eastern USA as far north as Boston. Withstood all the freezes on the western North American seaboard. Regenerates freely in a Northumberland garden.

Has a different corolla shape, shorter pedicels, fewer stamens and a smaller stigma than *calophytum*. Some plants in cultivation do appear to lie between these two but this could be due to hybridization in cultivation. Flowers of a typical *sutchuenense* do not have a blotch. × *geraldii* Chamb., merely *sutchuenense* × *praevernum*, intermediate between the two parents. L with persistent indumentum on midrib underneath and corolla with pronounced blotch. **AM**, 1971, 'Sunte Rose'.

The type is common in west Hupeh and east Szechwan, rare south of the Yangtsze, 1,500–2,400 m (5,000–8,000 ft) in woods, among evergreen oaks or bamboo.

January to April according to form and season

vernicosum Franch. 1898 (*adoxum* Balf.f. & Forr., *lucidum* Franch., *araliiforme* Balf.f. & Forr., *euanthum* Balf.f. & W.W. Sm., *hexamerum* Hand.-Mazz., *rhantum* Balf.f. & W.W. Sm. *sheltoniae* Hemsl. & Wils.) H3–4 usually 4 A – 15 to 0 L2–3 F2–3

Ht to 7.6 m (25 ft) usually much less. Habit often makes a rounded rigid bush. Bark rough or roughish, grey-brown and greenish-brown.
L 6–12 × 3–5 cm (2½–5 × 1¼–2 in.), 1.5–2.2 times as long as broad, elliptic to ovate to oblong-oval to oblong-elliptic, apex obtuse to round, base similar, pale glaucous green below but with minute hairs. L remain for 1 to 2 years. Petiole 1.5–3.5 cm.
Inflor six to twelve often quite compact, rachis 0.5–1 cm. Pedicel 2–3 cm glandular.
F palest pink, rose-lavender to bright rose, rarely white, ± crimson spotted, 3.8–5 cm (1½–2 in.) long, widely funnel-campanulate, lobes six to seven, sometimes reflexed.
Calyx fleshy about 2 mm densely glandular. Stamens fourteen *glabrous*. Ovary and style densely glandular, the latter with *dark red glands*.

A lovely species whose flowers are of a consistently high standard, often of a very delicate shade of pink, prettily spotted. Should be grown to complement *decorum* which blooms later. Varies a little in hardiness but most forms will succeed in all reasonably sheltered gardens. Sven Hedin and Harry Smith's collections from Kansu are hardy in sheltered positions in south Sweden. Also quite successful in Philadelphia and Pennsylvania, especially *R* 03788 (*R* field No. 18139) grown by Gable, known as *vernicosum* aff. In Oregon, it survived the 1972 freeze. The early growth is sometimes prone to frost damage. The upper leaf surface will become sticky-waxy and shiny when heated over a flame.

Differs from *decorum* in its glabrous stamens, generally earlier flowers and having little or no scent. Differs from *fortunei* in the red styler glands, usually smaller leaves, more compact truss and the lack of scent. The so-called geographal forms are abolished. 'Loch Eck' **AM**, white clone 1964, Benmore. 'Sidlaw' **PC**, 1969 Glendoick.

From Yunnan, Szechwan, south-east Tibet (Tsarong) and Kansu, 2,700–4,300 m (9,000–14,000 ft), fairly common and widespread but probably not as plentiful as *decorum*, in openings and margins of conifer and mixed forests, open rocky and bouldery meadows, dry situations and by streams. April–May

Probable hybrids formerly included in this subsection.

chlorops Cowan 1952

Ht to 3 m (10 ft). Habit inclined to be leggy. L 7.5–12.5 × 3.8–5 cm (3–5 × 1½–2 in.), oblong-elliptic. Inflor six to eight loose. F cream to pale yellow, green within at base, some spots, 3.8 cm (1½ in.) long, lobes seven. Stamens fourteen. Ovary and style glandular throughout.

This is almost certainly a natural hybrid, probably of *vernicosum* × *wardii* although this cross would be expected to produce better garden plants. Four clones are said to exist in Britain which may have come from F 16463 but this is an *Acer* sp. No herbarium specimen matches it. The RBG, Edinburgh clone has proved to be a poor plant, straggly and very prone to bark-split. The Lochinch clone may be of better value. An American plant known as *chlorops* 'Lackamas Cream' is probably a *wardii* hybrid of garden origin. Chamberlain says that *chlorops* is almost certainly a chance hybrid whose parentage remains uncertain. Yunnan?
May

planetum Balf.f. 1922 H4 L2–3 F2–3

Ht to 4.5 m (15 ft) or more. Young shoots ± white evanescent tomentum. Bark rough, flaking lightish-brown.
L 10–20 × 3–6 cm (4–8 × 1¼–2½ in.), elliptic to oblanceolate, apex cuspidate, base cuneate, vestiges of loose indumentum below ± persistent on midrib. Petiole about 2 cm.
Inflor about ten. F pink, usually without blotch or spots, 4–5 cm (1½–2 in.) long, funnel-campanulate, lobes six to seven.
Calyx very small ± glabrous. Stamens twelve to fourteen puberulous at base. Ovary and style glabrous, stigma broad.

Several clones of this occur in cultivation and all are free flowering. Some are good with larger flowers than others. Ours has poor chlorotic foliage. In my mind, this is a natural hybrid, perhaps between *sutchuenense* and *oreodoxa*. It originated from W 1882 which in Plantae Wilsonianae is not attached to a rhododendron. Cultivated plants do not apparently agree with the W description of ovate-cordate leaves. One specimen of Fang's could agree with this plant. Doubtful provenance.
From Szechwan 3,000–3,700 m (10,000–12,000 ft).   March–April

FULGENSIA SUBSECTION (CAMPANULATUM SERIES, PART) (E)

This rather unsatisfactory new subsection lies somewhere between Thomsonia and Neriiflora subsections. The presence of thick indumentum separates this from Thomsonia although *fulgens* is obviously close to *succothii* and *sherriffii* to *lopsangianum*. Even *fulgens* and *sherriffii* do not appear to be closely related and are only placed together for convenience. There is no obvious answer in how to place these species but they were undoubtedly wrongly positioned with *campanulatum*. All come from the eastern Himalayas. See Addendum *p.* 352.

fulgens Hook. 1849 H3–4 A + 5 L2–3 F2–3

Ht 1.5–3.7 m (5–12 ft). Habit usually fairly low and compact. Branchlets glabrous. L buds pointed, F buds rounded and conspicuous. Bark pinkish-grey to reddish-brown, smooth and peeling, as good as *barbatum*. Brilliant crimson bracts on young growth.
L 5.3–13 × 2.4–7 cm (2¼–5 × 1–2¾ in.), elliptic, broadly obovate, oval to oblong-obovate, apex rounded to obtuse, base rounded to cordulate, fairly glaucous young leaves above, polished dark green on maturity, indumentum below varies in denseness, *usually thick* though sometimes partly evanescent, white, fawn to tawny. L remain for 1 to 2 years. Petiole 0.3–2.8 cm glabrous, much longer than in *succathii*.
Inflor eight to fourteen, *compact and rounded*, rachis 0.8–2.4 cm. Pedicel 0.4–1.5 cm crimson tinted, glabrous.
F deep blood red to bright scarlet without spots and with very dark nectaries, 2–3.3 × 2.6–4.5 cm (¾–1½ × 1–1¾ in.), tubular-campanulate.
Calyx small 1–3 mm, crimson tinted, glabrous. Ovary glabrous, style glabrous, pinkish.

This handsome species has foliage of character and attractive, compact but small trusses. Closely related to *succothii* and blooms equally early in the season. The fasiculate hairs of this species and *hookeri* are very similar. Not all that variable although the leaves are sometimes fairly narrow. The flowers are often attacked by birds. Withstood the 1972 freeze in Oregon so is probably hardier than + 5 indicates. Some of Hooker's introduction survived at Lochinch until recently, over 100 years.

East Nepal, Sikkim, Bhutan, south Tibet and west Arunachal Pradesh, 3,200–4,600 m (10,500–15,000 ft), in conifer and rhododendron forest and open hillsides.   February–April

miniatum Cowan 1937 Not in cultivation (see RBG Notes 1937, p. 229)

Ht 1.50–4.60 m (5–15 ft). Shrub, branchlets floccose. L 3.3–5.5 × 1.5 cm (1⅓–2¼ × ⅜–1¼ in.), elliptic, obovate to oblong, apex obtuse to rounded, base cordulate to rounded, glabrous above, a thick woolly fawn indumentum below. Petiole tomentose or glabrescent. Inflor four to six, loose, rachis 5 mm. Pedicel 5–6 mm glabrous or sparsely hairy. F deep crimson, 2.8–3 cm (just over 1 in.) long, funnel-campanulate. Calyx *large to 1.4 cm*, crimson, unequal, glabrous. Ovary glabrous, rose or white.

Appears to be near *fulgens* and *sherriffii* and may connect these two although the calyx is sometimes larger than either. As the field notes of *L&S* 1627 mentions a small calyx, it is apparent that the large calyx is not a constant character, perhaps pointing to *miniatum* being a natural hybrid, possibly of *lopsangianum* which comes from the same area.

South Tibet, 3,200–3,700 m (10,500–12,000 ft), in and on edge of rhododendron zone, fir forest and cliffs. No seed collected.

sherriffii Cowan 1937 H3–4 L2–3 F2

Ht 1.80–6.10 m (6–20 ft). Habit bushy to rather erect. Branchlets thin, hairy and glandular. Bark red-brown to pinkish-grey, peeling.
L 4.5–7.5 × 2.5–4 cm (1¾–3 × 1–1½ in.), oval to obovate to oblong-elliptic, dark shiny above on maturity, apex rounded to obtuse, base rounded to obtuse, *thick chocolate-brown continuous indumentum* below. L remain for 1 to 3 years. Petiole 1.2–1.5 cm glabrous.
Inflor three to six, loose, rachis about 4 mm. Pedicel 1–2 cm flushed red on upper surface, glabrous.
F rich, deep carmine, 3.5–4 cm (about 1½ in.) long, 5.3 cm (2 in. +) across, funnel-campanulate, nectaries black.
Calyx 3–6 mm glabrous, carmine. Ovary glabrous, style glabrous carmine, stigma red.

A very distinct species, still rare in cultivation with unusual foliage and uniquely coloured indumentum. The small trusses of hanging flowers are rather different and quite attractive.

It is undoubtedly closely related to *lopsangianum* (see *Dwarf Rhododendrons*, p. 91) which has a ± glabrous leaf underside and comes from the same area. It is interesting that *lopsangianum* was collected several times on the 1938 *LS&T* expedition when *sherriffii* was not collected at all.

There are only two *L&S* numbers of *sherriffii* of which 2751 is the only one in cultivation so the distribution is apparently rather limited. Surely so distinct a plant is unlikely to be a natural hybrid. Shows some relationship with *fulgens* in its hair type. **AM**, 1966 *L&S* 2751 Crown Lands. South Tibet, 3,500–3,800 m (11,500–12,500 ft), in rhododendron forest, above bamboo and on steep hillsides near edge of fir and larch zone.   February–April

FULVA SUBSECTION (FULVUM SERIES) (E)

The two species in this subsection usually make nicely formed large shrubs or small trees with handsome foliage and compact to open topped trusses of white to deep rose usually blotched flowers in February to April. They are fairly hardy and long lived but both suffered in the 1972 freeze in Oregon.
Branchlets and petioles with short, usually dense tomentum. F campanulate to funnel-campanulate. Calyx small to minute. Stamens ten. Capsule narrow and curved.

There are possible relationships with Campanulata, Grandia (*uvarifolium*) and Lactea subsections.

fulvum Balf.f. & W.W. Sm. 1917 (*fulvoides* Balf.f. & Forr.) H3–4 A −5 to +5 L2–4 F2–3

Ht to 9 m (30 ft) in cultivation, 0.90–7.6 m (3–25 ft) in the wild. Habit shapely rounded tree. Branchlets tomentose. Bark moderately rough, greyish or grey-brown.
L 6–25 × 2–9 cm (6–10 × 1–3½ in.) (type only to 17 × 6 cm (7–2½ in.)),

R. uvarifolium

oblanceolate, oblong-lanceolate, obovate to ovate, apex shortly acuminate to obtuse, base narrowed to obtuse, shape very variable, dark green
above in type, sometimes paler in the Fulvoides Group, indumentum
below *granular, yellowish to deep crimson* made up of unusual capitellate
hairs with a short stem and mop-like head. L remain for 1 to 3 years.
Petiole 1.2–4 cm tomentose.
Inflor three to fifteen compact to fairly compact, rachis 0.6–2.2 cm.
Pedicel 1–3 cm hairy or glabrous.
F white, white flushed mauve or rose, pale lilac-pink outside almost white
within, pink to deep rose, usually with a crimson blotch and spots,
2.6–4.9 cm (1–2 in.) long, campanulate to funnel-campanulate, five to six
lobes.
Calyx minute 1–2 mm glabrous. Ovary usually glabrous, style glabrous.
Seed similar to *campanulatum* with extra tail at ends.
    A very reliable species for woodland gardens throughout Britain. Free
flowering on maturity and a good foliage plant. Starts blooming at a
comparatively young age for so large a plant. Young plants prone to
bark-split.
    The typical *fulvum* is the more desirable type in flowers and foliage; the
now synonymous *fulvoides* has a generally more easterly distribution.
While many intermediaries occur, the plant we used to recognize as
fulvoides has longer, narrower leaves and less continuous, lighter
coloured, coarser indumentum and often smaller, inferior flowers. This
plant appears to be more widespread and common in the wild. See
Addendum *p.* 352.

Wind turns up the leaves revealing the brilliant indumentum while frost curls up the leaves like cigarette paper. **AM**, 1933, Bodnant F pink.

East Arunachal Pradesh, Yunnan, Upper Burma, south-east Tibet and west Szechwan, 2,400–4,400 m (8,000–14,500 ft), in open thickets and bamboo brakes, openings in and on margins of forests usually conifer, cliffs, rocky and bouldery slopes.   March–April

uvariifolium Diels 1912 (*niphargum* Balf.f. & Ward, *dendritrichum* Balf.f. & Forr., *monbeigii* Rehd. & Wils.) H3–4 A L2–3 F1–3

Ht 1.20–10.60 m (4–35 ft). Habit shrub or tree, girths to 1.8–2.4 m (6–8 ft) in the wild. Branchlets tomentose, stout. Bark rough, greyish to brown.
L 7–27 × 2.2–7.2 cm (3–10½ × 1–3 in.), oblanceolate to oblong-oblanceolate to obovate, apex shortly acuminate to obtuse, base narrowed to obtuse, usually dark green and semi-rugulose above, indumentum below variable, *thin* or thicker, *white, ash-grey to fawn*, usually continuous, mat to woolly, occasionally sparse and patchy or even glabrous. L remain for 2 years. Petiole 1–2 cm tomentose.
Inflor six to eighteen or more, compact to loose, rachis 0.6–1.5 cm. Pedicel 1–3.1 cm hairy.
F white, white flushed rose, pink to pale rose, usually blotched and spotted, sometimes not, 2.7–4 cm (1–1½ in.) long, campanulate to funnel-campanulate. Lobes five.
Calyx minute 0.5–1 cm usually glabrous. Ovary usually glabrous, style glabrous.

A variable plant in many ways. While some forms have lovely full trusses of pink flowers, others are definitely inferior with poor, small trusses. The majority have impressive foliage, especially when young but many take years and years to bloom including several *R* numbers. The young growth is particularly attractive. Certain introductions lie between *fulvum* and *uvariifolium*. 'Yangtze Bend' **AM**, *F* pink, RBG, Edinburgh 1965, 'Reginald Childs' **AM**, 1976, *F* white, suffused rose, blotched, Wakehurst Place (RBG, Kew). Several recent reintroductions.

Very common in the wild in the Tsangpo Gorge, Pome and Kongbo in south Tibet, Tibet–Arunachal Pradesh frontier, Yunnan and west Szechwan, 2,100–4,300 m (7,000–14,000 ft) sometimes covers whole hillsides with little else growing or in shady or open conifer and mixed forest, forest margins and on limestone cliffs.   March–April

uvariifolium Griseum Group

L with almost matted, silky, closely knitted indumentum below, leaves often smaller than type, generally paler above, base rounded. Habit often compact. F white to white flushed pink, small blotch. Kongbo, south Tibet. Very variable in leaf width–breadth ratio and in number of flower per inflorescence. Some clones are horticulturally distinctive flowers and a ± large calyx.

GENESTIERANA SUBSECTION (Hutch.) Sleumer (*ex GLAUCOPHYLLUM SERIES*) (L)

The species *genestierianum* is unlike any other species, including *micromeres*, with which it was formerly grouped in a sub-series of the Glaucophyllum series.

L very glaucous underneath, apex acutely acuminate. Inflor four to fifteen, pedicel longer than corolla. F plum-purple with a distinctive glaucous bloom as has the calyx and capsule.

genestierianum Forr. (*mirabile* Ward) H2–3 L2–3 F1–2

Ht 1.20–4.60 m (4–15 ft). Habit tall and slim, generally erect in cultivation. Buds soft pink. Bark red, dark to light mahogany, peeling.
L 5–15.3 × 1.4–4.5 cm (2–6 × ½–1¾ in.), lanceolate to oblanceolate, apex *acutely acuminate*, base obtuse or narrowed, *very glaucous* below, scales minute, 4–10 times their own diameter apart, rarely more. Sometimes the glaucousness wears off. Petiole 0.5–2 cm sparsely scaly.
Inflor terminal four to fifteen; rachis 0.3–5 cm (⅛–2 in.). Pedicel slender, 1.6–3 cm (⅝–1¼ in.), *longer than corolla* ± glabrous.
F *dull plum-purple to deep port-wine* colour with *glaucous bloom*, 1.3–1.8 cm (½–⅔ in.) long, tubular-campanulate, fleshy, no scales outside. Calyx shallow fleshy cup 1–2 mm with *glaucous bloom*. Stamens eight to ten unequal, glabrous. Ovary densely scaly, style short, stout and sharply bent, glabrous. Calyx persistent on the glaucous capsule.

A most unusual species, too tender for most gardens in Britain. The attractive young growth comes early, thus increasing its tenderness. The high altitude forms have probably not been introduced. Its glaucous flowers, leaves and capsules and pretty bark make it worth cultivating. The flowers are very curious, often in large trusses on long pedicels. *KW* thought the flowers looked like plum-purple fruit from the distance; Farrer's opinion was that it is 'almost ugly' while *F* called it ' charming'. Grows luxuriantly at Brodick Castle, Isle of Arran and used to at Headfort, Ireland.

From Tsarong south-east Tibet, north-east Upper Burma and Yunnan. Is said to come from 2,400–4,400 m (8,000–14,500 ft). I am inclined to doubt the latter altitude although others are recorded from 3,700–4,000 m (12,000–13,000 ft). Most are found under 3,700 m (12,000 ft). Widely distributed. Apparently always terrestrial in the wild in and on margins of mixed and rhododendron thickets and mixed forest, in bamboo, on rocky slopes and in the alpine region.   April

GLISCHRA SUBSECTION (GLISCHRUM SUB-SERIES OF BARBATUM SERIES) (E)

This subsection comes from north-east Upper Burma, west Yunnan, south-east Tibet and Arunachal Pradesh, all neighbouring areas. The chief characters are glandular bristles, especially on young shoots, the pink to purple to white flowers, usually heavily blotched and/or spotted, the loose or fairly loose inflorescence and the large glandular calyx. Most have relatively large flowers and leaves. While several are attractive and/or interesting species, none can be termed really top ranking species for general cultivation.

There has been some reduction in this subsection although *crinigerum* and *recurvoides* have been added. *R. hirtipes* is moved to the Selensia subsection (Martinianum and Selense sub-series) as has *bainbridgeanum* from the old Crinigerum sub-series. *R. erosum* and *exasperatum* are moved to the Barbata subsection while *diphrocalyx* and *spilotum* are at present unplaced in any subsection. *R. crinigerum* shows some links with the large calyxed Talienses.

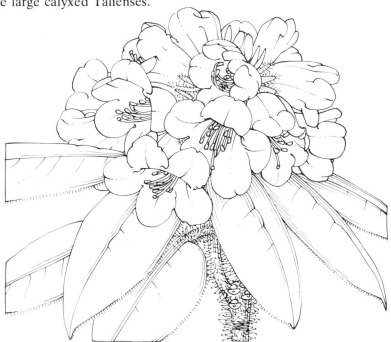

R. habrotrichum

adenosum Davidian 1978 (*glischrum* var. *adenosum* Cowan and Davidian *kuluense* Chamb. 1978) H3–4 L1–2 F2–3

Ht 2–5 m (6–17 ft) in wild, less in cultivation. Habit usually compact. Glands remaining on branches for 4 years. Bark greyish-brown.
L 7–10.5 × 2.4–3.4 cm (3–4¼ × 1–1½ in.) *c.* three times as long as broad stalked glands above and below ± persistent. L remain for 2 years. Petiole 1–1.3 cm, densely setose-glandular.
Inflor six to eight, rachis 0.5 mm. Pedicel 1.5–2.5 cm, densely setose-glandular.
F pale pink or white tinged pink, crimson spots, 3.8–5 cm (1½–2 in.) long, 5–6.3 cm (2–2½ in.) across, funnel-campanulate.

This plant has now quite correctly been given specific status. It is a neat, pretty plant in both pink and white forms and deserves to be better known. It has interesting very sticky (glandular) young growth, produced much earlier than the late growing *glischrum*. Distinguished from *glischrum* by its *short calyx*, short bristly glands on the leaf underside and the usually smaller, narrower leaves and fewer flowered inflorescence. The general appearance is quite different. Cultivated under *R* 18228. Comes from east of the range of *glischrum*.

From Muli, south-west Szechwan, 2,700–3,500 m (9,000–11,500 ft). The specimen of *L&S* placed under this name is not typical with red flowers and no glands on the leaf upper surface. In spruce forest and swamps. Late April–May

crinigerum Franch. 1898 (*ixeuticum* Balf.f. & W.W. Sm.) H3–4 A+5 L2–3 F1–3

Ht 1–5 m (3–16 ft). Habit usually spreading or compact. *Very sticky young growth and persistent bud-scales* though the latter varies. Bark greyish-brown, roughish. Number and size of hairs on branches variable. L 7.5–20 × 2–5 cm (3–8 × 1–2 in.), lanceolate, oblong-oblanceolate to elliptic, very variable, apex acuminate, base obtuse, usually *very shiny above*, *dark green*, sometimes bullate. The indumentum below has two types of hairs, coloured pale to deep buff or even darker, always fairly thick. Young leaves with evanescent woolly buff indumentum above. L remain for 2 to 4 years. Petiole with a variable number of sticky glands, about 1.5 cm.
Inflor ten to twenty, rachis red about 1.5 cm. Pedicel 3 cm glandular and hairy.
F white to pink to rose or white *and* pink in broad bands with blotch, spots and dashes (red forms may occur in the wild), 3–4 cm (about 1½ in.) long, campanulate.
Calyx split, to 1 cm long, densely glandular. Ovary densely glandular, style glandular.

There are mixed feelings about the value of this plant but the best forms are undoubtedly well worth growing for their flowers and/or foliage. *F* considered it the worst species he collected, but many introductions, especially those of *R* are attractive, some forming fine globular trusses. It blooms when reasonably young but the flowers are easily frosted. Hardiness is variable and many had leaves badly scorched in Oregon in the 1972 freeze. AM, 1935, Exbury.

From the Yunnan–Burma frontier, Arunachal Pradesh, Yunnan and south-east Tibet at 2,400–4,300 m (8,000–14,000 ft) where it can be exceedingly common (according to *KW* perhaps the commonest species in the Mishmi Hills) in open conifer forests, among boulders and on cliffs, rocky slopes and bamboo. April–May

crinigerum var. *euadenium* Tagg & Forr. 1931. This variety varies from near *glischrum* to being almost identical with *cringerum* (including the type specimen). Some specimens look like an almost glabrous *crinigerum*. Several variations are in cultivation and some of these are very good with excellent pink, blotched flowers. One with large leaves and truss was shown in London in 1976.

glischrum Balf.f. & W.W. Sm. 1916 H3–4 A + 5 L2–3 F1–3

Ht 6–7.6 m (20–25 ft) in the wild, rarely as tall in cultivation. *Branchlets densely bristly*. Bark roughish, greenish-grey-brown.
L 10–25 × 2.5–7 cm (4–10 × 1–1¾ in.), oblanceolate to occasionally obovate, apex acuminate, base cuneate to cordulate, covered with hairs below. L remain for about 3 years. Petiole about 2 cm glandular-bristly.
Inflor about ten to fifteen, rachis about 1 cm, bud-scales ± persistent during flowering. Pedicels about 3.5 cm red with dense silvery glands, sticky.
F deep rose through plum-rose, pink to almost white, some blotched and spotted, some not, about 4 cm (1⅜ in.) long, campanulate.
Calyx red, silvery hairs about 1.3 cm lobes unequal. Ovary glandular, style glandular at base, capsule with persistent calyx.

This can make a handsome plant though sometimes leggy but the flowers are liable to be somewhat uninteresting though it blooms when reasonably young. It makes a better plant in northern than southern Britain. It has been introduced under many collectors' numbers and the majority of these plants have been destroyed through lack of merit though some forms are really quite handsome in flower. *R. vesiculiferum*, *habrotrichum* and certain forms of *crinigerum* var. *euadenium* plus, of course, the two sub-species, are closely related.

From Yunnan, Upper Burma, south-east Tibet, common and widespread at 2,100–4,300 m (7,000–14,000 ft) in light woodland, conifer, mixed and margins of forest, thickets and open situations.

Late April–May

glischrum ssp. *glischroides* (Tagg & Forr. 1931) Chamb. 1978 H3–4 L2–3 F2–3

Ht 2–4.5 m (6–15 ft). Habit often more bushy than *glischrum*. Shoots *densely bristly*, bud-scales ± persistent. Bark light brown.
L 7–17 × 2.5–4.5 cm (3–7 × 1–2 in.), oblong-lanceolate to oblanceolate, apex acuminate, base rounded to cordate, very bullate above, not sticky, (young bud-scales very sticky) margins ciliate, two layers of hairs below. L remain for 1 to 2 years. Petiole with *dense red or purplish bristles*.
Inflor six to ten, loose, rachis about 1 cm. Pedicels *bristly red*.
F white washed rose through pale pink to rose-pink or mauve-pink, maroon blotch, 3.8–5 cm (1½–2 in.) long, campanulate.
Calyx to 2 cm purplish or red, cut into unequal glandular-ciliate lobes. Ovary densely glandular, style glabrous, capsule with persistent calyx.

A fine foliage plant and usually free flowering from a fairly young age. There are two different forms in cultivation, one with deeper coloured earlier flowers and earlier growth which is unsuitable for cold gardens, the other with paler flowers and later growth (the commoner form in cultivation) is hardier. Closely related to *vesiculiferum*.

From north-east Upper Burma–Tibet frontier at 3,000–3,700 m (10,000–12,000 ft) in thickets, on rocky and bouldery slopes and cliff ledges.

February–April

glischrum ssp.*rude* (Tagg & Forr. 1931) Chamb. 1978 H3–4 L2–3 F2–3

Ht about 2.7 m (9 ft). Habit as *glischrum*. Shoots bristly, bud-scales ±
persistent for 1 to 2 years. Bark as *glischrum*.
L 9–18 × 4.5–7.5 cm (3½–7 × 2–3 in.), broadly oblanceolate to oblong-
obovate, apex abruptly acuminate, base rounded or cordulate, margin
ciliate. Petiole 1.5–2 cm, bristly.
Inflor about ten, usually open topped, rachis about 1.5 cm. Pedicels about
3 cm glandular and hairy.
F pink through cherry-pink to purplish-pink with crimson markings,
2.5–3 cm (1–1½ in.) long, openly campanulate.
Calyx, ovary, style and capsule as *glischrum*.

I would make this a synonym of *glischrum* but it currently has subspecific status. Some specimens of *glischrum* have hairs on the upper leaf
surface as in *rude*. Plants in cultivation under *rude* are generally superior to
the average *glischrum* in flower and leaf. From *R* 8228 'Frank Kingdom
Ward' **AM**, 1969, Glenarn, flowers reddish-purple with crimson lines.

From Salween–Kiuchang divide, Yunnan, 3,400–3,700 m (11,000–
12,000 ft).

habrotrichum Balf.f. & W.W. Sm. 1916 H3–4 A+10 L2–3 F2–3

Ht 1.2–3 m (4–10 ft). Habit usually bushy but can become leggy with age.
Branchlets densely clad with reddish-purple glandular bristles. Bark
greyish-brown.
L 10–18 × 4–8 cm (4–7 × 1½–3 in.), elliptic or rarely elliptic-oblong,
apex abruptly acuminate, base cordate or rounded, margin with stalked
glands, slightly rugose above. L remain for 2 years. Petiole thick dense
reddish-purple bristles.
Inflor to twenty usually compact, rachis short. Pedicels about 2 cm glandular. F plum-rose to clear rose to white striped pink, spotted crimson; to
5 cm (2 in.) long, funnel-campanulate.
Calyx about 1.5 cm glandular-ciliate, five distinct lobes. Ovary densely
glandular, style glandular lower third.

This close ally of *glischrum* is usually more attractive in both flower and
foliage, the latter because of the coloured bristles. The leaves are broader
and shorter than *glischrum* and the leaf underside less glandular. Plants in
cultivation seem quite uniform. Just deserves to retain its specific rank.
Badly scorched in Oregon in 1972 freeze. **AM**, 1933, Sunningdale
Nurseries flowers pink.

From around the Yunnan–Burma frontier, Shweli–Salween area and
farther north, 2,700–3,700 m (9,000–12,000 ft) in open situations, thickets and among rocks. April–May

recurvoides Tagg & Ward 1932 see *Dwarf Rhododendrons* (*p.* 167) and
The Smaller Rhododendrons (*p.* 156).

vesiculiferum Tagg 1931 H3–4 L2–3 F2–3

Ht to 3 m (10 ft). Branchlets densely bristly.
L 8–16 × 2.5–5 cm (3–6 × 1–2 in), oblong-lanceolate to oblong-

oblanceolate, apex abruptly acuminate, base rounded to cordulate, margin ciliate, very hairy below especially on midrib, a few glandular hairs above at first making it sticky, bullate, base of midrib bristly. Petiole with bristles and white hairs.

Inflor seven to fifteen usually loose, rachis about 1 cm. Pedicels about 2.5 cm very glandular plus a few white hairs.

F almost white through pink to rosy-purple with deep blotch, 3–3.5 cm 1–1½ in.) long, campanulate.

Calyx about 1 cm very glandular, purplish with long lobes. Ovary with long stalked glands and shorter hairs, style stalked glands and hairy in lower third.

This is closely related to *glischrum* and its ssp. *glischroides*. The foliage is quite impressive but botanically and horticulturally it lies too close to these two to be of much consequence. 'High Flier' **AM**, 1968, Crown Lands.

From Yunnan and Burma–Tibet border, 2,400–3,400 m (8,000–11,000 ft) in thickets and *Abies-Rhododendron* forest. Distribution similar to ssp. *glischroides*.   April–May

GRANDIA SUBSECTION (GRANDE SERIES) (E)

Many species in this subsection have foliage reaching the utmost grandeur in the whole genus, also several are of very large stature. This subsection is closely allied to the Falconera subsection and should perhaps be amalgamated with it. Merging takes place in the *basilicum*, *rothschildii*, *semnoides*, *praestans* and *coryphaeum* alliance.

The chief characters are the plastered or fine woolly indumentum, the oblique or ventricose corolla with seven to ten lobes, a very small calyx, fourteen to twenty stamens and a tomentose ovary (except *watsonii*).

On account of their large leaves and stature, all need very sheltered positions and plenty of room to grow to their full glory. All take a number of years to bloom but their grand foliage, amongst the finest of all outdoor evergreens in this country, more than compensates for the lack of flowers in their early years. These are plants from heavy rainfall areas which need abundant moisture and humidity for good growth. They do *not* need heavy shade in places like the wetter parts of west Scotland with low summer temperatures. There, they will make better specimens if not drawn up below trees. These are plants for posterity; there are specimens of this and the Falconera subsections to be seen in British gardens well over 100 years old.

They look magnificent when viewed from above or across a valley but loose their effect when drawn up when the leaves and flowers can only be seen from below.

Members of this subsection are generally more tender than those of the Falconera, the majority being only really successful in the moister sheltered southern and western British gardens. All are susceptible to prolonged heat and strong sunshine. The 1955 and 1972 freezes in northwest North America hit this subsection very badly, with most being killed or severely damaged.

In the wild, the forest canopy can be made up entirely by these plants or they may be mixed up with other trees of a similar stature. Several extend to the tree line or a little higher. Distribution is from east Nepal to west Szechwan.

This subsection appears to fall into the following groups:

(1) *magnificum*, *protistum* very tender with early growth
(2) *praestans*, fairly hardy
(3) *grande*, *sidereum* tender, *grande* has early growth
(4) *montroseanum*, *pudorosum* moderately hardy
(5) *macabeanum*, *sinogrande* moderately hardy
(6) *watsonii* very hardy
(7) *watti* probably not in cultivation
(8) *wightii* hardy

Groups (1) and (2) are distinct enough and possibly there is only one broad spectrum species covering each; (3), (4) and (5) could be grouped wrongly. They are all fairly closely related and could be included in one group.

This grouping is largely my own unofficial arrangement. The inclusion of *wightii* is somewhat tentative and ahead of RBG, Edinburgh publications. See *p.* 354–5.

R. grande

praestans Balf.f. & W.W. Sm. (*coryphaeum* Balf.f. & Forr., *semnum* Balf.f. & Forr.) 1916 H4 L2–3 F2–3

Ht 6–9 m (20–30 ft), usually much less in cultivation. Bark light to dark brown, flaking.

L 18–38 × 7–14 cm (7–15 × 3–5½ in.), oblong-oblanceolate to oblong-obovate, apex rounded, base *cuneate*, *tapered*, typically plastered indumentum below, grey-white to fawn, sometimes slightly scurfy (near *basilicum*).

L remain for 2 to 4 years. Petiole *short and broad, flattish above.*

Inflor fifteen to thirty-two, rachis 2–4 cm, stout. Pedicel 4–5 cm, tomentose.

F white, white flushed pink, creamy-pink to magenta-rose or white flushed magenta-rose, with deep blotch, 3.5–4.5 cm (1½–2 in.) long, oblique-campanulate, eight lobes.

Calyx minute, tomentose. Stamens sixteen. Ovary tomentose, style glabrous.

Seems to be identical with *coryphaeum*, apart from some forms having deeper coloured flowers. The difference in flower colour used by Tagg to separate *coryphaeum* from *praestans* is of little significance especially since the flower colours of the respective type specimens are not known. Both have leaves tapered to the base and broad winged petioles, a character only shared by the *basilicum*, *semnoides*, *rothschildii* alliance and *watsonii*. This is one of the most wind resistant and hardy of the subsection and with a little protection, it forms a dense shrub with fine foliage. The best forms are those of a rich colour or white while the washy pinks are generally poor. Reasonably hardy in south Sweden. 'Sunte Rock' *PC* 1969 *R* 59480 Sunte House.

North-west and west Yunnan, Upper Burma, south-east Tibet, 2,700–4,300 m (9,000–14,000 ft), open conifer forests, shady cliffs.

March–May

R. *magnificum* and *protistum* in cultivation. It is sad that these dignified and handsome plants can only be grown successfully in a few of the most favoured gardens on the western seaboard of Britain. Not only are the early growth and flowers liable to be blasted by frost and the large leaves torn to shreds in the wind, but they are just not winter hardy below about −12°C (+10°F) for a day or two or −6°C (+20°F) for a longer spell (midwinter only).

The finest collection of these plants is to be seen at Brodick Castle, Isle of Arran and I was lucky enough to see them in full bloom on the 1 March 1976. As they are mostly unlabelled and unnumbered, it was necessary to come to one's own conclusions as to botanical relationships and how they fit into the categories of the present specific names. This is far from easy. I divided them into three groups, largely according to foliage as the flowers were reluctant to fit into any pattern.

(A) Wide leaves, usually completely lacking indumentum, rugose above, growth buds often red-tipped and beginning to elongate. No signs of ever having flowered. Fine foliage plants.

(B) Leaves rather similar to above but slightly narrower and often with a band of indumentum around the edge of the leaf underside but with others covered with a uniform pale brown indumentum, similar to C. Growth buds usually green. Most of these plants were flowering.

(C) Leaves of narrow to medium width, a darker green and less rugose above. The indumentum is ± plastered but never to the extent of *sidereum* and *montroseanum* and seems to be in two layers (Cowan says only one layer) with a ± loose upper layer sometimes in the form of dots or tufts. Growth is a little later.

A may just be an immature version of B although the plants are of a similar size and age and both are presumably *protistum* (*giganteum*). C tends to overlap with B but deserves some botanical status and fits our idea of *magnificum*. None have so far developed the woolly indumentum found on some herbarium specimens although they could do so yet. It is apparent that these plants (the old *giganteum* anyway) take longer to mature than any other rhododendron and are potentially the longest lived. They could be termed the elephants of the genus *Rhododendron*.

There is a great variation in the time these plants take to start flowering and there is a definite correlation between the forming of at least some indumentum and the production of flowers. *R. protistum* (*giganteum*) first flowered in cultivation at Arduaine, Argyll in 1936 in about 15 years from seed. In Australia it first flowered in 1971 at about 48 years old having started to form an indumentum 4 to 5 years prior to flowering. *R. magnificum* (C) generally forms indumentum and flowers younger. None are likely to ever reach 30 m (100 ft) in cultivation unless drawn up between large trees like the tallest specimens are in the wild.

Some clones have much superior flowers to others. The best have magnificent deep rose to crimson-purple flowers in full trusses which retain their colour well while others are of a washy colour and have a poor floppy truss. The young growth is most attractive with the elongating bud-like scarlet candles. It is odd that the earlier growing *protistum* tends to bloom later than the later growing *magnificum*.

J. Basford, head gardener at Brodick, says that these plants produce a smaller root system with thicker roots than most rhododendrons and should be planted (finally) early in life. If given space, they form a wide bush, broader than high, clothed to the ground for many years.

I will never forget seeing flourishing plants of this group growing in a shaded dell at the University of California garden at Berkley just 30 m (100 ft) away from their cactus garden in full sun. Where else in the world could this combination of moisture and drought loving plants be found growing successfully in such close proximity? Other areas in which they grow to their prime are the damper, milder parts of New Zealand.

protistum Balf.f. & Forr. 1920 (*giganteum* Forr. & Tagg 1926) H1–3 L2–4 F2–4

Ht to 24 or even 30 m (to 80 or 100 ft) in the wild, 2.1 m (7 ft) in girth, much less in cultivation, about 6 m (20 ft) so far. Habit, usually forms a large rounded shrub in the open, rarely tree-like in cultivation so far. Branchlets thin greyish-tomentose. Bright scarlet bud-scales, *growth very early*. Bark dark brown, roughish. Leaf buds prominent, elongated with conspicuous bud-scales (also in *magnificum*).

L to 56 × 25 cm (22 × 10 in.) on young plants, elliptic to oblanceolate, apex broadly acute, base narrowed, slightly auricled, *mat green, often rugulose above*, very variable below, often taking very many years to develop a thin to thicker indumentum which is usually greyish-brown, many semi-mature plants still have no indumentum at all or a band on the margin and are mat-green below. L remain for 2 years. Petiole stout, 2.5–4 cm.

Inflor twenty to thirty compact or lax, rachis stout 4.5 cm. Pedicel 2–3 cm tomentose.

F washy pink, pale to deep rose, mauve-pink, purple, crimson-rose to crimson-purple or creamy-white flushed rose, sometimes two-tone, pale and darker, 6–7.5 cm (2½–3 in.) long, and broad, funnel-campanulate *not ventricose*, with nectar pouches, lobes eight.

Calyx 2–3 mm tomentose. Stamens sixteen. Ovary densely tomentose, style glabrous, stout, stigma yellow or rarely red.

Specimens collected in the wild under the name *protistum* had largely glabrous leaves, although the plants were mature enough to bloom. In all probability the lack of indumentum (as seen in cultivation) has in this case little taxonimic significance. As *protistum* was described first, the better known and much more splendid name *giganteum* sadly has to go and I doubt if any horticultural distinction can enable us to retain it as a Group name. The typical *giganteum* as we all used to know it, was the 24–30 m (80–100 ft) giant, collected at low elevations.

FCC, 1953, *F* 19335 Brodick (as *giganteum*).

West Yunnan, Upper Burma, 2,700–4,000 m (9,000–13,000 ft) in open and heavy forest. February–March

protistum (*giganteum*) var. *seminudum* Tagg 1926. This has a band of indumentum around the leaf underside margin only (see B above). While an interesting phenomenon, I reckon that this feature has little botanical significance, although high altitude forms tend to have the most extreme foliage of var. *seminudum*.

magnificum Ward 1935 H2–3 L3–4 F2–4

Ht to fully 18 m (60 ft) in the wild, 6 m (20 ft) so far in cultivation. Bark ashy-white (Adung *KW*), dark brown in cultivation. Wine-red young leaves on young plants (Adung *KW*).

L to 46 × 23 cm (18 × 9 in.), oblong to oblong-obovate, longer and narrower than *protistum*, *thin grey to fawn plastered indumentum* below with floccose white hairs, often evanescent on maturity. L remain for 2 to 3 years.

Inflor to thirty, floppy and open topped to compact and dome shaped.

F pale to deep rose to rich purple and deep reddish-purple, 7.5 cm (3 in.) long, 6.3 cm (2½ in.) across, tubular-campanulate, *not ventricose*.

Calyx 4 mm–1.7 cm, uneven.

Appears to be nearer to *protistum* as we knew it (herbarium specimens) than the old *giganteum* in foliage and distribution.

Hardier and more floriferous than *protistum* at Brodick, the trusses are often larger. Does reasonably at Windsor (*KW* 21602). *KW* 13681 at Nymans has a noticeable fawn indumentum on long, narrow leaves, rugose above and rose coloured flowers with no blotch, still flowering in May 1975. Not typical. The type is *KW* 9200 of which there is only scanty herbarium material. There are many plants of this species at Mount Stewart, Northern Ireland. 'Kildonan' **FCC**, 1966, *KW* 9200 fuchsine-pink flowers Brodick.

Burma–Tibet frontier, Adung, 1,500–2,400 m (5,000–8,000 ft) in rhododendron and mixed forest, scattered, common but never truly gregarious.   February–March occasionally to May

grande Wight 1847 (*argenteum* Hook.f., *longifolium* Nutt., *Waldemarea argentea* Klotzsch.) H2–3 L2–3 F2–4

Ht 6–15 m (20–50 ft). Habit a loosely branched tree, often with a single trunk, to 60 cm (2 ft) in diameter at base. Bark rough, flaking medium-brown. Large rounded terminal buds with tightly appressed bud-scales.
L 15–46 × 8–13 cm (6–18 × 3–5 in.), oblong-lanceolate to oblanceolate to oblong-elliptic, apex obtuse to acuminate, base narrowed, obtuse to cuneate, slightly rugulose above, indumentum below plastered or loose woolly, white, *silvery* to fawn. L remain for 2 to 3 years. Petiole 4–5 cm thin whitish tomentose.
Inflor twenty to twenty-five usually rounded, rachis 4–5 cm. Pedicel 2–3 cm glandular, ± floccose. F cream, pale yellow to pink to deep rose with purple blotch and spots, 5–7 cm (2–3 in.) long, ventricose-campanulate, nectar pouches, lobes eight, sometimes scented.
Calyx short 1–2 mm. Ovary densely glandular ± tomentose, style stout, glabrous or few glands at base, stigma large, deep pink.

A fine plant in the few British gardens in which it can be well grown. The flowers are of nice, clean shades and there are lovely pink bud-scales on the young growth.

Most forms grow too early in the season, leading to frosted or distorted growth. The mature leaves are sensitive to wind damage and fail to acclimatize to lack of shelter. Only the most sheltered, mildest gardens are suitable for most forms. Very variable in foliage and flower, hence its synonyms. Related to *sidereum*. **FCC**, 1901, South Lodge.

East Nepal, Sikkim, Bhutan, south Tibet, and Arunachal Pradesh, 2,100–3,200 m (7,000–10,500 ft), evergreen and mixed forest, river banks, very common in Arunachal Pradesh (Subansiri Division) in dense temperate rain-forest covered in moss.   February–April

sidereum Balf.f. 1920 H2–3 A+5 to +15 L2–3 F2–4

Ht 6–9 m (20–30 ft). Habit erect to rounded. Branchlets unusually thin for this subsection with grey plastered tomentum. Bark greeny-brown, flaking.
L 9–23 × 3–7 cm (4–9 × 1–3 in.), oblong-elliptic, oblong-oblanceolate to oblong-lanceolate, apex acute to obtuse, base tapered usually cuneate,

mat grey above, indumentum below *silver-white to fawn* ± *plastered*. L remain for 2 to 5 years. Petiole 1.5–2.5 cm.

Inflor fifteen to twenty usually open topped, rachis 5–6 cm. Pedicel about 3 cm fawn tomentose.

F *creamy-yellow to primrose or clear yellow*, creamy-white to pale pink, with crimson ring or blotch in throat, about 5 cm (2 in.) long, 6.3 cm (2½ in.) across, ventricose-campanulate, lobes eight.

Calyx rim-like, oblique, tomentose. Stamens sixteen. Ovary densely tomentose, style glabrous. Capsule curved with grey to tawny tomentum.

A very rewarding yellow flowered species, hardy enough for most well sheltered western and southern British gardens although some forms are more tender than others. The leaves are small for the subsection and at first sight, the whole plant may appear like a large leaved *arboreum*. Various forms occur in cultivation, varying in leaf size and shape, flower colour, habit and horticultural value. The leaves may hang down for a greater part of the year than most other species. It is sometimes capable of sprouting from a stump after a hard winter. Said to be resistant to *Phytophthora*. Some forms open pale pink turning to a good shade of yellow with age. A free flowering plant makes a very fine sight, flowering as it does after most other large-leaved species are over.

Closely related to *grande* which usually has larger leaves and flowers and a much earlier blooming period and growth. It is possible that these two could either merge or hybridize naturally if and where their flowering period overlaps in Arunachal Pradesh. 'GlenRosa' **AM**, primrose yellow Brodick, 1964.

Arunachal Pradesh, Upper Burma and west Yunnan, 2,400–3,700 m (8,000–12,000 ft), in mixed and conifer forests, sometimes open, among other large rhododendrons, hemlock, maples and birch.   May–June

montroseanum Davidian 1979 (*mollyanum* Cowan & Davidian 1954) H2–3 A+15 to +5 L3–4 F2–4

Ht 12–15 m (40–50 ft) in the wild, to 9 m (30 ft) in cultivation so far. Bark very rough, dark brown, flaking. Bud-scales red.

L to 46 × 23 cm (18 × 9 in.) in cultivation, to 60 cm (2 ft) long in the wild, oblong to oblanceolate, apex rounded, base obtuse to narrowed, thick and rigid, *rugulose*, *dark green* and shiny above, indumentum below *silver to* silvery-white, plastered, shiny. L remain for 1 to 2 years. Petiole 2–4 cm sometimes slightly winged, thin grey tomentose.

Inflor about fifteen fairly compact to looser, rachis 2.5–3 cm. Pedicel 3–5 cm densely fawn tomentose.

F pale pink through a clear pink to purplish-pink, crimson veined and with a crimson blotch (*L&S* 13568 (not introduced) had white to pale mauve spotted flowers), 5 cm (2 in.) long, ventricose-companulate, lobes eight wavy margins.

Calyx short 1 mm, tomentose. Stamens sixteen. Ovary densely fawn tomentose, style glabrous.

A very fine recently named species, previously classified as a form of *sinogrande*. The best forms have the most beautiful pink flowers of any of the large species but some are definitely inferior. The leaves vary in shape but are amongst the most handsome of all. The name *mollianum* had been used earlier. This was considered too like *mollyanum* so the name *montroseanum* has been given instead.

The leaves are intermediate between *sinogrande* and *grande*, being larger and more coriaceous than *grande* and smaller and usually narrower than *sinogrande*. Has sixteen stamens while *sinogrande* has eighteen to twenty. The growth does not start until May. We find it slightly less winter hardy than *sinogrande* but generally hardier than *grande*. We lost it in 1981–2 at Glendoick, largely due to bark-split. 'Benmore' **FCC** 1957, lovely pink stained deeper, small blotch, Younger Botanic Garden, Benmore.

Described from *KW* 6261A from the Tsangpo Gorge, south-east Tibet, 2,400–2,700 m (8,000–9,000 ft), abundant, forming 50 per cent of part of the temperate rain-forest.   February–March

pudorosum Cowan H3–4 L2–3 F2–3

Ht 6–12 m (20–40 ft) in the wild. Slow growing so far in cultivation. *Bud scales persistent for 2 to several years*, giving stems a shaggy appearance. Bark roughish, brown.
L 8–30 × 3–12 cm (3–12 × 1–5 in.), oblanceolate to oblong, margins recurved, apex obtuse, base rounded to cordulate, usually glabrous above, indumentum below very slow to develop and even inclined to be absent on mature wild plants, when present it is slightly spongy but ± plastered. L remain for 2 to 3 years. Petiole stout 2.5–3 cm tomentose.
Inflor 16–25 cm, fairly compact, rachis 3 cm. Pedicel 2–3 cm rufous floccose.
F *bright pink to rose* or mauve-pink, with deep blotch, 3–3.5 cm (1¼–1½ in.) long, ventricose-campanulate, sometimes fragrant.
Calyx very small 2 mm. Stamens sixteen glabrous. Ovary white tommentose, not glandular, style glabrous rose to pink.

This species, very rare in cultivation, seems to be related to *montroseanum*, but is readily recognized by its persistent bud-scales.

I know of only three original plants in the RBG, Edinburgh which were no more than 1.2–1.5 m (4–5 ft) high at 37 years old when they first flowered in 1972, but the site is poor and dry. The flowers are beautiful shades of rose. The plant is evidently hardier than *montroseanum* which would be expected, coming from a considerably higher altitude. It is hoped that this species will become much more widespread in cultivation.

From Tsari and Chayul Chu, south Tibet, 3,400–3,800 m (11,000–12,500 ft) common in rhododendron and fir forest and about the upper limit of bamboo, often in shady sites; four *L&S* numbers, seed collected under *L&S* 2752 only, in 1936.
                              Flowered mid-March 1974, an early spring

macabeanum Watt ex Balf.f. 1920 H3–4 A+15 to +5 L3–4 F3–4

Ht to 14 m (45 ft) in the wild, 3–9 m (10–30 ft) in cultivation so far. Habit usually flat topped. Branchlets stout, tomentose. Bark rough, light brown.

L to 30 × 20 cm (12 × 8 in.), oblong-elliptic to broadly oval, apex rounded, base obtuse to rounded, usually *dark green and shiny above* ± vestiges of indumentum, indumentum below usually *white to greyish-cream* but sometimes fawn, pale buff, greyish-brown or orangy-fawn, *compact woolly*, some more woolly than others. This indumentum may take several years to develop and may be patchy at first. L remain for 1 to 2 years. Petiole about 2.5 cm ± tomentose.

Inflor to thirty, usually compact, sometimes rather floppy. Pedicel stout, about 2 cm white tomentose.

F *yellow to yellowish-white*, purple blotch, 5–7.5 cm (2–3 in.) long, ventricose-companulate, lobes eight.

Calyx almost obsolete, tomentose. Stamens sixteen, anthers black. Ovary tomentose, style glabrous, stigma orange-brown to bright red, large.

One of the finest of all species and surprisingly hardy, considering its low altitude in the wild. Starts to bloom earlier than most big-leaved species and is well worth attempting in all sheltered lowland gardens in Britain. Flowers consistently in the RBG, Edinburgh.

The expanding growth buds look like red candles and these develop into beautiful silvery young growth with contrasting bright scarlet bud-scales. The huge yellow trusses of the better forms are truly magnificent and it is usually noticeable that the better flowered forms also have the best foliage. The paler flowered forms should be avoided.

It varies appreciably, considering its limited natural distribution. Leaf shape, flower colour and shape all vary as does the colour and development of the indumentum. This juvenile stage with little or no indumentum can sometimes be seen on young growth sprouting from the trunks of mature specimens. A very distinct species; the combination of large yellow blotched flowers and dark green rounded shiny leaves with greyish-white indumentum below cannot be found in any other species. It is an easily grown plant able to withstand wind, frost and drought somewhat better than its near relatives. It will bloom successfully under trees but the habit will become leggy. **AM**, 1937 and **FCC**, 1938, Trengwainton.   March–May

Manipur and Nagaland only (so far), 2,400–2,700 m (8,000–9,000 ft), fairly common in the upper forest on steep slopes including the summit of Japvo, accompanied only by birch and forms almost pure stands by itself.

sinograndе Balf.f. & W.W. Sm. 1916 H3 occasionally 4 A+5 to +15 L4 F3–4

Ht to 12 m (40 ft) or more in the wild, to 9 m (30 ft) in cultivation so far. Habit tree-like with wide lower branches. Branchlets stout, thin grey tomentose. Bark roughish, greenish-brown or brown.

L *to 90 cm (3 ft) long* on vigorous young plants and 8–30 cm (3–12 in.) wide, oblong-lanceolate to oblong-elliptic, rarely to oval, apex obtuse to rounded, base cuneate to semi-rounded, *shiny and rugose above* sometimes with patchy persistent indumentum, indumentum below ± plastered, silvery to buff. L remain for 2 to 4 years. Petiole stout 3–5 cm.

Inflor twenty to fifty +, fairly compact, rachis thick 3–6 cm. Pedicel stout, dense felty-buff tomentose.

F creamy-white, creamy-yellow to pale yellow, with crimson blotch, 6.3–7.5 cm (2½–3 in.) long, ventricose-campanulate, lobes eight to ten. Calyx small, fleshy, tomentose. Stamens eighteen to twenty. Ovary densely tomentose, style glabrous, stigma large.

This magnificent plant with huge elephants ear leaves, the largest in the genus, has huge trusses to match. It does of course need shelter to attain its full glory. However, under moist, mild conditions, it may be planted in a fairly sunny position with plenty of space. A beautifully shaped specimen will result, often wider than high. The largest foliage is produced on healthy young plants growing under damp, rather shady conditions. It is rare that the best foliage for showing purposes goes with the best truss. Very variable in size and shape of leaves, some being almost round. Takes many years to bloom, especially on strong growing specimens in shade. Slow growing under dry east coast conditions. The time of growth varies greatly and in cold, dry areas the very late growers can be severely damaged so try to obtain the earlier growing forms.

We find this species surprisingly hardy in east Scotland once it gets over the tender juvenile stage at 5 to 6 years old. Two plants survived over 40 years but were killed in the 1981–2 winter. Not permanently successful in Oregon and Washington states.

It first flowered in cultivation on a forced and badly checked plant indoors in the RBG, Edinburgh. This unfortunate plant which was planted in the old (now destroyed) rhododendron house, never looked healthy since I first saw it. It took nearly 40 years to bloom again after its first effort: One of the earliest trusses opened out of doors was proudly born down Princes Street, Edinburgh en route for the RBG in April 1933 by Johnnie Holms of Larachmhor, Inverness-shire.

This species has the possibly unusual character of covering itself with flower simultaneously all over Britain from Inverewe, Ross-shire to Cornwall. I noticed this one year which was actually an off season of flowering for most other large species. Other species do have the same trait but with *sinogrande* it is more obvious as it only blooms really freely every 2 to 3 years. **AM**, 1922, South Lodge, Sussex, **FCC**, 1926 Trewithen. Re-introduced 1981, hopefully a hardier form.

East Arunachal Pradesh, Yunnan, Upper Burma, south-east Tibet, 2,100–4,300 m (7,000–14,000 ft), quite widespread and common in the wild in rhododendron, bamboo and mixed forest and uppermost rain-forest. Often slow growing (wild) with trunks frequently gnarled, bent and twisted.   April–May

sinogrande Boreale Group (var. *boreale*)

L perhaps smaller than type, indumentum similar range to type.
F clear pale yellow, *no blotch* (other herbarium specimens out of flower could also lack a blotch). Is in cultivation and may be hardier than type and possibly deserves to retain Group status.

More flowering specimens would need to be collected from the whole range of the species to prove if this is a good geographical variety. This has been collected in the northern part of the range of the species and at high altitudes.

Tsarong, south-east Tibet, 3,700–4,300 m (12,000–14,000 ft) in rhododendron forest and thickets.

watsonii Hemsl. & Wils. 1910 H4 L2–3 F1–2

Ht 2–6 m (7–20 ft). Habit usually a shrub rather than tree-like. Branchlets with scattered grey to fawn tomentum, stout. Bark greyish.
L 15–23 × 5–10 cm (6–9 × 2–4 in.), obovate oblong-elliptic to oblanceolate, apex usually obtusely rounded, base tapered ± rounded, midrib above often prominent, yellow, indumentum below ± plastered silvery-fawn but can be rubbed off and is sometimes glabrous. L remain for 1 to 2 years. *Petiole winged, very short.*
Inflor about fifteen, fairly loose, small for the subsection, rachis 3–5 cm. Pedicel 3–5 cm thinly tomentose.
F white or white flushed pink, spotted maroon, with or without blotch, 3–5 cm (1¼–2 in.) long, campanulate, lobes seven.
Calyx oblique, minute, glabrous to thinly tomentose. Stamens fourteen filaments puberulous. Ovary *glabrous*, style glabrous, stigma small.

This is undoubtedly the hardiest of the subsection but is unfortunately also the poorest in flower. The foliage is not impressive compared with some of the others but is worth growing in cold areas. For this subsection, it is very much an outlyer in its wild location and in its characters, perhaps showing some affinity with *calophytum*. Hardy enough for all sheltered British gardens and even parts of south Sweden.

North-west Szechwan only, 2,600–3,400 m (8,500–11,000 ft), in woods and thin conifer forest.   February–April

wattii Cowan 1936 Probably not in cultivation

Ht 3–6 m (10–20 ft)
L 5–15 × 2.5–5 cm (2–6 × 1–2 in.), oblong-ovate to elliptic to oblong to oblong-ovate, bullate above, brown beneath, convex.
Inflor sixteen in rounded truss.
F pink and purple with deep spots, 5 cm (2 in.) long, six to seven lobed.

Only known from type locality. From the plate at the RBG, Edinburgh drawn by Watt in the field, this plant is probably better placed in this subsection than in the Arborea subsection. The seven-lobed and more ventricose shaped corolla indicates this to be correct. Plants raised from seed collected by Watt at the type locality have a scarlet five lobed corolla, usually a more developed calyx and leaves from 6.5–12 cm (2½–5 in.) long. These plants were described as *arboreum* var. *kingianum* Hook.f. 1900 and are almost certainly hybrids with *arboreum* or *delavayi* and probably *wattii* as parents. The possibility arises that *wattii* itself is also a hybrid between *arboreum* and a member of subsection Grandia but there is no evidence to support this. On the unexplored peak of Saramati, nearby, unknown species may easily occur.

Other plants in cultivation under the name *kingianum* are *arboreum* ssp. *zelanicum*, these two often having been confused. The flowers of *kingianum* are said to be later than *zelanicum* but as many of the latter bloom into August, this claim is doubtful.

Rare in the wild in Manipur, east India, at 2,700 m (11,000 ft).

wightii Hook.f. 1851 H4 A+5 L2–3 F2–3

Ht 2–6 m (7–20 ft). Habit usually open and ungainly, sometimes tree-like. Young shoots almost white. Bark grey.
L 9–25 × 3.5–6.5 cm (3½–10 × 1½–2½ in.), 2–2.5 times as long as broad, broadly elliptic to obovate, apex rounded to shortly acuminate, base cuneate to rounded, indumentum fairly thin and moderately smooth below, buff to rich rusty colour, in two layers. L remain for 1 to 2 years. Petiole 1–2.5 cm sparsely tomentose or glabrescent.
Inflor twelve to twenty *lax one-sided truss*, rachis 1–5.5 cm. Pedicel 1.5–3 cm tomentose.
F pale to lemon-yellow with brown, red or purple spots and sometimes a crimson blotch, 4–4.5 cm (1½–1¾ in.) long, campanulate.
Calyx about 0.5 mm ± glabrous. Ovary densely red-brown tomentose, style glabrous.

A very distinct species which apparently varies little except in size of plant and truss which is according to elevation in the wild. The loose lopsided truss rather reduces its horticultural value as does its ungainly habit but it is none the less worth growing. While RBG Edinburgh places this species tentatively in the Taliensia subsection, it is freely admitted that it would be just as happily included in this subsection. It is one of the hardiest yellow-flowered species, being hardy with shelter throughout Britain and it survived the 1955 and 1972 freezes in Oregon and Washington states with no damage.
AM, 1913, pale sulphur-yellow, crimson blotch.

From east Nepal, Sikkim, Bhutan, 3,400–4,300 m (11,000–14,000 ft), often common especially above the tree line, forming dense thickets in the higher valleys, frequently on stony ground and covering whole hillsides. The truss is not always lopsided in the wild. See *p.* 354.

peregrinum Tagg 1930   April–May

Ht 3 m (10 ft) at Windsor Great Park.
L thin scurfy indumentum above, silvery-white slightly scurfy indumentum below. L wider than *galactinum*. F white.

This appeared as a rogue from the seed of *W* 4254 (*galactinum*) and could be a natural hybrid between *watsonii* and *galactinum*. Only appeared as a seedling at Lamellen, Cornwall so should never have been named.

GRIERSONIANA SUBSECTION (GRIERSONIANUM SERIES) (E)
griersonianum Balf.f. & Forr. 1919 H3–4 A+10 L2–3 F3–4

Ht 1.5–3 m (5–10 ft). Habit usually loose and often leggy. Branchlets densely to moderately bristly-glandular and floccose. Winter bud-scales elongated to well beyond the bud. Bark rough, brown.
L 6.4–20 × 1.2–5.3 cm (2½–8 × ½–2¼ in.), lanceolate, apex acute, base

R. griersonianum

obtuse, with *continuous* or occasionally patchy *fawn to light brown indumentum below*. L remain for 2 to 3 years. Petiole 1–3.5 cm glandular and floccose.

Inflor five to twelve usually loose, rachis 1–4 cm. Pedicel 1.6–4 cm deep red, glandular and tomentose.

F usually bright geranium-scarlet in cultivation (but said to vary from bright rose, soft geranium with vermilion shades to rich soft crimson in the wild; this is according to the native collectors as F himself never saw the fresh flowers) with or without spots, 5–8 cm (2–3 in.) long, funnel-shaped, hairy outside.

Calyx small 2–3 mm, tomentose and glandular. Stamens ten unequal, filaments deep red. Ovary densely white tomentose ± glandular, style deep red ± glandular and floccose at base.

This very distinct plant with its glowing freely produced flowers of unusual colour, is in the parentage of many of our best floriferous hybrids but it is certainly worth growing for its own merit. It is one of the most free flowering medium sized species, blooming in 5 years from seed. This valuable character plus its unique colour has given rise to such excellent F1 hybrids as 'Elizabeth', 'May Day', 'Vanessa' and many equally good F2 or subsequent generation hybrids.

While rather tender in most British gardens, it is worth attempting in the majority of sheltered lowland areas near the coast, avoiding frost pockets. It becomes hardier at flowering size. We find it susceptible to bark-split but it still carries on growing and flowering freely. Stands hot, sunny and dry conditions with surprising success and can also tolerate shade which lengthens its blooming season, although it is considered hardier in plenty of light. Can be pruned into compact bushes in mild localities such as coastal Cornwall. Not closely related to any other species. Very glandular (sticky). **FCC**, 1924.

West Yunnan and Burma–Yunnan frontier at 2,100–2,700 m (7,000–9,000 ft) in open situations in conifer and mixed forest, thickets and open glades amongst shrubs. Quite uniform with a small distribution. F reported that it grew as a symmetrical shrub in open country.

June–July (August in shade)

HELIOLEPIDA SUBSECTION (HELIOLEPIS SERIES) (L)

Evergreen shrubs or small trees to 9 m (30 ft). Bark grey to reddish-brown, roughish, uninteresting. Leaves densely scaly, usually very aromatic, only remaining on for 1 year. Several flowered terminal inflorescence. Flowers violet, mauve, rose, lavender to white, more or less funnel-shaped, corolla scaly outside, calyx very small. Stamens ten, usually pubescent towards base, ovary very scaly, style glabrous or pubescent towards base. All are polyploids, 2n = 52, 78 and 104.

Fairly closely related to the Triflora subsection but more heavily scaly and corolla always scaly outside; also related to the Scabrifolia and Caroliniana subsections.

These are mostly vigorous, easily grown plants, succeeding in a wide variation of soils including those often too dry or too heavy for most rhododendrons. They do not burn readily from heat in the San Francisco

R. rubiginosum

Bay area and the majority are hardy to fairly hardy in British gardens although *rubiginosum* is said to be intolerant of heat in other areas.

bracteatum Rehd. and Wils. 1913 H4 L1–2 F1–2

Ht about 1.8 m (6 ft). Branchlets not scaly. Persistent bracts in place of leaves on lower part of branchlets.
L 3.8–5 × 2–2.5 cm (1½–2 × ¾–1 in.), ovate-elliptic, rounded at base, scaly above, scales below one to two times their own diameter apart, unequal. Petiole 6 mm, sparingly scaly.
Inflor three to four. Pedicel slender 2 cm (¾ in.) with a few scattered scales.
F white or white flushed rose, with large maroon blotch and spots, 2 cm (¾ in.) long, campanulate, laxly scaly all over the outside, tube pubescent within.
Calyx about 2 mm, scaly. Ovary densely scaly, style a few hairs near base.

A neat plant but the flowers are rather small. Appears to be fairly well established in cultivation. Foliage smells like black currants when crushed. This distinct species, smaller in all its parts than the rest of the subsection, was formerly placed in the Oreotrephes sub-series of the Triflora subsection. From *W* 3421 (type) and 4253. Re-introduced, 1986.

Wild in north-west Szechwan only, Mupin and Wen-ch'uan Hsien, 2,100–3,000 m (7,000–10,000 ft), on cliffs and in woodlands.   June

heliolepis Franch. 1887 H(3)–4 A−5 L1–2 F1–3

Ht 2–4.5 m (6–15 ft). Habit usually compact but may become leggy with age. Branchlets scaly.
L 7.6–11 × 2.2–3.8 cm (3–4½ × ¾–1½ in.), oblong, ovate-oblong to oblong-elliptic, cuneate to rounded at base, scales below 1½ times their own diameter apart. Petiole 1.3 cm (½ in.) scaly.
Inflor four to ten. Pedicel 1.3 cm, densely scaly.
F white, off white, faintly flushed rose, soft to deep rose, cherry-red, rosy-purple to dull violet, the many spots may merge into a blotch, 2.5–3.8 cm (1–1½ in.) long, campanulate to widely funnel-shaped, scaly outside.
Calyx short 2 mm, loosely scaly. Ovary densely scaly, style as long as stamens, pubescent in lower half.

The best forms are useful and somewhat neglected late flowering plants. While not exactly spectacular in flower, they are pretty in a quiet way and are usually hardy and easily grown although one plant of ours has suffered from bark-split. Apart from white forms, the paler colours are the poorest. The very aromatic foliage varies much in strength and odour, some are sweet, others pungent and even rather nasty when crushed, while still others are hardly aromatic at all. Some are very free flowering. Survived the 1972 freeze in Oregon well. **AM**, 1954, Tower Court, white, green and brown spots (var. *heliolepis*).

From Szechwan, east Tibet, Yunnan–Tibet border, Upper Burma and north-east Yunnan, 2,400–3,800 m (8,000–12,500 ft), common and widespread in rocky gullies and conifer forest, forming even topped thickets, also on raw scree, in shade at base of cliffs and by rivers.

R. heliolepis is now divided into two varieties both of which include several former species.

heliolepis var. *brevistylum* (Franch. 1898) Cullen 1978 (*brevistylum*, *pholidotum* Balf.f. & W.W. Sm., *porrosquameum* Balf.f. & Forr.). Leaves with cuneate base, at least 2.7 cm (1⅛ in.) wide, inflor six to ten, Szechwan (mostly).

heliolepis var. *heliolepis* (*fumidum* Balf.f. & W.W. Sm., *oporinum* Balf.f. & Ward, *plebeium* Balf.f. & W.W. Sm.). Leaves with truncate or rounded base, 2.2–2.8 cm (occasionally to 3 cm) (¾–1⅛) (1¼ in.) wide, inflor five to eight, *not* Szechwan (mostly). There is some geographical mix up.

June–August

invictum Balf.f. & Farrer 1917 Not in cultivation

A frail bush of 1.20–2.1 m (4–7 ft). Inflor two. Flowers purple. Hairs on minor veins on leaf upper surface. Not uncommon in the alpine coppice of the Siku–Satanee ranges of Kansu at 2,400–2,700 m (8,000–9,000 ft), probably close to *heliolepis*.

rubiginosum Franch. 1887 (*catapastum* Balf.f. & Forr., *desquamatum* Balf.f. & Forr., *leclerei* Lévl., *leprosum*, *squarrosum* Balf.f., *stenoplastum* Balf.f. & Forr.), H3–4 A−5 to +5 L1–2 F2–3

Ht 6–9 m (20–30 ft). Habit erect to spreading, well branched. Branchlets scaly, purplish.
L 6.3–11.3 × 2.5–4.5 cm (2½–4½ × 1–1¾ in.), oblong-elliptic to elliptic-lanceolate, apex acute to acuminate, base narrowed, *rusty to brownish to brownish-green below*, *flaky* unequal sized scales, *variable* in size and shape, *dense, often overlapping*. Petiole 1.3 cm (½ in.) densely scaly.
Inflor four to eight or more in loose to moderately tight clusters. Pedicel 1.3–2.5 cm (½–1 in.) scaly.
F pale lavender-rose, lavender-purple deeper flush, deep rose-purple, pale to deep rose, mauve, pink to almost white, with purple, brown to crimson spots or flash, 3–3.8 cm (1¼–1½ in.) long, 3–5.5 cm (1¼–2¼ in.) wide, funnel to widely funnel-shaped, scaly outside, sometimes faintly scented.
Calyx very short, scaly. Ovary densely scaly, style glabrous.

A very free flowering, vigorous and wind hardy species, excellent for interior wind-breaks inside large gardens. Does particularly well with us in east Scotland reaching 6 m (20 ft) in dryish soil. Plants covered in flower are a fine sight. Will tolerate slight alkalinity if there is plenty of leafmould around its roots.

There are one or two introductions with large, wider open flowers which do not grow so tall with us. We have always called these *desquamatum* but a technical difficulty arises here. The type specimen of *desquamatum* cannot be separated from *rubiginosum* as it does not have the large, widely funnel-shaped flowers we have come to recognize horticulturally as *desquamatum*. This form is much more tender than *rubiginosum* (as we knew it) with very early easily frosted growth and a susceptibility to bark-split. At Glendoick, it lives but gets partially cut back and the growth damage leads to infrequent flowering compared with the hardier forms. A good plant for mild gardens which deserves some horticultural if not botanical status. It would appear to have a western distribution and includes Farrer 875. Plants from Rock's 1949 expedition which are average *rubiginosum*, survived the 1972 freeze in Oregon successfully. Apparently not heat resistant. 'Wakehurst' **AM**, 1960 (a hybrid) flowers in large tight trusses. **AM**, 1938, (*desquamatum*).

From Szechwan (Muli only), Yunnan, south-east Tibet, Upper Burma, common and widespread, 2,300–4,300 m (7,500–14,000 ft) in rhododendron, conifer and mixed forest, among bamboo, open thickets, hillsides and mountain pasture land, often dry; by streams in gullies and on granite boulders and limestone cliffs.

March–April

IRRORATA SUBSECTION (IRRORATUM SERIES) (E)

This is a large group of species, mostly from the China–Burma area but also the Himalayas and south into Thailand, Malaya and Sumatra. Closely related to the Barbata subsection but lacking the characteristic bristles. Also related to the Maculifera and Thomsonia subsections, although the leaf waxes do not indicate any particular affinity. Leaf upper surface usually tomentose when young, glabrous at maturity. Lower surface glabrous at maturity or with thin veil of persistent indumentum. Sessile glands usually overlying the veins. Calyx minute or cupular. Inflorescence four to twenty, usually loose, rachis 0.5–1 cm. Red glands on outside of corolla. Nectar pouches present. Stamens ten to fourteen glabrous or hairy near base. The presence or absence of glands and/or tomentum on the ovary may be of little significance while the glandular or glabrous style may be more important. Capsule cylindrical, sometimes curved. The persistent leaf indumentum may reflect no more than an increased number of glands on the young leaves.

Medium to large shrubs, the majority of which are of borderline hardiness in most British gardens. In many cases the growth is made very early and is frequently frosted. Only *aberconwayi* and *irroratum* itself can be classed as really good garden plants while certain colour forms of *anthosphaerum* are definitely ugly. All appreciate sheltered woodland conditions.

aberconwayi Cowan 1948 H4 A−15 to −5 L1–2 F2–4

Ht 1.5–2.5 m (5–8 ft). Habit usually upright with rigid branches. Young shoots sparingly clad with a few glands and hairs. Bark grey to brownish-grey.
L 3–7 × 1.2–3.3 cm (1¼–3 × ½–1½ in.), *thick, rigid and leathery*, somewhat rugulose above, oblong-elliptic to broadly lanceolate, margins often recurved, apex acute to obtuse, base obtuse to sub-rounded, distinctly

R. irroratum

mucronate, glaucous below with minute glands. L remain for 2 to 4 years. Petiole 0.5–1.3 cm, minutely hairy and glandular.

Inflor six to twelve, *erect truss*, rachis *often long* 0.8–5.4 cm. Pedicel 1.5–4.9 cm with short hairs and glands.

F white, white tinged pink, pale to blush pink, with few to many crimson spots, 2–3 cm (about 1 in.) long, 7 cm (3 in.) across, *flatly campanulate or saucer-shaped*.

Calyx small, about 1–2 mm, red tinged, glandular.

Ovary densely glandular, sparingly hairy, style glandular to tip.

This is one of the finest white flowered species with the most beautifully poised flattish flowers of outstanding merit. It is fairly hardy and its relatively small stature makes it ideal for the small garden. Should not be grown from seed or bought at random as some forms are of little value with small poorly shaped flowers. Do not plant in shade as it is apt to become very leggy. Prune if necessary to improve shape.

Very distinctive with its brittle, stiff leaves and saucer-shaped flowers in erect trusses. Probably closest to *annae*.

Hardy in most British gardens and survived in most of Oregon in the 1972 freeze. Not too hardy in Holland. Has some ability to tolerate heat. 'His Lordship' **AM**, 1945 is an excellent clone. We lost some 1981–2.

Only collected on one mountain location, probably in east Yunnan, by Forrest's collectors after he died. Could be fairly common in this limited area.   June in the wild, May–June in cultivation *agastum* Balf.f. & W.W. Sm. 1917 H3–4 L1–2 F1–3?

Ht 2.4–6 m (8–20 ft). Young shoots thinly floccose and ± glandular. Bark smooth to roughish, yellowish-brown to brown.

L 6–12.5 × 2–4.5 cm (2½–5 × 1–2 in.), oblong to obovate, apex rounded, base obtuse to rounded, indumentum below very thin, scurfy but continuous, with sessile glands overlying veins, not papillate, pale olive to fawn. L remain for 2 years. Petiole 1.5–2 cm.

Inflor ten to twenty, loose floppy to more compact, rachis 2–2.5 cm. Pedicel about 1.5 cm, densely glandular.

F pale to deep rose or white tinged pink, blotched, ± spotted, about 5 cm (2 in.) long, tubular-campanulate with nectar pouches, lobes five to seven. Calyx small cup shaped. Stamens ten to fourteen, filaments pubescent at base. Ovary glandular, style glandular or partially glandular.

It seems that this plant is rare in cultivation. Even most of the few plants labelled *agastum* are not *agastum*, some being just *irroratum*. Two plants of ours identified as this species, do not agree with the type on some characters and could be *agastum* × *anthosphaerum* or even *delavayi* × *anthosphaerum*. Some of the herbarium specimens look like natural hybrids. Our plants are quite attractive in very early spring with deep rose coloured flowers. *R. agastum* may have some affinity with *tanastylum* or possibly even *delavayi*. Now considered a natural hybrid, see Addendum p. 356.

From west Yunnan, 1,800–3,400 m (6,000–11,000 ft), open conifer and oak forests, forest margins and thickets.

February–March, perhaps to May

R. annae (laxiflorum)

annae Franch. 1898 (*laxiflorum* Balf.f. & Forr., *hardingii* Forr.) H3–4
A+5 L1–2 F2–3

Ht to 2.4 m (8 ft) in *annae* and the former *hardingii*, to 4.6 m (15 ft) or
more in the former *laxiflorum*. Habit rather upright and often straggly.
Young shoots thinly floccose ± glandular, young leaves sometimes
bronzed. Bark greyish-brown.
L 7–13.5 × 1.5–4 cm (3–5½ × ⅝–1½ in.), narrow-elongate-lanceolate to
oblong-elliptic, apex acute to broadly obtuse, base obtuse to cuneate,
slightly recurved, shiny above, smooth, light green and glabrous below,
minutely punctulate. L remain for 2 to 4 years. Petiole 1–2 cm *glabrous*.
Inflor eight to twelve, fairly loose, rachis 1–2.5 cm. Pedicel 2–2.5 cm
densely glandular.
F white to creamy-white flushed rose, not spotted or spotted purple to
pink, 2.5–3.8 cm (1–1½ in.) long, *cup-shaped to openly campanulate*.
Calyx minute 1–2 mm, densely glandular. Ovary and style densely glandular.
    A neat, small- to medium-sized member of this subsection with thin
growth and graceful foliage, certainly worth growing in more gardens.
The growth comes rather early but is otherwise reasonably hardy. Some
flower buds may get frosted and some forms are hardier than others, the
most tender being those formerly grown as *hardingii*. One of the better
species in the subsection. Related to *aberconwayi* and *araiophyllum*.
'Folks Wood' **AM**, 1977 (as *laxiflorum*) tender Sandling Park. See
Addendum *p*. 356.
    Found in south-west and mid-west Yunnan and Kwangsi,
1,300–3,400 m (4,500–11,000 ft), in mixed thickets, margins of thickets
and forests.   April–May

anthosphaerum Diels 1912 (*chawchiense* Balf.f. & Farrer, *eritimum*
Balf.f. & W.W. Sm., *gymnogynum* Balf.f. & Forr., *heptamerum* Balf.f.,
persicinum Hand.-Mazz.) H3 L1–2 F1–2

Ht 1.2–9 m (4–30 ft). Young branches with rufous glands and hairs. Bark
grey to brown, slightly rough.
L 8–18 × 2.5–5 cm (3–7 × 1–2 in.), narrowly oblong to obovate to
oblanceolate, apex acute to blunt, base obtuse to cuneate, margins sometimes recurved, *not* waxy above as in *lukiangense* and some *tanastylum*,
pale below, slightly floccose, papillate but may appear glabrous and
sometimes glaucous. L remain for 2 to 3 years. Petiole 1–2 cm.
Inflor seven to fifteen usually fairly compact, rachis about 1 cm. Pedicel
0.8–1.5 cm hairy.
F very variable in colour, pale pink to rose, pale lavender through mauve
and lilac to deep magenta, also white tinged pink, pink with darker
streaks, carmine and crimson, blotched and sometimes spotted, 3.8–5 cm
(1½–2 in.) long, tubular-campanulate, lobes five to seven, usually six to
seven.
Calyx 1–2 mm, uneven, floccose and glandular or glabrous. Stamens ten
to fourteen. Ovary usually glabrous, style glabrous.
    An extremely variable species now including *eritimum* and its sub-
species. There are many colour forms in cultivation in the older species

gardens; some are quite appealing while others are of unattractive shades. The best are probably the palest and the darkest. All have the annoying habit of very early growth making them unsuitable for cold gardens. These are plants that are unlikely to be propagated to any extent so may gradually disappear from cultivation but it would be worth producing replacements from the best selections. Several re-introductions.

Some forms approach *irroratum*. Certain groups within the species can be singled out but probably do not deserve taxonomic status. Plants matching the old *eritimum*, generally with narrow leaves, mostly come from the more northerly part of the range of the species. See Addendum *p.* 357.

Common and widespread in many parts of Yunnan at 2,700–4,000 m (9,000–13,000 ft), in open thickets and rocky pasture, above fir zone or in conifer, oak and mixed forest or in bamboo brakes.   February to May

araiophyllum Balf.f. & W.W. Sm. 1917 H2–3 L1–2 F2–3

Ht to 6 m (20 ft) in the wild, to 5 m (17 ft) in cultivation so far. Habit slender growth. Young branches ± white floccose, midrib woolly, young growth scarlet. Bark smoothish, slightly flaking.
L 5–11.5 × 2–3 cm (2–4½ × about 1 in.), lanceolate, narrowly elliptic, rarely to elliptic, apex acuminate, base cuneate, margin undulate, shiny below ± glabrous, midrib sometimes woolly. L remain for 1 to 2 years. Petiole 1 cm.
Inflor six to eight in small compact to loose truss, rachis 1.5 cm. Pedicel about 1.5 cm ± glabrous.
F snowy-white to white suffused rose or soft light pink, with crimson blotch and spots, 3.5–4 cm (1½–1¾ in.) long, *cupular* or openly campanulate, lobes five, slightly fragrant.
Calyx minute glabrous. *Ovary pubescent*, style glabrous, red.

An attractive species for mild gardens such as in Cornwall and parts of Sussex; more tender than *annae (laxiflorum)*. A very graceful plant in all ways. The flowers often have the blotch spreading brilliantly into spots. Growth comes early, adding to its tenderness. A good uniform species with rather narrower leaves than *irroratum* and completely lacking in glands. 'George Taylor' **AM**, 1971, Kew.

From the Shweli–Salween divide, west Yunnan and Yunnan–Burma frontier, 2,300–3,400 m (7,500–11,000 ft), obviously quite common over a limited area, in open thickets and conifer forest, mixed forest and in and on margins of bamboo brakes.   April–May

brevinerve Chun & Fang 1957 Not in cultivation

A little-known species from Kwangsi. F purple with darker stripes down the lobes. Doubtfully distinct from *annae* but has darker flowers and styles glabrous above.

excelsum Chev. 1929 Not in cultivation

Another little-known species, from Vietnam (central). F apparently white in six to twelve flowered inflorescence.

irroratum Franch. 1887 (*ningyuenense* Hand.-Mazz.) H3–4 A − 5 to + 5
L1–2 F2–4

Ht to 9 cm (30 ft) in the wild, usually 1.8–3.7 m (6–12 ft) in cultivation.
Habit erect to rather straggly. Young shoots thinly tomentose and glandular. Bark light greenish-brown, slightly rough with age.
L to 15 × 4.4 cm (6 × 1¾ in.), lanceolate, oblanceolate to narrowly elliptic, variable in size and shape, margins sometimes undulate, pale to deep
green above, paler below, apex acute, base obtuse to cuneate. L remain
for 2 to 3 years. Petiole 1.5–2 cm.
Inflor to fifteen truss mostly loose, rachis 1.5–3 cm. Pedicel 1.5–2.5 cm
densely glandular.
F very variable, pure white, pale yellow, pale shrimp-pink to dull rose, not
spotted to faint spotting to very heavily spotted, even on every lobe; most
forms are pale and ± heavily spotted; nectar pouches; 3–5 cm (1¼–2 in.)
long, tubular-campanulate.
Calyx small about 2 mm, densely glandular. Stamens ten. Ovary and style
densely stipitate-glandular.

This variable species varies considerably in horticultural merit. While
the heavily spotted forms are appealing to some people, the majority
prefer the non-spotted or slightly spotted paler forms, some of which are
very beautiful. It is often free flowering from quite a young age and should
be a much more popular species than it is at present. Selection is desirable
as many of the original plants seen in old gardens are the darker flowered
forms of limited garden value. While unsuitable for really cold gardens,
we find it does well at Glendoick and is an easily grown accommodating
species that we would not be without. All severely damaged 1981–2
winter.

Including its sub-species, this species is perhaps the widest distributed
of all, along with *arboreum* and its close relations. 'Polka Dot' **AM**, 1957
heavily spotted in a many flowered truss, perhaps a hybrid Exbury. **AM**,
1957 white Minterne. 'Spatter Paint' is a heavily spotted American clone
from Rock's last expedition.

Found mostly in Yunnan, also Szechwan, 2,400–3,700 m (8,000–
12,000 ft), usually a shrub plant apparently wanting support (Forrest),
shady conifer and rhododendron forest, open thickets and margins of
forests, often dry but also by streams. Very common and variable.

Early March–May

irroratum ssp. *kontumense* (Sleumer) Chamb. 1978 (*atjehense* Sleumer,
langbianense Chev. ex. Dop) Probably not in cultivation

Ht 5–7 m (17–23 ft).
F rose-lilac, 3–4 cm (about 1½ in.) long, spotted.
From South Vietnam and north Sumatra, 1,800–3,000 m (6,000–
10,000 ft) in mossy forest or sub-alpine brushwood, locally common.

January–February in the wild

irroratum ssp. *pogonostylum* (Balf.f. & W.W. Sm.) Chamb. 1978
(*adenostemonum*) This southerly ssp. is very close to *irroratum* with
pinker flowers; calyx and ovary tomentose and glandular.

From Mengtsz, south-east Yunnan, 2,100–2,600 m (7,000–8,500 ft), in forests.

kendrickii Nutt. 1853 (*pankimense* Cowan, *shepherdii* Nutt. (type only))
H2–3 L1–2 F1–2

Ht 3–7.6 m (10–25 ft). Habit rather erect, open and sparse. Branchlets slender. Bark light brown.
L 9–13 × 2–3 cm (3½–5 × about 1 in.), 4–6 times as long as broad, oblong-lanceolate to lanceolate-acuminate, apex acuminate, base narrowly cuneate, *wavy edges*, margins recurved, dark green above, paler smooth and somewhat shiny below. L remain for 1 to 2 years. Petiole 1–1.5 cm.
Inflor eight to twenty reasonably full truss, rachis 3 cm. Pedicel about 5 mm with strigose and floccose hairs.
F rose through deep rose to crimson, red and scarlet, ± spotted, prominent nectar pouches, 3–3.8 cm (1¼–1½ in.) long, tubular-campanulate.
Calyx minute, 1.5 mm floccose. Stamens ten. Ovary narrow with strigose and floccose hairs, style glabrous.

The flowers of this rather tender species are on the small side to be of much garden value. The growth is rather early, hence prone to frost damage. Its low elevation indicates a lack of winter hardiness although it is quite plentiful in some of the milder gardens of southern England. Some plants there labelled *tanastylum* seem to refer to this species. Differs from the closely related *ramsdenianum* in its narrower, less leathery leaves and the ovary being non-glandular. The type of *shepherdii* is now included here but cultivated plants under this name are apparently *barbatum*. R. *kendrickii* may be derived from the Parishia subsection.

From central and east Bhutan, Arunachal Prdesh and south Tibet, 2,100–2,700 m (7,000–9,000 ft), common in dense and evergreen rain forest, rhododendron and bamboo jungle, in open spruce and oak forest on heavy clay soil and amongst alder, hemlock, maple and birch or gregarious.   April–May

korthalsii Miq. 1863 Not in cultivation

L with waxy coating like *lukiangense*. F probably white. From central Sumatra, possibly Padang Highlands.

leptopeplum Balf.f. & Forr. 1919 Not in cultivation

L with a waxy upper surface like *lukiangense* and an indumentum more obvious than *agastum* but more patchy, narrower and more acute at each end. Style glabrous. Closely related to *tanastylum* var. *pennivenium*.

Only collected once on Mekong–Salween divide, Yunnan at 3,000 m (10,000 ft).

lukiangense Franch. 1898 (*admirable* Balf.f. – Forr., *adroserum* Balf.f. & Forr., *ceraceum* Balf.f. & W.W. Sm., *gymnanthum* Diels) H3–4 L1–2 F1–2

Ht 4.5–6 m (15–20 ft) in the wild, less in cultivation so far. Purplish young shoots. Bark roughish, greeny-grey.

L to 19 × 6 cm (7½ × 2¾ in.), oblong-lanceolate to oblanceolate, apex acute, base obtuse, dark above ± *waxy* and glossy, also ± glossy below. L remain for 1 to 2 years. Petiole about 1.5 cm slightly purplish.
Inflor eight to thirteen, rachis about 1.5 cm. Pedicel rarely over 1 cm ± glabrous.
F rose to magenta-rose to lilac, small blotch ± crimson spots, 4–4.5 cm (1½–1¾ in.) long, tubular-campanulate, lobes five.
Calyx 1.5 m ± glabrous. Ovary ± glabrous, style glabrous.
  While some rose-pink and lilac forms are quite attractive, the magenta shades rate amongst the poorest plants in the subsection. It is rather tender with early growth. Closely related to *irroratum*, differing in being non-glandular, having more shiny leaves and darker coloured flowers. Differs from *anthosphaerum* in the five lobed corolla and the leaves having a completely different (waxy) texture.
  From north-west Yunnan and south-east Tibet, 2,400–4,000 m (8,000–13,000 ft), in conifer and rhododendron forest, mixed thickets and open forest, on cliffs, among rocks and by streams.

March–April

mengtszense Balf.f. & W.W. Sm. 1917 Not in cultivation

L narrowly oblanceolate, 4–4.5 times as long as broad. F purplish-red, blotched, openly campanulate. Setose-glandular petiole, pedicel, ovary and style makes this different from the rest of the subsection. Found in south-east Yunnan (type only).

papillatum Balf.f. & Cooper 1922 (*epapillatum* Balf.f. & Cooper) Not in cultivation

Ht 1.8–9 m (6–30 ft). L with thin indumentum below without sessile glands and usually ± strongly papillate, 2–4 cm (1¼–1¾ in.) wide. F pale cream to pink, spotted, streaked and/or blotched.
  Differs from *kendrickii* in flower colour, indumentum on leaf underside and generally wider leaves. Found in Bhutan, 1,800–3,400 m (6,000–11,000 ft).

ramsdenianum Cowan 1936 H3 L1–2 F1–2

Ht to 12 m (40 ft), less in cultivation so far. Bark light brown.
L to 10 × 3.8 cm (4 × 1½ in.), broadly lanceolate to oblong-lanceolate, 2.8–3.5 times as long as broad, more leathery than *kendrickii*.
Inflor twelve to fifteen, funnel-campanulate.
F rich rose, dark pinkish-red to bright crimson, darker purplish-red and blood-red, with or without spots and blotch, about 3.9 cm (1½ in.) long, tubular-campanulate. Ovary densely hairy and glandular.
  Very close to *kendrickii* and could be treated as a sub-species. The leaves are wider and more leathery in *ramsdenianum* and the distribution is generally farther east, around the Tsangpo Gorge where it is common. Intervening territory is largely unexplored. Equally small flowers and

early growth as *kendrickii*, tender and only suitable for the milder western and southern British gardens.

From south-east Tibet, 2,400–3,000 m (8,000–10,000 ft), in deciduous and conifer forest, sometimes almost gregarious.   April

spanotrichum Balf.f. & W.W. Sm. 1917 Not in cultivation

Close to *tanastylum* but apparently differs in the shape of the corolla. The herbarium material is inadequate. One specimen of Henry and a very doubtful one of T. T. Yu. From an outlying little explored area of south-east Yunnan, 2,300 m (7,500 ft).

tanastylum Balf.f. & Ward (*cerochitum* Balf.f. & Forr., *ombrochares* Balf.f. & Ward) H2 L1–2 F2–3?

Ht 6–9 m (20–30 ft) in the wild. Habit loose spindly tree in the wild. Young branches slender, thinly floccose at first.
L to 18 × 6.3 cm (7 × 2½ in.), broadly lanceolate to oblanceolate, apex shortly acuminate to obtuse, base obtuse to subacute, margin undulate, somewhat glossy below on maturity ± glabrous. Petiole about 1.5 cm.
Inflor four to eight, rachis 1–2 cm. Pedicel about 1 cm ± with a few short hairs.
F rose-purple, magenta-crimson, purplish-crimson, black-crimson to rich crimson-scarlet, ± marked with deep spots, 4.5–5.5 cm (1¾–2¼ in.) long, tubular-campanulate.
Calyx minute fleshy, cupular, ± glabrous. Ovary and style glabrous.

A very tender species which has apparently died out in cultivation; efforts to locate the proper plant having failed so far, even at Caerhays, Cornwall. Several plants are labelled *tanastylum* at Nymans, Sussex but these appear to be *kendrickii*. These have far too many flowers to the truss and the leaves are too small. The average *tanastylum* has larger leaves and flowers than *kendrickii* and lacks the floccose and strigose hairs on the pedicel, calyx and ovary. Quite possibly merges or overlaps geographically with *kendrickii* and *ramsdenianum* in unexplored parts of Arunachal Pradesh. *R. cerochitum* = pink flowered variant of *tanastylum*. The flowers are sometimes hidden in the foliage.

Found wild in south-east Tibet, Upper Burma, west Yunnan, and Arunachal Pradesh, 1,800–3,400 m (6,000–11,000 ft) amongst scrub on rocky and bouldery slopes, conifer, oak and mixed forests and in shady places.   February in wild, April or earlier in cultivation

tanastylum var. *pennivenium* (Balf.f. & Forr.) Chamb. 1978

L. with persistent cobwebby semi-plastered indumentum below, often nearly glabrous. This indumentum may be due to a secretion from the more abundant glands on the young leaves as both this and *tanastylum* itself are apparently equally tomentose when young. Ovary tomentose. *R. ombrochares* has ± glabrous leaves but a tomentose ovary and lies between var. *pennivenium* and the type of *tanastylum*.

wrayi King & Gamble 1905 (*dubium* King & Gamble, *coruscum* Ridley)

Ht 3–12 m (10–40 ft). Habit shrub or lanky tree. Inflor ten to eighteen. F pink flushed buds opening white ± tinged pale pink, spotted or unspotted 5–7-lobed.

Was cultivated in California from seed collected by Michael Black, but all were killed in the 1972 freeze. It has been re-introduced by Peter Valder.

From the Malay Peninsular, 855–2,165 m (3,000–7,000 ft) on the main range in mossy forest, exposed ridges and on cliffs.

December–January in the wild opening sporadically

All these southern species of this subsection (*brevinerve, excelsum, irroratum* ssp. *pogonostylum* and ssp. *kontumense, korthalsii. mengtszense, spanotrichum* and *wrayi*) could be very useful for hybridization with other elepidotes to give heat tolerance for climates like lowland Japan, Gulf area of USA and warmer parts of Australia and New Zealand. It is doubtful if any would be hardy even in the mildest parts of Britain and in any case they would probably have no horticultural advantages over the hardier species of this subsection in cultivation. Some could of course be worth growing in their own right in warm climates. A few crosses of *wrayi* have already been made in Australia.

LACTEA SUBSECTION (LACTEUM SERIES) (E)

Only *lacteum* and *beesianum* remain in this subsection, all the other members of the old Lacteum series having been transferred to the Taliensia subsection to which they obviously belong, except *wightii* which goes tentatively to the Grandia subsection.

These two species have much in common. Both have the same stout, stiff branches, thick leathery leaves, thin compacted grey-brown indumentum, many flowered usually compact trusses, widely campanulate; flowers, tomentose ovary and glabrous style. They are also found wild in similar areas although *lacteum* is much more restricted. Lastly, both are difficult to grow successfully, more than likely for the same reasons. Both seem to survive best in cool, dry gardens. This subsection is tentative. At present (1989), they are officially in the Taliesia subsection. See Addendum *p.* 357.

beesianum Diels 1912 (*colletum* Balf.f. & Forr., *emaculatum* Balf.f. & Forr., *microterum* Balf.f.) H4 L2–3 F1–3

Ht to 9 m (30 ft). Habit shrub or tree, branches stiff and stout. Bark roughish, greenish-brown.
L 9–29 × 2.6–8.2 cm (3½–11½ × 1–3¼ in.), 3–5.3 times as long as broad, oblanceolate to elliptic, apex acuminate, base narrowed or rounded, ± glabrous above with thin compacted *grey, fawn to brown* single layered eglandular indumentum below. L remain for 1 to 2 years. Petiole 1.5–2 cm sometimes winged, glabrous or floccose.

R. lacteum

Inflor ten to twenty-five usually fairly compact, rachis 0.5–3 cm. Pedicel 1.5–2.5 cm sparsely hairy.

F white to deep rose or magenta-rose, purple or red, sometimes flushed or lined with rose, with or without purple or crimson spots and blotch, 3.5–5.3 cm (1½–2 in.) long, broadly campanulate.

Calyx 0.5–1 cm lobes rounded, glabrous. Ovary densely white to brown tomentose, style glabrous. Capsule cylindrical curved.

This species is now surprisingly scarce in cultivation, considering the number of times it was found and introduced. It has obviously proved rather difficult to grow and this was confirmed by L de Rothschild. Large, well flowered specimens are rarely seen which is sad as evidently many forms are very beautiful. *KW* named it 'Giant Rose' and said it made a wonderful sight when whole forests of it were in flower. There is a tremendous variation in leaf, size, indumentum thickness and colour. Good types have large leaves and flowers. Slow to reach blooming size. Fairly hardy but needs a very favourable site and probably needs perfect drainage. Several recent re-introductions.

Very common in the wild over wide areas of north-west Yunnan, south-west Szechwan, Tsarong, south-east Tibet and north-east Burma, 3,000–4,400 m (10,000–14,500 ft) especially on steep, cool, north facing slopes in dry districts, often socially with no other species of rhododendron, usually associated with fir and other conifers, also open rocky slopes, the foot of cliffs and among boulders.   April–May *lacteum* Franch. 1886 (*mairei* Lévl.) H4 A+5 L2–3 F2–4

Ht 2–7.5 m (7–25 ft). Habit stiff with thick, often sparse branches. Bark slightly rough, greyish-brown.
L 8–17 × 4.5–10 cm (3–7 × 1¾–4 in.), 2–2.5 times as long as broad, elliptic to obovate, apex rounded, base rounded to cordate, sparse indumentum on young leaves above, thin compacted grey-brown indumentum below, formed by partially radiate hairs. L remain for 1 to 2 years. Petiole 1–4.7 cm glabrescent sometimes with thickish red-brown tomentum.
Inflor fifteen to thirty forming trusses as much as 18 × 18 cm (7 × 7 in.), rachis 1.2–3.5 cm. Pedicel 2.5–3 cm floccose, evanescent.
F pale to clear canary-yellow, rarely white, with or without a crimson blotch, 4–5 cm (1½–2 in.) long, about 6.3 cm (2½ in.) across, margins of lobes wavy, broadly campanulate.
Calyx minute 0.5–1 mm usually glabrous. Ovary densely tomentose, style glabrous.

This famous yellow flowered species is about as well known for its miffyness as for its magnificent blooms. There is every indication that it succeeds better in a relatively dry climate, in other words, the more inland and eastern as opposed to maritime gardens. In the latter, it is all the more inclined to suffer from the aggravating habit of dying off bit by bit. It also apparently resents being moved and seems to do better when grafted on to a species such as *calophytum*. Avoid poor drainage and hot sun. Most seedlings (from cultivated plants), even those with typical foliage, usually produce pale or pinkish coloured flowers. Many of the most healthy and long lived plants in Britain are growing in some of our coldest gardens and it suffered little or no damage in the 1972 freeze in Oregon. Some forms are much superior to others, those without a blotch are considered the more desirable. **FCC**, 1926 sulphury-white flowers with crimson blotch. **FCC**, 'Blackhills' 1965 primrose-yellow, no blotch or spots. Several recent re-introductions.

From Yunnan, west and east flank of the Tali Range, Chienchuan–Mekong Divide and west flank Salween–Kiu–Chang Divide, north-east Upper Burma; limited distribution in the wild, 3,000–4,000 m (10,000–13,000 ft), in and on margins of conifer forest, rhododendron forest and rocky situations on very acid soil.   April–May

LANATA SUBSECTION (CAMPANULATUM SERIES, PART) (E)

A distinct new subsection taken from the old Campanulatum series. There is a relationship with *wasonii* and *wiltonii* but little connection with the new Campanulata and Fulgensia subsections.

They have densely tomentose branchlets and buds and a dense indumentum on the leaf underside and sometimes a semi-persistent indumentum above. The flowers are campanulate, yellow to pink spotted and are carried in loose trusses of two to ten. These two closely related species from the Himalayas are most attractive in both leaf and flower.

lanatum Hook.f. 1849 (*flinckii* Davidian) H4 L2–3 F2–3

Ht 30 cm–6 m (1–20 ft), usually around 1.8 m (6 ft). Habit erect and loose to bushy. Branchlets *densely tomentose*, white to brown. Distinctive *growth and flower buds, heavily tomentose*. Bark greyish-purple, slightly rough.

L 6–12 × 1.8–5 cm (2¼–5 × ¾–2 in.), narrowly elliptic, ovate, obovate to oblong-obovate, apex obtuse to rounded, base obtuse to narrowed. Young leaves with evanescent light reddish-brown indumentum above, indumentum grey-fawn, pinky-brown, brown to rust coloured below, variable in thickness. Hooker's form (from Sikkim) has soft grey-brown indumentum on both surfaces. L only remain for 1 to 2 years, often giving the plant a sparse appearance. Petiole tomentose, 0.5–2.6 cm.

Inflor five to ten, rachis 0.3–1 cm. Pedicel 0.9–2 cm dense white to brown tomentose.

F cream, pale to pale sulphur to near daffodil yellow, spotted maroon, sometimes with orange bands, 3.2–4.8 cm (1¼–2 in.) long, broadly campanulate.

Calyx minute 0.5–2 mm glabrous to densely hairy. Ovary densely tomentose, style glabrous. Capsule tomentose, occasionally evanescent.

A very distinct species apart from the closely allied *tsariense*. It has unusual foliage and exquisitely shaped and marked flowers. It is not too easy a plant to grow successfully and probably needs pure organic matter and perfect drainage. Very slow from seed and young plants are susceptible to spring frosts. Recently reintroduced from Sikkim and Bhutan. Several plants in cultivation lie midway between *lanatum* and *tsariense*. While they are reported to grow mixed up in the wild, herbarium specimens show them distinct enough to retain specific status. *R. flinckii* described by Davidian in 1975, is said to be distinguished by its thin felty rusty-brown indumentum, thin texture of leaves and somewhat by the structure of the hairs. These characters apparently lack significance and it has been made a synonym of *lanatum*. Likewise, *lanatum* var. *luciferum* Cowan. This and *flinckii* come from east and north-east of Hooker's original introduction. See Addendum *pp.* 358 and 359.

Plants survived the 1972 freeze in Oregon but flower buds were mostly killed. In the Himalayas, the indumentum is stripped off whole with the thumb-nail and twisted to use as lamp wicks.

Sikkim, Bhutan, south-east Tibet and Arunachal Pradesh, 3,000–4,300 m (10,000–14,000 ft), under birches, in rhododendron and bamboo forest, on very steep banks, among rocks and on cliffs.

April–May

tsariense Cowan, see *Dwarf Rhododendrons* (*p.* 91–2). See *p.* 359 for new taxa. *The Smaller Rhododendrons* (*p.* 188–9).

MACULIFERA SUBSECTION (BARBATUM SERIES MACULIFERUM SUB-SERIES) (E)

This subsection was formerly a sub-series of the old Barbatum series but these two really bear little relationship to each other and this lies closer to the Irrorata subsection. The distribution is to the east of the Barbata and Glischra subsections.

There is a general lack of bristles on most of these species but ± indumentum and/or sometimes bristles on all or the lower part of the midrib on the under surface of the leaf. The calyx is small except in the somewhat aberrant *longesquamatum*. The flower colour varies from crimson-scarlet to rose, pink and white, ± spotted or blotched. Several of these are splendid garden plants.

R. strigillosum

chihsinianum Chun & Fang Not in cultivation

L 19–23 × 5–7 cm (7½–9 × 2–3 in.).
Inflor *c.* eight. Corolla lobes seven.
Probably near *strigillosum*. Kwangsi 850 m (2,750 ft).

longesquamatum Schneider 1909 (*brettii* Hemsl. & Wils.) H4 L2–3 F1–3

Ht 2–6 m (6–20 ft). Habit compact when young, can become leggy when old. Young shoots covered with *coarse shaggy fawn turning to rusty branched hairs. Bud-scales persistent for several years* adding to the shaggy appearance. Bark shaggy for some years, rough purplish-brown. L 6–12 × 2–4 cm (2½–5 × 1–2 in.) crowded at ends of shoots, thick, dark green and lustrous above, convex, oblong, oblong-obovate to oblong-oblanceolate, apex obtuse to acute, base obtuse to rounded to auricled, pale green below with *shaggy tawny hairs on midrib* plus scattered pustile-like glands on the whole underside as in *edgeworthii*.

L remain for 1 to 2 years. Petiole stout 1–2 cm with *dense shaggy hairs*.

Inflor six to twelve loose, rachis short and stout. Pedicel 2–3 cm with dense stalked glands.

F pink to rose, crimson blotched, about 4 cm (1½ in.) long, openly campanulate.

Calyx 1–1.4 cm (about ½ in.) fleshy, lobes unequal, densely glandular. Ovary densely glandular, style glandular at base.

A most unusual foliage plant with strikingly shaggy shoots and other parts. Forms a slow growing bush, at first of rounded habit. It is often shy flowering but as the flowers can be a dirty rose colour, this is no drawback. It is very hardy but the growth comes rather early so some protection is necessary. Very distinct botanically. There is an interesting natural hybrid at Dawyck, Peeblesshire with no persistent bud-scales. Scarce in cultivation.

Common over a limited area in west Szechwan with *orbiculare* on Opien-hsien and Wa Shan (not Mt Omei), and possibly other parts of Szechwan at 2,300–3,500 m (7,500–11,500 ft) in woodlands, conifer forests and on grassy slopes. To July in the wild.   May

maculiferum Franch. 1895 H4 L1–2 F2–3

Ht to 6 m (20 ft) usually less. Habit often compact. Traces of thin tomentum on shoots. Bark grey-brown.

L 6–11 × 2.5–4.5 cm (2½–4½ × 1–2 in.), oblong-oval, elliptic to almost oval to obovate, apex obtuse to rounded to cordulate, dark green and glistening above, indumentum towards petiole below, fine textured matted or straggling, buff to white, otherwise rather shiny below. L remain for 1 to 2 years. Petiole 1.5–2.5 cm densely glandular.

Inflor seven to ten loose, rachis 1.5–2.5 cm. Pedicel 1.5–2 cm with whitish hairs.

F white to pale pink, dark crimson blotch sometimes a few lines and spots, about 3.5 cm (1½ in.) long, openly campanulate.

Calyx 2–3 mm small, very hairy. Ovary with whitish tomentum, style glabrous.

This hardy species has rather dainty flowers, the white, deep blotched type being the best. It blooms when quite young. A fairly distinct species, probably close to *pachytrichum* but with broader leaves. Undamaged by 1972 freeze in Oregon.

From Szechwan, Kweichow, and Hupeh, 2,100–3,000 m (7,000–10,000 ft). Very common in north-west Hupeh and east Szechwan in woodlands and on cliffs.   March–April

maculiferum ssp. *anhweiense* (Wils. 1925) Chamb. 1978 H4 A − 15 L1–2 F2–4

Ht rarely over 1.5–2.4 m (5–8 ft). Habit a spreading but compact and rounded shrub. Branchlets with evanescent white hairs. Leaf and flower buds rounded. Bark lightish-brown.

L 3–10 × 1.5–4 cm (1–4 × ½–1½ in.), thick, convex, ovate-lanceolate,

apex acute, base rounded to cuneate, mid-green above, white hairs on lower part of midrib below. L remain for 2 years. Petiole with white hairs or nearly glabrous.
Inflor six to ten. Pedicel ± glabrous.
F pink to white, flushed pink in bud with purplish-red spots, 2.5–4 cm (1–1½ in.) long, to 4.5 cm (1¾ in.) across, funnel-shaped.
Calyx with glandular-ciliate teeth 2 mm. Ovary ± glabrous. Capsule cylindric, curving, glabrous.

This excellent, relatively hardy sub-species is thoroughly recommended. It blooms freely when fairly young and is remarkably frost resistant in flower. The fine plant at Windsor Valley Gardens is a marvellous sight when full out. Other forms can be inferior. Comes from an isolated part of China. W considered it was related to *przewalskii* but the scanty herbarium material available seems to have misled him. Undamaged in Oregon in 1972 freeze but is not reliably hardy in Boskoop, Holland. **AM**, 1976, Crown Lands. May be given back specific status.

Found on Lion Ridge, Anhwei, 1,200–1,800 m (4,000–6,000 ft) on open rocky places, cliffs or shady thickets.   April–May

morii Hayata 1913 (*nakotaisanense* Hayata) H3–4 L1–2 F2–3

Ht to 10 m (33 ft), usually much less. Habit fairly erect to wider spreading. Branchlets evanescent tomentose. Bark greyish-brown.
L 6.5–15 × 2–3.5 cm (2½–6 × ¾–1½ in.), oblong-lanceolate, apex acuminate, base rounded to truncate, usually glossy below, midrib ± with indumentum or glands. L remain for 1 to 3 years. Petiole floccose-tomentose and glandular 2–3 cm.
Inflor five to twelve, loose to fairly compact, rachis often elongated 2 cm. Pedicels 3–4 cm, glandular-hairy.
F white to white flushed rose with variable degrees of spotting and blotch, even from flower to flower, sometimes no spots or blotch, 3.4–5 cm (1½–2 in.) long, widely campanulate.
Calyx small 2–3 mm, gland fringed unequal. Ovary with stalked glands and few hairs, *style glandular near base.*

A very fine, usually free flowering species. The flower markings are often exquisite. Well worth more extensive cultivation. Variable in hardiness, partly due to the early growth of some forms being liable to frost damage. Basically hardy but needs protection to flourish. Several new introductions have been made in recent years. May be related to *pachytrichum*. **AM**, 1956, Benenden.

Endemic to Taiwan where it is one of the commonest species, 1,650–3,500 m (5,500–11,500 ft), abundant as undergrowth in conifer forests in the central range of mountains where it sometimes hybridizes naturally with *pseudochrysanthum* and *pachysanthum*.   April–May

ochraceum Rehd. & Wils. 1913

The true plant is probably not in cultivation although Bodnant showed a truss under this name in the 1975 London Rhododendron Show with a thick woolly indumentum. Flowers appear similar to *strigillosum*.

The loose woolly indumentum and crimson flowers make this an aberrant species in this subsection. Although it could be near *strigillosum*, it lacks bristles and may be nearer the Neriiflora subsection. From south-east to west Szechwan, 2,400–3,000 m (8,000–10,000 ft) in thickets. Would make a worthwhile introduction.

pachysanthum Hayata 1913 H4 L3–4 F2–3? New introduction (see *Dwarf Rhododendrons* Sp. Nov., *p*. 154)

Ht 1.20 m (4 ft) in the wild. Habit globose in the wild, probably compact and symmetrical in cultivation. Bark rough, greyish-brown.
L 4–10.5 × 1.5–5 cm (1½–4¼ × ⅜–2 in.), lanceolate to ovate, apex acute, base rounded, truncate to cordulate, thick, dense indumentum, light to deep buff.
Inflor eleven or more, rachis 1–2 cm. Pedicel *c*. 2.5 cm.
F with strong purple flecks, *c*. 4 cm long, widely campanulate.
Calyx glandular-ciliate. Ovary densely stipitate-glandular. *Style glabrous*.

This very distinct plant was introduced for the first time in 1972. In *The Species of Rhododendron* it is placed as a synonym of *morii* which is ridiculous. Description here partly Hayata's original.

It grows intimately with *morii*. Natural hybrids occur. Related to *morii* and *pseudochrysanthum* although the thick indumentum makes one consider a link with the Taliensia subsection. First flowered at Glendoick April 1979. See Addendum for further information, *p*. 361.

If its early promise holds good, this could be one of the finest foliage plants of the genus. The combination of the flat dark green leaves covered with silvery-white to fawn indumentum above and thick fawn to brown indumentum below on a compact spreading bush, gives us a rival of *yakushimanum* for perfection. First introduced in 1972 by Patrick, under *RV* 72001.

From central Taiwan, Nan-fu-ta-shan (Cyn-Bajin) on fully exposed grassy ridges above *morii* and the tree line, 3,000–3,200 m (10,000–10,500 ft). Blooms earlier than *pseudochrysanthum*.

pachytrichum Franch. 1886 H4 L1–2 F1–3

Ht 1.5–12 m (4–40 ft). Habit large rounded bush, fairly quick growing. Bark grey-brown, rough.
L 6–13 × 2–4 cm (2½–5 × ¾–1½ in.), oblong to oblanceolate to obovate, apex obtuse to acuminate, base cuneate to somewhat cordate, margin reflexed, midrib below ± clothed with brownish shaggy hairs, otherwise smooth and shining. L remain for 1 to 2 years. Petiole about 1.5 cm with shaggy brown hairs.
Inflor seven to seventeen, loose to fuller, rachis 1–1.5 cm.
F white through pink to rose and rose-magenta with maroon blotch and ± spots, pink buds open to white, scarlet to pink or rose, 3.8–5 cm (1½–2 in.) long, campanulate.
Calyx about 1.5 mm five acute lobes ± sparse hairs. Ovary densely tomentose, style glabrous.

This species is the centre of a very variable cline ranging from what used to be called *monesematum* through *pachytrichum* to *strigillosum*. Their horticultural value is also very variable from fine pink to rose forms to ugly rose-magenta flowered plants with poor trusses. The latter are only fit for the bonfire. Easy to grow. Fairly hardy, being successful in parts of Scandinavia but suffered scorch in Oregon in the 1972 freeze. 'Sesame' **AM**, 1963, Bodnant, white tinged purple.

From west Szechwan, (Mt Omei and Mupin), 2,100–3,400 m (7,000–11,000 ft) growing with *calophytum* under mixed forest. Common. March–April

pseudochrysanthum Hayata described in *Dwarf Rhododendrons* (p. 81–82) and in *The Smaller Rhododendrons* (p. 158–9).

strigillosum Franch. 1886 H3–4 L1–3 F1–3

Ht 3–6 m (10–20 ft). Habit often a round symmetrical bush. Branchlets ± *thickly covered with long bristles*. Bark greenish-brown smoothish. L 8–18 × 2.5–4.5 cm (3–7 × 1–2 in.), oblong-lanceolate to oblanceolate, apex acuminate, base narrowly rounded to cordulate, margin often strongly recurved, bristles on young leaves frosty white, tinged red or green, somewhat glossy below, midrib with loose tawny indumentum and shortish stalked glands (variable). L remain for 1 to 3 years. Petiole 1–1.5 cm with *long bristles* and shorter hairs.
Inflor eight to twelve usually a *flat topped truss*, rachis very short. Pedicel about 1 cm with long reddish glands.
F *deep red to crimson scarlet* (in cultivation) with black-crimson nectar pouches, about 6.3 cm (2½ in.) long, tubular-campanulate.
Calyx very small thickened rim glandular. Ovary with *long reddish glands*, style glabrous, reddish.

A fine plant in foliage and flower when well grown. A large dome-shaped specimen with its long recurved medium green leaves makes a splendid bush. Fairly hardy. The young growth can be damaged by frost and it grows best in shade in Oregon. Mixed reports on the 1972 freeze from no damage to severe damage.

Leach shifts this species to the Glischra subsection on account of its simple bristly hairs but surely other factors have to be taken into account. Rose, purplish to white flowered forms were found in the wild and these may be hybrids with *pachytrichum* which comes from the same locality. The leaves of *strigillosum* are usually longer and more hairy. **AM**, 1923, Bodnant rich blood-red.

From west Szechwan (Mt Omei and Wa Shan) and north Yunnan, 2,100–3,400 m (7,000–11,000 ft) in thickets and open places on cliffs and slopes. February–May

Probable natural hybrid

monesematum Hutch. 1916 H4 L1–3 F1–3

Appears to be natural hybrid of *pachytrichum* and is similar to this species apart from being largely glandular instead of hairy. Some plants in cultivation labelled *monesematum* are in fact *pachytrichum*. All came from *W* 1521 from Wu Shan or perhaps Mt Omei, Szechwan. It is variable, there being several clones in cultivation, some of horticultural value, some not. No wild specimen.   February–April

MADDENIA SUBSECTION (MADDENII SERIES) (L)

Densely scaly shrubs or rarely small trees with evergreen leaves. Leaves ± densely scaly below. Flowers fairly to very large, usually several to a terminal inflorescence, ± funnel-shaped to tubular-campanulate, often waxy, lobes five. Calyx small to large, often fringed with hairs. Stamens ten to twenty-five. Ovary very scaly, style nearly always scaly for part of its length. Most members have a mucronate apex to the leaf and many have very hairy seedlings with leaves wider and shorter than on mature plants.

Mostly from the east Himalayas to west and south Yunnan, south-west China into Indo-China. The majority grow in densely forested areas where there is little frost and several have very long flowering seasons in the wild. Closest relations lie in the Edgeworthia, Moupinensia and Camelliiflora subsections and to a lesser extent to the Monantha and Triflora subsections. 2n = 26, 52, 78 and 156, the polyploids all coming from the Maddenii Alliance.

The majority of these species are rather straggly plants with beautiful, often scented, white or white flushed pink flowers with a yellow blotch or throat. Most are too tender for all but extreme coastal parts of Britain or sheltered walls. Many are well worth growing indoors in pots, beds, hanging baskets or even epiphytically. Several have the ability to grow again from the base after frost damage but this young growth must be carefully protected the following winter as it is usually very soft and vulnerable. Many are excellent in warm climates which have little or no winter frosts and fairly hot summers. Some may stand full sun while others need some shade to avoid leaf burn. There is some indication of *Phytophthora* resistance. Several of those that are epiphytic in nature need extra good drainage in cultivation, especially during winter. Most show some resistance to salt laden winds.

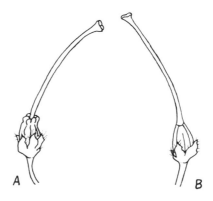

Pistils

Ciliicalyx Alliance (*Ciliicalyx sub-series*)

Divided into two parts. Difference easily seen when in flower.

(A) Impressed, *not* tapered style
amandum, *coxianum*, *crenulatum*, *cuffeanum*, *formosum*, *formosum* var. *inaequale*, *scopulorum*, (plus *burmanicum*, *ciliatum*, *fletcherianum* and *valentinianum* described in *Dwarf Rhododendrons* and *The Smaller Rhododendrons*.)
   Also in this part is the closely related *johnstoneanum* aggregate: *ciliipes*, *dendricola*, *johnstoneanum*, *rufosquamosum*, *walongense*.

(B) Tapering style
Ciliicalyx aggregate: *ciliicalyx*, *lyi*, *pachypodum*, *pseudociliipes*, *roseatum*.
   Also in this part: *carneum*, *fleuryi*, *horlickianum*, *ludwigianum*, *surasianum*, *veitchianum*, *yungchangense*.
   A generally tender group with few members able to survive outside in Britain except in extreme coastal districts. The majority have some scent and are free flowering plants of considerable horticultural merit. The results of the 1972 freeze in California showed that any Ciliicalyx Alliance members coming from south of the Tropic of Cancer or any below 1,800 m (6,000 ft) just to the north, are very tender.
   The type specimen of *cubittii* equals *veitchianum* so we will now refer to it as Cubittii Group. This is an attractive early flowering plant, white often flushed rose with an orange-yellow blotch. Slightly scented. 'Ashcombe' **FCC** 1962 Crown Lands **AM** 1935 Trengwainton. As cultivated plants are not typical *veitchianum*, I have not placed it under that species.

R. johnstoneanum

amandum Cowan 1937 Not in cultivation

Ht 1.2–1.5 m (4–5 ft). F pale lemon yellow, 3 × 3 cm (1¼ × 1¼ in.). Calyx about 6 mm, hairy. Looks distinct with leaves rather *cinnabarinum*-like in shape. One specimen only, *L&S* 1365 from Nat-rampa, south-east Tibet, at 3,500 m (11,500 ft) on steep banks among other smaller rhododendrons.

coxianum Davidian 1972 H1–2 L1–2 F2–3

Ht to 3 m (10 ft), often epiphytic when young. Habit straggly, branchlets moderately to sparsely bristly. Bark pale to creamy-brown.
L 5.3–11.5 × 1.5–3 cm (2¼–4½ × ⅗–1¼ in.), *oblanceolate*, apex acute, base tapered, scales below unequal, two to five times their own diameter apart. Petiole 0.5–1 cm with or without wings at margins, scaly ± bristly.
Inflor two to four. Pedicel 1.2–1.4 cm (about ½ in.), scaly, not bristly.
F creamy-white, greenish-yellow blotch at base, greenish tinge, two lower lobes of corolla sometimes broken, corolla curved, lobes *not* frilled as in *formosum* var. *inaequale* but with distinct 'potters thumb' marks, 7.3–7.5 cm (about 3 in.) long, tubular-funnel-shaped, ventricose, scaly outside, pubescent at base of tube.
Calyx 4–5 mm, unequal, ± hairy. Stamens ten, hairy at base. Style scaly in lower half.
   So far we have found this rather tricky to cultivate and liable to die off. The scent is good, rather similar to *formosum* var. *inaequale* to which it is obviously related.
   From south-east of Apa Tani Valley, Subansiri Division of Arunachal Pradesh, India at 1,700 m (5,500 ft) on marshy ground or epiphytic. *C&H* 396 and 475.   April–May

crenulatum Hutch. ex Sleumer Not in cultivation

L small, not lepidote above.
F pale yellow.
   Possibly near *burmanicum* (see *Dwarf Rhododendrons*, p. 125 and *The Smaller Rhododendrons*, p. 115–6) Laos, one collection only.

cuffeanum Craib ex Hutch. 1917 H1 A+25 L1–2 F2–3

Ht to 2.7 m (9 ft). Habit loosely branched, often straggly.
L to 10 × 3.8 cm (4 × 1½ in.), oblanceolate to oblong-lanceolate, apex shortly acuminate, base narrowed, scales below unequal, about their own diameter apart. Petiole 1.3 cm (½ in.), scaly.
Inflor about five. Pedicel 1.5 cm (⅗ in.), densely scaly.
F white with large yellow blotch, 6.3–7.5 cm (2½–3 in.) long, tubular-campanulate.
Calyx *long lobes*, leafy, about 8 mm long, lobes unequal, scaly with a few hairs. Stamens ten. Style scaly towards base.
   A fine plant, rare in cultivation. Flowered at Glasneven, Dublin in May 1915 from plants presented by Lady Wheeler Cuffe. Collected again by

KW in 1954 *KW* 21909 with very large fragrant flowers. These were all killed or cut back in 1972 freeze in California.

Collected by Lady Cuffe on Sindaung or 'Elephant Hill', 1,800 m (6,000 ft) at edge of Shan Plateau, *KW* 21909 found on Mt Victoria, both south-west Burma.   May

formosum Wall. 1832 (*assamicum, gibsonii* Paxton, *iteophyllum* Hutch). H2–3 A+15 L1–2 F2–3

Ht to 3 m (10 ft). Habit straggly to fairly compact. Young shoots finely scaly and bristly.
L 3–7 × 1–3 cm (1¼–2¾ × ⅖–1¼ in.), linear, oblanceolate to obovate, apex acute to subacute, base acute to narrowed, scales below 1–1½ their own diameter apart. Petiole *often fringed with hairs*.
Inflor two to three. Pedicel 6–13 mm (¼–½ in.).
F white or white tinged pink, yellow or rose, sometimes striped outside, scented but not nearly as strongly as var. *inaequale*, about 6.3 cm (2½ in.) long, scaly outside, funnel to widely funnel-shaped.
Calyx small, undulate. Stamens ten. Style scaly in lower half or three-quarters.

One of the hardier members of the Alliance, worth trying on walls or in sheltered corners in less cold areas. The more compact types make good pot plants. Very striking forms have been grown from seed from Kalimpong in RBG, Edinburgh with red or pink outsides to the corolla, white within except for orange-red blotch. Presumably the seed came from cultivated plants although other sources of *formosum* seed are reputed to have come from the Sikkim area.

Merges with var. *inaequale* in parts of the Khasia Hills although isolated populations of the latter are found at low elevations; *iteophyllum*, now merged with *formosum*, represents the narrowest leaf forms. **AM**, 1960, RBG, Edinburgh, white, tinged pink, orange throat.

From the Khasia Hills, north-east India, 600–1,800 m (2,000–6,000 ft), open areas mixed with other Ericaceous shrubs, windswept hillsides and river banks.   April–June

formosum var. *inaequale* (Hutch.) Cullen 1978 H1–2 A+20 L1–2 F2–4

Ht 0.90–1.8 m (3–6 ft). Habit usually rather open or straggly. Bark peeling, grey to reddish-brown.
L 6.3–12.5 × 2.5–5 cm (2½–5 × 1–2 in.), lanceolate to elliptic, apex acuminate to obtuse, base usually acute, scales below two to three times their own diameter apart. Petiole 1.5 cm (⅔ in.).
Inflor four to six.
F cream flushed green, deeper in throat, about 5 cm (2 in.) long, 12.5 cm (5 in.) across, widely funnel-shaped, lobes ± frilled.
Calyx 2 mm, oblique. Style very long, scaly lower half.

Has one of the best scents in the genus and makes an excellent greenhouse plant although inclined to be straggly. Very closely allied to *formosum* with which it merges but the average form is much larger in all parts, is less hairy and much stronger scented but also definitely more tender. Some variation in flower shape, those widest open being the best. All our *C&H* 301 introduction was killed by the 1972 freeze in California and it only succeeds in gardens like Trengwainton, Gigha and Brodick in Britain. **AM**, 1947, Bodnant.

From Khasia Hills, India, 1,200–1,750 m (4,000–5,600 ft) in occasional locations by stream sides or in forest, partly shaded.

April–May

scopulorum Hutch. 1930 H1 A+20 L1–2 F2–3

Ht to 4.5 m (15 ft), usually less.
L crowded, 5–6.3 × 2–3 cm (2–2½ × ¾–1¼ in.), obovate-lanceolate, apex rounded, base subacute, minutely scaly below, three to four times their own diameter apart. Petiole 1.3 cm (½ in.).
Inflor three to seven. Pedicel 6 mm.
F white, flushed rose or white with gold throat or pink or blush-pink, ± scented, 5 × 7.5 cm (2 × 3 in.), widely funnel-shaped, small scales outside and finely pubescent all over.
Calyx very small, 2 mm, slightly scaly, not hairy. Style ± scaly and hairy.

Seems to be a distinct species with a small distribution, tender. **AM**, 1936, Exbury.

From south-east Tibet, Pome and Tsangpo, 1,800–2,400 m (6,000–8,000 ft), sunny boulder screes, thickets on steep rocky slopes and cliffs, mixed and pine forest. April–May

johnstoneanum aggregate

ciliipes Hutch. Not in cultivation

Inflor one. F white, green or yellowish blotch, scented.
Yunnan, Shweli–Salween Divide, 3,000 m (10,000 ft).

dendricola Hutch. 1919 (*atentsienense* Hand-Mazz., *taronense* Hutch., *notatum* Hutch. + some old *ciliicalyx*) H1 A+25 L2–3 F2–3

Ht to 4.5 m (15 ft). Habit usually straggly. Bark smooth, dark purple to mahogany-red, peeling.
L 7.5–14 × 3–5 cm (3–5½ × 1¼–2 in.), oblong-elliptic, apex abruptly acuminate, base rounded obtuse, scales below not quite their own diameter apart to three to five times (*taronense*), variable in size and shape. Petiole 1.3 cm (½ in.) scaly.
Inflor two to five. Pedicel 8–13 mm (⅓–½ in.).
F white to white tinged pink, yellow flush or base or with broad bands of purple (*notatum* not in cultivation), 6.3–10 cm (2½–4 in.) long, widely funnel-shaped.
Calyx undulate rim, scaly and a few hairs. Stamens ten. Style scaly lower half.

A very fine plant in its best forms and excellent under glass. Barely hardy anywhere outside in Britain. Includes many old *ciliicalyx* forms.

Has hairy juvenile foliage like several other members of the Alliance. Killed or cut back in 1972 freeze in California. 'Walter Maynard'. **AM**, 1975, as *ciliicalyx* lined purple, yellowish base, Sunte House, probably now belongs here.

From north Burma and north-west Yunnan, 900–3,000 m (3,000–10,000 ft), usually epiphytic in the wild, often high on trees, also rocks, cliffs, margins of thickets and rocky slopes; common and widespread. Has a long, spasmodic flowering season in the wild.   May

johnstoneanum Watt ex Hutch. 1919 (*parryae* Hutch. type only) H2–3 A+15 L1–2 F2–3

Ht to 4.6 m (15 ft). Habit often forms a large, untidy bush. Branchlets bristly. Bark reddish-brown, smooth to shaggy, peeling.
L 5–10 × 2–3.8 cm (2–4 × ¾–1¼ in.), elliptic to slightly obovate-elliptic, apex rounded, bristly, scales dense and nearly contiguous below. Young leaves scented. Petiole to 1.3 cm (½ in.), hairy.
Inflor two to five. Pedicel 8 mm, densely scaly.
F creamy-white to cream flushed yellow, greenish-yellow or flushed pink, orange-red to yellow spots; colour variable in the wild from white to pink or rosy-purple flush along lobes, slightly fragrant, 5 cm (2 in.) or more long, funnel-campanulate, red scales on outside.
Calyx very short with long hairs. Stamens ten.

This is one of the hardiest of the Alliance. Survived outside at Glendoick for many years and often flowers successfully although it sometimes dies-back and was killed at Glendoick 1981–2. Stood up reasonably well to the 1972 freeze in California. Fairly heat resistant. Near *dendricola* botanically. **AM**, 1934.

The most desirable forms are pale yellow. We find the clone 'Double Diamond' more tender, always loosing its buds. The flower resembles a carnation. This **AM** clone is one of several doubles or semi-doubles. Another is 'Demi-john' **AM**, 1975 semi-double white flushed green, Leonardslee. 'Rubeotinctum' **AM**, is a seedling from *KW* 7732, white with a deep pink stripe along the middle of each lobe (outside). *KW* 22200 from Mindat Ridge, central Burma, lies botanically between *johnstoneanum* and *burmanicum* and is more tender than the former.

From Manipur and Nagaland, 1,300–3,400 m (6,000–11,000 ft) where it is quite widespread and common, in open scrub on margins of forests and on grassy slopes or epiphytic.   May

rufosquamosum Hutch. Not in cultivation

Ht to 1 m (3 ft). F white, pink in bud, about 7 cm (2¾ in.) long.
From south-east Yunnan, Szemao Hills, 1,400 m (4,800 ft).

walongense Ward 1953 H1–2 L2–3 F2–3

Medium bush 2–3 m (7–10 ft). Habit *KW* rarely epiphytic. *C&H* always epiphytic.
L. *c.* 10 cm (4 in.) long, elliptic.

Inflor three to four. Pedicels 1.5 cm ($\frac{2}{3}$ in.).
F cream with green flash, 6–7 cm (2½–3 in.) long, 6 cm (2½ in.) across, hairy.
Calyx inconspicuous.

A plant we collected in north-east India in 1965 under *C&H* 373 is very closely related to if not this species. The scales are very similar although ours tends to have deciduous scales towards the midrib. This has good, shiny foliage and a beautiful deep mahogany bark. The flowers are medium sized and have a distinct rather spicy scent. Originally recognized as *parryae*. *KW*'s may not be in cultivation.

From Arunachal Pradesh near Lohit and Delei. Ours from the Subansiri Division, 1,500–2,100 m (5,000–7,000 ft), in thin mixed forest or forest ravines, on rocks, cliffs or epiphytic (all ours high in forest trees).   April–May (ours)

Part 2 *Tapering Style*

Ciliicalyx aggregate

ciliicalyx Franch. 1886 (*missionarum* Lévl., *pseudociliicalyx* Hutch.)

The true plant is probably not in cultivation.

Those plants formerly grown under this name are probably *pseudociliipes* and *dendricola*. A plant we acquired labelled *ciliicalyx* is probably a hybrid. This is a pity for here we are with a first rate plant and with no name for it.

Restricted distribution near Tali, Yunnan, 2,200–2,700 m (7,300–9,000 ft), sides of rocky hills.

lyi Lévl. 1914 H1–2 A+25 L1–2 F2–3

Ht to 1.8 m (6 ft) or more. Habit very lanky. Branchlets scaly and bristly. Bark tawny-brown.
L to 8.5 × 3 cm (3½ × 1¼ in.), oblanceolate to oblong-oblanceolate, apex bluntly acute, narrowed at base, with evanescent hairs. Petiole 6 mm, hairs evanescent.
Inflor to five. Pedicel 4 mm.
F white with green or yellowish blotch, 5 cm (2 in.) long, widely funnel-shaped, partly scaly outside, scented.
Calyx minute, 2–3 mm, densely scaly and a few long hairs. Stamens ten. Style much longer than corolla, scaly lower two-thirds.

The leaves and flowers are roughly similar in size to *formosum*, that is smaller than most of this Alliance. Recently reintroduced by P. G. Valder from Thailand. Very tender, all died in 1972 freeze in California except under lath or very protected sites but flowered successfully at Lamellen, Cornwall about 1923. Not worthy of indoor culture.

From Kweichow, Indo-China and Thailand, 1,200–2,800 m (4,000–9,300 ft), in dense woods and dry broken limestone plateau.

April–June

pachypodum Balf.f. & W.W. Sm., 1916 (*pilicalyx* Hutch., *scottianum* Hutch., *supranubium* Hutch.) H2–3 L1–2 F2–3

Ht 1.2–7.6 m (4–25 ft). Branchlets scaly, not hairy.
L 3–10 × 1.3–3 cm (1¼–4 × ½–1½ in.), obovate, elliptic-obovate to oblanceolate, rarely elliptic, apex abruptly acute, narrowed at base, densely
scaly below, less than their own diameter apart, glaucous, sometimes
bristly. Petiole 8 mm, sometimes evanescent hairy.
Inflor one to four. Pedicel 0.8–1.6 cm (⅓–⅔ in.).
F white, dull white to white, flushed pink, rose, pale green or pinkish-
brown, sometimes with brown to yellow blotch, *never yellow*, 3.8–10 cm
(1½–4 in.) long, widely funnel-shaped, scaly outside, pubescent within,
fragrant or scentless.
Calyx usually small but sometimes has one long lobe, scaly and hairy.
Stamens ten to eleven. Style scaly lower half to two-thirds.

This species now includes some *scottianum* and *supranubium* and
covers a wide variation in flower size. *R. scottianum* types have large
flowers of considerable garden value while some forms of *supranubium*
have rather small, inferior flowers and are hardly worthy of indoor
culture. Many introductions are of moderate hardiness for the Alliance
and will survive out of doors in the mildest parts of Britain and withstood
the 1972 freeze in California quite well and can also tolerate heat if
shaded and sheltered. Several recent re-introductions.

From west Yunnan, Kwangtung and Upper Burma, 1,800–3,700 m
(6,000–12,000 ft), dry rocky situations, cliff ledges, open scrub and stony
pastures or epiphytic.   March–June

pseudociliipes Cullen 1978 probably H2–3 L1–2 F2–3

Ht 0.6–2 m (2–7 ft). Branchlets setose at first.
L 4–6 × 1.6–2.7 cm (1½–2¼ × ⅔–1 in.), narrowly elliptic to narrowly obo-
vate, apex acute, base cuneate, brown and loosely scaly below.
Inflor one, occasionally two.
F white to pinkish, 5–7 cm (2–3 in.) long.
Calyx lobes variable, disc-like, ciliate. Stamens ten.

This newly described species includes various specimens (some probably in cultivation) previously identified as *ciliicalyx*, *scottianum*, *ciliipes*
(a paratype!), *dendricola*, *notatum* and *supranubium*. It is very close to
the old description of *supranubium* Hutch. but unfortunately the type
does not agree, hence the necessity of the new name.

roseatum Hutch. (*lasiopodum* Hutch.) (also *parryae* **AM** form) H1–2
L1–2 F2–3

Ht to 5 m (16 ft). Bark red, peeling.
L 5.5–10.5 × 3–5.5 cm (2¼–4¼ × 1¼–2¼ in.), broadly elliptic, usually
rounded at both ends, scales below unequal, less than their own diameter
apart. Petiole 8 mm.
Inflor two to four. Pedicel length variable, tomentose at base.
F white, base yellow to yellowish-orange or white flushed purple, often

fragrant, 7–8 cm (about 3 in.) long, narrowly funnel-shaped, scaly outside (widely funnel-shaped in *parryi* **AM**).
Calyx hairy. Stamens ten. Style scaly in lower half.

Includes *parryae* **AM**, a fine plant although very straggly with flowers 7.5 × 11.3 cm (3 × 4½ in.), large for the Group, tender. *R. parryae* **FCC**, 1973, white, yellow-green blotch, Sunte House, may fit here although its petiole seems to be too long.

From Upper Burma, west Yunnan, 1,500–2,700 m (5,000–9,000 ft), margins of mixed and conifer forests, rocky and bouldery slopes, scrub and open thickets, larva bed, on rocks and epiphytic on tree tops.

carneum Hutch. H1–2 A + 20 L1–2 F3

Ht about 1 m (3 ft). Habit can be compact in some situations but may be trained to a pillar or wall. Branchlets densely scaly.
L 5–11.4 × 3.2–3.8 cm (2–4½ × 1¼–1½ in.), elliptic-obovate, apex sub-acute, slightly wedge-shaped at base. Petiole to 1.5 cm (⅔ in.), densely scaly.
Inflor three to seven. Pedicel scaly.
F flesh-pink fading to almost white, subtle scent, not strong, 6.3–7.5 cm (2½–3 in.) long, 8½ cm (3½ in.) across, tube scaly outside, funnel-shaped.
Calyx scaly and fringed with hairs. Stamens usually twelve. Style densely scaly, pink.

One of the few pinkish members of the Alliance, a delicate shade, quite pretty, especially when first out. Only known in cultivation and is possibly all one clone although several plants were raised from the original seed. First flowered in 1914, having been collected in 1909. **AM**, 1927, Exbury.

Said to be from the Shan States, Burma at 2,300 m (7,500 ft), on open grassy hillsides away from large trees.   April–May

fleuryi Dop. Not in cultivation

F five yellow lines on corolla tube. Pedicel recurved in fruit.
From Laos.

horlickianum Davidian 1972 probably H1–2 L1–2 F2–3

Ht 1.5–3 m (5–10 ft). Habit straggly. Branchlets scaly, not bristly.
L   5.3–11.5 × 1.8–4.5 cm   (2–4½ × ⅔–1¼ in.), elliptic-lanceolate to obovate-lanceolate, apex ± acuminate, base obtuse to tapered, scales below unequal, *1–1½* times their own diameter apart, ± bristles on margin. Petiole 0.4–1.6 cm, ± bristly.
Inflor two to four. Pedicel 5–8 mm, densely scaly, not bristly.
F white to creamy-white, strongly flushed rose, orange flair, ± no scent, scaly and *pubescent* outside, 6.5–7 cm (about 2¾ in.) long, about 7 cm (3 in.) across, widely funnel-shaped.
Calyx minute, 1 mm, ± fringed with long bristles. Stamens ten to eleven. Style scaly at base.

A recently named, distinct species, related to *formosum* var. *inaequale* (Davidian). Free flowering with early growth. Unfortunately the original plants in cultivation were lost and those now grown are seedlings from these. Introduced under *KW* 9403. The strongly flushed flowers are attractive.

From north Burma, 1,200–2,100 m (4,000–7,000 ft), in thickets, on cliffs or epiphytic high in trees. March–April

ludwigianum Hossens H1 A+25 L1–2 F3

Ht to 1.4 m (4½ft). Habit straggly. Bark peeling with age, purplish-pink.
L to 10 × 5 cm (4 × 2 in.), obovate, apex triangular, base narrowed, margins ciliate at first, later glabrous, scales below about half their own diameter apart. Petiole 4 mm.
Inflor two to four. *Pedicel hairy*, scarcely 6 mm long.
F white with yellow blotch or rose, rose-coloured bud, nearly 7 cm (3 in.) long and 10–12.5 cm (4–5 in.) across, funnel-shaped, pubescent inside, partially scaly outside, *not* scented.
Calyx small, hairy. Stamens ten. Style one-eighth to one-half from base scaly, *usually hairy*.

A very fine species as seen in the RBG, Edinburgh but the strange lack of scent rather takes from its overall effect. A large white flower in a rhododendron is usually scented and a rude disappointment awaits anyone who sticks their nose into this one! Very tender, all died in 1972 freeze in California except under lath or in very protected sites. From Thailand, 2,000 m (6,500 ft). March–April

surasianum Balf.f. & Craib H1–2 L1–2 F2–3

Ht to 3.6 m (12 ft). Branchlets finely scaly.
L 5.5–10 × 2.5–3.8 cm (2¼–4 × 1–1½in.), elliptic-obovate to oblong-obovate, apex acute, base rounded to shortly cuneate, densely scaly below, contiguous or overlapping. Petiole 8 mm.
Inflor two to three. Pedicel 1.5 cm (⅔in.).
F pale pink, about 7.5 cm (3 in.) long, widely funnel-shaped, densely scaly outside and finely pubescent near base.
Calyx small, 2 mm, scaly and bristly. Stamens ten. Style scaly lower two-thirds.

Was in cultivation in Trinity College, Dublin and RBG, Edinburgh; not any longer in Edinburgh. From north Indo-China, 1,300 m (4,500 ft), rocky ground in evergreen jungle. June?

veitchianum Hook. 1857 (*smilesii* Hutch., *cubittii* Hutch. (type specimen)) H1 A+25 L2–3 F3–4

Ht 1 m (3 ft) or more. Habit often more compact than most of the Group.
Bark fairly smooth, reddish-brown.
L 5–10 × 2–4 cm (2–4 × ¾–1½in.), obovate to elliptic-obovate; apex obtusely acuminate narrowed to base, scales below 1–1½ times their own diameter apart. Petiole 1 cm (⅜ in.).
Inflor to five. Pedicel 1 cm (⅖ in.).
F white, white, yellow throat, white slightly tinged green, often frilled or

wavy edges to lobes, 7.5 cm (3 in.) long and up to 12.5 cm (5 in.) or even more across, widely funnel-shaped, sweet scented, sometimes reminiscent of lemon scented verbena. Lobes often deeply cut. Calyx variable, often hairy and scaly. Stamens ten. Style scaly lower half.

One of the finest of the Group and was a very popular greenhouse plant in Victorian times, later becoming quite rare in cultivation, having lost favour. Flowers very large and elegant in some forms and freely produced. Recently reintroduced by P. G. Valder from Thailand under three numbers and also by Sir Peter Smithers. Sometimes forms lignotubers in the wild to withstand dry periods. P.G.V. 29 and 30 have strongly scented flowers while P.G.V. 42 has very large flowers and little scent. Barely hardy anywhere in Britain and all died in 1972 freeze in California except under lath and very protected sites. Survives in lath houses in Melbourne, Australia. Variable flowering season.

From southern and central Burma, Thailand and Indo-China, 900–2,400 m (3,000–8,000 ft), usually epiphytic, on such trees as birch, oak, and chestnut or in dry, evergreen forest.   February–July

yungchangense Cullen 1978 Not in cultivation

Ht 0.8–1.3 m (2½–4½ ft). L 7–10 × 2.8–3.8 cm (3–4 × 1–1½ in.). Inflor two to four.
F white, faintly flushed rose, fragrant. Calyx conspicuous, about 7 mm long, ciliate. Only known from F specimens 25446 and 25772. Plants in cultivation under F 25446 are quite different, being *chrysodoron*.

Distinct with very individual calyx, glabrous and elepidote corolla and elepidote style. From Yunnan north of Yungchang-fu, 2,100–2,400 m (7,000–8,000 ft) on cliffs and in side valleys.

Dalhousiae Alliance (Megacalyx sub-series) (part)

Horticulturally, this Group can be regarded as the finest of the subsection although the habit is usually straggly. The flowers are often magnificent, like large white to yellow trumpet-shaped lilies and the scent is frequently superb. Certain introductions are hardier than is generally realized and these are well worth attempting on semi-shaded walls and very sheltered corners even with us in east Scotland. The 1972 freeze in west North America caused only superficial damage except where the temperature dropped below −9.5°C (15°F). Most of these species have few, long shoots and do not respond well to pruning to make them more bushy although pinching the tips of vigorous shoots may lead to one to two extra growth breaks. These species may be grafted on to *ponticum* giving vigorous growth but personally I do not recommend this practice.

Marks of the 'potter's thumb' at the base of corolla is also found in the Ciliicalyx Group. Calyx large and ± leafy with broadish lobes, 1 cm (⅖ in.) or more long. Leaf stalks not grooved on upper side. Stamens ten. *R. megacalyx* has been moved to a separate Group on account of its deeply sunk scales, sunken veins, large calyx and short capsule.

chunienii Chun & Fang Not in cultivation. Discovered 1955, Kwangsi.

dalhousiae Hook. 1849 H1–2 A+15 L2–3 F2–4

Ht to 3 m (10 ft). Habit usually untidy and leggy, erect or sprawling. Often epiphytic in the wild. Leaves at ends of branches. Bark brown cinnamon, peeling.
L 6.3–20 × 2.5–7.5 cm (2½–8 × 1–3 in.), obovate to oblanceolate, apex rounded to obtuse, base cuneate, edges sometimes retain vestiges of hairs. Petiole 1–1.5 cm (⅖–⅗ in.).
Inflor two to six. Pedicel 1–1.5 cm (⅖–⅗ in.), softly pubescent and scaly.
F *usually greeny-yellow in bud, eventually fading to cream* when mature, sometimes lemon-yellow, cream or white, scent usually slight but occasionally strong, about 10 cm (4 in.) long, tubular-campanulate.
Calyx about 1 cm (⅖ in.), glabrous. Style scaly lower two-thirds.

A superb species in its best coloured, large flowered forms, those showing a strong green tinge being particularly exciting. It is hardy enough for protected sites in places like Cornwall and extreme western seaboard areas of Scotland, especially against a partly shaded wall. While it often looses its buds from hard frost, it is frequently more frost resistant than its notoriously bud-tender hybrid 'Countess of Haddington'. At Brodick, Isle of Arran, it grows through an *orbiculare* giving a striking combination of colour as they generally flower together. Perfect drainage is essential. Is apparently resistant to heat and drought in hot climates such as parts of Australia. First flowered in cultivation in 1853, 3 years from seed, having been inarched on to *ponticum*. Two double flowered clones were once much praised but have probably disappeared.

Related to *lindleyi* but has generally larger, wider leaves and some hairs on leaf margins and *lindleyi* has no hint of yellow in the corolla except from the base. **AM**, 1930, 'Frank Ludlow' **FCC**, 1974 *LS&T* 6694 Sandling Park.

From east Nepal, Sikkim, Bhutan and south-east Tibet, 1,800–2,700 m (6,000–9,000 ft), usually epiphytic on trees or stumps or on rocks, and boulders and on steep dry hillsides.   April–July

dalhousiae var. *rhabdotum* (Balf.f. & Cooper) Cullen 1978

Ht to 3.6 m (12 ft). Inflor two to six. F creamy-white to pale yellow with *bold red stripes down each lobe*, yellow to orange base, little scent or sometimes very fragrant.

This astonishing plant looks too good to be true. Several rhododendrons have lines or stripes on the corolla to a greater or lesser degree but none of these are half so resplendent as this. Some people may consider it garish, in fact *KW* did not admire it and considered it more than a little absurd with its military red stripe down each of its five trouser legs! Does very well out of doors at Brodick Castle, Isle of Arran but even there it sometimes looses its buds. In the 1972 freeze in California, only some buds were lost where the minimum was −7°C (20°F) or higher.

Very closely related to and now made a variety of *dalhousiae* but there is no evidence that the two merge as no plants have been recorded that have anything but bold red lines or none at all. Comes true from hand-pollinated seed. Has been found several times in the wild and the red lines are always remarkably uniform. Relatively common in places. **FCC**, 1934, Exbury, **AM**, 1931, Bodnant.

From Bhutan and Arunachal Pradesh, 1,500–2,700 m (5,000–9,000 ft) in rain forest, dry rock faces, open hillsides, pine-oak forest, epiphytic or terrestial. Usually flowers later than *dalhousiae*.

Late June–August

excellens Hemsl. & Wils. 1910. Rare in cultivation. See *p.* 363.

Ht to 3 m (10 ft). L 15–20 × 3.8–13.3 cm (6–8 × 1½–2¼ in.), lateral nerves eighteen to twenty pairs, louped and branched towards margin.
F white, 7.5 cm (3 in.) long and across, tubular. Stamens fifteen.

Possibly distinct but these funny leaf nerve patterns can occur in other rhododendrons and are probably due to some type of fasciation. Moved to this Alliance from the Maddenii sub-series by Cullen. An isolated distribution in south Yunnan, south of Mengtze, rare. Collected by Henry from one specimen brought in by a native collector.   July in the wild

levinei Merrill. Rare in cultivation. See *p.* 364.

Thin peeling bark, red-brown young shoots. L with ciliate margins. Shoots and petioles with strigose hairs. Calyx with large membranceous lobes. May have some connection with Ciliicalyx Group. Kwangtung.

liliiflorum Lévl. 1913. Recently introduced. See *p.* 365.

Bark reddish, peeling. F white, fragrant. The herbarium specimen looks like *taggianum* to me. From Kweichow and Kwangsi, 600–1,400 m (2,000–4,800 ft) in light woods, open scrubby ridges and rocky shaded slopes.

kiangsiense Fang 1958 Not in cultivation

Ht 1 m (3 ft). L oblong-elliptic. Petiole very short. F white, stigma red. Style short. Stamens eight. Smaller and more glabrous than the closely related *liliiflorum*. No specimen in RBG, Edinburgh. Kiangsi 1,100 m (3,500 ft).

lindleyi T Moore 1864 (*bhotanicum* Clarke, *grathausii* Davidian) H1–3 L1–2 F3–4
Ht to 4.5 m (15 ft). Habit straggly, few shoots, usually epiphytic in the wild. Bark reddish-brown, peeling. Young leaves sometimes tinged red. L 5.5–15 × 1.5–5.5 cm (2¼–6 × ⅗–2¼ in.), elliptic to elongate-oblong-elliptic, rounded to acute at both ends, sometimes slightly rugulose above, sometimes recurved, scales below smallish, unequal, two to three times their own diameter apart. L remain for 2 years. Petiole 1.5–2 cm (about ¾ in.).
Inflor two to twelve commonly three to seven. Pedicel 1–1.5 cm (⅖–⅗ in.), rusty scaly.

F white, white with yellow or orange base, sometimes tinged pink, about 10 cm (49 in.) long, widely tubular, sweetly scented.
Calyx purplish-green, *densely fringed with hairs*. Style scaly only at base. Capsule about 5 cm (2 in.) long, calyx persistent.

This marvellous plant has been introduced many times from over its wide distribution in the wild and varies considerably in cultivation. The early introductions are mostly tender with few large flowers to the truss. Undoubtedly the best garden plant is *L&S* 6562, surprisingly collected as low as 2,600 m (8,500 ft) in south Tibet. It has proved remarkably hardy in cultivation, having flowered successfully most years (recently) in the open at Glendoick. There is a fine group of these at Glenarn, Rhu, Dunbartonshire. Second and third generations of these from seed have given particularly good forms with many flowers to the truss. Our own *C&H* 399 is also excellent, frequently winning prizes in shows but is more tender than *L&S* 6562 (*grothausii*). See Addendum *p.* 364.

L&S 6562 is worth attempting on a sheltered wall in part shade in all but the colder British gardens while the others require a west coast climate. Superb groups are to be seen at Caerhays Castle, Cornwall. As it is always straggly, plant closely together in groups or where they can grow up behind or through another plant. Another alternative is to place on tree stumps, moss covered rocks and cliffs or in forks in trees, provided enough moisture and shelter are available. From seed, it will flower in 3 to 5 years. Hardy in most of New Zealand. Occasional cultivated plants have compact habits, these are almost certainly garden hybrids. More flowers per truss are often produced in cultivation than in the wild. **FCC**, 1937, **AM**, 1935; **AM**, 1969, 'Geordie Sherriff' Glenarn, heavily flushed pink. Closely related to *taggianum* which has a more easterly distribution. **AM**, 1965, 'Dame Edith Sitwell' Sunte House.

A wide distribution from east Nepal eastwards to Arunachal Pradesh, adjacent parts of south Tibet, and Manipur, at 1,800–3,400 m (6,000–11,000 ft). Usually epiphytic in upper temperate rainforest, sometimes on the tops of large trees and also hanging over cliffs and river banks. Late April–May

nuttallii Booth 1853 (*sinonuttallii* Balf.f. & Forr, *goreri* Davidian.) H1 occasionally 2 A+30 L2–4 F4

Ht to 9 m (30 ft). Habit usually sprawly but quite compact in full sun, sometimes epiphytic. Branchlets nearly glabrous. Bark smooth. Some forms have attractive puce, purple to deep purple-red young growth.
L 10–24 × 5.5–12.4 cm (4–10 × 2¾–5 in.), elliptic, rounded at both ends, *heavily bullate-reticulate* above, fairly densely scaly below, 1½–2 times their own diameter apart, unequal. L remain for 3 to 4 years. Petiole 2 cm (¾ in.), sparingly scaly.
Inflor three to nine. Pedicel about 3 cm (1¼ in.).
F white flushed yellow or orange within tube or deep creamy-yellow, often tinged pink. *12.5 cm (5 in.) or more long*, tubular-funnel-shaped, usually strongly fragrant, margins sometimes wavy and/or reflexed.
Calyx to 2.5 cm (1 in.). Style densely scaly towards base. Capsule over 5 cm (2 in.) long, very large.

Where grown successfully, this is perhaps the most magnificent rhododendron of all. The enormous flowers are only rivalled by the Vireya *leucogigas*. Unfortunately, it is seldom a permanent feature outside in British gardens but has flowered in the open for many years at Mount Stewart, Northern Ireland (*sinonuttallii*) and has flowered or survived on walls at Trengwainton and Caerhays, Cornwall and Brodick, Scotland. It grows too strongly for all but large greenhouses and is apt to look rather coarse indoors where the scent may prove to be rather strong (a lady with a sensitive nose likened it to horse piss!).

This species flourishes in many parts of New Zealand, in the mountains around Melbourne, Australia and San Francisco, California, where it makes a quite compact specimen in full sun which it stands very well. I was lucky to see the gorgeous spectacle of a group in full bloom in the Golden Gate Park, San Francisco in May 1956 growing fully exposed on a south slope, buffeted by prevailing westerly winds, and also wild plants in India.

It normally takes some years to flower. C. P. Raffill of Kew grafted it on to *ponticum* and it flowered in 4 to 5 years with as many as nine flowers to the truss.

Now includes *sinonuttallii*. Plants grown under this name have sometimes proved to be slightly hardier. High altitude forms may not be in cultivation. In the 1972 freeze in California, there was only some bud loss where temperatures did not drop below −7°C (20°F). Capsules take about 1 year to ripen. **FCC**, 1864, **AM**, 1936 (var. *stellatum*), **AM**, 1955 (*sinonuttallii*), Sunningdale Nurseries see *p.* 363 under *goreri*; 'Lhasa' *PC* 1971 Crown Lands, *L&S* 12117.

A form known as var. *stellatum KW* 6333 with smaller flowers than the type and apple-green starry calyces may possibly be hardier than type.

Widely distributed but often sparingly (we only found three to four plants growing at the edge of a bog when in Arunachal Pradesh), from Bhutan through Arunachal Pradesh to south-east Tibet, Yunnan and Kweichow, at 1,100–3,700 m (3,500–12,000 ft), usually only epiphytic when young, otherwise in thickets, margins of mixed forest, on boulders in river beds, rocky slopes, edge of bog, in open or dense forest.

April–May

taggianum Hutch. 1931 (*headfortianum* Hutch.) H1–2 L1–2 F3–4

Ht 2.1–3 m (7–10 ft). Leggy shrub with very few branches. Branchlets glandular-scaly. Bark dark reddish-brown and grey, peeling.
L to 12.5 × 6.3 cm (to 5 × 2½ in.), oblong-lanceolate to oval, apex obtuse to rounded, base rounded, small glandular scales below, two to three times their own diameter apart, sometimes recurved as in the former *headfortianum*. L remain for 1 to two years. Petiole 1.3 cm (½ in.).
Inflor three to eight, usually three to four or one to three in the former *headfortianum*. Pedicel 2 cm (¾ in.).
F light amber to cream in bud opening pure white with yellow throat, usually very fragrant, nearly 10 cm (4 in.) long, broadly tubular-funnel-shaped.
Calyx 1.5 cm (⅝ in.), *scaly* rather than hairy. Style scaly lower two-thirds.

A lovely plant, similar to *lindleyi* in many ways only differing in the scaly rather than hairy calyx, the larger, wider lobes of the corolla and often wider leaves except in the former *headfortianum* which has narrower leaves and smaller flowers. Hardiness equals the more tender forms of *lindleyi* and it should be similarly treated. Buds are often frosted or flowers poor after a hard winter. The texture of the flowers looks like fine porcelain and are often frilled. One of the most beautiful species when flourishing. Flowers from seed in 3 to 4 years. Vigorous when grafted on to *ponticum*. **FCC**, 1943, **AM**, 1932.

The plant formerly called *headfortianum* was found by *KW* in the Tsangpo Gorge, south Tibet, and Delei Valley, Arunachal Pradesh. The first plants to flower in cultivation had only one flower per inflorescence but all the original ones died. Subsequent generations from seed have two to three, but retain the narrower recurved leaves.

From south and south-east Tibet, Arunachal Pradesh, Upper Burma and west Yunnan with slight overlap in distribution with *lindleyi*, 1,800–3,700 m (6,000–12,000 ft), in and on margins of conifer forests, among scrub on rocky slopes and margins or thickets or epiphytic on high trees.

Megacalyx Alliance

megacalyx Balf.f. & Ward 1916 H2–3 A+15 L2–3 F3–4

Ht variable 2–7.6 m (7–25 ft). Habit loose floppy bush to small straggly tree. Bark light brown, peeling, fairly smooth.
L to 19 × 7.6 cm (7½ × 3 in.), elliptic to obovate-elliptic, apex and base rounded, *sunken veins above*, glaucous and densely scaly below, scales small and *sunken*, about their own diameter apart. Petiole 1.3 cm (½ in.), rounded except for *shallow groove* above.
Inflor to five. Pedicel 2.5–3.8 cm (1–1½ in.), quite glabrous.
F often flushed purple in bud, opening pure white, yellow or greenish base with 'potter's thumb' marks, nutmeg scented, to 8.9 cm (3½ in.) long, tubular-funnel-shaped with longer lower two lobes.
Calyx *consistently large*, green or pinkish-green, quite decorative through summer, to 2.5 cm (1 in.), glabrous. Stamens ten. Style scaly towards base. Capsule *very short*, only 2 cm (¾ in.), hidden by calyx.

A splendid scented species which should be much more widely grown in really mild areas. Of greater stature than *lindleyi* and *taggianum* and may form a more shapely bush in full sun. Leaves of thicker texture. About equal to the more tender forms of *lindleyi* in hardiness although occasional plants have succeeded in quite cool gardens. These may have come from the higher altitude collections. Harder to propagate and slower to bloom than *lindleyi*.

Recently transferred to a separate Alliance on account of its deeply sunk scales, sunken veins, large calyx and short capsule, **AM**, 1937.

Often very abundant in the wild in north-west Yunnan, east and south-east Tibet and Upper Burma, 1,800–4,000 m (6,000–13,000 ft) usually on steep cliffs and banks, often hanging over water, also in bamboo forest, rain forest, thickets and forest margins, usually mixed with other shrubs, very rarely epiphytic. May

Maddenii Group (*Maddenii sub-series*)

A very variable species, formerly divided into several closely related species which all merge botanically and horticulturally into one another.

It is generally late flowering with white to pink, rarely yellow or purple tinged flowers, heavily scented. The flowers often do not all open at once and therefore there is a long but not very spectacular flowering season. Forms dense, straggly thickets in shade and shelter. Leaves are usually dark green, hard and thick and are very densely scaly below; much thicker and more rigid than the Ciliicalyx Alliance.

Some introductions are relatively hardy in most British gardens once mature but they often loose their buds in cold winters. The flowers are easily damaged by rain and strong sun.

maddenii Hook.f. 1851 H2–3 A+15–25 L1–3 F2–4

Ht 1–9 m (3–30 ft). Habit sometimes compact in the open, straggly in shade, erect or sprawling. Bark rough flaking or sometimes papery, grey to grey-brown.
L 10–20 × 2.5–8 cm (4–8 × 1–3¼ in.), lanceolate to oblong-lanceolate to obovate to elliptic, apex acute to rounded, base obtuse, subacute to rather blunt, scales below dense, nearly contiguous to overlapping; very variable in size and shape, sometimes rugose above. L remain for 2 to 4 years. Petiole 1.3–3 cm (½–1¼ in.).
Inflor two to eleven. Pedicel stout, 1–2 cm (⅕–⅖ in.).
F white, white flushed pink, rose or purple, white lined pink, white with pink or purplish base, cream various shades of pink, pink outside white within, with or without greenish or yellow base or rarely yellow, 5–12.5 cm (2–5 in.) long and up to 12.5 cm (5 in.) across, tubular-funnel-shaped, sweetly scented, partly or covered with scales outside.
Calyx 2–8 mm, not hairy. Stamens fifteen to twenty-five. Style scaly half to whole length.

The whole of this Alliance are now correctly merged into one species containing two sub-species, *maddenii* and *crassum*.

ssp. *crassum* (Franch.) Cullen 1978 (*chapaense* P. Dop, *manipurense* Balf.f. & Watt, *odoriferum* Hutch.). This is the eastern ssp. from Yunnan, south-east Tibet, Upper Burma, Indo-China, Manipur and Nagaland. Capsule rounded at apex, not cut off.

Many forms of this are relatively hardy once mature. Some clones survive at Glendoick and succeed in flowering most years. Plant in enough shade and shelter to reduce frost and sun damage but not so shady that the habit becomes too straggly or flowers are rarely produced. Many plants formerly called *manipurense* have larger than average leaves for the whole species and one form is a dodecaploid 2n = 156 while *odoriferum* often had smaller than average leaves and flowers.

ssp. *maddenii* Hook.f. (*brevitubum* Balf.f. & Cooper, *brachysiphon* Balf.f., *calophyllum* Nutt., *jenkinsii* Nutt., *polyandrum* Hutch.). The western form from western Arunachal Pradesh to Sikkim. Capsule with cut off top.

The larger growing types formerly called *maddenii* are often rather tender and only really suitable for the mildest of British gardens while some of those under *polyandrum* with rather long, narrow leaves and dwarfer habit and *brachysiphon* often with pink flowers, tend to be slightly hardier but all are totally mixed up. *R. calophyllum* was frequently referred to by Mangles as being different from *maddenii* and was widely cultivated under that name at one time, later to largely disappear. The whole Alliance is utterly confusing. Anyone cultivating a large selection is in agreement that it is almost impossible to separate and classify these plants under the former specific names. The type of confusion that occurred was that the supposedly large-leaved and flowered *manipurense* has a type specimen with leaves only 10×4 cm ($4 \times 1\frac{1}{2}$ in.).

The yellow form (possibly only one clone) originated at Nymans. The same seed number at Exbury produced white flowers. The plant at Gigha, if the same as the Nymans, has very large lemon coloured flowers and is unfortunately rather tender.

Taken all over, they vary very much in every way, size, habit, shape and size of flowers, leaves and flower colour and hardiness. We saw all shapes of plant and leaf mixed together on the ridge we explored in Arunachal Pradesh. Many have lovely flowers, especially those with pink, purple or yellow in all or part of the corolla. Most are rather vigorous for indoor culture but are worth trying in sheltered corners or partly shaded walls in most milder parts of Britain. Their scent is one of their chief virtues and all are worth the effort of growing them successfully. They show promise of being heat resistant in such places as Melbourne, Australia and San Diego, California, if given shade, while in the Golden Gate Park, San Francisco, they were moved from shade to sun with very good results, making more compact growth and being more floriferous. **AM**, 1924, white flowers (*crassum*); **AM**, 1928, white, greenish within tube (*maddenii*); **AM**, 1933 white, yellow in throat; **AM**, 1938, rose-pink (*polyandrum*).

Found form 1,500–3,700 m (5,000–12,000 ft) in a great variety of habitats, often in dense forest where it tends to grow horizontally with vertical branchlets, also on open ridges and slopes, rocks in river bed, cliffs (limestone and granite), dry hillsides, humus covered boulders, conifer forests, mixed and bamboo thickets. May–July

MICRANTHA SUBSECTION (MICRANTHUM SERIES) (L)

micranthum Turcz. 1848 (*pritzelianum* Diels, *rosthornii* Diels) H4 A–5 L1–2 F1–2

Ht to 1.8 m (6 ft) or more in cultivation, to 5 m (17 ft) in the wild. Habit rather straggly with occasional long vigorous shoots. Bark grey, pale brown to brown.
L 3.2–4.4 × 0.6–1.3 cm ($1\frac{1}{4}$–$1\frac{3}{4}$ × $\frac{1}{4}$–$\frac{1}{2}$ in.), oblanceolate, gradually narrowed to base, with prominent overlapping light brown scales below. L remain for 1 year. Petiole 3 mm.
Inflor many flowered. Pedicel about 8 mm.
F milky-white, 6–8 mm ($\frac{1}{4}$–$\frac{1}{3}$ in.) long, campanulate.

Calyx about 1.5 mm ciliate. Stamens ten. Ovary scaly, style shorter than stamens, glabrous. Capsule 6 mm long.

This distinct species resembles a ledum but the latter have no scales. It is free flowering and hardy. While useful for its late blooming season, it does not create much of a spectacle even when covered with flowers. Has no close relationship with any other subsection. Shows little variation over its wide distribution.

From Shangtung to Kansu in north China, also west Hupeh, west Szechwan and rarely in north-east Yunnan, 1,600–3,200 m (5,200–10,500 ft), thickets, dry gorges, cliffs, ridges, grassy slopes and under forests.

May–July

MONANTHA SUBSECTION (Cullen 1978) *(UNIFLORUM SERIES PART, TRIFLORUM SERIES PART)* (L)

This new subsection contains *concinnoides, flavantherum* and *kasoense* from the Triflorum series and *monanthum* from the Uniflorum series (formerly placed in the Boothii series).

These are all little-known species, none of which are in cultivation although *concinnoides* was.

Relationship is probably with the Triflora, Moupinensia and the new Tephropepla subsections.

concinnoides Hutch. & Ward 1932 Probably not in cultivation

Habit small shrub, often epiphytic.
L 2.3–4.5 × 1–2.5 cm $(1–1\frac{3}{4} × \frac{2}{5}–1$ in.), elliptic to obovate-elliptic. Petiole 3–6 mm.
Inflor terminal three. Pedicel 0.5–1 cm.
F purplish-pink fading to white at base, darker spotting inside, 1.6–2.6 cm $(\frac{3}{5}–1$ in.) long, tubular-campanulate.

This plant was cultivated in Britain including Exbury but is probably lost. Said to be growing in California (E. H. Long, Oakland). *KW* said it was a scraggy little plant with small bronzed leaves and tiny flowers produced near the ends of the rains in September–October with capsules which take nearly a year to ripen. L. de Rothschild said it was 'not of special note'. Both Cullen and Davidian have said that it might be just *tephropeplum*.

From Arunachal Pradesh, Delei Valley, 2,700–3,400 m (9,000–11,000 ft) abundant on big firs, usually quite low down, in rhododendron forest and on rocks and tree stumps in rhododendron thickets on an exposed ridge.

flavantherum Hutch. & Ward 1931 Not in cultivation

Ht 2–3 m (6–10 ft). F bright, clear yellow, tubular-campanulate, anthers deep orange. Was probably never in cultivation (L. de Rothschild never saw it in flower). There is one specimen in the RBG herbarium, Edinburgh. Both Cullen and Davidian say it is near *xanthostephanum*.

From south-east Tibet, Tsangpo Gorge, 2,400–2,700 m (8,000–9,000 ft) on vertical cliffs facing north.

kasoense Hutch. & Ward 1931 Not in cultivation

F yellow, tubular-campanulate. Very close to *flavantherum* but with a smaller calyx. Like the above, Rothschild never saw it in flower.

From south-east Tibet, Pachakshiri, *L&S* 6583, also Arunachal Pradesh, Kaso peak, *KW* 8522, 2,100–2,700 m (7,000–9,000 ft) in dense mixed forests, on rocks, in thickets and epiphytic.

monanthum Balf.f. & W.W. Sm. Not in cultivation

Ht 30 cm–1.20 m (1–4 ft). Habit straggly, often epiphytic. L 2.5–3.8 × 0.6–1.8 cm (1–1½ × ¼–¾ in.) long, usually elliptic, densely scaly below. Inflor *one flowered*. Pedicel short. F bright lemon to sulphur-yellow, 1.3–1.9 cm (½–¾ in.) long, widely funnel-shaped. Calyx very small. Anthers brick-red to red-brown. Ovary densely scaly, style glabrous.

An interesting species, quite widespread in the wild and surprisingly never introduced. Although the flowers are very small and solitary, the colour is rich and this species was frequently reported as having bloomed twice a year in the wild.

South-east Tibet, Upper Burma, north-west Yunnan, 2,700–4,400 m (9,000–14,500 ft), epiphytic on conifers and other moss-clad trees and scrub, also open situations, margins of thickets and bamboo brakes, on rocks and cliffs.   Spring and September–November in the wild

MUMEAZALEA SECTION (SEMIBARBATUM SERIES) (E)

One distinct species with solitary flowers from lateral buds; five unequal stamens.

Related to Azaleastrum section (Ovatum series) which contains only evergreen species.

semibarbatum Maxim 1870 (*Azalea semibarbata* Kuntze, *Azaleastrum semibarbatum* Makino, *Mumeazalea semibarbata* Makino) H4 L1–3 F1

Ht 0.60–3 m (2–10 ft). Habit bushy, fairly erect with irregulary whorled slender spreading branches. Branchlets pubescent and glandular, evanescent. Branches yellowish-grey or grey to dark brown.
L deciduous, thin 2–5 × 0.7–2.5 cm (¾–2 × ¼–1 in.), elliptic to elliptic-ovate to elliptic-oblong, *bristle-tipped serrations at edge*. Petiole 4–7 mm pubescent and setose-glandular.
Inflor *solitary from lateral buds only*, crowded at ends of branchlets, opening after leaves. Pedicel about 4 mm pubescent and glandular.
F white, yellowish-white or white flushed pink, spotted red, 1.5–2 cm (⅜–¾ in.) across, rotate-funnel-shaped, short tube about 6 mm (¼ in.) long. Calyx minute, 2 mm pubescent and glandular. Stamens five, very unequal. Ovary glandular-setose, style shorter than stamens glabrous. Capsule very short as in Azaleastrum section (Ovatum series).

This plant is grown for its foliage only, the flowers being small and hidden in the foliage. The leaves are often attractively tinted during the summer and turn yellow, orange or more commonly red or crimson in the autumn. A very glandular species covered with stipulate glands. The terminal bud develops into a leafy shoot.

From Japan, south Hokkaido, Honshu, Shikoku and Kyushu in open areas and thickets in the mountains.   June–July in Japan   June

NERIIFLORA SUBSECTION (E)

mallotum Balf.f. & Ward 1917 (*aemulorum* Balf.f.) H3–4 A+5 L3–4 F2–3

Ht 1.5–4.5 m (5–15 ft). Habit shrub or small tree, usually narrow and stiff, said to be scraggy in the wild but often of good shape in cultivation. Branchlets tomentose. Bark roughish, flaking, purplish-grey to grey-green.
L 7–22 × 3.5–7 cm (3–9 × 1½–3 in.), obovate, apex rounded to retuse, base obtuse, *very thick and stiff, dark green and rugose above*, glabrous at maturity, *dense woolly cinnamon-brown indumentum below*. L remain for 1 to 3 years. Petiole stout, about 1.3 cm tomentose.
Inflor *to fifteen fairly compact*, rachis about 1 cm. Pedicel stout to 1.3 cm densely woolly.
F scarlet, cherry-red to dark crimson, 3.7–5 cm (1½–2 in.) long, tubular-campanulate, fleshy.
Calyx very small with woolly teeth. Ovary woolly, style glabrous. Capsule short about 1 cm densely tomentose-woolly.

One of the best foliage plants in the genus, especially with vigorous young specimens. The flowers are very fine when they get a chance to open properly as they open early in the season and are often destroyed by titmice. Hardy enough for most woodland gardens in Britain, but badly cut back at Glendoick in 1981–2 and killed at Dawyck, Peeblesshire.

While an aberrant species in the Neriiflora subsection with its large rugose leaves, fairly compact truss, very small calyx and larger than usual stature, it does not fit happily into any other subsection. The small capsule and surprisingly small seed makes it distinct from the Falconera subsection to which the foliage bears some resemblance. Hutchinson suggests a relationship with *lanatum* which has a similar densely tomentose ovary but I see little else to connect them.

An excellent example of a distinct species with a limited (known) distribution. Farrer and my father said it was the only species that they saw growing solitary that could cope with the bamboo. It made squat, sturdy specimens around 5 m (16 ft), very uniform, standing out of a sea of bamboo in exposed situations. They observed that the flowers were resistant to rain or sleet but we have not found this so in cultivation. **AM,** 1933 Borde Hill.

Found only around the north-east Upper Burma–Yunnan frontier at 3,400–3,700 m (11,000–12,000 ft) on open hillsides and rocky slopes, margins of thickets and bamboo brakes.   February–April

PARISHIA SUBSECTION (IRRORATUM SERIES, SUB-SERIES PARISHII) (E)

Recently made into a separate subsection.

The chief distinctions of this subsection are the presence of stellate hairs, fleshy predominantly red flowers with five lobes, ten stamens tomentose and often glandular ovary and style, the late flowering period and distinctive long-tailed bud-scales. The capsules are stout, blunt and tomentose. All come from low altitudes in wet areas in Burma, Yunnan and Nagaland. This appears to be a primitive subsection.

These red-flowered species are amongst the finest of this colour and are magnificent in mid to late summer in the mild localities where they can be successfully grown. Plant in their final positions when fairly young as they grow very late in the season and dislike being moved.

The number of species in this subsection have been reduced. *R. cookeianum* is a species of uncertain relationships and has therefore been placed after the end of the subsections. *R. venator* has no close affinities and is given its own subsection. *R. agapetum* becomes a synonym of *kyawii* and *eriogynum* a synonym of *facetum*.

elliottii Watt ex W.W. Sm. 1914 H2–3 A+15 L2–3 F3–4

Ht 3–9 m (10–30 ft). Habit upright, often rather straggly. Young branches tomentose and glandular. Buds rounded and prominent.
L to 25 × 10 cm (10– × 4 in.), elliptic-oblong, apex obtuse, base broadly cuneate to rounded, glossy above, glabrous on maturity, glossy below, glabrous or with vestiges of stellate indumentum, especially on midrib. Petiole 2.5 cm thinly floccose and glandular at first, ± glabrous on maturity.
Inflor ten to twenty in compact truss, rachis about 1 cm. Pedicel 1 cm minutely glandular.
F scarlet to crimson with deeper spots, sometimes purplish-red to deep rose-purple, with nectar pouches, to 7.5 cm (3 in.) long and wide, tubular-campanulate.
Calyx 3–4 cupular, hairy and glandular. Ovary densely rufous hairy, style hairy and glandular.

This magnificent species was originally introduced by Watt and later by *KW*. Watt's plants all had purple flowers and the first introductions into the USA had lilac-rose to deep rose-purple flowers and probably came from seed off Watt's plants. These apparently all died in the 1950s as a result of a freeze but were considered quite attractive. Wild seed was later sent there under *KW* 19083 and some of these are said to show some hardiness. The brilliant red flowers have led to this species being much used in hybridizing.

It has the typical buds and hairy style of this subsection but has generally more glabrous leaves.

This species is unfortunately tender throughout most of Britain, being just as hardy enough to survive in a few milder gardens in the south of England. The very late growth is easily frosted and it is hard to propagate. Rare in cultivation but a big group grows at Mount Stewart, Northern

Ireland. 'War Paint', an American clone grown from open pollinated British seed of *KW* 7725 is said to be a hybrid. **AM**, 1934, Embley Park, Hampshire, **FCC**, 1937, Clyne Castle, Wales.

Found on Japvo, Nagaland and Manipur, north-east India, 2,400–2,700 m (8,000–9,000 ft).   May to late June

facetum Balf.f. & Ward 1917 *eriogynum* Balf.f. & W.W. Sm. 1917 H2–3 L2–3 F3–4

Ht 2.4–4.5 m (8–15 ft) to 12 m (40 ft) in the wild. Habit compact to leggy. Branchlets with white hairs at first. Bark roughish, flaking, slightly reddish-brown.
L 12–20 × 5–7.5 cm (5–8 × 2–3 in.), oblong-elliptic to oblong lanceolate, apex obtuse, base cuneate to rounded or truncate, white to light brown indumentum above at first, glabrous on maturity; similar below, shiny with patches of easily rubbed off indumentum remaining for a while. L remain for 2 years. Petiole 2.5–3 cm.
Inflor twelve to twenty, rachis 1–1.5 cm. Pedicel 1.5 cm hairy.
F deep rose to clear, bright red with nectar pouches, to 7.5 cm (3 in.) long, tubular-campanulate.
Calyx 4–5 mm, fleshy, reddish, hairy. Ovary densely hairy, style hairy at base, glandular to tip.

One of the loveliest red flowered species but only fit for mild localities such as the western British seaboard and the mildest southern gardens. Not suitable for hot climates. It looks best planted on a woodland fringe, just out of strong sunshine. Shelter and moisture are needed in the late growing season and the flowers are long lasting provided they do not collapse in the heat.

Cut to the ground in 1955 freeze in Seattle but grew again. Undamaged in California in 1972 freeze although the growth was still soft. Generally easier than the closely related *kyawii*. My father, who saw it flowering in Burma, reckoned this the finest red of any rhododendron. **AM**, 1924, Sunninghill, Berks. (as *eriogynum*). **AM**, 1938 Clyne Castle, Wales.

Common at low elevations on Burma–Yunnan frontier and a little farther east, 2,400–3,400 m (8,000–11,000 ft), open conifer, deciduous and mixed forests, thickets, stony slopes and amongst scrub in moist areas. Sometimes the first species met with at low elevations.

June to August or later in shade

kyawii Lace & W.W. Sm. 1914 (*agapetum* Balf.f. & Ward *prophantum* Balf.f. & Forr.) H2–3 L2–3 F3–4

Ht 4.5–7.6 m (15–25 ft). Habit small scraggy tree or shrub. Branchlets tomentose and glandular at first.
L 10–30 × 3.5–10 cm (4–12 × 1½–4 in.), oblong to oblong-oval, apex and base rounded, reddish-brown indumentum and glands at first above, sometimes semi-persistent, otherwise bright green; similar below, indumentum easily rubbed off. Petiole 3–6 cm hairy and glandular at first.
Inflor ten to twenty, rachis 2.5–4 cm. Pedicel densely glandular and sparsely hairy.

F bright rose-scarlet, scarlet to crimson, not spotted to faintly spotted, 4.5–6 cm (1¾–2½ in.) long, tubular-campanulate with nectar pouches. Calyx about 5 mm, glandular and hairy. Ovary densely hairy ± glandular, style crimson, hairy and glandular.

Larger in most parts than *facetum* with broader and larger leaves, rounded at both ends and more glandular. However, they do appear to merge in some herbarium specimens with a pointed leaf apex. Could be worth some separate status. Just as fine horticulturally but possibly even more tender with still later growth.

Upper Burma and Burma–Yunnan frontier, 1,500–3,700 m (5,000–12,000 ft), deep wooded gorges, limestone cliffs, mixed thickets and forests. Apparently flowers twice or over a very long period in the wild.   June–July–August

parishii C. B. Clarke 1882 H1 L2–3 F2–3?

Ht 5.5–7.6 m (18–25 ft). Young shoots rusty-tomentose at first.
L broadly elliptic to obovate 7–12 × 4–7 cm (3–5 × 1½–3 in.), much wider for their length than other members of the subsection, apex pointed to rounded, base broadly cuneate, indumentum as others.
F red with deeper lines, 3.5 cm (1½ in.) long, tubular-campanulate.

Appears to be closely related to *kyawii* but with much wider leaves for their length. Probably not in cultivation. Lower Burma, 1,900 m (6,200 ft)

schistocalyx Balf.f. & Forr. 1920 H3 L1–2 F2–3

Ht 3.6–4.5 m (12–15 ft).
F bright rose crimson.
Calyx to 2 cm, split on one side almost to base, otherwise uneven and ragged.

Very similar to *facetum* apart from irregular large calyx but as *facetum* has a fairly large, uneven calyx itself, it is doubtful if this character warrants specific status alone. West Yunnan, 3,000–3,400 m (10,000–11,000 ft).

PONTICA SUBSECTION (HYMENANTHES SUBSECTION, PONTICUM SERIES) (E) See Addendum *p.* 366.

This is a rather odd assemblage of species which has been dealt with (botanically) in many different ways by botanists and horticulturalists from Japan, USA, Sweden and Britain. Who has got nearest to the most correct or best interpretation of this group, it is hard to say and botanists will no doubt go on juggling with them for years to come. See *p.* 366–7.

The chief characters used in the *Species of Rhododendron* are (1) the elongated or candelabroid inflorescences; (2) the erect pedicels and capsules; and (3) the deeply cut corolla lobes.

Horticulturally this subsection contains amongst the hardiest, most heat tolerant and easiest grown species. Some have been invaluable for hybridizing for hardiness and will be for heat tolerance in the future. All survived the 1972 freeze in Oregon with no damage.

Leach claimed that the Japanese members of the old Caucasicum sub-series have entirely different indumentum to those from the Caucasus and therefore should be placed in another subsection but what other characters warrant this theory if any?

The old division into two sub-series has been abolished. Characters separating out the old Ponticum sub-series were the ± lack of indumentum on the soft leathery leaves. Neither are sufficient nor indeed reliable as some indumentum is frequently present on all four species except *ponticum* and the texture of the leaves is not distinctive. The species not described in this book were covered in *Dwarf Rhododendrons* and *The Smaller Rhododendrons*.

R. catawbiense

adenopodum transferred to Argyrophylla subsection. See *Dwarf Rhododendrons p.* 149.

brachycarpum D. Don ex G. Don 1834 H4 A–15 L1–2 F1–3

Ht 2.5–4 m (8–13 ft). Habit rounded and compact when young and to older in the open, looser growth in shade. *Pointed growth buds.* Bark roughish, greyish-brown. Young foliage densely clad with hairs which are evanescent during the first year except on the underside.
L 7–15 × 3–7 cm (3–6 × 1¼–3 in.), oblong, oblong-elliptic to oblong-obovate, indumentum below thin felty, variable in thickness, pale fawn to

brownish; often convex. L remain for 1 to 2 years. Petiole 1.5–2 cm ± glabrous on maturity.

Inflor ten to twenty, elongated, rachis 2–3 cm. Pedicel unequal, 2–4 cm sparsely tomentose.

F pink to white, sometimes deep rose to yellowish with *brownish-green spots and flushed green, often in lines*, hairy at base of tube, about 2.5 cm (1 in.) long and 3–5 cm (1¼–2 in.) across, broadly funnel-shaped.

Calyx small, about 2 mm. Ovary densely tomentose, *style shorter than stamens*, glabrous.

A useful, very hardy late flowering species. The flowers are attractively marked but are rather small in contrast with the foliage and are sometimes partially hidden under the leaves on young plants. These make fine symmetrical bushes when growing on an open site. Doleshy suggests that this species is an immigrant from farther north as it awaits for long days to flower, growth comes early before the flowers and seed ripens quickly.

Hardy in much of eastern USA and south Sweden where it grows well and stands wind and dried up mineral soil better than most other rhododendrons. The early growth of young plants sometimes suffers from frost damage in Britain. Even grows in Iceland. Double flowered clones are known in Japan. A very distinct species (with ssp. *fauriei*) which might be better placed by itself.

Common at high altitudes in mid-Honshu to Hokkaido, south Kuriles and mid to south Korea, often above the tree-line at 1,700–2,300 m (5,500–7,500 ft); also on the two highest peaks on Shikoko where it grows with *degronianum* var. *heptamerum* and dwarf bamboo; also on rocky slopes, larva flows with conifers or as a continuous scrub cover above the tree-line. May–July

brachycarpum ssp. *fauriei* Franch. 1883–6 H4 L1–2 F1–2

This is typically glabrous on both leaf surfaces and is otherwise virtually identical with *brachycarpum*. In the wild, they grow mixed in some locations and separately in others. Little difference horticulturally.

brachycarpum ssp. *tigerstedtii* Nitz. Not recognized by Chamberlain.

Ht 5 m + (17 ft +). Young shoots with sparse covering of radiate hairs. L 15–25 × 5–9 cm (6–10 × 2–3½ in.) with radiate hairs below.

F white, greenish spots, 7 cm (nearly 3 in.) across. Calyx larger than type.

This variety is apparently larger in all parts than the type with thicker shoots, larger growth and larger leaves and flowers. Has withstood −45°C (−49°F) at Mustila Arboretum, Finland and is probably the hardiest rhododendron in the world. Could be very useful for increasing hardiness in hybrids. Named for Dr Carl Tigerstedt who introduced it. Said to bloom 2 to 3 weeks earlier than type. See *p.* 366.

From central and north Korea at 200–1,600 m (660–5,300 ft), common in fir forests and on cliffs in woods.

catawbiense Michaux 1803 H4 A – 25 L1–2 F1–3

Ht to 3 m (10 ft) or more. Habit spreading, rounded in the open, generally wider than tall. Young shoots tomentose, later glabrous. Bark roughish brownish-grey.
L 7–15 × 3–5 cm (3–6 × 1–2 in.), elliptic, broadly elliptic, oblong-oval to oval, apex rounded to acuminate, base cordate to rounded, *convex*, glabrous below to naked eye but with vestiges of indumentum, especially on midrib, almost glaucous. L remain for 2 to 3 years.
Petiole 2–3 cm ± woolly at first, later glabrous.
Inflor fifteen to twenty fairly compact to compact, generally elongated, rachis 3–4 cm, pedicel 3.5 cm ± floccose.
F lilac-purple, light to darker pink, rosy-pink or occasionally white, faintly spotted, about 4 cm (1½ in.) long, funnel-campanulate, puberulous in throat.
Calyx small 1 mm, slightly floccose. Ovary *densely tomentose*, fawn to rufous, style glabrous.

One of the toughest of all species and used as a parent in a great many of our best-known hardy hybrids. Quite attractive itself. The true species seems rare in Britain and should be grown more often, especially to replace the ubiquitous *ponticum* where it is liable to be damaged in severe winters. Excellent white forms which apparently breed true from seed have been raised by growing several generations of seedlings and always selecting the best and hardiest white to breed from again. One of these is 'Powell Glass', a fifth generation selection. This is proving an ideal parent for hardy whites and cleaner colours, avoiding the 'blue' tones common in early *catawbiense* hybrids. Succeeds in most of eastern USA although some hotter lowland regions are not too satisfactory. Survives in Iceland.

Natural groups of dwarf *catawbiense* are *not* apparently to be found, even on top of Mt Mitchell and Roan Mt. Several distinct shades are growing on the latter peak which appear to be identical to named clones (hybrids?) such as 'Boursault', 'Roseum Elegans' and 'Catawbiense Grandiflorum'. Natural hybrids with *maximum* are reported to be quite common, known sometimes as 'Wellesleyanum'.

Summits of mountains of North Carolina around 1,800 m (6,000 ft) and mountain sides in Virginia at 1,200 m (4,000 ft) associated with firs, lycopodiums, rowans and at slightly lower elevations, *calendulaceum*.

June

catawbiense Insularis Group (apparently not officially described).

This lowland *catawbiense* has only recently come to people's attention. It probably evolved from isolated colonies left behind by an ice age and has adapted to the warmer and present day torrid conditions of the coastal plains. It is found in a few places on steep hillsides in North Carolina and Georgia where it grows to 2.4–4.5 m (8–15 ft) high at 45–300 m (150–1,000 ft) above sea-level.
F light to darker or even rosy-pink, one white (so far discovered) to the more typical type with bluish to violet, lavender and magenta shades.

Could be highly resistant to heat and root-rot together with being very useful as a garden plant and for hybridization.

macrophyllum G. Don 1834 (*californicum* Hook.) H4 A − 5 L1–2 F1–3

Ht 3–9 m (10–39 ft). Habit open tree-like shrub, often erect. Bark fairly rough, dark grey.
L 7–23 × 3–7.5 cm (3–9 × 1¼–3 in.), oblong-obovate to elliptic, apex rounded to acuminate, base tapered, glabrous apart from vestiges of brown indumentum below. L remain for 2 to 3 years. Petiole 1–2 cm.
Inflor about twenty fairly compact, rachis about 2 cm. Pedicel 3.5–5 cm.
F usually *deep rose to rosy-purple*, more rarely clear pink, white or even nearly red; reddish-brown to reddish spots, 3–4 cm (about 1½ in.) long, broadly campanulate, lobes often crinkly.
Calyx 1 mm slightly hairy. Ovary tomentose, style glabrous.

Along with *occidentale* and the peculiar *albiflorum*, this is the only rhododendron from western North America. It is very widespread and obviously extremely drought and heat resistant, which should make it a valuable parent for hybridizing. It is also very free flowering in an open position. The flowers are quite pretty but most forms are apt to become leggy. Hard to propagate from cuttings.

Grows best on the Oregon coast and parts of the Olympic Peninsula, especially along Hood Canal. Does well on gravelly soil, often coming up quickly after clearing or burning. Stands salt spray.

We find it not easy to satisfy at Glendoick, usually having a poor root system and chlorotic foliage. A compact form with pink flowers from the Portland Test Garden has though, grown happily for many years. Seems to stand the climate of Iceland.

From California north to British Columbia, sea-level to 1,200 m (4,000 ft), in sun or semi-shade, often on the edge of conifer forest or *Lithocarpus* sp. or mixed with *Arctostaphylos*, *Vaccinium*, *Gaultheria* and *Ledum* species. White flowered plants used to be relatively common on the Oregon coast but have been largely destroyed by developers.

May–June

maximum L. 1753 (*procerum* Salisb., *purpureum* G. Don, *purshii* G. Don) H4 A − 25 L1–2 F1–2 'Rosebay', 'Great Rhododendron' or 'Great Laurel'.

Ht to 12 m (40 ft) in the wild, a shrub in cultivation. Young shoots with evanescent glandular hairs. Bark slightly rough, dark greyish.
L 10–30 × 4–7 cm (4–12 × 1½–3 in.), *ovate-lanceolate to obovate-lanceolate*, oblanceolate to narrowly obovate, apex acute, base narrowed to rounded; young leaves have indumentum on both surfaces, white and sticky, leaving a thin film-like indumentum below on maturity, midrib glandular.
L remain for 3 to 6 years. Often has very small dendroid-type hairs.
Petiole 2.5–4 cm, tomentose and glandular, later ± glabrous.
Inflor sixteen to twenty-four, elongated truss. Pedicel 2–3 cm glandular.
F light to deeper pink or purplish or white flushed pink, deeper at edges,

rarely white; with greenish spots, about 3 cm (1¼ in.) long and 3.8–5 cm (1½–2 in.) across, campanulate.

Calyx *about 5 mm, glandular*. Stamens eight to twelve. Ovary glandular and hairy, style glabrous.

Rare in Britain and considered to be of little garden value. While late flowering, the flowers are on the small side often of a poor, anaemic colour. So far, it has proved to be an inferior parent to *catawbiense* but it is a heat resistant very hardy species which stands heavy shade. Has survived on a poor site at Glendoick for many years. 'Summer Time' **AM**, 1974 Crown Lands.

'Leachii' is a curiosity with compact growth, undulating leaves and globular flower buds which is said to come more or less true from seed. Another odd form is a reddish flowered variation with a red cambium layer which looses its pigment at low elevations. Some of these change their flower colour from year to year from white to pink or red and back again, probably due to an extreme example of the often reported minor degrees in colour change which result from weather and other variable conditions. 'Roseum' is most likely a *ponticum* or *maximum* hybrid. 'Ashleyi' is an extreme mutant from North Carolina.

Common and widespread in many parts of eastern North America from Georgia and Alabama to Nova Scotia to 900 m (3,000 ft). Grows best in hollows and along stream sides and in raised areas in bogs and swamps, but can survive on drier, poorer and higher sites. Forms dense thickets known by mountaineers as 'hells' or 'slicks'. Often associated with mountain laurel, *Kalmia latifolia* and in conifer forest or deciduous woods. Occurs in scattered colonies, frequently some distance apart, appearing to be relic populations. Young shoots are often effected by lacewing fly.

July

ponticum L. 1762 (*baeticum* Boiss & Reuter) H4 A–5 L1–2 F1–3

Ht to 4.5 m (15 ft) or more. Habit dense in open sites, leggy in shade. Bark rough, brown to dark brown.
L 10–20 × 3–7.5 cm (4–8 × 1¼–3 in.), narrowly obovate, elliptic, oblong to oblanceolate, usually *flattish*, glabrous. L remain for 2 to 4 years. Petiole 1–2 cm.
Inflor ten to fifteen fairly compact to compact, rachis usually glabrous. Pedicel 3–3.5 cm glabrous.
F lilac-pink to pinkish-purple, pale to deep shades and occasionally white?, often spotted, 4–5 cm (1½–2 in.) long, campanulate.
Calyx small, about 3 mm. Ovary *glabrous*, style glabrous.

This, the 'common' rhododendron of Britain which has naturalized itself widely, is capable of growing happily and spreading by layers and seed over a much larger range of conditions than any other species. It has become a serious pest of silviculture and its ability to sucker and resist weedkillers is well known. It is still used all too much as an understock and its versatility goes as far as to make a good hedging plant in wet, mild locations. Contrary to many beliefs, it is not a native of Britain and is by no means the frost hardiest species, frequently suffering minor damage in hard winters even at Glendoick.

Huge areas in full flower make a vivid mass of colour and are a charming sight scattered through wooded hillsides. Some forms are better coloured than others, even to the extent of reaching near 'blue' and rivalling *augustinii*.

Not reliably hardy in south Sweden where it does not flower too freely. Slight damage was found on terminal shoots in Seattle in the 1955 freeze. Survives sub-tropical heat in lowland Japan. Some success in Iceland.

Various queer forms occur: 'Variegatum' wavy variegated edge to leaf; 'Aucubifolium' yellow spotted leaves; 'Lancifolium' small narrow leaves, flat, not wavy, small flowers; 'Cheiranthifolium' narrow leaves with wavy margins, small disappointing flowers, probably a hybrid; a double found in a German park, flowers hose-in-hose with about twenty sterile anthers, some with petaloid enlargements, no pistil, 'Folius Purpureus' has greenish leaves in summer turning to a copper colour in winter. FCC, 1895.

R. ponticum has a most interesting distribution. This is centred in Turkey with relic populations in Turkey in Europe, south-east Bulgaria, Caucasus, Lebanon and southern Iberian Peninsular. Some of these have been given separate names in the past but really do not warrant any botanical status. The Lebanon form was called variety or ssp. *brachycarpum* (not to be confused with the species *brachycarpum*) while the Iberian form was known as *baeticum*. From my own observations of wild *ponticum* in Portugal and Turkey, I would say that the most usual type of plant in cultivation is nearer the Portuguese than the Turkish forms. These observations were very limited and a much more thorough study is necessary to prove this point or otherwise. Many 'ponticum' have become contaminated with the blood of *maximum* and *catawbiense* plus various hybrids and botanical examination has confirmed this.

Turkey, from sea-level to 1,800 m (to 6,000 ft) in mixed deciduous, mixed beech, fir and spruce forest, hornbeam and alder forest with laurel, vaccinium and other woody plants. Lebanon, 700–1,100 m (2,300–3,500 ft), sandy soil in pinewoods on sandstone. Iberian Peninsula, near Cadiz and Algeciras in Spain; Monchique and other peaks in central and south Portugal in shrub on granite slopes and wooded valleys beside rivers. Those from low elevations are likely to be the most heat resistant.

× *sochadzeae* Char. & Davlian 1967 (*ponticum* var. *artvinense* [not published]) (*ponticum* × *caucasicum*)

This is a splendid example of natural hybridity which I was lucky enough to observe myself in the wild in 1962. The whole range of expected variations in a hybrid population have been found and there is an excellent representative collection of these in the herbarium in the RBG, Edinburgh.

R. ponticum typical has a glabrous ovary and this character holds good in all the areas where no other rhododendron species are present, plus all specimens collected below 1,750 m (5,700 ft) where only the occasional *ungernii* and *smirnowii* are found but no *caucasicum*. *R. ponticum* has a long flowering season which overlaps with the other Turkish species throughout their range up to the lower stands of *caucasicum*. Most F1 hybrids and obvious back crosses and subsequent generations are located just below *caucasicum* proper at about 1,800–2,100 m (6,000–7,000 ft). All this swarm has a ± amount of hairs on the ovary and it is obvious from the herbarium specimens that the nearer they are to *caucasicum*, the more hairs there are on the ovary. What is more, many of these have vestiges of the plastered indumentum of that species. At the other extreme, pale pink or white flowered plants may be found with glabrous leaves shaped like *ponticum* but again with hairy ovaries.

In most cases, the two parents are to be found in the vicinity but in certain places, these hybrids may have perpetuated themselves by seedlings. Some of these show evidence of being back crosses on to either parent like the plants mentioned above while others could be in the gradual process of speciation with hybrids forming colonies breeding amongst themselves. We saw no evidence ourselves where hybrids were apparently breeding true to type. Seed collected from a wild white flowered plant near to *ponticum* gave us seedlings showing the whole range between both species. We saw two large clumps, each consisting of one clonal hybrid with dirty pink and dirty cream coloured flowers. Both showed strong *caucasicum* influence with regards to habit, leaf and flower shapes but had no indumentum. This would be expected in all but back crosses on to *caucasicum* as it is a known fact that when an indumentumed species is crossed with a glabrous one, the F1 hybrids are invariably glabrous. Only back crosses, F2 or subsequent generations might throw a certain percentage of seedlings with an indumentum present. On the other hand, the hairs on the ovary must be a dominant feature which are present to some extent on all this hybrid group.

Hybrids between *ponticum* and *ungernii* and *smirnowii* probably also occur.

smirnowii Traut 1886 H4 A−15 L2–3 F2–3

Ht 1–3 m (3–10 ft). Habit often compact in the open, more upright in shade. Young shoots clothed with white felty tomentum which may last a year or two; bud-scales ± persistent for some years. Bark roughish, brown.
L 6.5–17.5 × 2–3.5 cm (2½–7 × ¾–1½ in.), oblong, oblanceolate to oblong-obovate, apex obtuse to semi-rounded, base tapered, cuneate, young leaves white woolly with scattered glands, soon glabrous above, dense thick woolly indumentum below, pale fawn to pale brown on maturity, margins recurved. L remain for 3 to 5 years. Petiole 1–1.5 cm with white evanescent tomentum.
Inflor ten to twelve loose to fairly compact, rachis 1.5 cm. Pedicel 3–5 cm densely glandular and with fewer floccose hairs.
F mauve-pink, deep pink to rose-purple, rarely very pale pink or white, all with brown to yellow spots, about 4 cm (1½ in.) long, funnel-campanulate puberulous inside.
Calyx minute 2–3 mm, tomentose and glandular. *Ovary white tomentose*, style glabrous.

A very useful hardy species with attractive pale densely woolly indumentum. The flowers with softer, paler colours are the more desirable. Should be grown in open sites to avoid it becoming untidy and leggy.

It is probably the hardiest species with a thick indumentum, being successful in south Sweden and many cold eastern North American districts where it is inclined to open its flowers in autumn. Survived the severe freezes in Oregon and Washington States and shows some promise of being heat and drought resistant. Reported to grow slowly but steadily in Iceland. Closely related to *ungernii*, the chief differences are shown in italics.

The Caucasus (Georgia) and north-east Turkey, 800–2,300 m (2,800–7,500 ft), abundant on igneous and limestone outcrops, often at the edge of spruce forest or just above the tree-line. Overlaps with *caucasicum*, *luteum*, *ponticum* and *ungernii* and sometimes hybridizes naturally with the three other rhododendrons. Like other species in the wild (and in gardens) in some years it may fail to flower. When I was in Turkey in 1962, it was covered with flower and had been the previous year.   May–June

ungernii Traut 1886 H4 L2–3 F1–2

Ht 2.4–6 m (8–20 ft) in the wild, usually less in cultivation. Habit generally looser than *smirnowii*. Young shoots white evanescent tomentose. Bark brown, slightly flaking.
L *10–25 × 4–9 cm (4–10 × 1½–3½in.)*, oblong-oblanceolate, narrowly obovate, narrowly elliptic to oblong, apex rounded, base tapered, cuneate, indumentum below white to grey to fawn, thick and woolly with sparsely scattered long stalked glands. L remain for 2 to 3 years. Petiole 2–3 cm with evanescent tomentum.
Inflor twenty to thirty compact or elongated, rachis 3–4 cm.
Pedicel 3–4 cm with glands and fewer hairs.
F white, white flushed pink, pink to pale rose with pale green spots, 3.5 cm (nearly 1½ in.) long, funnel-campanulate, puberulous within.
Calyx 5–7 mm unequal lobes, densely glandular. *Ovary densely glandular.*

An excellent foliage plant when flourishing; we find it rather fastidious. It seems to resent sunlight in the wild and in cultivation and needs a moist, shady position to succeed. Quite pretty and is useful for its late flowering period though the flowers are small.

Differs from *smirnowii* in its larger leaves, not as shiny or as dark above, indumentum not as dense and the flowers are more bell-shaped. Other differences are in italics. Probably not quite as hardy as *smirnowii* although reports indicate that it will survive in any well sheltered and shaded garden in Britain and in the east USA as far north as the Arnold Arboretum, Mass.

Caucasus and north-east Turkey, 800–2,200 m (2,800–7,300 ft), usually in shady positions among laurel, alder, beech, spruce and fir, often associated with *ponticum* and *smirnowii* and hybridizes naturally with *smirnowii*.   July–August

RHODORASTRA SUBSECTION (DAURICUM SERIES) (L)

Small to medium shrubs with thin scaly branchlets. L deciduous to semi-evergreen, scaly below, thin textured. Inflor terminal and sometimes axillary, often with clusters of buds. F mauve to pink with several white (albino) clones, thin textured, pubescent outside. Calyx very small, stamens ten pubescent, ovary scaly, style glabrous, capsule small. Young growth comes from below the flowers.

Two closely related species from east and central Asia. Chemically related to subsections Rhododendron (Ferrugineum series), Lepidota, Lapponica and Micrantha.

These are invaluable, easily grown species which are especially good in cold areas, bursting into flower at the first hint of spring. They also appear to be heat tolerant. Their abundant small flowers are produced from mid-winter onwards in Britain, according to available mild spells and the many newly introduced forms can give a succession of flowers from December to April in mild winters. The flowers stand frost better than most rhododendrons. These are amongst the finest of all winter flowering shrubs. While growth often comes early and gets frosted, this is readily replaced and plenty of flower buds will still be set.

E.M.S.

R. mucronulatum

dauricum L. 1753 (*fittianum* Balf.f. in cultivation a ? *racemosum* hybrid), (*ledebourii* Poyark, *sichotensis* Pojark 1952) H4 A − 25 L1–2 F2–3

Ht to 2.4 m (8 ft) or more. Habit usually erect. Branchlets scaly and pubescent. Bark light grey.
L *semi-deciduous* with a varying number of persistent leaves, 2–3 × 1–1.5 cm ($\frac{3}{4}$–$1\frac{1}{4}$ × $\frac{2}{5}$–$\frac{3}{5}$ in.), *elliptic, rounded at each end*, loosely

scaly above, densely scaly below, ± contiguous. Leaves sometimes turn purplish-brown during winter. Petiole 1.6 mm.
Inflor terminal and axillary one to three. Pedicel 1 cm softly puberulous.
F various shades of pale to deep rosy-purple to purple, almost pink or white, about 1 cm (⅜ in.) long, 2–5 cm (¾–2 in.) wide, widely funnel-shaped.
Calyx very short, densely scaly. Ovary densely scaly, style glabrous, slightly longer than stamens.

This species in all its new forms is sure to become a much more popular garden plant. The early blooming clones like 'Midwinter' **FCC**, are lovely planted with *Hamamelis mollis*. As well as numerous forms of the normal colours, some with very much larger flowers than others, a fine dwarf clone has been recently introduced from Japan where it is much used in containers. Several white clones have come from Hokkaido, north Japan from pure white to white with a tinted centre and inconspicuous green spots to a pale yellow throat with conspicuous green spots. These have flowers from 2–5 cm (¾–2 in.) across and bloom from February to April, according to clone. Another clone has white flowers with red stripes. These often come white from seed.

While generally winter hardy, young plants are occasionally killed by unseasonable frosts, having suffered bark-split. Good in Scandinavia in mild winters. Best planted in groups for effect.

Var. *sempervirens* refers to plants that retain a higher percentage of leaves during winter than average. The plant named *ledebourii* of which recent introductions have been made is said to come from an isolated area in the Altai and east Siberia but does not apparently have any real botanical significance. Some seedlings are almost pink. 'Midwinter' **FCC**, 1969, Crown Lands.

Very widely distributed; Altai east to Korea, north China and east Siberia, central Manchuria, Kamtschatica, Daurica, Hokkaido and Sakhalin. Forms extensive thickets in larch, alder and pine forests, river valleys and woods and even survives on moving sand dunes on an island in Lake Baikal. In pine forests the organic matter is often very sparse and it appears to be happy on acid mineral soils. In the spring, whole hillsides around Lake Baikal are covered with the rosy-purple flowers. An important nectar plant in the wild, often covered with bees.
Blooms in June in central Manchuria, December–April in cultivation.

mucronulatum Turcz. (*dauricum* var. *mucronulatum*, *taquetii* Lévl.) H4
A – 15 L1–2 F2–3

Ht to 2.7 m (9 ft). Habit erect to somewhat sprawly. Branchlets sparingly scaly, thin. Bark light grey to light brown, flaking.
L *deciduous*, 3–7.5 × to 3 cm (1¼–3 × to 1¼ in.), elliptic-lanceolate to lanceolate, usually thin texture, *acute* at both ends, scales below *two to three times* their own diameter apart. Petiole about 2 mm scaly.
Inflor terminal and occasionally axillary, one flower per bud. Pedicel 0.6 cm loosely scaly.

F deep rosy-purple to mauve-pink and rose-pink or white, precocious, 3–5 cm (1¼–2 in.) across, widely funnel-shaped.
Calyx very short densely scaly. Ovary scaly, style glabrous, about half as long as the longest stamens.

Very closely related to *dauricum*, differing in the usually thinner texture of the leaves which are deciduous, larger and acute at both ends. The flowers are often larger and the habit is often more spreading. Japanese plants mostly have appressed hairs on leaves and petioles. Responds well to pruning. Flourishes in many areas of eastern North America including Great Lakes, Philadelphia and Pennsylvania areas. The pink forms especially, succeed in Scandinavia and it promises to be heat resistant and dry air tolerant in places like San Diego and Washington DC. 'Cornell Pink' **AM**, rose-pink is an excellent clone, grown in 1946 as a selection from 1,000 seedlings. Seedling strains have been raised from this and it has been much used for hybridizing in eastern USA. Often later flowering than other clones. 'Mahogany Red' collected in wild by Wada has deep purplish-red flowers. Two to three times the average pigment content. 'Winter Sunset' **FCC**, 1957, flowers rich purplish-rose. **AM**, 1924. **AM**, 1935, 'Roseum' mauve-pink. White forms were recently introduced. The type specimen probably came from a cultivated plant.

From north-east China and Ussuri, Tsushima Island, west Honshu and north Kyushu, Cheju Island (Quelpaert) Korea, Manchuria and north Japan. Range generally more easterly than *dauricum* although the two may overlap and merge in places. 300–1,700 m (1,000–5,500 ft) often in dry, stony situations, rocky slopes and larch forests, very abundant in North Korea. The dwarf form growing en masse on the highest parts of Cheju Island was introduced in 1976 by Berg (seed); it retains this low habit in cultivation and flowers in 2 years from seed. This introduction is late flowering and has fine autumn colour.   January–April

SCABRIFOLIA SUBSECTION ((Hutch.) Cullen 1978) *(SCABRIFOLIUM SERIES)* (L)

The rest is described in *Dwarf Rhododendrons*.

spinuliferum Franch. 1895 (*duclouxii* Lévl., *fuchsiiflorum* Lévl.) Hc3 A + 10 L1–2 F2–3

Ht 2.4 m (8 ft) or more. Habit often rather straggly. Branchlets softly pubescent. Bark fairly smooth, dark purple-brown.
L 3–9 × 1.5–4 cm (1¼–3½ × ⅖–1½ in.), oblanceolate to obovate, sometimes nearly lanceolate, bullate above, reticulate below, pubescent. Petiole 1 cm pubescent.
Inflor terminal and axillary towards apex of shoots, usually in compact bunches. Pedicel 6 mm softly pubescent.
F pink, orange, peach-red, brick-red, crimson-red to crimson, about 2.5 cm (1 in.) long, *tubular, erect, contracted at each end*, glabrous outside. Calyx small densely pubescent. Stamens glabrous protruding from corolla about 6 mm (¼ in.). Ovary densely tomentose, style glabrous, protruding from corolla.

A most unusual species with unique upright tubular flowers. Considering how distinct it is, it is surprising how readily it crosses with other species. The orange-red to crimson forms are the most desirable. Variable in hardiness. Best in the milder western areas of Britain but some forms survive for years in places like the RBG, Edinburgh and Glendoick. It is odd how tough it is coming from such low elevations in the wild. Cut to the ground in the 1972 freeze in Oregon but regrew in 1973. Has much nectar, in common with *cinnabarinum*. 'Jack Hext' **AM**, 1974, Chyverton; 'Blackwater' **AM**, 1977, Brodick.

From south Yunnan Tali to Kunming, 1,700–2,400 m (5,500–8,000 ft). Grows in dry dense scrub and shady thickets and is quite common. Not collected by *F, KW* or *R*.   April–May

SELENSIA SUBSECTION (THOMSONII SERIES, SUB-SERIES SELENSE) (E)

This group of rather undecisive species, usually merging into one another and probably having hybrid ancestry with the Campylocarpa subsection. L oblong, elliptic to oblong-oval. F usually funnel-shaped. Calyx usually small. Stamens ten. Style ± glandular for part of its length but never glandular to tip. Capsule slender, curved. The leaves have a ± amount of indumentum or vestiges of hairs present on the underside.

Two species have been added to this subsection from the old Barbatum series to which it has a definite relationship. These are *bainbridgeanum* and *hirtipes*. This subsection may be derived from Irrorata.

The majority have an attractive compact habit if grown in the open and small, neat foliage. The flowers are predominately rose, pink to white and sometimes yellow (yellow probably shows hybridity). Some are very pretty but *selense* and its sub-species can have the unfortunate trait of not starting to bloom until 20 years old plus.

bainbridgeanum Tagg & Forr. 1931 H4 L1–2 F2–3

Ht 1–2 m (3–6 ft). Habit fairly compact but may become straggly with age. Branchlets with evanescent glands and a few hairs. Bark roughish, greyish-brown. Bud-scales ± persistent.
L 6–12 × 2–4.5 cm (2½–5 × 1–2 in.), variable in shape, oblong-lanceolate to obovate to sub-elliptic, apex obtuse, base obtuse or rounded, a few white hairs below, especially around the midrib while the *loose woolly* indumentum which can be scurfy or spotted and tawny in colour, can sometimes be evanescent. L remain for 1 to 2 years. Petiole 1–1.5 cm, with thick stalked brown glands and long thin white hairs.
Inflor six to eight, rachis about 5 mm. Pedicel about 2.5 cm with different lengths of glands.
F white, creamy-white flushed or margined pink or rose, yellow, reddish-yellow to orange, pale to deep pink or pinkish-red, spotted and/or blotched, about 3.8 cm (1½ in.) long, campanulate.
Calyx variable 4–9 mm split into lobes, glandular. Ovary densely glandular, style ± glandular at base.

R. erythrocalyx

Considering the number of collections from the wild, this species is surprisingly rare in cultivation and several of the colour forms listed above are not apparently grown. Some forms are free flowering and attractive but it is very easily frosted even in the bud and leaves were badly scorched in Oregon in the 1972 freeze. The indumentum is usually more noticeable and the leaves longer and thicker than in *dasycladum* and *erythrocalyx*. There may be some relationship with *crinigerum* with which *bainbridgeanum* was previously placed, but affinities mostly lie in this subsection.

Found wild only in south-east Tibet at 3,000–4,000 m (10,000–13,000 ft), common and widespread in open thickets and margins of conifer forest, mixed scrub, among boulders, rocks and on cliffs.

March–April

calvescens Balf.f. & Forr. 1919 Probably not in cultivation

Ht 0.90–1.80 m (3–6 ft). Branchlets glandular and tomentose.
L 6–10 × 2.5–3.5 cm (2½–5 × 1–1½ in.), apex obtuse, base trunculate thin, matted indumentum below. Petiole with thin, matted indumentum.
Inflor eight, loose, rachis *c*. 5 mm. Pedicel *c*. 1.3 cm.
Ovary tomentose or tomentose-glandular. Shoots coarser than its rela-

tions. Special characters are dendroid hairs on narrow leaves. Probably a hybrid.

This species was excluded from this subsection in the 1951–1952 review but has been returned by Chamberlain. South-east Tibet in open thickets.

calvescens var. *duseimatum* (Balf.f. & Forr.) Chamb. 1978 Probably not in cultivation

L 7–10 cm (3–4 in.) long, oblong-lanceolate.
F rose with crimson blotch. Ovary tomentose.
Only one herbarium number.

dasycladoides Hand.-Mazz. 1936 Said to be not in cultivation

Smallish shrub.
L stalked glands below, especially on mid-rib and primary veins including some along mid-rib above, sparse white indumentum below. Petiole dense stalked glands. F pale pink to pinkish-purple.
Calyx, ovary, lower half of stamens and lower half of inside of corolla also covered with stalked glands.

A little-known species near *dasycladum*, but has dendroid hairs. *R. selense* ssp. *dasycladum* has a glandular but not tomentose ovary and has no stalked glands on the leaf underside. Wild in south-west Szechwan.

erythocalyx Balf.f. & Forr. 1920 (*beimaense* Balf.f. & Forr., *cymbomorphum* Balf.f. & Forr., *eucallum* Balf.f. & Forr., *docimum* Balf.f., *truncatulum* Balf.f. & Forr.) H3–4 L1–2 F1–3

Ht 90 cm–2.4 m (3–8 ft). Habit twiggy. Branchlets ± with stalked glands. Bark greyish-brown.
L 3–10.6 × 2.1–5.3 cm (1¼–4¼ × ¾–2 in.), elliptic, oval, oblong-elliptic to ovate, apex rounded to broadly obtuse, base cordulate to rounded, ± glabrous above, glabrous or minutely hairy below. Petiole 1–1.3 cm ± glandular. L remain for 1 year.
Inflor four to ten loose, rachis 0.3–1 cm. Pedicel 1.3–3 cm glandular. F usually white or pink, with or without a crimson blotch, sometimes creamy yellow or yellow, often flushed rose, c. 4.5 cm (1¾ in.) long, funnel-campanulate.
Calyx 1–7 mm red to green, very variable in size, glandular. Ovary densely glandular, style ± glandular at base.

This is often a better garden plant than *selense* and its ssp. although closely related. Some forms have larger flowers which are more freely produced from a younger age and can be very pretty. Subject to bark-split.

Much less glandular on average than the near relative *selense* ssp. *dasycladum* and generally has a larger calyx but the two probably merge. Both may have originated from a hybrid swarm of *wardii* × *selense*.

From north-west Yunnan and south-east Tibet, 3,400–4,000 m (11,000–13,000 ft), in and on margins of conifer forests, in open thickets and scrub.
April–May

esetulosum Balf.f. & Forr. (*manopeplum* Balf.f. & Forr.) H4 L1–3 F1–2

Ht 1.2–1.8 m (4–6 ft).
L 5–9.4 × 2.3–5.1 cm (2–3¾ × 1–2 in.), oblong to elliptic to oblong-ovate, apex shortly acuminate to broadly obtuse, base rounded to cordulate, ± glabrous above and with a *thin veil of hairs below*, coriaceous texture to leaves. Petiole 1–2 cm ± glandular.
Inflor eight to ten loose, rachis 0.1–1 cm. Pedicel 1–2.4 cm glandular.
F white to rose flushed to purple, ± spotted crimson, 3.1–5 cm (1¼–2 in.), broadly funnel-campanulate.
Calyx to 1 cm glandular. Ovary densely glandular, style glandular for *most of its length from base.*

Close to *selense* and *erythocalyx* but more glandular, especially on the style and with a larger calyx. The leaves are coriaceous and have a slight indumentum on the underside.

Harry Smith's and R's Beima Shan introductions are both hardy in southern Scandinavia.

From north-west Yunnan and south-east Tibet, 3,000–4,300 m (10,000–14,000 ft), in scrub and margins of thickets and on bouldery slopes.   April–May

hirtipes Tagg 1931 H3–4 L1–3 F1–3

Ht dwarf shrub to tree of 7.6 m (25 ft), rarely over 3 m (10 ft) in cultivation. Habit rounded.
Shoots with *bristly glands*. Bud-scales not very persistent. Bark roughish.
L 6.3–13 × 3.8–7.5 cm (2½–5 × 1½–3 in.), oblong-oval, oval to broadly elliptic, apex rounded, base rounded to cordulate; young leaves hairy above towards base, evanescent; indumentum below usually consisting of brown dots, buff to dark brown, sometimes only near midrib or almost glabrous.
L remain for 1–2 years. Petiole 1–2 cm *bristly*.
Inflor two to seven, usually three to four, loose. Pedicel with red hairs, about 1 cm.
F colour very variable in the wild, almost white, through pale yellow to pale or deeper pink, with or without flush, stripes, blotch or spots, 4–5 cm (about 2 in.) long, *widely funnel-shaped.*
Calyx about 8 mm lobes unequal with *pink to reddish-brown hairs*. Ovary densely glandular, style glandular at base, red.

It is a great pity that our fitful springs do not enable this very pretty species to flower properly. The wide open flowers as *KW* rightly says, give a beautiful effect. He thought this was the most bewitching rhododendron he saw on the Tsangpo Gorge expedition. The early opening flowers are all too easily frosted and/or weather beaten.

This distinct species has just been moved from the Barbatum series, sub-series Glischrum and undoubtedly fits better into this subsection. Rare in cultivation with most colour forms not yet introduced. 'Ita' **AM**, 1965, *LS&T* 3624 flowers phlox pink, flushed deeper pink, Glenarn. Those in cultivation mostly pink.

From both sides of the Tsangpo in south-west Tibet, common over a wide range of elevation and rare in west Bhutan, 3,000–4,700 m (10,000–15,000 ft), usually a forest plant on mossy heavily wooded cliffs and shady ravines, conifer and thick rain-forest but also among rocks above the forest.   February–March–April

martinianum Balf.f. & Forr. 1919 H4 L1–2 F2–3

Ht to 2.1 m (7 ft). Habit erect and sometimes rather leggy in cultivation. *KW* 21557 more compact. Branchlets ± setose-glandular. Bark grey to greyish-brown.
L 1.9–5.4 × 0.8–2.5 cm (¾–2¼ × ⅓–1 in.), oblong, elliptic to oblong-elliptic, apex rounded to broadly obtuse, base broadly obtuse to rounded, rather thick and rigid, ± glabrous above, glabrous below with minute punctulations, usually glaucous. L remain for 1 to 2 years. Petiole 3–7 mm ± glandular.
Inflor *one to three*, rarely more, rachis 2–8 mm. Pedicel 1.5–3.5 cm slender and glandular.
F pale to deep pink or rose with deep crimson spots or pure white with ± crimson markings, 2.5–4 cm (1–1½ in.) long, funnel-campanulate.
Calyx 1–3 mm ± glandular. Ovary densely glandular, style ± densely glandular at base.
   A distinctive little plant with thin growth and dainty foliage and flowers. Horticulturally, this could be the best of the subsection and is a charming species, suitable for small gardens. There are several introductions in cultivation including a white form. The best should be widely distributed. Prefers an open habitat in the wild. Akin to *selense* but with smaller leaves, longer pedicels, a smaller inflorescence and usually setose-glandular branchlets. *KW* 21557 often has almost sessile leaves, a more compact habit and a two-flowered inflorescence. Rather tender.
   From north-west Yunnan, south-east Tibet, Upper Burma, 3,000–4,300 m (10,000–14,000 ft), alpine moorland and meadows, among rocks, open thickets and scrub, margins of conifer forest, dry open slopes and bamboo brakes; on granite or limestone.   April–May

selense Franch. 1898 (*axium* Balf.f. & Forr., *chalarocladum* Balf.f. & Forr., *metrium* Forr., *nanothamnum* Balf.f. & Forr., *pagophyllum* Balf.f. & Ward, *probum* Balf.f. & Forr.) H4 L1–3 F1–3

Ht 60 cm–2.7 m (2–9 ft). Habit usually dense when young, becoming leggy with age, especially in woodland. Bark fairly smooth to roughish, grey. Rounded flower buds.
L 2.6–8.2 × 1.5–3.9 m (1–3⅓ × ⅗–1½ in.), oblong, obovate, oblong-oval to elliptic, apex obtuse to rounded, base similar, ± glabrous above and below. L remain for 1 year. Petiole 0.6–3 cm ± glandular and hairy.
Inflor three to eight loose, rachis 2–4 mm. Pedicel long, 1–3 cm ± glandular and hairy.
F usually pink to rose, occasionally white, ivory to pale yellow sometimes flushed rose, with or without a basal blotch, 2.2–4 cm (¾–1½ in.) long, funnel-campanulate.

Calyx 1–3 mm glandular. Ovary glandular, style eglandular or glandular at base.

This is a disappointing plant in cultivation on account of its slowness to bloom and the foliage is not good enough alone to warrant its space in the garden. It can obviously flower very freely in the wild and often received praise from collectors. It should be grown on an open but sheltered site to retain the neat habit. When it does produce flowers, these are frequently hidden in the foliage.

This is the centre species of a large collection of closely related, very variable plants, many of which show signs of hybridity. Overlaps with *erythocalyx*.

From south-east Tibet, north-west Yunnan and south-west Szechwan, 2,700–4,400 m (9,000–14,500 ft), on open meadows, thickets, margins of conifer forest, alpine regions, rocky pasture by streams and in bamboo scrub. Obviously common and widespread.   April–May

selense ssp. *dasycladum* (Balf.f. & W.W. Sm.) Chamb. 1978 (*dolerium* Balf.f. & Forr., *rhaibocarpum* Balf.f. & W.W. Sm.) H4 A + 5 L1–2 F1–2

Ht 90 cm–3.6 m (3–12 ft). Branchlets *usually moderately to densely setose-glandular* or sometimes hairy.
L 3–12.5 × 1.5–4.7 cm (1¼–5 × ⅝–1¾ in.), oblong to oblong-elliptic, apex obtuse, base obtuse to rounded, cordulate or truncate, ± glabrous above, glabrous or with thin veil of hairs below. Petiole usually setose-glandular.
F white to white flushed rose to rose, funnel-shaped to funnel-campanulate. Calyx small 1–2 mm.

This very variable sub-species is close to *erythocalyx* and *bainbridgeanum*, the leaves tend to be thinner than ssp. *setiferum* while it is not quite as glandular as *dasycladoides*. It is often superior to *selense* itself. The southern forms are distinct but overlap with others farther north.

Very common and widespread in north-west Yunnan and south-east Tibet away from the wettest areas. Best around Wei Hsi area.

selense ssp. *jucundum* (Balf.f. & W.W. Sm.) Chamb. 1978 H4 L1–2 F1–2

Ht 60 cm to 6 m (2–20 ft). Branchlets usually setose-glandular.
L ± glabrous above, glabrous or minutely hairy below.
F slightly more open than the other sub-species of *selense*.

Rare in cultivation. Geographically distinct, coming from the Tali Range and to the south, north-west Yunnan. Re-introduced 1981. See Addendum *p.* 368.

selense ssp. *setiferum* (Balf.f. & Forr.) Chamb. 1978 (*vestitum* Tagg & Forr.)

Ht 1.5–2.7 m (5–9 ft). Branchlets setose-glandular.
L 5–9 × 2–3.7 cm (2–3½ × ¾–1½ in.), thin veil of hairs or patchy (*vestitum*) below. Petiole setose-glandular and hairy.

F creamy-white, heavily spotted crimson. Calyx 0.3–*1 cm.*

This is perhaps a *selense* × *bainbridgeanum* natural hybrid. Differs from the other sub-species in the usually larger calyx and fairly long bristles. *KW* says it was named off only one bush of *KW* 7190 and he considered it a hybrid. Now includes *vestitum*, which was only collected in one place.

TALIENSIA SUBSECTION (LACTEUM (PART) AND TALIENSE SERIES) (E). See Addendum *p.* 368.

Dwarf shrubs to small trees, often compact and shapely. L ± glabrous on maturity above, often sparsely hairy when young; indumentum usually present below, occasionally glabrescent. This indumentum occurs in one layer of loose to compacted compound hairs, sometimes with stipitate glands, or in two layers, the lower one with an understory of appressed hairs embedded within a whitish film. Inflor terminal five to twenty, rachis lacking or to *c*. Icm. F white to pink to purplish or yellow, nearly always spotted purple and sometimes blotched, campanulate to funnel-campanulate, lobes usually five, occasionally to seven, nectaries absent. Calyx usually minute though sometimes well developed with large lobes. Stamens usually ten, puberulous near base. Ovary glabrous to tomentose and/or glandular, style glabrous or occasionally glandular. Capsule shortly cylindrical, sometimes curved. In the following descriptions, corollas are five-lobed and stamens ten unless otherwise stated.

Geographical range extends from east Bhutan to the Tali Range in central Yunnan, through south-west Szechwan to Kansu. On the edge of the distribution, species tend to be clear cut. However, within the triangle bounded by Dokar La on the Tibet–Yunnan border, the Tali Range and the Muli district in south-west Szechwan, there is a confusing array of ill-defined species, particularly around *alutaceum, bathyphyllum, proteoides, roxieanum* and *taliense.* Although the taxa within this species complex which have been maintained, do have some validity, their exact relationships remain uncertain. Further information is needed, particularly on the variations in wild populations, before a classification can be made that is anything more than provisional.

The four former sub-series and the former Lacteum series have obscured the relationships between the different species within the two former series. The distinguishing characters were not mutual to each sub-series and series and none formed a distinct group.

These plants have been rather neglected horticulturally. People growing these from the masses of *F* and *R* seed became fed up with their apparent sombreness and slowness to bloom. It is only recently that many have shown their true value, having made fine mature foliage plants and having started to flower freely. Owing to the difficulty of rooting cuttings, even the more desirable species have been scarce in the trade. The majority are hardy, adaptable, long-lived, shapely species, well worth planting for posterity. All seemed to survive the 1972 freeze in Oregon. *KW* mistakenly told people to avoid these plants and at least in North America, they are becoming more popular.

R. adenogynum

adenogynum Diels 1912 (*adenophorum* Balf.f. & W.W. Sm.) H4 L2–3
FI–3

Ht 50 cm–4 m (2–13 ft). Habit usually semi-dwarf and slow growing.
Bark grey-brown, rough.
L 6–11 × 2–4 cm (2½–4½ × ¾–1½ in.), 2.2–5 times as long as broad, narrowly elliptic to elliptic, apex acute, base usually rounded, usually dark
green, slightly rugulose and almost glabrous above, *dense woolly
indumentum below*, yellowish turning to *olive-brown* on maturity, inter-
mixed with glands, leathery. L remain for 2 to 4 years. Petiole 1–2 cm
glabrescent or with persistent tomentum and glands.
Inflor four to twelve generally loose. Pedicel long, 2–3 cm, densely
tomentose and glandular.
F white, white tinged pink on exterior, pale rose, rose fading to white,
bright rose to rose-purple or magenta-rose, ± crimson or purple markings, 3–4.5 cm (1¼–1¾ in.) long, funnel-shaped, viscid base.
Calyx usually *0.8–1.5 cm*, unequally lobed, glandular. Ovary densely
glandular, style usually glandular in lower half.
   A good plant in foliage and also in flower if the purple tinted forms are
avoided. White, tinged pink and rose coloured forms are all attractive.
Hardy enough for south Sweden.
   Closely related to *balfourianum*, having the large calyx in common.
Intermediate plants occur but the chief differences are in the broader

leaves and more plastered indumentum of *balfourianum*. 'Kirsty' **AM**, 1976 white, suffused purple Borde Hill. Recently re-introduced.

From south-east Tibet (Tsarong), west and north-west Yunnan and south-west Szechwan, 3,000–4,300 m (10,000–14,000 ft), rhododendron and mixed thickets, often in clumps of three to four, open alpine and rocky pasture, in and on margins of conifer forest, on rocks and cliffs, often limestone, amongst scrub, boulders and bamboo.   March–May

aganniphum Balf.f. & Ward (*doshongense* Tagg, *fissotectum* Balf.f. & Forr., *glaucopeplum* Balf.f. & Forr., *schizopeplum* Balf.f. & Forr.) H4 L1–2 F1–2

Ht 30 cm–3 m (1–10 ft). Habit generally dwarf. Bark rough, grey-brown. L 4–12 × 2–5 cm (1½–5 × ¾–2 in.), 1.7–2.8 times as long as broad, elliptic to broadly ovate-lanceolate, dense ± compacted to spongy indumentum below, *whitish to yellowish to pale pinkish-brown when young, becoming deep red-brown at maturity*, sometimes splitting but not into a pattern as in var. *flavorufum*. Petiole 1–2 cm tomentose, evanescent.
Inflor ten to twenty, rachis short. Pedicel 1–3 cm sparsely tomentose to glabrescent.
F white, creamy-white, white flushed or streaked rose, pink to rose with ± number of markings, 3–3.5 cm (1¼–1½ in.) long, funnel-campanulate.
Calyx *0.5–1 mm*, lobes rounded, glabrous or with a few scattered glands. Ovary and style glabrous.

This is basically a wider-leaved version of *adenogynum* with a slighter, thinner indumentum, smaller flowers and calyx and generally shorter pedicels. The indumentum is thicker than the average *phaeochrysum* var. *levistratum* (*dryophyllum*) and leaves are more elliptic. Intergrades completely with var. *flavorufum* with many intermediaries but the extremes are clearly distinct. Distribution virtually identical. Now includes *glaucopeplum* which was said to differ only in the presence of glands on the leaf undersurface and petiole.

Some forms have good large flowers while others are inferior. There are perhaps more herbarium specimens of this species than any other which gives some indication to its abundance in the wild.

From south-east Tibet (Tsarong), north-west Yunnan and south-west Szechwan, 3,400–4,600 m (11,000–15,000 ft), open rocky and bouldery moorland and moist meadows, open thickets and scrub-clad slopes, openings and margins of conifer forests, by streams, in bamboo breaks and on boulders and cliff ledges.   April–June

aganniphum var. *flavorufum* (Balf.f. & Forr.) Chamb. 1978

L indumentum white turning to buff, brown or reddish on maturity, *splitting, sometimes irregularly*.
Differs from *aganniphum* with which it merges, in the indumentum which splits on maturity into irregular patches (also sometimes on young leaves).

alutaceum Balf.f. & W. W. Sm. *globigerum* Balf.f. & Forr., *roxieanum* Forr. var. *globigerum* (Balf.f. & Forr.) Chamb. H4 L2–3 F1–3.

Ht 60 cm–4.5 m (2–15 ft). Habit usually fairly dwarf. Bark rough, brown. L 5–18 ×2–4 cm (2–7 × ¾–1½ in.) 2–6.2 times as long as broad, oblong to oblanceolate, apex acuminate, base rounded to cuneate, *dense persistent to evanescent olive-brown to rust-brown indumentum* below. L remain for 2 to 3 years. Petiole 0.8–2 cm, usually persistently brown tomentose.
Inflor ten to twenty fairly dense. Pedicel 1–2 cm tomentose.
F white to pink to lilac-mauve or white flushed rose, with or without blotch or spots, 3–4 cm (1¼–1½ in.) long, funnel-campanulate.
Calyx *minute, 0.5–1 mm* with a few glands. Ovary glandular and tomentose, style glabrous.

Quite an attractive plant. Rather similar in appearance to *adenogynum* in some forms but lacks the large calyx. May merge with *phaeochrysum* var. *levistratum* but the leaves of *alutaceum* tend to be longer and narrower with indumentum coarser, looser and generally darker.

From south-east Tibet (Tsarong), west and north-west Yunnan and bordering Szechwan (Yung-ning), 2,700–4,300 m (9,000–14,00 ft), open pasture, bouldery and rocky slopes and thickets, in bamboo, rhododendron and conifer forest, usually open; fairly common in the wild. April

alutaceum var. *russotinctum* (Balf.f. & Forr.) Chamb. 1978 (*triplonaevium* Balf.f. & Forr., *tritifolium* Balf.f. & Forr.) see *Dwarf Rhododendrons* (*p.* 168), *The Smaller Rhododendrons* (*p.* 183).

balfourianum Diels 1912 H4 A−5 to +5 L1–3 F1–3

Ht 1–4.5 m (3–15 ft). Habit rounded and compact under good conditions. Bark rough, greyish-brown.
L 4.5–12 × 2–4 cm (1¾–5 × ¾–1½ in.), 2.2–3 times as long as broad, ovate-lanceolate to elliptic, apex acute, base rounded, *dense compacted to spongy* indumentum below, silvery-white turning to pale pinkish-cinnamon to grey at maturity, usually shining and with broken surface film, sometimes splits. L remain for 1 to 3 years. Petiole 1–2 cm glabrescent.
Inflor six to twelve, loose to fairly compact. Pedicel 1–2 cm sparsely hairy and glandular.
F pale to deep rose, purplish-pink to rose-pink to white or white flushed rose with crimson markings, 3.5–4 cm (about 1½ in.) long, funnel-campanulate, sometimes slightly fragrant.
Calyx *0.6–1 cm* split to base, lobes uneven, glandular. Ovary glandular.

A hardy, easily grown species, slow to flower but free flowering on maturity and attractive in its larger, fuller trussed forms. Many fine plants are to be seen at Corsock, Dumfriesshire and in other cold gardens. The flowers are usually long lasting though not of heavy substance. Survived the 1972 western American freeze. Closely related to *adenogynum* in its foliage which has narrower leaves and a more woolly indumentum. The foliage of *aganniphum* is also similar but this species has a short calyx and glabrous ovary. The old name var. *aganniphoides* is merged into *balfourianum*. The former had a more spongy indumentum but there is no clear dividing line between the two.

A fairly common species in the wild in west Yunnan, Tali district, and the Muli district of south-west Szechwan, 3,000–4,600 m (10,000–15,000 ft), on open rocky slopes, among bamboos and scrub, in and on margins of conifer forest, in thickets, sometimes gregarious and on limestone cliffs. March–May

bathyphyllum Balf.f. & Forr. (*iodes* Balf.f. & Forr.), see *Dwarf Rhododendrons* (*p.* 164)

bureavii Franch. 1887 (*bureavioides* Balf.f., *cruentum* Lévl.) H4 −15 to −5 L3–4 F2–3
Ht 1–7.6 m (3–25 ft), usually not over 3 m (10 ft). Habit compact and shapely in the open, more tree-like in shade. *1 year shoots covered with thick rusty-red indumentum*, stout. Bark roughish, greyish-brown.
L 4.5–19 × 2–7 cm (1¾–7½ × ¾–2¾ in.), 1.7–3 times as long as broad, elliptic, apex ± acuminate, base rounded to cuneate, usually glabrous at maturity above, *dense indumentum below, deep salmon-pink turning to rich rusty-red at maturity*. L remain for 3 to 4 years. Petiole 1–2 cm densely tomentose.
Inflor ten to twenty usually rather loose to 12.5 cm (5 in.) across. Pedicel 1–2 cm densely tomentose and glandular.
F white flushed rose, sometimes fading to white, apple-blossom-pink to rose, crimson to purple spotted, 2.5–4 cm (1–1½ in.) long, tubular-campanulate.
Calyx *0.5–1 cm* lobes fleshy or membranous, densely glandular. Ovary densely glandular ± tomentose, style usually glandular, at least at base.

A superb foliage plant, undoubtedly one of the finest in the genus. Hardy and quite easily grown in Britain. Very distinctive, not easily confused with any other species. Should be in every collection but the demand always exceeds the supply. Somewhat tender in Stockholm, Sweden. Some forms have larger, superior flowers.

R. bureavioides which is now merged into *bureavii* was reputed to have leaves of a different shape and paler, less thick indumentum while *cruentum* was said to have smaller flowers and a fleshy calyx but the differences are hardly significant. There is some variation in the foliage of *bureavii* and some forms are definitely superior. **AM**, 1939, Exbury.

McLaren AD 77 and 106 have smaller leaves similar to *wasonii* but white flowers more like *bureavii*. The indumentum is dark, thick and woolly. These may be *wasonii* × *bureavii* natural hybrids and perhaps deserve varietal or cultivar recognition.

A limited distribution in Szechwan near Tatsienlu and in north-west Yunnan north of Tali Lake, 2,700–4,400 m (9,000–14,500 ft), alpine region, open pasture, rhododendron forest and on margins of and above conifer forest. April–May *clementinae* Forr. 1915 H4 L2–4 F2

Ht 1–3 m (3–10 ft). Habit usually rounded and compact with stiff, stout shoots. Bark rough, brown to grey-brown.
L 6.5–14 × 3–8 cm (2½–5½ × 1¼–3¼ in.), 1.5–2 times as long as broad, ovate-lanceolate to oval, apex rounded, base ± cordate, *leaves usually convex, thick spongy whitish to buff indumentum below*. L remain for 2 to 5 years. Petiole 1.5–2 cm glabrous when mature.
Inflor ten to fifteen compact. Pedicel 1.5–3 cm glabrous, stout.
F white to creamy-white, usually flushed rose to rose with deeper markings, *seven lobed*, 4–5 cm (1½–2 in.) long, funnel-campanulate. Calyx about 1 mm. Stamens twelve to fourteen. Ovary and style glabrous.

A fairly distinct slow growing species with beautiful foliage especially when young and steely-blue. This foliage strongly resembles that of *campanulatum* var. *aeruginosum*. Flowers take many years to appear and the buds are apt to abhort. Hard to propagate and always likely to remain scarce. It is reasonably uniform with several collectors' numbers in cultivation. Very hardy in Britain. Young leaves sometimes scented.

From north-west Yunnan, south-west Szechwan (Muli) and south-east Tibet, quite widespread and common, 3,400–4,300 m (11,000–14,000 ft), on open rocky and bouldery slopes and moorland, margins of conifer forests and thickets and cliff ledges.   April–May

codonanthum Balf.f. & Forr. 1922 Not in cultivation
    Ht 0.3–1.3 m (1–4½ ft). Dwarf shrub. L 4–6.5 × 1–1.8 cm (1½–2¾ × ⅖–¾ in.), 3.5–4.5 times as long as broad, margins recurved, base cuneate, sparse reddish indumentum below with glands. Petiole 6.5 mm tomentose. Inflor about six. Pedicel 2.5–3 cm sparsely glandular. F bright yellow with crimson markings, about 3 cm (1¼ in.) long, campanulate. Calyx cupular 4 mm, glandular-ciliate. Ovary and style glandular.
    Forrest said it was shy flowering in the wild. Only four herbarium specimens. Where does it fit in?
    From north-west Yunnan, 3,650–4,250 m (12,000–14,000 ft) on rocky hillsides and cliffs.

coeloneurum Diels 1900 Not in cultivation. See Addendum *p.* 369.
    Has been photographed by Chinese and resembles *wiltonii*. Szechwan.

detersile Franch. 1896. Said to be in cultivation in RHS Handbook, which is very doubtful.

Ht 30 cm–1 m (1–3½ ft). Dwarf shrub. L small, 4–5 × 1.5–1.8 cm (1½–2 × ⅗–¾ in.), apex acute, base cuneate, bullate above, very loose, thick woolly rust-brown indumentum below, patchy. Petiole about 5 mm.
Inflor about ten. Pedicel about 1 cm densely glandular and hairy.
F pinkish, 2.5–3 cm funnel-campanulate.

Calyx about 3 mm densely hairy and glandular. Ovary hairy and glandular, style glandular lower half.

Only said to have been collected by Farges but other specimens may occur in undetermined group in herbarium. Perhaps near *citriniflorum*. Szechwan, about 2,500 m (8,300 ft) on rocky slopes.

detonsum Balf.f. & Forr. 1919 H4 L2–3 F2–3

Ht 1–4 m (3–13 ft). Habit spreading or bushy. Branchlets stout, glabrous at 1 year old. Bark rough, grey to greyish-brown.
L 6–15 × 3–5 cm (2½–6 × 1¼–2 in.), 2.3–2.8 times as long as broad, obovate to broadly elliptic, apex acuminate, base rounded, *sparse brown evanescent* indumentum below. L remain for 2 to 3 years. Petiole 1.5–2 cm glabrescent.
Inflor six to eleven fairly compact. Pedicel 2–6.5 cm sparsely glandular. F fleshy, pink to rose-pink with a few purple spots, 4–5 cm (1½–2 in.) long, 7–8 cm (2¾–3¼ in.) across, funnel-campanulate, lobes *five to seven*, fragrant, like *decorum*.
Calyx 3–6 mm glandular. Stamens *ten to fourteen*. Ovary glandular and with a few hairs, style glandular for three-quarters of its length.

The plant we cultivate under this name has bigger leaves and flowers than any other member of the subsection. The herbarium specimens of which there are only two (I F I Delavay) and three possibles have smaller leaves but large flowers with long pedicels. This may be a natural hybrid of *adenogynum* or related species, perhaps with a member of the Fortunea subsection. The five to seven lobed corolla and the ten to fourteen stamens point to this being so. It is none the less a handsome plant with large flowers. New flower buds are formed by mid-June.

From west Yunnan, 3,000–4,000 m (10,000–13,000 ft), margins of mixed forests, thickets and rocky slopes.   May

dignabile Cowan 1937 Not in cultivation

Ht 60 cm–6 m (2–20 ft).
L 7.5–18 × 4–6.5 cm (3–7 × 1½–2½ in.), elliptic to obovate-lanceolate, apex obtuse to shortly acuminate, base cordate to ± rounded, scattered brown hairs and glands below.
Inflor five to fifteen. F white, cream, white flushed red or purple, lemon-yellow tinged pink, pale pink flushed blush-pink, with or without blotch or spots, also a white base with rose-pink lobes, 2.5–4.5 cm (1–1⅘ in.) campanulate to funnel-campanulate. Ovary very variable amount of tomentum.

This very variable species is said to be most handsome. It is sad that it was not introduced by *L&S* who found it relatively widespread and common in south-west and south Tibet. Shows some resemblance to *beesianum* but the extreme variability suggests a possible hybrid swarm with perhaps *wardii* or *campylocarpum* in the parentage. Other very variable plants have been found in the same area such as *hirtipes* and *bainbridgeanum*. Those from open habitats have significantly smaller flowers, leaves and stature. 3,400–4,400 m (11,000–14,500 ft), in rhododendron and conifer forest, deep forest and on rocks and hillsides.

elegantulum Tagg & Forr. 1927 H4 L2–3 F1–3

Ht 1–1.6 m (3–5½ ft). Usually fairly compact. Light red-brown tomentum on upper surface of young leaves and petiole. Bark rough, grey-brown. L 7–13 × 2.4–3.5 cm (2¾–5 × 1–1½ in.), *3–3.7* times as long as broad, elliptic oblong, apex acute, base rounded, *dense somewhat woolly indumentum below, deep pink turning to a rich rufous brown* on maturity. L remain for 3 years. Petiole 1–1.5 cm evanescent tomentose.
Inflor ten to twenty, fairly compact. Pedicel about 2 cm rufous tomentose, sometimes evanescent.
F cream flushed pink to pale pink flushed deeper pink to pale pinkish-purple, small crimson spots, 3–4 cm (1¼–1¾ in.) long, over 5 cm (2 in.) across.
Calyx silky-tomentose, about 1.2 cm glandular and hairy. Stamens hairy lower quarter. Ovary silky-tomentose, style hairy lower quarter, a few glands at base.

A fine foliage plant that has only recently been recognized in cultivation. Beautiful light red-brown tomentum on young foliage. Tagg's description in *The Species of Rhododendron* (*p.* 644), seems to agree with plants now cultivated as this species. Rather to my surprise, I saw several plants of this species correctly named in the Seattle area so it may be more plentiful in America than Britain. Some forms have better flowers and foliage than others. Closely akin to *bureavii*. The leaves of *elegantulum* are narrower with more velvety and less woolly indumentum.

From south-west Szechwan near Yung-ning, 3,650–3,950 m (12,000–13,000 ft) on rocky slopes, meadows and among conifers.

March–April

faberi Hemsl. 1889 (*faberioides* Balf.f., *wuense* Balf.f.) H4 L1–2 F1–2

Ht 1–3 m (3–10 ft). Habit dwarf thickets in the wild. Young leaves with rust coloured fine textured indumentum which rather unusually turns paler on older leaves and wears off.
L 6–17 × 2.8–8 cm (2½–6½ × 1–3 in.), 2–2.5 times as long as broad, elliptic, apex acuminate, base rounded to cuneate, thick and leathery, loose rust-red juvenile indumentum below and *whitish dense appressed ± permanent adult indumentum*. L remain for 3 years. Petiole 0.5–2 cm densely tomentose. Indumentum takes some years to develop.
Inflor seven to twenty. Pedicel 1.5–3 cm densely glandular.
F white, sometimes spotted pink with scarlet blotch, 3–4 cm (1¼–1½ in.) campanulate.
Calyx 7–10 mm lobes broad, almost divided to base, sparsely glandular. Ovary densely glandular ± hairy, style glabrous or glandular at base.

A scarce plant, cultivated at Windsor Park under the name *wuense* which has leaves somewhat shiny above and thin, patchy indumentum below. It has attractive apple-blossom like flowers. Re-introduced.

Apparently only collected on Mt Omei, Wa and Wu Shan, south-west Szechwan, 2,540–4,400 m (8,300–14,500 ft), rare in the wild, usually associated with *ambiguum* and *concinnum* in thickets and on cliffs but plentiful on summit of Mt. Omei. May

faberi ssp. *prattii* (Franch.) Chamb. 1978 H4 L2–3 F1–3

Ht to 3 m (10 ft). Fairly compact to rather leggy. Bark very rough, greyish-brown.
L 8–19 × 5–8 cm (3–7½ × 2–3 in.), broadly ovate to elongate-elliptic, shiny above, indumentum below thin brown, loose and sheds easily. Leaves thick and leathery, rigid and convex. L remain for 1 to 2 years. Petiole 1.5–2.5 cm tomentose and glandular.
Inflor twelve to twenty. Pedicel 1.5–2.5 cm rufous hairy and glandular.
F white, large scarlet blotch or spotted pink, 4–5 cm (1½–2 in.) long, funnel-campanulate.
Calyx about *1 cm persistent as faberi*. Ovary and style as *faberi*.
   A fine foliage plant when well grown which has large shiny leaves. The flowers are pretty but unspectacular against the foliage. Leaves usually larger than *faberi* with stouter branches. Hardy in Britain and probably in southern Scandinavia. 'Perrywood' **AM**, *W* 3758A 1967 Sandling Park.
   From Szechwan, around Tatsienlu, 2,700–4,300 m (9,000–14,000 ft), in thickets and woods. April-May

kansuense Millais 1924 Not in cultivation

Little is known about this plant, the sterile specimen being totally inadequate.

leei Fang 1933 Not in cultivation

F white to purplish-white. Near *prattii*. Central Szechwan.

mimetes Tagg & Forr. H4 L1–2 F1–2

Ht 1–2 m (3–6½ ft).
L 6–11 × 3–4.7 cm (2½–4½ × 1¼–1¾ in.), 2–2.8 times as long as broad, ovate-lanceolate to elliptic, apex acuminate, base rounded, matted or loose persistent or evanescent indumentum below. Petiole 1.5–2 cm glabrescent.
Inflor about six. Pedicel 2–2.5 cm sparsely glandular.
F white to rose with crimson or purple markings, about 3.5 cm (1½ in.) long, funnel-campanulate.
Calyx 3–8 mm lobes narrow, reflexed, glandular. Ovary densely hairy with some glands, style glabrous.
   An unimportant species of doubtful distinction.
   From south-west Szechwan near Muli and possibly Yunnan, 3,350–3,650 m (11,000–12,000 ft) among rocks and shrub, thickets and forest margins. May

mimetes var. *simulans* Tagg & Forr. Resembles *sphaeroblastum* vegetatively but it has very different floral parts. Might be of hybrid origin.

L 6–11 ×3–4.7 cm (2½–4½ × 1¾–1¾ in.) indumentum loose sometimes evanescent in mimetes. L 8–10 × 4–4.7 cm (3¼–4 × 1½–1¾ in.) indumentum matted, persistent in var. simulans. Indumentum not nearly so split as in *aganniphum* var. *flavorufum*, suède-like.

nakotiltum Balf.f. & Forr. 1920 Probably not in cultivation

Ht 1–3.5 m (3–12 ft). L 8–11 × 3–4.3 cm (3¾–4½ × 1¼–1¾ in.), elliptic, apex acuminate, base ± rounded, two layered indumentum below, the upper loose and floccose, the lower compacted, long rayed hairs. Petiole about 1.5 cm glabrescent. Inflor twelve to fifteen rachis about 1 cm. Pedicel about 1.5 cm sparsely pubescent. F white flushed rose to pale pink with purple markings, ± with basal blotch, 3–3.5 cm (1¼–1½ in.) long, openly funnel-campanulate. Calyx about 1 mm, glabrous, lobes rounded. Ovary densely rufous tomentose. Capsule not known.

There is no record of this species being introduced and flowering, herbarium specimens only would confirm this. The type specimen does not appear to agree with the plant named *nakotiltum* at Blackhills, Morayshire which has a granular indumentum; *F* 14068 looks a little closer but the flowers white flushed rose with deep crimson markings and lines at base do not match the pale creamy-yellow Blackhills plant which in my belief is a form or hybrid of *lacteum*.

From north-west Yunnan, 3,400–4,000 m (11,000–3,000 ft), conifer forests and open scrub.

nigroglandulosum Nitzelius 1975 H4

Ht 1–1.5 m (3–5 ft) ±. Habit upright. Branchlets thick, tomentose plus dark purple shortly stalked glands.

L 14–20 × 3.5–5.5 cm (5½–8 × 1¼–2¼ in.), oblanceolate, apex shortly acuminate, base cuneate, dark green and glossy with dense glands above, loose woolly tawny indumentum below in two layers. Petiole 2.5–3 cm floccose-tomentose at first.

Inflor *c*. ten, rachis 1–1.5 cm. Pedicel 2–3 cm pubescent.

F opening carmine fading to yellowish-pink ± spotted carmine, 3.5–4 cm (1¼–1½ in.) long, 4.5–5 cm (1¾–2 in.) across, campanulate, lobes five.

Calyx small, unequal lobes. Ovary glandular, style glabrous.

This new species was described from material grown in Gothenburg Botanic Garden from seed collected by Dr Harry Smith in 1934 under No.13979. It has foliage resembling *alutaceum* and *adengynum* but has a loose tawny indumentum like *rufum*. But *nigroglandulosum* has larger glossier leaves than *rufum*. As it survives in Gothenburg, it must be very hardy.

Found on a mountain north of Kangting (Tatsienlu), north-west Szechwan at 3,500 m (11,500 ft).

phaeochrysum Balf.f. & W.W. Sm. 1917 (*dryophyllum* Balf.f. & Forr.)
H4 L2–3 F1–3

Ht 1–4.5 m (3–15 ft). Habit compact to upright. Bark rough, shaggy,
flaking, greenish-brown.
L 8–14 ×1–6.5 cm (3¼–5½ × ½–2½ in.), 1.7–3 times as long as broad, elliptic to ovate-oblong, apex obtuse to acute, base cordate to rounded, ±
glabrous above, *dense compacted, sometimes agglutinated pale fawn to
rufous-brown indumentum* below, not splitting. L remain for 2 years.
Petiole 1.5–2 cm floccose.
Inflor eight to fifteen fairly compact, rachis 0.5–1.5 cm. Pedicel 1–2.5 cm
glabrescent.
F white, white flushed pink to pink, with crimson markings, *3.2–5 cm*
(1¼–2 in.) long, funnel-campanulate.
Calyx about 1 mm, usually glabrous. Ovary and style glabrous.

A hardy, quite attractive plant, which often blooms freely when
mature. The foliage is usually worthwhile alone with lovely pale grey to
almost white young growth. The flower trusses are neat and the plants
lend an air of charm and grace in a woodland garden. A hardy species.
'Greenmantle' **AM**, 1977 *R* 59229, Borde Hill.

Leaves larger than var. *agglutinatum* but they do merge. Close to
aganniphum. A very variable and common species in the wild.

From Yunnan, Szechwan 3,400–4,700 m (11,000–15,500 ft), open
stony pastures and moorland, thickets and rhododendron scrub, openings
and margins of conifer and mixed forest, bamboo brakes, on rocks and
cliffs.   March–April

phaeochrysum var. *agglutinatum* (Balf.f. & Forr.) Chamb. 1978 (*dic-
hropeplum* Balf.f. & Forr., *dumulosum* Balf.f. & Forr., *lophophorum*
Balf.f. & Forr., *syncollum* Balf.f. & Forr.) L1–2 F1–2

Habit usually low and compact.
L *4–9 cm* (1½–3½ in.) long, very variable in size and shape, indumentum
felted or agglutinate, sometimes splitting, big variation in thickness and
colour.
F white, creamy-white, white flushed rose, pale lilac-pink, bright rose-
pink, with or without crimson markings, *2–3.5 cm* (¾–1 ⅖ in.) long.

Completely intergrades with *phaeochrysum* although the extremes are
distinct. Also close to *sphaeroblastum*.

Very common and widespread in Szechwan, south-east Tibet and
Yunnan.

phaeochrysum var. *levistratum* (Balf.f. & Forr.) Chamb. 1978 (*aiolopep-
lum* Balf.f. & Forr., *dryophyllum* part, *helvolum* Balf.f. & Forr., *intortum*
Balf.f. & Forr., *sigillatum* Balf.f. & Forr., *vicinum* Balf.f. & Forr.) H4
L1–2 F1–3

Habit usually a smallish shrub, often only 30–45 cm (1–1½ ft) in the
wild. L 5–14 ×1.4–5.2 cm (2–5½ × ½–2 in.), oblong-elliptic to lanceolate, thin suède-like continuous indumentum below, fawn, brown,

yellowish-brown, yellowish to cinnamon coloured, a great variation in shape, size and width, colour and consistency of indumentum and length of petiole, stiff.

F white to pink to rose-pink or pinkish-purple, with or without crimson spots and sometimes blotched.

This variety represents a dwarfer edition of *phaeochrysum* itself. Very hardy in Britain and also south Sweden (from Szechwan and Kansu). Some forms have very small flowers while others are larger, the best forms being quite desirable.

Very common and widespread in the wild. It is so variable that it might be possible to divide these different forms into several groups such as thick indumentum and short petiole, thin indumentum and long petiole and so on but there are full gradations between these too.

From Yunnan, Szechwan, Kansu and perhaps Burma, 3,000–4,400 m (10,000–14,500 ft).

pomense Cowan & Davidian 1953 Not in cultivation

Shrub 0.6–1.2 m (2–5½ ft). L 8.5–10 × 3.5–4.7 cm (3½–4 × 1¼–1¾ in.), oblong-oval, thin compacted brown indumentum below, *long rayed hairs*. Inflor *c*. five. F pink, 3.8 cm (1½ in.) long.
Calyx *c*. 1.2 cm, lobes unequal. *Ovary densely tomentose.*

A distinct species, possibly allied to *adenogynum*. Only one specimen from Pome, south-east Tibet above Showa Dzong, 3,400 m (11,000 ft).

principis Bur. & Franch. (*vellereum* Hutch. ex Tagg) H4 L1–2 F1–3

Ht 2–6 m (6–20 ft). Habit bushy rounded topped shrub to small tree. Bark rough, greyish.
L 6–14 × 1.8–5 cm (2½–5½ × ¾–2 in.), 2–3.6 times as long as broad, oblong to ovate-lanceolate, apex acute, base rounded to ± cordate, *thick spongy white to fawn indumentum* below. L remain for 2 years. Petiole 1–2 cm tomentose at first, usually glabrous, evanescent.
Inflor *ten to thirty* truss full or flat topped. Pedicel 1.5–2 cm glabrous, slender.
F white, white flushed rose, blush-pink, bluish-pink, rich rose to reddish-magenta, spotted purple or maroon or unspotted, 2.5–3.7 cm (1–1¾ in.) long, more campanulate than most of the subsection.
Calyx minute, about 1 mm, fringed with glands. Ovary and style glabrous. Capsule narrowly cylindrical, curved, glabrous.

A distinctive species in foliage and flower with its pale suède-like indumentum and many flowered trusses of rather bell-shaped flowers. Some forms are much better than others. Often starts blooming a little younger than average for the subsection and is free flowering on maturity. Is very hardy in Britain and apparently succeeds in south Sweden. The growth is sometimes rather early and can occasionally be damaged. Tolerates dry conditions in the wild.

R. principis type was discovered by Prince Henry D. Orleáns farther east than *vellereum* has been found, probably in an area otherwise unexplored. Chamberlain considers this synonymous with *vellereum* and the

Prince's name takes presidence. There are two specimens intermediate between this species and *aganniphum* in the Edinburgh Herbarium. *R. vellereum* is incorrectly placed under *aganniphum* in the new Bean. 'Lost Horizon' **AM**, 1976, white suffused purple, Borde Hill.

Comes from a more westerly distribution than its relatives, in south Tibet, being common on both sides of the Tsangpo for nearly 320 km (200 miles) at 2,700–4,600 m (9,000–15,000 ft), river banks, dry open stony hillsides, often socially in conifer forest below the dry plateau region, lake sides, limestone cliffs and in various types of deciduous and evergreen forest. March–April

pronum Tagg & Forr. 1927, see *Dwarf Rhododendrons* (*p.* 166), *The Smaller Rhododendrons* (*p.* 184).

proteoides Balf.f. & W. W. Sm. 1916 (*lampropeplum* Balf.f. & Forr.), see *Dwarf Rhododendrons* (*p.* 166), *The Smaller Rhododendrons* (*p.* 184–5).

przewalskii Maxim. 1877 (*kialense* Franch.) H4 L1–2 F1–2

Ht 1–2.7 m (3–9 ft). Habit usually compact and rounded.
L 4.5–10 ×2–4.5 cm (1¾–4 × ¾–1¾ in.), 1.8–3 times as long as broad, broadly elliptic, apex obtuse to shortly acuminate, base ± rounded, ± glabrous above, compacted whitish to pale brown indumentum below, often hard to see with the naked eye, sometimes glabrescent. L remain for 2 years. Petiole about 1 cm glabrous. L often with metallic sheen above. Inflor ten to fifteen compact, rachis 0.4–1.5 cm. Pedicel 1.5–2 cm glabrous.
F white (usually) to pale pink, with or without crimson spots, 2.5–3.5 cm (1–1½ in.) long, funnel-campanulate to campanulate.
Calyx about 0.5 mm glabrous. Ovary and style glabrous.

A very hardy species which flourishes in cold climates such as Scandinavia. While it makes a neat bush, the flowers are rather small. Rare in Britain but re-introduced in 1986–8.

A distinct species, especially geographically, being relatively common over a wide area of north China producing many different flowering forms. Related to *phaeochrysum*, sharing the compacted, often agglutinate indumentum. Usually has a distinctive yellow midrib on L above.

From Szechwan, Kansu and east Tibet, 3,000–4,300 m (10,000–14,000 ft), high ridges, grassy and rocky alpine slopes often facing north-east, among limestone rocks and in conifer forest.

April–May

purdomii Rehd. & Wils 1913. Said to be introduced.

Robust shrub. L coriaceous, 6–9 ×2.5–3.5 cm (2½–3½ × 1–1½ in.), oblong-lanceolate to oblong, glabrous and shining above, ± glabrous beneath.
Inflor ten to twelve. Pedicel slender 1–1.6 cm densely villous-tomentose.
F campanulate, 2.5–3 cm (1–1¼ in.) long.
Calyx 1–1.5 mm. Ovary sparsely white-villous, style glabrous.

Only known from type specimen. Possibly related to *przewalskii* or *brachycarpum*, but affinites remain in doubt. Plants labelled *purdomii* in cultivation are wrongly named. From Shensi, mid-China.

recurvoides Tagg & Ward 1932, see *Dwarf Rhododendrons* (*p.* 167), *The Smaller Rhododendrons* (*p.* 184–6). Chemical tests have shown this to be related to *crinigerum* and it has been transferred to the Glischra subsection.

roxieanum Forr. 1915 (var. *oreonastes* Balf.f. & Forr., *poecilodermum* Balf.f & Forr.), see *Dwarf Rhododendrons* (*p.* 167–8), *The Smaller Rhododendrons* (*p.* 185).

roxieanum var. *cucullatum* (Hand.-Mazz.) Chamb. 1978 (*coccinopeplum* Balf.f. & Forr., *porphyroblastum* Balf.f. & Forr.)

Var. *cucullatum* and *coccinopeplum* were formerly synonyms of *roxieanum* while *porphyroblastum* was a synonym of *globigerum*.

roxieanum var. *globigerum* (Balf.f. & Forr.) Chamb. 1978, see *Dwarf Rhododendrons* (*p.* 164) see *p.* 266.

rufum Batal 1891 (*weldianum* Rehd. & Wils.) H4 L2–3 F1–2

Ht 1.3–6 m (4–20 ft), usually not over 4.5 m (20 ft). Habit tends to be leggy. Bark greyish, slightly rough.
L 6.5–11 ×2.5–5 cm (2½–4½ × 1–2 in.), 2.3–3 times as long as broad, narrowly obovate to elliptic, apex acute, base cuneate to ± rounded, *dense reddish-brown indumentum below with an understory of appressed hairs embedded within a whitish film*. Leaves usually white when young. L remain for 2 years. Petiole about 1 cm tomentose.
Inflor six to twelve. Pedicel 0.7–1.5 cm densely tomentose.
F white to deep pink, sometimes with a stripe down the centre of each lobe, crimson spotted, 2–3.2 cm (¾–1¼ in.) long, funnel-campanulate.
Calyx about 0.5 mm very small, tomentose. Ovary densely reddish-tomentose with a few glands, style ± glabrous.

A good foliage plant whose indumentum almost rivals *bureavii* in some forms but it is not quite so dense or so dark. The flowers are rather small. A distinct species which now includes *weldianum* which was only separated by its cuneate as opposed to rounded leaf base, not sufficient to maintain it as a species. Very hardy including Scandinavia as far north as Stockholm and even Iceland. Recently re-introduced.

From Szechwan and Kansu (mostly south-west), 2,400–4,000 m (8,000–13,000 ft) in conifer forests.   April

sphaeroblastum Balf.f. & Forr. 1920 H4 L2–3 F1–3

Ht 1–3 rarely to 7 m (3–10–23 ft). Habit often a small fairly compact shrub. Bark very rough, brown to brownish-grey.
L 6–12 × 3.6–6.2 cm (2½–5 × 1½–2½ in.), 1.7–2.3 times as long as broad, oval to elliptic to broadly ovate-lanceolate, apex obtuse, base rounded to

cordate, *dense, felted, usually rust coloured indumentum* below. L remain for 2 to 3 years. Petiole 1–1.5 cm glabrescent.
Inflor ten to twenty. Pedicel 1–1.5 cm ± glabrous when mature.
F white, creamy-white, white flushed rose to pink, marked or lined with crimson or purple, 3–4 cm (1¼–1½ in.) long, funnel-campanulate.
Calyx 1.5–2 mm glabrous. Ovary and style glabrous.

Makes a handsome foliage plant when well grown and the flowers are usually neat and attractive. Hardy throughout Britain. The leaves are generally flatter than *clementinae*. Merges with *phaeochrysum* in the narrower leaved forms of *sphaeroblastum*.

Mostly south-west Szechwan and also north-west Yunnan, 3,000–4,500 m (10,000–14,500 ft), open rocky meadows and slopes, open scrub and among boulders, in thickets and in openings in conifer forests and in rhododendron thickets.   April–May

taliense Franch. 1886. H4 L1–3 F1–3.
Ht 0.8–4 m (2½–13 ft). Habit usually fairly dwarf and compact.
L 5–11 × 2–4 cm (2–4½ × ¾–1½ in.), 2.2–3.5 times as long as broad, oblong-ovate to broadly lanceolate, apex acute, base rounded to ± cuneate, *dense tawny-brown to rufous indumentum* below. L remain for 3 to 4 years. Petiole 0.5–1 cm tomentose.
Inflor ten to twenty. Pedicel 1–2 cm *tomentose and glandular.*
F white, creamy-yellow to pinkish-white, often marked, flushed or lined with rose and crimson spots, 3–3.5 cm (1¼–1½ in.) long, funnel-campanulate.
Calyx 0.5–2 mm glabrous. Ovary glabrous or white glandular.

This is the centre plant in a very complex group of closely related species. Those closest are *alutaceum, phaeochrysum, roxieanum, proteoides, aganniphum* and *sphaeroblastum*. It is usually an attractive plant with a compact habit and good, dark indumentum. Some forms have pretty flowers in neat trusses. Differs from *phaeochrysum* var. *levistratum* in its more convex leaves.

Occurs on both the dry east and moist west of the Tali Range, Yunnan, 3,000–4,000 m (10,000–13,000 ft), dry and moist rocky situations on mountain meadows and on cliffs.   April–May

traillianum Forr. & W.W. Sm. 1914 (*aberrans* Tagg & Forr., *theiophyllum* Balf.f. & Forr.) H4 L2–3 F1–3

Ht 60 cm–8 m (2–26 ft). Habit usually a stiff upright shrub. Bark rough, grey to greyish-brown.
L 7–13 × 3–6.5 cm (2¾–5 × 1¼–2½ in.), 2–3 times as long as broad, obovate to elliptic, apex obtuse to shortly acuminate, base rounded, *compacted rust-brown indumentum of short rayed, radiate hairs* below. L remain for 2 to 3 years. Petiole 1–2.5 cm floccose.
Inflor six to fifteen, rachis 0.5–1.3 cm. Pedicel 1–1.5 cm tomentose.
F white sometimes flushed rose to rose, with or without spots or blotch, 2.5–3.5 cm (1–1½ in.) long, funnel-campanulate.
Calyx about 1 mm glabrous. Ovary glabrous or sparsely red-brown tomentose, style glabrous.

A good foliage plant with indumentum of a very fine texture. The flowers are inclined to be rather small for the size of the leaves. Not very different from *phaeochrysum*. Indumentum usually less plastered.

A very common and fairly uniform species in the wild, often growing socially in huge quantities forming forests by itself. Re-introduced.

From south-west Szechwan, south-east Tibet and west Yunnan, 3,000–4,600 m (10,000–15,000 ft), open thickets and margins of conifer forest, rhododendron scrub and on limestone cliffs.   April–May

traillianum var. *dictyotum* (Balf.f. & Tagg) Chamb. 1978

Ht 1.2–1.8 m (4–6 ft). Habit a relatively small shrub.
L 5–13.5 × 2–5.5 cm (2–5½ × ¾–2¼ in.), oblong-elliptic to oblanceolate, thin felty continuous brown indumentum below.
F white to white flushed rose, with or without crimson spots, 3.2–5 cm (1⅓–2 in.), campanulate.
Ovary tomentose, style glabrous.

A fairly rare plant which L. de Rothschild considered rare and difficult to grow. The indumentum is generally darker, coarser and looser than *traillianum* with ribbon-like arms on indumentum hairs. The type vaguely resembles *wasonii* while Cowan and Davidian considered it near *nakotiltum*. 'Kathmandu' **AM**, 1966 flowers with crimson blotch and some spots. Exbury.

From south-east Tibet, south-west Szechwan and north-west Yunnan, 3,400–4,300 m (11,000–14,000 ft), open rhododendron scrub and thickets, scrub-clad slopes and in and on margins of conifer forests.

May

wallaceanum Millais 1924 Not in cultivation

A little-known species.

wasonii Hemsl. & Wils. 1910, see *Dwarf Rhododendrons* (*p.* 170), *The Smaller Rhododendrons* (*p.* 187).

wiltonii Hemsl. & Wils. 1910 H4 A − 5 L2–3 F2–3

Ht 1–4.5 m (3–15 ft). Habit upright but often compact. Young shoots tomentose for 3 to 4 years. Bark light to dark brown, roughening with age.
L 5–12 × 1.5–4 cm (2–5 × ⅝–1½ in.), 2.5–6 times as long as broad, apex oblanceolate to broadly elliptic, apex obtuse, base cuneate, *bullate with deeply impressed veins* above and dense one layered *cinnamon to rusty-red indumentum* below, eglandular. L remain for 2 to 3 years. Petiole 1.5–3 cm tomentose, becoming glabrescent.
Inflor about ten, loose. Pedicel 1.5–2.5 cm densely woolly tomentose.
F white to pink, often flushed irregularly with deeper pink and with red spots and crimson blotch, 3–4 cm (1¼–1½ in.) long, funnel-campanulate to campanulate.
Calyx 2–3 mm densely tomentose. Ovary densely rust-red woolly tomentose, eglandular, style glabrous or hairy at base.

A very distinctive species with fine bullate foliage and prettily marked flowers. There is quite a variation in foliage on cultivated plants in width and size. Generally hardy in Britain and fairly successful in southern Scandinavia. Is very different from the rest of the subsection and shows no close resemblance to any other species. Out on its own chemically. **AM**, 1957. Exbury white, flushed pink, crimson blotch.

From west Szechwan, 2,400–3,400 m (8,000–11,000 ft), in woods, thickets, under conifers, often along very windy northern ridges and on cliffs. April–May

TEPHROPEPLA SUBSECTION (L)

longistylum Rehd. & Wils. 1913 H3–4 L1–2 F1–2

Ht 50 cm–2 m (2–7 ft). Habit erect but inclined to sprawl.
Young shoots ± scaly, usually minutely puberulous.
L evergreen, 1.6–6 × 0.6–1.5 cm (⅗–2½ × ¼–⅗ in.), oblanceolate, lanceolate to oblong-lanceolate, apex acute, narrowed to base to obtuse, not hairy, scales below unequal, brown, two to four times their own diameter apart. Petiole 2–6 mm scaly, minutely puberulous.
Inflor terminal or terminal and axillary in upper one to two leaves, three to ten per bud. Pedicel 0.6–1.5 cm.
F white, white tinged pink, 1.3–1.8 cm (½–¾ in.) long, about 1.8 (¾ in.) across, usually not scaly outside.
Calyx green, 1–3 mm, margin ciliate. Ovary densely scaly, style long and slender, glabrous, often bright red.

A very distinct species, previously placed in the Triflorum series. Makes a pretty little bush with small leaves and flowers to match. Dainty and graceful. This plant is inclined to be both wood and bud tender.

From west Szechwan, 900–2,300 m (3,000–7,500 ft), scrub-clad rocky slopes in full sun, in thickets and on cliffs. May

THOMSONIA SUBSECTION (THOMSONII SUB-SERIES) (E)

This subsection can be divided into four Alliances centred around the following species. (a) *cerasinum*, (b) *thomsonii*, (c) *hookeri*, (d) *eclecteum*.

These are shrubs or small trees, 60 cm–14 m (2–45 ft) with smooth or peeling bark. L 2.7–18 × 1.5–9 cm (1–7 × ⅗–3⅗ in.), orbicular, broadly elliptic, obovate to oblong to oval. Inflor terminal, three to twelve, usually loose, F crimson to pink, white and yellow, campanulate to tubular-campanulate, calyx 0.1–2 cm usually large, stamens ten often glabrous, ovary glabrous to glandular to densely tomentose, style usually glabrous, capsule straight.

They are found wild from the Himalayas eastwards just into Szechwan. Several have fine foliage and bark as well as flowers. They have been proved biochemically distinct from the rest of the old Thomsonii series. The majority are reasonably hardy in all but the coldest British gardens but suffered badly in the 1972 freeze in Oregon.

Several species of this subsection are amongst the most susceptible of the elepidotes to powdery mildew.

(a) *bonvalotii, cerasinum* and (possibly) *populare* Alliance

A distinctive Alliance, both morphologically and biochemically. Erect shrubs, occasionally forming small trees in the wild. Branchlets not setose-glandular. L oblong to oblong-elliptic. Inflor five to seven.

bonvalotii Bur. & Franch. 1891 Not in cultivation

L rather small and narrow. F rose? campanulate. Style glandular to tip. Little is known of this plant, there being only one inadequate specimen but it appears to be related to *cerasinum* with smaller flowers and leaves. From south-west Szechwan near Tatsienlu.

cerasinum Tagg 1931 H4 L1–2 F1–3

Ht 1.80–3.60 m (6–12 ft). Habit stout thick set bush.
Bark fairly smooth, orange-brown, slightly flaking.

L 5–10 × 2–4 cm (2–4 × ¾–1½ in.), oblong to oblanceolate to oblong-elliptic, apex obtuse to rounded, base obtuse to rounded, glabrous above and below. L remain for 1 year. Petiole 0.7–2 cm.
Inflor three to five very loose, sometimes hanging between leaves. Pedicel 1.6–2 cm glandular.
F usually cherry-red, or creamy-white to pale pink with a broad cherry band around the edge of the lobes, rarely scarlet or pink, deep purple nectaries, to 5 cm (2 in.) long, campanulate.
Calyx 1–5 mm, undulate ± glandular. Ovary densely glandular, style glandular to tip.
   The rimmed forms have a most unusual and striking appearance and always create quite a stir. When young, the flowers may be partially hidden by the foliage but give a good show on mature specimens. Long lasting. The rimmed form was named 'Cherry brandy' by *KW* and the cherry-red form 'Coals of fire'. The darker forms sometimes have darker petioles.
   This very distinct species was collected a few times by *KW* and *L&S* and is probably common and widespread over much of the unexplored territory near where their collections were made. It is interesting that both collectors found the self and bicolor forms growing together in different areas. **AM**, 1938 bicolor form. Some clones flower twice.
   From south-east Tibet, Arunachal Pradesh and Upper Burma, at 3,000–3,700 m (10,000–12,000 ft), quite common in dense thickets, often tangled or impenetrable in sheltered dips and hollows or ridges, by streams, in and on margins of conifer forests.   May–June

populare Cowan 1937 Not in cultivation

Ht 90 cm–4.60 m (3–15 ft). L 3.5 × 1.5–3.5 cm (1½–3 × ⅜–1½ in.), oblong to elliptic. Inflor three to five. F blood-red to crimson with ± deeper spots, 2.5–3.8 cm (1–1½ in.) long, funnel-campanulate to campanulate. Calyx 0.1–1 cm crimson to greenish-pink.

Seems to be a distinct species, although it could possibly be a natural hybrid; three *L&S* numbers from Chayul Chu and Pemakochung, Tsangpo Gorge, south-east Tibet, 2,900–3,700 m (9,500–12,000 ft) in rhododendron and bamboo forest. The Tsangpo Gorge form has rougher, wider leaves than the others with a less pointed apex.

(b) *lopsangianum, thomsonii, viscidifolium* Alliance

A small group, closely related to the well-known *thomsonii* with orbicular to oblong-elliptic leaves, leathery, ± glaucous below, all from the Himalayan region. Probably related to *neriiflorum*.

lopsangianum, see *Dwarf Rhododendrons* (*p.* 90–1). *The Smaller Rhododenrons* (*p.* 187). Considered a subspecies of *thomsonii* by chamberlain.

thomsonii Hook.f. 1851 H3–4 A+5 L2–4 F2–4

Ht 60 cm–7 m (2–23 ft). Habit bushy to tree-like with age. Bark smooth and peeling, usually mixed colours; pink, creamy-brown, fawn, grey, green, maroon and orange.
L thick and leathery, 4–11.3 × 3–7.5 cm (1½–4½ × 1¼–3 in.), orbicular, ovate to broadly elliptic, apex rounded, base rounded to truncate, dark to medium-green above, glabrous, sometimes very glaucous when young; glaucous to pale glaucous-green below, glabrous. L remain for 1 to 2 years. Petiole 1–2.6 cm usually eglandular.
Inflor six to twelve loose, rachis 0.5–1.8 cm. Pedicel 0.8–2.7 cm, usually eglandular.
F *deep blood-red to dark wine-red*, ± spotted, 3.5–6 cm (1½–2½ in.) long, campanulate, fleshy, often with a bloom.
Calyx *large*, cup-shaped 0.6–2 cm, whitish-green, greenish-scarlet to greenish-purple to various shades of red. Ovary eglandular, style eglandular.

A species of many virtues with its fine, dark red flowers, often brilliantly glaucous young leaves and lovely peeling, smooth colourful bark. Some forms have much finer foliage than others and likewise the flowers vary in their merit, the best forms having large flowers in many flowered trusses. It takes a few years for it to flower freely but it is well worth waiting for. Unfortunately often susceptible to powdery mildew.

Hardy enough for most British woodland gardens but may be damaged in cold gardens in very hard winters. Suffered severely in the winters of 1955 and 1972 in north-western North America, where they find *L&S* 2847 to be hardier than most introductions. Several re-introductions.

First flowered in Britain at Sunningdale Nursery and Edinburgh in 1857. It appreciates being dead-headed as it often sets an abundance of seed. Honey from the nectar of this species is said to be non-poisonous and the Tibetans sometimes eat the flowers. Some fine hybrids have been raised using this species. **AGM**, 1925, **AM**, 1973 Crown Lands.

From east Nepal, Sikkim, Bhutan, south Tibet, Arunachal Pradesh and doubtfully Upper Burma, 2,400–4,300 m (8,000–14,000 ft), dense rhododendron and conifer forest, among bamboo, upper limits of conifers and open hillsides, bogs and stream sides, sometimes gregarious and sometimes mixed with other species.

L&S sometimes March, April–May

thomsonii ssp. *candelabrum* (Hook.f.) Chamb. 1978 (*thomsonii* var. *pallidum* Cowan)

This plant has every appearance of being a natural hybrid between *thomsonii* and *campylocarpum*. These two species often grow together in the wild and the morphology of ssp. *candelabrum* points to intermediate characters between the two. Chamberlain says that although natural hybridity is very likely, these plants may have undergone the process of speciation for generations and therefore deserve subspecific rank until field studies have a chance to prove otherwise. I would say that the reverse should be applied and treat it as a natural hybrid until it can be proved otherwise. I saw several plants of this in Nepal.

The chief characters of a glandular ovary and smaller calyx do not appear to be constant factors and both vary all the way between the supposed parents. Also, cultivated plants sometimes show the blotch often found in *campylocarpum* and the bark is not always smooth. What is more, the man-made hybrid 'Exminster' is very similar to the plants of ssp. *candelabrum* in cultivation.

F rosy-pink, pink spotted red, pale vermilion; some approach the deep colour of *thomsonii* which could be a back cross, F2 or subsequent generation showing a tendency towards *thomsonii* which I admit does seem to be the dominant parent. Many *KW* collections of the Thomsonia subsection at Nymans, Sussex, are hybrids.

Morphologically, *thomsonii* var. *pallidum* does not differ from ssp. *candelabrum* although no *thomsonii* occurs in its habitat in south Tibet. The probable answer is that *lopsangianum* is the other parent with *campylocarpum* instead of *thomsonii*. Only *L&S* 1728 and 1730 belong here. Ssp. *candelabrum* is found in Sikkim. Bhutan and probably Arunachal Pradesh.

viscidifolium Davidian 1967 H3–4 L2–3 F2

Ht 60 cm–2.40 m (2–8 ft). Habit usually rounded and compact, twigs slender. Bark *not* smooth like *thomsonii*, pale brown.
L 4–9.7 × 2.8–6.6 cm (1½–4 × 1–2½ in.), oval to rounded, apex rounded, base rounded to truncate, glabrous above, *densely glandular (sticky) below, white*. L remain for 1 year. Petiole 1–2.5 cm.
Inflor one to three, very loose, rachis 1–3 mm. Pedicel 0.8–1 cm, reddish.
F *copper-red to coppery-orange*, spotted crimson, crimson nectaries, 3.6–4.6 cm (1½–1¾ in.) long, tubular-campanulate.
Calyx cup-shaped 4–9 mm, green or copper-red, margin hairy. Ovary *densely tomentose* and glandular, style crimson, glabrous.

A very distinctive species, neat, attractive and unusual. This recently named plant is still rare in gardens. While hardly spectacular in flower, the colour is so out of the ordinary that it frequently brings comment. The old leaves often drop when in flower, turning nearly the same colour as the flowers. Subject to bark-split; lost upper leaves in Oregon in 1972 freeze.

Collected twice by *L&S* in south Tibet and bloomed in 7 years from seed at Glenarn, west Scotland. From 2,700–3,400 m (9,000–11,000 ft), close to streams, usually on cliff faces near waterfalls.   May

(c) *faucium, hookeri, hylaeum, subansiriense, succothii* Alliance

This is distinguished botanically by the red punctulate glands which sometimes form hairs. These five related species, two of them newly described, form compact or large upright shrubs or trees with beautiful smooth bark. The inflorescence tends to be tighter than the rest of the Thomsonia subsection. Affinity also lies with the Irrorata subsection and comes nearest to *anthosphaerum*.

faucium Chamb. 1978 Sp. nov. probably H3–4 L2–3 F1–2

Ht 1.5–6.5 m (5–21 ft) or more. Habit erect, often tree-like. Bark as *hylaeum*.
L 7–12 × 2.5–3.5 cm (3–5 × 1–1½ in.), oblanceolate, apex rounded, base tapered, cuneate. Petiole 0.7–1.5 cm, stipitate-glandular.
Inflor five to ten, often dense, rachis 8–10 mm. Pedicel 5–10 mm.
F pale rose or white suffused rose, rarely yellow; spotted purple, 3.5–4.5 cm (1½–1¾ in.) long, campanulate.
Ovary densely stipitate-glandular.

It is apparent that most of the *hylaeum* in cultivation are in fact this new species. This makes a fine specimen plant in mild gardens including Sussex with a lovely smooth bark but the flowers are usually a poor dingy rose. These can make a good splash of colour where freely produced. The growth comes early (but not as early as *subansiriense*) and this leads to mostly rather stunted plants in cold places like Edinburgh. Only really separated from *hylaeum* by botanical details. These are the narrower leaf, flattened or winged petiole and the glandular ovary. Also includes some plants formerly under *eclecteum* and var. *brachyandrum*.

Only from south Tibet from *L&S* and *KW* collections   March–May

hookeri Nutt. 1853 H3–4 A+15 L2–3 F1–4

Ht 3–6 m (10–20 ft). Habit usually upright. Bark smooth, grey and maroon.
L 6.3–17 × 3–7.5 cm (2½–7 × 1¼–3 in.), oblong to oblong-oval, apex rounded to obtuse, base obtuse to truncate, glabrous above, *isolated tufts of hairs on lateral veins below*. L remain for 1 to 2 years. Petiole 1.5–2.6 cm eglandular.
Inflor eight to eighteen fairly loose to compact, rachis 1.4–1.6 cm. Pedicel 0.7–1.6 cm eglandular.
F bright to blood to cherry-red to deep crimson with dark crimson nectaries at base. *KW* 8238 carmine to pinkish-purple to amethyst-purple; 3.5–4.4 cm (1½–1¾ in.) long, tubular-campanulate to funnel-shaped, fleshy.
Calyx 0.5–2 cm eglandular. Ovary and style eglandular.

In its best forms, this is one of the most gorgeous scarlet rhododendrons. All forms of this colour are unfortunately rather tender and suffer severe bark-split and frosted growth if attempted in the colder parts of Britain. The new growth comes early so adequate shelter and tree protection is needed for good growth, which is like tapering red candles. The tufted hairs (hooks!) are a very good identifying character.

KW 8238 is considerably hardier, makes later growth and has wider leaves. Unfortunately it is only of botanical interest in my opinion; the flowers of any I have seen are of a decidedly dirty colour and only fit for the bonfire anywhere but in a specialized species collection. This form appears to be closely related to *hylaeum* and *faucium*. It has a green or yellowish calyx. **FCC**, Bodnant dark red flowers and calyx (type).

From Bhutan and Arunachal Pradesh, 3,000–3,700 m (10,000–12,000 ft). The red form at least would seem to be uncommon in the wild; *Abies-Rhododendron* forest on sheltered slopes.   March–April

hylaeum Balf.f. & Farrer 1922 H3–4 L2–3 F1–2

Ht to 12 m (40 ft) in the wild. Bark *smooth* almost glistening (*KW*), silvery, grey-brown to purplish-red.
L 6–17.5 × 3.5–5.7 cm (2½–7 × 1½–2¼ in.), oblong-lanceolate, apex rounded to obtuse, base narrowed, obtuse to cordulate, broadest about middle, old leaves glabrous, minutely punctulate below.
Petiole 1–2.4 cm eglandular.
Inflor ten to twelve, moderately compact, rachis about 2 cm. Pedicel 0.8–1.5 cm eglandular.
F pale to deep pink, rose to rose-purple or almost white, lightly to heavily spotted, with basal nectaries, 3.6–4.5 cm (1½–1¾ in.) long, tubular-campanulate, fleshy.
Calyx cup-like 4–8 mm, undulating, eglandular. Ovary and style *glabrous*, the latter flesh-pink like corolla.

Most plants in cultivation are probably the newly described *faucium* and not *hylaeum* at all. Shows a relationship with the Irrorata subsection and to *eclecteum*.

From Upper Burma, south-east Tibet and north-west Yunnan, 2,100–3,700 m (7,000–12,000 ft).   March–May

subansiriense Chamb. & Cox 1978 H3–4? L1–2? F2–3?

Ht to 14 m (45 ft) in the wild. Habit erect shrub or tree.
Trunk to 60 cm (2 ft) in diameter in the wild. Bark smooth or peeling, grey to red. L buds *c.* 3 × 0.8 cm cupidate. F buds rounded.
L 7–13 × 2–4 cm (3–5 × ¾–1½ in.), 3–3.5 times as long as broad, apex rounded and apiculate, base ± rounded, *numerous sessile glands overlying the veins below each with vestige of a dendroid hair*, otherwise glabrous. L remain for 1 year. Petiole 1–1.5 cm glabrous.
Inflor ten to fifteen + fairly dense, rachis *c.* 5 mm. Pedicel 0.7–1 cm glabrous.
F *crimson-scarlet*, shining with a few spots, about 4 cm (1½ in.) long tubular-campanulate with nectar pouches.
Calyx 4–5 mm cupular, lobes ciliate. Ovary densely *tomentose*.

Collected as plants and seed in 1965. First flowered in a cool house at

Glendoick in 1976. While the flowers are rather small, the colour is excellent and the smooth bark quite a feature. Seems to be reasonably winter hardy at Glendoick but the very early growth is easily damaged. Is related to *hylaeum* and *faucium*, which have a similar bark, habit and leaf shape. Shows some relationship with *kendrickii*, and *ramsdenianum* but differs in the leaf texture, shape and glands with persistent dendroid hair. Killed at Glendoick 1981–2.

Collected in the Subansiri Division of Arunachal Pradesh, 2,550–2,750 m (8,400–9,200 ft), common on and below top of ridge in moss forest with *grande* and *eximium*.   March

succothii Davidian 1966 (*nishiokae* Hara) H4 L2–3 F2–3

Ht 1–4.6 m (3–15 ft). Habit often rounded and compact. Bark very attractive red-brown and purplish-grey, peeling right up to 2-year-old shoots. Branchlets glabrous.

L in *whorls* at ends of branches, often *upturned* in an unusual manner, 5.3–13.5 × 2.6–6.4 cm (2–5½ × 1–2½ in.), oblong-obovate to elliptic, apex rounded to broadly obtuse, base broadly obtuse or rounded, *cordulate, auricled*, dark and glossy above, glabrous or rarely hairy below. L remain for 1 to 2 years. Petiole *short*, 2–5 mm.

Inflor ten to fifteen compact and rounded, rachis 1–1.5 cm. Pedicel 0.4–1.3 cm.

F crimson or scarlet, 2.3–3.5 cm (about 1–1½ in.) long, nectar pouches at base, tubular-campanulate.

Calyx minute 1 mm glabrous. Ovary and style glabrous.

The combination of a compact rounded bush with dark glossy leaves and compact deep red trusses makes a fine sight in early spring. It takes a number of years to start flowering. Hardy in most parts of Britain. This is undoubtedly closely related to *fulgens* and could be regarded as a glabrous leaved equivalent of that species. Recently moved by Chamberlain to this subsection on account of the compact inflorescence, nectar pouches, bark and other characters. Lies botanically between Thomsonia, Fulgensia and Barbata subsections. One of the most susceptible species to powdery mildew. Recently re-introduced.

From Bhutan and west Arunachal Pradesh at 3,400–4,100 m (11,000–13,500 ft), common in places in rhododendron and mixed scrub forest, sometimes gregarious, fir forest or edge of moorland.

February–April

(d) *cyanocarpum, eclecteum, eurysiphon, meddianum, stewartianum* Alliance

This group comes from the eastern end of the distribution of this subsection. These are small to large shrubs with largely glabrous leaves. The flowers are remarkably variable in colour in three of the five species and are in rather loose trusses of two to twelve. These mostly open early in the season so are very prone to frost damage although the plants themselves are generally hardy enough for sheltered gardens in Britain. The bark is usually peeling.

Distribution is south-east Tibet, Burma, Yunnan and Szechwan.

R. meddianum var. *atrokermesinum*

cyanocarpum (Franch.) W.W. Sm. 1914 H4 L2–3 F1–3

Ht 1.2–7.6 m (4–25 ft). Habit a stiff shrub, sometimes tree-like. Bark yellowish to greyish-pink peeling.

L thick, 5–12.6 × 4–9 cm (2–5 × 1½–3½ in.), broadly elliptic to orbicular, apex rounded, base rounded to truncate, glabrous and usually glaucous above, glabrous or minutely hairy below. L remain for 1 year. Petiole 1.5–3 cm ± glandular.

Inflor six to ten usually loose, rachis 0.5–1 cm. Pedicel 1–2 cm eglandular.

F pure white to creamy-white, pink to rose-pink, flushed rose to purplish-rose, 4–6 cm (1½–2½ in.) long, campanulate to widely funnel-campanulate, fragrant.

Calyx 0.2–1.1 cm cup-shaped, greenish or slightly coloured, eglandular. Ovary glabrous or sparsely stipitate-glandular, style glabrous.

   The foliage somewhat resembles *thomsonii* but the flower colour is quite different and it is widely separated geographically. The white flow-ered forms are the most attractive, some of the others being rather a poor colour. Foliage was damaged in 1972 freeze in Oregon but undamaged in the 1955 freeze in Seattle. Var. *eriphyllum* is possibly a natural hybrid. **AM**, 1938 Leonardslee flowers white flushed rose. Powdery mildew prone.

   From north-west Yunnan, Tali Range only at 3,000–4,000 m

(10,000–13,000 ft), rocky ravines and open pasture, moist alpine meadows and margins of conifer forest. Common there. March–April

eclecteum Balf.f. & Forr. (var. *brachyandrum* Balf.f. & Forr.) 1920 H3–4 A+5 L2–3 F1–3

Ht 60 cm–2.40 m (2–8 ft). Habit bushy to sparse with age. Bark reddish-brown, greyish-pink to greyish-fawn, fairly smooth flaking. Vivid red bud-scales with new growth.
L 5–15 × 2–6 cm (2–6 × ¾–2½ in.) obovate to *oblong-obovate* and oblong, apex rounded, base cordulate, obtuse to truncate, glabrous and often glaucous above, usually glabrous below but midrib sometimes pubescent. L remain for 1 to 2 years. Petiole usually very short, *almost sessile*, 0.3–1.8 cm, often broad.
Inflor six to twelve loose to fairly compact, rachis 0.4–1.5 cm. Pedicel 0.8–2 cm usually eglandular.
F very variable in colour, white, pale purple, pale pink to rose, purple, salmon-pink, red or yellow; not marked or speckled or heavily spotted or stained or blotched and various bicolors such as buff and yellow edged rose-red and white, margined rose; also variable in size and shape 3–5.3 cm (1¾–2⅛ in.) long, tubular-campanulate, fleshy.
Calyx 0.2–2 cm glabrous. Ovary glandular, style eglandular.
   This is one of the most variable of all species as to flower colour and has been introduced many times. All bloom early and are not really suitable for cold areas. Several of the self colours such as yellow and bicolors are most attractive and well worth attempting. Some of the purple shaded forms are decidedly ugly and not worthy of cultivation.
   Closely related to *stewartianum* which has a less elongate leaf which is usually smaller, a generally longer petiole and thinner, weaker growth. May merge with *hylaeum* or *faucium* in the former var. *brachyandrum*.
   Grow on a well-drained site in partial shade, avoiding if possible, the early morning sun. **AM**, 1949, Exbury F yellow, **AM**, 1978 *KW 6869* Borde Hill.
   From north-west and west Yunnan, south-east Tibet, south-west Szechwan, Upper Burma and possibly Arunachal Pradesh in a non-typical form. *R* found many colour forms all mixed together in places while elsewhere the colours were more uniform and segregated. 3,000–4,300 m (10,000–14,000 ft) usually in open situations amongst scrub, edges of thickets, among boulders and rocks, alpine ridges, among bamboo and in and on margins of conifer forest. January–April

eclecteum var. *bellatulum* Tagg L with longer petiole than type, oblong.

eurysiphon Tagg & Forr. 1930 H4 L2–3? F1–3?

Ht 90 cm–1.5 m. Branchlets ± setose-glandular.
L 2.6–7.5 × 1.3–2.8 cm (1–3 × ½–1 in.), oblong to oblong-elliptic, apex ± rounded, base rounded or obtuse, glabrous above, glabrous below, minutely ± glandular. Petiole 0.5–1.2 cm ± setose-glandular.

Inflor three to five, loose, rachis 3–5 mm. Pedicel 1.2–2.5 cm glandular.
F creamy-white, blush-pink or pale rose flushed deep magenta, heavily
spotted crimson, 3–4 cm (about 1½ in.) long, campanulate.
Calyx 2–4 mm, glandular. Ovary densely glandular, style eglandular.

This rare plant seems to be half-way between the Selensia and Thomsonia subsections and could be a natural hybrid between *martinianum* and
stewartianum. Only one finding of F in south-east Tibet at 4,000 m
(13,000 ft).   May

meddianum Forr. 1920 H3–4 A+5 L1–2 F2–4

Ht 90 cm–1.8 m (3–6 ft). Habit upright, rather a poor grower. Bark
pinkish-fawn, peeling, roughish when old.
L 5.5–18 × 3.5–8 cm (2¼–7 × 1½–3 in.), oval to oblong-oval to obovate,
rarely oblong, apex rounded, truncate to retuse, base rounded to
truncate, glabrous above and below. L remain for 1 to 2 years. Petiole
1–3 cm usually eglandular.
Inflor five to ten, usually fairly loose, rachis 0.2–1.8 cm. Pedicel 1–2.4 cm
reddish, eglandular.
F scarlet to crimson or almost black-crimson, nectaries at base, 4–6.3 cm
(1½–2½ in.) long, tubular-campanulate, fleshy.
Calyx cup-shaped, fleshy, red, 0.4–1.8 cm lobes unequal eglandular.
Ovary and style eglandular.

The type form as cultivated, *F* 24219 is a dwarfish plant and all I have
seen lack vigor. This is a pity as the fine scarlet flowers are freely produced
and are brighter than *thomsonii*. It is reasonably hardy with growth made
fairly late in the season. 'Machrie' **AM**, 1965, Brodick, is probably a
hybrid.

Has a limited wild distribution on the Shweli–Salween divide on west
Yunnan–Burma frontier at 3,000–3,400 m (10,000–11,000 ft) in open
rhododendron scrub, open rocky slopes and margins of thickets. April

meddianum var. *atrokermesinum* Tagg

Ht 3–9 m (10–30 ft). Habit more vigorous than type.
L often larger than type. Differs botanically in its glandular branchlets,
pedicels and ovary.

There are two distinct forms in cultivation. The first introduction (*F*
26495) is a splendid plant for mild gardens with large scarlet to crimson
flowers. It grows early in the season and is very prone to bark-split in cold
gardens. Our last plant was killed in 1981–2. **AM**, 1954 Logan.
From the Di-Chu, Upper Burma and Burma–Yunnan frontier,
2,400–3,700 m (8,000–12,000 ft).

The later introduction, *KW* 21006A from the Triangle, Upper Burma
grows much later in the season and has proved hardy, except for foliage
damage in 1978–9 winter. It forms rather a gawky specimen as the leaves
only remain for 1 year but the large flowers are so magnificent that it is a
plant well worth being extensively cultivated. It must be classed about the

top of all hardier red flowered species forms. 'Bennan' **AM**, 1977, Brodick. Unfortunately proved tender in 1981–2 winter.

stewartianum Diels 1912 (*aiolosalpinx* Balf.f. & Farrer, *niphobolum* Balf.f. & Farrer) H3–4 L1–2 F1–3

Ht 60 cm–2.70 m (2–9 ft). Habit usually a thin branched upright small shrub. Bark fawn, peeling.
L 5–12 ×2.5–6.5 cm (2–5 × 1–2½ in.), obovate to *elliptic* to oblong-obovate, apex rounded, base obtuse to truncate, bright green and glabrous above, sometimes glaucous, glabrous or a thin veil of hairs below. L remain for 1 year. Petiole *0.6–1.9 cm* usually eglandular.
Inflor two to seven, loose, rachis 2–6 mm. Pedicel 0.8–2.5 cm ± eglandular.
F very variable in colour, various shades of yellow, pink, rose, red and crimson, often flushed or margined a different colour or darker on the exterior, usually unmarked but occasionally heavily spotted, 3.6–5.4 cm (1½–2¼ in.) long, tubular-campanulate.
Calyx variable 0.1–1.4 cm. Ovary glandular, style glabrous.

A pretty, rather dainty species. While the flowers rather hang between the leaves, the whole plant has a light and elegant nature and the best colour forms such as apple-blossom pinks, yellows and bicolors are very attractive. Unfortunately, the majority of cultivated plants I have seen in flower are a rather washy pink. Often lacks vigour and might grow best planted en masse in a fairly open situation to attempt to simulate its natural habit of growing gregariously, forming flat-topped thickets.

Closely related to *eclecteum* but has a longer petiole and generally thinner twigs and shorter more elliptic leaves. Early flowering. Perhaps slightly hardier than *eclecteum* on average but not suitable for the coldest British gardens. **AM**, 1934, Exbury.

From Upper Burma, south-east Tibet and north-west Yunnan, 3,000–4,300 m (10,000–14,000 ft), common on windswept hillsides, streamsides, rocky and bouldery slopes, in bamboo brakes and occasionally in mixed forests.   February–April

TRIFLORA SUBSECTION (TRIFLORUM SERIES) (L)

This large subsection has been revised recently by Cullen, RBG, Edinburgh and considerable changes made. Several previously recognized as species have become synonyms or are considered to be natural hybrids while others have been removed from the subsection altogether.

These are relatively small-leaved and flowered but quite tall growing species. They come chiefly from west China with outlyers into Burma, Arunachal Pradesh to Nepal and south-east Tibet (plus the dwarf species *keiskei* from Japan).

The chief characters are: the zygomorphic corolla (a flower that can be divided into two equal parts in one plane only, in this case vertically), which is usually widely funnel-shaped with long exserted stamens and style. The inflorescence is often terminal and axillary in the uppermost 1 to 2 leaves. The leaves are sometimes partially deciduous but this character is now considered to be of little importance as it is too inconsistent. The calyx is usually minute, a mere rim or five-lobed, 0.5–1 mm, rarely longer and the lobes are seldom bristly (only in *tricanthum* and sometimes *amesiae*); stamens ten, usually unequal and pubescent towards base. The ovary is densely scaly and the style non-scaly. The capsule is oblong, ovoid or oblong-ovoid, small.

The large majority of these species are very common in their natural haunts and show considerable variations in elevation and choice of habitat. They are also very variable in flower colour and size, leaf size and even in the presence or absence of aromaticness. This variation means there are great differences in hardiness and horticultural value in species such as *augustinii*, *lutescens*, *yunnanense* and *davidsonianum*. Special clones have been selected either from wild seed or careful breeding programmes and are vegetatively propagated. Some of these may be untypical of the average wild specimens.

Of the plants retained at specific status, several are closely related to *yunnanense* and can be classed as aggregate species which could be termed microspecies. These are divided into two Alliances: (1) *tatsienense* with the very closely related *davidsonianum* and *siderophyllum* and (2) *yunnanense* with *pleistanthum* and *rigidum*.

Biochemical analyses have separated *augustinii* and the yellow flowered species from the rest. Chromosome counts 2n = 26, 52 and 78 and I find this a limiting factor in hybridization as the different chromosome counts are often hard to bridge.

Spots on the flowers can vary considerably from flower to flower on one plant, even in colour. The bark is uninteresting in all Triflorums except some introductions of *triflorum* and *zaleucum*.

These are generally plants from relatively dry areas and are in the main vigorous, easily grown species which can succeed better in soil too heavy for the average rhododendron. The majority start into growth rather too early and therefore suffer from frosted growth and bark-split. Most flower freely from a fairly to very young age and are best grown in comparatively open, sunny situations to avoid undue legginess. Most will respond well to hard pruning but in cold areas the resulting vigorous growth may be damaged by frost. Likewise plants cut back by hard weather like in 1972 in the freeze in Oregon are very vulnerable the winter following regrowth.

ambiguum Hemsl. 1911 (*chengshienianum* Fang (*wongii* Hemsl. & Wils. probably)) H4 A − 5 L1–2 F2–3

Ht 50 cm–5.7 m (1½–18 ft). Habit neater than *triflorum*, usually fairly compact. Bark *rather rough*.
L 2.3–8 × 1.2–3.2 cm (1–3¼ × ½–1¼ in.), lanceolate, oblong-lanceolate, ovate-lanceolate to elliptic, apex obtuse to acute, base rounded to obtuse, scaly above, usually dark green, midrib usually hairy; glaucous below, the unequal brownish scales are contiguous to their own diameter apart. Petiole 0.5–1.3 cm scaly.

R. augustinii

Inflor usually terminal only, two to seven, rachis 2–4 mm. Pedicel 0.6–2 cm ($\frac{1}{4}$–$\frac{3}{4}$ in.).
F greenish-yellow to pale yellow, 2–3.4 cm ($\frac{3}{4}$–1$\frac{1}{2}$ in.) long, scaly outside, widely funnel-shaped.
Calyx minute, margins hairy or glabrous. Style not scaly, slender.
    This is the hardiest of the larger yellow Triflorums and makes a good foil in its taller forms for the 'blues' of *augustinii*. The best forms are pretty in a sober way. There are fairly dwarf clones which bloom at a younger age than the taller ones. The closest relation is *triflorum*; *wongii* of which there is only a very poor inadequate herbarium specimen is probably *ambiguum*. Plants cultivated under *wongii* are most likely hybrids. 'Jane Banks' **AM**, 1976, Hergest Croft.
    From west Szechwan, Mt Omei and near Tatsienlu, 2,600–4,500 m (8,500–14,700 ft), very abundant in thickets, on rocks in woods and on rocky exposed slopes.   April–May

amesiae Rehd. & Wils. 1913 H4 L1–2 F1–2

Ht 2–4 m (7–13 ft). Branchlets sometimes bristly.
L 2.8–7 × 1.5–3.4 cm (1–3 × $\frac{3}{8}$–1$\frac{1}{2}$ in.), ovate to elliptic, apex obtuse, to acute, base usually rounded, pale green below, scales unequal, brownish, about half their own diameter apart. Petiole *bristly*, 0.5–1.1 cm.

Inflor two to five. Pedicel 1.1–1.8 cm, sometimes bristly.
F purple to dark reddish-purple ± darker spots, 3–4 cm (1¼–1½ in.) long,
widely funnel-shaped.
Calyx minute, sometimes with bristly margins. Style not scaly.

A plant of no special merit, closely related to *concinnum*. Setose petiole
and glabrous corolla separates this from *searsiae* and *tricanthum*.

From west Szechwan, Mupin, W 3444, 2,300–3,000 m (7,500–
10,000 ft) in woods.   Late May

augustinii Hemsl. 1889 (*vilmorinianum* Balf.f. type specimen only) H3–4
A − 5 to +5 L1–2 F2–4

Ht 1–7 m (3–23 ft). Habit usually erect. Branchlets often hairy. Young
foliage *hairy above* and below, often tinted red.
L 3.3–12 × 1.1–4.5 cm (1⅓–5 × ½–1¾ in.), lanceolate to oblong and
somewhat obovate, apex acuminate, base narrowed to obtuse, scales
unequal, half to three times their own diameter apart, *midrib usually
hairy for a large part of its length*. Petiole *fringed with long hairs*,
0.5–1.4 cm.
Inflor two to six, rachis 2–8 mm. Pedicel 0.6–2.7 cm (¼–1 in.) usually
minutely puberulous.
F pale blue, lavender to light purple, lavender-blue, deep lavender to
deep mauve and violet-mauve are the usual cultivated colours (but in the
wild pale to rosy-purple or even pink are the most common), with various
coloured spots and eye, olive, green, purple and ochre, scaly outside,
2–4.3 cm (¾–1¾ in.) long, widely funnel-shaped.
Calyx 0.5–1 mm, rarely 2–4 mm, usually fringed with long hairs. Ovary ±
pubescent. Stamens pale, pinkish to pale mauve to purple to almost
red.

This fine species is widely planted in gardens in southern England
where it makes a splendid show in various shades of near blue. It is
especially effective when grown in bold clumps. In the north, it is not quite
so successful, sometimes having poor foliage and young growth which is
frequently frosted but the hardier, paler-coloured forms succeed. Very
wet conditions are not usually suitable.

Many of the best clones were raised by crossing the rather tender
deepest colours with the hardier pale forms and selecting the best
seedlings. If there is enough space, plant different clones as one clone may
be especially good one year and another one the next. The colour of the
filaments alters the tone of the whole flower, reddish filaments give a
more purple look so paler ones are usually more desirable. Further
breeding would be worthwhile by crossing the best green-eyed clones.
Many good clones originated at Tower Court, Exbury and Bodnant plus
Barto in America. The bluest forms are inclined to develop the poorest
foliage with us and are sometimes partly deciduous.

Often tender when young. Varying reports have come from the freezes
in Oregon and Washington States in 1955 and 1972 but generally the
bigger and paler forms survived the best. Said to be susceptible to
Phytophthora root-rot in San Francisco area but is fairly successful on
heavy soils in some places.

This species and its sub-species have a unique type of long, straight hair. Separated from ssp. *chasmanthum* by the hairs being continued from the midrib (below) right down the petiole. **AM**, 1926, **AGM**, 1924.

Very common in Hupeh and far into Szechwan, not Yunnan, 1,200–4,000 m (4,000–13,000 ft), margins of woods but happiest in open rocky situations in full sun. Introduced by *W* in 1900, 1907 and 1908.

April–May

augustinii ssp. *chasmanthum* (Diels 1912) Cullen 1978 (*chasmanthoides* Balf.f. & Forr., *hirsutocostatum* Hand.-Mazz.)

Branchlets glabrous to minutely puberulous.
L often wider than ssp. *augustinii*. Hairs on the midrib and veins below and midrib above, otherwise not hairy above, dark and lighter scales below well apart, very loose, three to five times their own diameter apart. Petiole *glabrous or minutely hairy*.
Inflor usually more compact than ssp. *augustinii*. Pedicel usually glabrous. F soft to rose-lavender, clear violet-blue, mauve and occasionally white, marked olive or yellow, very widely funnel-shaped, often frilled and partly reflexed. Ovary usually glabrous.

This is often an equally fine plant in cultivation as ssp. *augustinii*. The flowers usually open later, have more reflexed corolla lobes forming a tighter truss and the leaves are often wider. Ssp. *augustinii* and ssp. *chasmanthum* may merge in *hirsutocostatum*. **AM**, 1930, **FCC**, 1932 both Exbury.

Comes from Yunnan, south-east Tibet and west Szechwan, to the west of locations of ssp. *augustinii*.

augustinii ssp. *hardyi* (Davidian 1974) Cullen 1978 H3–4 L1–2 F2

Ht 1.20–3 m (4–10 ft). Branchlets scaly, ± minutely puberulous.
L *nearly completely deciduous*, but this varies from plant to plant and year to year, 4.5–8.2 × 1.8–2.9 cm ($1\frac{3}{4}$–$3\frac{1}{4}$ × $\frac{3}{4}$–$1\frac{1}{4}$ in.), lanceolate to oblong-lanceolate, apex acute to acuminate, base obtuse to tapered, scaly above, midrib puberulous, scales unequal below, brown, three to six times their own diameter apart, midrib hairy for two to three times its entire length. Petiole 5–9 mm ± minutely puberulous.
Inflor terminal or terminal and axillary, two to four. Pedicel 1.2–3 cm ($\frac{1}{2}$–$1\frac{1}{4}$ in.).
F *white* or greenish-white, faintly tinged lavender with yellow-greenish spots, 2.3–3.3 cm (1–$1\frac{1}{3}$ in.) long, widely funnel-shaped, scaly outside, ± hairy towards base of tube. Calyx margins ciliate.

A nice white flowered plant. We find the flowers tend to vary in size from year to year. The light bronze coloured young foliage is attractive. Sometimes suffers from frosted growth and bark-split at Glendoick.

Introduced by *R* in 1949, probably from north-west Yunnan. May *augustinii* ssp. *rubrum* (Davidian 1963) Cullen 1978 (*bergii* Davidian 1976) H3–4 L1–2 F1–2

Habit *compact*. L much darker green than the average *augustinii*.
F not red as described by Davidian but a poor shade of slightly reddish-purple.

This distinct plant is of limited horticultural value. It blooms much earlier than its relatives and we find it rather tender at Glendoick. **AM**, 1978, Borde Hill. Perhaps deserves specific status.

From north-west Yunnan collected under *F* 25914 at 4,000 m (13,000 ft) in thickets and amongst scrub on rocky slopes.

March–early May

concinnum Hemsl. 1910 (*apiculatum* Rehd. & Wils., *atroviride* Dunn, *benthamianum* Hemsl., *coombense* Hemsl., *hutchinsonianum* Fang, *laetevirens* Balf.f. ex Hutch., *pseudoyanthinum* Balf.f. ex Hutch., *yanthinum* Bur. & Franch.) H4 A−15 to −5 L1–2 F1–3
Ht 60 cm–4.50 m (2–15 ft). Habit fairly neat without the long 'water sprouts' common in *yunnanense*.
L 2.5–8.5 × 1.2–3.5 cm (1–3$\frac{2}{5}$ × $\frac{1}{2}$–1$\frac{1}{2}$ in.), oblong-lanceolate, oblong-elliptic, ovate to ovate-lanceolate, apex usually acute to obtuse, base obtuse to rounded, scaly above, midrib puberulous; pale glaucous-green to green below, scales unequal, brownish, half their own diameter apart to contiguous, rarely wider apart. Petiole 0.5–1.3 cm densely scaly.
Inflor terminal or terminal and axillary in upper one to two leaves, two to five. Pedicel 0.4–1.8 cm scaly.
F lavender-pink, mauvy-pink, white spotted brown, deep to reddish-purple, with or without green to crimson spots, 1.5–3.2 cm ($\frac{3}{5}$–1$\frac{1}{4}$ in.) long, widely funnel-shaped, scaly outside.
Calyx 0.5–1.5 mm, rarely 4–6 mm, margin scaly ± ciliate. Style not scaly.

A very variable species, hence all its synonyms. Quite commonly cultivated and generally hardy. The best deep coloured forms are often grown under the Pseudoyanthinum Group and vary from deep purple to ruby-red and are attractive garden plants. There are two American named clones of this: 'Purple Flake' and 'Chief Paulina', the latter a compact form with royal-purple flowers. The Tower Court selection is very fine with ruby-red flowers, while Benthamianum Group usually has paler leaves than average and flowers more of a violet-blue to lavender-purple, often a good colour. Some of the paler forms are quite nice while others are not worth growing. Starts to bloom in 3 to 6 years from a cutting. One of the hardiest of the subsection being quite successful in southern Scandinavia and came through the 1972 freeze in Oregon unharmed. **AM**, 1951, RHS Garden, Wisley.

From west Szechwan, west Hupeh, also Shensi and Sikang, very common in west Szechwan, rarer elsewhere, 1,500–4,400 m (5,000–14,500 ft) in woodlands, margins of thickets and woods, conifer forest floor and on cliffs.

April–May

lutescens Franch. 1886 (*blinii* Lévl., *costulatum* Franch., *lemeei* Lévl.)
H3–4 A–5 to +5 L1–3 F1–4

Ht 90 cm–6 m (3–20 ft). Habit upright and often straggly. Bark grey to
light grey. Young growth often bronzy-red.
L 4.8–9.3 × 1.3–3.7 cm (2–3¾ × ½–1½ in.), lanceolate, oblong-lanceolate,
to ovate-lanceolate, apex acutely acuminate, base rounded to obtuse, ±
scaly above, large unequal scales below, half to five times their own
diameter apart. Petiole 0.6–1.2 cm (¼–½ in.).
Inflor terminal and axillary in uppermost few leaves, one to three per bud.
Pedicel 0.4–1.5 cm.
F *pale to deeper primrose-yellow* with green spots, 1.3–2.6 cm (½–1 in.)
long, to 5 cm (2 in.) wide, widely funnel-shaped, ± scaly and *pubescent*
outside.
Calyx minute 0.5–1 mm, margin ± ciliate.

A lovely early blooming yellow, most attractive in early spring, having a
very airy, graceful appearance and the young foliage is often an eye-
catching bronzy-red which may last through the summer. Unfortunately
the large flowered **FCC** clone is the most tender and suffers from bark-
split at Glendoick. 'Bagshot Sands' **AM** also has large flowers but is
slightly hardier; the young foliage is not quite so striking. Most other
forms I have seen are relatively hardy but the majority have much
smaller, poorer flowers. Sometimes produces a succession of flowers after
being lightly frosted. Most plants were unharmed in 1972 western American freeze. Stands hard pruning. **FCC**, Exbury 1938, **AM**, 'Bagshot
Sands' Tower Court 1953.

Found wild in western Szechwan and Yunnan, 550–3,000 m
(1,500–10,000 ft), quite a common species with a wide altitudinal distribution which is borne out by differences in hardiness in cultivation.
Large and small flowered forms occur in the wild but the latter predomi-
nate. Grows in thickets in fairly open places, in and under trees, hill slopes
and bamboo thickets, usually isolated from other rhododendron species.

February–April

oreotrephes W.W. Sm. 1914 (*artosquameum* Balf.f. & Forr., *cardioeides*
Balf.f. & Forr., *depile* Balf.f. & Forr., *exquisetum* Hutch., *hypotrichotum*
Balf.f. & Forr., *oreotrephoides* Balf.f., *phaeochlorum* Balf.f. & Forr.,
pubigerum Balf.f. & Forr., *siderophylloides* Hutch., *timeteum* Balf.f. &
Forr., *trichopodum* Balf.f. & Forr.) H4 A0 L1–3 F2–4

Ht 60 cm–7.6 m (2–25 ft). Habit usually quite compact in open, sunny
situations but can become very leggy in shade.
L evergreen to semi-deciduous, 1.8–8.9 × 1.2–4.3 cm (¾–3½ × ½–1¾ in.),
oblong-elliptic, elliptic, oblong, ovate to almost orbicular, apex usually
obtuse to rounded, base rounded to obtuse to cordulate, usually medium
to palish green above, often glaucous; glaucous to pale glaucous-green to
brown below, scales ± equal sized, contiguous to three to four times their
own diameter apart, slightly aromatic to non-aromatic. Petiole 0.5–2 cm.
Inflor terminal or terminal and axillary in upper one to two leaves, three
to ten per bud. Pedicel 0.5–3 cm.

F pale grey-mauve, light purple, pink to rosy-purple, bright rose, deep-lavender-rose, bright purple, whitish-pink or even yellowish-pink and apricot-yellow (the latter two colours are probably not in cultivation), with ± number of spots on corolla, fleshy, 1.8–4 cm ($\frac{3}{4}$–1$\frac{1}{2}$ in.) long, widely to narrowly funnel-shaped to sometimes funnel-campanulate. Calyx 0.5–2 mm.

In some ways, this is the best plant in the subsection as it is usually reliably hardy, often has good glaucous foliage, a neat habit (in the open) and very pretty consistently good flowers of various shades. This is the connecting link between *cinnabarinum* and the Triflorums but lacks the nectar of the former species. Forms tending to be semi-deciduous are best avoided as this takes from the normally attractive winter foliage. Many have flowers of especially good shades, such as *exquisetum* F 20489; a semi-dwarf with pale flowers and some of the rich rose or pink coloured clones including one known as 'Exbury form'. Has proved reasonably hardy in Oregon, Media Pennsylvania and is said to withstand heat if sheltered.

There are several herbarium specimens in the RBG, Edinburgh of probable natural hybrids, perhaps with *zaleucum* and *concinnum*. Some special colour forms, notably *L&S* from Pome, south-east Tibet, would be thoroughly worthy of introduction. **AM**, 1932, Exbury (*timeteum*), **AM**, 1935, Embley Park (*siderophylloides*), **AM**, 1937, Exbury (*exquisetum*) light mauvish-pink, red spotted.

An exceedingly common, widespread and variable species found over large areas of south-east Tibet, Szechwan, Yunnan and Burma, 2,700–4,300 m (9,000–14,000 ft), alpine regions, open rocky slopes amongst scrub, in and on margins of thickets, exposed granite ridges, limestone cliffs, among bamboo, by streams, in thin and thick forest, conifer or mixed and forest margins and sides of swamp.   April–May

polylepis Franch. 1886 (*harrovianum* Hemsl.) H4 L1–2 F1–2

Ht 90 cm–5 m (3–17 ft). Branchlets with dense flaky scales. Bark grey to brownish-grey.
L 4.5–10.2 × 1.2–3.7 cm (1$\frac{3}{4}$–4 × $\frac{1}{2}$–1$\frac{1}{2}$ in.), oblong-lanceolate, lanceolate to oblanceolate, apex usually acute, narrowed to base, dull and usually glabrous above, large unequal *brown flaky scales below*, overlapping to contiguous, rarely wider, usually convex. Petiole 0.5–1 cm densely scaly. Inflor terminal or rarely terminal and axillary in upper one to two leaves, three to five per bud. Pedicel 0.6–2 cm scaly.
F *usually pale to deep purple* to purplish-violet, or rosy-mauve, ± yellow spots, 2.1–3.5 cm ($\frac{3}{4}$–1$\frac{2}{5}$ in.) long, widely funnel-shaped.
Calyx 0.5–1 mm, margin scaly, rarely ciliate. Stamens variable in length.

Horticulturally, this is one of the poorer members of the subsection with rather dingy flowers like an inferior coloured *ponticum*. We grow a (probable) *polylepis* hybrid, perhaps with *virgatum* with pinker flowers, axillary all down the vigorous shoots which is quite attractive. Buds of *polylepis* may be damaged in really severe winters in Britain.

From west Szechwan, 2,000–3,000 m (6,500–10,000 ft), a common plant in woodlands, thickets and on cliffs.   April *searsiae* Rehd. & Wils. 1913 H4 A−5 L1−2 F1−2

Ht 2.50–5 m (8–17 ft).
L 2.5–8 × 1–2.6 cm (1–3¼ ×⅖–1 in.), lanceolate, oblong-lanceolate, oblanceolate to rarely oblong-elliptic, apex acuminate, usually narrowed to base, scaly above, *bluish-glaucous below*, scales brown, half to rarely their own diameter apart, 3 sizes of scales. Petiole 0.3–1 cm scaly.
Inflor terminal or terminal and axillary in upper leaves, three to eight per bud. Pedicel 0.5–1.6 cm scaly.
F white to pale rose-purple, light green spots, 2–3.4 cm (¾–1⅓ in.) long, widely funnel-shaped.
Calyx minute, 0.5–1 mm, rarely 4–5 mm, margins scaly.

Quite an attractive, free-flowering species. Distinctive for its long, narrow pointed leaves with very obvious scales below. Close to *polylepis* which has a fulvous-brown leaf underside, anthers exserted and smaller capsule; also near *concinnum* which has shorter oblong-oval leaves, flowers scaly outside pubescent within and slenderer capsules.

From west Szechwan, Wa Shan only, 2,300–3,000 m (7,500–10,000 ft). April–May

tricanthum Rehd. 1945 (*villosum* Hemsl. & Wils. not Roth) H4 A−5 to +5 L1−2 F1−3

Ht 1–6 m (3–20 ft). Branchlets *bristly* and often pubescent. Young growth very soft to touch.
L 4–11 × 1.5–3.7 cm (1½–4⅜ × ⅗–1½ in.), oblong-lanceolate, lanceolate to ovate-lanceolate, apex acuminate, base obtuse to cordulate, scaly, bristly and often pubescent above; scales unequal below, brown, one to four times their own diameter apart. Petiole 0.4–1 cm scaly, *bristly* and often pubescent.
Inflor terminal three to five. Pedicel 1–1.5 cm, scaly and *bristly*.
F very variable in colour, the best forms a rich, deep plum-purple to dark red-purple or deep purple (in the wild, the majority are a pale washy purple to bluish-mauve), sometimes with olive-green to brown flair, 2.8–3.8 cm (1–1½ in.) long, widely funnel-shaped, scaly outside, *bristly* on tube.
Calyx *bristly*. Ovary scaly and *bristly*.

A useful late flowering species in its deeper coloured forms. Needs care in placing owing to the deep colour but it does flower later than other Triflorums. All wild collected herbarium specimens suffer from leaf spot just like ours at Glendoick but several cultivated specimens show little or no spots. It is likely that it prefers excellent drainage and light soil. We find it liable to die suddenly for no apparent reason. The name had to be changed from *villosum* Roth to *tricanthum* because *villosum* Roth was a synonym of *Clerodendrum fragrans*.

Closely related to *amesiae* and *concinnum* and is really just a hairy version of the latter species. The hairs are a type distinct from those of *augustinii* but nevertheless can be said to be a link between this and *concinnum*. **AM**, 'Honey Wood' 1971 raised at Tower Court.

Found in west Szechwan, Mupin, Wa Shan and elsewhere,

1,200–3,400 m (4,000–11,000 ft) where it is very common in woodlands often forming dense thickets.   May–June

triflorum Hook. 1849 (*triflorum* var. *mahogani* Hutch.) H3–4 L1–2 F1–3

Ht 60 cm–4.60 m (2–15 ft). Habit usually loose. Bark sometimes smooth, peeling, fawn, pinky-chestnut to reddish-brown, sometimes just dull and non-peeling.
L 3–7.2 × 1.3–2 cm ($1\frac{1}{4}$–$2\frac{3}{4}$ × $\frac{1}{2}$–$\frac{3}{4}$ in.), oblong-lanceolate to elliptic, apex acuminate to obtuse, base rounded to cordulate, *glabrous* above; glaucous to pale green below, scales very small, ± equal, half to their own diameter apart, slightly to very aromatic. Petiole 0.5–1.3 cm.
Inflor two to four, usually three. Pedicel 0.6–1.6 cm.
F cream to pale, greenish or bright yellow, greenish-yellow spots, or suffused with various colours (Mahogani Group), 2–3.3 cm ($\frac{3}{4}$–$1\frac{1}{3}$ in.) long, about 2 cm ($\frac{3}{4}$ in.) across, widely funnel-shaped, scaly and ± pubescent outside.

This variable and widespread species differs considerably in flower colour and size, hardiness, bark and garden value. It is apparent that the western forms have the best bark and are the more tender while the eastern types are hardier, tend to lack a peeling bark and have much more variable flowers. The good barked forms are worth growing for this character alone, while never as impressive as the beautiful barked tree-like species; it is none the less very attractive, being best on middle aged wood. These western collections are just hardy enough to grow at Glendoick while a pale creamy *L&S* form we grow is definitely hardier. The flowers tend to be rather small but can be quite pretty. So called var. *mahogani* Hutch. 1937 is extremely variable with yellowish flowers lightly to strongly suffused with salmon-pink, burnt sienna, apricot, orange, pink, mahogany-red, spotted or splashed mahogany. Some of these colours may not be in cultivation. Good salmon-pink forms are said to be attractive but I have yet to see one of these that I did not consider muddy. The coloured forms are often all mixed up with the plain yellows in the wild. These eastern introductions often have shorter, broader leaves than those from Nepal and Bhutan.

From Nepal, Sikkim, Bhutan, south-east Tibet, Arunachal Pradesh and the Burma–Tibet frontier, 2,100–4,000 m (7,000–13,000 ft) on dry or damp hillsides, rhododendrons, mixed and conifer forest, edges of streams and rivers, on cliffs and rocks, scrub jungle, bamboo thickets, bogs, in the open or in shade, Mahogani Group south-east Tibet only.

                                                                                   May–June

triflorum var. *bauhiniiflorum* (Watt ex Hutch. 1930) Cullen 1978 H3–4 A+5 L1–2 F2–3

F greenish to a clear yellow ± darker greenish-yellow spots, *flat, saucer-shaped*, 2.2–2.8 cm ($\frac{3}{4}$–$1\frac{1}{4}$ in.) long, 3.8–4.3 cm ($1\frac{1}{2}$–$1\frac{3}{4}$ in.) across.

This geographical variant of *triflorum* has wider open flowers which are usually superior to *triflorum* type and are often very pretty and quite showy. While the bark does peel, it is rarely as good as the best *triflorum* in this respect and we found it really too tender for Glendoick in the clone that we grew.

Common in the mountains of Nagaland and Manipur, 2,400–2,900 m (8,000–9,500 ft). May–June

yunnanense aggregate (1) *davidsonianum, siderophyllum, tatsienense*

davidsonianum Rehd. & Wils. 1913 (*charianthum* Hutch.) H3–4 A − 5 to + 5 L1–2 F1–4

Ht 90 cm–3 m + (3–10 ft +). Habit erect or angular, becoming leggy in too much shade. Branchlets scaly. Bark yellowish-brown with age. L 2.3–7.8 × 0.8–2.6 cm (1–3 × ⅓–1 in.), lanceolate to oblong, apex usually acute narrowed to base to obtuse, often concave, scaly above; unequal scales below, brown contiguous to their own diameter apart, rarely wider (*much more prominent scales than yunnanense*). Petiole 0.3–1 cm scaly.
Inflor terminal or terminal and axillary in top one to two leaves, three to six rarely to ten per bud. Pedicel 0.6–1.8 cm scaly.
F plants from wild seed mostly mauve to pale lavender to white tinged pink; selected clones have pink to rich pink flowers with or without purple to red spots and/or blotch, 1.9–3.3 cm (¾–1⅓ in.) long, widely funnel-shaped.

A very floriferous species which starts blooming almost from a rooted cutting. There are several really fine selected pink clones but far too many very inferior forms are still widely grown in Britain and America. Varies in hardiness, the **FCC**; Bodnant clone being somewhat tender although it has grown and flowered successfully at Glendoick for many years. Other clones seem hardier but the majority suffered in the 1972 freeze in north-west North America, many being cut to the ground. Said to be heat resistant in Australia but burns easily around San Francisco. This may depend on the clone.

Closely related to *tatsienense* and merges with *yunnanense* in the north-east corner of the latters distribution. Named clones are: 'Serenade' apparently hardy in Media, Pennsylvania; 'Ruth Lyons' upright habit and lovely rich almost unspotted rich pink flowers; 'Bodnant' form **FCC**, 1955, **AM**, 1935, sometimes called 'Bonfires of Delight' an unregistered name, **AGM,** 1969.

From Szechwan only, 1,800–3,500 m (6,000–11,500 ft), very common in exposed, sunny situations, also in thickets, open glades and conifer forest and woodlands, on cliffs and stream banks. April–May

siderophyllum Franch. 1898 (*ioanthum* Balf.f., *jahandiezii* Lévl., *leucandrum* Lévl., *obscurum* Franch. ex Balf.f., *rubro-punctatum* Lévl. & Vent., *sequini* Lévl. (part)) H3–4 L1–2 F2–3

Ht 90 cm–3 m (3–10 ft).
L 3–9 × 1.5–4 cm (1¼–3⅝ × ⅝–1½ in.), oblong-lanceolate, elliptic to lanceolate, apex acuminate to obtuse, narrowed to base to obtuse, scaly

above; densely scaly below, unequal, brown, contiguous to 1½ times their own diameter apart, not hairy. Petiole 0.6–1.5 cm densely scaly.
Inflor terminal and axillary, three to six per bud forming *dense many flowered clusters*. Pedicel 0.4–1.5 or more cm scaly.
F white, white tinged pink, pink, pale lavender-blue, mauve, purple or rose, ± yellow to rose spots, 1.5–3 cm (⅜–1¼ in.) long, widely funnel-shaped.
Calyx 0.5–1 mm or more, margin scaly.

Distinct for its dense inflorescences of small flowers; closely related to *davidsonianum, tatsieninse* and *yunnanense*. **AM**, 1945, Exbury.

From south-west Szechwan, Kweichow and south-west Yunnan, 1,800–3,400 m (6,000–11,000 ft) in dry woods or scrub covered hills or in mixed thickets by streams.   May

tatsienense Franch. 1898 (*heishuiense* Fang, *hypophaeum* Balf.f. & Forr., *leilungense* Balf.f. & Forr., *stereophyllum* Balf.f. & W.W. Sm., *tapelouense* Lévl.) H3–4 L1–2 F1–2

Ht 30 cm–2.70 m (1–9 ft). Habit spreading to erect rather untidy shrub. Branchlets red to deep crimson.
L 1.6–6 × 1–3.1 cm (⅜–2⅔ × ⅖–1¼ in.), elliptic, obovate, oval, oblong to oblong-lanceolate, apex rounded, obtuse to rarely acute, base obtuse, rounded to rarely truncate, rigid and leathery, usually scaly above; pale to glaucous-green below, scales unequal half to their own diameter apart, rarely wider. Petiole 0.3–1.4 cm scaly.
Inflor terminal or terminal and axillary in upper one to two leaves, one to six per bud. Pedicel 0.4–1.9 cm usually scaly.
F blush-white, blush-pink, rose-pink to rose-lavender or purple, ± red spots. 1.4–3 cm (½–1¼ in.) long, widely funnel-shaped.
Calyx minute 0.5–1 mm.

This variable species is fairly often seen in old collections. While quite pretty, the flowers are rather small and horticulturally, it does not compare with the better forms of *davidsonianum* or *yunnanense* to which it is closely related. Very variable in leaf shape, prominence of scales on leaf underside, size of flowers and size of bush. Probably merges with *siderophyllum* and sometimes bears some resemblance to *racemosum*.

Quite a common species in Yunnan, 2,100–3,700 m (7,000–12,000 ft), open dry rocky hillsides, open and mixed thickets, margins of open forests including conifers and open moist stony meadows.
                                                                    March–May

yunnanense aggregate (2) *pleistanthum, rigidum, yunnanense*

pleistanthum (Balf.f. ex) Wilding (*yunnanense* Hort. *hormophorum* part)

L not scaly above, scales three to four times their own diameter apart. Pedicel not scaly.
F white, white flushed pink or lilac.
Calyx not scaly.

Similar to *yunnanense* but with no bristles and a westerly and northern distribution compared with than species. Some forms of *hormophorum* transferred here.

rigidum Franch. 1886 (*caeruleum* Lévl., *eriandrum* Lévl. ex Hutch., *hesperium* Balf.f. & Forr., *rarosquameum* Balf.f., *sycanthum* Balf.f. & W.W. Sm.) H4 A − 5 L1–2 F2–3

Ht 60 cm–3 m (2–10 ft). Habit usually upright.
L evergreen, *leathery*, 2.5–6.8 × 1–3.2 cm (1–2¾ × ⅖–1⅓ in.), elliptic, oblong-elliptic, oblong-lanceolate, oblanceolate, oblong to lanceolate, apex acute to rounded, narrowed to base to rounded, usually *glaucous* above and below, scales unequal below two to eight times their own diameter apart. Petiole 0.2–1.2 cm.
Inflor terminal or terminal and axillary in upper one to two leaves, two to six per bud. Pedicel 0.5–2 cm.
F white tinged pale pink, lilac-rose, pinkish-violet, deep rose-lavender or white with faint gold, olive-brown to reddish-brown spots or markings, 1.8–3.1 cm (¾–1¼ in.) long, widely funnel-shaped, fragrant.
Calyx 0.5–1 mm slightly scaly.

The white forms are those most commonly cultivated, formerly under the name *caeruleum* 'Album' or *album*. These are first rate, free flowering garden plants. Some have relatively few larger flowers while others have a multitude of smaller flowers which form dense inflorescences. These white forms are said to be all from one *R* number 59207. The lilac-rose forms are also worth growing. The name *rigidum* is appropriate in both habit and foliage. Differs from *yunnanense* in its bluish-green young leaves which usually have a thicker texture. Equal to or perhaps slightly hardier than the average *yunnanense*. **AM**, 1939 Exbury white speckled red.

Occurs south of *pleistanthum* and is very common in north Yunnan and into Szechwan, 800–3,400 m (2,500–11,000 ft) in open scrub and thickets, margins of thickets and forests, bamboo thickets, cliffs, rocky slopes, among boulders and in conifer forests.   March–May

yunnanense Franch. 1886 (*aechmophyllum* Balf.f. & Forr., *bodinieri* Franch., *chartophyllum* Franch., *hormophorum* Balf.f. & Forr., *seguini* Lévl. (part), *strictum, suberosum* Balf.f. & Forr., *hesperium* (part)) H3–4 A − 5 to + 5 L1–2 F2–4

Ht 90 cm–3.60 m (3–12 ft) in the wild, often taller in cultivation. Habit straggly with 'water sprout' growths.
L evergreen to deciduous, 2.5–10.4 × 0.8–2.8 cm (1–4¾ × ⅓–1¼ in.), oblanceolate, oblong-lanceolate to lanceolate-elliptic, narrowly obovate, narrowly elliptic and obovate, often with a great variation of shape on one plant, *usually rather thin, not rigid*, ± scaly above, ± bristly, pale glaucous-green to green below, scales unequal, brown, two to six times their own diameter apart. Petiole 0.3–1.1 cm ± bristly and puberulous.
Inflor terminal or terminal and axillary in upper one to two leaves, three to five per bud. Pedicel 0.5–2 cm.
F usually white to pale pink to pale purple, also white flushed pink, pale

rose to rose, pinkish-purple to blue-lavender, with olive, deep green, deep rose to brownish-crimson spots or markings, occasionally not marked, sometimes slightly fragrant, 1.8–3.4 cm ($\frac{3}{4}$–1$\frac{2}{8}$ in.) long, widely funnel-shaped.

Calyx 0.5–1 mm, scaly.

One of the best of the subsection, easily grown and very floriferous from a rooted cutting onwards. While liable to bark-split (at Glendoick) and inclined to be straggly, it responds to pruning. Best grown in a fairly sunny position to obtain a shapely bush and/or planted in clumps. One of the most successful species on alkaline soils. Vigorous.

A very variable species with generally bristly, long and thinly textured leaves. Now includes the deciduous *hormophorum*. Varies in hardiness, most forms being too tender for south Sweden and the majority may be damaged in cold parts of Britain and freezes like 1955 and 1972 in north-west North America. F reported that the flowers were ruined in the wild in May one year. The leaves sometimes colour in the autumn in the more deciduous forms. **AM**, 1903, **AGM**, 1934, **AM** (*hormophorum*), 1943. Several recent re-introductions.

Has one of the widest altitudinal ranges of any species and is very widespread and common and versatile as to habitat. Often a matted shrub in the wild, even at low elevations. Found in south-west Szechwan, Yunnan, Burma, south-east Tibet, and Kweichow, 900–4,300 m (3,000–14,000 ft), dry and moist situations in the open or in the shade, on rocky slopes, thickets, forest (usually conifer) margins and openings, among boulders, moorland, by streams, bamboo breaks and cliffs, often limestone, many out of the bare rock.   May

zaleucum Balf.f. & W.W. Sm. 1917 (*erileucum* Balf.f. & Forr.) H3 rarely 4 L1–2 F2–3

Ht 60 cm–10.6 m (2–35 ft) in the wild, intermediary in cultivation. Habit fairly compact to straggly.

L 3.2–8.8 × 1–3 cm (1$\frac{1}{3}$–3$\frac{1}{2}$ × $\frac{2}{8}$–1$\frac{1}{4}$ in.), usually lanceolate to oblong-lanceolate, rarely oblong, elliptic to obovate, apex usually acuminate to acute narrowed to base or obtuse to rounded, usually not scaly above dark green, margins ± bristly; *very glaucous below* which sometimes wears off, scales unequal, large, brown, 1$\frac{1}{2}$–4 times their own diameter apart, aromatic. Petiole 0.4–1.5 cm scaly.

Inflor terminal or terminal and axillary in upper leaves, three to five per bud. Pedicel 0.8–2.8 cm scaly.

F colour very variable, white, white flushed lilac, purple or rose or margined rose, pale lilac, pink to almost salmon ± crimson spotted, sometimes fragrant, 2–4.8 cm ($\frac{3}{4}$–1$\frac{3}{4}$ in.) long, widely funnel-shaped, scaly outside.

Calyx minute, 0.5–rarely to 2 mm.

It is unfortunate that this attractive species is usually only hardy in the milder parts of Britain. Many forms are good with large flowers of delicate shades and some have fine young foliage rivalling a *Pieris* in colour. Not as free flowering as most other Triflorums. Liable to loose its leaves in cold gardens. The growth is often very early and therefore liable to be damaged.

A distinctive species easily identified by its very glaucous leaf under-side, showing some relationship with the Maddenia subsection, especially *pachypodum* (*supranubium*). **AM**, 1932, mauve-pink, slightly spotted.

From west Yunnan and Burma, 1,800–4,000 m (6,000–13,000 ft) mostly from on or near the Burma–Yunnan frontier at low elevations, on dry rocky slopes, among dwarf scrub, in thickets in open conifer or deciduous forest and in damp rain forest or rhododendron forest.

March–April–May

zaleucum var. *flaviflorum* Davidian 1978 H3

Collected under *KW* 20837 in the Triangle, Upper Burma at 2,700 m (9,000 ft). L larger than type, dark green. F pale yellow. Attractive, vigorous but tender.

Probable natural hybrids

lochmium Balf.f. & Forr. 1919

Possibly *tricanthum* × *davidsonianum*; originated from seed of *W* 1220, (*tricanthum*) and described from a cultivated plant with bristless parts and flowers white tinged pink. Balf.f. thought it might be *searsiae* × *polylepis*.

pallescens Hutch. 1933

Probably *davidsonianum* × *racemosum* although to me it looks like *tatsienense*. A stray from *R* 59574 ((*eritimum*) *anthosphaerum*) and described from a cultivated plant.

trichophorum Balf.f.

From seed of *W* 4242 (*tricanthum*), several seedlings appeared which are apparently *tricanthum* × *augustinii* but it looks like *tricanthum* to me.

vilmorinianum Balf.f. 1920

There is some confusion over this plant. The type specimens equal *augustinii* but cultivated plants appear to be *augustinii* × *yunnanense*. The seed supposedly came from Farges 2306 from east Szechwan and the few clones in cultivation have yellowish-white or pink flowers and rather small leaves with few or no hairs. Not of much horticultural value.

bivelatum Balf.f.

Known only from one poor specimen and may be a chance hybrid between *augustinii* ssp. *chasmanthum* and some other species. Flowers rose.

bodinieri Franch.

Possibly a hybrid between *rigidum* and *siderophyllum*. Only one specimen. *F* rose spotted purple. A funny looking plant in the RBG, Edinburgh = *yunnanense*.

VENATORA SUBSECTION (IRRORATUM SERIES, SUB-SERIES PARISHII PART) (E)

A new monotypic subsection containing the very distinct *venator* which apparently has no close relation.

venator Tagg 1934 H3–4 A + 5 L1–2 F2–3

Ht 1.5–2.7 m (5–9 ft). Habit often rather straggly, especially in shade. Branchlets with white hairs and glands. Bark grey-brown, roughish.
L to 15 × 4.5 cm (6 × 1¾ in.), oblong-lanceolate to oblanceolate, rugulose above, pale green below with scattered hairs. L remain for 3 years. Petiole about 1.3 cm stout.
Inflor four to ten loose. Pedicel about 1.3 cm glandular and hairy, fawn to rusty.
F scarlet to reddish-orange, 3.8 cm (1½ in.) long, tubular-campanulate with nectar pouches.
Calyx 3–4 mm, glandular. Stamens ten. Ovary hairy and glandular, style hairy at base.

A distinctive species, attractive when not too leggy. Prune if necessary. Hardy enough for most favoured lowland gardens in Britain. Difficult to place in any subsection. It does not appear to have any characters to fit into the Parishia subsection, even the stellate hairs look wrong to me. It might fit better into the Barbata subsection although the bark, late flowering and habit do not agree. **AM**, 1933 Bodnant.

Only found in a limited area in the Tsangpo Gorge, south-east Tibet, 2,400–2,600 m (8,000–8,500 ft) in thickets, in swamps and on rock faces.

May–June

SPECIES AT PRESENT UNPLACED

asterochnoum Diels 1921. See Addendum.

A probable ally of *calophytum* but the indumentum is like the Parishia subsection. Little known and not in cultivation. Szechwan.

sikangense Fang 1952 (*cookeanum* Davidian 1962) H4 L1–2 F2–3. See Addendum *p*. 362.

Ht 1.2–8 m (4–26 ft). Habit shrub or tree, fairly upright. Branchlets densely to moderately tomentose, white to fawn. Bark greenish-brown.
L 6.5–15 × 2.4–6.5 cm (2½–6 × 1–2½ in.), oblong-lanceolate to oblong-elliptic, apex acute to shortly acuminate, base obtuse to rounded, glabrous above and below on maturity. Petiole 1–2.8 cm ± tomentose.
Inflor eight to fifteen, rachis 1–2.5 cm. Pedicel 0.8–3.2 cm floccose.
F white, pink to red-purple (R's description), ± blotch, 3–5 cm (1–2 in.) long, campanulate.

Calyx minute 0.5–1 mm glandular. Stamens ten. Ovary tomentose, rarely glandular, style glabrous or floccose or glandular at base.

Fairly rare in cultivation but what I have seen of it points to a rather characterless plant which is shy flowering.

Appears to agree with the Parishia subsection in the stellate hairs on young leaves, pedicel, calyx and ovary; somewhat resembles *facetum* in growth and leaves but differs in flower colour, sparsely hairy young leaves, minute calyx, style being usually glabrous, slender curved capsule and in its very distant natural location and altitude. Immature capsules do not appear to have similar stellate hairs to *facetum*. Chamberlain has made *cookeanum* a synonym of *sikangense* which he has placed in the Maculifera subsection where it seems to fit best, especially on flower characters.

Muli, south-west Szechwan, 3,700–4,400 m (12,000–14,500 ft) in conifer forest, among alpine rocks, on alpine meadows and forming forests on alpine ridges and spurs.   June–July

dimitrum Balf.f. & Forr. 1919. An aberrant species lying somewhere between the Neriiflora and Irrorata subsections. F deep rose, large calyx. Yunnan.

diphrocalyx Balf.f. 1919 (*burrifolium* Balf.f. & Forr.) H3–4 L1–2 F1–3

Ht 1.5–4.6 m (5–15 ft). Habit bushy but inclined to become leggy. 1-year-old shoots almost glabrous. Bark rough, greenish-brown.
L 6–15 × 2.5–5.5 cm (2½–6 × 1–2¼ in.), oblong-oval, oval or obovate, very small floccose hairs below although it appears to be glabrous, apex obtuse, base obtuse or rounded. L remain for 1 to 2 years. Petiole with hairs and glands which shed easily.
Inflor ten to twenty rather loose, rachis red, about 1.5 cm. Pedicels densely hairy, about 2 cm.
F rosy-red through rose to pink or pale cerise, with dark blotch and some flecking, about 4 cm (1½ in.) long, broadly tubular-campanulate.
Calyx *very large, variable in size and length of lobes 1–2 mm to 2.5 cm, coloured.* Stamens ten. Ovary usually hairy and sometimes glandular, style ⅔ hairy.

An interesting and unusual species on account of its large, variable calyx, giving an almost double effect. It is quite attractive and free flowering and some forms have flowers of nice pink shades. It was cut to the ground or killed in Oregon in the 1972 freeze. Tender at Glendoick.

At first sight, it seems that this oddity is a likely natural hybrid between the often large calyxed Neriiflora subsection and the Glischra subsection but examination of the herbarium specimens and the distribution appear to discount that theory. It could of course have undergone the process of speciation a while ago having originated as a group of hybrids.

It is fairly uniform with a small distribution on the Shweli–Salween Divide, west Yunnan, 3,000–3,400 m (10,000–11,000 ft) in open thickets and on hillsides.   April

potanini Batalin 1890–1892 Not in cultivation and no specimens available. Seems to lie near to *rufum*. Kansu.

spilotum Balf.f. & Farrer 1922 H3–4 L1–2 F2–3

Habit shrub or small tree in the wild, shrub in cultivation.
Branches thin, branchlets densely glandular.
L 6–12 × 2–4 cm (2¼–5 × ¾–1½ in.), oblong-lanceolate to oblong-elliptic, apex obtuse apiculate, base obtuse to rounded, slightly rugulose above, glistening, minute glands below. Petiole about 1 cm.
Inflor about eight, loose, rachis about 1 cm. Pedicel slender 2–3 cm glandular.
F pink to white tinged pink with small crimson blotch, about 4 cm (1½ in.) long, funnel-campanulate.
Calyx about 8 mm, glandular elongated lobes. Ovary dense long-stalked glands, style glandular at base.

Usually a rather uninteresting plant but one individual in the RBG, Edinburgh under this name is very beautiful with daintly marked flowers, freely produced.

This plant has been removed from the Glischra subsection as it does not really fit there. I suggest this is a natural hybrid and Farrer's field notes support this theory. He reported that it occurred as rare and isolated specimens which would indicate natural hybridity, perhaps between *habrotrichum* and *martinianum* which occurred near by. Only under Farrer 1539 who apparently introduced it, although that was the year he died.

North-east Upper Burma in alpine woodlands.   April–May

6 *Propagation*

This is the only method of reproducing a young plant exactly similar to its parent. If a special clone is to be propagated, cuttings, grafting, micropropagation or layering need to be resorted to. Great improvements have been made in the ease of rooting cuttings, but with the more difficult subjects, few people can guarantee continual success. Modern methods must still be combined with good husbandry. Sharp knives or razor blades, cleanliness and careful observation are still just as necessary.

What method to use depends on a multitude of circumstances. Facilities already available, the number of young plants wanted and what type of species is to be propagated. Is it easy or difficult to reproduce, will seedlings be as satisfactory as vegetative reproduction or will low branches be available for ground layering?

It is most interesting to see the different approach to propagating in the USA compared with Britain. In Britain, few amateurs take up cutting propagation really seriously and treat it at all scientifically. In the USA, I was most impressed with the small basement units, often fitted out with pucka growing-room conditions where seedlings, cuttings and grafts can be raised almost throughout the year. In Britain, most amateurs resort to layering and perhaps a few seedlings. The latter are usually grown very slowly and take many years to reach a size fit for their permanent positions in the garden. I have even heard of some Americans who started with propagating as their hobby, only taking up gardening as an afterthought when they found nowhere to put their young stock!

For those with some knowledge of propagating, take heed of the advice of that old pioneer of rhododendrons in eastern USA, G. G. Nearing: 'Listen to everybody's advice, but be exceedingly wary about following it. Nearly all my disasters have resulted from advice taken from experts. ...' I can truthfully say that this has happened to me on several occasions, much to my annoyance. In endeavouring to increase one's successes by trying out a new rooting method, medium or rooting 'hormone', I have had years where my percentage take has dropped considerably, sometimes with whole batches of cuttings rotting off. In other words, if your present system gives fair results, do not hurriedly change it. If you want to make improvements, try small experiments first.

Cuttings

It is difficult to find any hard and fast rules over rooting cuttings other than that they should never be allowed to wilt and that they should be placed in a free draining, loose, friable medium, in which the base of the cutting can remain healthy. It is most important that sufficient light reaches the cuttings and that the rooting medium does not become either too dry or too wet. Most subjects have an optimum time for taking the cuttings to give the highest rooting percentage. The most difficult may be in a suitable condition for only a few days while the easier ones may root well when taken at widely differing times.

Equipment

For rooting a few cuttings, a small propagating unit can either be bought or made at home. Even such simple containers as glass jars, pots or boxes placed in sealed polythene bags or in outdoor frames facing north, can produce reasonable results. For larger numbers of cuttings, heated thermostatically controlled frames, pits or mist units, are desirable. Bottom heat at a controlled temperature is of great benefit for the more difficult subjects. A mist unit must be capable of spraying the cuttings with a very fine spray. This can be controlled manually, by a time clock or an electronic 'leaf' or balance which turns the mist on when it dries out. Time clocks are used in many hot climates where the weather is more predictable than our fickle conditions here. Whatever way the mist is controlled, saturation of the rooting medium should be avoided. This means that the run off the foliage should be negligible. I now turn off the spray at night during much of the winter period, as long as there is no chance of wilting overnight.

For all cuttings, cool tops and warm bottoms is a very desirable but often hard to achieve ideal, especially during hot summer days. The usual recommendation for bottom heat temperature is 21–24°C (70–75°F). Recent experiments have shown that such a high temperature leads to more cuttings rotting off than say 15–18°C (60–65°F). Whether the percentage lost from rotting at 21–24°C (70–75°F) is more serious than the slower formation of roots at 15–18°C (60–65°F) would need many controlled experiments with different subjects. If the thermostat was set at the lower level during the summer months, the heat would rarely come on, resulting in little or no bottom heat. The higher temperature should be reduced after a few weeks by 5½°C (10°F). Several propagators advocate air circulation through the rooting medium by having air holes underneath and small spaces above to allow the air to pass through the medium and foliage from below. A good supply of oxygen at the base of the cuttings is essential. Some people have gone as far as to use an oxygen cylinder for giving extra aeration from below with encouraging results.

Where frames are used, it is most important to have a level covering over the cuttings. This allows condensation to drip back evenly on to the cuttings which helps to give an even moisture content in the rooting medium thus avoiding the necessity for frequent watering. The covering used may be glass, polythene in a framework or just polythene laid down directly on to the cuttings. The last is proving highly successful with the cuttings suffering the least stress. Some of my frames have glass with a polythene lining underneath with an air space in between. The polythene may be cut larger than the lid of the frame so that the overlap can be stuck down with water on to the side of the frame, thus making it more airtight.

A regular re-damping and sticking down is all that is needed each time the cuttings are watered and inspected. It can be stapled on or fixed with strips of wood. Keep it as taut and level as possible.

Outside frames of the Nearing type are often successful (see *Rhododendrons of the World*, David Leach, *p*. 322). These and other cold frames may need protective covering in cold weather.

Fogging systems giving a smaller droplet than mist are proving successful.

Lighting

If cuttings are to be rooted in frames in daylight, all direct sunlight must be kept off them or they will wilt and deteriorate. Where shading is needed, it is difficult not to overshade and this accentuates any rotting of the cuttings and leads to poorer, slower rooting. North-facing frames if properly orientated, can exclude direct sunlight but plenty of light must be available. Painting the insides of the frame white can help a little. Various types of shading may be used such as white polythene, thin hessian (burlap), woven plastic, sheets of newspaper, rolls of split bamboo or reeds or a shading substance painted on to the glass or polythene. Cuttings under mist can be lightly shaded in the early part of the season. If the mist can be applied in very short, frequent bursts, no shading may be needed at all. Plenty of light helps photosynthesis, hence better rooting.

Cuttings rooted under artificial light only, have the advantage of no shading being necessary and a greater control being possible over lighting and moisture. Various lights can be used and the most simple are tubes. A good combination is 1 warm white to 1 white (cool white or 'daylight' are similar). Tubes should be placed 23–30 cm (9–12 in.) apart and either 18 or 24 hours of light can be applied. I use 18 hours. Other good lighting combinations are cool white and incandescent or incandescent and Grolux. Recent American trials have found that low pressure sodium lamps and incandescent have been much more effective for increasing growth than the above.

Other more sophisticated lights are available but these are mostly much more expensive to install and run. Vita-lite, made by Duro-Test Corporation, North Bergen, New Jersey, USA is said to be an excellent light for plants, having a spectrum of 92 per cent of natural daylight. Flash lighting can speed up growth. One second in every 60 seconds for 8 to 12 hours a night is all that is needed and therefore much cheaper to run.

Rooting mediums

Many different mediums are used, largely depending on local availability. Over the years, the standard medium in Britain has been 50/50 peat and sand and provided these are both of top quality, it is a suitable mixture. The peat should be high grade sphagnum peat, not too fine and if dry, it must be moistened before use. The sand is the chief difficulty. We find it almost impossible to get the best sharp washed grit and have suffered many losses through using either alkaline sand or unwashed grit containing silt and salts. I like grit of about 3 mm ($\frac{1}{8}$ in.) diameter but I have had reasonable results using 6 mm ($\frac{1}{4}$ in.) gravel with peat under mist. Sand or grit under 3 mm (⅛ in.) if clean, may prove satisfactory. It is well worth searching for good grit even if expensive. Some people use one-third grit to two-thirds peat with good results.

Alternatives to sand or grit are styrofoam, perlite, washed china clay sand. Avoid dusty perlite if possible. Vermiculite tends to hold too much moisture, leading to rotting.

The excellent peat from Germany is or was still available in the USA but is very expensive. Irish peat is of good quality, while Scandinavian and Russian peats tend to be rather young, over acid peats which may break down rather too quickly. Some British peat is good, but the quality is liable to vary too much for propagation purposes.

Ground pine bark and sawdust can be used as alternatives to peat. The former has given results as good as quality peat but sawdust is too variable a product to chance any but a known good source suitable for propagating. My own trials with it gave a very poor rooting percentage.

Other combinations are peat/perlite, peat/pine-bark, styrofoam/ peat and pure peat. Many people root all their rhododendrons in the last but I find it hard to manage, especially on a small scale. It requires extra careful management to avoid it becoming too wet or too dry. If it dries out underneath, it is very difficult to re-wet it. Wetting agents can help get over this problem.

The pH of the medium should be between 4 and 4.5 if possible. If lower, add lime to the mix. Adding slow release fertilizer saves having to move cuttings quickly after rooting.

All mixtures should be carefully levelled but never firmed as this spoils the essential air flow through the medium. The depth of the rooting medium should be at least 7.6 cm (3 in.) deep, especially if lying over electric warming cables where uneven drying out may occur. A layer of sand or other inert material can be sprinkled on top of the medium which helps to check the growth of moss and algae. Always renew the medium at least once a year but preferably after each batch of cuttings.

Free drainage is essential except in airtight containers where overhead watering is virtually unnecessary. The rooting medium can lie either on a layer of gravel with bigger gravel below that, or on a mesh which allows water to pass through readily. I prefer to root my larger cuttings directly into a frame or bench fitted with the medium rather than into boxes in which the moisture is more difficult to control.

Always look after hygiene and clean out all frames, boxes and other containers after each batch of cuttings. I use Jeyes Fluid. Another disinfectant is copper naphthale but many proprietary brands are equally good. If containers are made of wood, treat the wood with a suitable preservative every year or two. Green Cuprinol is good but avoid the brown which burns the foliage.

Preparation of stock plants and collection of cuttings

There is little doubt that the time of propagating from cuttings should vary according to the climate in the locality. In warm countries or areas where the temperatures remain high until well on into autumn, it is hard to keep the top of the cuttings cool enough under greenhouse conditions.

Thus, we are able to keep ours cool at an earlier date than in the USA and Australia. The longer warm autumns and higher light intensity probably keeps the wood softer for longer than here, enabling the successful taking of cuttings of the larger species to a later date. Also, where only natural light is used, the stronger winter light nearer the equator no doubt leads to better winter rooting.

I would again (*Dwarf Rhododendrons*) like to draw the nurseryman's attention to the possible dangers of repeatedly propagating from young stock, thus getting more and more generations (vegetatively) away from the original seedling from which all members of a clone have arisen. Several shrubs other than rhododendrons have become noticeably weaker over the years. While this could in some cases be due to virus infection, there is little doubt that there is a danger of loss of vigour. From the propagator's angle, this is annoying because many items do root significantly better off young stock plants. One suggestion is to keep one or two old stock plants and to re-propagate young stock plants off these originals and not off subsequent generations. Partially blanched stock plants under sheets of black polythene for a week or two up to collecting the cuttings could be beneficial. I have not had a chance to try this yet. Or find a method of keeping growth in a juvenile state by pruning or by the use of chemicals for adequate rootability. Remove flower buds on stock plants just as they are swelling. To produce extra shoots from growth buds, the emerging growth may be pinched out as it elongates. Where only a limited number of cuttings are needed, it is still worthwhile removing the occasional flower or growth bud on garden specimens to produce better quality cuttings, but never more than about a third of the young growth per season or the health of the parent plants will deteriorate.

Thick cuttings are often hardier to root than thinner ones although the stouter ones will make more young shoots at an early age. Cuttings taken from low down on the shaded side may root easier than those in full sunlight on the top of a bush. The ability to root seems to vary from season to season for no accountable reason. Another variability appears to be in the type of soil, locality or individual treatment of the stock plants. Healthy plants undoubtedly give better cuttings and in dry weather, stock plants should be watered 2 days before collecting cuttings. Poor, short growth on old specimens is not recommended, and it is hard to propagate from a plant one wants to perpetuate when it appears to be dying. Another pitfall can be propagating from stock recently treated with weedkiller. If any foliar damage is visible, however slight, the cuttings are sure to rot off more readily than usual. Keep stock plants free of *Phytophthora* (see *p.* 326) and avoid shoots spattered with soil.

Collect cuttings into polythene bags when they are turgid, preferably in the early morning. They may be stored under refrigeration or refrigeration plus low pressure $\frac{1}{30}$ of an atmosphere at 1–2°C (34–36°F), prolonging their life considerably. Cuttings can be sent considerable distances by post if placed dry in polythene bags which are sealed. Air should be added to the bags to avoid the cuttings being crushed. Do not treat with fungicide or moisten before packing as they may rot if damp. Do not crush the base of the cuttings when removing them from the parent plant with secateurs. Most cuttings should be taken when nearly firm, from July to

October with us. Exceptions are deciduous azaleas of the *Pentanthera section* (Luteum sub-series) and species like *dauricum* which should be taken soft from April to June. Some azaleas root better if the cuttings are taken off stock plants forced on under glass in spring.

Preparation and insertion of cuttings

Prepare in a cool place. The leaves may be trimmed if space in the bench is at a premium. Cuttings should not be too long. I do not like them more than 10 cm (4 in.) on the larger-leaved species and prefer them shorter on the others. Always use sharp clean instruments for cutting leaves and making the final cuts on the stem. Remove all flower buds as they may reduce rooting ability and very often rot off anyway, which may spread to the whole cutting. Try to make the final preparations shortly before insertion.

Wounding is beneficial to all but the softest, thinnest and smallest of rhododendron cuttings. A slice down one or both sides depending on thickness, is the best and simplest method. Cut just through the bark and cambium layers to the wood. The wound can be up to 2.5 cm (1 in.) or more long, according to the length of the cuttings and is preferably made not quite down to the base. Indumentum on the stems may sometimes hinder rooting. This may be rubbed off using paper towelling.

All cuttings other than very soft ones can be pushed into the medium without injuring them. There is no need to firm the cuttings after insertion and they should not be pushed in too deep, only just far enough to prevent them toppling over. Avoid overlapping the foliage where possible, especially in closed frames. Where one leaf is under another, particularly when touching, the lower is inclined to rot (turn black) and this rot may spread all too rapidly. Do not place cuttings in dark corners of frames or directly under partitions, these will often rot completely due to lack of light. Water after insertion but do not soak medium.

Always keep a constant check on the water content of the rooting medium. It is better to keep it slightly on the dry side, especially if the cuttings have become well established and have started to root. Carefully regulate the amount of water applied with each watering to the moisture content of the medium and only lightly syringe the foliage if the medium is moist enough. Indoor frames need watering only very occasionally once the cuttings are established if they have well fitting covers but all need regular inspection to remove any rotted leaves or whole cuttings. While it is not normally necessary to leave cuttings uncovered for a spell every week or so, it does help to reduce rotting if frames are left open for a period during very dull, damp winter weather.

All mist units require regular inspection too and perhaps adjustments to make sure the correct amount of water is being applied and that all nozzles are in working order. The same applies to fog.

Rooting 'hormones' and fungicides

These 'hormones' are undoubtedly beneficial in rooting the more difficult rhododendrons although they are no magic potion and in no way replace the necessary skill of a good propagator. These substances are based on several chemicals related to 'hormone' weedkillers and are themselves lethal when over applied. Their application is still rather by trial and error. Many proprietary brands are either too strong without dilution, or not strong enough in the case of a few of the harder to root species. In this instance, it may be necessary to make up one's own mixture; powder in talc and liquid in alcohol.

Indolebutyric (IBA), indoleacetic and naphthaline acetic acids are the most usual active ingredients and may be applied in powder or liquid form. Various chemicals, fungicides and diluters are added in the brands available to the public. Makers instructions should be followed with caution and newly tried brands should not be applied to whole batches of valuable and rare cuttings. Experiment with different strengths and leave some untreated. Where powder is used, it may be desirable to make little holes for each cutting so as not to rub off all the powder, when pushing them into the medium.

There are various theories such as the value of applying the substance only to the very base and allowing it to soak up the stem. Naturally, the softer the cutting, the weaker the strength of the substance should be. Certain harder to root cuttings may benefit from an overhead spray of liquid 'hormone'. Another variability is whether the cuttings are turgid or nearer wilting. The less sap in the cutting, the more 'hormone' will be assimilated, therefore the more effect it will have. Thus if the strength is suitable for a cutting in a turgid state, it may be too strong if it is deficient in sap.

There are now many conflicting opinions over the use of fungicides on cuttings. It may be true to say that really good hygiene and near ideal conditions for rooting are far superior to using a fungicide of any sort. For a while, Benomyl (Benlate) was considered to be the answer to a propagator's prayers but it is now considered too wide in its fungicidal properties, thus effecting beneficial as well as pathenogenic fungi. Good newer fungicides are Rovral (Iprodione) and Octave (Prochlorag). Naturally, if any outbreaks of a fungus disease takes place, it should be treated accordingly but I must admit that I often have better results using no precautionary fungicide. The above fungicides may be used as a spray or drench every two to three weeks but too frequent applications may inhibit rooting. Fongarid (Furalaxyl) for controlling Pythium may be used as a drench or compost mix.

The stem rotting of cuttings is caused by various fungi and the following are those most frequently found. *Cylindrocarpon destructans*, *Fusarium* sp., and *Botrytis cineria*. Experiments have shown that Benomyl can reduce rotting by about 15 per cent if used as both an immersion before insertion and a rooting medium drench.

Deciduous azalea cuttings

These need to be divided into groups and they all need some special treatment.

Many of the Pentanthera section (Luteum sub-series) root from soft or semi-soft cuttings taken in May–July from out of door plants. Better results are obtained from plants brought into growth under cover and also by taking cuttings off tips of young plants being grown on indoors at almost any time of the year. These cuttings should be taken before the buds (growth or flower) have formed at the apex. If buds have formed, these should be cut off. Make sure that the cuttings do not wilt before insertion. They may be rooted in mist or frames and can be successful with no bottom heat.

There are two main methods of growing on rooted azalea cuttings. The first is under supplementary lighting and heat to force growth prior to going into winter dormancy. This makes it much easier to over-winter rooted azaleas and get a good growth the following spring. If growth is made, the young plants may be transplanted into pots, boxes or benches before winter. We now use the second method. Leave the rooted cuttings in the containers they were rooted in and give them at least a 3 month cool period in a cold frame or cold greenhouse. They may be returned to heat in March if desired. This method leads to a reasonable growth break in spring after which they should be transplanted. Mix a slow release fertilizer into the base of rooting medium. If transplanted with no new growth or kept in heat over winter, they will fail to grow and then die. Transplanted rooted cuttings may also be given a cool period.

Pentanthera azaleas of the stoloniferous types may be propagated from root cuttings. These can be taken at almost any season, should be about pencil thickness and about 10 cm (4 in.) long. Lay horizontally and cover lightly with sphagnum or sphagnum and sand.

Some species may be rooted from hardwood cuttings such as *occidentale* but the percentage success is small with the experiments so far. Leafless cuttings may be taken in late December and treated with IBA. Wounding and artificial light are probably beneficial.

R. schlippenbachii is hard to root. One method that gives some success is to take hardwood cuttings in the spring just as the leaf buds are starting to burst. The percentage may be small and roots may take some time to emerge. Soft cuttings of *reticulatum* have rooted easily.

Other types of rhododendron cuttings

It is suggested that leaf-bud cuttings need a higher temperature than normal to make the bud break and stop it from rotting off. Alternatively after rooting, a cooling period of at least 3 months may force the bud break. This type of cutting is at present only recommended when material is very scarce. The use of 'hormones' may inhibit bud break.

Quicker growth is often made with seedlings if they are cut off at soil level and treated as cuttings when the second set of leaves shows.

Research into the use of meristem tissue culture has often been talked about in recent years. Now at last success has been achieved with rhododendrons and in a few years it may become possible to propagate even the most difficult to root species in quantity by this method. Basically, this involves taking minute portions of the growing tips and placing them in cultural solutions under laboratory conditions. These start to grow and produce juvenile multiple shoots which are divided, grown on and re-divided. These are then rooted and grown on normally.

Hardening off and transplanting rooted cuttings

Many rooted cuttings are lost after their first move. There are various reasons for this. If rooted cuttings are transplanted without any attempt to wean them off from full misting or airtight frame conditions, they will wilt and die. They should be put back into a similar environment for 2 to 3 weeks before gradually hardening off. At no time should they be allowed to wilt. If the rooted cuttings are hardened off for a period before being removed from the rooting medium, they need less humid conditions after transplanting. Never try to move cuttings with inadequate root balls. For small-leaved species like Triflorums, at least 2.5 cm (1 in.) diameter root balls are necessary while larger-leaved species should be at least 5 cm (2 in.).

Rooted cuttings can be treated in a variety of ways depending on quantities and the facilities that are available. They can be potted singly, boxed, planted into greenhouse beds or frames or plastic tunnel houses. Manually operated mist lines are excellent for establishing quantities of rooted cuttings while smaller lots may be covered temporarily with polythene sheets. Compost should consist of a high percentage of peat, leafmould and/or ground bark and conifer needles. Care should be taken over the use of fertilizer, especially in the late summer, autumn and winter as the release of nitrogen into the soil can scorch and kill when growth is not vigorous. Be careful not to over water before growth starts.

Grafting

For rhododendron species, grafting should only be resorted to if all other methods of propagation are out of the question. I only graft when wanting to reproduce special clones of the larger or harder to root species. Two good uses for grafting are for scions introduced from abroad, especially those wild collected and for budded scions for use in hybridizing. The latter can be grafted over winter and then brought into flower indoors and used for hybridizing or cross pollinating with another clone of the same species.

I do not propose to describe the different types of grafts which may be used with rhododendrons. This information is readily available in specialist books on propagating.

Grafting can be done at nearly any time of the year with a good chance of success. I prefer February. Good-quality under-stocks are best established for a while before doing the actual grafting. While *ponticum* is excellent for easy results, the disadvantages of the continual sucker problem, its dislike of alkaline soil and its susceptibility to root rot leads me to recommend the use of other stocks wherever possible. I have used a variety of seedlings and some easily rooted hybrids with varying results but I do like to use a close relative of the scion where possible. For instance, the Falconera and Grandia subsections are best on to seedlings from the same subsections. I like 'Cunninghams White' *decorum* or *fortunei* for general purposes as they are vigorous with nice clean stems.

Be careful to select only good healthy, vigorous stocks, place them in a bed of peat having cleaned up the stems and removed any unwanted leaves and side-shoots. It is important that the stems are roughly the same thickness as the proposed scions which can of course vary greatly from species to species. I have had losses from the stock dying off some weeks after grafting, due to poor root conditions. Do not let the roots of the stock become sodden. To ensure vigorous root growth on the stock, bury it in peat to cover the root ball when the stocks are initially brought indoors but keep them on the dry side.

A clean, sharp knife is essential for the actual grafting. Raffia, polythene strips or rubber strips can be used for tying. It is advisable to keep some leaves below the union. This should be low down so that it can ultimately be buried below ground level to enable roots to develop on the scion. The completed grafts must be kept turgid with no direct sun on them. They may be placed in frames or in polythene tents or individual polythene bags. Hardening off after callousing must be done very slowly as any wilting usually proved fatal. Long leaves of both scions and under-stocks may be cut and some difficult scions may be helped by removing the terminal bud.

There are many variations of this theme. In New Zealand, success has been had out of doors in shady sites using polythene bags over the scion and union using semi-soft material. An American friend was successful using no covering material at all.

Rooted or unrooted cuttings may be used as understocks. When unrooted cuttings are used, these need to be easily rooted subjects. I had a fair success using the latter method but was much bothered with growth repeatedly sprouting on the stock while none developed on the scion.

Some people graft indoors in summer using soft wood. The scion should be a little thicker than the stock as it shrinks a little and brings the cambium together. Callousing should be rapid using soft growth. One successful American propagator advocates cutting the base of a scion on a wedge graft with a square rather than a tapered base which is liable to rot off.

An American friend buds rhododendrons in February. He cuts a shield 1.9 cm ($\frac{3}{4}$ in.) long, just deep enough to take some wood which should be peeled out. Remove the top of the stock leaving three or more leaves. Cut a T in the stock just above a bud on a remaining leaf, with two or more leaves above the scion bud. After gently placing the bud in the T cut, bind with light rubber and coat with tree seal. Rub out buds on the stock above the bud scion and cut off above it when the bud starts to swell. After care as with other grafts. Chip budding has also proved successful.

C. P. Raffill of Kew used to graft Maddeniis on to *ponticum*. He said that they all do well on *ponticum* (surprisingly) and apparently the numbers of flowers in the truss were increased and strong growing, free flowering specimens resulted.

Layering

This is the commonest and often the best way for the amateur to propagate when just one or two extra plants are required. Any pliable branch in easy reach of the ground can be layered and where there are no low branches, aerial layering using polythene and moss can be resorted to.

Layering is more rapid and more successful in wet districts and where there is plenty of organic matter that does not dry out readily. Many people layer into wooden boxes. The great advantage of this is that the root system of the parent plant is not damaged or disturbed. I have heard of a case where the layering into the ground inside the parent's root system has been successful but to the detriment of the parent whose roots were so injured that it died.

Low branches can be held down with forked sticks or large stones. The latter help to retain moisture. The shoot to be layered may be twisted, sliced or grooved and rooting powder can be added. Personally, I usually do none of these but try to bend the stem round into as upright a position as possible. Layers may produce sufficient roots in one season under ideal conditions but can on the other hand take several years. In our rather poor, dry soil, the more difficult subjects take ages to form satisfactory roots. It is well worthwhile adding a liberal amount of peat, leafmould or shredded bark and if the ground is at all heavy, sand. Mix it into the trench dug out to receive the branch. It is better to avoid attempting to root large branches and of course several tips of one branch may be layered at a time.

In the old days before advances in propagation from cuttings, nurseries layered whole plants. These were usually laid on their sides and as many shoots as possible were spaced out and bent upright with the idea of making a young plant out of each shoot. Likewise deciduous azaleas were made into stools with each crop of young shoots being bent over and layered. Some of these old stool beds are still used but by and large this method of propagation is dying out. Grafted plants do not make good subjects to throw on their sides and layer.

It is usually good practice to sever the layer a season before lifting it rather than give it the double shock of severing and lifting at the same time. Extra peat and/or leafmould can be added to boost the root system of the layer but if the foliage on the layer is very over-shadowed or the ground is liable to dry out, it is advisable to sever and lift in one operation and transfer the layer to a good position in a shady nursery bed. All layers should in fact, be grown on in a nursery before planting in final positions.

Aerial layering

This involves wrapping a branch with sphagnum moss and (and/or peat) and surrounding this with polythene to keep in the moisture. It is very hard to make this watertight and therefore water (rain) should be allowed to run through and drain out at the lower end. The stem should be slit on the underside and a rooting powder may be applied. Sever when well rooted. Considerable care needs to be taken in establishing in soil in shaded humid conditions.

SEED

Seed of species should either be from hand-pollinated or wild collected sources, if at all possible. Only isolated specimens or groups of one species which flower at a different time from others near by are likely to come consistently true. Nearly all evergreen rhododendrons hybridize readily with at least some of their neighbours in any collection of more than a handful of plants. Only certain rather remote species that have so far proved impossible to hybridize such as *semibarbatum*, *albiflorum* and the azaleas *schlippenbachii* and *vaseyi*, invariably come true from seed. Even wild collected seed often produces a number of natural hybrids.

If collected when it is ripening, that is October–January depending on the species, rhododendron seed should keep for up to 3 years or even more when stored dry in an airtight tin. Under refrigeration, it will keep for at least 5 years. The exception is seed of the Vireya section which will fail to germinate at all after a few weeks. Ripening capsules may start to turn brown or black or may split open green. Most species hold a proportion of the seed in their capsules for some months. As rough guide, large-leaved species, Maddeniis and Pentanthera (Luteum) azaleas are the last to ripen their seeds but all should be checked weekly from October onwards.

Hand-pollinating is really quite an easy operation and I cannot understand why more people do not make use of this way of reproducing species. I find that the majority are not self fertile, therefore another plant of the same species (not the same clone) needs to be found. All I do is to remove stamens and corollas from unopened buds, usually preparing three to five flowers per truss and picking off any opened flowers and any buds not prepared. Each truss or branch should be carefully labelled and noted in a book. I used to pollinate 2–3 times over intervals of 1–2 days to ensure the stigma being ripe. Now, a Danish friend suggests applying ripe pollen immediately (without the destruction of the flower being necessary) and covering the stigma with a small piece of micropore (surgical) tape. This not only keeps the pollen in place but allows air to circulate, protects from the weather, provides 100% protection from unintended pollination and saves time. Only collect pollen from flowers just about to open to avoid contamination.

Pollen (still enclosed in the anthers) travels well, dry, in envelopes and may be stored dry in gelatine capsules over calcium chloride in a jar for some months (powdered milk wrapped in paper handkerchiefs also works as a desiccant). For longer storing, pre-dry the pollen in a refrigerator for 2 to 3 days, then place in a freezer at about $-17°C$ ($0°F$). Warm before use and refreeze several times if desired.

Seed can be picked green (as long as the capsule is fully developed), opened in gentle heat and still give good germination. Most species, particularly those with large capsules, produce vast quantities of seed. Even the contents of one to two capsules can give an amount of seedlings which might embarrass a nurseryman wanting a hundred or more plants. Nearly all rhododendrons ripen their seed well in our climate out of doors and the germination is generally excellent. Seed collected in spring may be scarce but will germinate just as well, producing plants of full vigor. Old seed may give a proportion of weak seedlings which die off in infancy. There are a few golden rules in growing rhododendrons from seed. Always sow thinly, always keep the seed compost moist, and always watch for signs of grey mould, the greatest killer of rhododendron seedlings.

There are many different mediums that the seed can be sown on and most can give a fair degree of success. I have seen various combinations of peat, leafmould, rotten bark (sterilized), sphagnum moss (dried or fresh), perlite, vermiculite and loam used. I use either finely sifted peat or for especially tricky items, riddled live sphagnum. I recently started adding a few granules of slow release fertilizer two thirds the way down the seed pan. The roots of the seedlings utilize this fertilizer once they are well established and this considerably increases growth, allowing thinly sown seedlings to remain in the pan for a year of more.

I sow my seeds in pans which have been filled to the top with peat, soaked in a trough and allowed to drain off. The seeds are never covered initially but may benefit from a careful sifting of fine peat through a sieve once the roots are well developed. The pans are placed in a frame and covered with newspaper with bottom heat of about 18–21°C (65–70°F).

Light is gradually increased once the cotyledons start to open. Actual germination at this temperature usually takes from 9 to 20 days. A few may take longer and the cotyledons vary in the time they take to develop. Air is also gradually given once the cotyledons are opened.

I then take the pans out of the frame and place them on a bench under supplementary light and cover the pans with a sheet of polythene with holes cut in it 1.3 cm ($\frac{1}{2}$ in.) across and 7.6 cm (3 in.) apart. This helps to keep the pans from drying out and yet allows a circulation of air which is so important for avoiding botrytis (grey mould). The lights are the same as mentioned on *p*. 309 (under cuttings) and should be about 45 cm (18 in.) above the seedlings. If any scorching is noticed, raise the lights a few inches. Shade with newspaper in bright sunlight. Remove polythene at night.

When bottom heat and artificial light are available, seed may be sown as soon as it ripens. I usually sow all my own seed in late December–early January but seed from other sources generally arrives later. Some people have had success with germinating Ericaceous seeds under red spectrum fluorescent lighting.

If there is bottom heat but no lights, sow in late January–early February. Where there is neither, sow in March–April.

Various other containers may be used. Some people use boxes and others are successful in plastic dishes with clear tops. Seedlings can be grown in the latter for some considerable time provided there is sufficient head room for growth. No watering is needed for a long time. If they are sprayed overhead, allow the leaves to dry before replacing the lid. Personally, I do not like seedlings grown in this way because they tend to be soft and drawn and hard to transplant but this is a useful method for those with no greenhouse or basement growing room.

Watering is generally not needed for some weeks and should be done from underneath. Once the seedlings have developed two to three true leaves, an occasional overhead syringing is all right and this can include a fortnightly dilute liquid feed. Remember to watch carefully for mould, especially where the seedlings are close together. Remove any mouldy seedlings promptly and treat the area with a mould controlling fungicide such as Rovral.

Seedlings can be pricked out as soon as they are easily handled or may be left for some months if widely spaced. Be very careful not to damage either the foliage or the thread-like roots. Boxes, pots, frames or peat benches can be used. Small rhododendron seedlings are vulnerable to direct sunlight at all times and all the more so after pricking out but on the other hand too much shading encourages mould so light shading is desirable. Never allow the young seedlings to dry out and try to keep the atmosphere humid during the hotter months.

I have yet to find the ideal compost for pricking out seedlings into even after years of experimenting. Various combinations of peat, oak or beech (acid) leafmould, ground pine bark, rotten wood (sterilized), acid loam, rotted chopped bracken and pine needles may all be satisfactory. I generally use ¼ peat, ¼ leafmould, ¼ rotted spruce needles and ¼ pulverized bark. I used to add grit but as it is so hard to find a good supply, I no longer use it. Care must be taken with many species over the amount of fertilizer added. Too much nitrogen often leads to leaf scorch, especially in early winter. I now use a little Osmocote Plus placed near the base of the trays. This helps avoid growth of moss and algae which would occur if mixed through the compost.

Various types of fungi are liable to form on the organic matter used for growing on seedlings in and are often hard to control. If a serious attack develops, it is usually better to re-box the seedlings into fresh compost.

Further notes on seeds

Liquid fertilizer should not be given after August (July in Scotland). Use at half recommended strength (USA) every 2 to 3 weeks.

Seed can be germinated under mist. I find that it is hard to avoid the compost becoming saturated and it is noticeable how the cooling effect of the mist slows down the germination and growth compared with a heated frame.

Too much fungicide such as Captan on seed or seedlings may inhibit germination and growth.

Hot water gives good penetration of the medium before sowing.

Kingdon Ward had a theory that wild collected seeds give rise to hardier plants than from cultivated plants in exile. I think this most unlikely and in any case he can have had little chance to test this theory by growing seedlings himself.

Avoid using boxes (wooden) newly treated with wood preservative. The fumes can burn young seedlings (or cuttings). Only use green Cuprinol not brown. All containers for sowing seeds or pricking out seedlings into should be thoroughly washed and sterilized before using again.

Some people advise an overhead watering after seeds are sown to settle them into the medium. This must be carefully done to avoid washing the seeds into heaps.

Sphagnum is often hard to keep at the right moisture content. I find that a layer of sphagnum over peat dries out at the edges and curls upwards. Dried sphagnum is available in the USA, but I find it goes mouldy.

Short growing mosses are to be encouraged among seedlings as they help to control disease and avoid the undesirable liverworts, algae and fungi which should be removed or promptly treated with a suitable chemical. The fungicide Thiram helps to control liverwort and algae and other algaesides are now available. These mosses may be encouraged by rubbing through a sieve over the surface of the seedling container.

When seedlings are being grown on in a polythene tent, a fan inside greatly helps air circulation and thus reduces disease problems. '

GROWING ON OF YOUNG PLANTS

The best plants are always those which have been grown on steadily without a check at any stage of their development. Checked growth can be caused by a multitude of mishaps such as scorching from sunburn, too much fertilizer, a bad balance of nutrients, starvation, overheating, draughts, drying out or waterlogging, overcrowding, frost damage, fungus and insect attacks.

It is well worth transplanting seedlings or rooted cuttings twice in a season if the young plants start to look overcrowded by July–August or earlier. The amount of growth that can be hoped for the first season varies tremendously from species to species. The most vigorous are usually members of the Fortunea, Rhodorastra (Dauricum), Triflora, Heliolepida and Pentanthera subsections (Luteum). Given ideal growing room conditions and the correct balance of nutrients, truly remarkable growth can be achieved in one year, 60 cm (2 ft) or more in some cases. Personally, I am satisfied if I have seedlings large enough to plant out in the nursery in the early summer at 16 months old. To produce larger seedlings would cost far more in heating, lighting and labour, let alone greenhouse or frame space. I never attempt to grow on seedlings continuously until ready to plant outside. If I am in a hurry, I carry out the following procedure.

Sow seeds in December, prick out in March, re-box July, grow on in heat and under supplementary lights until November, harden off and give a cooling period in a cold house or frame from January to March. Bring indoors again in March, re-box again if necessary, grow on under lights and heat, harden off and plant out in June. The cooling period is all important for seedlings and many rooted cuttings. If seedlings are over-wintered in a heated house, set at say 7–10°C (45–50°F), they may not start into growth again until May–June and then do so erratically. The 3 to 4 month cooling leads to an even, vigorous flush of spring growth.

Likewise cuttings. Many species, especially elepidotes, may fail to make any growth at all if over-wintered in heat, more so if rooted and potted in October–November. Early rooted cuttings (before January) if showing no growth, should be placed in a carefully looked after cold frame before February. I plunge all the pots in peat. Heavy hessian or equivalent may be needed to guard against hard frost, particularly just after shifting out of a heated house. Attempting to give a cooling period from February onwards does not work, it is too late.

Carbon dioxide (CO_2) enrichment of the atmosphere is often advocated nowadays. If the normal 300 ppm. CO_2 is increased to about 2000 ppm., greatly increased growth may result, provided other conditions such as light, nutrients and temperature are boosted accordingly, if necessary. This CO_2 can be applied indoors by dry ice, from cylinders or by burning alcohol and is most effective in early spring on young seedings.

I over-winter many of my hardier seedlings in a cold house on the floor in boxes. They remain there from November to May when they are placed in a partly shaded area outside prior to lining out in June–July. An alternative to over-wintering in boxes is to line out the hardier, more vigorous species directly into soil in a frame, shade-house or tunnel-house in July–August which gives them time to become established before winter. These require the usual care over watering, ventilation, frost protection and botrytis control. Growth is often superior to that achieved in boxes. Frequent examinations of all seedlings should be carried out to watch for rodent and insect attack, scratching by birds and loosening by moles. Ventilation should be given daily in all but the coldest weather and water should only be given sparingly and then only on really sunny days capable of drying off the foliage. More liberal watering can start in February–March and some shading may be needed from March to May.

The alternative to a cooling period for rooted cuttings is a high temperature in February to April. I find that newly potted rooted cuttings usually respond well to these high temperatures which can be largely achieved by not ventilating on sunny days. Naturally, direct sunlight on newly potted cuttings from February onwards can cause severe wilting and/or scorch, so some shading and/or misting is necessary.

Seedlings and rooted cuttings should respond to further liquid feeding in the spring. Ventilation can be given on warm days from late February onwards but avoid cold draughts. I turn off the heating in mid to late April depending on the weather. Leave the ventilators open all the time from mid-May onwards. Then the young plants can be finally hardened off out of doors in a partially shaded site prior to planting out in June–July. In 1975, some young plants at Glendoick put out just before the May 15th frost suffered severe damage but the majority ultimately recovered, albeit smaller than they should have been. This was an exceptional frost but these nasty cold spells have an unpleasant habit of occurring when least expected. Colder and warmer areas than us will of course need to vary their hardening off and planting accordingly.

Nursery, frame, lath or polythene house should all have well proportioned beds with at least 50% of peat, leafmould and/or conifer needles thoroughly mixed-in with the local soil. An alternative, particularly if the soil is heavy or otherwise unsuitable, is to use pure peat or peat plus one or both of the other ingredients mentioned above.

It is most important to plant out young stock at the correct depth. If too shallow, they dry out readily or get thrown out by birds and moles. If too deep, they gradually die off. Always make sure that the root balls are well moistened before planting and do not plant into ground when the surface is dry as the dry soil will fall into the holes. Always water thoroughly after planting. If the weather is at all dry and hot, frequent sprinklings will be necessary to ensure good establishment. Shading is essential in hotter climates than Scotland. Most of my nursery area is partially shaded by trees and I gave up artificial shading of newly planted stock some years ago.

The majority of large species appreciate some shade from trees when young, the degree of shade depends on the species and the climate. Most species do not have to be protected during their first winter outside if there is good air drainage and shelter where the frost rarely drops below

−12°C (10°F). We do protect the more tender big-leaved species in a lath house, cold frame or under cloche their second winter and perhaps their third. Others may require similar protection such as the more tender Triflorums and Irroratums.

I give a light feed of a 20/10/10 organic fertilizer when planting and another the following spring of about one medium handful (about 50 grams) per 3 square metres followed by another in mid summer. Some cold climates necessitate a phosphate and potassium or phosphate alone fertilizer late in the year to help ripen growth.

As stated under pruning, the great majority of species should not be pruned when young and should be allowed to grow into their natural form. Avoid overcrowding and stake the more lanky species where necessary.

Even in warmer climates than ours, Maddeniis should be grown on under protection in a cold, cool or lath house until they reach flowering size before placing in their final position.

I do not like growing on species in containers to a saleable or plantable size. They require more attention in containers, good growth is harder to attain and foliage and the root systems are never as good.

Growth retardants may be applied to either container or field grown plants. Their effect on larger rhododendron species is almost unknown.

While the hardier species over-winter satisfactorily outside or in a cold frame, they are very vulnerable to early autumn and late spring frosts. In the early spring of 1981, I lost hundreds of small seedlings that had started into growth as a result of the hard frost in late April–early May. It is well worth going to some trouble to give extra protection, especially after a mild winter and/or early spring when growth flushes as early as March on some species. Glass usually proves adequate but a new substance called Agryl (spun-bonded crop cover) now readily available, is also good for covering these seedlings or rooted cuttings.

7 Pests, diseases and disorders

There is no doubt that pests in general are more of a problem to those living in the country as opposed to built-up areas. The only pests liable to be worse in the town are human ones in the form of vandals and stray dogs and cats which can break and urinate on one's plants.

As stated in *Dwarf Rhododendrons* and *The Smaller Rhododendrons*, pests can be divided into two categories; vertebrates and invertebrates. Very often the former are more troublesome and harder to control than the latter.

So many people suffer from deer damage these days, even on the outskirts of villages where it can be dangerous to attempt to shoot them. If practicable, it is well worth going to the expense of erecting a deer fence around the boundary, 2–2.5 m (6 ft 6 in.–8 ft) being the necessary height, depending on the species of deer. While *any* rhododendrons may be eaten, their favourites are small-leaved species like Cinnabarinums and Triflorums. We have even had *eximium* attacked on two occasions. Once they start on an individual plant, it is usually eaten to the bone so as soon as eaten foliage is spotted, surround the plant with wire-netting. In addition to eating, the bucks rub their horns to mark their territories; in this case youngish rhododendrons with bare stems are popular and these can be completely ruined. Plastic tree-guards are good for stopping this. Various deterrent compounds are now available but these can only work very short term at the best. Tie on bags of human hair! With us, most of the eating is done between January and April.

Rabbits are only a problem on young and dwarf rhododendrons although they do occasionally de-bark a larger specimen in very cold, snowy winters. Deciduous azaleas are very vulnerable to rabbits and need permanent rabbit protection until mature in badly infested districts like our own. Likewise hares if plentiful. Wire-netting is the only real solution.

Beware of moles loosening up anything newly planted and birds can scratch out surprisingly large young plants. Titmice can strip or severely damage flowers, especially early flowering red species when looking for nectar.

Insect pests

We are lucky in Britain that insects rarely cause severe injury to rhododendrons. In America, especially, more devastating attacks do occur. I have never found it necessary so far to carry out any regular spraying programme against invertebrates. It is hoped that the wholesale spraying of everything in America in by gone days is now over. Not that pests have diminished in any way but much more thought is now put into biological control and the use of systemic insecticides which only kill those insects causing the actual damage to the plants.

Weevils

These are the most talked about pest of rhododendrons. Several species attack foliage in the adult form and roots as larvae. In Britain these pests are rarely as serious as in America, especially with the larval root damage. We have the vine, clay coloured and strawberry weevils but in America they have the common woods and obscure woods or root weevils as well as the introduced Japanese weevil.

The usual foliar injury is a notched edge which can be very unsightly. Where roots are badly eaten, the foliage may become unhealthy and even wilting may occur. Seedlings and rooted cuttings can have all their roots and bark eaten off below soil level. Weevils are associated with conifers and certain deciduous trees, especially birch.

Control This has always been difficult, especially since the nasty persistent poisonous organochlorine insecticides such as aldrin have been largely banned. There is a promising new systematic insecticide called Orthene (Chevron Chemical Co.) which should be sprayed over the foliage once a month during the danger period for leaf damage. Fenitrothion is effective on adult weevils. Spray foliage when these are active in about May and August. Foliar sprays of Malathion or Diazinon monthly also help to control adult woods and Japanese weevils during their active periods. I find Diazinon very effective on weevil grubs in containers without damaging the plants. It has been suggested that bantams kept amongst rhododendrons during the summer will keep weevils under control. I have not tried them out so far!

Aphids

While usually only troublesome on young seedlings and rooted cuttings, larger plants out of doors may become infested during dry weather on young growth. Spray, dust or fumigate with Malathion or Diazinon.

Caterpillars

These have been more bothersome in recent years, probably because of our series of mild winters. I have seen young Triflorums under woodland conditions almost defoliated. Most other species can be attacked but those with soft indumentumed young leaves are special favourites. Many different species of caterpillar are responsible. As soon as damage is located, spray or where a few small plants are involved, hand pick. Suitable insecticides are Derris and Trichlorphon.

It is important to spray thoroughly on both sides and well into the unfolding young leaves so that the insecticide comes into contact with the caterpillars.

Various other insects can be troublesome, especially in warmer climates than our own. These include Rhododendron whitefly, thrips, symphyllids, scales, Rhododendron bug and even grasshoppers in California. Plants in shade are less prone to attacks from whitefly and bug. Red spider mites and thrips are more inclined to attack hardy rhododendrons being grown indoors for grafting and forcing than they are tender species. These can mostly be controlled by Malathion, Diazinon and Derris.

Naturally occurring pests

R. ungernii and other species were severely attacked by the Rhododendron bug, *Stephanitis rhododendri* in north-east Turkey when I was there in 1962, especially in the open.

Capsules of *R. nuttallii* were eaten out by grubs in north-east India in 1965 and other collectors have reported similar occurrences on different species.

A caterpillar eats the flower buds of *R. periclymenoides* in east USA but does not appear to be abundant.

No doubt other insects attack wild rhododendrons and it is important to see that these do not get introduced into gardens. Here they could become much more troublesome and destructive than is noticeable on natural plants.

DISEASES

Diseases have unfortunately become more troublesome in recent years, especially powdery mildew (see Addendum *p.* 375–6). This first appeared in the U.K. about 1982–3 and has now spread to most parts of the country. It can actually prove fatal in a few cases. The death of elms has aggravated the honey fungus problem and I have lost some newly planted items near to elm stumps.

Root rot (wilt) Phytophthora sp. particularly cinnamoni

Much has been written and said on this disease in recent years. It is always worst where high temperatures are combined with over abundant moisture. The increased use of containers for growing many types of plants has led to its overall spread.

Many factors can encourage this killer such as bad drainage, over-watering, the over-use of the weedkillers Casoron G and Prefix and root damage by eelworms (nematodes). The usual symptoms are a dulling and yellowing of the foliage followed by wilting and subsequent death.

It has been stated that *R. ponticum* and *griersonianum* are particularly susceptible as are species from high elevations while selected clones of certain species such as *racemosum, delavayi, sidereum* and even *ponticum* have shown some resistance. Rhododendrons can be infected even when not showing visual aerial symptoms. Thus with well-drained soils plus cool conditions, they may be infected, yet show no symptoms, but if these same plants are moved to poorly drained, hot locations, they may succumb. These 'carriers' may show browning of the root tips.

Control Improve drainage, avoid over-watering especially during high temperatures. Many new chemicals are being released which show promise in controlling this problem. Two new systematic fungicides are Dynone (Prothiocarb) and Aaterra (Etridiazole). Both are fairly safe to use, the former as a drench, the latter for use in composts. Nina and Aliette (both May and Baker) are also new. These are claimed to be capable of killing the pathogen completely. Other materials are Dexon, Fongarid (Furalaxyl) and Terrazole. Control eelworm with Nemagon or Nemafos (Thionazin). This is best done when the soil temperature is above 18 °C (65°F) and water in heavily as it must penetrate the soil thoroughly.

Stem and tip blight or die-back (Phytophthora cactorum)

Leaves become discoloured and wilt and stems wilt and shrivel. This can spread through a whole bush. Does not seem to be troublesome in Britain although always plant away from plants susceptible to the disease, such as lilacs.

Control Good drainage and sanitation. Prune out infected wood and allow in more air and light. Various fungicides may be applied after flowering especially copper fungicides. Crown rot is caused by a related fungus *P. crytogea*; infected plants should be removed with the surrounded soil and all destroyed; the larger species are apparently more susceptible.

Honey fungus (Armillaria mellea or Armillariella)

This is a very troublesome fungus in Britain, especially the wetter areas like west Scotland and south-west England. It seems that some form of damage such as caused by waterlogging, drought, windshake, scythe, spade or mowing machine, is necessary before the fungus can enter the plant. While only parts of plants may die, the commonest characteristic symptoms are sudden collapse and death, often during the growing season. This disease usually only strikes within the area covered by the dead roots of tree stumps or effected trees. The tell-tale fructifications may be seen on or some distance away from the actual stumps in the late autumn. The fungus spreads by long underground brown or black bootlace-like strands called rhizomorphs. Experiments have shown that the disease rarely if ever attacks healthy undamaged plants in containers into which it has been deliberately introduced. Mulches of sawdust have been said to encourage attacks in certain places although there is little real experimental evidence to support this. Try to keep the health of the plants at a high state of vigour, those in good condition rarely become affected.

Control No suitable chemical has been found yet to treat rhododendrons with. Wooded areas with stumps are always the worst affected areas. All dead rhododendrons should be removed promptly, roots and all as should as many tree stumps as is practical. In very small areas it might be worth renewing the soil or sterilizing it with 2 per cent formalin.

The insertion of thick gauge black polythene about 50 cm (20 in.) deep around the root system of a bush to form a vertical wall is effective although only practical for single or small groups of plants of special value.

Petal blight

Commonest on evergreen (Obtusum) azaleas, but may attack large rhododendrons during wet or damp spells. Brown spots develop on the flowers which spread, turning the whole flower to pulp which sticks to leaves and branches and looks very unsightly. Grey mould (botrytis) may produce similar symptoms and is far commoner. Also indoors.

Control   Avoid overhead watering during flowering. Various fungicides may help the control including Benlate (Benomyl) applied once a week during wet weather. Heavy mulches may stop the spores from developing out of the resting bodies although it is best to remove any old leaves with flowers sticking to them before mulching. Apply a fungicidal spray to the mulch. Indoors use a fungicidal smoke.

Rusts

Different groups of rhododendrons are attacked by different rusts and often have alternate hosts, especially *Picea* and *Ledum* sp. Luckily, some have not yet been introduced and those that have been are not at present widespread in cultivation anyway. The one most commonly met with usually attacks *cinnabarinum* and its hybrids and is especially prevalent in Cornwall. Rusts occur as patches of loose orange powder on the leaf undersides. Another rust affects the native *macrophyllum* in western North America. Only certain rhododendrons are susceptible to each species of rust.

Control   Affected plants or leaves should either be burnt or the disease should be treated with fungicides such as Benlate or Flowers of Sulphur until eradicated. Always thoroughly inspect plants or cuttings with *cinnabarinum* blood from outside sources on arrival. Plant susceptible varieties (in an infected area) away from ledums and American spruces and plant in open well aerated locations.

Bud blast

Much fuss was made of this disease some years ago but the true disease is rarely troublesome as it only affects a few rhododendrons, mainly those with *caucasicum* or *ponticum* blood in them. It is most frequent in old neglected collections. Does not occur in areas with heavy atmospheric pollution from sulphur and soot. W. R. Sykes noticed a little bud blast on *arboreum* during the monsoon in Nepal. This disease may largely occur as a secondary attack and is usually encouraged by poor husbandry. It is probably spread by a leaf hopper.

Control   If serious, spray against the leaf hopper and with a fungicide such as one containing sulphur, against the disease. Normally, the collection of dead buds and burning them gives adequate control.

Leaf spot

This may be caused by one of at least fifteen different pathogens but is only really serious in areas such as parts of eastern North America and in old neglected collections. Usually caused by too much moisture, shade or poor root conditions.

Control   Improve drainage on heavy soils, thin out overhanging trees or branches and reduce insect attack. Spray with Zineb or a related fungicide immediately buds burst and at 10 to 14 day intervals thereafter.

Cylindrocladum wilt and blight

This is another disease which appears where temperatures are high and is especially serious on azaleas in the USA. Sclerotia or black bodies are formed on the leaves and these in turn produce conidial spores that infest and kill the roots.

Control   A similar procedure as with petal blight is recommended.

Mildew See Addendum *p.* 329.

Common on azaleas in America especially on *luteum* and *occidentale* and also attacks rhododendron seedlings to which it can prove fatal. Eastern American azaleas show high levels of resistance.

Control   Benlate or Karathane used according to instructions or spray with wettable sulphur.

Botrytis grey mould

This is the worst killer of young seedlings that I know and once it attacks boxes of seedlings, it is rather difficult to stop it spreading and killing most of them. It can also attack frosted young growth as a secondary parasite. Slight injury in otherwise healthy stock can be aggravated by colonization by grey mould. *Pestalotia* attack resembles grey mould and also follows winter damage, sun scald or mechanical injury to leaves.

Control   Avoid feeding late in the season or the use of slow release fertilizers which can lead to scorch. Scorch allows mould to get a start. Adequate hygiene, light and ventilation both winter and summer are most important in avoiding this trouble on seedlings. Captan, Rovral (Iprodione) or Benlate sprayed on the foliage regularly are a great help. Avoid watering in the evening or on dull days. Remove badly frosted growth in spring as this may even start botrytis on old leaves underneath.

Leaf spot and stem disease

Lophodermium maculare was first reported in Scotland in 1937 and grows on Vaccinium, *L. rhododendri* on *ponticum* and allies and *L. vagulum* on Chinese rhododendrons. These are fairly widespread but do little real damage except on neglected collections.

Control   Treat as leaf spot.

Crown gall Agrobacterium tumaefacens

An uncommon bacteral disease forming enlarged tumor-like swellings; this bacterium attacks a whole range of garden plants.

Control   Cut out gall with sharp knife and treat with a proprietary wound dressing. Mulch and encourage vigorous growth to bring natural callus formation.

Damping off

Various fungi cause stem rots at the soil level when young plants are overcrowded and over-watered, and are grown in poorly aerated and illuminated conditions. A general fungicide can be applied before planting.

Exobasidum leaf gall

Pick off young galls and destroy, spray before the leaves unfurl, either with Ferban or Zineb. These galls may be found in greenhouse or outdoors.

Naturally occurring diseases

Several diseases or strains of diseases occur on wild rhododendrons in various parts of the world which have so far not been introduced or have not become established in cultivation. It is important for us to make sure that these are not introduced on live collected material. Examples are the rust already mentioned on *macrophyllum* in western North America; also 'Blister blight' (*Exobasidum* sp.) attacks *arboreum* and *johnstoneanum* in Manipur, *rubiginosum* and *decorum* in China.

For future control of diseases, it is hoped that the up and coming systemic fungicides may be of benefit, even to the extent of prohibiting the entry of such troubles as honey fungus. Some fungicides in common use, such as Benlate, are partially systemic.

NATURAL INJURY

Bark-split

This usually results from unseasonable early autumn or late spring frosts although severe mid-winter frosts can damage the bark of tender species.

The worst type of bark-split occurs just above soil level where the whole of the bark may lift off the wood. This often results in death although some species may send up fresh shoots from ground level, even as late as the following year. These shoots need special frost protection the following one to two winters (see *p.* 49 and 76). Bark-split is not always noticeable for some days or weeks after the frost has done its damage as the bark only starts to peel back when it begins to dry out. It can also occur up the stems to well above the ground.

Little can be done once the bark is split other than applying a protective paint to prevent the entry of fungal or insect attack. I have found that taping the wound to be of little help. One suggestion is to wrap clay around the split and bind this with hessian or another binding material. This would have to be done immediately after the frost before the bark starts peeling.

To help prevent basal bark-split, try mounding up soil around the stems or trunks on susceptible species, remembering to remove it again in the spring once the dangers of frost are over. Various mulching materials could also be used such as 7.5–10 cm (3–4 in.) of wood chips (see *p.* 78). Any of the following suggestions are worth a trial. Wrap soft fibreglass around the stems. Nothing eats it and it helps to keep the stem at an even temperature. Cover the base of the stems with a mulch of polystyrene foam but it might be difficult to dispose of this in the spring. Paint stems with the cheapest white latex paint. The white paint reflects the light and minimises rapid temperature fluctuations known to be responsible for much of the bark-splitting that occurs. Wrap anti-rot treated paper or burlap around the stems.

Bud and growth damage

Both leaf and flower buds are very vulnerable to sudden early autumn frosts, particularly after a warm, moist spell. Aborted growth buds and partly killed flower buds may result. Spring frosts can cause all sorts of distortions to young growth as soon as growth buds start to elongate (see photograph, 53). Very badly frosted young growth is best sprayed or totally removed (see *p.* 329 on diseases). These damaged shoots are usually replaced without difficulty provided there is no severe bark-split or destruction of secondary buds by early autumn frosts.

Chlorosis

This can be caused by over-wet or over-dry conditions at the roots, in addition to the lack of some essential major or minor element in the soil. Deficiences and toxicities are hard to treat. A professional soil analysis is recommended.

8 Recommended Lists

These lists should only be used as a rough guide, bearing in mind that many species are extremely variable in such characters as hardiness, flower colour and stature. Also they can behave in different ways in various parts of the world. Closely related species to those included may have been omitted but may be of equal value horticulturally. Where individual species vary very much in their merits, those listed refer to superior forms. Some former species now classed as sub-species, varieties or synonyms are left under the former name for easier reference. Many listed are not at present available from nurseries but hopefully will become so.

Easy species

augustinii, calendulaceum, catawbiense, dauricum, decorum, fictolacteum, japonicum, luteum, maximum, occidentale, oreotrephes, ponticum, rubiginosum, vernicosum, wardii L&S, yunnanense.

Hardiest

brachycarpum, catawbiense, dauricum, fortunei, maximum, micranthum, mucronulatum, prezwalskii, prinophyllum, schlippenbachii, smirnowii, viscosum.

Heat tolerant

arboreum (lowland), *catawbiense* Insularis Group, *championiae, fortunei, irroratum* ssp. *kontumense, japonicum, korthalsii, macrophyllum, oblongifolium, ovatum, ponticum* (lowland), *serrulatum, simiarum, stamineum, tashiroi, westlandii, wrayi.*

Lime tolerant

ambiguum, decorum, fargesii, fortunei, insigne, lutescens, rubiginosum, traillianum, vernicosum.

Species for the smaller woodland garden

augustinii, bakeri, campylocarpum, Concatenans, *luteum, mucronulatum, orbiculare, oreotrephes, souliei, thomsonii, wardii L&S, yunnanense.*

For the connoisseur

adenosum, cerasinum, crinigerum, exasperatum, hirtipes, hookeri, insigne, keysii, lacteum, lanatum, lanigerum, martinianum, pudorosum, sherriffii, spinuliferum, taliense, thayerianum, venator, wiltonii.

My choice (limited to 12)

aberconwayi, bureavii, hemsleyanum, lindleyi, niveum, occidentale, pachysanthum, schlippenbachii, souliei, thomsonii, wardii, yunnanense.

Large growing for cool climates (to −18°C (0°F)

arboreum (pink and white), *argyrophyllum, calendulaceum, calophytum, fulvum, galactinum, occidentale, oreodoxa, sutchuenense, rex, ungernii, watsonii.*

Large growing for mildest British climates and similar (to −10°C (14°F)

arboreum (red), *delavayi, diaprepes, grande, griffithianum, kyawi, magnificum, montroseanum, protistum, sinogrande.*

Early flowering

barbatum, calophytum, Cubittii Group, *dauricum, eclecteum, fulgens, glischroides, grande, hirtipes, kendrickii, lanigerum, lutescens, mallotum, meddianum* var. *atrokermesinum, mucronulatum, oreodoxa, protistum, ririei, sherriffii, stewartianum, strigillosum, sutchuenense, succothii, uvarifolium.*

Late flowering

amagianum, arborescens, auriculatum, discolor, griersonianum, heliolepis, hemsleyanum, insigne, kyawi, maddenii, maximum, micranthum, occidentale, serrulatum, serotinum, thayerianum, ungernii, zelanicum.

Free flowering

anhweiense, catawbiense, davidsonianum, dauricum, formosum, fulvum, griersonianum, johnstoneanum, irroratum, morii, occidentale, oreodoxa, ponticum, rigidum, rubiginosum, souliei, yunnanense.

Best red to crimsons

arboreum (red), *barbatum, cinnabarinum roylei, concinnum* Pseudoyanthinum, *elliottii, facetum, fulgens, griersonianum, hookeri, kyawi, lanigerum* (red), *mallotum, meddianum* var. *atrokermesinum, prunifolium, spinuliferum, strigillosum, thomsonii, venator.*

Best pinks

anhweiense, argyrophyllum, crinigerum, davidsonianum, fulvum, hodgsonii (pink), *insigne, montroseanum, orbiculare, oreodoxa, principis, prinophyllum, schlippenbachii, souliei, sutchuenense, vaseyi, vernicosum, wiltonii.*

Best whites and creams

aberconwayi, annae (laxiflorum), auriculatum, calophytum (white), *decorum, falconeri, fictolacteum, hemsleyanum, irroratum, lindleyi, megacalyx, morii, occidentale, phaeochrysum, puralbum, quinquefolium, rigidum, sphaeroblastum, taggianum, yunnanense.*

Best lavender to purple

augustinii, campanulatum, floribundum, hodgsonii (purple forms), *niveum, reticulatum, ririei, rubiginosum (desquamatum), wallichii.*

Best yellow and orange shades

campylocarpum, Concatenans, *dalhousiae, lacteum, lanatum, lutescens, luteum, macabeanum, sidereum, wardii, wightii, xanthocodon.*

Variable coloured species

arizelum, calendulaceum, cerasinum, eclecteum, flammeum, lanigerum, occidentale, stewartianum.

Best flowers

aberconwayi, arboreum, augustinii, cinnabarinum, griersonianum, griffithianum, insigne, macabeanum, montroseanum, nuttallii, rubiginosum (desquamatum), schlippenbachii, souliei, taggianum, wardii, yunnanense.

Best azaleas

albrechtii, calendulaceum, japonicum, luteum, occidentale, pentaphyllum, prunifolium, quinquefolium, reticulatum, schlippenbachii, vaseyi.

Largest leaves

auriculatum, basilicum, calophytum, grande, griffithianum, hemsleyanum, magnificum, montroseanum, nuttallii, praestans, prattii, protistum, rex, sinogrande, ungernii, uvarifolium.

Best foliage

adenogynum, arizelum, basilicum, bureavii, clementinae, Concatenans, *eximium, falconeri, glischroides, hemsleyanum, hodgsonii, longes-*

quamatum, macabeanum, mallotum, nuttallii, orbiculare, pachysanthum, rex, sinogrande, sphaeroblastum, strigillosum, ungernii, watsonii, wiltonii.

Glaucous foliage

atlanticum, campanulatum (some), *cinnabarinum, clementinae,* Concatenans, *cyanocarpum, fulgens, genestierianum, luteum* (some), *oreotrephes, souliei, thomsonii, wardii* (some).

Finest young foliage

campanulatum (some), *clementinae, coriaceum, elegantulum, exasperatum, eximium, leptothrium, lutescens, macabeanum, nuttallii, pachysanthum, protistum, rex, sinogrande, argipeplum, thomsonii, uvarifolium.*

Best indumentum

arboreum ssp. *cinnamomeum, arizelum, bureavii, elegantulum, eximium, falconeri, fictolacteum, fulvum, lanatum, mallotum, pachysanthum, phaeochrysum, sherriffii, traillianum.*

Best bark

arboreum, barbatum, falconeri, faucium (hylaeum), fulgens, griffithianum, hodgsonii, argipeplum, stenaulum, subansiriense, succothii, thomsonni, triflorum, zelanicum.

Best Maddeniis

dalhousiae, dendricola (ciliicalyx), inaequale, lindleyi, maddenii, megacalyx, nuttallii, rhabdotum, taggianum, veitchianum.

Scented

arborescens, auriculatum, coxianum, decorum, fortunei, griffithianum, inaequale, lindleyi, luteum, maddenii, megacalyx, nuttallii (some), *occidentale, stenaulum, taggianum, viscosum.*

Autumn colour

calendulaceum, luteum, nipponicum, occidentale, pentaphyllum, prinophyllum, quinquefolium, schlippenbachii, semibarbatum.

Newly introduced

bhutanense, coxianum, ellipiticum, excellens, formosanum, hemsleyanum, hongkongense, kesangiae, levinei, liliiflorum, ludwigianum, pachysanthum, sanctum, subansiriense, tashiroi, walongense, westlandii, wrayi.

Appendix A

LIST OF RHODODENDRON SOCIETIES

AUSTRALIA: Australian Rhododendron Society, Mrs L. Eaton, P.O. Box 21, Olinda, Victoria, 3788, Australia.
The International Rhododendron Union, Hon. Membership Secretary, c/o 67 Strabane Avenue, Box Hill North, Australia 3129.

CANADA: Rhododendron Society of Canada, Dr H. G. Hedges, 4271 Lakeshore Rd, Burlington, Ont., Canada.

CHINA: Chinese Rhododendron Society, Prof. Feng Guomei (K. M. Feng), Kunming Institute of Botany Academia Sinica, Heilongtan, Kunming, Yunnan, China.

DENMARK: The Danish Chapter of the American Rhododendron Society, Ole. Packendah, Hejrebakken 3, DK 3500 Vaerloese, Denmark.

GERMANY: German Rhododendron Society, Dr L. Heft, Rhododendron Park, 28 Bremen 17, Marcusallee 60, West Germany.

GREAT BRITAIN: The Rhododendron and Camellia Group of the R.H.S., Hon. Secretary, Mrs B. Jackson, 2 Essex Court, Temple, London EC4Y 9AP, England.
The Scottish Rhododendron Society (Scottish Chapter of the American Rhododendron Society), Mr Hubert Andrew, Stron Ailne, Colintrave, Argyll PA22 3AS, Scotland.

JAPAN: Japanese Rhododendron Society, Teruo Takeuchi, 8–5, 2-chome Goshozuka, Takatsuk, Kawasaki, Japan.

NEW ZEALAND: New Zealand Rhododendron Association, P.O. Box 28, Palmerston North, New Zealand.
Dunedin Rhododendron Group, S. J. Grant, 25 Pollack St, Dunedin, New Zealand.

SWEDEN: The Swedish Rhododendron Society, Botaniska Trådgården, Carl Skothsbergs Gata 22, 41319 Goteborg, Sweden.

USA: The American Rhododendron Society, Executive Secretary, 14885 S.W. Sunrise Lane, Tigard, OR 97224, USA.
Pacific Rhododendron Society, P.O. Box 297. Puyallup, WA 98371, USA.
The Rhododendron Species Foundation, P.O. Box 3798, Federal Way, WA 98003, USA.

Appendix B

Great Britain

Burncoose & South Down Nurseries, Gwennap, Redruth, Cornwall TR16 6BJ.

Glendoick Gardens Ltd, Glencarse, Perth PH2 7NS, Scotland.

Hydon Nurseries Ltd, Clock Barn Lane, Hydon Heath, nr. Godalming, Surrey GU8 4AZ.

Leonardslee Gardens Nurseries, Lower Beeding, Horsham, Sussex RH13 6PP.

Millais Nurseries, Crosswater Farm, Churt, Farnham, Surrey GU10 2JN.

Reuthe Ltd, Crown Point Nursery, Ightham, nr. Sevenoaks, Kent TN15 0HB.

Wall Cottage Nursery, Lockengate, Bugle, St Austell, Cornwall.

Continental Europe

Firma C. Esveld, Rijneveld 72, 2771 XS, Boskoop, Holland.

Tue Jorgensen, Rijvej 10, DK 2830, Virum, Denmark.

Joh. Wieting, Omorikastrasse 6, 1910 Gieselhorst, Westerstede 1, West Germany.

Pieter Zwijnenburg Jr., Halve Raak 18, 2771 AD Boskoop, Holland.

Australia

Lapoinya Rhodo Gardens, R.S.D. 106A, Lapoinya, Tasmania, 7325.

New Zealand

Cross Hills Gardens, R.D. 54, Kimbolton.

Riverwood Gardens, Main Road, Little River, Banks Peninsula.

USA

Benjamins Rhododendrons, 18402–A North Tapps Highway, Sumner, WA 98390.

The Bovee Nursery, 1737 S.W. Coronado Street, Portland, OR 97219.

Eastern Plant Specialities, Dept. R, P.O. Box 40, Colonia, NJ 07067.

Ellanhurst Gardens, Rt. 3, Box 233–b, Sherwood, OR 97140.

Greer Gardens, 1280 Goodpasture Island Rd, Eugene, OR 97401.
Stan & Dody Hall, 1280 Quince Drive, Junction City, OR 97448.
Mowbray Gardens, 3318 Mowbray Lane, Cincinnati, OH 45226.
North Coast Rhododendron Nursery, P.O. Box 308, Bodega, CA 94922.
Rhododendron Species Foundation, Box 3798, Federal Way, WA 98063.
Sonoma Horticultural Nursery, 3970 Azalea Avenue, Sebastopol, CA 95472.
The Greenery, 14450 N.E. 16th Place, Bellevue, WA 98007.
Trillium Lane Nursery, 18855 Trillium Lane, Fert Bragg, CA 95437.
Van Veen Nursery, 4201 Franklin Street, P.O. Box 06444, Portland, OR 97206.
Westgate Gardens Nursery, 751 Westgate Drive, Eureka, CA.
Whitney Gardens, P.O. Box F, Brinnon, WA 98320.

Glossary

The definitions given here apply to use of terms in this book.

aberrant characteristics different from type
agglutinate indumentum glued or joined together
appressed lying flat
axillary in angle of leaf and stem (below terminal bud)
bullate blistered or puckered
capitellate having a small head
chlorosis leaves partly or wholly pale green or yellow
chromosome rod-like objects in a cell-nucleus which hold hereditary characteristics. In multiples of thirteen in rhododendrons
ciliate fringed with hairs
cline plants that merge with every gradation between them
clone the vegetatively produced progeny of a single individual
contiguous neighbouring parts in contact
coriaceous leathery
cotyledon seed leaf
cultivar a cultivated variety as opposed to other varieties
dendroid hairs hairs tree-like in form
eglandular destitute of glands
elepidote without scales
epiphyte growing on another plant without being parasitic
evanescent soon disappearing
exserted projecting beyond (stamens from corolla)
fasciculate hairs hairs clustered from one point
flavonoid certain natural colouring compounds in a plant
floccose bearing loose-tufted soft wool
gene the inheritance of a given unit character
glabrescent becoming glabrous
glabrous hairless
gland a protuberance on leaves and other parts, often secreting and viscid
glandular possessing glands
glaucous greyish-blue; covered with bluish or grey bloom
grex all the seedlings of one cross in hybridizing
hirsute with rather coarse or long hairs
hybrid swarm a large group of natural hybrids in the wild showing much variation
indemic native of a specified country or area only
indumentum a woolly or hairy covering found on leaves
inflorescence the flowers arising from one bud
lepidote covering of small scurfy scales
morphological the study of living plants or their parts
mucronate a sharply pointed tip (to leaf)

nectar pouches or *nectary* a nectar secreting gland at base of corolla
nodal the part of a stem where a leaf is attached
papillate soft superficial glands or protuberances
perulae leaf-bud scales
plastered indumentum indumentum stuck down having a smooth finish
polyploid having more than the usual number of chromosomes
potter's thumb mark indentations like a thumb mark
precocious flowering before the leaves appear
puberulous slightly covered with short soft hairs
pubescent clothed with short soft hairs
punctate with translucent or coloured dots or depressior.s
punctulate minutely punctate
radiate hairs hairs spreading from a common centre
reflexed abruptly bent backwards or downwards
reticulate like a network
rugose wrinkled or rough
rugulose slightly wrinkled or rough
scabrid somewhat rough
scale small disc-like dots found on leaves, shoots and flower parts
serrulate minutely saw-toothed
sessile not stalked
setose covered with bristles
splitting indumentum indumentum dividing into patches
spreading limb outward expanding petal lobes of a tubular flower
stipitate having a stalk
stoloniferous sending out suckers from the main plant
strigose clothed with sharp pointed appressed bristle-like hairs
taxa unit of classification
taxonomic classification
terminal tip of a shoot (bud)
tomentum dense woolly pubescence (on all parts except leaves)
triploid three sets of chromosomes
ventricose enlarged on one side
vestige the remaining trace of an organ
villous-tomentose clad with long weak hairs
viscid sticky from a secretion or coating
water sprouts long, vigorous, sappy shoots

Bibliography

BEAN, W. J., *Trees and Shrubs Hardy in the British Isles*, Vol. III, 8th Revised Edition, John Murray, London, 1976.

CHAMBERLAIN, D. F., *Notes from the Royal Botanic Garden, Edinburgh, Vol. 39, No. 2, Revision of Rhododendron II, Subgenus Hymenanthes*. Her Majesty's Stationery Office, 1982.

COX, E. H. M., *Farrer's Last Journey*, Dulau, London, 1926.

COX, P. A., *Dwarf Rhododendrons*, Batsford, London, 1973.

COX, P. A., *The Larger Species of Rhododendron*, 1st Edition, Batsford, London, 1979.

COX, P. A., *The Smaller Rhododendrons*, Batsford, London, 1985.

CROIZAT, L., *Manual of Phytogeography*, Uitgeverij Dr. W. Junk, The Hague, 1952.

CULLEN, J., *Notes from the Royal Botanic Garden, Edinburgh, Vol. 39, No. 1, Revision of Rhododendron I, Subgenus Rhododendron, sections Rhododendron & Pogonanthum*. Her Majesty's Stationery Office, 1980.

DAVIDIAN, H. H., *The Rhododendron Species, Vol. I, Lepidotes*, Batsford, London, 1982.

DAVIDIAN, H. H., *The Rhododendron Species, Vol. II, Part I, Elepidotes*, Batsford, London, 1989.

FANG, WENPEI (edited), *Sichuan Rhododendron of China*, Science Press, Beijing, 1986.

FENG, GUOMEI (edited), *Rhododendrons of China Vol. I*, Science Press, Beijing, 1988 Batsford, London, 1989.

FENG, GUOMEI, *Rhododendrons of Yunnan*, title and text in Chinese script, 1981; 2nd ed. 1983.

GOOD, RONALD, *The Geography of Flowering Plants*, Longman, Green and Co., 1947, since reprinted.

GREER, H. E., *Greer's Guidebook to Available Rhododendrons*, Revised 2nd Edition, Offshoot Publications, Eugene, 1988.

HOOKER, J. D., *Himalayan Journals*, Ward Lock, Bowden Co., London, Melbourne, New York.

HOSIE, SIR A., *On the Trail of the Opium Poppy*, Vol. I and II, George Philip & Son, London 1914.

HUNTINGDON, E., *The Pulse of Asia*, Houghton Mifflin C., Boston & New York, 1919.

KEHR, A., 'Research – What's New in '72', AMRS–QB, Oct. 1972, pp. 223–34.

KINGDON WARD, F., *A Plant Hunter in Tibet*, Jonathan Cape, London, 1934.

KINGDON, WARD, F., *Plant Hunters Paradise*, Jonathan Cape, London, 1937.

KINGDON WARD, F. *Return to the Irrawaddy*, Andrew Melrose, London, 1956.

LEACH, D. G., *Rhododendrons of the World*, Allen & Unwin, London, 1962.

LEPPIK, E. E., 'Evolutionary interactions between Rhododendrons, Pollinating Insects and Rust Fungi', *AMRS–QB*, April 1974, pp. 70–89.

LESLIE, A. (compiler), *The Rhododendron Handbook, 1980, Species in cultivation*, The Royal Horticultural Society, London, 1980.

MILLAIS, J. G., *Rhododendrons and the Various Hybrids,* Longmans, Green & Co. London, 1917.

MILLAIS, J. G., *Rhododendrons and the Various Hybrids Second Series,* Longmans, Green & Co. London, 1924.

PHILIPSON, W. R., *Notes from the Royal Botanic Garden, Edinburgh*, 1973.

STAINTON, J. D. A., *Forests of Nepal*, John Murray, London 1972.

URQUHART, B. LESLIE, *The Rhododendron*, Vol. I, The Leslie Urquhart Press, Sharpthorne, Sussex, 1958.

YOUNG, J., & LU-SHENG CHONG (translated), *Rhododendrons of China*, Binford & More, Portland, 1980.

Periodicals and Year Books

AMERICAN RHODODENDRON SOCIETY, *Quarterly Bulletin*, Portland, Oregon, 1947–81.

AMERICAN RHODODENDRON SOCIETY, *Quarterly Journal*, Portland, Oregon, 1982 onwards.

ROYAL HORTICULTURAL SOCIETY, *Rhododendron Year Book*, London 1946–53.

ROYAL HORTICULTURAL SOCIETY, *Rhododendron and Camellia Year Book*, 1954–71.

ROYAL HORTICULTURAL SOCIETY, *Rhododendrons*, 1972–3.

ROYAL HORITCULTURAL SOCIETY, *Rhododendrons with Magnolias and Camellias*, 1974 onwards.

Addendum

Introduction: changes since 1979

Most of the new species and changes in status in this addendum have been described by the Chinese. There is an overall tendency amongst Chinese taxonomists to be 'splitters', resulting in a number of taxa that we do not recognize in Britain. Many of these taxa have been described off just one or two herbarium specimens and from botanical characters that are horticulturally of little or no significance. It is unfortunate that with their relatively easy access to wild locations, they have not made more use of what I would term 'horticultural' characters such as bark, growth habit, flowering and growth periods, poise of foliage and the difference if any between juvenile and adult foliage. For example, the new taxa in the Heliolepida subsection all appear to me to have nothing to separate them horticulturally from existing taxa but on the other hand, some could have important characters that are not included in the Chinese descriptions. Also, I am rather suspicious of some of their suggested relationships. They may say how a taxon differs from one given species, when it is clear in our minds that it is more closely related to another species or even synonymous with it.

These criticisms of Chinese taxonomic work are supposed to be constructive rather than destructive. Many Chinese botanists are now coming over to Britain and spending several months in British herbaria. This should result in much more of a consensus of opinion on classification between the British and Chinese. I believe it is a question of deciding which characters are most important in rhododendron taxonomy. I feel that the Chinese have been giving too much emphasis to characters like presence to absence of different types of hairs on flower parts, leaves and branchlets, and also to some extent size and shape of flowers, leaves etc. It could be true to say that different characters are of importance in different subsections. It all ends up by being just an individual taxonomist's or horticulturalist's matter of opinion and everyone who claims to have any knowledge of the subject will come up with different conclusions.

The descriptions vary considerably in length. Those species recently described, but not in cultivation, are just given a few lines. Those newly introduced are dealt with at greater length as are species I have been able to study myself in the wild or in my own collection.

ARBOREA SUBSECTION

arboreum Wight 1850

It is well-known what an extremely variable species this is and my own observations in the wild in east Nepal, Bhutan, north-east India and Yunnan have given me a fairly good idea of the overall complexity of this species. Any attempts to divide this species into separate species as Davidian has done in *The Rhododendron Species, Volume II, Part 1*, or to divide it into subspecies and varieties as in Chamberlain's *Revision of Rhododendron 11, Subgenus Hymenanthes*, may be useful horticulturally but are unsatisfactory taxonomically apart from those isolated geographically. The variation in foliage in Bhutan was quite astonishing and made a mockery of any attempt to pigeon-hole them into separate taxa. I accept the classification of Chamberlain as making the best compromise of a difficult problem.

arboreum ssp. *delavayi* (Franch. 1886) Chamb. See *p.* 96

There is some argument as to how far west this subspecies occurs. Chamberlain gives it as Meghalaya, Assam and Arunachal Pradesh and var. *peramoenum* to Arunachal Pradesh. I would agree that the apparently uniform population that I saw in Meghalaya (around Shillong) is closer to ssp. *delavayi* than to low-elevation *arboreum* as found in east Nepal and Bhutan. Long has included ssp. *delavayi* as occurring in Bhutan and herbarium specimens from east Bhutan do resemble this subspecies. Plants I saw in west and central Bhutan, with spongy indumentum, were scattered amongst others with plastered indumentum with no uniform population apparent so it would appear that from central Bhutan westwards to east Nepal, *arboreum* as a whole is at its most variable with relatively stable populations to the east and west. There is no doubt that *arboreum* and its subspecies and their varieties all merge with considerable overlapping and mixing in some areas.

arboreum ssp. *delavayi* var. *albotomentosum* Davidian 1989

KW 21976 (see *p.* 96). I think that Davidian has been correct in giving this distinct form varietal status although collections would need to be made in Thailand and other neighbouring areas to ascertain how distinct it is. It does have particularly white indumentum and usually smaller leaves than the type.

arboreum ssp. *delavayi* var. *pilostylum* K. M. Feng 1983

Only seems to differ from the type by its floccose base to style. Yunnan, 1,550 m (5,000 ft).

ARGYROPHYLLA SUBSECTION

argyrophyllum ssp. *hejeiangense* Fang 1983. Not in cultivation

Differs from the type in its glabrous branchlets, inconspicuous leaf veins, shorter pedicels, more flowers to the truss and fewer glabrous stamens (8–10). Szechwan, 740–1,740 m (2,250–5,500 ft).

argyrophyllum ssp. *omeiense*, see *p.* 101.

This was introduced from Mt Omei in 1980. Leaves are smaller and narrower than the type. First flowered 1988 with small white flowers. We are not finding it very easy to grow so far.

ebianense Fang f.1986. Not in cultivation

Differs from *argyrophyllum* in its fairly large calyx and stout pedicels. Unlikely to be of any special merit or distinction. Illustrated in *Sichuan Rhododendron of China*, *p.* 123–5. Only found wild in Ebian county in southwestern Szechwan in thickets at around 1,600 m (5,250 ft).

fangchengense Tam 1983. Not in cultivation

Closely related to *simiarum* but differing in its long and narrow leaves, inflor about 10 and style densely pubescent at base. Kwangsi. Little known.

longipes, see *p.* 106.

Davidian reckons this is closely related to *argyrophyllum*, differing in its long acuminate leaf apex. The photographs in *Sichuan Rhododendron of China* (*p.* 118–9) show these narrow, pointed leaves and quite attractive rose-coloured flowers. South-central Szechwan, 2,000–2,500 m (6,500–8,250 ft).

longipes var. *chienianum*, see *p.* 106.

Davidian and the Chinese give this specific status. The photographs in *Sichuan Rhododendron of China* show a plant with much wider leaves than *longipes* and with a yellowish-brown thicker indumentum. The flowers look quite good. South-east Szechwan.

pingianum, see *p.* 106. Not in cultivation

I thought that this close relation of *argyrophyllum* was introduced from Mt Omei in 1980 by Keith Rushforth but the seedlings which first flowered in 1987 do not agree with the description of *pingianum*. The main difference is in the ovary which is white floccose in *argyrophyllum* (really just appearing green on these Rushforth introductions) and is densely rufous-tomentose in *pingianum*. Edward Millais reports seeing *pingianum* in flower on Mt Omei with a distinctly deeper purplish tinge. So it appears that *pingianum* has still to be introduced.

simiarum var. *deltoideum* Tam 1983. Not in cultivation

Differs from *simiarum* in its purplish-red flowers and its disc-like calyx with triangular reflexed lobes. Kwangtung (Hainan only) 1,840 m (6,000 ft).

BARBATA SUBSECTION

argipeplum Balf.f. & Cooper 1916 (*smithii* Hook.f. non Sweet, *macro-smithii* (Davidian))

There has been a good deal of confusion in recent years between *argipeplum* and *smithii*. Chamberlain sank *argipeplum* into *smithii* in 1982. Since then he has realized that this was a mistake; but it has also been found that *smithii* is an invalid name and has to go anyway, which is perhaps convenient. Davidian, who has also realized the invalidity of *smithii* but wishes to retain the plant at specific status, has called it *macrosmithii*.

The plant we have regarded as *smithii* in cultivation has leaves closely resembling *barbatum* apart from a thin usually discontinuous indumentum on the leaf lower surface. The plant that we have been regarding as *argipeplum* has a broader leaf with a distinctive cordulate base. The former plant comes from Sikkim while the latter is found in south Tibet and Arunachal Pradesh. In between, in Bhutan, are to be found numerous populations with leaves varying (often within one population) from near *smithii* to *argipeplum* as we have known them, though none were seen with the cordulate base so prominent. The colour of the indumentum varied from buff to white and in density. Most of what we saw could be placed in either taxa so it is obviously incorrect to retain *smithii (macrosmithii)* as a separate species. There is an overlap in distribution between *argipeplum* and the closely related *barbatum* from Sikkim to central Bhutan.

BOOTHIA SUBSECTION

leptocarpum Nutt. 1854 (*micromeres* Tagg 1931) (see *p.* 138)

David Long of the RBG, Edinburgh has decided that the herbarium specimen labelled *leptocarpum* equals *micromeres* and as *leptocarpum* was named much earlier, it takes precedence over *micromeres*. The specimen of *leptocarpum* was collected by Booth in Arunachal Pradesh.

CAMPANULATA SUBSECTION

aeruginosum Hook. 1849 (see *p.* 141)

Davidian has changed the status of this plant from Chamberlain's subspecies to full species as described by Hooker. It was known from 1949 to 1982 as *campanulatum* var. *aeruginosum*. I agree with Davidian that this is better at full specific rank. Chamberlain did not give it specific rank due to apparent intermediary plants between this and ssp. *campanulatum* in east Nepal and Sikkim. There are also herbarium specimens classified under *wallichii* that look closely related to ssp. *aeruginosum* (see *The Smaller Rhododendrons p.* 155 for description).

jorgensenii Davidian 1989

Here is a doubtful species if there ever was one. Davidian says it was first collected by Stainton under *S.* 245 in the Arun Valley, east Nepal in 1956 and then says that it was possibly introduced by Stainton, Sykes and Williams which I believe impossible. For one thing *SS&W* collected in central Nepal 1954; and for another, *wallichii*, with which this plant is undoubtedly synonymous, only occurs in east Nepal, through Bhutan and just into south Tibet and east Arunachal Pradesh. The white-flowered plants that he based this so-called species on grew in the RBG, Edinburgh and no longer exist. Stainton rarely if ever collected seed while collecting on his own. Davidian writes that it is said to be uncommon in its native home. New species should not be described from one herbarium specimen and some doubtful cultivated plants of unknown provenance. It is also unwise to describe a white-flowered variant. Occasional white-flowered plants of *wallichii* occur in the wild and I have grown *wallichii* from seed collected in Sikkim with a thick leathery leaf, shiny above and a glabrous leaf underside. These characters are all that he bases this so-called new species on.

CAMPYLOCARPA SUBSECTION

henanense Fang f. 1983. Not in cultivation

Inflor 12–13, F white, campanulate. Shows some affinity with *souliei* and *callimorphum* according to Fang. Pedicel, calyx and style all eglandular which is unusual in this largely glandular subsection. Could be an interesting and hardy species, coming from Honan in central east China at around 1,800 m (6,000 ft), an area unknown to western collectors.

henanense ssp. *lingbaoense* Fang f. 1983. Not in cultivation

Differs from *henanense* in its thinner, less coriaceous smaller more slender leaves, usually oblong, apex rounded to apiculate, base rounded. Also smaller flowers. Honan.

longicalyx Fang f. 1986. Not in cultivation

This looks to me to be quite a distinct species, perhaps closest related to *souliei* but with pink campanulate flowers, 9–13 to the truss. From central western Szechwan, growing in valleys at around 2,900 m (9,500 ft).

CHONIASTRUM SECTION

The Chinese have been describing several new species and varieties in this little-known section. As so few species in this section are familiar to us, and very few of us are able to cultivate them, I have kept the descriptions to a minimum. This is not to say that many are not good species or that they are not worthy of cultivation. I endorse what I said in 1979 – that many of these should make first-rate garden subjects for those in more or less frost-free climates.

championae var. *ovalifolium* Tam 1983. Not in cultivation

F white. Differs from type in its style being sparsely puberulent at base. Kwangtung, about 750 m (2,500 ft), rare.

dentampullum Chun ex Tam 1983 (kosepangii Chun) Not in cultivation

F lilac. Similar to *cavaleriei* but differs in the 4-flowered inflor, densely pubescent calyx with 5 tooth-like lobes and the puberulous filaments. Kwangtung.

henryi var. *pubescens* K. M. Feng & A. L. Chang 1982. Not in cultivation

Differs from *henryi* in its glabrous petiole and pubescent calyx. From Malipo, Maguan and Funing, Yunnan, 1,300–1,500 m (4,500–5,000 ft) in mixed forest.

hukwangense Tam 1982 (huguangense). Not in cultivation

Related to *moulmainense* from which it differs in its setulose petioles, whitish-yellow corolla and two types of calyx.

kaliense Fang & M. Y. He 1982. Not in cultivation

Differs from *stamineum* and *moulmainense* in its much longer cylindric capsule, only 2.5–3.8 cm (1–1½ in) long in the other two species. Kweichow.

linearicupulare Tam 1983. Not in cultivation

Related to *moulmainense* from which it differs in its leaf shape and long, narrow calyx lobes. Kwangsi, 340 m (1,115 ft).

shiwandashanense Tam 1983. Not in cultivation

Related to *henryi* but differing in its non-ciliate juvenile leaves, only sparsely setose petiole, more slender glandular-setose pedicel, fimbriate calyx and ovary and base of style sparsely setulose. Kwangsi 410 m (1,300 ft).

stamineum var. *lasiocarpum* Mrs R. C. Fang & C. H. Yang 1982. Not in cultivation

Differs from type in its tomentose ovary and pubescent pedicels. From Guangnan, Yunnan, at 1,450 m (5,000 ft) in mixed forest.

subestipitatum Chun ex Tam 1983 (*brevipes* Chun)

F red. Related to *championae* but differs in its thin papery leaves, very small lobes on calyx and tomentose ovary. Kwangtung.

tutcherae var. *gymnocarpum* A. L. Chang 1982. Not in cultivation

Differs from type in its glabrous ovary and pedicels. From Yunnan, 1,200 m (4,000 ft).

wilsonae var. *ionanthum* Fang 1983. Not in cultivation

Differs from *wilsonae* in its persistent perulae, smaller oblong-elliptic leaves, the abruptly acuminate apex, broadly cuneate base and smaller violet flowers. Hunan and Kwangsi.

CINNABARINA SUBSECTION

cinnabarinum var. *breviforme* Davidian 1982

Cullen made a wise move when he lumped most varieties and relations of *cinnabarinum* under three subspecies. Having seen numerous plants in east Nepal and Bhutan, I can endorse the extreme variability of this species. Here, Davidian has attempted to name a clone as a variety of the species. *R. cinnabarinum* 'Nepal' A.M. *LS&H* 21283, a misnomer as it was actually collected in north-east Bhutan. Cullen says that the leaf characters are closer to ssp. *xanthocodon* but most people would place it in the Blandfordiiflorum Group.

laterifolium Mrs R. C. Fang & A. L. Chang 1983. Not in cultivation

F not seen. Probably closely allied to *keysii* but the latter has never been found further east than the Bhutan-Arunachal Pradesh border and a part of Tibet to the north-east. Should be worth introducing. From Yunnan, Gongshan, around 3,400 m (11,000 ft).

tenuifolium Mrs R. C. Fang & S. H. Huang 1986

Tibet (no other information).

FALCONERA SUBSECTION

Most of this subsection have their indumentum on the lower side of the leaf made up of so-called cup-shaped hairs but it is only in the cases where the hairs are broadly cup-shaped and hardly fimbriated that the cups are easily recognized (under moderate magnification). The species with these broadly cup-shaped hairs are *hodgsonii*, *coriaceum*, *basilicum* and also *sinofalconeri* which is not in cultivation. In *coriaceum* the hairs tend to be rather glued together while in *basilicum*, the hairs are less distinctly broadly cup-shaped than in the first two.

gratum T. L. Ming 1981

Both Chamberlain and Davidian think that this is probably a synonym of *basilicum*. From its description, photographs in *Rhododendrons of China Vol. 1*, and from the one herbarium specimen in Edinburgh, I would be inclined to agree. It could be intermediate between *basilicum* and *rex* ssp. *arizelum*. The flowers are said to be from white, through light yellow to rose with the usual crimson blotch. T. L. Ming himself says that it is related to *rex* from which it differs in its upper layer of indumentum on the leaf underside in which the hairs are funnel-form, appressed, not continuous, and the flowers are without spots. The leaf shape looks much nearer *basilicum* and it comes from within the area where this is recorded in west Yunnan and within the altitudinal range at around 3,200 m (10,500 ft).

rex ssp. *fictolacteum* var. *miniforme* Davidian 1989

According to Davidian, there are two *F* and two *R* numbers, all collected at fairly high elevations. Davidian says that it has small leaves and flowers and makes a small plant. There are no less than 25 herbarium specimens in the RBG, Edinburgh which have rather smaller-than-average-sized leaves, about a third of the total number of this subspecies. Where size of plant was recorded, the majority were given as being 4 m (13 ft) and under in height, and the trusses do appear to be generally smaller than average. Most came from above-average elevation. Overall, I doubt if the trend in plant height, truss size and altitude is really significant. There is no correlation on locality. Actually, Davidian's type number *F* 25512, of which there are three specimens, is recorded as growing to 6 m (20 ft)! All have uniformly small leaves. Several small-leaved specimens appear to be half-way between ssp. *fictolacteum* and ssp. *arizelum*. These could either be hybrids or from intermediary populations. There does seem to be little doubt that ssp. *fictolacteum* and *arizelum* do merge in the wild.

   I have seen a few distinctly dwarf plants in cultivation but nothing like the percentage among cultivated plants that there is among herbarium specimens. I will not be entirely satisfied with this new variety until I have seen either genetically dwarf wild populations or have grown even batches of dwarf seedlings. An old plant of *F* 25512 in the RBG, Edinburgh has grown to about 3 m (10 ft) and has certainly retained its small leaves but would probably grow to 6 m (20 ft) in western Scotland. It flowers freely.

hodgsonii aff. Cox, Hutchison & Maxwell Macdonald 3093

We found this plant at 3,900 m (12,750 ft) on the Rudong La, central west Bhutan on 30 September 1988. The leaves were generally shorter and smaller than *hodgsonii*, often with a cordate apex and *thick, dark chocolate-rufous-brown indumentum* below. The indumentum was made up of broadly cup-shaped hairs, identical to those of *hodgsonii*, but far denser and thicker. The buds were like those of *hodgsonii* with short-tailed scales and the bark was similar to *hodgsonii*. The smallish, almost straight capsules, covered with dense rufous fimbriated hairs, were exactly like those of *arizelum*.

   This plant was quite plentiful over a limited area and was very uniform with no other big-leaved species in the immediate locality. In other localities, we did see occasional plants of *kesangiae* X *hodgsonii* which, to our surprise, had similarly coloured dark indumentum, much darker than the indumentum of either parent. Could this *CH&M* 3093 be a stabilized population of this hybrid? Whether it is or not, I feel that it deserves some botanical status, perhaps as a variety of *hodgsonii* which is undoubtedly its nearest relative.

Ludlow & Sherriff failed to notice this plant when they went over the Rudong La in 1933 and 1949.

FORTUNEA SUBSECTION

asterochnoum Diels 1921 see *p.* 304

Said to differ from *calophytum* in the stellate hairs on the leaf underside (the only species to have these in the subsection) and the funnel-campanulate flowers. In spring 1989 I visited Wolong Panda Reserve in Szechwan which according to *Sichuan Rhododendron of China* is a location for *asterochnoum* and not *calophytum*. Many plants were examined both in and out of flower. The amount of indumentum present was very small, usually just on the midrib on the leaf underside but sometimes a little scattered on the lower surface. The reported difference in the flower shape was not noticeable. Chamberlain and I came to the conclusion that if all so called *asterochnoum* is similar to what we saw, it is not worth botanical status. It is reported from other parts of Szechwan so the presence of indumentum and the different flower shape could be more pronounced elsewhere.   May in the wild.

asterochnoum var. *brevipedicellatum* W. K. Hu 1986. Not in cultivation

Said to differ from the type in its oblong leaves, short pedicels and smaller flowers. Comes from the type location of *asterochnoum* so its distinctness is doubtful; could it be a hybrid, perhaps with *oreodoxa*?

calophytum var. *pauciflorum* W. K. Hu 1986. Not in cultivation

This is found in a fairly isolated region in south-east Szechwan. According to *Sichuan Rhododendron of China*, it differs from *calophytum* in having broadly oblanceolate to oblong leaves, shortly acuminate at apex, only 5–7 or rarely to 11 flowers per truss, bowl-like-campanulate in shape, always 5-lobed and 21–22 stamens. In the photographs, the flowers are pink but this could vary. This could be a distinct variety but apparently typical *calophytum* is also recorded on the same mountain which makes one suspicious that it might be a hybrid. It does look attractive and worth introducing.

decorum Franch. ssp. *diaprepes* (Balf.f. & W. W. Smith) T. L. Ming (date?)

Chamberlain in a footnote below *diaprepes* in *Revision of Rhododendron*

II came to the conclusion that *diaprepes* is better treated as a subspecies of *decorum* and in fact this had already been done by T. L. Ming in China. On Cang Shan, Yunnan, we found populations of intermediate forms with large leaves at low elevations which could really be placed in either species. I think this placing of *diaprepes* as a subspecies is a correct move. See *p.* 168.

huianum see *p.* 172. Illustrated in *Sichuan Rhododendron of China*, *p.* 17–19, this looks a distinct species worth introducing. South-central and south-west Szechwan, also Yunnan and Kweichow.

jiangangshanicum Tam 1982. Not in cultivation

Related to *fortunei* from which *jiangangshanicum* differs in its long narrow leaves, 5 lobed corolla of a different shape, larger calyx and stamens and style puberulous at base. From Kiangsi and Hunan at around 1,150 m (3,900 ft).

maoerense Fang & G. Z. Li 1984

no information except Kwangsi

platypodum, see *p.* 175

As illustrated in *Sichuan Rhododendron of China*, *p.* 8–9, this looks like one of the finest of the Fortunea subsection and well worth introducing. Splendid-looking pink flowers in fairly full trusses.

FULGENSIA SUBSECTION

I fully endorse Davidian's move to place *succothii* with *fulgens* (see *p.* 178) and wish Chamberlain would do likewise. Davidian has made a separate Sherriffii series which in addition to *sherriffii*, includes the little known *miniatum*. This I feel is also a good move but I would have preferred to see *lopsangianum* somehow placed in the same subsection (series) as *sherriffii*.

FULVA SUBSECTION

fulvoides Balf f. & Forr. 1920, see *p.* 181

Davidian has for long talked about resurrecting this plant to specific status and I am happy to see him doing so. While it does apparently merge with *fulvum*, most herbarium specimens and cultivated plants are sufficiently distinct for it to warrant specific status.

GRANDIA SUBSECTION

kesangiae Long & Rushforth 1989

Ht 8–12 m. Tree or large shrub, single- or multi-trunked. Bark mid-brown, not peeling, encouraging moss in the wild. Young shoots often closely white floccose. Terminal buds *rounded*, green, through reddish to nearly black.

L 20–30 × 10–16 cm, broadly elliptic to almost obovate, apex rounded, base cuneate or rounded, glabrous above with *prominent lateral veins*, indumentum below variable, woolly floccose to almost plastered, fawn to silvery white on young leaves *without cup-shaped hairs, uniformly grey-white on old*. L remain about 2 years. Petiole 2–3.5 cm.

Inflor 15–25, usually compact. Pedicels 1.5–2.5 cm, glandular.

F *Rose to pink, fading to pale pink*, 3–4.7 cm long, campanulate *with nectar pouches*.

Calyx small, ovary densely glandular and also sometimes thinly tomentose, style glabrous. Capsule usually long, thin and curved.

This is one of the most important species to be described in recent years. It is quite amazing that what is perhaps the commonest big-leaved species in Bhutan should not have been recognized as being distinct by previous collectors. It was Keith Rushforth, really an authority on conifers and other trees, who realized that this was a distinct species during recent trips to Bhutan. There were various herbarium specimens of this species collected by Cooper, L&S and other collectors which had mostly been labelled *hodgsonii* X *falconeri*. I am not necessarily blaming taxonomists for this lapse, as having examined these specimens myself, I can see that the chief characters of this species are not really in evidence, nor was it made clear in the field notes how plentiful it really is in the wild.

To my knowledge, there are no mature specimens of this species in cultivation and it was not introduced until 1967 by Simon Bowes-Lyon from seedlings given to him by the Kesang, Queen Mother of Bhutan, under two numbers collected in west Bhutan. It has been named in her honour. The plants are cultivated at Wakehurst Place and elsewhere. One number is fairly typical *kesangiae* but the other has a strange grey-brown indumentum, referred to by Tony Schilling (deputy curator of Wakehurst) as being slightly sinister in appearance. Examinations of countless plants in the wild failed to show anything quite like this plant but several with indumentum approaching it. I do not consider it to be a natural hybrid as the fairly numerous *kesangiae* X *falconeri* and *kesangiae* X *hodgsonii* that I saw were quite different with much deeper coloured indumentum, consistently deeper in fact than either parent in both cases. From my own observations of 8 different wild populations, this species does change gradually from west to east. In the west, the indumentum is mixed, from light brownish to greyish-white, floccose to plastered. Further east the indumentum tends to be a more uniform grey-plastered which may take longer to develop on young seedlings, many 60–90 cm (2–3 ft) being glabrous or having the curious ring of indumentum around the margin, as is sometimes seen in *protistum*. The furthest-east population we saw on the Thrumsing La had me worried. One of the chief characters of the species, its very distinctive rounded buds, were all elongated (conical) but without the long tails of *hodgsonii*. Typical *hodgsonii* occurred in quantity on top of the pass and a short search revealed no intermediaries or natural hybrids. At first I thought that this form of *kesangiae* was mid-way between the two species but in retrospect I doubt it. Keith Rushforth reports that this population had pale-pink flowers fading to near-white. Examinations of populations further east would be very interesting.

This species generally lies in altitude between *falconeri* and *hodgsonii* although there is often a considerable overlap in both cases, resulting in the natural hybrids mentioned above. *R. kesangiae* seems to prefer wetter conditions than *hodgsonii*, as far as rainfall is concerned, and also it seems to tolerate damper soil conditions: three times we found it growing in really boggy, almost level ground. While *hodgsonii* can be found slightly higher than *kesangiae*, the dominance of one or the other appears to depend on the climatic and soil conditions. Hardiness-wise *kesangiae* should prove about equal to or slightly less hardy than *hodgsonii*. The clear rose to pink to pale-pink flowers are obviously of considerable merit, especially as they evidently do not pass through the rather muddy phase that often characterizes both *hodgsonii* and *falconeri* ssp. *eximium* between first opening and finally fading out. At Wakehurst, *kesangiae* is comparatively slow-growing and slow to bloom but the conditions are some way from perfect there for large-leaved species. It is also of course impressive as a foliage plant, so could become one of the most satisfactory big-leaved species in cultivation. One plant first flowered at Wakehurst in 1985, see cover and photograph no. 34. Growth may be rather early.

Only known from Bhutan so far, 2,900–3,500 m (9,500–11,500 ft), in fir or hemlock forest, often with other rhododendrons and bamboo.

April–May

There seems to be at least one unnamed taxa in east Bhutan and the neighbouring Kameng Division of Arunachal Pradesh. *KW* 13681 (see *p.* 81) is one of these which has been grown under *magnificum*. Further collections are needed from this region.

wightii, see *p.* 199

In the first edition, I tentatively placed this species in the Grandia subsection. Chamberlain in *The Revision of Rhododendron II, subgenus Hymenanthes*, has left it tentatively in Taliensia. Davidian has left it in the Lacteum Series but admits that it might be better placed in a series on its own. This species has been observed in the wild on several occasions recently, in Nepal, Sikkim and Bhutan and everyone seeing these wild plants agree that the plant normally cultivated is something very different. According to Millais in 1917, there were apparently only two old plants including one at Littleworth in Surrey (**AM** clone) and the majority if not all the plants now grown may have originated from these. Many were raised from seed by Gill, and the RBG, Edinburgh received its original plant from this source in 1917. The old Littleworth plant still exists but is of unknown origin. In Millais's second volume (1924) he mentions one plant grown by Gill from Sikkim seed which went to Borde

Hill (where it seems this plant no longer exists) and a graft off this went to RBG, Edinburgh but has also disappeared. Millais wrote that this had much larger leaves than the Littleworth plant which he refers to as var. *minor*. I have not heard of any plants in cultivation from Cooper or L&S introductions but there are a very few from Beer, Lancaster and Morris No. 92 collected in 1971. My experience of growing three Nepal introductions from seed are that they germinate quite easily but are extremely slow and hard to grow on, especially the first few years.

There is no doubt that this is a variable species and it could be that the old cultivated plant is an extreme form. The fact that it appears to come true from seed points to it not being of hybrid origin. On the other hand, assuming it was originally introduced by Hooker in 1849, the 68 years between introduction and Millais's comments of 1917 leaves a long time for funny things to happen. Could it be that the cultivated *wightii* is in fact an open-pollinated seedling or seedlings that somehow breed true? Could the putative parents perhaps be *wightii* and either *grande* or *falconeri*, also both Hooker's introductions? Either cross could give a yellow flower. Alternatively, have we in fact got two species here? This question is difficult to answer without seeing many different wild populations. I have only seen two populations close together in east Bhutan. These appeared to be quite uniform in themselves but differed from BLM 92 in wider, shorter leaves and a more plastered indumentum. All have the distinctive character of very sticky buds while the old form has non-sticky buds and more recurved leaves. One plant of BLM 92 flowered at Glendoick in 1990 with creamy-yellow flowers in a normal-shaped truss. I have not seen flowers of Bhutan plants yet. It could be that the indumentum becomes more plastered and lighter in colour the further east the species goes. I would suggest that this species would be better returned to my own tentative Lactea subsection or perhaps put into a subsection on its own.

HELIOLEPIDA SUBSECTION

The Chinese seem to have gone overboard in 'splitting hairs' in all the plants described below. I feel we can largely forget about them, especially from a horticultural point of view.

heliolepis var. *fumidum* (Balf.f. & W.W.Sm.) A. L. Chang 1982

The differences between this and the type are given as dark-brown upper leaf surface and brown lower surface of dried leaves, purplish-red corolla spotted reddish-brown and the absence of hairs on the style. From north-east Yunnan.

heliolepis var. *oporinum* (Balf.f. & Ward) A. L. Chang 1982

Only differs from the type in its finely pubescent exterior to the corolla, except where it is scaly.

hirsutipetiolatum R. C. Fang & A. L. Zhang 1983. Not in cultivation?

It would appear from the time of flowering that this comes out at about the same time as *rubiginosum* and, apart from its puberulous midrib and puberulous and bristly petiole, is probably very similar to this species. Yunnan, 3,400 m (11,155 ft).

rubiginosum var. *leclerei* (Levl.) R. C. Fang 1982

Regarded as a synonym of *rubiginosum* in Britain. Davidian says that the only difference appears to be in the size of the flower which is very variable in *rubiginosum* anyway. In contrast, R. C. Fang says that the difference is in that the stamens are devoid of hairs and the calyx lobes have no scales or a few on the margins. West Yunnan.

rubiginosum var. *ptilostylum* R. C. Fang 1982

Only differs from type in its puberulous lower part of the style Central Yunnan, 3,300 m (10,750 ft).

IRRORATA SUBSECTION

agastum Balf.f. & W.W. Sm. 1917 (see *p.* 206)

When I wrote the first edition in 1978, I had my suspicions that at least some herbarium specimens were natural hybrids. On our 1981 Cang Shan Expedition, Chamberlain and I virtually confirmed that this 'species' consists entirely of natural hybrids, many between *arboreum* ssp. *delavayi* and *decorum*. We found several plants including one in flower with deep pink flowers with 7-lobed corollas. There were also several apparent hybrids amongst *irroratum* which I feel must be *irroratum X delavayi*. This latter hybrid would appear to be a more likely combination on account that these two species are more inclined to bloom together than *delavayi* and *decorum*. Some plants in cultivation labelled *agastum* are just *irroratum* which would perhaps show that the latter is the more frequent parent.

agastum var. *pennivenium* T. L. Ming

Chamberlain makes this a variety of *tanastylum*. It seems very likely that this variety is just another natural hybrid.

annae ssp. *laxiflorum* (Balf.f. & Forr.) T. L. Ming 1984 (see *p.* 207)

Chamberlain now suspects that *annae* is probably a natural hybrid or cultivar and does not come from Kweichow. The plant we grow as *annae* is perfectly hardy (in contrast to what Davidian says) while *laxiflorum* 'Folks Wood', no doubt originating from Yunnan, has been killed both at Sandling and Glendoick in recent hard winters.

anthosphaerum var. *eritimum* (Balf.f. & W.W. Sm.) Davidian 1989 (see p. 208)

This has been resuscitated by Davidian who says it differs from the type by its deep plum-crimson or crimson flowers and often larger leaves. These are poor characters in such a variable species and it is better to continue to regard *eritimum* as a synonym of *anthosphaerum*.

gongshanense T. L. Ming 1984. Not in cultivation

Thought to be related to *kendrickii* which only has hairs on the leaf midrib below, this species being sparsely setose-glandular on the whole surface. Yunnan.

guizhouense M. Y. Fang 1988, described at Australian conference, 1988. Not in cultivation. No other information available.

laojunense T. L. Ming 1984. Not in cultivation

Probably related to *aberconwayi*, differing in the blackish-purple spots on the corolla, densely tomentose eglandular ovary and glabrous style. Yunnan, around 2,500 m (8,250 ft), stony and bamboo forests, April in the wild.

lapidosum T. L. Ming 1981. Not in cultivation

Only known from the type specimen. Similar to *araiophyllum* from which it differs in narrower leaves on which the midrib is glabrous below, the pedicel is sparsely glandular and the stamens are nearly glabrous. May also be close to *irroratum* ssp. *pogonostylum*, differing in its glabrous style. North-east Yunnan.

rubro-punctatum T. L. Ming 1984. Not in cultivation

Probably allied to *tanastylum* but with more papery oblong leaves, paler flowers and slightly pubescent ovary. Tibet, around 3,700 m (12,000 ft) in forests. Late April in the wild.

ziyuanense Tam 1983. Not in cultivation

Said to be related to *anhweiense* and *maculiferum*. Differs from the former in its oblong lanceolate leaves and its puberulous ovary; from the latter, leaves with cuneate or near cuneate bases, usually smooth above and in the not markedly triangular calyx lobes; from both in its fewer-flowered inflor. Kwangsi.

LACTEUM SUBSECTION, see *p.* 213–5.

I still maintain that I made the best compromise in the First Edition by placing *lacteum* and *beesianum* in their own subsection. Chamberlain has moved all the old Lacteum series into the Taliensia subsection while Davidian has left it as it was which is totally unsatisfactory. Having now seen *wightii* in the wild and several recently introduced seedlings, I feel perhaps that this would be the best place for *wightii* as well. See *p.* 199 and *p.* 354–5.

LANATA SUBSECTION

There has been considerable reorganization in this subsection recently. First, Chamberlain hived off this new subsection from the old Campanulatum series, quite correctly, as *lanatum* and *tsariense* have virtually nothing in common with *campanulatum* or for that matter *sherriffii*. Chamberlain also added a new species *lanatoides*. Now in 1989, Davidian has made a subseries Lanatum of the Campanulatum series and has added a new species and two new varieties plus resurrecting *luciferum* to specific status. This is a complex group of closely related (except *lanatoides*) species which may make up a cline in the wild but a thorough study of wild populations would be necessary to prove this one way or the other. I am certainly of the opinion that Davidian has split these into too many different taxa.

flinckii Davidian 1975 H4 L2–3 F2–3 see *p.* 216

Ht to 4 m (13 ft), a rounded bush. Branchlets densely tomentose.
L 4–10 × 2–4.5 cm (1⅗–4 × ⅘–1⅘ in), *thinner* than in *lanatum*, being usually narrowly elliptic to oblong-elliptic, apex usually shortly acuminate, base obtuse, palish green above with fairly persistent light rusty-brown indumentum for the first few months, dense *but thin felted orangy-brown* indumentum below. Petiole tomentose, 0.8–1.5 cm (⅓–⅗ in).
Inflor 3–8, rachis 3–88 mm. Pedicel 0.5–1.6 cm (⅕–⅗ in), densely tomentose.
F pale yellow, cream to pale pink, spotted crimson, 3.5–5 cm (1⅗–2 in) long, campanulate.
Calyx minute. Ovary densely tomentose, style glabrous.
    D. Long in *Flora of Bhutan* has given this specific status but states that it might be better as a subspecies of *lanatum*. Chamberlain had sunk it into *lanatum*. Having seen four populations of this in the wild in central east Bhutan, I am happy with Long's classification. Without further explorations to the west and east of where we were, it is difficult to ascertain whether intermediate populations occur between *lanatum* and *flinckii* and also *flinckii* and *tsariense*. Reports of *flinckii* in flower tell of both pale yellow and pale-pink flowers so Davidian is wrong to say that *flinckii* is always yellow. I do not think it is correct to attempt to separate *flinckii* and *tsariense* on flower colour and I feel that there is little doubt that these two merge in east Bhutan. What we saw were quite uniform in foliage and certainly distinct from *lanatum* from Sikkim and east Bhutan. *R. lanatum* has a thicker leaf, more of a rounded apex and thicker more coffee-coloured indumentum which turns rusty in west Bhutan; it also has a darker leaf upper surface with less indumentum. *R. flinckii* is an

attractive plant in the wild and considering the variety of habitats it grows in, it may prove easier to cultivate than *lanatum*. Central east and north east Bhutan only, 3,000–4,000 m+ (10,000–13,000 ft+), common on the edges of fir forest and above the tree line, often among rocks but also in bogs.

April–May

lanatoides Chamb. 1982 H4 L3 F2

Ht 2–4 m (6–13 ft). Habit upright bush.
L 9–11 × 2.1–2.7 cm (3⅗–4⅖ × about 1 in), *lanceolate*, dark green with slightly persistent indumentum above, otherwise glabrous and shiny, dense thick dark fawn to light brown made up of +/− straight dendroid hairs (curled dendroid hairs in *lanatum*). Petiole 1–1.5 cm (⅕–⅗ in), densely light brown or whitish-tomentose.
Inflor compact, 10–15, rachis 7–10 mm. Pedicel 0.7–1.5 cm (⅓–⅗ in), densely brownish-tomentose.
F white flushed pink with faint flecks, fading to white, 3.5–4 cm (1⅖–1⅗ in) long, campanulate.
Calyx *c.* 1 mm sparsely tomentose. Ovary densely brown tomentose, style glabrous.

When I wrote *The Smaller Rhododendrons* in 1984, it was thought that this species was not in cultivation but since then at least four plants have been found in different gardens. This is a very distinctive species which might be happier placed in the Taliensia subsection although the type of indumentum is different. It is a first-rate foliage plant, rivalling the best of the Talienses. The flowers open exceptionally early so they usually get frosted and are small in relation to the foliage. The leaves resemble those of *principis* but this has a glabrous ovary. Plants in cultivation from *KW* introduction. From a limited area of south-east Tibet on the north side of the Tsangpo near the gorge, 3,200–3,650 m (10,500–12,000 ft) among rocks.   February–March

luciferum (Cowan) Cowan 1953 (*lanatum* var. luciferum Cowan 1937)

Davidian has given this specific status but I doubt if it deserves any status other than as a synonym of *lanatum*. The leaves tend to be larger than *lanatum* and *flinckii* and have a more pointed apex. The indumentum is a light to dark slightly greenish fawny-brown while in *lanatum* it is more coffee or rust-coloured. In *flinckii* it is a bright orangy-brown.
South and south east Tibet, 3,300–4000 m (11,000–13,000 ft).

poluninii Davidian 1989

This has been described off one cultivated plant in the RBG, Edinburgh and a not particularly good herbarium specimen. There is considerable doubt if the cultivated plant came from the same collection as the herbarium specimen, L&S 3089 which was apparently not a seed number. According to Davidian, it differs from *tsariense* in its lanceolate-to-oblong unusually large leaves, 6.2–8 cm (2½–3¼ in) long, its pale rusty brown indumentum and the larger numbers of flowers in the truss, 5–11.

In my opinion, apart from insignificantly thicker indumentum, the type specimen is identical to *flinckii*. The cultivated plant does not really agree with the herbarium specimen, having thicker indumentum, more oblong-elliptic leaves, with a more acuminate apex and a slightly cordulate base as opposed to a rounded base on the herbarium specimen. The cultivated plant really looks like a larger edition of *tsariense* with longer more oblong leaves, white flushed pink, heavily spotted crimson flowers and does appear not to warrant any botanical rank.

L&S 3089 comes from Black Mountain, central Bhutan at 4,000 m (13,000 ft).

tsariense var. *magnum* Davidian 1989

R. tsariense var. *magnum* is larger in plant and leaf size than the type with the same thick woolly cinnamon-coloured indumentum. It comes from the same area as *flinckii* and is probably just a pink-flowered form of this species despite the apparent difference in Davidian's description of the thickness of the indumentum. *R. flinckii*, when growing on rocks and cliffs, tends to have smaller leaves and probably merges with *tsariense*. From the Bumthang area of central Bhutan, 3,800–4,100 m (12,500–13,500 ft).

tsariense var. *trimoense* Davidian 1989 H3–4 L2 F2

This has much paler-coloured leaves and indumentum than the type. I have grown a plant (with no collector's number) for many years and with its less compact habit and pale indumentum, it is an inferior plant to the type. Davidian assumes this to be from L&S 2894 from Trimo at around 3,400 m (11,000 ft), a part of south Tibet very close to north-east Bhutan, some distance west of where the typical small-leaved, deep-indumented *tsariense* comes from. As there are four specimens in the RBG, Edinburgh herbarium with pale indumentum, all from Trimo, this plant does appear to be worth varietal status. There is also a specimen of KW 13663 in the herbarium from west Arunachal Pradesh with similar pale indumentum.

MACULIFERA SUBSECTION

oligocarpum Fang & X. S. Zhang 1983. Not in cultivation

Related to *maculiferum* from which it differs in its small leaves, fewer flowers to the truss and densely yellow pubescent calyx and pedicels. With small leaves and trusses on a relatively large plant, it cannot be of much horticultural merit.

From Kweichow and Kwangsi 1,800–2,500 m (6,000–8,250 ft).

pachyphyllum Fang 1983. Not in cultivation

Again related to *maculiferum* from which it differs in its thicker leaves which are oblong to oblong-elliptic with acuminate apices. These seem rather trivial distinctions so it might be sunk into *maculiferum*.

Hunan, around 1,800 m (6,000 ft).

pachysanthum Hayata 1913 H4 L3–4 F2–3

The description below is supplementary to the one on *p.* 220.
Ht our biggest plants are now 1.5 m (5 ft) high and 2.4 m (8 ft) across after 17 years but could ultimately reach 3 m (10 ft) as they are putting on up to 18 cm (7 in) a year on the strongest shoots. Habit mound forming and good branch retention.
L up to 11 × 6 cm (4½ × 2½ in), very conspicuous indumentum above, brown to silvery, some even retained on 3-year-old leaves; indumentum below pale at first, turning to a rich rusty-brown on maturity. Leaves retained for 3 years.
F funnel-campanulate, the lobes not being so fanned as in *pseudo-chrysanthum*. Buds usually open various shades of rose or occasionally white, fading to very pale rose, with a crimson to green blotch, flare or spots or almost no markings at all.

The early promises of being a first-rate garden plant have been fully fulfilled, especially in its marvellous foliage. While our best group from *RV* 72001 are in half-shade, it usually grows satisfactorily in a fairly sunny site. It is easy to cultivate but we have had some leaf-tip burn similar to that found in *pseudochrysanthum* which seems to be due to too much sun or/and drought plus perhaps too much fertilizer. We received a second packet of seed in 1977 as *RV* 77077 which have turned out rather differently. Several are natural hybrids with *morii* while others seem to be mid-way (hybrids?) between *pachysanthum* and *pseudochrysanthum*. The former are vigorous with less indumentum while the latter are slower-growing with darker leaves and smaller flowers.

On *p.* 220 I stated that the flowers are similar to *pseudochrysanthum* but they are in fact a different shape (see above). Most plants have attractive flowers but not as beautiful as in the best forms of *pseudo-chrysanthum*. While the presence of a dense indumentum makes this species rather aberrant in this subsection, its closest relations definitely appear to be *pseudochrysanthum* and *morii*, having much in common. Davidian has moved *pachysanthum* to the Taliense series, subseries Wasonii. Everyone knows what an unsatisfactory *mélange* of species this subseries contained and although in some ways *pachysanthum* does look like a Taliensia and has a lot in common with *bureavii* for instance, especially its thick indumentum of ramiform hairs, it makes the Wasonii subseries even more of a dumping ground of misfits.   April

polytrichum Fang 1983. Not in cultivation

Differs from *strigillosum* in its more oblong leaves, its branchlets, petiole and pedicel being reddish-brown setose glanduar, and in its pinkish flowers. Again these characters seem too trivial to separate this species from *strigillosum*. From Hunan and Kwangsi, around 1,100 m (3,500 ft).

sikangense Fang 1951 (*cookeanum* Davidian 1962), see *p.* 304–6

Fang's name has preference over Davidian's. Chamberlain is happiest with this species in the Maculifera subsection, mostly due to its flower characters. Davidian keeps it in the Parishii series under *cookeanum*. Since writing the description on *p.* 304, we have flowered a plant of this species very nicely in our Argyll garden but only once so far. It is illustrated in *Sichuan Rhododendron of China*, *p.* 97–100. It is also found as far north as central Szechwan. The Chinese give the altitude much lower than we do at 2,800–3,200 m (9,250–10,500 ft).

sikangense var. *exquisitum* T. L. Ming 1981

Differs from the type in the apparently persistent indumentum on the leaf underside and the stellate-tomentose young shoots and pedicels. Chamberlain reckons this is synonymous with *sikangense*. North-east Yunnan, 3,500–4,500 m (11,500–14,750 ft).

strigillosum var. *monesematum* (Hutch.) T. L. Ming

A new arrangement which seems to be unsatisfactory. *R. monesematum* is undoubtedly closer to *pachytrichum* than *strigillosum* so we can forget about this move.

MADDENIA SUBSECTION

Ciliicalyx Alliance

Five species and a variety have been described recently in China. I give the names of them all but only attempt to describe two as the others are all too dwarf to include here. I also add some notes on three other species which have now been introduced into cultivation.

changii (Fang) Fang 1983. Not in cultivation

Now given specific status. See *The Smaller Rhododendrons*, *p.* 117.

linearilobum R. C. Fang & A. L. Chang 1982. Not in cultivation

Said to be related to *valentinianum*, Yunnan. Too dwarf to describe here.

nemorosum R. C. Fang 1984. Not in cultivation

Said to be related to *pachypodum* but smaller in all parts, Yunnan. Too dwarf to describe here.

rhombifolium R. C. Fang 1982. Not in cultivation

Said to be related to *formosum* from which it differs in its location, leaf shape and possibly also related to *chrysodoron* from which it differs in leaf shapes and different scales. Described from a specimen collected out of flower in 1937 at Gongshan, west Yunnan, *c.* 1,800 m (6,000 ft) in dense forest.

valentinianum var. *oblongilobatum* R. C. Fang 1982. Not in cultivation

Too dwarf to describe here, Yunnan.

wumingense Fang 1983. Not in cultivation

Said to be related to *lyi* but with smaller leaves. Probably of little merit and very tender, coming from only 1,000 m (3,250 ft) in Kwangsi.

Dalhousiae Alliance

basfordii Davidian 1979

This is a very doubtful species. Long in *The Flora of Bhutan* says that the herbarium specimen is *cinnabarinum* and does not match the cultivated plant at Brodick, Isle of Arran from where Davidian got his material to name it. The herbarium specimen is so poor that it is hard to identify it. I had hoped to see this plant in the wild in autumn 1988 but alas, we got no closer than a few miles. Davidian says that it differs from *lindleyi* in its smaller funnel-shaped as opposed to tubular-campanulate flowers, scaly all over outside as opposed to scaly only at base of tube or glabrous, smaller flower parts and leaves more densely scaly below.

Found (if the herbarium specimen *does* match the cultivated plants) on the east side of the Rudong La in central east Bhutan at 1,600 m (8,500 ft).

excellens Hemsl. & Wils. 1910, see *p.* 234

I have seen one plant of this in the Kunming Botanic Garden and I have seedlings from this plant. Large robust foliage, perhaps closest to *nuttallii* but appears to be distinct. Seed has recently been introduced. See *p.* 234. Said to be closely related to *dalhousiae* but has larger leaves, a glabrous calyx and corolla scaly outside. Highly rated by the few that have seen it.

goreri Davidian 1980, see *p.* 235

I do not accept this as a separate species, considering it to be a synonym of *nuttallii* from which it was removed.

Davidian gives as his characters: young growth pale green as opposed to crimson-purple, leaf surface not nearly so bullate, calyx and pedicel not pubescent, and flower parts smaller. *R. nuttallii*, like most other species, is quite variable. The plant Davidian describes as *nuttallii* is the extreme form with large coarse bullate leaves and large flowers but there are plants in cultivation and herbarium specimens which would fit half-way between *nuttallii* and *goreri*. Davidian's illustration in *The Rhododendron Species Vol. 1* and the one in *RHS–RSHB* 156 of the AM plant, LS&E 12117, show plants with bullate leaves, which contradicts one of the chief characters he used to warrant it being a separate species. I grew some seedlings from the AM plant, one of which produced a truss that nearly won the best in show award at the 1988 Glasgow Festival show. This has moderately bullate leaves. LS&E 12117 and 13077 were collected in south-east Tibet, 2,100–2,300 m (7,000–7,500 ft), in dense mixed forest.

grothausii Davidian 1980

Again, I do not accept this as a species. It was previously known (and still is by most people) as *lindleyi* *L&S* form (6562) (see *p*. 235) and is now widely distributed in gardens, mostly as seedlings, sometimes several generations from the originals. We lost all our plants outside in the exceptionally cold winter of 1981–2 (down to −18°C [0°F]), but these were immediately replaced. Davidian's characters separating this plant from *lindleyi* are: smaller flowers, leaves usually smaller and bullate above, flower buds reddish-brown turning to crimson purple and a hardier plant. The extreme western form of *lindleyi* agrees with Davidian's description of *lindleyi* and appears fairly distinct. Plants in the middle of the distribution are intermediate in character. For example, our C&H 399 from the Subansiri, collected just a little to the south of L&S 6562 which was from a northern tributary of the same river, has similar rugose foliage, slightly larger flowers and green buds. Actually, bud colour is often of no significance, many species showing great variations on adjacent plants in the wild. Seedlings of L&S 6562 show a considerable variation in bud colour from purple to green, tending to be less coloured in shady sites. From Migyitun, Tsari Chu, south Tibet, 2,600 m (8,500 ft), and two locations in Bhutan. It is noticeable that Davidian still gives the distribution of *lindleyi* as being Nepal to Assam (Arunachal Pradesh) including Tibet and Bhutan, thus covering the area that so called *grothausii* comes from.

levinei Merrill 1918 H1 L2 F2, see *p*. 234

Ht 3–4 m (10–13 ft), less in cultivation? Habit loose arching growth on a small scale. Bark mahogany, peeling or smooth, branchlets sparsely hairy.
L 5–10 × 2–5 cm (2–4 × ⅘–2 in), obovate to lanceolate, apex acute, base cuneate to rounded, upper surface at first mostly covered with long hairs, partly glabrous on maturity, scaly below, the golden scales 1–2 × their own diameter apart, margins hairy, the hairy being up to 4 mm (⅛ in) long. Petiole moderately hairy
Inflor 2–3. Pedicel *c*.1 cm (⅖ in), scaly.
F white, 5–7 cm (2–nearly 3 in) long, funnel-campanulate, very fragrant. Calyx about 8 mm, deeply lobed. Ovary densely scaly, tapering into style which is scaly at base.
We have now grown this for eight years and flowered it for three, from seed collected in the wild in Kwangtung province. This is very distinct species with exceptionally hairy leaves which are retained into adulthood.

The flowers are an unusual shape for the Megacalyx Alliance and are comparatively small but match the equally small leaves. Not spectacular like some of its relatives but worth growing. Requires exceptionally good drainage.   April–May

liliiflorum Leveille 1913 H1? L1–2 F?, see *p.* 234

Ht to 3 m (10 ft) or more (1.5 m [5 ft] for Guiz 163). Habit erect. Branchlets red to green, scaly.
L 4–11+ × 2–4+ cm 1⅗–4⅖ × ⅘–1⅗ in), narrowly obovate to oblong-lanceolate, apex obtuse to broadly acute, base cuneate to obtuse, not scaly above, scales two sizes below, larger ones scarce, all 2–4 × their own diameter apart, veins raised. Petiole 1–2 cm (⅖–⅘ in), densely scaly.
Inflor 2–3. Pedicel 1–1.5 cm (⅖–⅗ in), densely scaly.
F white, 6–9 cm (2⅖–3⅗ in) long, narrowly funnel-campanulate, densely scaly outside.
Calyx 0.8–1 cm (⅓–⅖ in), conspicuous, lobes. Ovary scaly, style scaly on lower part.

This was introduced by the Guiz Expedition in autumn 1985 and seedlings are now being distributed (1988–9). One or two of our seedlings are budded. I endorse what I said on *p.* 234 about it probably being closest related to *taggianum* but it appears to be a distinct species.

Collected as Guiz 163 on Fan-jin-shan, north-east Kweichow at 1,500 m (5,000 ft) on boulders.

PARISHIA SUBSECTION

brevipetiolatum Fang f. 1986. Not in cultivation

Differs from *facetum* in being smaller in all parts and in its pubescent and stipitate-glandular young shoots. Should be relatively hardy from southern central Szechwan, 1,900 m (6,250 ft) in forests.

flavoflorum T. L. Ming 1984. Not in cultivation

Related to *facetum* but obviously could be interesting on account of its pale yellow flowers, spotted red, unique to this subsection. Yunnan, 2,700 m (9,000 ft) in mixed forest.

huidongense T. L. Ming 1981. Not in cultivation

Said to be related to *elliottii* but much smaller in all part and lacks gland-tipped bristles on branchlets and petioles. Should be fairly hardy from south Szechwan, 3,200 m (10,500 ft) in forest.

urophyllum Fang f. 1983. Not in cultivation

Differs from *brevipetiolatum* in its narrower leaves and glabrous young shoots. Rather small flowers. Likely to be tender. South Szechwan, 1,200–1,600 m (4,000–5,250 ft), in evergreen forest.

PONTICA SUBSECTION (see p. 245)

There have been numerous deliberations on how to classify this subsection in recent years. Different classifications have been produced in Japan where about half of the species grow wild. Our own taxonomists have also been uncertain what to do but by a pooling of opinions, including those of the American Frank Doleshy who has travelled much in Japan, a fairly satisfactory conclusion (or at least compromise) has been reached. As the species we are concerned with are described in *The Smaller Rhododendrons*, p. 177–9, listed below are just the species as now published, with a few comments. Davidian has now also abolished the separate subseries but has retained *adenopodum* here instead of moving it back to the Argyrophylla subsection and has also retained the name *metternichii* against the International Rules of Nomenclature and sunk the name *degronianum* into *metternichii* var. *pentamerum*.

brachycarpum ssp. *fauriei* (Franch) Chamberlain 1979

There is further confirmation that ssp. *fauriei* and the type are often completely mixed up in the wild, thus giving ssp. *fauriei* no botanical standing.

brachycarpum var. *tigerstedtii* (Nitz) Davidian 1989, see *p.* 247

I tentatively gave this subspecific status, following Nitzelius's description from a cultivated plant. Chamberlain sank it into *brachycarpum*, reckoning the differences were trivial, while Davidian has now given it varietal status – perhaps the best solution. I have now grown seedlings from wild seed for some years and can vouch for their added vigour and size compared with several introductions of Japanese *brachycarpum*. It comes from Dagelet Island off the Korean coast in addition to mainland Korea.

degronianum ssp. *degronianum* Hara 1986
This only includes the plants formerly grown as *degronianum* or *japonicum* var. *pentamerum* or *metternichii* ssp. *pentamerum*.

degronianum ssp. *yakushimanum* Hara 1986

This only includes the plants formerly grown as *yakushimanum*. I am sure that most horticulturists will continue to call this simply *yakushimanum*. The reason why *yakushimanum* has not been retained at full specific rank is due to low elevation populations (var. *'intermedium'*) which are nearly identical to some forms of *degronianum* ssp. *degronianum*.

degronianum ssp. *heptamerum* var. *heptamerum* Hara 1986 (synonyms *japonicum* [Blume] Schneider, *metternichii* Siebold & Zuccarine, 'Degronianum' var. '*Metternichii*' in *The Smaller Rhododendrons*)

This was formerly known as *metternichii* and it is here that the real trouble has lain. Several years ago it was found that *metternichii* was an invalid name. This is due to the type description citing an earlier valid specific epithet, *Hymenathes japonica* Blume, in synonymy. This leaves *degronianum* as the earliest valid name at specific rank. So regrettably, the name *metternichii* has to go to be replaced by the cumbersome name above. I would suggest that horticulturalists should refer to it as *heptamerum* when not wanting to refer to it in full. At least we can be thankful that we can still use the name *japonicum* for the well-known azalea species.

degronianum ssp. *heptamerum* var. *hondoense* Hara 1986

This only includes plants formerly known as *metternichii* var. *hondoense* or *degronianum* var. *hondoense*.

degronianum ssp. *heptamerum* var. *kyomaruense* Hara 1986

This only includes plants formerly known as *metternichii* var. *kyomaruense*. There is still some doubt whether this plant warrants even varietal rank.

makinoi Tagg

This has now been returned to its former specific status and will not be known as *yakushimanum* ssp. *makinoi*.

RHODORASTRA SUBSECTION

mucronulatum var. *chejuense* Davidian 1989, see *The Smaller Rhododendrons*, p. 122.

Davidian has, quite rightly I feel, described this introduction as a variety as all plants from Cheju appear to be dwarf, later flowering and over all, very distinctive.

SCABRIFOLIA SUBSECTION

spinuliferum var. *glabrescens* K. M. Feng 1982. Not in cultivation

Differs from *spinuliferum* in its leaf above and below, pedicel, calyx and ovary are all almost glabrous or have a few soft hairs scattered along the midrib on leaf below. Yunnan.

SELENSIA SUBSECTION

selense var. *jucundum* T. L. Ming (see *p.* 262)

Just a change of status by the Chinese which Chamberlain is maintaining at subspecific rank.

TALIENSIA SUBSECTION

Several interesting new species have been described in this subsection recently, most of which sound worth introducing. Davidian does not list any of these in *Rhododendron Species Vol. 2, (Elepidote Species, Series Arboreum-Lacteum)*, Davidian has retained the old Lacteum series in its entirety which is highly debatable, as apart from *lacteum*, *beesianum* and *wightii*, there is no way of separating the rest of the species from the Taliensia subsection. Also, he has retained the old subseries which again make, in my view and Chamberlain's, unnatural subdivisions. See *p.* 263.

balangense Fang 1983. Not in cultivation

Ht 5–8 m (16–26 ft). Habit fairly open, almost tree-like. *Leaf bud scales persistent.*
L 6–15 × 3.5–8 cm (2½–6 × 1½–2¾ in), obovate to elliptic-obovate, apex acute, base obtuse or rounded, glabrous above, loose, *floccose greyish-white indumentum* below. Petiole 1–1.5 cm (⅓–⅔ in), glabrous, *winged*.
Inflor 13–15. Pedicels 3–4 cm (about 1½ in).
F tinged pink in bud, opening to white or white with pink stripe on lobes with a few small spots. Calyx small 1–2 mm, stamens puberlous lower half, style and ovary glabrous.

I was lucky to see a quantity of this new species in full bloom in spring 1989 in Wolong Panda Reserve. Both Chamberlain and I were well satisfied that this is a very distinct species but that it has been incorrectly placed in the Taliensia subsection. It is one of these species that defies classification, but would appear to be closest related to *watsonii* which grew on the hillside some 1,200 m (3,800 ft) above *balangense*. The leaf shape, indumentum, truss and flower shape make it appear different from members of Taliensia. While distinct, unusual and obviously worth introducing, it is unlikely to be classed as one of the best species.

So far only found at the foot of Balang Mountain, Wenchuan County, Szechwan, 2,350–3,400 m (nearly 8,000–11,000 ft) on steep wooded banks above river, scattered fairly plentifully through the forest in a limited area, either on its own or accompanied in places by *galactinum*, *concinnum* and *ambiguum*.   June in the wild.

barkamense Chamb. 1982. Not in cultivation

Related to *lacteum* with pale yellow flowers with purple flecks and same type of leaf hairs but differs in its smaller leaves with cordate bases and smaller flowers with glabrous ovaries. Another interesting new species.
north Szechwan, a little to the north-west of *balangense*.

bhutanense Long 1989 H4? L2–3

Ht 60 cm–3 m (2½–10 ft). Habit quite compact.
L 6–12.5 × 3–5 cm (2½–5 × 1¼–2 in), broadly elliptic to obovate, base cordate, glabrous above except some floccose hairs at base of midrib, plastered greyish-brown to orange-brown indumentum below. Petiole 0.3–1 cm (⅛–⅖ in), floccose above, tomentose below.
Inflor 10–15. Pedicel 0.8–1.3 cm (⅓–½ in), glabrous or puberulous.
F Deep pink buds open to pale pink, 3–3.5 cm (1⅕–1⅖ in), campanulate. Stamens glabrous, ovary glabrous.

This new species was previously named *agglutinatum* on herbarium specimens from which it differs in the presence of hairs on the midrib above, shorter petiole and glabrous stamens. It is common in central and east Bhutan above the tree line, often associated with *wightii*, *flinckii* and *campanulatum* ssp. *aeruginosum* where it is easily identified from a distance by the upward posture of its foliage (in autumn anyway). I saw quantities of this species in the Rudong La, central-east Bhutan in late September 1988. This is the furthest west Taliensia proper and looks an attractive and distinct species. Introduced recently although there may be a few old plants in cultivation.

Bhutan and perhaps south Tibet, 3,800–4,300 m (12,500–14,000 ft) amongst scrub just above the tree line to open hillsides further up.

coeloneuron, see *p.* 268. This is illustrated in *Sichuan Rhododendron of China*, *p.* 140–1. This seems to me closely related to *wiltonii*, in fact the descriptions fail to give much to separate them except that *coeloneuron* has a bistrate indumentum and *wiltonii* a unistrate indumentum. From the photographs, *coeloneuron* has especially bullate leaves. The distribution is similar except that *coeloneuron* also occurs in south-east Szechwan.

dabanshanense Fang & Wang 1978 (synonym of *przewalskii*)

Chamberlain gives this as being a glabrous-leaved *przewalskii* which I saw in north Szechwan in 1986 above the tree line and again in 1989. The type specimen of *dabanshanense* comes from Chinghai which borders north-west Szechwan.

danbaense L. C. Hu 1986

From the photographs and the description in *Sichuan Rhododendron of China*, I cannot see any difference between this and *bureavii*. This so called species is recorded as coming from western Szechwan within the same area as that in which *bureavii* (*bureavioides*) is found. In *The Species of Rhododendron*, the difference between *bureavii* and *bureavioides* is in the former having hairs and glands on the ovary and base of style and the latter having glands but no hairs on the ovary and glands but no hairs on the style. *R. danbaense* is said to have glands and hairs on both ovary and style. This is 'splitting hairs' and a detailed examination of a large number of plants of each would probably show no distinctions between the three 'species'. W. Berg found what is probably this plant in 1983 and I saw it in 1989. We find this noticeably slow to develop its indumentum compared with typical *bureavii*. Davidian retains *bureavioides*.

faberi var. *glabratum* K. M. Feng date?

Presumably a glabrous-leaved form of *faberi*. I have found *faberi* one of the slowest of the subsection to develop its indumentum as a seedling which makes me wonder if the leaf underside of var. *glabratum* is not just a juvenile state.

montiganum T. L. Ming 1984. Not in cultivation

Said to be related to the newly described *pubicostatum* from which it differs in its elliptic leaves, slightly hairy leaf underside, glabrous rachis and pedicel, ovary sparsely glandular and style glabrous. It certainly seems to be a peculiar species for the Taliensia subsection and perhaps it could be a hybrid or in the wrong subsection. Yunnan, 4,000 m (13,000 ft) in rhododendron thickets.

pubicostatum T. L. Ming 1981. Not in cultivation

Probably related to *montaginum* (see *montaginum* above). Chamberlain suggests that it might be related to *detersile* due to its distinctive floccose indumentum. North-east Yunnan.

roxieoides Chamb. 1982 (see *The Smaller Rhododendrons*, p. 186)

With its height of 2.5 m (8 ft), this would have been better described in this volume. This sounds an interesting plant worth introducing, coming from a little-explored area of east Szechwan.

shanii Fang 1983. Not in cultivation

This is found in Anhwei in east China, very remote from other Taliensia. No other information available.

sphaeroblastum var. wumengense K. M. Feng 1983

Differs from the type in its thinner leaf and greyish indumentum. Feng says it is related to *traillianum*. Has white to rose flowers. Yunnan, 3,700–4,000 m (12,000–13,000 ft).

wasonii var. *wenchuanense* L. C. Hu 1986. Possibly not in cultivation.

Differs from the type in its more plastered, thinner yellowish-brown to dark-brown indumentum on leaf underside, smaller funnel-campanulate pink to white flowers and style hairy at base. There are different pink-flowered forms of *wasonii* in cultivation, some with thinner indumentum than others. This is said to be endemic to Wenchuan County in *Sichuan Rhododendron of China*. I saw a few plants of *wasonii* out of flower in the above locality in spring 1990 and the indumentum was not noticeably plastered or thinner than plants in cultivation. All *wasonii* and var. *wenchuanense* illustrated in *Sichuan Rhododendron of China* have white or pale pink flowers.

TEPHROPEPLA SUBSECTION

longistylum ssp. *decumbens* R. C. Fang 1982

Differs from the type (see *p.* 279) in its absence of pubescence on the young branchlets, petioles and pedicels and also in its distribution in north-east Yunnan at 1,700 m (5,500 ft). There are nice photographs of pink-flowered forms of the type in *Sichuan Rhododendron of China, p.* 266–9.

THOMSONIA SUBSECTION

ramipilosum T. L. Ming 1984. Not in cultivation

Differs from other members of the subsection in the tawny punctulations on the leaf underside, the large calyx with narrow lobes and the sparsely hairy and glandular ovary. I am not happy with a description from only one specimen without even any flowers. Only recorded once in Tibet in alpine forest.

TRIFLORA SUBSECTION

brachypodum Fang & Liu 1982. Not in cultivation

Differs from *augustinii* in the young branchlets being slightly pubescent and glandular at first, the short 5–7 mm petiole and the densely scaly and sparsely glandular pedicel. From its description it would seem to be too close to *augustinii* to be of much distinction horticulturally. It does though come from an isolated location in south-east Szechwan so could be more distinct than it appears. At low elevations of 1,000–1,500 m (3,250–5,000 ft), so might be tender.

guangnanense R. C. Fang 1982. Not in cultivation

Mrs Fang gives this as being related to *bivelatum*, a little known species collected only once in north-east Yunnan. Davidian gives *bivelatum* as being closest related to *tatsienense*. Cullen thinks it is probably a chance hybrid of *augustinii* ssp. *chasmanthum*, Yunnan, 1,500 m (5,000 ft), on rocky hillside.

shaanxiense Fang & Zhao 1982. Not in cultivation

Said to show some relationship with *lutescens* from which it differs in its more papery foliage and purple flowers. Shensi, 1,500–2,000 m (5,000–6,500 ft), Probably distinct, coming from a remote area.

shimianense Fang & P. S. Liu 1982. Not in cultivation

Related to *lutescens* but differing in its leaf midrib below being minutely white pubescent and the flowers being pale yellow. May be little different from *lutescens*. Szechwan, 2,800 m (9,250 ft).

tatsienense var. *nudatum* R. C. Fang 1982. Not in cultivation

Differs from type in its absence of scales on young branchlets, petioles, pedicels and calyces. Type specimen collected by Forrest. Lichiang, Yunnan, 3,600 m (11,750 ft), in thickets below pines.

triflorum var. *multiflorum* R. C. Fang 1982

Differs from type in having 4–5 flowers per inflor. As normal *triflorum* can have up to 4 flowers per inflor, I cannot see the point of this variety but it does seem to be of interest that this is the first *triflorum* to be discovered in Yunnan at 2,500 m (8,250 ft).

zaleucum var. *pubifolium* R. C. Fang 1982

Differs from the type in a conspicuously pubescent lower leaf surface. A glabrous style is also given but the style is usually glabrous anyway. Yunnan, 3,100 m (10,250 ft), below fir and larch.

INTRODUCTION INTO CULTIVATION

A few years ago we were all rejoicing that China, Tibet and Bhutan were opening up to tourism and plant-hunting, at least to a limited extent. The idea of being able to see so many of the species that are familiar in gardens out in the wild certainly thrilled me, especially as a few years earlier, the prospects looked so bleak. Also, we naturally looked forward to being able to collect a few seeds of perhaps new forms of species or even species that had never been introduced.

Alas this rosy state of affairs has in one way been soured. The Chinese, Indians and Bhutanese have decided that people have been taking advantage of the opening up of their territories and have been plundering them for plants and seeds, often with purely commercial gain in mind. At first the Chinese were happy for people to collect a very limited amount of seed and a few plants but things got rather out of hand. The real trouble I feel has its roots in the wholesale exploitation of rare orchids by the Japanese and others. These often have a very limited distribution. Also, I have seen first-hand an unscrupulous Chinese man collecting many trays of orchids. Catalogues received from Japan make it clear what the destination of these orchids has been.

It is now extremely difficult to get permission to collect anything. It is sad from our point of view and also the host country's point of view as it may discourage would-be tourists-cum-plant-hunters from visiting. The collection of a few seeds and even for that matter a few seedlings is not going to have the slightest effect on the conservation of the rhododendron species that are being collected, although collecting can easily wipe out some plants such as orchids. Nature is indeed bountiful in its production of rhododendron seed and the chances of more than one in every several thousand seeds ever growing to maturity in the wild is about nil. The same to a lesser extent goes for seedlings in the wild. For instance, where big-leaved species grow, no seedlings have a hope of growing on until an old plant either dies or is blown over or is chopped by man. This brings me to another point, the conservation of the forest. The destruction of forests including rhododendrons is taking place at an alarming rate, especially in China, Tibet and Nepal. One Chinese or Nepalese with an axe and/or saw is going to do more damage to conservation in a week than all foreign plant-hunters in ten years.

Why do they object to us collecting a few seeds? The past history of our collectors coming home with pounds of rhododendron seed does not help. They ask themselves 'why should these foreigners come to our countries, collect, and then sell the proceeds for commercial gain? Perhaps we could export seed and seedlings ourselves and make some badly needed foreign exchange. Why should foreigners come and discover new species in our countries, name them themselves and then take all the credit for them?'

We cannot blame them for these feelings. We would feel likewise if they came here and did what we do in their countries. Actually, I feel that they do not realize the full implications involved. Most people collect simply to grow on a very few plants for their own gardens, surely a harmless state of affairs. Yes, some seeds are collected by specialist nurserymen, which may end in a few hundred plants which have been grown from those seeds, being sold to enthusiasts. However, this is on a very small scale. Wild seed is a good alternative to hand-pollinated seed with the added bonus of the chance of producing something superior, different or even new. We can hand pollinate our own species as an alternative and we already have most species in cultivation. A nurseryman collecting his own seed is never going to make a fortune on the proceeds; he is only making enough to pay for part of the cost of the trip. Travelling in these countries is expensive, especially as a result of the extra charges tourists have to pay. All anyone is hoping to do by, say, selling seed subscriptions, is help to pay these costs. Indeed, some travellers could not afford to go to these countries unless they could recoup some of their expenses by selling a few seeds or plants.

What are the chances of these countries themselves being able to make something worthwhile by exporting seed and plants? I would say very little. Rhododendron species are just not big business. There is a scattering of enthusiasts throughout rhododendron-growing areas of the world and the likelihood of ever increasing the demand for species by any significance is very low.

I would suggest that if a very limited amount of seed were permitted to be collected in these countries, it would do no harm to anyone. Much effort is needed in conserving the forests and their accompanying flowering plants: and these are what tourists like to see. Many tourists would not want to collect seed anyway.

POWDERY MILDEW (see *p*. 329)

This can now be considered the most serious rhododendron disease. When I wrote the First Edition, it was virtually unheard of, at least in the present form which seems capable of attacking a very wide spectrum of hardy rhododendrons, both species and hybrids. First symptoms are light areas, usually in the form of dots or circular patches appearing on the leaf upper surface, with corresponding brown patches below. Other parts of the leaf may turn yellow, leading to leaf fall. Sometimes, the whole of the leaf underside may be covered with white or grey powder, even though there is little evidence on the upper side. In really severe cases, a plant may be completely defoliated. In this case, some plants may die while others develop fresh young growth the following year or even that autumn. If the season is relatively dry and unfavourable to the fungus or if a thorough spraying programme is carried out, there may be a complete recovery.

At first, it was thought that only a few species and rather more hybrids within certain relationships were susceptible but alas, this has proved not to be the case. Very susceptible plants act as a centre of infection and if the weather is wet with moisture hanging on the leaves over long periods, the fungus will gradually spread on to neighbouring plants, even on to some normally considered fairly resistant. There is no doubt that the wettest and mildest geographical locations are the most easily effected and gardens or parts of gardens with many overhanging trees, much shade and good shelter, are the places most liable to severe infection. The lower leaves on a larger plant are especially prone to attack as are smaller plants growing partially under larger ones or right under the drip of trees. This may make us have to rethink our ideas on shade and shelter for rhododendrons and consider growing all but the most tender and largest-leaved species and their hybrids in much more open airy situations.

The most susceptible species are *cinnabarinum*, especially orange-flowered forms including Blandfordiiflorum Group, *keysii*, *succothii*, *cyanocarpum*, *thomsonii*, *eclecteum*, and *hookeri*. Slightly less susceptible are other members of the Thomsonia subsection, *barbatum*, *argipeplum*, *wiltonii*, *glaucophyllum*, *rubiginosum*, *wallichii*, and many others, partly depending on location. Some clones of these species seem to be more susceptible than others. On the whole, indumentumed species are less susceptible but by no means immune. Much depends on the stage of growth when there are the most spores on the move. It is apparent that only young growth is capable of being infected.

Control

At first we considered that a monthly spray, starting in mid-summer, and just treating those we considered the most susceptible, would prove adequate for a satisfactory control. In a season when the disease is not rampant, this might prove adequate but if there are many infected plants around and the season proves a bad one for spreading the fungus, it may be necessary to start much earlier. At the Benmore outstation of the Royal Botanic Garden, Edinburgh, where the rainfall approaches 250 cm (100 in), many species have become infected and they started spraying in the exceptionally mild winter of 1989 in mid-January. They are using two new powered knapsack sprayers and are spraying all the rhododendrons from top to bottom every three weeks. Getting over everything takes a week. It is obviously not feasible for most people to carry out a programme like this but it may be the only way to achieve good control. It is important to use at least two unrelated fungicides alternately to prevent the fungus from building up a resistance. There is a difficulty in knowing what fungicides to recommend at present with all the changes taking place in the use of pesticides. Several cereal fungicides (for powdery mildew) are successful on rhododendrons such as Bayleton (Triadimefon), Repulse (Chlorothalonil), Sportak and Octave (Prochloraz), plus Topaz (Penconazole), Fungaflor (Imazalil), Benlate (Benomyl) and Nimrod (Bupirimate). It is during very wet spells like July–August 1988 that the mildew runs rampant and yet spraying is next to impossible to accomplish. Also, during very mild winters like 1989–90, the disease may continue to spread, necessitating spraying every month. Do not use systemic fungicides during the winter months as they are not effective then.

Changes from Wade-Giles Romanization to Pinyin *(see p. 92)*

Since the publication of the First Edition in 1979, the use of Pinyin spelling of Chinese place names has become more or less standard so I used Pinyin in *The Smaller Rhododendrons* in 1985. As it would have been quite an upheaval to change all the names throughout the text, I have not been able to alter the spelling in this Second Edition. So as to be consistent throughout the book, I have continued to use the old Wade-Giles spelling in the Addendum. Some names like Yunnan have not changed at all while others have become almost unrecognizable. The following is a guide to the chief changes, Wade-Giles given first.

Provinces

Anhwei	Anhui
Chekiang	Zhejiang
Fukien	Fujian
Kansu	Gansu
Kwangtung	Guangdong
Kwangsi	Guangxi
Kweichow	Guizhou
Honan	Henan
Hupeh	Hubei
Kiangsi	Jiangxi
Shensi	Shaanxi
Shangtung	Shandong
Szechwan	Sichuan
Tibet	Xizang

Rivers

Yangtze River	Chang Jiang
Salween River	Nu Jiang
Tsangpo River	Zangbo Jiang

Places or mountains

Tali	Dali
Lichiang	Lijiang
Mt Omei	Emei Shan

General Index

Africa 41
American Rhododendron Society 336
aphids 325
Armillaria 53, 54, 69, 327–8
Asia 43
Australia 41
Australian Rhododendron Society 336
Avraham, Dr Zvi Ben 12
awards 65, 92

barks 59
bark-split 46, 48, 330–1
Basford, J. 191
Bayley Balfour, Sir Isaac 9, 19, 84
Beadle, Chauncy 81
Berg, Warren 370
bird pollination 27
Black, Michael 15, 34
blister blight 29, 330
BLM expedition 29
botrytis 48, 319, 322, 329
Bowes-Lyon, Simon 353
Britain 39–40
bud-blast 328–9

caterpillars 325
Chamberlain, Dr D. F. 9, 82, 137, 159, 274, 282, 344, 346, 349, 351, 352, 354, 356, 357, 358, 362, 366, 368
Chinese Rhododendron Society 336
Chinese taxonomists 343
chlorosis 331
choice of site 37–9
Christie, Sylvester 104
coastal influences 50
Coe, Dr Frederick, 81
Coleman, S. D. 32
collecting wild rhododendrons 32–6, 373–4
colour 60–1
conservation, in gardens 84–7
    in the wild 30–2
continental drift 11
Cooper, R. E. 25
Cowan, Dr J.M. 9, 82, 83, 84
Cox, E. H. M. 242, 244
Cox, P. A. 30
Croizat, Leon 13
crown gall 330
Cullen, Dr J. 9, 139, 240, 371
cuttings 307–11
    collection 310–12
    deciduous azaleas 313–14
    equipment 308–9
    fungicides 312–13
    growing on 321–3

hardening off 315
'hormones' 312–13
lighting 309
preparation and insertion 312
rooting mediums 309–10
stock plants 310–11
Cylindrocladium 329

damping off 330
Danish Chapter of the American Rhododendron Society 336
Davidian, H. H. 9, 83, 240, 344, 346, 347, 349, 350, 352, 354, 356, 357, 358, 359, 360, 362, 363, 364, 366, 367, 368, 370, 371
dead-heading 75
deer 324
Dilleniaceae 16
diseases 313, 326–30
    in the wild 29
Doleshy, Frank 366
drainage 67–8
Dunedin Rhododendron Group 336
Dwarf Rhododendrons 9, 10, 28, 82, 88, 143, 146, 246

ecology 17, 24
Ericaceae 13, 16
Europe 40–1

Fang, Dr W. 167
Farrer, R. 242
fertilizers 70–3, 320, 322
Fletcher, Dr Harold 85
foliage 58–9
Forrest, George 24, 29, 35, 36, 69, 84
fossils 11, 17
frost damage 45–9, 330–1
fungicides 376

German Rhododendron Society 336
Glass, Powell 87
Glendoick 10, 16, 26, 44, 45, 50, 51, 73, 99, 125, 126, 132, 152, 153, 195, 209, 235, 249, 250, 284, 285, 295, 297, 298, 299
Good, Ronald 13
Gorer, Geoffrey 38, 61, 173
grafting 315–16
grey mould 48, 319, 321, 329
growth in the wild 24–5
growth regulators 62

Hara, Dr H. 133
hardiness 45–54
Harrison, General E. 60
Harrison, Mrs R. 87

Index of Rhododendrons

Note: Main page references of species names appear bold. No species described in *Dwarf Rhododendrons* and *The Smaller Rhododendrons* is described in this book.